KOVELS'
AMERICAN
SILVER MARKS

BOOKS BY
RALPH AND TERRY KOVEL

American Country Furniture 1780–1875
Dictionary of Marks—Pottery & Porcelain
Kovels' Advertising Collectibles Price List
Kovels' American Silver Marks
Kovels' Antiques & Collectibles Price List
Kovels' Book of Antique Labels
Kovels' Bottles Price List
Kovels' Collector's Guide to American Art Pottery
Kovels' Collectors' Source Book
Kovels' Depression Glass & American Dinnerware Price List
Kovels' Guide to Selling Your Antiques & Collectibles
Kovels' Illustrated Price Guide to Royal Doulton
Kovels' Know Your Antiques
Kovels' Know Your Collectibles
Kovels' New Dictionary of Marks—Pottery & Porcelain
Kovels' Organizer for Collectors
Kovels' Price Guide for Collector Plates, Figurines, Paperweights,
    and Other Limited Editions

KOVELS'
AMERICAN
SILVER MARKS

RALPH & TERRY KOVEL

Crown Publishers, Inc., New York

ACKNOWLEDGMENTS

We would like to thank, once again, those who helped us with research beyond the expected limits of their jobs: Gebelein Silversmiths, Inc., Jack Kellmer Co., Kirk Stieff Co. (Charles C. Stieff II), Stuart Nye Silver Shop, Orleans Silver Co., Potter & Mellon, Inc., Dorothy T. Rainwater, Reed & Barton (Ray Haverstroh and Lisa Mellian), and Ernest Thompson Jr.

Combining the information from a *A Directory of American Silver, Pewter and Silver Plate,* our 1961 book, with the additional information we have been able to locate has been a complex and sometimes baffling job. Those who struggled with the problems and made this the book it is include Ann Cahn, Milt Wackerow, Joan Denman, and Deborah Kerner at Crown Publishers and our staff, including Sandy Brady, Grace Clyde, Marcia Goldberg, Harriet Goldner, Gay Hunter, Susan Otto, Nancy Saada, and Edie Smrekar. Special thanks to Jeff Clark, who did the drawings of the silver pieces.

Portions of this book originally appeared in *A Directory of American Silver, Pewter and Silver Plate,* © 1961 by Crown Publishers, Inc.

Published by Crown Publishers, Inc., 201 East 50th Street, New York, New York 10022.
Member of the Crown Publishing Group.
CROWN is a trademark of Crown Publishers, Inc.
Manufactured in the United States of America

Library of Congress Cataloging-in-Publication Data

Kovel, Ralph M.
[American silver marks, 1650 to the present]
Kovels' American silver marks, 1650 to the present / Ralph & Terry Kovel.—1st ed.
 p. cm.
 Portions of this book originally appeared in A directory of American silver, pewter and silver plate.
 ISBN 0-517-56882-9
 1. Silverwork—United States. 2. Hallmarks—United States. I. Kovel, Terry H. II. Kovel, Ralph M. Directory of American silver, pewter and silver plate. III. Title. IV. Title: American silver marks, 1650 to the present.
NK7210.K68 1989
739.2'3'0278—dc20   89–9999

Book design by Deborah Kerner
10 9 8 7 6 5 4

This book is dedicated to
K I M
who wrote long ago:

> A Book
>
> A book is a thing to read,
> Or to look at,
> Or to balance on your head.
>
> But the very best book is a book about
>   silver,
> Dedicated to me.
>
>   by
>   Kim
>   Kovel

INTRODUCTION

The marks on the bottom of a piece of silver can be an indication of the age, maker, and origin of the piece. A single mark usually indicates that the piece of silver was made in America, although there are some Irish and Scottish pieces with just the maker's name. This is a book about American silver marks and solid American silver. It will not help you to identify other silver. Four or five small pictorial marks usually indicate England as the country of origin. For example, the leopard's head indicates England. Become familiar with the English king or queen's head mark as an indication of age. If the king's head faces right, it was made before 1850. Queen Victoria faces left. Queen Elizabeth faces left. Silver was stamped with a lion for London, a thistle for Edinburgh. The harp indicated the piece was made in Dublin. Glasgow silver-smiths used a fish or tree. Ornate capital letters or the fleur-de-lis were used in France. A hand indicates Antwerp, a spread eagle Germany or Russia. The word STERLING indicates Ireland as well as America. COIN, DOLLAR, and STANDARD were usually American terms, but some Irish makers also used them. The words quadruple, triple, double, EPNS, and EPWM indicate that the ware is silver plated. "800" is usually found on Continental silver.

If a piece is not American, refer to the books written about English or Continental silver. If it seems to be American, this book will help.

The earliest silversmiths in the colonies used their initials. Many makers used their last name, or first initial and last name. Pseudo-hallmarks were used about 1800.

They were meant to mislead the public into believing that the silver was of English origin. Many unmarked pieces of American silver were made by 1825. The pieces were later marked with the store name. By 1830 the words COIN, PURE COIN, DOLLAR, STANDARD, PREMIUM, or the letters "C" or "D" were placed on silver to indicate that it was 900 out of 1000 parts silver. The word STERLING was frequently used by 1860. STERLING means that 925 out of 1000 parts are silver. This is still the standard for sterling silver. Gorham Silver Company used a special mark for their Martelé silver from 1899 to 1912. Martelé was made of silver of sterling or better quality, some with 950 parts silver to each 1000 parts.

Silversmiths in Baltimore, Maryland, had a maker-date system from 1814 to 1830. An assay office was legally established in 1814, and marks were placed on all silver sold. The head of liberty indicated quality; a date letter, the arms of the city of Baltimore, and the maker's initials or name were included. The dating system was discontinued in 1830 when the silversmiths developed another system. Numbers like 10.15, 112, or 11/12 were stamped on the silver to indicate the percentage of pure silver in the metal.

When the American silversmiths were first "discovered" in the early 1900s, most collectors felt that only the eighteenth-century makers were important. Now, years later, we have learned that fine American silver was also made during the nineteenth and twentieth centuries.

Any collection is only as good as the collector's knowledge of the subject. This book is a guide to makers. Learn to know good work by its shape, feel, and construction.

Look up its maker and determine its age and origin. This book should make it easier to identify Grandma's spoon or a dish in an antiques shop. Remember, a mark can easily be copied.

The information in this book is as accurate and complete as possible. The authoritative sources indicated in our Bibliography have been used. Readers of our nationally syndicated newspaper column "Kovels: Antiques and Collecting," dealers, and collectors have also helped furnish information not previously available.

Each entry in the book includes numbers ranging from 1 to 160. These numbers indicate the book or article that was used as a source of information. At the end of the book is a Bibliography. It is as complete as possible. We have omitted current articles from magazines and newspapers that are not devoted to antiques. We have also omitted some books which are glamorized biographies. The Bibliography notation 89 refers to original research information obtained through our collection, talks with former workers or relatives of silversmiths, and unpublished material made available to us through historical societies, museums, and collectors. Primary source material not available to the general public has also been included under the 89 listing.

Numbers in parentheses are shown after each entry. The numbers refer to the birth or death dates of the craftsman or the most accurate working dates known. Dates that are based on information compiled in earlier studies have been corrected only for blatant errors. For example: One silversmith was listed as living to 140 years old. This type of misinformation has been corrected. Some early books list incorrect information and later studies have furnished more accurate information. If we were unable to prove that an error existed, we listed all available information. Because of this, you may find a silversmith listed as working in two cities during the same years. Some books list silversmiths, watchmakers, and jewelers separately. We have included all three as silversmiths if there is not enough evidence to determine their trades. Some later pieces of silver are marked with the store owner's name, not the maker's. These names have been included.

Many entries are followed by a drawing of the craftsman's mark. Pictorial marks were drawn by an artist; many company logos have been reproduced from actual marks; but marks which are just names or initials are set in type. Letters set in type surrounded by a line drawing of a box indicate that the actual mark was incised or stamped into the silver with a punch. The box is the outline of the indentation. Marks that were incised letters are indicated by simple letters set in type. The form of type—all capitals, or capitals and small letters—is an indication of how the original mark appeared. Marks comprised of just initials have periods between the letters only if they appeared that way on the silver. Pseudo-hallmarks and small separate symbols are not included. Symbols indicative of a specific city, such as the Baltimore assay marks or city names, are not included. Unusual descriptive marks such as "OPPO THE POST OFFICE" or "JOYS BUILDING" are included.

If your piece is marked with a name beginning with I or J, look in the I *and* J sections, since those letters were frequently interchanged. There may be confusion when looking up a maker whose last name begins with a vowel. For example: G. Eoff used a mark that might appear as GEOFF. Always check that possibility. Marks that contain the beginning M' are listed as Mc; consequently, the name M'Donnell will appear in the listing for McDonnell.

During the past years the names of cities have been changed. Wherever possible we have used the most recent city name, but confusion still exists. For example, three settlements in Virginia were named Charleston.

1640 to 1850

The history of silver in America began in Boston, Massachusetts, with Richard Sanderson (1608–1693) and John Hull (1624–1683). Sanderson, trained as a silversmith in England, arrived in the colonies in 1638. Hull had been trained by his half-brother, Richard Storer. Hull and Sanderson worked together and made the earliest American silver pieces known to exist. The first American-born silversmith was Jeremiah Dummer, born in 1645.

John Hull first gained fame when he was chosen to start the mint in Boston. England had forbidden the colonists to mint their own money, but in 1652 the general court of Massachusetts ordered the first silver money to be minted for use in local trading. Hull designed and made the now famous pine-tree shilling.

Few families in seventeenth-century America had enough money or leisure to desire wares made from silver. Most early silver was made for churches. The lines were simple and the pieces plain. New England (Boston), the state of New York (especially New York City), Pennsylvania (especially Philadelphia), and later Delaware and South Carolina were the centers for the silversmithing trade. Each city developed its own designs and characteristics, which were influenced by the heritage of the colonists. Silver design in Boston echoed the English, while New York silversmiths received their inspiration from the Dutch.

A law was passed in Boston in 1660 forbidding a maker to mark his silverwork alone until he reached the age of twenty-one. There were many other rules, but the silversmiths in America were never controlled as rigidly as the English with their guilds. There was very little cheating and only a few smiths ever got into trouble with their customers or the law. The silversmith was a successful businessman, well respected in the community. He handled the wealth of the community and was trusted to give a fair accounting of the amount of silver he used. This was during a period when it was difficult to keep money safely hidden. A family of means quickly learned it was safer to have a silversmith melt the coins and make a large teapot than it was to keep money under the bed. Each teapot or sugar bowl was unique in design and marked by the maker so it could be identified. A thief had more trouble disposing of a teapot than coins.

Most silversmiths only produced the pieces of silver ordered by their customers. Many wealthy customers requested drinking vessels, which indicates the important position liquor played in the daily living of our ancestors. Liquor was a part of the celebration for marriage, death, and business discussions. A silver tankard usually helped add to the enjoyment.

Coffee, tea, and chocolate became important beverages in the colonies by the early eighteenth century. Pots, sugar bowls, creamers, and other utensils were made to fit the need. The design of these utensils changed to reflect the style of the period. Silver shapes changed from colonial to classical, then Federal, Empire, Victorian, Art Nouveau, Arts and Crafts, Art Deco, and modern.

Silver was made by machine by 1840, but there were some silvermakers who continued making silver by hand. Victorian tastes and the machine age converted simple silver designs to a mass of decoration by 1875. However, plain lines and simple decorations gradually reappeared in the twentieth century.

The history of silver in America covers many years and many men. Families passed their knowledge and skills on to future generations. Paul Revere, one of the most famous American silversmiths, was the father and son of a silversmith. The Reveres, Burts, and Hurds of Boston, the Richardsons and Syngs of Philadelphia, the Faris family of Annapolis, the Ten Eyck family of Albany, the Moultons of Newburyport, and the Kirks of Baltimore were all famous for their silversmiths. Silversmithing requires years of training, inherent skill, and artistic talent.

The marks used by most pre-1850 American silversmiths were composed of the maker's name or initials. Letters or names were usually stamped inside the many characteristic shapes shown. Makers also used other marks, which were made to resemble the guild marks used by English silversmiths. A head, bird, hand, star, arm, or letter often appeared in the pseudo-marks, along with the maker's mark.

1850 to 1980

Designs of the Victorian period were inspired by the Greek Revival of the earlier decades and the repoussé (raised) decorations newly in vogue. Classical forms were decorated with cast bands of trim, sculptured figures, floral patterns, and Oriental and Indian motifs. The silver reflected the rococo patterns of the furniture in the 1850s and the Renaissance Gothic rectangular patterns of the 1880s. Ideas were borrowed freely, and a tea set could have repoussé roses, ram's head handles, a seated Indian as a knob on the teapot, deer's feet and legs, plus an engraved initial. New technologies had great influence on silverware made after 1850. Silver plating was introduced in 1840 and inexpensive plated wares became available in quantity. The drop hammer, the rolling mill, and other improvements changed the skill and time required to make a spoon or a bowl.

Jabez Gorham, after apprenticing for seven years, then working with four partners for five years, formed his own company in 1818. It eventually became Gorham & Company and later Gorham Manufacturing Company. This was one of the first silver manufacturers to use mass-production methods. Silverware, hollowware, and jewelry were made by many companies. Baby cups, tea services, pitchers, goblets, and many different serving pieces were popular. Elaborate figural napkin rings, tilting water pitchers, and other pieces were popular with silver plate makers. Souvenir spoons were made in sterling and in silver plate. The traditional flatware patterns of Plain Thread, Shell, Grape, and Tip't continued into the 1850s. Ribbon pattern was introduced about 1865; Medallion pattern was made by the 1860s. Many elaborate floral patterns soon followed, and in the 1870s Japanese styles became popular. The famous Audubon pattern by Tiffany & Company was first made in 1871.

Art Nouveau designs were introduced in the late 1880s. The handmade Martelé silver by Gorham and the commercially produced sets by Tiffany & Company and Gorham were sold in all parts of the country. By the early 1900s the Arts and Crafts movement was in fashion and a few makers produced silver with plain solid lines that went well with Stickley furniture. Copper became a popular metal for many vases and decorative pieces, and silver was in less demand.

The Art Deco movement in France influenced the silversmiths of America after World War I. Simple lines and plain surfaces were popular with those who made silver by hand. Designs were inspired by the work of the Danish silversmith Georg Jensen. A few areas of the country had artisans producing special handmade silver. Chicago, Cleveland, New York, San Francisco, Boston, and some smaller Massachusetts towns had artists making important silver pieces.

The tradition of handmade silver made in small workshops has continued in America to the present. Artists exhibiting at museums or craft shows still sell unique pieces of silver made in the latest styles. Large commercial companies have continued making silver in old and new patterns. New ideas are expressed in unfamiliar shapes for silver teapots, vases, spoons, and even sculpture.

Ralph and Terry Kovel
March 1989

A

A & G W
(See A. G Welles)

A & R
(See Andras & Richard)

A & S
(See Abrecht & Sulsberger)

A & S Co.
(See Adams & Shaw)

A B
(See Adrian Bancker,
Andrew Billings, Asa
Blanchard, Abel Buel)

A C
(See Alexander Cameron,
Abraham Carlisle, Aaron
Cleveland, Albert Cole,
Arnold Collins, A. Cuyler)

A D
(See Antoine Danjen, Amos
Doolittel, Abraham
Dubois)

A E
(See John Aaron Elliott)

A E W
(See Andrew Ellicott
Warner)

A F
(See Abraham Forbes)

A G F
(See Abraham G. Forbes)

A H
(See Ahasuerus Hendricks)

A J & Co.
(See A. Jacobs & Co.)

A K
(See Amos Kay, Alexander
Kerr)

A K Co.
(See Archibald-Klement Co.,
Inc.)

A L
(see Aaron Lane)

A N
(See Abijah Northey)

A O
(See Andrew Oliver, Antoine
Oneille)

A P
(See Alexander Petrie,
Abraham Pontran)

A R
(See Anthony Rasch)

A R G
(See Arthur R. Geoffroy)

A. R. S. Sterling (c. 1926)
Boston, Mass.
Frederick J. R. Gyllenberg
Alfred H. Swanson
Bibl. 127

F. ℒ
A.R.S.

A S
(See Amity Silver Inc.,
Anthony Simmons, Adam
Stone)

A. S. & M. Co.
(See Art Stamping & Mfg.
Co.)

A T
(See Andrew A. Taylor,
Armistead Truslow,
Andrew Tyler)

A U
(See Andrew Underhill)

A W
(See Ambrose Ward, Antipas
Woodward)

Joseph Aaron (c. 1798)
Philadelphia, Pa.
Bibl. 3, 23, 36, 44

George Abbott (c. 1822)
Philadelphia, Pa.
Bibl. 3

J. S. Abbott
Location unknown
Bibl. 28, 29, 44, 114

J. S. ABBOTT

John S. Abbott (1860)
Bethel, Me
Bibl. 105

John W. Abbott
(b. 1790–d. 1850)
Portsmouth, N.H. (c. 1839)
*Bibl. 3, 15, 23, 25, 28, 36,
44, 91, 94, 110, 114, 125*

J ABBOT   J W ABBOTT

S. H. Abbott (1875)
Providence, R.I.
Bibl. 108

Robert K. Abel
(c. 1840–1850)
Philadelphia, Pa.
Bibl. 3

John D. Abercrombie
(c. 1823–1843)
Philadelphia, Pa.
Bibl. 3

Henry Abraham (c. 1844)
New York, N.Y.
Bibl. 23, 124, 138

Abrecht & Sulsberger
(c. 1896)
Newark, N.J.
Abrecht & Co.
(1896–c. 1904)
Albert Abrecht
(c. 1915–c. 1937)
Bibl. 14, 127, 157   A & S

Albert Abrecht   A&A
(c. 1915–1937)
Newark, N.J.
Successor to Abrecht &
Sulsberger (c. 1896)

Abrecht & Co.
    (c. 1876–1915)
Bibl. 127, 157

Academy Silver
    (c. 1951–1961)
New York, N.Y.
Bibl. 127

F. W. (M.) Ackerly
(See Francis W. Ackley)

David Ackerman
New York, N.Y.
    (c. 1818–1825)
Bibl. 23, 36, 44, 124, 138

E. Ackley (c. 1800)
Alexandria, Va.
Bibl. 24, 28 | E ACKLEY |

Francis M. Ackley
    (c. 1797–1800)
New York, N.Y.
Bibl. 15, 21, 23, 29, 36, 114,
    122, 135, 138

Thad Ackley (c. 1840)
Warren, Ohio
Bibl. 89

George Acton
    (c. 1795–1797)
New York, N.Y.
Bibl. 23, 36, 44, 124

R. C. Acton & Sons
    (c. 1905)
Alexandria, Va.
R. C. Acton (c. 1888–1889)
Richard E. Acton (d. 1893)
Bibl. 130

Robert F. Adair
Paris, Ky. (to 1796)
Lexington, Ky. (after 1796)
Bibl. 32, 54, 90, 93

Charles Adam
    (b. 1848–d. 1925)
Alexandria, Va.
Bibl. 54

James Adam
    (b. 1755–d. 1798)
Alexandria, Va.
Bibl. 19, 54

John Adam
    (b. 1780–d. 1846)
Alexandria, Va. (c. 1799)
Bibl. 15, 19, 28, 29, 44, 54,
    72, 78, 91, 95, 114

John B. Adam (c. 1822)
New Orleans, La.
Bibl. 23, 36, 44

L. Adam (d. 1731)
Location unknown
Bibl. 28, 29

Robert L. Adam
    (c. 1846–1898)
Alexandria, Va.
Bibl. 54

William Wallace Adam
    (b. 1817–d. 1877)
Alexandria, Va.
    (c. 1846–?)
Charles Adam
Robert L. Adam
Bibl. 19, 54

Adams & Buttre
    (c. 1836–?)
Elmira, N.Y.
Henry B. Adams
Bibl. 20, 91, 124

Adams & Farnsworth
Location unknown
Bibl. 80

| ADAMS AND FARNSWORTH |

Adams & Shaw
    (c. 1874–1880)
Providence, R.I.
New York, N.Y.
Newark, N.J.
Became Dominick & Haff
Bibl. 127, 135

Benjamin F. Adams
    (c. 1845)
Troy, N.Y.
Bibl. 23, 124

C. J. Adams (c. 1840)
Frankfort, Ky.
Bibl. 32

C. J. Adams & Co.
    (c. 1870)
Bowling Green, Ky.
Bibl. 54, 93

Dunlap Adams (c. 1764)
Philadelphia, Pa.
Bibl. 3, 28

Henry B. Adams (c. 1842)
Elmira, N.Y.
Adams & Buttre
    (c. 1836–?)
Hamilton & Adams
    (c. 1837–c. 1842)
Bibl. 20, 124

Henry B. Adams (c. 1848)
Philadelphia, Pa.
Bibl. 3, 23, 124

J. S. Adams (1860)
Providence, R.I.
Bibl. 108

John Adams (c. 1829)
Alexandria, Va.
District of Columbia
Bibl. 23, 36, 102, 151

John B. Adams (1860)
Winthrop, Me.
Bibl. 105

Jonathan Adams (c. 1783)
Philadelphia, Pa.
Bibl. 3, 23, 36, 44

Lucien Adams (1860)
Biddeford, Me.
Bibl. 105

Nathan Adams
    (b. 1755–d. 1855)
Maine, Mass.
Bibl. 15, 91, 114

| ADAMS |

Nathaniel Adams
(c. 1797–1813)
Troy, N.Y.
Bibl. 20, 124, 138

Nathaniel W. Adams
(c. 1842–1844)
Buffalo, N.Y.
Sibley & Adams
(c. 1847–1848)
Bibl. 20, 124

Pygan Adams
(b. 1712–d. 1776)
New London, Conn.
(c. 1735)
Bibl. 15, 16, 22, 23, 28, 29,
36, 44, 54, 61, 72, 92, 94,
102, 110, 114, 151

Robert Adams (c. 1800)
Baltimore, Md.
Bibl. 15, 44

Thomas F. Adams
Baltimore, Md. (c. 1804)
Petersburg, Va. (c. 1807)
Edenton, N.C. (c. 1809)
Bibl. 19, 21

Welcome K. Adams
(1860)
Providence, R.I.
Bibl. 108

Wesley Adams
(c. 1849–1850)
Philadelphia, Pa.
Bibl. 3

William Adams
(See also Towle Silversmiths)

William Adams
(c. 1831–1842)
New York, N.Y.
Bibl. 4, 15, 22, 23, 28, 29,
35, 36, 44, 54, 79, 83, 114,
116, 122, 124, 134, 138

William L. Adams
(c. 1842–c. 1850)
Troy, N.Y.
Bibl. 20, 23, 44, 124

George Mitchell Addison
(c. 1798–1804, d. 1810)
Baltimore, Md.
Bibl. 23, 28, 44

William Addison
(c. 1845–1850)
Philadelphia, Pa.
Bibl. 3

Eldridge I. Adell (1875)
Lewiston, Me.
Bibl. 105

Adelphi Silver Plate Co.
(c. 1890–1915)
New York, N.Y.
John Schimpf & Sons
Bibl. 127, 131, 135, 157

William Adgate
(b. 1744–d. 1779)
Norwich, Conn.
Bibl. 16, 22, 23, 28, 36, 44,
110

Allan Adler, Inc.
(1939–present)
Los Angeles, Calif.
Allan W. Adler (b. 1916)
Bibl. 104, 127, 141, 144

Duff Adolph (c. 1837)
Philadelphia, Pa.
Bibl. 3

Adriance & Cook
(c. 1814–1815)
Poughkeepsie, N.Y.
John Adriance (?)
Harry Cook
Bibl. 20, 124

Charles Platt Adriance
(b. 1790–d. 1874)
Poughkeepsie, N.Y.
Richmond, Va.
(c. 1816–1832)
Bibl. 15, 19, 44, 114, 124

Edwin Adriance
Ithaca, N.Y. (c. 1832–1835)
St. Louis, Mo.
(c. 1835–1870)
Mead, Adriance & Co.
(c. 1831–1832)
Mead & Adriance
(c. 1836–1852)
Bibl. 15, 20, 23, 25, 28, 36,
44, 54, 91, 114, 124, 134

John Adriance
(c. 1814–1828)
Poughkeepsie, N.Y.
Adriance & Cook
(c. 1814–1815) (?)
Hayes & Adriance
(c. 1816–1826)
Bibl. 15, 20, 91, 95, 124

William Adriance
(c. 1835)
Natchez, Miss.
Bibl. 19

Aertsen & Eichbaum
(c. 1829)
Nashville, Tenn.
Bibl. 54

Thomas Agnis
(c. 1761–1762)
Edenton, N.C.
Bibl. 21

Adolph Aherns (c. 1837)
Philadelphia, Pa.
Bibl. 3

Ahrendt & Taylor Co., Inc.
(c. 1922–1943)
Newark, N. J.
Wm. G. Ahrendt
Bibl. 127

Anthony Aigron
(c. 1732–1745)
Charleston, S.C.
Bibl. 5

Charles G. Aiken (c. 1850)
Cleveland, Ohio
Bibl. 54

George Aiken
(b. 1765–d. 1832)
Baltimore, Md.
(w. 1787–c. 1823)
*Bibl. 15, 23, 28, 29, 36, 39,
44, 50, 91, 95, 114, 151*

J. Aiken
(See John Aitken)

Michael Ainsworth
(c. 1755)
Fredericks County, Va.
Winchester, Va.
Bibl. 3, 19, 23, 36, 44

**John Aitken (Aitkin)
(Aiken)** (c. 1785–1814)
Philadelphia, Pa.
*Bibl. 3, 4, 22, 25, 28, 29, 36,
44, 91, 102, 114*

William Aitken (w. 1802)
Baltimore, Md.
Bibl. 38

William Aitken (c. 1825)
Philadelphia, Pa.
Bibl. 3, 22, 44

John Aitkin
(See John Aitken)

W. Aitkins (c. 1802)
Baltimore, Md.
Bibl. 23, 28, 36

Akerly & Briggs
(c. 1845–1851)
New York, N.Y.
*Bibl. 15, 44, 91, 114, 124,
138*

**John B. Akin (Brent
Akin)** (c. 1820–1860)
Danville, Ky.
*Bibl. 25, 32, 44, 54, 68, 93,
114*

J. B. AKIN   JOHN B. AKIN
STANDARD
JOHN B AKIN DANVILLE KY.

William Akin (d. 1824)
Danville, Ky. (c. 1812–1820)
Bibl. 32, 54, 68, 93

Samuel Akins
(c. 1841–1842)
Philadelphia, Pa.
Bibl. 3

John L. Albert
Shepherdstown, Va (c. 1826)
Winchester, Va. (c. 1827)
George B. Graves
Bibl. 19

Anthony Albertson
(c. 1848)
Philadelphia, Pa.
Bibl. 3

Joseph P. Albertson
New York, N.Y.
Cleveland, Ohio
(c. 1849–1858)
Cowles & Albertson
(c. 1849–1858)
Bibl. 54, 124

Thomas F. Albright
(c. 1835–1847)
Philadelphia, Pa.
Bibl. 3

Alcock & Allen (c. 1810)
Location unknown
Bibl. 28

ALCOCK & ALLEN

George Alcorn
(c. 1830–1833)
Philadelphia, Pa.
Bibl. 3

Alden Brothers (1875)
Waterville, Me.
Bibl. 105

A. J. Alden (1861)
Waterville, Me.
Bibl. 105

Charles Aldis (c. 1814)
New York, N.Y.
*Bibl. 15, 23, 25, 36, 44, 114,
124, 138*

C. ALDIS

Carlos Bernerdo Alemany
(c. 1950–1968)
New York, N.Y.
Bibl. 117

Alexander
(See Brasher & Alexander)

Alexander & Riker
(See Riker & Alexander)

**Alexander & Riter
(Riker)**
(See Riker & Alexander)

A. Alexander (c. 1802)
Philadelphia, Pa.
Bibl. 3, 36, 44

Isaac Alexander
(b. 1812–d. 1855)
New York, N.Y. (c. 1850)
*Bibl. 15, 23, 25, 44, 114,
124, 138*

I. ALEXANDER

Isaac B. Alexander
(b. 1812–d. 1885)
Camden, S.C. (c. 1841)
Bibl. 5

Moses Alexander
(c. 1851–1859)
York, S.C.
Bibl. 5

Philip Alexander
Location unknown
Bibl. 10

Robert Alexander
(b. 1825–d. 1862)
Rochester, N.Y.
(c. 1847–1850)
Bibl. 20, 41, 44, 114, 124

Alexander & Simmons
(See Simmons & Alexander)

Samuel Alexander
(c. 1797–1808)
Philadelphia, Pa.
Wiltberger & Alexander
(c. 1797–1808)
Simmon(s) & Alexander
(c. 1798–1804)
*Bibl. 3, 4, 22, 25, 28, 29, 36,
44, 54, 91, 95, 114*

S. ALEXANDER

Samuel P. Alexander
(b. 1810–d. 1900)
Charlotte, N.C.
Trotter & Alexander
(c. 1837–1838)
Brem & Alexander (c. 1848)
Bibl. 21

Zenas Alexander (d. 1826)
Mecklenburg County, N.C.
(c. 1805–1810)
(near Charlotte, N.C.)
Bibl. 21

Samuel Alford
(c. 1759–1762)
Philadelphia, Pa.
Bibl. 3, 22, 28, 36

Samuel Alford (c. 1840)
Philadelphia, Pa.
Bibl. 44

Thomas Alford
(c. 1762–1764)
Philadelphia, Pa.
Bibl. 3, 22, 23, 28, 36, 44

Samuel Allardice
(d. 1798)
Philadelphia, Pa.
Bibl. 3

Allcock & Allen
(c. 1810–1820)
New York, N.Y.
*Bibl. 25, 44, 79, 114, 124,
138*

ALLCOCK & ALLEN

Allen
(See Allcock & Allen,
Evans & Allen)

**Allen & Edwards
(Edwards & Allen)**
(c. 1700–1707)
Boston, Mass.
John Allen
John Edwards
*Bibl. 23, 25, 28, 29, 36, 44,
54, 80, 91, 94, 110, 114*

Allen, Rhodes & Co
(c. 1837)
Cincinnati, Ohio
Bibl. 89

A. C. Allen (c. 1836)
Cincinnati, Ohio
Bibl. 34, 152

Alexander Allen (c. 1850)
Rochester, N. Y.
Bibl. 20, 135, 138

Cairns Allen
(c. 1837–1848)
Philadelphia, Pa.
Bibl. 3

Caleb Allen
(b. 1808–d. 1873)
Cincinnati, Ohio
(1833–1873)
Bibl. 54, 90

Charles Allen
(b. 1731–d. 1767)
Boston, Mass. (c. 1760)
*Bibl. 25, 29, 36, 44, 91, 110,
114, 124*

C ALLEN

G. W. Allen (c. 1836)
Batavia, N.Y.
Bibl. 20, 124

George W. Allen (1860)
Waldenboro, Me.
Bibl. 105

J. T. Allen (c. 1832–1836)
Batavia, N.Y.
Bibl. 20, 124

James Allen (c. 1720)
Philadelphia, Pa.
Bibl. 3, 4, 22, 23, 28, 36, 44

Jared T. Allen
(c. 1844–1846)
Rochester, N.Y.
Bibl. 20, 41, 44

Joel Allen
(b. 1755–d. 1825)
Middletown, Conn.
(c. 1787)
Plantsville, Conn.
Southington, Conn.
*Bibl. 16, 22, 23, 28, 36, 44,
92, 110*

John Allen
(b. 1671–d. 1760)
Boston, Mass.
Allen & Edwards
(c. 1700–1707)
*Bibl. 2, 15, 22, 23, 25, 28,
29, 44, 50, 54, 69, 94, 102,
110, 114, 116, 119*

John Allen (c. 1814)
Philadelphia, Pa.
Bibl. 3, 23, 36, 44

L. C. Allen (b. 1826)
Utica, N.Y. (c. 1850)
Bibl. 18, 20

Luther A. Allen
(c. 1844–c. 1850)
Rochester, N.Y.
Bibl. 20, 124, 158

Oliver Allen (c. 1830)
Lyons, N.Y.
Bibl. 20, 124

Philo Allen (c. 1844)
Buffalo, N.Y.
Chedell & Allen
Bibl. 20, 124

Allen Rhodes & Co.
(1834–1837)
Cincinnati, Ohio
Bibl. 54, 90

Richard Allen
(c. 1816–1817)
Philadelphia, Pa.
Bibl. 3, 23, 36, 44

Richard Allen (c. 1850)
Auburn, N.Y.
Bibl. 20, 124

Robert Allen
(b. 1755–d. 1825)
Philadelphia, Pa.
(c. 1787–1796)
Bibl. 3, 22, 28, 36, 44

S. Allen & Co. (1875)
Providence, R.I.
Bibl. 108

Samuel Allen (1860)
Providence, R.I.
Bibl. 108

Thomas Allen (c. 1758)
Boston, Mass.
Bibl. 22, 23, 28, 36, 44, 110

William Allen (w. 1772)
Annapolis, Md.
Bibl. 38

Marc Alleoud (c. 1820)
Augusta, Ga.
Morand, Alleoud & Co.
Bibl. 17

W. A. Allibone
(c. 1828–1833)
Philadelphia, Pa.
Bibl. 3

John Allies
(w. 1782–1796,
d. 1796)
Elkton, Md.
Bibl. 38

Peter Allison
(c. 1791–1800)
New York, N.Y.
Bibl. 22, 23, 36, 44, 124, 138

William N. Allison
Albany, N.Y. (c. 1831–1834)
New York, N.Y.
(c. 1834–1837)
Philadelphia, Pa.
Bibl. 3, 15, 20, 124, 138

William Alloway (c. 1823)
Ithaca, N.Y.
Bibl. 20, 124

Allsopp-Steller, Inc.
(1943–1973)
Newark, N.J.
Successor to
Wordly, Allsopp & Bliss Co.,
Inc. (c. 1915–1927)
Allsopp & Allsopp
(c. 1927–1931)
Allsopp-Bliss
(c. 1927–1931)
Allsopp Bros.
(c. 1927–1931)
Allsopp-Bliss Co.
(c. 1931–1943)
Allsopp Bros.
(c. 1931–1943)
Bibl. 127,157   **YYB**

**J. N. Alrich & S. W.
Warriner** (c. 1848)
Louisville, Ky.
Jacob N. Alrich
S. W. Warriner
Bibl. 32

Jacob N. Alrich (c. 1848)
Louisville, Ky.
J. N. Alrich & S. W.
Warriner
Bibl. 32, 93

Wessell Alrichs
(b. 1670–d. 1734)
Salem, N.J. (c. 1719)
Delaware (after 1725)
Bibl. 30, 46, 54

Thomas Alsop
(c. 1842–1850)
Philadelphia, Pa.
Bibl. 3

Jeromimus Alstyne
(c. 1787–1798)
New York, N.Y.
*Bibl. 15, 22, 25, 28, 35, 36,
44, 83, 91, 114, 124, 138*

ꝺ Alstyne	IA	IA

Alvin Corporation
(1928–present)
Providence, R.I.
Division of Gorham
Corporation
Alvin Mfg. Co. (1886–1893)
Alvin-Beiderhase Co.
(1893–1919)
Alvin Silver Co.   ALVIN STERLING
(1919–1928)
*Bibl. 114, 120, 127, 130, 135,
146, 147, 152, 157*

ALVIN

Philo G. Alvord
(b. 1812–d. 1878)
Utica, N.Y. (c. 1834)
Buffalo, N.Y. (c. 1837–1848)
Bibl. 18, 20, 124, 158

Fester Amant (c. 1794)
Philadelphia, Pa.
Bibl. 3

American Beauty
(See William B. Kerr & Co.)

American Classic
(See Easterling Company)

Ames Mfg. Company
(1829–1920)
Chicopee, Mass.
Bibl. 127, 135

Cornelius Ames
(See Amos)

H. R. Ames & Co.
(c. 1850)
Potsdam, N.Y.
Bibl. 20, 124

Cornelius Amiss
(See Amos)

Amity Silver Inc. (c. 1950)
Brooklyn, N.Y.
Bibl. 127

Amory
Location unknown
Bibl. 28

| AMORY |

Cornelius Amos (Ames)
(Amiss)(c. 1840)
Louisville, Ky.
E. C. Beard & Co.
   (c. 1831–c. 1852)
Bibl. 32, 93

Amston Silver Co., Inc.
   (c. 1960)
Meriden, Conn.
Division of Ellmore Silver
   Co. (c. 1965)
Dies bought by Crown Silver
   Co., Inc.
Bibl. 127, 147   *Amston*

Amston Sterling

Martin Anatotte (c. 1818)
Philadelphia, Pa.
Bibl. 3

Adolph Ancker
   (c. 1806–1807)
Philadelphia, Pa.
Bibl. 3

Anco Silver Co.
   (c. 1920–1927)
New York, N.Y.
Bibl. 127

Anderson
(See Buckley & Anderson,
   Woolworth & Anderson)

—— **Anderson**
Greensboro, N.C.
Scott & Anderson (c. 1829)
Woolworth & Anderson
   (c. 1829–1830)
(might be James S.
   Anderson)
Bibl. 21

Anderson & Whitteker
   (c. 1831–1835)
Charleston, Va.
Henry C. Anderson
—— Whitteker
Bibl. 19

Albert A. Anderson
   (c. 1837)
Philadelphia, Pa.
Bibl. 3

Alex Anderson
   (c. 1860–1868)
Danville, Ky.
Bibl. 54, 93

Alexander J. Anderson
   (c. 1848)
Philadelphia, Pa.
Bibl. 3

Andrew Anderson
   (b. 1793)
Danville, Ky. (c. 1814–1844)
Bibl. 32, 68, 93

David Rush Anderson
   (b. 1795–d. 1855)
Cincinnati, Ohio (c. 1825)
Marietta, Ohio
Bibl. 34, 152

Edward Anderson
   (c. 1854, d. 1886)
Laurens, S.C.
H. C. Anderson & Co.
Bibl. 5

Henry C. Anderson
Charleston, Va.
   (c. 1828–1839)
Lewisburg, Va.
Anderson & Whitteker
   (c. 1831–1835)
H. C. Anderson & Co.
   (c. 1839)
Bibl. 19

L. D. Anderson Jly. Co.
   (c. 1910–1944)
Reading, Pa.
Bibl. 127   **L.D.A.**

Stephen Anderson
   (c. 1802)
Philadelphia, Pa.
Bibl. 3

Thomas & William
Anderson
   (c. 1814–1817)
Philadelphia, Pa.
Bibl. 3

William Anderson
   (c. 1746)
New York, N.Y. | W A |
Bibl. 4, 15, 22, 23, 25, 28,
   29, 35, 36, 44, 54, 83, 114,
   119, 124, 138

William S. Anderson
   (b. 1820–d. 1871)
Wilmington, N.C.
Brown & Anderson
   (c. 1850–1871)
Bibl. 21

Andras & Co. (c. 1800)
New York, N.Y.
Bibl. 25, 44, 124

| ANDRAS & CO |

Andras & Richard | A&R |
   (c. 1797–1799)
New York, N.Y.
Bibl. 15, 23, 25, 29, 36, 44,
   114, 124, 135, 138

William Andras (c. 1795)
New York, N.Y.
Bibl. 23, 25, 29, 36, 44, 124,
   135, 138

| ANDRAS |

Abraham Andreas
   (c. 1780)
Bethlehem, Pa.
Bibl. 36, 44

Abraham Andrew(s)
   (c. 1795–1796)
Philadelphia, Pa.
Bibl. 3, 23, 36, 44

John Andrew
   (b. 1747–d. 1791)
Salem, Mass.
Bibl. 2, 22, 23, 28, 29, 36,
   44, 91

| I. ANDREW |

| J. Andrew |

Elon Andrews
  (b. 1790–d. 1855)
Utica, N.Y.
Murdock & Andrews
  (c. 1822–1826,
  c. 1838–1849)
James Murdock & Co.
  (c. 1826–1838)
*Bibl. 15, 18, 20, 91, 124,
  135, 158*

F. B. Andrews (1875)
Oxford, Me.
Bibl. 105

Henry Andrews   H. A.
  (c. 1795–1800)
Philadelphia, Pa.
*Bibl. 3, 22, 23, 25, 28, 29,
  36, 44, 91, 114*

Henry Andrews   H A
  (c. 1830–1847)
Boston, Mass.
Haddock & Andrews
  (c. 1838–1847)
Bibl. 3, 6, 22, 23, 28, 44

John Andrews
  (b. 1749– d. 1791)
Salem, Mass.
Windham, Me.
Bibl. 28, 110, 114

  J ANDREWS

Jeremiah Andrews
  (c. 1817)
New York, N.Y. (c. 1774)
Philadelphia, Pa.
  (c. 1776–1780)
Savannah, Ga. (c. 1788)
Norfolk, Va. (c. 1791–1817)
*Bibl. 3, 17, 19, 22, 23, 36,
  44, 50, 91, 102, 114, 124,
  138*

  J ANDREWS

  J Andrews

  I ANDREWS

Joseph Andrews (c. 1800)
Norfolk, Va.
Bibl. 23, 25, 29, 36, 44, 114

  I ANDREWS   J. ANDREWS

Jr. Andrews (c. 1746)
Philadelphia, Pa.
Bibl. 28, 44

M. C. Andrews (1860)
Rockland, Me.
Bibl. 105

N. Andrus & Co.
  (c. 1834–1837)
New York, N.Y.
Nelson Andrus
Bibl. 15, 25, 44, 114, 124

  N ANDRUS & CO

Solomon Ange
  (b. 1788–d. 1861)
New York, N.Y.
  (1827–1828)
Cincinnati, Ohio
  (1834–1861)
Bibl. 15, 90, 124, 138

Angell & Holden (1870)
Providence, R.I.
Bibl. 108

James F. Angell (1860)
Providence, R.I.
Bibl. 108

W. H. Angell (1875)
S. Kingstown, Mass.
Bibl. 108

Joseph Anglaire
  (1827–1853)
New Orleans, La
Bibl. 141

James Angram
  (c. 1835–1836)
Albany, N.Y.
Bibl. 20, 124

William James Angus
  (c. 1841)
New York, N.Y.
Bibl. 15, 124, 138

Isaac Aniston (c. 1785)
Philadelphia, Pa.
Bibl. 3

C. H. Ankeny
  (c. 1868–1892)
Richmond and Lafayette,
  Ind.   ANKENY
Bibl. 133

William F. Annelly
  (c. 1850)
Philadelphia, Pa.
Bibl. 3, 23

Robert M. Anners
  (c. 1824)
Philadelphia, Pa.
Bibl. 3

Annin & Dreer
  (c. 1837–1841)
Philadelphia, Pa.
John Annin
Ferdinand J. Dreer
Bibl. 3

**Ansbey & McEwen
(McEuen)**
  (c. 1825)
Philadelphia, Pa.
George Ansbey
——— McEwen
Bibl. 3

George Ansbey
  (c. 1837–1850)
Philadelphia, Pa.
Ansbey & McEwen (c. 1825)
Bibl. 3

**(Monsieur) Jean B.
  Anthiaume** (c. 1790)
Gallipolis, Ohio
Bibl. 34

**Anthony & Carey (Carey
  & Anthony)** (c. 1837)
Cincinnati, Ohio
Bibl. 34, 152

Edwin Anthony
  (c. 1835–1836)
Troy, N.Y.
Bibl. 20, 124

Isaac Anthony
  (b. 1690–d. 1773)
Swansea, Mass.
Newport, R.I.

  I A

Bibl. 15, 25, 28, 54, 56, 94,
106, 110, 114

Isaac Anthony
Troy, N.Y. (c. 1807–1808)
Augusta, Ga. (c. 1812)
Bibl. 17, 20, 29, 44, 124

J. Anthony (c. 1815)
Washington, Ga.
Bibl. 17

Joseph Anthony
(See next entry)

Joseph Anthony Jr.
(b. 1762–d. 1814)
Philadelphia, Pa.
Bibl. 2, 3, 4, 15, 22, 23, 25,
28, 29, 36, 39, 44, 54, 81,
91, 102, 104, 114, 116, 122

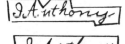

Joseph Anthony & Son
(c. 1810–1814)
Philadelphia, Pa.
Bibl. 3, 4, 22, 23, 25, 28, 29,
36, 44, 114

Lorenzo D. Anthony
(c. 1805)
Providence, R.I.
Bibl. 22, 23, 36, 44, 110

M. H. & T. Anthony
(c. 1814)
Philadelphia, Pa.
Michael H. Anthony (?)
Thomas Anthony (?)
Bibl. 36

Michael H. Anthony
(c. 1810–1814)

Philadelphia, Pa.
M. H. & T. Anthony
(c. 1814) (?)
Michael H. & Thomas
Anthony (c. 1816–1817)
Bibl. 3, 23, 36, 44

**Michael H. & Thomas
Anthony**
(c. 1816–1817)
Philadelphia, Pa.
Michael H. Anthony
Thomas Anthony
Bibl. 3, 23, 44

Susan B. Anthony
(See Millie B. Logan)

Thomas Anthony
(c. 1810)
Philadelphia, Pa.
M. H. & T. Anthony
(c. 1814) (?)
Michael H. & Thomas
Anthony (c. 1816–1817)
Bibl. 23, 36, 44

William Anthony
New York, N.Y. (c. 1800)
Ballston Spa, N.Y.
(c. 1809–1810)
Bibl. 20, 23, 36, 44, 124, 138

A. W. Antoine (1875)
Minot, Me.
Bibl. 105

Charles Antrim
(c. 1837–1847)
Philadelphia, Pa.
Bibl. 3

Ernest Antz (c. 1880)
New Orleans, La.
Bibl. 141

George Antz (1838–1854)
New Orleans, La.
Bibl. 141

Kenrick Anwyl (b. 1748)
Baltimore, Md. (c. 1775)
Bibl. 23, 28, 36, 38, 44

Apollo Silver Co.
(c. 1899–1904)
Became Bernard Rice's Sons

Dies bought by Garden
Silver Co.
Bibl. 127

Samuel App
(c. 1837–1850)
Philadelphia, Pa.
Bibl. 3, 91

George B. Appleton
Salem, Mass. (1855–1857)
Bibl. 15, 25, 44, 91, 106, 114

APPLETON

William Applewhite
Columbia, S.C.
(c. 1824–1828)
Camden, S.C.
(c. 1828–1837)
Bibl. 5

Joseph Arans (b. 1782)
New Orleans, La. (1822)
Bibl. 141

John Arbuckle (c. 1843)
Philadelphia, Pa.
Bibl. 3

Joseph Arbuckle
(c. 1847–1848)
Philadelphia, Pa.
Bibl. 3

John Archer (c. 1798)
Halifax, N.C.
Bibl. 21

**Archibald-Klement Co.,
Inc.** (c. 1909–1922)
Newark, N.J.
Successor to C. F. Kees &
Co.
Bibl. 127

Dumm Archibald
(c. 1837)
Philadelphia, Pa.
Bibl. 3

John Archibald (c. 1843)
Philadelphia, Pa.
Bibl. 3

John Archie (c. 1759)
New York, N.Y.
*Bibl. 22, 23, 28, 36, 44, 124,
138*

**Argentum Silver   DEKRA
Company**
(c. 1958–1973)
New York, N.Y.
Bibl. 127

Ariston Silversmith Corp.
(c. 1931)
New York, N.Y.
Bibl. 127   ⟨ARISTON⟩

D. P. Armer (c. 1850)
Richmond, Ky.
Bibl. 32, 54, 93

George Armitage
(c. 1800–1825)
Philadelphia, Pa.
Bibl. 3

Robert Armitage (c. 1797)
Charleston, S.C.
Bibl. 5

Nelson T. Arms
(c. 1837–1850)
Albany, N.Y.
Bibl. 20, 44, 124

T. N. Arms
(See preceding entry)
Bibl. 22, 23, 28

Allen Armstrong
(c. 1806–1817)
Philadelphia, Pa.
*Bibl. 3, 15, 23, 25, 28, 29,
36, 44, 54, 91, 95, 114*

| A Armstrong |
| A ARMSTRONG |

John Armstrong
(c. 1810–1813)
Philadelphia, Pa., New York,
N.Y. (c. 1814)
Bibl. 3, 4, 22, 23, 28, 36, 138

Thomas S. Armstrong
(c. 1839–1840)
New York, N.Y.
Bibl. 15, 124, 135

William Armstrong
(c. 1750, d. 1775)
Philadelphia, Pa.
Bibl. 23, 36, 44

D. Arn
Delaware (?)
Bibl. 30

| D. ARN |

John M. Arnault
(c. 1848–1850)
New York, N.Y.
Bibl. 23, 124, 138

—————— **Arnold**
(See Howell & Arnold)

George Arnold (c. 1820)
Uxbridge, Mass.
Bibl. 24, 89, 110

| G: ARNOLD |

H. B. Arnold
(c. 1840–1844)
Rome, N.Y.
Bibl. 15, 20, 44, 114, 124

| H. B. Arnold |

| H.B. Arnold. |

Jacob Arnold (c. 1848)
Philadelphia, Pa.
Bibl. 3

Peleg Arnold (1860–1875)
E. Greenwich, Conn.
Bibl. 108

Thomas Arnold
(b. 1739–d. 1828)
Newport, R.I.
(c. 1751–1828)
*Bibl. 22, 23, 29, 44, 54, 56,
94, 104, 110, 114*

| T.ARNOLD | | TA |

| ARNOLD |

Thomas Arnold (c. 1760)
Philadelphia, Pa.
*Bibl. 15, 25, 28, 36, 78, 91,
119*

| T A | | T ARNOLD |
| | ARNOLD |

John Arrison (c. 1837)
Philadelphia, Pa.
Bibl. 3

Arrowsmith Silver Corp.
(c. 1960–1966)
Brooklyn, N.Y.
Became Garden Silversmiths
Ltd.
Bibl. 127   ⟨ARROWSMITH STERLING⟩

Art Metal Studios
(1934–c. 1977)
Chicago, Ill.
Edmund Boker (b. 1886)
Ernest Gould
(b. 1884–d. 1954)
Successor to
Chicago Art Silver Shop
(1912–1918)
Art Silver Shop (1918–1934)
Bibl. 98, 127

Art Silver Shop
(See Art Metal Studios)

Art Stamping & Mfg. Co.
(c. 1909–1915)
Philadelphia, Penn.
Bibl. 127, 157

A.S. & M. CO.

**Artcraft Silversmith Co.,
Inc.** (c. 1927–1931)
New York, N.Y.
Bibl. 127 | ARTCRAFT STERLING |

William Arwin
(c. 1837–1838)
Albany, N.Y.
Bibl. 20, 124

Lawrence Ash
(c. 1762–1763)
Baltimore, Md. (c. 1773)
Philadelphia, Pa.
Bibl. 3, 38

Ashburn & Shannon
  (c. 1841)
Philadelphia, Pa.
James C. Ashburn (?)
Robert Shannon
Bibl. 3

James C. Ashburn
  (c. 1841–1850)
Philadelphia, Pa.
Ashburn & Shannon
  (c. 1841) (?)
Clements & Ashburn
  (c. 1847)
Bibl. 3

John Ashburner
  (c. 1840–1841)
Philadelphia, Pa.
Bibl. 3

James Ashman
  (c. 1831–1841)
Philadelphia, Pa.
Bibl. 3

James J. Ashman
  (c. 1839–1841)
Philadelphia, Pa.
Bibl. 3.

William Ashmead
  (c. 1797)
Philadelphia, Pa.
Bibl. 3, 22, 23, 28, 36, 44

Isaac Ashton
  (c. 1790–1797)
Philadelphia, Pa.
Bibl. 3

William Ashton
  (c. 1845–1873,
  d. 1873)
Charleston, S.C.
Bibl. 5

James Askew (1785)
Philadelphia, Pa.
Bibl. 44

James Askew (d. 1800)
Charleston, S.C.
  (c. 1776–1800)
Bibl. 5

Aspinwall & Griffing
  (c. 1831–1832)
Oswego, N.Y.
Chauncy B. Aspinwall
Edward Griffing
Bibl. 20, 90, 124

Chauncy B. Aspinwall
  (b. 1801–d. 1882)
Oswego, N.Y.
Cincinnati, Ohio
Aspinwall & Griffing
Bibl. 20, 90, 124

Gravling Astle (1860)
Providence, R.I.
Bibl. 108

Athenic
(See Gorham Manufacturing
  Co.)

Matthew Atherton
  (c. 1837–1840)
Philadelphia, Pa.
Bibl. 3

Nathan Atherton Jr.
  (c. 1825–1850)
Philadelphia, Pa.
Bibl. 3, 22, 23, 28, 36, 44

John H. Atkin
  (c. 1831–1838)
New York, N.Y.
Hinsdale & Atkin
  (c. 1830–1838)
Bibl. 15, 91, 124, 138

Alvin S. Atkins (c. 1850)
Rochester, N.Y.
Bibl. 20, 124

Atkinson Mfg. Co. (1895)
Biddeford, Me.
Bibl. 105

Anne Maria Atkinson
  (c. 1790–1816)
Baltimore, Md.
Bibl. 38

Harrison Atkinson
  (c. 1823–1824)
Philadelphia, Pa.
Bibl. 3

Isaac Atkinson
  (c. 1825–1833)
Philadelphia, Pa.
Bibl. 3, 23, 36, 44

Leroy Atkinson
  (w. 1824–1830)
Baltimore, Md.
Bibl. 38

**Matthew & William
  Atkinson** (w. 1787)
Baltimore, Md.
Bibl. 38

William O. Atkinson
  (c. 1848)
Louisville, Ky.
Bibl. 32, 93

Charles Atlee (c. 1837)
Philadelphia, Pa.
Bibl. 3, 23, 36, 44

Atmar & Monk
  (c. 1797–1799)
Charleston, S.C.
Ralph Atmar Jr.
James Monk
Bibl. 5

Ralph Atmar Jr.
  (c. 1793–1803)
Charleston, S.C.
Atmar & Monk
  (c. 1797–1799)
Bibl. 5, 102

Edward W. Atmore
  (c. 1846–1850)
Philadelphia, Pa.
Bibl. 3

J. A. (J.) Atterbury
  (c. 1799)
New Haven, Conn.
*Bibl. 22, 23, 28, 36, 44, 110,
  143*

Attleboro Chain Co.
  (c. 1909–1915)
Attleboro, Mass.
Bibl. 127, 157

Attleboro Mfg. Co.
  (c. 1898–1915)
Attleboro, Mass.
Bibl. 127, 157

Marshall Attmore
(c. 1821–1837)
Philadelphia, Pa.
Bibl. 3, 91

George E. Atwell
(c. 1830–1838)
Charleston, S.C.
Bibl. 5

A. H. Atwood (1875)
Portland, Me.
Bibl. 105

David Austen
(c. 1837–1839)
Philadelphia, Pa.
Bibl. 3, 23, 36, 44

————**Austin** (before 1750)
Boston, Mass.
Bibl. 70, 110

Austin & Boyer (Boyer & Austin)
(c. 1750–1770)
Boston, Mass.
Josiah Austin
Daniel Boyer
Bibl. 25, 36, 44, 114

I. Austin

Benjamin Austin (c. 1775)
Portsmouth, N.H.
Bibl. 22, 23, 28, 36, 44, 110, 125

Ebenezer Austin   E A
(b. 1733–d. 1818)
Hartford, Conn. (c. 1764)
New York, N.Y. (c. 1788)
Boston, Mass. (c. 1790)
Charlestown, Mass.
*Bibl. 2, 16, 22, 23, 25, 28,
29, 36, 44, 61, 92, 94, 106,
110, 114, 124*

E J AUSTIN   AUSTIN

Isaac Austin (d. 1801)
Philadelphia, Pa.
(c. 1781–1801)
Bibl. 3

James Austin (b. 1750)
Charlestown, Mass.
Bibl. 28, 44, 106, 110

John Austin
(b. 1757–d. 1825)
Philadelphia, Pa.
(c. 1802–1809)
Charleston, S. C.
(c. 1809–1820)
Bibl. 3, 5, 23, 25, 36, 44

I. AUSTIN

John Austin (c. 1770)
Hartford, Conn.
Bibl. 28, 110

Joseph Austin (c. 1740)
Hartford, Conn.
Bibl. 44, 110

Josiah John Austin   I A
(b. 1719–d. 1780)
Boston, Mass.   IA
(c. 1760–1770)
Charlestown, Mass.
Austin & Boyer
(c. 1750–1770)
Minott & Austin
(c. 1760–1769)
*Bibl. 2, 15, 22, 23, 25, 29,
36, 44, 50, 54, 69, 94, 106,
110, 114, 116*

J. AUSTIN

Nathaniel Austin
(b. 1734–d. 1818)
Boston, Mass.
Charlestown, Mass.
*Bibl. 15, 22, 23, 25, 28, 29,
36, 44, 91, 106, 110, 114*

N A
AUSTIN

Seymour Austin
(b. 1787–d. 1847)
Hartford, Conn.
Geauga County, Ohio
Bibl. 34, 110

Avery, Willis & Billis
(c. 1820)
Salisbury, N.Y.
Bibl. 20, 23, 36, 124

James Avery, Craftsman, Inc. (1954–present)
Kerrville, Texas
Bibl. 127

John Avery
(b. 1732–d. 1794)
Preston, Conn. (c. 1762)
*Bibl. 15, 16, 22, 23, 25, 28,
29, 36, 44, 61, 92, 94, 110,
114*

I A
I. AVERY
JA

John Avery Jr.
(b. 1755–d. 1815)
Preston, Conn. (c. 1776)
*Bibl. 16, 22, 23, 28, 36, 44,
91, 94, 110*

Robert Staunton Avery
(b. 1771–d. 1846)
Preston, Conn. (c. 1794)
*Bibl. 16, 22, 23, 28, 36, 44,
110*

Samuel Avery
(b. 1760–d. 1836)
Preston, Conn. (c. 1781)
*Bibl. 15, 16, 22, 23, 25, 28,
36, 44, 61, 91, 92, 94, 110,
114*

S A   SA
S AVERY

W. & B. Avery (c. 1820)
Salisbury, N.Y.
Bibl. 20, 23, 36

William Avery
(b. 1765–d. 1798)
Preston, Conn. (c. 1786)
*Bibl. 16, 22, 23, 28, 36, 44,
91, 110*

Avice & Pottier (c. 1818)
Savannah, Ga.
Francis J. Avice
Francis Pottier
Bibl. 17

Avice & Raulin
(c. 1818–1819)
Savannah, Ga.
Francis J. Avice
Anthony R. Raulin
Bibl. 17

Francis J. Avice
(c. 1818–1820)
Savannah, Ga.
Avice & Pottier (c. 1818)
Avice & Raulin
(c. 1818–1819)
Bibl. 17

Candide Avinenc
(b. 1804–d. 1861)
New Orleans, La.
(1832–1861)
Bibl. 141

Charles Avisse (w. 1812)
Baltimore, Md.
Bibl. 38

Avon
(See Weidlich Bros. Mfg.
Co.)

Hugues Avril
(b. 1776–d. 1842)
New Orleans, La.
(1811–1832)
Bibl. 141

Ayers (c. 1839)
Penn Yan, N.Y.
Ayers & Dunning
Bibl. 20

Ayers & Badger (c. 1835)
Elmira, N.Y.
Socrates Ayers (?)
A. M. Badger
Bibl. 20, 91, 124

Ayers & Dunning
(c. 1839)
Penn Yan, N.Y.
Bibl. 20, 124

Ayers & Hall (c. 1800)
Newburgh, N.Y.
Ebenezer B. Ayers
George W. Hall (?)
Bibl. 20, 124

B. Ayers (c. 1790)
Location unknown
Bibl. 24, 44

B. Ayers

Ebenezer Bryan Ayers
(c. 1799–1800)
Newburgh, N.Y.
Ayers & Hall (c. 1800)
Bibl. 20, 124

John Ayers (c. 1817–1819)
Philadelphia, Pa.
Bibl. 3

Socrates Ayers
(c. 1845–after 1850)
Elmira, N.Y.
Ayers & Badger (c. 1835) (?)
Bibl. 20, 91, 114, 124

Ayres & Beard
(See Beard & Ayres)

Ayres & Hiter (c. 1813)
Lexington, Ky.
Samuel Ayres
John G. Hiter
Bibl. 32

Ayres & Warden (c. 1817)
Philadelphia, Pa.
——— Ayres
——— Warden
Bibl. 3

E. Ayres & Company
(c. 1816–1828)
Louisville, Ky.
Ebenezer Bryam Ayres
Bibl. 32, 54, 68

Ebenezer Bryam Ayres
(c. 1816–1828)
Louisville, Ky.
E. Ayres & Company
Bibl. 32

Elias Ayres
(b. 1791–d. 1842)
Louisville, Ky.
Beard & Ayres
(c. 1828–1831)
Bibl. 32

Samuel Ayres
(b. 1767–d. 1824)
Lexington, Ky.
(c. 1790–1823)
Danville, Ky. (c. 1823–1824)
Ayres & Hiter (c. 1813)

*Bibl. 23, 25, 29, 32, 36, 44,
54, 84, 89, 91, 93, 114*

S AYRES . LEX. K

Thomas R. J. Ayres
(c. 1823–1861)
Danville, Ky.
*Bibl. 29, 32, 44, 54, 68, 88,
93*

T AYRES

B

B
(See Theophilus Bradbury)

B. & C. (c. 1815)
Location unknown
Bibl. 24

B & C

B & D
(See Barrington &
Davenport)

B & H
(See Brinsmaid & Hildreth)

B & I
(See Boyce & Jones)

B & J
(See Boyce & Jones)

B & K
(See Bailey & Kitchen)

B & M
(See Bradley & Merriman)

B & P
(See Barton & Porter)

B. & P. (c. 1800) [B & P]
New York State
Bibl. 24, 72

B & R
(See Brower & Rusher,
   Burnet & Ryder)

B & S
(See Beach & Sanford)

B & W
(See Beach & Ward)

B B
(See Barzillai Benjamin,
   Benjamin Benjamin,
   Binder Bros. Inc.,
   Benjamin Brenon,
   Benjamin Brenton,
   Benjamin Bunker,
   Benjamin Bussey)

B. B. & Co.
(See Barden, Blake & Co.)

B. B. S. Ld
(See Barker Bros. Silver Co.,
   Inc.)

B C
(See Beriah Chittenden)

B C G
(See Benjamin Clark
   Gilman)

B G
(See Baldwin Gardiner)

B G & Co.
(See B. Gardiner & Co.)

B H
(See Becht & Hartl, Inc.,
   Benjamin Hurd)

B L
(See Matthias Lamar,
   Benjamin Lemaire)

B P
(See Benjamin Pierpont)

B S
(See Bay State Silver Co.,
   Benjamin Sanderson,
   Bartholomew Schaats)

B W
(See Barstow & Williams,
   Billious Ward, Barnabas
   Webb, Barnard Wenman,
   Bancroft Woodcock,
   Benjamin Wynkoop Jr.)

Charles Babbitt
   (b. 1798–d. 1890)
Taunton, Mass.
Providence, R.I. (c. 1815)
Davis & Babbitt (c. 1815) (?)
*Bibl. 15, 25, 44, 91, 106,
   110, 114*

[C BABBITT]

Babcock & Co.
   (c. 1831–1833)
Philadelphia, Pa.
Bibl. 3

Charles Babcock
   (c. 1832–1833)
Albany, N.Y.
Bibl. 20, 124

George W. Babcock (1835)
Providence, R.I.
Bibl. 108

Samuel Babcock
   (b. 1788–d. 1857)
Middletown, Conn.
   (c. 1812)
Saybrook, Conn.
*Bibl. 16, 22, 23, 28, 29, 36,
   44, 92, 110, 114*

[Babcock]

Thomas Bacall
   (c. 1836–1850)
Boston, Mass.
Pear & Bacall (c. 1850)
Bibl. 23, 36, 44, 91

Valentine Bach (w. 1798)
Frederick, Md.
Bibl. 29, 38

Charles Bachelard
   (c. 1774)
Savannah, Ga.
Bibl. 17

Bachelder
Bachlader
Bachlander
(See Batchelder)

A. Bachman (c. 1848)
New York State
Bibl. 25, 44, 114, 124

Joseph Bachman
(1855-c. 1870)
New York, N.Y.
Bibl. 89

Bachrach & Freedman
   (c. 1896–1900)
New York, N.Y.
Became E. & J. Bass
Bibl. 114, 127, 157

Bachus
(See Backus)

**John Peter Francis
   Backes** (c. 1852–1858)
Charleston, S.C.
Bibl. 5

Delucine Backus (Bachus)
   (c. 1792)
New York, N.Y.
Cady & Backus
   (c. 1792–1796)
*Bibl. 22, 23, 25, 28, 29, 36,
   44, 114, 124, 138*

[D. Backus]   [D.Backus]

Simon Backus (d. 1805)
Burlington, Vt. (c. 1793)
Bibl. 54, 110

Bacon & Minter
   (c. 1855–1860)
Indianapolis, Ind.
Robert Bacon
George W. Minter
Bibl. 133

Bacon & Smith (c. 1830)
Boston, Mass.
   (c. 1845–1857)
Bibl. 28, 91

[BACON & SMITH]

Robert Bacon
Indianapolis, Ind.
Bacon & Minter
   (c. 1855–c. 1859)
Bibl. 133

Samuel Bacon (w. 1752)
Annapolis, Md.
Bibl. 38

Badger & Lillie (c. 1837)
Elmira, N.Y.
A. M. Badger
J. H. Lillie
Bibl. 20, 124

A. M. Badger (c. 1836)
Elmira, N.Y.
Ayers & Badger (c. 1835)
Badger & Lillie (c. 1837) (?)
Bibl. 20, 124

John Baen (c. 1849–1850)
Philadelphia, Pa.
Bibl. 3

Agnes Baer (c. 1933–1980)
St. Louis, Mo.
Bibl. 155

William Baggs (c. 1850)
Philadelphia, Pa.
Bibl. 3, 23

Abbot G. Bagley
   (c. 1840–1842)
Buffalo, N.Y.
Bibl. 20, 124

Benjamin Bagnall
   (c. 1749–1753)
Philadelphia, Pa.
Bibl. 3

Benjamin Bagnall
   (c. 1770)
Boston, Mass.
Bibl. 3

Lewis Baielle (c. 1799)
Baltimore, Md.
Bibl. 22, 28, 36

Bailey & Brothers
   (c. 1846–1852)
Utica, N.Y.
Hugh Bailey
James Bailey

Thomas Bailey
William Bailey
John J. Brown
Thomas C. Stephens
Bibl. 18, 20, 124, 135, 158

| BAILEY & BROTHERS |

Bailey & Co. (1846–1878)
Philadelphia, Pa.
Joseph T. Bailey
F. W. Bailey
Jeremiah Robbins
James Gallagher
Joseph T. Bailey II
Bibl. 3, 15, 25, 44, 79, 91,
   104, 114, 122, 127, 135

| BAILEY & CO. |

Bailey & Kitchen
   (1832–1846)
Philadelphia, Pa.
Joseph T. Bailey
Andrew B. Kitchen
Became Bailey & Co.
   (1846–1878)
Bailey, Banks & Biddle
   (1878–1894)
Bailey, Banks & Biddle Co.
   (1894–present)
Bibl. 3, 15, 28, 29, 39, 44,
   72, 91, 104, 114, 122, 127,
   135

| B & K |

| BAILEY & KITCHEN |

Bailey & Owen
   (c. 1848–1850)
Abbeville, S.C.
Edward S. Bailey
M. T. Owen
Bibl. 5

Bailey & Parker (c. 1845)
Owen, Vt.
Bibl. 23

Bailey & Parmenter
   (c. 1849)
Rutland, Vt.
Bibl. 23

Bailey, Banks & Biddle
   (1878–1894)
(See Bailey, Banks & Biddle
   Co.)

**Bailey, Banks & Biddle
   Co.** (1894–present)
Philadelphia, Pa.
James Trowbridge Bailey
Andrew B. Kitchen
George Banks
Samuel Biddle
Bailey & Kitchen
   (1832–1846)
Bailey & Company
   (1846–1878)
Bailey, Banks & Biddle
   (1878–1894)
Bibl. 113, 127, 130, 131

B. M. Bailey
   (b. 1824–d. 1913)
New York, N.Y.
Ludlow, Vt. (1848–1852)
Rutland, Vt. (1852–1875)
Bibl. 23, 25, 44

Benjamin Bailey
   (c. 1800–1820)
Boston, Mass.
Bibl. 22, 23, 28, 36, 44, 110

Ebenezer Eaton Bailey
   (d. 1862)
Claremont, N.H.
E. E. & S. C. Bailey
   (c. 1825–1830)
Bibl. 15, 23, 25, 91, 105,
   110, 114, 125

| E. E BAILEY |

E. E. BAILEY & CO.

E. E. & S. C. Bailey
   (1825–1862)
West Unity, N.H.
   (1825–1844)
Claremont, N.H.
   (1836–1862)
Bibl. 25, 28, 29, 36, 44, 91,
   104, 105, 114, 125

| E E & S C BAILEY |

E. L. Bailey (c. 1835)
Woodstock, Vt. (?)
Bibl. 25, 44, 114

| E. L. BAILEY & CO. |

E. S. Bailey & Co.
(c. 1854)
Newberry, S. C.
Edward S. Bailey
Bibl. 5

Edward Bailey (b. 1753)
Baltimore, Md. (c. 1774)
Bibl. 23, 28, 36, 38, 44

Edward S. Bailey
Abbeville, S. C. (c. 1847)
Newberry, S. C.
(c. 1852–1860)
Bailey & Owen
(c. 1848–1850)
E. S. Bailey & Co. (c. 1854)
Bibl. 5

Gamaliel Bailey
Mt. Holly, N.J.
(c. 1807–1821)
Philadelphia, Pa.
(c. 1828–1833)
Bibl. 3, 46, 54, 90

Henry Bailey | H B |
(c. 1780–1808)
Boston, Mass.
*Bibl. 22, 25, 28, 36, 44, 72,
110, 114*

Hugh Bailey (b. 1830)
Utica, N.Y.
Bailey & Brothers
(c. 1846–1852)
Bibl. 18, 20, 124, 158

I. Bailey
(See John Bailey)

Joseph Trowbridge Bailey
(d. 1854)
Philadelphia, Pa.
Bailey & Kitchen
(c. 1832–1846)
Bailey & Co. (c. 1846–1878)
Bibl. 3

James Bailey (b. 1825)
Utica, N.Y.
Bailey & Brothers
(c. 1846–1852)
Bibl. 18, 20, 124, 158

**John Bailey (Baily)
(Bayly) (Bayley)**
Philadelphia, Pa.

(c. 1754–1783)
New York, N.Y.
(c. 1762–1771)
*Bibl. 3, 15, 22, 23, 25, 28,
29, 36, 39, 44, 54, 91, 102,
114, 124, 138*

Loring Bailey | L B |
(b. 1740–d. 1814)
Hingham, Mass. (b. 1780)
Hull, Mass.
*Bibl. 22, 23, 28, 29, 36, 44,
54, 110, 114*

Lyman C. Bailey (1860)
Calais, Me.
Bibl. 105

Roswell H. Bailey
(b. 1804–d. 1886)
Woodstock, Vt. (1839–1872)
Claremont, N.H.
*Bibl. 15, 23, 25, 28, 29, 36,
91, 114, 125*

| R. H. BAILEY |

Samuel P. Bailey
(b. 1822–d. 1863)
Woodstock, Vt. (c. 1851)
Indianapolis, Ind.
(c. 1851–1860)
Bibl. 23, 133

**Simon (Simeon) A. Bailey
(Bayley?)** (c. 1789)
New York, N.Y.
Bibl. 22, 23, 28, 36, 44, 124

T. A. Bailey (c. 1843–1845)
Philadelphia, Pa.
Bibl. 3

Thomas Bailey (b. 1826)
Utica, N.Y.
Bailey & Brothers
(c. 1846–1852)
Bibl. 18, 20, 124, 135, 158

T. BAILEY

Westcott E. J. Bailey
(c. 1842)
Philadelphia, Pa.
Bibl. 3

William Bailey
(See William Baily, William
Baily Jr.)

William Bailey (b. 1818)
Utica, N.Y.
Bailey & Brothers
(c. 1846–1852)
*Bibl. 18, 20, 25, 44, 114,
124, 158*

Baily
(See also Bailey)

William Baily (Bailey)
(c. 1820–1850)
Philadelphia, Pa.
New York, N.Y. (c. 1810) (?)
Bibl. 3, 15, 29, 36, 44, 114

   W BAILY

William Baily Jr. (Bailey)
(1816–1843)
Philadelphia, Pa.
Bibl. 3, 15, 44, 72, 91

Henry Bain (c. 1849)
Philadelphia, Pa.
Bibl. 3

——— **Baird** (c. 1805)
Raleigh, N.C.
Might be David Baird.
Bibl. 21

David Baird (c. 1804)
Raleigh, N.C.
Glass & Baird
Bibl. 21

Pleasant H. Baird
Paris, Ky.
(c. 1813–1817)
Maysville, Ky.
(c. 1817–1838)
Bibl. 32, 54, 68

Pleasant H. Baird
(c. 1802)
Petersburg, Va.
Bibl. 19

Baker
(See Baldwin & Baker,
   Knorr & Baker)

—————— **Baker** (c. 1765)
Boston, Mass.
Bibl. 28, 44

**Baker-Manchester Mfg.
   Co.**
   (c. 1914–1930)
Providence, R.I.
Bibl. 127, 135, 147

Baker & Shriver
   (c. 1837–1841)
Philadelphia, Pa.
Edwin G. A. Baker
Thomas H. Shriver
Bibl. 3

Anson Baker
   (c. 1820–1837)
New York, N.Y.
*Bibl. 15, 22, 23, 36, 44, 124,
   138*

Benjamin H. Baker
   (c. 1823–1825)
Philadelphia, Pa.
Bibl. 3

E. Baker
(See Eleazer Baker)

E. Baker (1740–1790)
New York, N.Y.
Bibl. 29

| E. BAKER |

Edward Baker (1860)
Belfast, Me.
Bibl. 105

Edwin G. A. Baker
   (c. 1837–1850)
Philadelphia, Pa.
Baker & Shriver
   (c. 1837–1841)
Bibl. 3

Eleazer Baker
   (b. 1764–d. 1849)
Ashford, Conn.

*Bibl. 15, 23, 25, 36, 44, 54,
   61, 91, 92, 110, 114*

| E BAKER |

Elias Baker
   (b. 1815–d. 1874)
New Brunswick, N.J.
   (c. 1840)
Bibl. 46

George Baker | G. BAKER |
Providence, R. I.
   (1824–1867)
Salem, Mass.
*Bibl. 15, 22, 23, 25, 28, 29,
   36, 44, 56, 91, 94, 110,
   114*

George A. Baker
   (c. 1841–1843)
Philadelphia, Pa.
Bibl. 3

George M. Baker (c. 1840)
Philadelphia, Pa.
Bibl. 3

J. G. A. Baker (c. 1835)
Philadelphia, Pa.
Bibl. 3

J. M. S. Baker
   (c. 1828–1831)
Philadelphia, Pa.
Bibl. 3

James M. Baker (c. 1842)
Philadelphia, Pa.
Bibl. 3

L. Baker (c. 1821)
Batavia, N.Y.
Bibl. 20, 124

L. Baker & Co. (c. 1826)
Auburn, N.Y.
Bibl. 20, 124

Nehemiah Baker (c. 1816)
Philadelphia, Pa.
Plattsburg, N.Y.
Bibl. 3, 20, 124

S. Baker (c. 1830–1840)
Location unknown
Bibl. 15

| S BAKER |

Samuel Baker
   (b. 1787–d. 1858)
New Brunswick, N.J.
   (c. 1822)
Bibl. 46, 54

Stephen Baker
   (c. 1817–1818)
Wilmington, N.C.
Bibl. 22, 91, 110, 114

Stephen Baker
   (b. 1787–d. 1856)
New York, N.Y.
   (c. 1819–1825)
*Bibl. 25, 44, 91, 114, 124,
   138*

| S. BAKER |

Balch & Fryer (c. 1784)
Albany, N.Y.
Joseph Balch
John W. Fryer
*Bibl. 4, 20, 22, 23, 28, 36,
   44, 124*

Ebenezer Balch
   (b. 1723–d. 1808)
Hartford, Conn. (c. 1744)
Wethersfield, Conn.
Boston, Mass.
*Bibl. 16, 22, 23, 25, 28, 29,
   36, 44, 61, 92, 94, 110,
   114*

| E. BALCH |

Baldwin
(See Downing & Baldwin,
   Shinn & Baldwin, Stiles &
   Baldwin)

Baldwin & Baker
   (c. 1817)
Providence, R.I.
Bibl. 22, 23, 28, 36, 44, 110

Baldwin & Co.
   (c. 1840–1869)
Newark, N.J.
New York, N.Y.
*Bibl. 23, 25, 36, 44, 102,
   114, 124, 127, 135, 138*

Baldwin & Jones (c. 1813)
Boston, Mass.
Jabez L. Baldwin
John B. Jones

Bibl. 4, 15, 22, 23, 25, 28,
29, 36, 44, 110, 114, 155

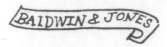

BALDWIN & JONES

Baldwin & Miller Inc.
(1920–present)
Newark, N.J.   **B & M**
Fred W. Miller, Sr.
Milton Baldwin
Bibl. 127

Baldwin & Smith
(1850–1853)
Newark, N. J.
Samuel Baldwin
Richard Smith
Bibl. 91, 135

Baldwin & Storrs
(c. 1792–1794)
Northampton, Mass.
Jedediah Baldwin
Nathan Storrs
Bibl. 41, 44, 84, 91, 110

Baldwin, Ford & Co.
(c. 1896–1904)
New York, N.Y.
Became Ford & Carpenter
(c. 1904–1915)
Cohen & Rosenberg
(c. 1915–1943)
Bibl. 114, 127, 157

Baldwin, Miller Co., Inc.
(1883–present)
Indianapolis, Ind.
Bibl. 127

     B. M. CO.

E. J. Baldwin
(c. 1851–1859)
Columbus, Ohio
Indianapolis, Ind.
Bibl. 133

E.J. BALDWIN & CO.

Ebenezer Baldwin
(c. 1810)
Hartford, Conn.   `BALDWIN`
Bibl. 15, 23, 25, 36, 44, 92,
110, 114

Edgar Baldwin
(c. 1848–c. 1850)
Troy, N.Y.
Bibl. 20, 124

H. E. Baldwin & Co.
(c. 1825)
New Orleans, La.
Bibl. 15, 24, 44, 104, 114

Isaac Baldwin (c. 1825)
Newark, N.J.
Taylor & Baldwin (c. 1825)
Bibl. 54

J. & S. Baldwin
(c. 1861–c. 1862)
Newark, N. J.
John Baldwin
Samuel Baldwin
Bibl. 15, 91, 110, 114

`J. & S. BALDWIN`

Jabez L. Baldwin
(b. 1777–d. 1819)
Boston, Mass. (c. 1813)
Salem, Mass.
Baldwin & Jones (c. 1813)
Bibl. 22, 23, 25, 28, 29, 36,
44, 54, 91, 102, 104, 110,
114, 125

`J. BALDWIN`   `BALDWIN`

Jedediah Baldwin
(b. 1768–d. 1849)
Northampton, Mass. (1791)
Norwich, Conn. (1791)
Hanner, N.H. (1793)
Fairfield, N.Y. (1811)
Monisville, N.Y.
(1817–1820)
Rochester, N.Y. (1834–1844)
Stiles & Baldwin
(c. 1791–1792)

Baldwin & Storrs
(c. 1792–1794)
Bibl. 15, 20, 22, 23, 25, 28,
29, 36, 41, 44, 84, 91, 110,
114, 124, 125

`J. BALDWIN`

Jedediah & Storrs
Baldwin (c. 1800)
Rochester, N.Y.
(probably Baldwin & Storrs)
Bibl. 25

Jobey Baldwin (c. 1805)
Salem, Va.
Bibl. 19

Joseph Baldwin
(c. 1823–1824)
Philadelphia, Pa.
Bibl. 3

Matthias Baldwin
(c. 1819–1822)
Philadelphia, Pa.
Bibl. 3

S. Baldwin (c. 1810)
Boston, Mass.
Bibl. 22, 110   `S BALDWIN`

Samuel Baldwin
(c. 1850–1853)
Newark, N. J.
Baldwin & Smith
Bibl. 89, 91, 135

Stanley S. Baldwin
(c. 1820–1837)
New York, N.Y.
Bibl. 15, 23, 25, 29, 36, 44,
91, 114, 124, 135

`STANLEY S BALDWIN`

Ball
(See Jones, Low(s) & Ball)

Ball, Black & Co.
(c. 1851–1876)
New York, N.Y.
Henry Ball
William Black
Bibl. 15, 23, 25, 44, 54, 78,
104, 114, 116, 122, 124,
135, 138

`BALL, BLACK & CO.`

Ball & Heald
(c. 1811–1812)
Baltimore, Md.
William Ball
J. S. Heald
Bibl. 15, 25, 29, 38, 114

Ball, Tompkins & Black
(c. 1839–1851)
New York, N.Y.
Henry Ball
Erastus O. Tompkins
William Black
Bibl. 15, 22, 23, 36, 44, 78,
91, 95, 114, 116, 122, 124,
135

Albert Ball (d. 1875)
Poughkeepsie, N.Y.
(c. 1832–1835)
Bibl. 20, 124

Calvin S. Ball (b. 1798)
Pompey, N.Y. (c. 1825)
Bibl. 20, 124

Calvin S. Ball Jr. (c. 1850)
Syracuse, N.Y.
Stone & Ball
Bibl. 20, 124

Charles Ball
(c. 1840–1848)
Poughkeepsie, N.Y.
Bibl. 20, 124

David Ball (c. 1845–1846)
Rochester, N.Y.
Bibl. 20, 41, 44, 124

Edward Ball Co.
(c. 1918–1919)
New York, N.Y.
Bibl. 127

Gideon I. Ball (c. 1832)
Buffalo, N.Y.
Bibl. 20, 124

Henry Ball (c. 1833–1837)
New York, N.Y.
Marquand & Co.
(c. 1834–1839)
Ball, Tompkins & Black
(c. 1839–1851)

Ball, Black & Co.
(c. 1851–1876)
Bibl. 15, 23, 36, 44, 138

John Ball
Philadelphia, Pa. (c. 1760)
Concord, Mass.
(c. 1763–1767)
Boston, Mass. (c. 1770)
Bibl. 15, 22, 23, 25, 28, 29,
36, 44, 50, 91, 94, 110,
114, 124

S. Ball (c. 1826)
Black Rock, N.Y.
Bibl. 20

S. S. Ball (w. 1838)
Boston, Mass.
John B. Jones & Co.
Low(s), Ball & Co. (?)
Jones, Ball & Poor
Jones, Ball & Co.
Bibl. 28, 44

Sheldon Ball
(w. 1821–1836)
Buffalo, N.Y.
Bibl. 20, 25, 44, 114, 124

True M. Ball
(b. 1815–d. 1890)
Boston, Mass.
Bibl. 28, 44, 91, 104

William Ball
(b. 1729–d. 1810)
Philadelphia, Pa.
Bibl. 3, 4, 15, 22, 23, 25, 28,
29, 36, 39, 44, 91, 102,
114, 122

William Ball Jr.
(b. 1763–d. 1815)
Baltimore, Md.
Johnson & Ball
(c. 1785–1790)
Ball & Heald (c. 1811–1812)

Bibl. 4, 15, 22, 25, 28, 29,
38, 44, 91, 95, 104, 114,
122

William H. Ball
Utica, N.Y.
Bingham, Ball & Co.
(?–1833)
Bibl. 18, 20, 124

James Ballantine
(c. 1772–1785)
Norfolk, Va.
Skinker & Ballantine
(c. 1772–)
Bibl. 19

The Ballou Mfg. Co.
(c. 1915–1927)
Attleboro, Mass.
Bibl. 127

Baltes-Chance Co., Inc.
(c. 1920–1927)
Became Baltes Mfg. Co.
(c. 1927)
Bibl. 127

Baltimore Silversmiths
Mfg. Co.
(c. 1903–1905)
Baltimore, Md.
Frank M. Schofield
Became Heer-Schofield Co.
(c. 1905–1928)
Frank M. Schofield Co.
(c. 1928–1930)
Schofield Co. (c. 1930)
Schofield Co., Inc.
(c. 1933–1967)
Bought by Stieff Co. (1967)
Bibl. 127, 157

Baltimore Sterling Silver Co. (1892–1904)
Baltimore, Md.
(See Kirk Stieff Company)
Became Stieff Company
(1904)
Bibl. 114, 127, 128, 131, 157

Adrian Bancher
(See Adrian Bancker)

Adrian Bancker
(b. 1703–d. 1772)
New York, N.Y.
*Bibl. 2, 4, 22, 23, 25, 28, 29,
35, 44, 54, 91, 95, 102,
114, 119, 124, 135, 138,
139*

Bancroft, Redfield & Rice
(c. 1857–1865)
New York, N. Y.
Became Redfield & Rice
Bibl. 127

Bangs
(See Dunbar & Bangs)

John J. Bangs
(c. 1825–1840)
Cincinnati, Ohio
*Bibl. 23, 24, 25, 34, 36, 44,
54, 90, 114, 152*

J. J BANGS

Benjamin B. Banker
(c. 1834–1836)
Albany, N.Y.
Bibl. 20, 124

Joseph Banks (c. 1819)
Philadelphia, Pa.
Bibl. 3

John Banstein (c. 1791)
Philadelphia, Pa.
Bibl. 3

Edward Baptista
(c. 1841–1843)
New York, N.Y.
Bibl. 15, 124, 138

Jean Baptiste (c. 1807)
Charleston, S.C.
Bibl. 5

C. G. Barbeck (c. 1835)
Philadelphia, Pa.
Bibl. 3

J. C. Barber
(c. 1844–1846)
Philadelphia, Pa.
Bibl. 3

James Barber
(c. 1842–1850)
Philadelphia, Pa.
Bibl. 3

Lemuel D. Barber
(c. 1850)
Syracuse, N.Y.
Bibl. 20, 23, 124

William Barber (c. 1843)
Hartford, Conn.
Bibl. 23, 151

Stephen Barbere (c. 1841)
Philadelphia, Pa.
Bibl. 3

Theon Barberet (c. 1822)
New Orleans, La.
Bibl. 23, 36, 44

G. Barbier (c. 1837–1842)
Philadelphia, Pa.
Bibl. 3

Peter Barbier
(c. 1823–1824)
Philadelphia, Pa.
Bibl. 3, 23, 36, 44

Stephen Barbier (c. 1847)
Philadelphia, Pa.
Bibl. 3

Stephen P. Barbier
(c. 1810–1843)
Philadelphia, Pa.
Bibl. 3

Charles M. Barchett
(c. 1824)
Clarksburg, Va.
Bibl. 19

James Barclay (c. 1848)
Philadelphia, Pa.
Bibl. 3

Orin Barclay (c. 1849)
Philadelphia, Pa.
Bibl. 3

**Bard & Hoffman (Bird &
Hoffman)** (c. 1837)
Philadelphia, Pa.
Conrad Bard (Bird)
Christian Frederick Hoffman
Bibl. 3, 4, 22, 23, 36, 44

Bard & Lamont
(c. 1841–1845)
Philadelphia, Pa.
Conrad Bard
Robert Lamont
*Bibl. 3, 4, 22, 23, 25, 28, 29,
44, 54, 91, 114, 116*

BARD & LAMONT

Conrad Bard & Son
(c. 1850)
Philadelphia, Pa.
Conrad Bard
*Bibl. 3, 4, 22, 23, 28, 44, 95,
114*

Conrad Bard (Bird)
(c. 1825–1854)
Philadelphia, Pa.
Bard & Hoffman (c. 1837)
Bard & Lamont
(c. 1841–1845)
C. Bard & Son
*Bibl. 3, 15, 20, 23, 25, 29,
36, 44, 54, 91*

C.BARD

J. Bard (c. 1800)
Philadelphia, Pa.
Bibl. 22, 23, 36, 44

Connard Bardeer
(c. 1830–1833)
Philadelphia, Pa.
Bibl. 3, 23, 36, 44

Barden, Blake & Co.
(c. 1896–1915)
Plainville, Mass.
Attleboro, Mass.

Became Chapman & Barden
Bibl. 114, 127, 157

B. B. & CO.
STERLING.

George Bardick
(c. 1790–1802)
Philadelphia, Pa.
Bibl. 23, 25, 29, 36, 44, 114

G B

John Bardick
(c. 1805–1808)
Philadelphia, Pa.
Bibl. 3, 23, 36, 44

Stephen Bardon (c. 1785)
Philadelphia, Pa.
Bibl. 3, 23, 36, 44

Thomas Barge (w. 1848)
Philadelphia, Pa.
Bibl. 3

George Barger (w. 1844)
Philadelphia, Pa.
Bibl. 3

Willam Baria (c. 1805)
New York, N.Y.
Bibl. 23, 36, 44, 124, 138

Barker & Mumford
(c. 1825)
Newport, R.I.
Bibl. 25, 28, 44, 110, 114

BARKER &
MUMFORD

Barker Bros. Silver Co.,
Inc.
New York, N.Y.
William & Matthias Barker
(c. 1860, Birmingham,
England)
American branch (1897)
Bibl. 127

Ezra W. Barker (1875)
Corinth, Me.
Bibl. 105

James F. Barker (c. 1826)
Palmyra, N.Y.
Bibl. 20, 124

Joseph Barker (1860)
Gorham, Me.
Bibl. 105

J. Barklay (w. 1812–1824)
Baltimore, Md.
J. & S. Barklay
(1812–1816)
Bibl. 38

J. & S. Barklay
(1812–1816)
Baltimore, Md.
Bibl. 38

Edward C. Barlow
(c. 1850)
Georgetown, Ky.
Bibl. 32, 54, 68, 93

James Madison Barlow
(c. 1812)
Lexington, Ky.
Bibl. 32, 54, 68, 93

S. S. Barnaby
(c. 1852–1853)
Utica, N.Y.
Bibl. 18, 124, 158

Barnard
(See Morrow & Barnard)

E. Barnard (c. 1834)
Geneva, N.Y.
Bibl. 20, 124, 138

Samuel Barnard
(c. 1844–1845)
Utica, N.Y.
Bibl. 18, 20, 124, 158

Abraham Barnes (c. 1716)
Boston, Mass.
Bibl. 22, 23, 28, 36, 44, 110

James Barnes
(c. 1841–1844)
Philadelphia, Pa.
Bibl. 3

James M. Barnes
(c. 1845–1850)

Philadelphia, Pa.
Bibl. 3

James P. Barnes
(c. 1848–1869)
Louisville, Ky.
Bibl. 32, 54, 68, 91, 93

Moses D. Barnes
(d. 1858)
Macon, Ga.
Bibl. 17

Archibald Barnet
(w. 1781)
Baltimore, Md.
Bibl. 38

Joseph Barnett
(See Joseph Barrett)

Barney & Valentine
(c. 1850)
Syracuse, N.Y.
George Barney
Dennis Valentine
Bibl. 20, 124

Edmund G. Barney (1875)
Brunswick, Me.
Bibl. 105

George Barney (c. 1850)
Syracuse, N.Y.
Barney & Valentine
Bibl. 20, 124

James Barney (c. 1840)
Syracuse, N.Y.
Bibl. 20, 124

Robert Barnhill
(c. 1776–1778)
Philadelphia, Pa.
Bibl. 3

Barnhurst & Walker
(1814)
Philadelphia, Pa.
Joseph Barnhurst
———— Walker
Bibl. 3

Joseph Barnhurst
Philadelphia, Pa.
Barnhurst & Walker (1814)
Bibl. 3

Laurent Baron
(c. 1841–c. 1850)
Rochester, N.Y.
Bibl. 20

Louis (Lewis) Baron
(b. 1792)
Rochester, N.Y.
(c. 1841–1867)
Bibl. 11, 20, 44, 124

John J. Barralet
(w. 1794–1798)
Philadelphia, Pa.
Bibl. 3

Joseph J. Barras
(w. 1833–1850)
Philadelphia, Pa.
Bibl. 3

Joshua L. Barrass
(w. 1837)
Philadelphia, Pa.
Bibl. 3

James Barret (c. 1717)
Norwich, Conn.
Bibl. 23, 36, 44

James Barret(t) (c. 1805)
New York, N.Y.
Bibl. 22, 25, 28, 29, 36, 44, 114, 124

Robert Barret(t)
(b. 1765–d. 1821)
Green County, Ky.
(c. 1816–1818)
Greensburg, Ky.
Bibl. 32, 54, 68, 93

Joseph Barrett (Barnett)
(c. 1753)
Nantucket Island, Mass.
Bibl. 11, 14, 110

J BARRETT

Samuel Barrett
(c. 1760–1800)
Hingham, Mass.
Hull, Mass.
Nantucket, Mass.

Providence, R.I.
Bibl. 2, 12, 22, 23, 25, 28, 36, 44, 72, 91, 110, 114

David Barriere
(w. 1799–1817)
Baltimore, Md.
Bibl. 25, 29, 38, 44, 114

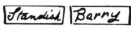

George Barringer (c. 1842)
St. Louis, Mo.
Bibl. 54

Barrington & Davenport
(c. 1806–1807)
Philadelphia, Pa.
——— Barrington
Robert Davenport
Bibl. 3, 23, 25, 29, 36, 44, 114

Joseph Barrington
Dumfries, Va. (c. 1792)
Salisbury, N.C. (c. 1826)
Tarboro, N.C. (c. 1832)
Bibl. 19, 21

T. Barrington (c. 1839)
Tarboro, N.C.
Bibl. 21

Henry Barrow
(c. 1833–1841)
New York, N.Y.
Bibl. 15, 124, 138

Samuel Barrow (c. 1771)
Philadelphia, Pa.
Bibl. 3

H. F. Barrows & Co.
(c. 1851–present)
North Attleboro, Mass.
Henry F. Barrows
James Sturdy
Bibl. 114, 127

James Madison Barrows
(b. 1809)
Tolland, Conn. (w. 1832)
Eddy & Barrows (c. 1832)
(?)
Bibl. 15, 16, 22, 23, 25, 28, 29, 36, 44, 91, 92, 114

J. M. BARROWS

Barrowss
(See Twedy & Barrowss)

Ruth Barry (c. 1920–1942)
St. Louis, Mo.
Bibl. 155

Standish Barry
(b. 1763–d. 1844)
Baltimore, Md.
(w. 1784–1810)
Rice & Barry (c. 1785–1787)
Bibl. 15, 22, 23, 25, 28, 29, 36, 38, 39, 44, 54, 72, 78, 91, 95, 114

Standish   Barry

BARRY   S.B

William Barry
Philadelphia, Pa.
(c. 1801–1802)
New York, N.Y. (c. 1803)
Charleston, S.C. (c. 1809)
Bibl. 3, 5, 138

Barstow & Williams
(c. 1888–1904)
Providence, R.I.
Became N. Barstow & Co.
(c. 1904)
Bibl. 127

N. Barstow & Co.
(c. 1904–1915)
Providence, R.I.
Successor to Barstow & Williams
Bibl. 127, 157

Charles Barthe (c. 1750)
Detroit, Mich.
Bibl. 58

Charles Bartholomew
(w. 1843–1846)
Philadelphia, Pa.
Bibl. 3

John Bartholomew
(w. 1846–1848)
Philadelphia, Pa.
Bibl. 3

Joseph Bartholomew
(w. 1818)
Philadelphia, Pa.
Bibl. 3

Joseph Bartholomew
(w. 1833–1835)
Philadelphia, Pa.
Bibl. 3, 23, 36, 44

Leroux Bartholomew
(See Bartholomew Le Roux)

Roswell Bartholomew
(b. 1781–d. 1830)
Hartford, Conn.
Ward & Bartholomew
(c. 1804–1809)
Ward, Bartholomew &
Brainard (c. 1809–1830)
*Bibl. 16, 22, 23, 25, 28, 36,
44, 91, 92, 110, 114*

Israel Bartlet(t)
(b. 1748–d. 1838)
Haverhill, Mass.
Newbury, Mass.
Bibl. 15, 25, 44, 91, 110, 114

Bartlett & Knapp (1860)
Providence, R.I.
Bibl. 108

Asa Bartlett (1875)
Woonsocket, R.I.
Bibl. 108

Edward Bartlett (c. 1833)
Philadelphia, Pa.
Bibl. 23, 36

Edward M. Bartlett
(w. 1843–1850)
Philadelphia, Pa.
Bibl. 3, 44

Nathanial Bartlet(t)
(c. 1760)
Concord, Mass.
*Bibl. 23, 25, 28, 29, 36, 44,
72, 91, 94, 110, 114*

N BARTLETT

Samuel Bartlett
(b. 1752–d. 1821)
Boston, Mass.
Concord, Mass.
*Bibl. 4, 15, 22, 23, 25, 28,
29, 36, 44, 54, 69, 91, 94,
110, 114*

S.B.   SB

S.BARTLETT

S. Bartley (c. 1841)
Philadelphia, Pa.
Bibl. 3, 23

Samuel Bartley
(b. 1788, w. 1801)
Baltimore, Md.
Bibl. 29, 38

Barton & Butler
(c. 1831–1832)
Utica, N.Y.
Joseph Barton
———— Butler
Bibl. 15, 18, 20, 25, 44, 124

Barton & Clark (c. 1826)
Utica, N.Y.
Joseph Barton
William Barton Clark
Bibl. 15, 18, 20, 25, 44, 124

Barton & Porter
(c. 1811–1816)
Utica, N.Y.
Joseph Barton
Joseph S. Porter
Bibl. 18, 20, 91, 124, 158

Barton & Smith
(c. 1829–1831)
Utica, N.Y.
Joseph Barton
———— Smith
Bibl. 15, 18, 20, 25, 44, 124

Benjamin Barton
(d. 1816)
Alexandria, Va.
(c. 1801–1816)
Bibl. 15, 19, 44, 54, 114

B BARTON

Benjamin Barton (2d)
(c. 1821–1841)
Alexandria, Va.
Bibl. 19

Erastus Barton (d. 1823)
New York, N.Y.
Bibl. 23, 36, 44, 114, 124

Erastus Barton & Co.
(1815–1830)
New York, N.Y.
Erastus Barton
Isaac Marquand
Bibl. 25, 44, 114, 124, 138

E B & CO

Joseph Barton
(b. 1764–d. 1832)
Stockbridge, Mass.
(c. 1764–1804)
Utica, N.Y. (c. 1804–1832)
Barton & Porter
(c. 1811–1816)
Barton & Clark (c. 1826)
Barton & Smith
(c. 1829–1831)
Barton & Butler
(c. 1831–1832)
*Bibl. 15, 18, 20, 25, 44, 110,
114, 124, 158*

Thomas Barton
  (c. 1816–1821)
Alexandria, Va.
Bibl. 19, 54, 102

William Barton (Bartram)
  (c. 1769)
Philadelphia, Pa.
*Bibl. 3, 22, 23, 25, 28, 36,
  39, 44*

Basch Bros. & Co.
  (c. 1904–1915)
New York, N.Y.
Bibl. 127, 157

A. W. Bascom
Kentucky
Bibl. 54, 93

Hiram B. Bascom
  (c. 1838–1842)
St. Louis, Mo.
Bibl. 54, 134

E. & J. Bass (c. 1900–1930)
New York, N.Y.
Bachrach & Freedman
  (c. 1896–1900)
Bibl. 127, 157

Francis Basset(t)
Charlestown, Mass.
  (c. 1678–1715)
New York, N.Y.
  (c. 1764–1774)
*Bibl. 23, 25, 28, 29, 36, 44,
  114, 124*

George Francis Basset
  (c. 1797)
Philadelphia, Pa.
Bibl. 3

John Francis Basset
  (c. 1798)
Philadelphia, Pa.
Bibl. 3

Bassett & Warford
  (c. 1800–1806)
Albany, N.Y.
Bibl. 15, 20, 25, 44, 114, 124

Bassett Jewelry Co.
  (c. 1896–1943)
Newark, N.J.
Providence, R.I.
(See Kent & Stanley)
Bibl. 114, 127, 157

J. & W. H. Bassett
  (c. 1815–c. 1826)
Cortland, N.Y.
Joshua Bassett
William H. Bassett
Bibl. 20, 124

Joshua Bassett
  (b. 1756–d. 1836)
Cortland, N.Y.
J. & W. H. Bassett
Bibl. 20, 124

Nehemiah B. Bassett
  (d. 1844)
Schenectady, N.Y.
  (1800–1805)
Albany, N.Y.
  (1795–1800, 1813–1819)
Bibl. 20, 91, 124

William H. Bassett
  (d. 1834)
Cortland, N.Y.
J. & W. H. Bassett
Bibl. 20, 124

Joseph Bastid (1822–1827)
New Orleans, La.
Bibl. 141

Joseph Bastien
  (1822–1823)
New Orleans, La.
Bibl. 141

—— **Batchelder**
(Bachelder) (Bachlader)

(Bachlander)
Boston, Mass. (c. 1850)
New York, N.Y. (?)
Palmer & Batchelder
  (c. 1850)
*Bibl. 23, 24, 25, 28, 29, 36,
  44*

Nathaniel A. Batchellor
  (c. 1825–1839)
New York, N.Y.
Bibl. 22, 23, 36, 44, 124, 138

William Bateman
  (c. 1774–1876)
New York, N.Y.
Bibl. 28, 102, 124, 138

Bates & Klinke, Inc.
  (1919–present)
Attleboro, Mass.
Harold Bates
Oscar F. Klinke
Bibl. 127

Baton
(See Dubosq & Baton)

Augustine Baton Jr.
  (w. 1828–1837)
Philadelphia, Pa.
Bibl. 3

Augustus Baton
  (w. 1839–1845)
Philadelphia, Pa.
Bibl. 3

Charles Baton
  (w. 1833–1835)
Philadelphia, Pa.
Bibl. 3

**A. T. Battel (Battle) &
  Co.** (1846–1850)
Utica, N.Y.
Albert T. Battel(s)
Bibl. 18, 20, 114, 124, 158

**Albert T. Battel(s)
  (Battle[s])** (b. 1795)
Utica, N.Y.
Davies & Battel (1844–1850)
A. T. Battel & Co. (1846)
*Bibl. 18, 22, 23, 25, 28, 44,
  124, 158*

John Batterson (w. 1723)
Annapolis, Md.
Bibl. 38

Battin & Co.
(c. 1896–1922)
Newark, N.J.
Bibl. 114, 127, 157

STERLING **B.**

STERLING
—∞—€

Joseph Batting (w. 1850)
Philadelphia, Pa.
Bibl. 3

Battle(s)
(See Battel[s])

Jean Baptiste Baudry
(w.c. 1750, d. 1755)
Detroit, Mich.
Bibl. 58

Valentine Baugh (c. 1800)
Abingdon, Va.
Bibl. 19

Bauman & Kurtzborn
(c. 1850)
St. Louis, Mo.
Louis Bauman
———— Kurtzborn
Bibl. 54

BAUMAN & KURTZBORN

Louis Bauman
(b. 1843–d. 1870)
St. Louis, Mo.
Bauman & Kurtzborn
(c. 1850)
Bibl. 54, 134

Henry Baumford
(w. 1806–1807)
Philadelphia, Pa.
Bibl. 3

DeWitt Baxter (w. 1850)
Philadelphia, Pa.
Bibl. 3

**Bay State Jewelry &
Silversmiths Co.**
(c. 1914)
Attleboro, Mass.
Bibl. 127

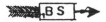

Bay State Silver Co.
(c. 1890–1893)
North Attleboro, Mass.
Bibl. 127, 157

〉〉〉〉〉| B S |→

A. S. Bay (w. 1786)
New York, N.Y.
Bibl. 22, 23, 36, 44, 124, 138

Bayeaux & Co.
(1839–1842)
Troy, N.Y.
Bibl. 20, 124

H. Bayeaux & Son
(c. 1825–1833)
Troy, N.Y.
Bibl. 20, 124

Henry Bayeaux
(c. 1801–1812)
Troy, N.Y.
Bibl. 20, 24, 25, 44

| BAYEAUX |

**Henry F. Bayeaux
(Baycux)**
(w. 1833–1839)
(d. 1839)
Troy, N.Y.
Bibl. 20, 91, 114, 124

Bayley & Douglas(s)
(c. 1798)
New York, N.Y.
*Bibl. 4, 22, 23, 25, 28, 29,
36, 114, 124, 135, 138*

| D B & A D |

Alexander Bayley
(c. 1790)
New York, N.Y.
Bibl. 23, 36, 44

E. E. Bayley (1875)
Burnham, Me.
Bibl. 105

John Bayley
(See John Bailey)

S. H. Bayley (c. 1790)
New York, N.Y.
Bibl. 22, 36

**Simeon and Alexander
Bayley (Bailey?)**
(c. 1791)
New York, N.Y.
Bibl. 23, 36, 44, 138

**Simon (Simeon) A.
Bayley** (c. 1796)
New York, N.Y.
(w. 1789–1796)
May be Simon A. Bailey.
*Bibl. 15, 23, 25, 28, 29, 30,
35, 36, 44, 54, 91, 95, 114,
116, 124, 135, 138*

| BAYLEY |

Simeon C. Bayley
(w. 1794)
Philadelphia, Pa.
Bibl. 3

J. Bayly
(See John Bailey)

Joseph Baysset (c. 1822)
New Orleans, La.
Bibl. 36, 44

Beach, Ives (Ivers) & Co.
(c. 1820)
New York, N.Y.
Bibl. 23, 36, 44, 124, 138

**Beach & Sanford
(Sanford & Beach)**
(c. 1785–1788)
Hartford, Conn.
Miles Beach
Isaac Sanford
*Bibl. 22, 23, 25, 28, 29, 36,
44, 74, 92, 110, 114*

| B & S |

Beach & Ward
(c. 1790–1797)
Hartford, Conn.
Miles Beach
James Ward
*Bibl. 15, 22, 23, 28, 29, 36,
44, 92, 110, 114*

| B & W |

A. Beach (c. 1823)
Hartford, Conn.
Nashville, Tenn.
(1841–1855)
Bibl. 15, 23, 25, 29, 36, 44,
92, 110, 114

Isaac Beach (c. 1788–1794)
New Milford, Conn.
Noadiah Mygatt
Bibl. 16, 22, 23, 28, 36, 44,
110

John Beach (c. 1813)
Hartford, Conn.
Miles Beach
Bibl. 15, 110

Miles Beach
(b. 1743–d. 1828)
Hartford, Conn.
(c. 1780–1797, c. 1813)
Goshen, Conn.
Litchfield, Conn.
Beach & Sanford
(c. 1785–1788)
Beach & Ward
(c. 1790–1797)
Bibl. 5, 15, 22, 23, 25, 28,
29, 36, 44, 54, 61, 89, 91,
92, 94, 110, 114

Caleb Beal
(b. 1746–d. 1801)
Boston, Mass. (1796–1800)
Hingham, Mass.
(c. 1746–1801)
Bibl. 15, 22, 23, 28, 29, 35,
36, 44, 78, 91, 94, 110,
114

[BEAL]
[C B]

John J. Beal
(c. 1845–1846)
Louisville, Ky.
Bibl. 32, 93

Theodore L. Beal
(c. 1845–1846)
Louisville, Ky.
Bibl. 32, 93

John Beale
(b. 1749–d. 1837)
Baltimore, Md. (c. 1771)
Petersburg, Va. (c. 1791)
Lynchburg, Va. (c. 1793)
Alexandria, Va. (c. 1797)
Richmond, Va.
(c. 1798–1808)
Bibl. 19, 54

Jacob Beam (c. 1821–1822)
Philadelphia, Pa.
Bibl. 3

Jacob C. Beam
(c. 1818–1820)
Philadelphia, Pa.
Bibl. 3, 23, 36, 44

Amos G. Bean (1875)
Albany, Me.
Bibl. 105

H. L. Bean
Skaneateles, N. Y.
Smith & Bean (c. 1844) (?)
H. L. Bean & Co. (c. 1846)
Bibl. 20, 124

H. L. Bean & Co. (c. 1846)
Skaneateles, N.Y.
Bibl. 20, 124

Henry Bean (c. 1848)
Philadelphia, Pa.
Bibl. 3

Jacob Bean (c. 1819–1822)
Philadelphia, Pa.
Bibl. 3

N. P. Bean (1860)
Scarsmouth, Me.
Bibl. 105

Bear & Conrad
(c. 1846–1851)
Charlottesville, Va.
Harrisonburg, Va.
Luray, Va.
Jehu W. Bear
George Oliver Conrad
Bibl. 19

David S. Bear
(c. 1847–1857)
Staunton, Va.
Bibl. 19

Jacob Bear (c. 1839)
Lexington, Va.
Philadelphia, Pa.
Bibl. 19

Jehu W. Bear
(c. 1842–c. 1852)
Harrisonburg, Va. (c. 1842)
Charlottesville, Va. (c. 1852)
Luray, Va.
Harry & Bear (c. 1842)
Bear & Conrad
(c. 1846–1851)
Bibl. 19

Beard & Ayres (Ayres &
Beard) (c. 1828–1831)
Louisville, Ky.
Evans C. Beard
Elias Ayres
Thomas Jefferson Shepard
Bibl. 32, 54, 68

B. E. Beard (c. 1800)
Philadelphia, Pa.
Bibl. 15, 44, 114

[B. E. BEARD]

Duncan Beard (d. 1797)
Appoquinimink Hundred,
Del. (c. 1771–1790)
Bibl. 25, 30, 44, 114   [D B]

E. Beard (c. 1800)
Philadelphia, Pa.
Bibl. 25

E. C. Beard & Co.
(c. 1831–c. 1852)
Louisville, Ky.
Evans C. Beard
Cornelius Amos
William Kendrick
George A. Zumar
Bibl. 32, 68, 93

Evans C. Beard
(c. 1824–1875)
Louisville, Ky.
Beard & Ayres
(c. 1828–1831)

E. C. Beard & Co.
  (c. 1831–c. 1852)
Bibl. 32, 54, 93

Robert Beard
  (b. 1753, w. 1774)
Maryland
Bibl. 38

Beasley & Houston
  (c. 1886–c. 1890)
Fayetteville, N.C.
Benjamin Franklin Beasley
J. C. Houston
Bibl. 21

**Benjamin Franklin
  Beasley**
Fayetteville, N.C.
Beasley & Houston
  (c. 1886–c. 1890)
Bibl. 21

John M. Beasley
  (b. 1815–d. 1889)
Fayetteville, N.C.
  (c. 1838–?)
Bibl. 21

Beasom & Reed
(See Bleasom & Reed)

J. Beaton
(See James B. Eaton)

Albert L. Beatty (c. 1833)
Philadelphia, Pa.
Bibl. 3

G. Beatty
Location unknown
Bibl. 15, 44, 114

John Anthony Beau
New York, N.Y. (c. 1770)
Philadelphia, Pa. (c. 1772)
Bibl. 3, 28, 44, 124, 138

J. Beauchamp
  (c. 1840–1850)
Bowling Green, Ky.
Bibl. 32, 54, 93

Samuel Beauchamp
  (c. 1840–1844)
Buffalo, N.Y.
Bibl. 20, 124

Beaucraft Inc.   BEAU
  (1947–present)
Providence, R.I.
New York, N.Y. (showroom)
Bibl. 127, 146

B–STER

BEAUCRAFT

BEAU–STERLING

Augustus Beauvais
  (c. 1850)
St. Louis, Mo.
R. & A. Beauvais
Bibl. 54

E. A. Beauvais (c. 1840)
St. Louis, Mo.
Bibl. 25, 44, 114, 134

E.A.BEAVAIS

R. & A. Beauvais (c. 1850)
St. Louis, Mo.
Rene Beauvais
Augustus Beauvais
Bibl. 54, 91

R & A BEAUVAIS   ST. LOUIS

Rene Beauvais
  (c. 1838–1898)
St. Louis, Mo.
R. & A. Beauvais (c. 1850)
Bibl. 25, 44, 89, 91, 114

R BEAUVAIS

Mathias Beaver (c. 1793)
Augusta, Ga.
Wittich & Beaver
Bibl. 17

—— **Becham** (c. 1740)
Location unknown
Bibl. 28, 29, 44   BECHAM

G. Bechler
(See G. Bichler)

Becht & Hartl, Inc.
  (c. 1935–1950)
Newark, N.J.
Bibl. 127

George Bechtel (c. 1865)
Kansas City, Ks.
Bibl. 89

Henry Bechtel (c. 1817)
Philadelphia, Pa.
Bibl. 3

Augustus Bechtler
  (b. 1813–d. 1846)
Rutherfordton, N.C.
  (c. 1830–?)
Bibl. 21

C. Bechtler & Son
  (c. 1857)
Spartanburg, S. C.
Bibl. 21

Christopher Bechtler (Sr.)
  (b. 1780–d. 1842)
Philadelphia, Pa.
  (c. 1830–1831)
Rutherfordton, N.C.
  (c. 1832–1842)
Bibl. 3, 21

Christopher Bechtler Jr.
  (c. 1830–1857)
Rutherfordton, N.C.
Spartanburg, S.C. (c. 1857)
Sometimes confused with
  Christopher Bechtler Sr.
Bibl. 5, 21

Henry Beck (c. 1837–1839)
Philadelphia, Pa.
Bibl. 3

John O. Beck (c. 1847)
Philadelphia, Pa.
Bibl. 3

Thomas Beck
Philadelphia, Pa.
  (c. 1773–1777)
Trenton, N.J. (c. 1784)
Bibl. 3, 23, 36, 44, 46, 54

Moses Beckel
  (c. 1848–1853)
Albany, N.Y.
Simpson & Beckel (c. 1848)
Bibl. 20, 124

Albert Becker (c. 1850)
Syracuse, N.Y.
Bibl. 20, 124

D. Becker & Co. (c. 1850)
Syracuse, N.Y.
Daniel Becker
Bibl. 20, 124

Daniel Becker (c. 1850)
Syracuse, N.Y.
D. Becker & Co. (?)
Bibl. 20, 124

Fredrick Becker (c. 1736)
New York, N.Y.
Bibl. 23, 36, 44, 124, 138

Philip Becker (c. 1764)
Lancaster, Pa.
*Bibl. 22, 23, 25, 28, 36, 44,
    112, 114*

P B

Beckwith & Brittain
    (c. 1858)
Charlotte, N.C.
Robert W. Beckwith
————— Brittain
Bibl. 21

Robert W. Beckwith
Raleigh, N.C.
New Bern, N.C.
Tarboro, N.C. (1850)
Charlotte, N.C.
    (c. 1858–1868)
Thomson & Beckwith
    (c. 1837–1839)
Ramsay & Beckwith
    (c. 1840–1843)
Beckwith & Brittain
    (c. 1858)
Bibl. 21

E. Bedford (c. 1816)
Batavia, N.Y.
Bibl. 20, 124

John Bedford
    (b. 1757–1834)
Fishkill, N.Y.
*Bibl. 15, 20, 22, 23, 25, 28,
    29, 30, 44, 91, 95, 114,
    124*

J Bedford

Morton Bedford (w. 1796)
Baltimore, Md.
Bibl. 38

Bedwell
(See Norman & Bedwell)

J. W. Beebe & Co.
    (c. 1844)
New York, N.Y.
*Bibl. 15, 23, 25, 29, 44, 114,
    124, 138*

J. W. BEEBE & CO.

James W. Beebe
    (c. 1835–1841)
New York, N.Y.
James W. & L. Beebe
    (c. 1836–1840)
J. W. Beebe & Co. (c. 1844)
*Bibl. 15, 23, 25, 29, 36, 44,
    91, 114, 124, 138*

J W BEEBE

James W. & L. Beebe
    (c. 1836–1840)
New York, N.Y.
Bibl. 15, 91, 124, 138

John O. Beebe
    (c. 1833–1835)
New York, N.Y.
Bibl. 15, 124, 138

Lemuel D. Beebe (c. 1850)
Syracuse, N.Y.
Bibl. 20, 124

Samuel Beebe (d. 1819)
Onondaga, N.Y.
Bibl. 20, 124

Stanton Beebe
    (b. 1796)
Providence, R.I.
    (c. 1818–1824)
Gorham & Beebe
    (c. 1825–1831)
Bibl. 22, 23, 28, 36, 44, 110

William Beebe   BEEBE
    (c. 1848–1850)
New York, N.Y.
*Bibl. 21, 23, 25, 44, 114,
    124, 138*

A. S. Beech (c. 1855)
Nashville, Ky.
Bibl, 54

Patrick Beech
    (c. 1773–1774)
Williamsburg, Va.
Bibl. 19, 153

C. Beecher & Co. (c. 1820)
Meriden, Conn.
Clement Beecher
Bibl. 23, 36, 44, 110

Clement Beecher
    (b. 1778–d. 1869)
Berlin, Conn.
Cheshire, Conn.
Meriden, Conn.
Clement Beecher & Co.
    (c. 1801–1820)
C. Beecher & Co. (c. 1820)
*Bibl. 16, 22, 23, 25, 28, 30,
    44, 91, 92, 110, 114*

C B

Clement Beecher & Co.
    (c. 1801–1820)
Berlin, Conn.
Cheshire, Conn.
Meriden, Conn.
Bibl. 16, 110

Isaac Beers
    (b. 1742–d. 1813)
New Haven, Conn. (c. 1800)
Henry Dagget
Bibl. 23, 110, 143

J. B. Beers (c. 1838–1839)
Honeoye Falls, N.Y.
Bibl. 20, 124

John Beesleyhaven
    (c. 1839–1840)
Philadelphia, Pa.
Bibl. 3

**Beggs & Smith (Smith &
    Beggs)** (c. 1848–1861)
Louisville, Ky.
William Beggs (?)
————— Smith
Bibl. 32, 54, 90, 93, 114

William Beggs
  (c. 1841–1844)
Louisville, Ky.
Beggs & Smith (1848–1861)?
McGrew & Beggs (c. 1850)
Bibl. 32, 54, 68, 90, 93

Julius Beidt (c. 1848)
Philadelphia, Pa.
Bibl. 3

Henry Beigel
  (c. 1816–1817)
Philadelphia, Pa.
Bibl. 3

Gilbert Belcher
Albany, N.Y. (1700's)
Massachusetts
Bibl. 54, 110

Maxim Belgord (c. 1848)
Philadelphia, Pa.
Bibl. 3

Lewis Belin (c. 1818–1819)
Philadelphia, Pa.
Bibl. 3, 23, 36, 44

William Belk
  (c. 1797–1800)
Philadelphia, Pa.
Bibl. 3

Samuel Belknap
  (b. 1751–d. 1821)
Boston, Mass.
*Bibl. 22, 23, 28, 36, 44, 102,
  110*

Stephen Belknap
  (Belnap)
  (c. 1818–1850)
Philadelphia, Pa.
Bibl. 3

Bell & Co. (c. 1825)
Location unknown
(Probably S. W. Bell)
Bibl. 28

Bell Trading Post
  (1932–present)
Albuquerque, N.M.
Division of Sunbell
  Corporation
Bibl. 127

Andrew Bell
  (b. 1712–d. 1752)
Beaufort, S.C.
Bibl. 5

George Bell Co.
  (c. 1904–1922)
Denver, Colo.
Bibl. 127

Joseph Bell (c. 1817–1824)
New York, N.Y.
Bibl. 15, 44, 114, 124

J BELL

J. & S. Bell (c. 1850)
San Antonio, Tex.
S. Bell
Bibl. 54

S. Bell (c. 1846)
San Antonio, Tex.
J. & S. Bell (c. 1850)
Bibl. 54

S. W. Bell (c. 1837)
Philadelphia, Pa.
Bibl. 3, 15, 25, 44, 114

Thomas W. Bell
Philadelphia, Pa. (c. 1837)
Petersburg, Va.
  (c. 1838–1848)
Bibl. 3, 19

T. W. BELL

W. Bell & Company
  (1950–present)
Rockville, Md.
Walter Bell
Bibl. 127

Warwick

William Bell (c. 1805)
Philadelphia, Pa.
Bibl. 3

Jean P. Bellanger
  (1810–1827)
New Orleans, La.
Bibl. 141

Francois Belliard
  (c. 1822)
New Orleans, La.
Bibl. 36, 44

John O. Bellis (c. 1910)
California
Bibl. 120, 140

JOHN O. BELLIS STERLING

Belloni & Durandeau
  (c. 1835–1836)
New York, N.Y.
Louis J. Belloni
John Durandeau
*Bibl. 15, 23, 36, 44, 72, 124,
  138*

BELLONI & DURAND

Louis J. Belloni (c. 1835)
New York, N.Y.
Belloni & Durandeau
  (c. 1835–1836)
Bibl. 23, 36, 44, 124, 138

Stephen Belnap
(See Stephen Belknap)

Butler Bement
  (b. 1784–d. 1869)
Pittsfield, Mass.
  (c. 1810–1818)
Bibl. 25, 44, 91, 94, 110

B. BEMENT

B E N
(See Benjamin F. Lowell)

Benedict & Scudder
  (c. 1827–1837)
New York, N.Y.
Andrew C. Benedict
Egbert Scudder
*Bibl. 15, 79, 91, 124, 135,
  138*

Benedict & Son (c. 1840)
New York, N.Y.
Bibl. 23, 36, 44, 124, 135

Benedict & Squire
(c. 1825–1839)
New York, N.Y.
Martin Benedict
Bela S. Squire Jr.
*Bibl. 15, 23, 25, 29, 36, 44,
114, 124, 135, 138*

BENEDICT & SQUIRE

A. Benedict (c. 1835)
Syracuse, N.Y.
Bibl. 20, 124

Andrew C. Benedict
(c. 1827–1840)
New York, N.Y.
Benedict & Scudder
(c. 1827–1837)
*Bibl. 15, 23, 25, 29, 36, 44,
89, 91, 114, 124, 135, 138*

A. C. BENEDICT

Isaac H. Benedict
(c. 1837–1854,
d. 1854)
Greenville, S.C.
Mr. Burns
Bibl. 5

J. H. Benedict
Auburn, N.Y.
New York, N.Y.
Skaneateles, N.Y.
Munger & Benedict
(c. 1826–1828)
Bibl. 20, 23, 36, 44, 124

Martin Benedict
(c. 1823–1839)
New York, N.Y.
Benedict & Squire
(c. 1825–1839)
Bibl. 15, 89, 124, 135, 138

Samuel Benedict (c. 1845)
New York, N.Y.
Bibl. 35, 83, 124

Morris Benham (c. 1843)
Hartford, Conn.
Bibl. 23

Benjamin & Co.
New York, N.Y. (?)
Barzillai Benjamin
(b. 1774–d. 1844)
*Bibl. 15, 16, 23, 25, 28, 29,
36, 44*

Benjamin & Ford
(c. 1828–1874?)
New Haven, Conn.
Everard Benjamin
George H. Ford
Bibl. 28

B. Benjamin
(See Benjamin Benjamin)

Barzillai Benjamin
(b. 1774–d. 1844)
New Haven, Conn. (c. 1799)
Bridgeport, Conn.
Milford, Conn.
New York, N.Y.
Benjamin & Co.
*Bibl. 15, 16, 23, 25, 28, 29,
36, 44, 91, 92, 94, 110,
114, 122, 124, 138, 143*

B BENJAMIN   B B

Benjamin Benjamin
(c. 1825)
New Haven, Conn.
New York, N.Y.
Bibl. 15, 23, 29, 44

B BENJAMIN   B B

Everard Benjamin
(b. 1807–d. 1874)
New Haven, Conn.
Benjamin & Ford
(c. 1828–1874?)
*Bibl. 16, 23, 25, 28, 29, 36,
44, 91, 92, 114, 143*

E BENJAMIN

Everard Benjamin & Co.
(c. 1830–1840)
New Haven, Conn.
*Bibl. 15, 44, 54, 61, 91, 92,
94, 114, 143*

E BENJAMIN & CO

E B & CO

John Benjamin
(b. 1699–d. 1773)
Stratford, Conn.
*Bibl. 25, 28, 44, 54, 61, 91,
92, 110, 114*

John Benjamin
(b. 1730–d. 1796)
Stratford, Conn.
Bibl. 16, 23, 29, 36

Luther W. Benjamin
(c. 1803)
Canandaigua, N.Y.
Thompson & Benjamin
Bibl. 20, 124

Samuel C. Benjamin
(c. 1801–1831, c. 1819)
New Haven, Conn.
*Bibl. 16, 23, 28, 36, 44, 110,
143*

Solomon Benjamin
(w. 1816–1818)
Baltimore, Md.
Bibl. 23, 28, 36, 38, 44

Theodore Benjamin
(c. 1823–1824)
Philadelphia, Pa.
Bibl. 3

Whiteman Benner
(c. 1818–1824)
Philadelphia, Pa.
Bibl. 3

Bennet
(See Hall & Bennet)

Bennett (c. 1811)
Philadelphia, Pa.
Bibl. 3

Bennett & Caldwell
(c. 1843–1848)
Philadelphia, Pa.
——— Bennett
James E. Caldwell
Bibl. 3, 91

Bennett & Cook (c. 1820)
New York, N.Y.
Bibl. 78

Bennett, Cooke & Co.
  (c. 1823–1827)
Charleston, S.C.
John Bennett Sr.
D. C. Cooke
Maltby Pelletreau
Bibl. 5

Bennett & Fletcher
  (Fletcher & Bennett)
  (1830–1894)
Louisville, Ky.
Philadelphia, Pa.
___ Bennett
Henry Fletcher
Bibl. 3, 23, 32, 36, 44, 54,
  68, 93

FLETCHER & BENNETT

Bennett, Fletcher & Co.
(See Bennett & Fletcher)

Bennett, Lewis & Co.
  (c. 1856)
York, S.C.
Jordan Bennett
J. N. Lewis
Bibl. 5

Bennett & Thomas
  (c. 1812–1819)
Petersburg, Va.
John Bennett
Ebenezer Thomas
John Warren Thomas
Bibl. 19

BENNETT & THOMAS

Bennett, Wilson & Co.
  (c. 1856)
York, S.C.
Jordan Bennett
D. W. Wilson
Bibl. 5

Alfred Bennett
  (c. 1837–1847)
Location unknown
Bibl. 3, 125

Charles Fletcher Bennett
  (c. 1843–1848, d. 1876)
Louisville, Ky.
Bibl. 32, 54, 93

Dwight H. Bennett, Jr.
  (c. 1975–1980)
St. Louis, Mo.
Bibl. 155

J. D. Bennett (c. 1847)
J. D. Bennett & Co.
  (c. 1849)
Petersburg, Va.
Bibl. 19

Jacob Bennett
  (c. 1825–1850)
Philadelphia, Pa.
Bibl. 3, 23, 36, 44

James Bennett (d. 1783)
New York, N.Y.
  (c. 1769–1773)
Bibl. 23, 36, 44, 114, 124,
  138

James Bennett (c. 1839)
Philadelphia, Pa.
Bibl. 3

John Bennett
Richmond, Va.
  (c. 1811–1812)
Petersburg, Va.
  (c. 1812–1827)
Bennett & Thomas
  (c. 1812–1819)
John W. Thomas & Co.
  (c. 1819)
Bibl. 19

John Bennett Sr.
  (c. 1815–1827)
Charleston, S.C.
New York, N.Y.
Pelletreau, Bennett & Cooke
  (c. 1826–c. 1827)
Bennett, Cooke & Co.
  (c. 1823–c. 1826)
Pelletreau, Bennett & Co.
  (c. 1827–1829)
Bibl. 5, 91, 124

Jordan Bennett
  (c. 1824–?)
York, S. C. (c. 1854–1856)
Chester, S.C.
J. N. Lewis & Co. (c. 1854)
  (?)
Bennett, Lewis & Co.
  (c. 1856)

Bennett, Wilson & Co.
  (c. 1856)
Bibl. 5

L. M. Bennett
  (c. 1856–1860)
Utica, N.Y.
Leach & Bennett
  (c. 1856–1858)
Bibl. 18, 124, 158

Purden (Purnell) Bennett
  (c. 1835–1843)
Philadelphia, Pa.
Bibl. 3

Robert H. Bennett
  (c. 1849–1850)
Philadelphia, Pa.
Bibl. 3

Benneville
(See De Benneville)

Jonathan Benny
  (w. 1798)
Easton, Md.
Bibl. 38

Jean Baptiste Benoit
  (w. 1796)
Baltimore, Md.
Bibl. 38

Wm. Bens Co., Inc.
  (c. 1915–1920)
Providence, R.I.
Bibl. 127, 157

G. L. Benson (c. 1818)
Cincinnati, Ohio
Bibl. 34, 152

Thomas Bentley
  (b. 1764–d. 1804)
Boston, Mass.
Bibl. 4, 23, 25, 28, 29, 36,
  44, 54, 91, 110, 114, 119

J. Benton (c. 1810)
Location unknown
Bibl. 24, 89

J. BENTON

Lucius Benton (c. 1850)
Cleveland, Ohio
Bibl. 54, 89

Peter Bentson (Bentzon)
(c. 1817–1849)
Philadelphia, Pa.
Bibl. 3, 23, 36, 44

Eugene C. Benyard
(c. 1839–1849)
Philadelphia, Pa.
Bibl. 3

Hugh G. Benyard
(c. 1841)
Philadelphia, Pa.
Bibl. 3

Ferdinand Bera (Bero)
(c. 1839–1850)
Philadelphia, Pa.
Bibl. 3

Andrew Berard (c. 1797)
Philadelphia, Pa.
Bibl. 3, 23, 28, 36

E. Berard (c. 1800)
Philadelphia, Pa.
Bibl. 29, 36, 44, 114

E B ERARD

Samuel Berd (c. 1840)
Philadelphia, Pa.
Bibl. 3

Frederick Berenbroick
(c. 1839–1841)
New York, N.Y.
Frederick Berenbroick & Co.
(c. 1850)
Bibl. 15, 124, 138

**Frederick Berenbroick &
Co.** (c. 1850)
New York, N.Y.
Bibl. 23, 124

Peter W. Bergantz
(c. 1848–1852)
Louisville, Ky.
Bibl. 32, 93

Joseph Berger
(c. 1829–1833)
Philadelphia, Pa.
Bibl. 3

I B

John Bering
(c. 1790–1807)
Charleston, S.C.
Bibl. 5, 44, 54

Charles H. Berkenbush
(c. 1825)
New York, N.Y.
Bibl. 15, 23, 36, 44, 124, 138

Henry Bermingham
(b. 1904)(1917–1950)
New Orleans, La.
Bibl. 141

A. & J. Berniard
(c. 1806–1807)
Philadelphia, Pa.
Bibl. 3

Ferdinand Bero
(See Ferdinand Bera)

Peter Berrgant
(c. 1829–1833)
Philadelphia, Pa.
Bibl. 3

A. & J. Berringer
(c. 1834–1835)
Albany, N.Y.
Bibl. 20, 124

Jacob Berringer
(c. 1835–1843)
Albany, N.Y.
Bibl. 20, 124

James Berry (w. 1803)
Easton, Md.
Bibl. 38

William Berry (c. 1805)
New York, N.Y.
Bibl. 23, 36, 44, 124

Solomon Berson
(1834–1858)
Brownsville, Tenn.
Bibl. 89

William Berson Sr.
(1834–1838)
Franklin, Tenn.
Brownsville, Tenn.
Bibl. 89

**Ferdinand Berstardus
(Besterdes)** (1836–1840)
New York, N.Y.
Bibl. 15, 124, 138

George Bertie
(c. 1808–1814)
Baltimore, Md.
Bibl. 38

Harry Bertoia (b. 1920)
Bally, Pa. (c. 1945–1955)
Bibl. 117

Tousaint Bertrand
(w. 1795–1796)
Baltimore, Md.
Bibl. 38

John Besher
(c. 1827–1832)
New York, N.Y.
Bibl. 15, 124, 138

Thauvet Besley (Besly)
(d. 1757)
New York, N.Y.
(c. 1727–1757)
*Bibl. 4, 23, 25, 28, 29, 30,
35, 36, 44, 54, 91, 102,
114, 119, 124, 138*

B

H. W. Bessac (c. 1823)
Hudson, N.Y.
Bibl. 15, 20, 44, 91, 114, 124

H. W. Bessac

John Besselievre
(c. 1825–1840)
Philadelphia, Pa.
Bibl. 3

John A. Besselievre
(c. 1841–1850)
Philadelphia, Pa.
Bibl. 3

Thomas Besselievre
  (c. 1829–1833)
Philadelphia, Pa.
Bibl. 3, 23, 36, 44

A. Besselievre (c. 1837)
Philadelphia, Pa.
Bibl. 3

B. Best & Co. (after 1850)
Louisville, Ky.
Bibl. 32, 54

John Best (c. 1794)
Lexington, Ky.
Shelby County, Ky.
Bibl. 32, 54, 93

Joseph Best (c. 1723)
Philadelphia, Pa.
Bibl. 3, 23, 28, 36, 44

Robert Best
  (b. 1790–d. 1831)
Cincinnati, Ohio
  (c. 1812–1819)
Bibl. 34, 44, 90, 152

Samuel Best
  (b. 1776–d. 1859)
Cincinnati, Ohio
  (c. 1802–1818)
Bibl. 34, 90, 114, 133, 152

Besterdes
(See Berstardus)

W. J. Bettinger
  (c. 1853–1854)
Utica, N.Y.
Bibl. 18, 124, 158

Samuel Bettle (c. 1803)
Philadelphia, Pa.
Bibl. 3

Charles Betton (c. 1850)
Philadelphia, Pa.
Bibl. 3

Thomas W. Betton
  (c. 1830–1833)
Philadelphia, Pa.
Bibl. 3

Richard Bevan
  (w. 1803–1804)

Baltimore, Md.
Bibl. 23, 28, 36, 38, 44

William Bevans
  (c. 1810–1813)
Philadelphia, Pa.
Bibl. 3

John K. Bevin
  (c. 1786–1825)
Charleston, S.C.
Bibl. 5, 54

G. Bichler (Bechler)
  (b. 1807)
Utica, N.Y.
  (c. 1858–?)
Bibl. 18, 124, 158

Francis Bicknell
  (c. 1818–1859)
Rome, N.Y.
Bibl. 15, 20, 25, 44, 91, 114, 124

F.BICKNELL

Biddle
(See Krider & Biddle)

John S. Biddle (c. 1807)
Wheeling, Va.
Bibl. 19

Owen Biddle (d. 1799)
Philadelphia, Pa.
  (c. 1764–1770)
Bibl. 3

C. Frances Bieber
  (b. 1886)
Santa Fe. N.M.
Bibl. 117

Henry Biegel
  (c. 1810–1813)
Philadelphia, Pa.
Bibl. 3

Henry Biershing   [H B]
  (b. 1790–d. 1843)
Hagerstown, Md.
  (w. 1815–1843)
Bibl. 25, 29, 38, 44, 114

Bigelow (c. 1830)
Location unknown

Bibl. 54

[BIGELOW]

Bigelow & Bros.
  (c. 1840–1850)
Boston, Mass
John Bigelow
Abram O. Bigelow
Alanson Bigelow
Bibl. 15, 23, 25, 29, 36, 44, 114

[BIGELOW & BROS.]

Bigelow Bros. & Kennard
  (c. 1845)
Boston, Mass.
Bibl. 89

[BIGELOW BROS. & KENNARD]

Bigelow, Kennard & Co.
  (c. 1863)
Boston, Mass.
Bibl. 15, 91, 122

Bigelow, Kennard & Co., Inc.
Boston, Mass.
Bibl. 15, 91

Abram O. Bigelow
Boston, Mass.
Bigelow & Bros.
  (c. 1840–1850)
Bibl. 23

Alanson Bigelow (c. 1832)
Boston, Mass.
Bigelow & Brothers
  (c. 1840–1850)
Bibl. 23

John Bigelow (c. 1830)
Boston, Mass.
Bigelow & Bros.
  (c. 1840–1850)
Bibl. 23, 25, 29, 36, 44, 91, 114

[JOHN BIGELOW]

Bigger & Clarke
  (c. 1783–1784)
Baltimore, Md. (1783–1784)
Philadelphia, Pa.
———— Bigger
Ambrose Clarke
Bibl. 3, 38

Gilbert Bigger
(w. 1783–1816)
Baltimore, Md.
Bibl. 38

Biggins-Rodgers Co.   D
(c. 1894–1915)
Wallingford, Conn.
Henry E. Biggins
Frank L. Rodgers
Henry B. Hall
Became Dowd-Rodgers Co.
(silverplate)
Bibl. 127

Joseph Biggs
(c. 1827–1835)
New York, N.Y.
Bibl. 15, 23, 36, 44, 124, 138

**Silvian A. Bijotal
(Bigotut?)** (c. 1795)
New York, N.Y.
Bibl. 23, 36, 44, 124, 138

Andrew Billings
(b. 1743–d. 1808)
Preston, Conn.
Fishkill, N.Y.
Poughkeepsie, N.Y.
*Bibl. 15, 20, 23, 25, 28, 29,
36, 44, 54, 91, 102, 110,
114, 122, 124*

Daniel Billings (b. 1749)
New London County, Conn.
Preston, Conn. (c. 1795)
*Bibl. 16, 23, 25, 28, 29, 36,
44, 61, 91, 92, 110, 114*

Joseph Billings (b. 1720)
Reading, Pa. (c. 1770)
Bibl. 3, 28

L. Billings (c. 1832)
Bloody Brook, Mass.
Bibl. 84

Billon & Co.
(c. 1795–1797)
Philadelphia, Pa.
Charles Billon
Bibl. 3

Charles Billon
(c. 1795–1819)
Philadelphia, Pa.
Billon & Co. (c. 1795–1797)
Bibl. 3, 91

Charles Billon
(c. 1818–1822)
St. Louis, Mo.
Bibl. 25, 44, 54, 91, 114, 134

Richard Bilton
(w. 1800–1801)
Baltimore, Md.
Bibl. 38

Binder Bros. Inc.
(1919–present)
New York, N.Y.
Bibl. 127

Bingham & Breorbey
(c. 1799)
Philadelphia, Pa.
Thomas Bingham
——— Breorbey
Bibl. 3

Bingham, Ball & Co.
(?–1833)
Utica, N.Y.
George W. Bingham
William H. Ball
John D. Douglass
Bibl. 18, 20, 124

Flavel Bingham
(b. 1781–d. 1804)
Utica, N.Y. (c. 1802–1804)
Bibl. 18, 20, 124, 158

George W. Bingham
Utica, N.Y.
Bingham, Ball & Co.
(?–1833)
Bibl. 18, 20, 124, 158

James Bingham
(c. 1839–1850)
Philadelphia, Pa.
Bibl. 3

James Bingham
(c. 1896–1910)
Philadelphia, Pa.
Bibl. 127, 157

John Bingham (c. 1678)
Boston, Mass.
Bibl. 4, 28, 110

John Bingham (c. 1664)
Newark, N.J.
Bibl. 23, 36, 44

Thomas Bingham
(c. 1797–1811)
Philadelphia, Pa.
Bingham & Breorbey
Bibl. 3

Wheelock P. Bingham
(c. 1859–1881)
Indianapolis, Ind.
Bibl. 133

W.P. BINGHAM

——— **Bingley** (c. 1790)
Connecticut (?)
Bibl. 28, 92   BINGLEY

Theodore Binneau
(c. 1820–1822)
Philadelphia, Pa.
Bibl. 3, 23, 36, 44

John Bioren
(c. 1829–1833)
Philadelphia, Pa.
Bibl. 3

Fred M. Birch Co., Inc.
(1959–present)
Providence, R.I.
Bibl. 127

Bird & Hoffman
(See Bard & Hoffman)

Conrad Bird
(See Conrad Bard)

Albert G. Bird
(c. 1829–1850)

Philadelphia, Pa.
Bibl. 3

John Stiles Bird
   (b. 1794–d. 1887)
Charleston, S.C.
   (c. 1820–1861)
Bibl. 5, 25, 44, 114

Joseph Bird
Location unknown
Bibl. 15, 44, 114, 124

Thomas Bird (c. 1791)
Alexandria, Va.
Bibl. 19, 54

William Bird
   (c. 1848–1850)
Philadelphia, Pa.
Bibl. 3

Birmingham Silver Co., Inc. (c. 1932–present)
Yalesville, Conn.
New York, N.Y.
Sol Goldfeder
Bibl. 127, 146

Lawrence Birnie
(See Lawrence Burney)

Frank G. Birtel
   (1880–1912)
New Orleans, La.
Bibl. 141

Bishop (1875)
Bethel, Me.
Bibl. 105

Benjamin F. Bishop
   (c. 1846–1847)
Philadelphia, Pa.
Bibl. 3

Edward Bishop (c. 1839)
Philadelphia, Pa.
Bibl. 3

Edwin Bishop
   (c. 1825–1833)
Philadelphia, Pa.
Bibl. 3

Erwin Bishop
   (c. 1835–1837)
Philadelphia, Pa.
Bibl. 3

Joachim Bishop (c. 1835)
Philadelphia, Pa.
Bibl. 3

Jodquin Bishop (c. 1837)
Philadelphia, Pa.
Bibl. 3

John Bishop
   (c. 1839–1851)
Wheeling, Va.
Bibl. 19

Joseph Bishop
Wilmington, N.C.
   (c. 1817–1822)
Philadelphia Pa.
   (c. 1829–1833)
Bibl. 3, 21, 114

Josiah Bishop (c. 1830)
Columbia, S. C.
Bibl. 5

Peter S. Bishop (c. 1837)
Philadelphia, Pa.
Bibl. 3

Thomas Bissbrown
   (c. 1788–1790)
Albany, N.Y.
Bibl. 20, 23, 36, 44, 124

Bitterman Brothers
   (c. 1869–1881)
Vincennes and Evansville, Ind.
Bibl. 133

BITTERMAN BROS.

Bittrolff Brothers
   (c. 1860–1875)
Evansville, Ind.
Bibl. 133

BITTROLFF BROS.

George A. Bittrolff & Co.
   (c. 1860–1875)
Evansville, Ind.
Bibl. 133

G.A. BITTROLFF & CO.

John Louis Bittrolff
   (1834–1875)
Evansville and Princeton, Ind.
Herman, Mo.
Bittrolff & Son
   (c. 1857–1875)
Became J. L. Bittrolff & Sons
   (c. 1853–1857)
Bibl. 133

Bixby Silver Co.
   (c. 1896–1909)
Providence, R.I.
Bibl. 114, 127, 157

    B. S. C.

Christian Bixler (c. 1784)
Easton, Pa.
Bibl. 25, 44

Black, Starr & Frost, Ltd.
   (1962–present)
New York, N.Y.
Successor to
Marquand & Co.
   (1834–1839)
Ball, Tompkins & Black
   (1839–1851)
Ball, Black & Co.
   (1851–1876)
Black, Starr & Frost
   (1876–1929)
Black, Starr, Frost-Gorham
Inc. (1929–1940)
Black, Starr & Gorham, Inc.
   (1940–1962)
Bibl. 15, 23, 72, 111, 117, 127, 131, 157

B S & F

Black Starr

Black, Starr & Frost Ltd

I. Black (c. 1795–1822)
Philadelphia, Pa.
Perhaps James or John
  Black
Bibl. 15, 91, 114, 122, 135

| I. BLACK |

James Black
  (c. 1795–1822)
Philadelphia, Pa.
Bibl. 3, 23, 25, 29, 36, 44, 91

| J B | | J BLACK |

John Black (c. 1811–1819)
Philadelphia, Pa.
McMullin & Black (c. 1811)
Bibl. 3, 4, 23, 28, 36, 44

| J B | | I BLACK |

John Black (c. 1839–1850)
Philadelphia, Pa.
Bibl. 3

William Black
  (c. 1833–1840)
New York, N.Y.
Ball, Tompkins & Black
  (c. 1839–1851)
Ball, Black & Co.
  (c. 1851–1876)
*Bibl. 15, 23, 36, 44, 91, 124,
138*

**William Nelson
  Blackburn** (c. 1812)
Shelbyville, Ky.
Bibl. 32, 54, 68, 93

Blackington & Balcom
  (1875)
Providence, R.I.
Bibl. 108

R. Blackinton & Co.
  (1862–1967)
North Attleboro, Mass.
Walter Ballou
Roswell Blackinton
Became Wells, Inc.
Bibl. 114, 120, 127, 147, 157

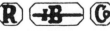

MARIE LOUISE   PONTIFEX

F. S. Blackman & Co.
  (1856–1859)
Danbury, Conn.
Frederick Starr Blackman
*Bibl. 15, 23, 25, 29, 36, 91,
92, 114*

| F. S. B. & Co. |

Frederick Starr Blackman
  (b. 1811–d. 1898)
Danbury, Conn. (c. 1832)
Bridgeport, Conn.
F. S. Blackman & Co.
*Bibl. 16, 23, 25, 28, 29, 36,
44, 91, 112, 114*

| J. C. B. & Co |

| J.C. BLACKMAN & CO. |

J. C. Blackman & Co.
  (c. 1835)
Bridgeport, Conn.
John Clark Blackman
Bibl. 15, 25, 91, 92

John Clark Blackman
  (b. 1808–d. 1872)
Danbury, Conn. (c. 1829)
Bridgeport, Conn. (c. 1835)
J. C. Blackman & Co.
  (c. 1835)
*Bibl. 15, 16, 23, 25, 36, 44,
91, 92, 114*

John Starr Blackman
  (b. 1777–d. 1851)   (J S B)
Danbury, Conn.
*Bibl. 16, 23, 25, 28, 29, 36,
44, 91, 92, 110*

Redman Blackwell
  (d. 1812)
Bethlehem Township, N.J.
Bibl. 46

Blackwood & Brooks
  (c. 1828–1830)
Utica, N.Y.
William Blackwood
Benjamin Franklin Brooks
Bibl. 18, 20, 124

William Blackwood
  (c. 1836–1838)

Utica, N.Y.
Blackwood & Brooks
  (c. 1828–1830)
H. S. Bradley & Co.
  (c. 1836–1850)
Bibl. 18, 20, 124, 158

Daniel Blair
St. Louis, Mo.
  (c. 1817–1821)
New Orleans, La.
  (1830–1842)
Daggett & Blair (c. 1821)
Harland & Blair
  (1830–1833)
Bibl. 54

D. B. Blake (1875)
Providence, R.I.
Bibl. 108

D. B. Blake & Co. (1860)
Providence, R.I.
Bibl. 108

E. G. Blake (1860–1875)
Farmington, Me.
Bibl. 105

Frederick Blake
  (c. 1840–1844)
Albany, N.Y.
Bibl. 20, 124

George H. Blake
  (w. 1842–1849,
  d. 1849)
Troy, N.Y.
Bibl. 20, 124

Isaac Blake
  (c. 1846–c. 1850)
Troy, N.Y.
Bibl. 20, 124

James E. Blake Co.
  (1898–1936)
Attleboro, Mass.
Bibl. 127, 157   Sterlin E

Peter Blake (c. 1807)
Charleston, S.C.
Bibl. 5

C. Blakeslee (c. 1820)
Vermont (?)
Bibl. 28

| C BLAKESLEE |

Blakesley
(See Willey & Blakesley)

Harper Blakesley
   (1829–1836)
Cincinnati, Ohio
Bibl. 54, 90

Collins Blakley (c. 1845)
Troy, N.Y.
Bibl. 23

William Bla(c)kslee
   (b. 1795–d. 1879)
Newtown, Conn.
Bibl. 16, 23, 28, 36, 44, 110

Ziba (Zeba) Bla(c)kslee
   (b. 1768–d. 1825)
Newtown, Conn.
Bibl. 23, 28, 36, 44, 92, 110

Lewis Blanc (c. 1810)
Philadelphia, Pa.
Bibl. 3

P. Blancan (c. 1811–1813)
Philadelphia, Pa.
Bibl. 3

Thomas Blanch
   (b. 1793, w. 1827)
Baltimore, Md.
Bibl. 38

A. Blanchard (c. 1800)
Lexington, Ky.
Bibl. 30

Asa Blanchard
   (c. 1808–1838)
Lexington, Ky.
*Bibl. 23, 25, 28, 29, 32, 36,
   44, 54, 68, 91, 93, 95, 114,
   151*

A BLANCHARD	A. B

Joshua Blanchard
   (c. 1829)
Cincinnati, Ohio
Bibl. 54, 90

Thomas Blanche
   (b. 1793, w. 1805)
Baltimore, Md.
Bibl. 38

Peter Blancjour (c. 1838)
Richmond, Va.
Bibl. 19

**Jurian (Jeurisen)
   (Jeuriaen) Blanck Jr.**
   (b. 1665–d. 1714)
New York, N.Y.
*Bibl. 25, 44, 54, 95, 104,
   114, 116, 119, 124, 138,
   151*

Samuel Bland
   (c. 1837–1850)
Philadelphia, Pa.
Bibl. 3

William Bland
   (c. 1845–1848)
St. Louis, Mo.
Bibl. 54

Victor G. Blandin
   (c. 1831–?)
Charlotte, N.C.
Bibl. 21

Charles Blank (c. 1850)
Philadelphia, Pa.
Bibl. 3

John Blank (c. 1837–1839)
Philadelphia, Pa.
Bibl. 3

Asa Blansett (c. 1795)
Dumfries, Va.
Bibl. 19

John Blatt (c. 1841)
Philadelphia, Pa.
Bibl. 3

John W. Blauvelt
   (c. 1831–1844)
New York, N.Y.
Bibl. 15, 23, 36, 44, 124

Joseph Blauvelt (c. 1819)
New York, N.Y.
Bibl. 15, 124, 138

Spencer Blauvelt
   (c. 1836–1840)
New York, N.Y.
Bibl. 15, 124, 138

**Bleasom (Beasom?) &
   Reed** (c. 1830)
Nassau, N.H.
Portsmouth, N.H.
*Bibl. 23, 25, 29, 36, 44, 107,
   114, 125*

A. A. & A. G. Blethen
   (1875)
Dover, Me.
Bibl. 105

Bliss
(See also Hall & Bliss
   Napier)

E. A. Bliss Co.
   (c. 1883–1920)
North Attleboro, Mass.
   (1883–1890)
Meriden, Conn.
   (1890–1920)
E. A. Bliss (1883)
J. E. Carpenter
Successor to Carpenter &
   Bliss (1875–1883)
Became Napier-Bliss Co.
   (1920–1922)
Napier Company
   (1920–present)
Bibl. 127

H. Bliss (d. 1830)
New Orleans, La. (1830)
Bibl. 141

Jonathan Bliss
Middletown, Conn.
Hart & Bliss (c. 1803–1804)
Hughes & Bliss (c. 1806)
*Bibl. 23, 25, 36, 44, 92, 110,
   114*

William Bliss
   (c. 1812–1828)
Middletown, Conn.
Cleveland, Ohio
Bibl. 34, 54, 110

George Blome (c. 1845)
Philadelphia, Pa.
Bibl. 3

Blondell (Blondel) & Descuret
(c. 1798–1799)
Philadelphia, Pa.
Anthony Blondell
Louis Descuret
Bibl. 3, 23, 36, 44

Anthony Blondell (Blondel)
Philadelphia, Pa.
(c. 1797–1813)
Baltimore, Md.
(w. 1814–1827)
Martinsburg, Va.
(c. 1819–1840)
Blondell & Descuret
(c. 1798–1799)
Bibl. 3, 19, 23, 28, 36, 38, 44

John M. Blondell (Blondel)
(c. 1814–1824)
Baltimore, Md.
Bibl. 19, 38, 91

Blood & Hix (1875)
Rockland, Me.
Bibl. 105

Blood, Hix & Sumner
(1875)
Thomaston, Me.
Bibl. 105

Frederick Blood (1860)
Westboro, Me.
Bibl. 105

Simeon Blood (1860)
Rockland, Me.
Bibl. 105

William H. Blood (1860)
Thomaston, Me.
Bibl. 105

James & L. Bloodgood
(c. 1805–1810)
Utica, N.Y.
James A. Bloodgood
Lynott Bloodgood
Bibl. 18, 20, 124, 158

Lynott Bloodgood
(c. 1805)
Albany, N.Y.
Utica, N.Y.

James & L. Bloodgood
(c. 1805–1810)
Bibl. 18, 20, 54, 124, 158

Charles Bloomer (c. 1850)
Syracuse, N.Y.
Bibl. 20, 124

George Blowe
(c. 1837–1850)
Philadelphia, Pa.
Bibl. 3

John Blowers
(c. 1710–1748)
Boston, Mass.
Bibl. 2, 15, 23, 25, 28, 29, 36, 44, 54, 69, 70, 91, 94, 110, 114, 119

BLOWERS   I BLOWERS

Samuel Bluis (c. 1791)
Norfolk, Va.
Bibl. 19

Charles Blundy (d. 1766)
Charleston, S.C. (c. 1760)
Savannah, Ga. (c. 1766)
Bibl. 17

Luther Boardman & Son
(1820–1905)
East Haddam, Conn.
Bibl. 127

L. BOARDMAN & SON

John Bochler
(c. 1796–1820)
Savannah, Ga.
Bibl. 17

Joseph Bock
(c. 1859–1891)
Charleston, S.C.
Bibl. 5, 44, 54

Daniel Bockius (Buckius) (Buckins)
(c. 1792–1798)
Martinsburg, Va.
Young & Bockius (c. 1798)
Bibl. 19, 91

William Bode
(c. 1796–1798)
Philadelphia, Pa.
Bibl. 3

Lorenzo Bodoano
(c. 1819)
Philadelphia, Pa.
Bibl. 3

Andreas W. Boehler
(c. 1784)
New York, N.Y.
Bibl. 23, 36, 44, 124

Charles Louis Boehme
(b. 1774–d. 1868)
(w. 1799–1812)
Baltimore, Md.
Bibl. 15, 23, 25, 28, 29, 36, 38, 44, 54, 78, 114, 122

Hendrik Boelen I
(b. 1661–d. 1691)
Hendrik (Henricus) Boelen II
(b. 1697–d. 1755)
New York, N.Y.
These men are often confused.
Bibl. 2, 15, 23, 25, 28, 29, 30, 35, 36, 44, 54, 91, 95, 114, 116, 118, 119, 124, 135, 138

Jacob Boelen
(b. 1654–d. 1729)
New York, N.Y.
Bibl. 2, 4, 15, 23, 25, 28, 29, 30, 35, 36, 44, 54, 67, 91, 95, 102, 104, 114, 116, 118, 119, 124, 135, 138, 139

Jacob Boelen II
(c. 1733–1786)
New York, N.Y.
Bibl. 15, 23, 25, 35, 36, 44, 67, 91, 95, 114, 124, 135, 138

Abraham Boemper
(c. 1780–1793)
Bethlehem, Pa.
Bibl. 3, 23, 36, 44

Charles Bofenchen
(c. 1854–1857)
Camden, S.C.
Bibl. 5

Everadus Bogardus | E B |
(b. 1675)
New York, N.Y.
*Bibl. 4, 15, 23, 25, 28, 29,
35, 36, 44, 95, 114, 124,
138*

Peter S. Bogardus
(c. 1833–1834)
Albany, N.Y.
Bibl. 20, 124

Albert Bogart
(See Albert Bogert)

William Bogart
(c. 1839–1847)
Albany, N.Y.
Bibl. 20, 124

Boger & Wilson
(c. 1846–1853)
Salisbury, N.C.
John E. Boger
William Rowan Wilson
Bibl. 21

John E. Boger
(c. 1845–c. 1853)
Salisbury, N.C.
Boger & Wilson
(c. 1846–1853)
Bibl. 21

Albert Bogert (Bogart?)
(c. 1815–1830)
New York, N.Y.
*Bibl. 15, 23, 25, 28, 29, 36,
44, 124, 138*

**Widow of Albert Bogert
(Bogart?)**
(c. 1834–1836)
New York, N.Y.
Bibl. 15

**Nicholas J. Bogert
(Bogirt)** (c. 1801)
New York, N.Y.
*Bibl. 15, 23, 25, 28, 29, 36,
44, 114, 124, 138*

| N. J. BOGERT |

| N. BOGERT |

William Bogert (c. 1842)
Albany, N.Y.
Bibl. 23

Thomas Boggs (c. 1849)
Philadelphia, Pa.
Bibl. 3

Nicholas Bogirt
(See Nicholas Bogert)

Thomas H. Boguc & Co.
(c. 1844)
Philadelphia, Pa.
Bibl. 3

L. T. Boland (c. 1844)
Columbia, S.C.
Bibl. 5

Bolland
(See Gottschalk & Bolland)

Bolles & Childs
(See Bulles & Childs)

Bolles & Hasting
(c. 1840–1850)
Hartford, Conn.
Bibl. 89, 91, 114

Bolton & Horn (c. 1808)
Philadelphia, Pa.
William Bolton
Henry Horn
Bibl. 3

James Bolton (c. 1789)
New York, N.Y.
Bibl. 23, 28, 36, 44, 124, 138

**William Bolton (Botton)
(Boulton)**
(c. 1797–1813)
Philadelphia, Pa.
Bolton & Horn (c. 1808)
Bibl. 3

John Bonaus (c. 1809)
Charleston, S.C.
Bibl. 5

C. Bond (c. 1840)
Location unknown
Bibl. 28

| C BOND |

William Bond (c. 1765)
Portland, Me.
Boston, Mass.
Bibl. 28, 29, 44, 110

| W. Bond |

Boning & Co. (c. 1843)
Philadelphia, Pa.
William Boning
Bibl. 3

William Boning
(c. 1844–1850)
Philadelphia, Pa.
Boning & Co. (c. 1843)
Holden & Boning (c. 1843)
Bibl. 3

Victor Bonjean (c. 1822)
New Orleans, La.
Bibl. 36, 44

——— Bonnaud (c. 1799)
Philadelphia, Pa.
Bibl. 3

Bonnet & Co. (1879)
New Orleans, La.
Bibl. 141

James Bonnet (c. 1769)
New York, N.Y.
Bibl. 44

Bonsall & Jacot (c. 1849)
Philadelphia, Pa.
Edmund C. Bonsall
Julius Jacot
Bibl. 3

Bonsall & Scheer
(c. 1845–1847)
Philadelphia, Pa.
Edmund C. Bonsall
John C. Scheer (?)
Bibl. 3

Edmund C. Bonsall
(c. 1844–1850)
Philadelphia, Pa.
Bonsall & Jacot
Bonsall & Scheer
Bibl. 3

Edward C. Bonsall
(c. 1839–1840)
Philadelphia, Pa.
Bibl. 3

**Roswell Bontecou
(Bonticou) (Bounticou)**
(c. 1784–1805)
New Haven, Conn.
Augusta, Ga.
Gregory & Bontecou
(c. 1802–1805)
Bibl. 17, 110

Timothy Bontecou
(w. 1791–1815)
Savannah, Ga.
Bibl. 89

T B

Timothy Bontecou Sr.
(b. 1693–d. 1784)
Hartford, Conn.
Stratford, Conn.
New York, N.Y.
*Bibl. 15, 16, 23, 25, 28, 29,
36, 44, 61, 92, 94, 110,
114, 143*

T B

T B

R. Bonticou
(See R. Bontecou)

Boon
(See Webb & Boon)

Boon & Ormsby
(c. 1832–1834)
Cortland, N.Y.
Sanford Boon
Daniel D. R. Ormsby
Bibl. 20, 124

Timothy Bontecou Jr.
(b. 1723–d. 1789)
New Haven, Conn.
Stratford, Conn.
*Bibl. 15, 16, 17, 23, 25, 28,
29, 36, 44, 61, 92, 110,
114, 143*

Michael Boon (c. 1840)
Philadelphia, Pa.
Bibl. 3

Sanford Boon
(c. 1822–1844)
Hamilton, N.Y.
Boon & Ormsby
Bibl. 20, 124

Jeremiah Boone
(c. 1790–1796)
Philadelphia, Pa.
*Bibl. 3, 23, 25, 29, 36, 44,
114*

Ezra B. Booth
(b. 1805–d. 1888)
Rochester, N.Y.
(c. 1838–1888)
Vergennes, Vt.
Erastus Cook
*Bibl. 20, 25, 41, 44, 91, 110,
114, 124*

E. B. BOOTH

Thomas Booth (c. 1841)
Philadelphia, Pa.
Bibl. 3

Borde & Pettit (c. 1803)
Charleston, S.C.
Augustus Borde
——— Pettit
Bibl. 5

Augustine Bordeaux
(c. 1798–1799)
Philadelphia, Pa.
Bibl. 3, 23, 36, 44

Christian Bordersen
(c. 1850)
Russellville, Ky.
Bibl. 32, 54

George Bordick
(See George Burdick)

Charles G. Borhek
(c. 1829–1840)
Philadelphia, Pa.
Bibl. 3

Edward Borhek
(c. 1835–1850)
Philadelphia, Pa.
Bibl. 3, 25, 44, 114

**Frederick Bos(s)ardet
(Boshardt) (Bussarec)**
(c. 1840–1847)
Philadelphia, Pa.
Bibl. 3

——— Bosier (c. 1811)
Philadelphia, Pa.
Bibl. 3

Boss & Kindell (c. 1794)
New York, N.Y.
Bibl. 23, 36, 44, 138

Boss & Peterman (c. 1841)
Rochester, N.Y.
Philip Boss
Jefferson Peterman
Bibl. 20, 124

James Boss (c. 1846–1847)
Philadelphia, Pa.
Bibl. 3

Philip Boss (c. 1841)
Rochester, N.Y.
Boss & Peterman
Bibl. 20, 124

Peter Bossordet
(c. 1847–1849)
Philadelphia, Pa.
Bibl. 3

Zalmon Bostwick
(c. 1846–1852)
New York, N.Y.
*Bibl. 15, 23, 25, 29, 44,
114, 124, 138*

Z. BOSTWICK

Samuel Bosworth
(c. 1816–1837)
Buffalo, N.Y.
*Bibl. 20, 23, 25, 29, 36, 44,
114, 124, 133*

[BOSWORTH]

Gideon B. Botsford
(b. 1776–d. 1856)
Woodbury, Conn.
*Bibl. 15, 16, 23, 25, 28, 29,
36, 44, 91, 92, 110, 114*

[G B BOTSFORD]

J. S. Botsford
(c. 1840–1849)
Schenectady, N.Y.
Troy, N.Y.
Bibl. 20, 124

L. F. Botsford
(c. 1830–1831)
Albany, N.Y.
Bibl. 2, 124

Samuel N. Botsford
(c. 1839–1842)
Norfolk, Va.
Bibl. 19

William Botton
(See William Bolton)

Joseph Boudar (c. 1800)
New York, N.Y.
Bibl. 23, 36, 44, 124, 138

**Elias (Ellas) Boudinot
(Buddinott)**
(b. 1706–d. 1770)
Philadelphia, Pa.
(c. 1733–1752)
Princeton, N.J.
(c. 1753–1762)
*Bibl. 3, 23, 25, 28, 29, 36,
44, 46, 54, 81, 114, 124*

[BOUDINOT]

[EB] [BOUDINOT]

Heloise Boudo
(c. 1827–1837,
d. 1837)   [H BOUDO]

Charleston, S.C.
Bibl. 5, 25, 44, 54, 95, 114

Louis Boudo
(b. 1786–d. 1827)
Charleston, S.C.   [Lˢ BOUDO]
(1819–1827)
Maurel & Boudo (c. 1810)
*Bibl. 5, 15, 23, 25, 29, 36,
44, 54, 72, 91, 95, 102,
114*

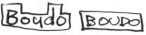

[L.P BOUDO]

[Boudo] [BOUDO]

Joseph Bouju
(w. 1812–1849)
St. Louis, Mo.
Bibl. 54, 134   [J BOUJU]

———— **Boullien** (c. 1811)
Philadelphia, Pa.
Bibl. 3

Mousier Boullien (c. 1811)
Philadelphia, Pa.
Bibl. 23, 36, 44

William Boulton
(See William Bolton)

Bounticou
(See Bontecou)

Stephen Bourdet(t)
(c. 1730)   (S.B)
New York, N.Y.
*Bibl. 4, 23, 25, 28, 35, 36,
44, 83, 114, 119, 124, 138*

Phelix Bourge (w. 1804)
Baltimore, Md.
Bibl. 38

Francis Bourgeois
(c. 1799)
Philadelphia, Pa.
Bibl. 3

Mary Bourgeois (c. 1801)
Charleston, S.C.
Bibl. 5

D. C. Bourquin
(c. 1904–1909)   ᐯᐯ
Port Richmond, N.Y.
Bibl. 127, 157

Joseph Bourreus (c. 1820)
Charleston, S.C.
Bibl. 5

Lewis Charles Boute
(c. 1839)
Philadelphia, Pa.
Bibl. 3

**James Boutelle
(Bowtelle)**
(c. 1783–1787)
Worcester, Mass.
Bibl. 23, 28, 36, 44, 121

(Widow) Boutier
(c. 1824–1826)
New York, N.Y.
Bibl. 15

John Boutier
(c. 1805–1824)
New York, N.Y.
*Bibl. 15, 23, 25, 29, 36, 44,
72, 91, 114, 124, 138*

(J BOUTIER)

Joseph Bouvar (c. 1797)
Philadelphia, Pa.
Bibl. 3, 23, 36, 44

Daniel Bouvier (c. 1816)
Putnam, Ohio
Bibl. 34, 44

Bowdle & Needles
(w. 1798)
Easton, Md.
James Bowdle
William Needles
Bibl. 38

James Bowdle
(c. 1790–1798)
Easton, Md.
Bowdle & Needles (c. 1798)
Bibl. 38

John Bowen (c. 1809)
Philadelphia, Pa.
Bibl. 3

**Joseph Morgan Bowene
and Mr. Prentice**
(w. 1788)
Baltimore, Md.
Bibl. 38

C. Bower (c. 1828–1833)
Philadelphia, Pa.
Bibl. 3, 23, 25, 36, 44, 114

BOWER

Michael Bower (c. 1799)
Philadelphia, Pa.
Bibl. 3

George Bowers (c. 1850)
Philadelphia, Pa.
Bibl. 3

Bowler & Burdick Co.
(c. 1890–c. 1922)
Cleveland, Ohio
Bibl. 127

Daniel Bowler (c. 1815)
Providence, R.I.
Bibl. 28, 110

Bowles & Phelps
(c. 1828–1829)
Albany, N.Y.
Bibl. 20, 124

H. H. Bowles (1875)
Cherryfield, Me.
Bibl. 105

Janet Payne Bowles
(b. 1876)
Indianapolis, Ind. (c. 1948)
New York, N.Y.
Bibl. 89

Jack Bowling
(c. 1940–1980)
Philadelphia, Pa.
Bibl. 127

Elias Bowman (c. 1834)
Rochester, N.Y.
*Bibl. 15, 20, 25, 41, 44, 114,
124*

Samuel Bowne (d. 1819)
New York, N.Y.
(c. 1780–1819)

*Bibl. 4, 15, 23, 25, 28, 29,
35, 36, 44, 83, 114, 124,
138*

S BOWNE

(Widow) Samuel Bowne
(c. 1825–1826)
New York, N.Y.
Bibl. 15, 138

Bowtelle
(See Boutelle)

Boyce & Jones   B & J
(c. 1825–1830)
New York, N.Y.
Geradus Boyce
William Jones (?)
*Bibl. 15, 23, 25, 29, 36, 44,
66, 91, 114, 122, 124*

BOYCE & JONES

**Geradus (Gheradus)
(Jared) Boyce**
(b. 1795–1797–d. 1880)
New York, N.Y.   G B
(c. 1814–1854)
Boyce & Jones   G. BOYCE
(c. 1825–1830)
*Bibl. 4, 15, 23, 25, 28, 29,
35, 36, 44, 91, 95, 114,
116, 122, 124, 138*

James Boyce
(c. 1825–1841)
New York, N.Y.
Philadelphia, Pa. (c. 1849)
James Boyce & Co.
(c. 1836–1838)
Bibl. 3, 15, 23, 36, 124, 138

James Boyce & Co.
(c. 1836–1838)
New York, N.Y.
Bibl. 15, 124, 138

Jared Boyce
(See Geradus Boyce)

John Boyce (c. 1801)   J B
New York, N.Y.
Bibl. 23, 25, 29, 36, 44, 114

Joseph Boyce
(c. 1802–1810)
Philadelphia, Pa.
Bibl. 3

William Boyce (w. 1806)
Baltimore, Md.
Bibl. 38

Boyd & Hoyt
(c. 1830–1842)
Albany, N.Y.
William Boyd
George B. Hoyt
*Bibl. 20, 23, 25, 28, 36, 44,
61, 114, 124*

Boyd & Mulford
(c. 1832–1842)
Albany, N.Y.
William Boyd
John H. Mulford
*Bibl. 20, 23, 25, 28, 36, 44,
114, 124*

BOYD & MULFORD

Boyd & Richards (c. 1808)
Philadelphia, Pa.
Thomas Boyd
——— Richards
Bibl. 3

Ezekiel C. Boyd
(c. 1830–1833)
Philadelphia, Pa.
Coats & Boyd (c. 1831) (?)
Bibl. 3

Joseph W. Boyd
(1816–1820)
New York, N.Y.
*Bibl. 23, 25, 29, 36, 44, 114,
124*

J W B

Thomas Boyd
(c. 1807–1809)
Philadelphia, Pa.
Boyd & Richards (c. 1808)
Bibl. 3

William Boyd
(b. 1775–d. 1840)
Albany, N.Y. (c. 1809–1840)
Sheperd & Boyd
(c. 1810–1830)
Boyd & Hoyt (c. 1830–1842)
Boyd & Mulford
(c. 1832–1842)
*Bibl. 20, 23, 28, 36, 44, 91,
95, 102, 119, 124, 135*

Boyden-Minuth Company
(1918–present)
Chicago, Ill.
Successor to Frank S.
Boyden Company
(1903–1918)
Bibl. 98, 146

Boyden & Fenno (c. 1825)
Worcester, Mass.
Bibl. 54, 110

———— **Boyer** (c. 1748)
Boston, Mass.
Bibl. 4

Boyer & Austin
(See Austin & Boyer)

Daniel Boyer
(b. 1725–d. 1779)
Boston, Mass.
Austin & Boyer
(c. 1750–1770)
*Bibl. 2, 15, 23, 25, 28, 29,
36, 44, 54, 69, 91, 94, 110,
114*

James Boyer
(c. 1700–1741)
Boston, Mass.
Bibl. 2, 23, 44, 70, 110

Edward Boylston
(b. 1765–d. 1836)
Stockbridge, Mass. (c. 1789)
Catskill, N.Y.
Manlius, N.Y.
Bibl. 20, 28, 44, 110, 124

Wm. N. Boynton (c. 1882)
Manchester, Ia.
(See Guild)
Bibl. 127

Daniel Boyter (c. 1803)
Poughkeepsie, N.Y.
Bibl. 20, 124

Isaac Brabant (d. 1764)
Savannah, Ga.
Bibl. 17, 23, 36, 44

**Brackett, Crosby &
Brown** (c. 1850)
Boston, Mass.
Jeffrey R. Brackett
Samuel T. Crosby
———— Brown
Bibl. 28

Jeffrey R. Brackett
(c. 1815–1876)
Boston, Mass.
Brackett, Crosby & Brown
(c. 1850)
Bibl. 25, 28, 44, 91, 114

JEFFREY BRACKETT

Francis Braconnier
(c. 1826)
New York, N.Y.
Bibl. 15, 124, 138

Bradbury & Brother
(c. 1810)
Newburyport, Mass.
Bibl. 23, 28, 36, 44, 110

Edward Bradbury
(c. 1819–1822)
Philadelphia, Pa.
Bibl. 3

Capt. Phineas Bradbury
(c. 1779)
New Haven, Conn.
Bibl. 28

Theophilus Bradbury
(c. 1815)
Newburyport, Mass.
Moulton & Bradbury
(c. 1830)
*Bibl. 15, 23, 25, 28, 29, 36,
44, 91, 94, 102, 110, 114*

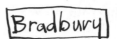

Charles H. Bradford
(c. 1855–1894)
Massachusetts
Westerley, R.I.
New Albany, Ind.
Owensboro, Ky.
Bibl. 28, 44, 110, 133

C.H. BRADFORD

Joseph Bradford
(c. 1842–1843)
Philadelphia, Pa.
Bibl. 3

O. C. Bradford (c. 1841)
Binghamton, N.Y.
Bibl. 20, 124

Simon Bradford (b. 1797)
Lexington, Ky
(c. 1814–1819)
Bibl. 32, 54, 68, 93

John Bradier
(c. 1802–1804)
Philadelphia, Pa.
Bibl. 3

———— **Bradley**
Hartford, Conn.
Bradley & Bunce
(1830–1835)
Bibl. 16, 23, 36, 44

Bradley & Bunce
(c. 1830–1835)
Hartford, Conn.
———— Bradley
———— Bunce
Bibl. 16, 23, 36, 44

Bradley & Merriman
(c. 1826–1847)
New Haven, Conn.
Zebul Bradley
Marcus Merriman Jr.
*Bibl. 16, 23, 25, 28, 29, 36,
44, 143*

Aner (Abner) Bradley
  (b. 1753–d. 1824)
New Haven, Conn.
Watertown, Conn.
Bibl. 16, 23, 25, 28, 29, 36,
  44, 54, 91, 92, 110, 114,
  143

[A BRADLEY]

G. C. Bradley
Binghamton, N.Y. (c. 1841)
Kingston, N.Y.
  (c. 1842–1843)
Bibl. 20

Gustavus Bradley
  (c. 1848)
New Haven, Conn.
Zebul Bradley & Son
Bibl. 16, 23, 143

H. G. Bradley (c. 1810)
Mantua, Ohio
Bibl. 34, 44, 88

H. S. Bradley & Co.
  (c. 1836–1850)
Utica, N.Y.
Horace S. Bradley
William Blackwood
  (c. 1836–1838)
Bibl. 18, 20, 124

Horace P. Bradley
  (c. 1832–1841)
Utica, N.Y.
Storrs & Cooley
  (c. 1831–1839)
Tanner & Cooley
  (c. 1840–1842)
Bibl. 18, 20, 124

Horace S. Bradley
  (b. 1805)
Utica, N.Y. (c. 1828–1850)
Leach & Bradley
  (c. 1832–1835)
H. S. Bradley & Co.
  (c. 1836–1850)
Bibl. 18, 91, 124, 158

Luther Bradley
  (c. 1772–1830)
New Haven, Conn.
Bibl. 15, 23, 25, 28, 36, 44,
  61, 91, 92, 94, 110, 114,
  143

Phineas Bradley [P B]
  (c. 1745–1797)
New Haven, Conn.
Bibl. 15, 16, 23, 25, 28, 29,
  36, 39, 44, 91, 92, 110,
  114, 143

Richard Bradley
  (b. 1787–d. 1867)
Hartford, Conn.
  (c. 1825–1828)
Bibl. 16, 23, 28, 36, 44, 110

Zebul Bradley
  (b. 1780–d. 1859)
New Haven, Conn.
Marcus Merriman & Co.
  (c. 1802–1817)
Merriman & Bradley
  (c. 1817–1820)
Bradley & Merriman
  (c. 1826–1847)
Zebul Bradley & Son
  (c. 1848)
Bibl. 15, 16, 23, 25, 28, 29,
  36, 44, 61, 91, 92, 94, 110,
  114, 143

[Z.BRADLEY]

Zebul Bradley & Son
  (c. 1848)
New Haven, Conn.
Zebul Bradley
Gustavus Bradley
Bibl. 16, 23, 91, 92, 110, 143

William Bradshaw
  (c. 1809–1810)
Philadelphia, Pa.
Bibl. 3

E. Brady (c. 1825)
New York, N.Y.
Bibl. 23, 25, 29, 36, 44, 114,
  124

[E.BRADY]

[BRADY]

John Brady (c. 1835)
Philadelphia, Pa.
Bibl. 3

William Brady (c. 1835)
New York, N.Y.
Bibl. 4, 28

William Vermilyea Brady
  (c. 1834–1841)
New York, N.Y.
Bibl. 15, 23, 36, 44, 124, 138

**Frederick Adolphus
  Brahe** (d. 1892)
Albany, N.Y. (c. 1840–1844)
Augusta, Ga. (c. 1845)
Bibl. 17, 124

[F A BRAHE]

C. Brainard & Son (1830)
Hartford, Conn.
Charles Brainard
Charles H. Brainard
Bibl. 16, 25, 28, 36, 44

Charles Brainard
  (b. 1787–d. 1850)
Hartford, Conn.
Ward, Bartholomew &
  Brainard (c. 1809–1830)
C. Brainard & Son (Charles
  H.)
Bibl. 16, 23, 28, 36, 44, 110

W. J. Braitsch & Co.
  (c. 1895–1922)
Providence, R.I.
Bibl. 114, 127, 157

[TRADE MARK
STERLING]

Barnet Brakman (c. 1840)
Philadelphia, Pa.
Bibl. 3

E. Braman (c. 1830)
Location unknown
Bibl. 24

[E. Braman]

S. D. Bramhall (1875)
Camden, Me.
Bibl. 105

Sylvanus Bramhall
  (b. 1776)
Plymouth, Mass. (c. 1790)

Bibl. 23, 25, 28, 29, 36, 44, 91, 110, 114

S BRAMHALL

Bartlett M. Bramhill
(c. 1820)
Boston, Mass.
Davis, Watson & Co.
Bibl. 25, 28, 29, 110

C. Brand (c. 1820)
Philadelphia, Pa. (?)
Bibl. 89

Thomas Brand
(c. 1837–1842)
Troy, N.Y.
Bibl. 20, 124

Charles Branda
Philadelphia, Pa. (c. 1817)
Norfolk, Va (c. 1818–1829)
Bibl. 19

C. BRANDA

James Brander (c. 1813)
Charleston, S.C.
Bibl. 5

Brandt & Mathey
(c. 1795–1799)
Philadelphia, Pa.
———— Brandt
Lewis Mathey
Bibl. 3

Brandt (Brant), Brown & Lewis (c. 1795–1796)
Philadelphia, Pa.
Bibl. 3

Aime Brandt
(c. 1816–1831)
Philadelphia, Pa.
Aime & Charles Brandt
(c. 1800–1814)
Bibl. 3

Aime & Charles Brandt
(c. 1800–1814)
Philadelphia, Pa.
Bibl. 3, 25, 44, 54, 114

A & C BRANDT

Charles Brandt
Philadelphia, Pa.
Aime & Charles Brandt
(c. 1800–1814)
Charles Brandt & Co.
(c. 1816–1818)
Bibl. 3

Charles Brandt & Co.
(c. 1816–1818)
Philadelphia, Pa.
Bibl. 3

Barnet Brannan
(c. 1840)
Philadelphia, Pa.
Bibl. 3

Bernard Brannan
(c. 1842–1848)
Philadelphia, Pa.
Bibl. 3

Rees Branson (b. 1771)
Martinsburg, Va.
(c. 1802–1809)
Bibl. 19

Brant
(See Brandt, Brown & Lewis)

Brasher & Alexander
(c. 1800)
New York, N.Y.
Bibl. 23, 36, 44, 124, 138

Amable Brasher
(See Amable Brasier)

E. Brasher & Co. (c. 1790)
New York, N.Y.
Ephraim Brasher
Bibl. 23, 36, 44, 124

E B & Co

Ephraim Brasher
(b. 1744–d. 1810)
New York, N.Y.
E. Brasher & Co. (c. 1790)
Bibl. 4, 15, 23, 25, 28, 29, 30, 35, 36, 44, 54, 91, 95, 102, 114, 116, 118, 124, 135, 138, 151

EB

Amable Brasier (Brasher)
(c. 1790–1840)
Philadelphia, Pa.
New York, N.Y.
A BRASIER
Bibl. 3, 15, 23, 25, 28, 29, 36, 44, 72, 78, 79, 91, 102, 114

A. BRASHER

Francis Brasier (c. 1824)
Philadelphia, Pa.
Bibl. 3

John Brassington
(c. 1820–?)
Alexandria, Va.
Bibl. 19

Bray & Redfield
(c. 1850–1857)
New York, N.Y.
Became Bancroft, Redfield & Rice
Bibl. 127

Henry Bray (c. 1799–1813)
Philadelphia, Pa.
Bibl. 3, 23, 36, 44

Thomas Bray (c. 1799)
Augusta, Ga.
Bibl. 17

C. L. Bready (c. 1808)
Philadelphia, Pa.
Bibl. 3

John Breans (c. 1825)
Philadelphia, Pa.
Bibl. 3

James Brearley
(c. 1795–1822)
Philadelphia, Pa.
Bibl. 3

Louis Brechémin
(c. 1816–1850)
Philadelphia, Pa.
Laret & Brechémin
(c. 1816–1818)
Bibl. 3

Joseph Hunt Breck
(b. 1766–d. 1801)
Northampton, Mass.
(c. 1789–1801)
Bibl. 84, 110

John Breed
  (b. 1752–d. 1803)
Colchester, Conn.
Bibl. 16, 23, 28, 36, 44, 110

William Breed (b. 1719)
Boston, Mass. (c. 1750)
*Bibl. 15, 23, 25, 28, 29, 36,
  44, 69, 94, 110, 114*

Lamon Brees (c. 1837)
Wellsburg, Va.
Bibl. 19

Edward H. Breese
  (1921–1940)
Chicago, Ill.
Bibl. 98

L. Breidenbauch (c. 1807)
Philadelphia, Pa.
Bibl. 3

Brelet, Wearer & Co.
  (c. 1825)
Augusta, Ga.
Francis Brelet
William Wearer
John Guimarin
Bibl. 17

Francis Brelet
  (c. 1824–?)
Augusta, Ga.
Guimarin & Brelet (c. 1824)
Brelet, Wearer & Co.
  (c. 1825)
Bibl. 17

Brem & Alexander
  (c. 1848)
Charlotte, N.C.
—————— Brem
Samuel P. Alexander
Bibl. 21

Barnabas Brennan
  (c. 1843)
Philadelphia, Pa.
Bibl. 3

Raymond Brenner, Inc.
  (c. 1949–present)
Youngstown, Ohio
Bibl. 127

Brenno & Co. (c. 1818)
Philadelphia, Pa.
John Brenno
Bibl. 3

John Brenno (c. 1824)
Philadelphia, Pa.
Brenno & Co. (c. 1818)
Bibl. 3

Benjamin Brenon
(See B. Brenton)

**Benjamin Brenton
(Brenon)**
  (b. 1710–d. 1766)
Newport, R.I.
(See preceding entry)
*Bibl. 15, 23, 25, 28, 29, 36,
  44, 54, 56, 72, 110, 114,
  118*

—————— **Breorbey** (c. 1799)
Philadelphia, Pa.
Bingham & Breorbey
Bibl. 3

John Breslin
  (c. 1828–1833)
Philadelphia, Pa.
Bibl. 3

John Brevoort
  (b. 1715–d. 1775)
New York, N.Y.
*Bibl. 4, 15, 23, 25, 28, 29,
  35, 36, 44, 54, 91, 95, 102,
  114, 119, 124, 138, 142*

Brewer & Mann
  (c. 1803–1805)
Middletown, Conn.
Charles Brewer

Alexander Mann
*Bibl. 16, 23, 28, 36, 44, 91,
  110*

C. Brewer & Co. (c. 1810)
Middletown, Conn.
*Bibl. 15, 23, 25, 36, 91, 92,
  110, 114*

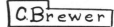

Charles Brewer
  (b. 1778–d. 1860)
Middletown, Conn.
Hart & Brewer
  (c. 1800–1803)
Brewer & Mann
  (c. 1803–1805)
*Bibl. 15, 16, 25, 28, 29, 36,
  61, 78, 91, 92, 94, 110,
  114, 122*

Charles Brewer (c. 1824)
New York, N.Y.
Moore & Brewer
  (c. 1824–1837)
Jared L. Moore & Co.
  (c. 1837–1844)
Bibl. 15, 44, 124, 135, 138

N. Alexander F. Brewer
  (c. 1842–1847)
Charlotte, N.C.
Lawing & Brewer
  (c. 1842–1843)
Bibl. 5, 21

Thomas A. Brewer
  (c. 1830–1850)
Philadelphia, Pa.
Bibl. 3

William Brewer
  (c. 1774–1824)
Philadelphia, Pa.
Bibl. 3

—————— **Brewington**
  (c. 1711)
Charleston, S.C.
Bibl. 5

Abel Brewster
  (b. 1775, c. 1797–1805)
Canterbury, Conn.
Norwich, Conn.
*Bibl. 16, 23, 25, 28, 36, 44,
  92, 110, 114*

Samuel Bricknall (c. 1817)
Philadelphia, Pa.
Bibl. 3

Chas. C. Briddell, Inc.
  (c. 1900–present)
Crisfield, Md.
(Carvel Hall Division of
  Towle Silversmiths)
Bibl. 127

Bride & Tinckler
  (c. 1896–1922)
New York, N.Y.
Bibl. 114, 127

Benjamin Bridge (c. 1797)
Rutland, Vt.
Bibl. 54, 110

John Bridge
  (b. 1723, c. 1751)
Boston, Mass.
*Bibl. 2, 4, 15, 23, 25, 28, 29,
  36, 44, 110, 114*

Joseph Brier
  (c. 1849–1850)
Philadelphia, Pa.
Bibl. 3, 23

Robert Brier (c. 1848)
Philadelphia, Pa.
Bibl. 3, 23

Thomas Brigan (c. 1832)
Louisville, Ky.
Bibl. 32, 54, 93

C. Brigden (c. 1770)
Boston, Mass.
Bibl. 23, 29, 36, 44

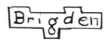

**Timothy Brigden
(Brigdon)**
  (c. 1774–1819)
Albany, N.Y.
*Bibl. 15, 20, 23, 25, 28, 36,
  44, 54, 102, 114, 124*

Zachariah Brigden
  (b. 1734–d. 1787)
Boston, Mass.
*Bibl. 2, 15, 23, 25, 28, 29,
  36, 39, 44, 54, 72, 91, 94,
  102, 114, 116, 119, 151*

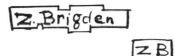

C. Brigdens (c. 1770)
Boston, Mass.
Bibl. 4, 28, 91

Brigdon
(See Timothy Brigden)

Briggs
(See Akerly & Briggs)

Briggs & Harlow
Location unknown
Bibl. 89

Daniel Briggs (c. 1836)
New York, N.Y.
Bibl. 15, 124, 138

William W. Briggs
  (c. 1834–1836)
New York, N.Y.
Bibl. 15, 91, 124, 138

John Brigham (c. 1678)
Location unknown
Bibl. 28

Anthony Bright (d. 1749)
Philadelphia, Pa. (c. 1739)
Bibl. 3, 23, 28, 36, 44

A. A. Brimmer (1860)
Ellsworth, Me.
Bibl. 105

Brindsmaid
(See also Brinsmaid)

Abraham Brindsmaid
  (c. 1815)
Burlington, Vt.
Bibl. 44, 114

—— Bringhurst
  (c. 1850)
Maine or New Hampshire
Bibl. 28, 105

Joseph Bringhurst
  (c. 1813)
Philadelphia, Pa.
Bibl. 3

William Brinkley
  (c. 1802–1810)
New York, N.Y.
Bibl. 23, 28, 36, 44, 124, 138

Brin(d)smaid & Hildreth
  (c. 1830)
Burlington, Vt.
Bibl. 24, 25, 54, 89

Brinsmaid's
(See Brin[d]smaid &
  Hildreth, Pangborn &
  Brinsmaid)

Henry Brinsmaid
  (c. 1847–c. 1850)
Rochester, N.Y.
Bibl. 20, 124

Brinton, Gordon & Quick (Quirk) (c. 1780)
Boston, Mass.
Bibl. 23, 28, 36, 44

F. Brintzinghoffer
(c. 1804)
Philadelphia, Pa.
Bibl. 3

Bristol Brass & Clock Co.
(1856–1901)
Bristol, Conn.
Successor to Holmes & Tuttle
Mfg. Co. (1857)
Became American Silver Co.
(1901)
Bought by International
Silver Co. (1935)
Bibl. 127

Bristol Silver Company
(c. 1915)
Attleboro, Mass.
Successor to Bristol Mfg. Co.
Bibl. 127, 157

Bristol Silver Corp.
(c. 1950–present)
Taunton, Mass.
(See Poole Silver Co., E. J.
Towle Mfg. Co.)
Bibl. 127, 146

John S. Britain (c. 1855)
Nashville, Tenn.
Bibl. 54

Britannia Artistic Silver
(See M. T. Goldsmith)

Brittain
(See Beckwith & Brittain)

**Isaac Britton (Brittin)
(Britten)**
(c. 1811–1816)
New York, N.Y.
Philadelphia, Pa.
*Bibl. 3, 23, 36, 44, 91, 124,
138*

**Jacob Britton (Brittin)
(Britten)**
(c. 1807–1850)

Philadelphia, Pa.
Bibl. 3, 23, 36, 39, 44

John Britton (c. 1855)
Nashville, Tenn.
Bibl. 54

Thomas Britton (Brittin)
(c. 1848–1850)
Philadelphia, Pa.
Bibl. 3, 91

James Broadbridge
(c. 1806–1832)
Newburgh, N.Y.
Bibl. 20, 124

Samuel Broadhurst
(d.c. 1735)
New York, N.Y. (c. 1724)
*Bibl. 4, 23, 28, 36, 44, 124,
138*

Charles P. Brocha
(c. 1833)
Philadelphia, Pa.
Bibl. 3

Charles Brochet
(c. 1819–1822)
Philadelphia, Pa.
Bibl. 3

Charles B. Brochett
(c. 1831)
Philadelphia, Pa.
Bibl. 3

John Brock (c. 1831–1849)
New York, N.Y.
*Bibl. 4, 15, 23, 25, 28, 29,
36, 44, 91, 114, 124, 138*

L. Brock (c. 1830)
New York, N.Y.
(May be John Brock)
Bibl. 23, 25, 29, 36, 44

| L. BROCK |

F. C. Brockman
(b. 1814–d. 1898)
Cincinnati, Ohio

(1839–1858)
Bibl. 34, 90, 152

John Brodnox
(b. 1668–d. 1719)
Williamsburg, Va.
Bibl. 19, 53

Thomas F. Brogan Co.
(c. 1896–1930)
New York, N.Y.
Bibl. 114, 127

John Bronaugh
(c. 1817–1827)
Richmond, Va.
Bibl. 19, 54

| BRONAUGH |

Robert Brookhouse
(b. 1779–d. 1866)
Salem, Mass. (c. 1750)
*Bibl. 15, 23, 25, 28, 29, 36,
44, 91, 110, 114*

Brooks
(See Trott & Brooks)

Brooks & Dold
(c. 1866–1874)
Madison, Ind.
Frederick O. Brooks
Godfried Dold
Bibl. 133

BROOKS & DOLD

Brooks & Griswold
(c. 1832)
Utica, N.Y.
Benjamin Franklin Brooks
Joab Griswold
Bibl. 18, 20, 124

Brooks & Hone (c. 1858)
Utica, N.Y.
Benjamin Franklin Brooks
——— Hone
Bibl. 18, 20, 124

Brooks & Van Voorhis
(c. 1843)
Utica, N.Y.
Benjamin Franklin Brooks
——— Van Voorhis
Bibl. 18, 20

Brooks & Warrock
(c. 1795–?)
Norfolk, Va.
Samuel Brooks
William Warrock
Bibl. 19

BROOKS & WARROCK

B. F. Brooks & Co.
(c. 1829–1831)
Utica, N.Y.
Benjamin Franklin Brooks
Gaylord Griswold
Bibl. 18, 20, 124

B. F. Brooks & Son
(c. 1855)
Utica, N.Y.
Benjamin Franklin Brooks
Bibl. 18, 20, 124

Benjamin Franklin
Brooks (c. 1828–1858)
Utica, N.Y.
Blackwood & Brooks
(c. 1828–1830)
B. F. Brooks & Co.
(c. 1829–1831)
Brooks & Griswold (c. 1832)
Brooks & Van Voorhis
(c. 1843)
B. F. Brooks & Son
(c. 1855)
Brooks & Hone (c. 1858)
Bibl. 18, 20, 124, 158

Charles V. Brooks
(c. 1834–1840)
Utica, N. Y.
Bibl. 18, 20, 124, 158

Frederick O. Brooks
(c. 1853–1900)
Madison, Ind.
Brooks & Dold
Bibl. 133

BROOKS

F.O. BROOKS

Nicholas Brooks (1775)
Philadelphia, Pa.
Bibl. 44

Samuel Brooks
Philadelphia, Pa. (c. 1790)
Norfolk, Va. (c. 1794)
Richmond, Va.
(c. 1803–1820)

Brooks & Warrock
(c. 1795–?)
*Bibl. 3, 19, 23, 25, 29, 36,
44, 102, 114*

{BROOKS}

Brookway & Bacon
(c. 1836)
Louisville, Ky.
Bibl. 32, 93

Broom & Clement
(c. 1837)
Philadelphia, Pa.
William Broom (?)
James W. Clement (?)
Bibl. 3

William Broom
(c. 1833–1837)
Philadelphia, Pa.
Broom & Clement (c. 1837)
(?)
Bibl. 3

William Broom Jr.
(c. 1835)
Philadelphia, Pa.
Bibl. 3

Lewis R. Broomall
(c. 1846–1850)
Philadelphia, Pa.
Bibl. 4, 91

William Broome
(c. 1825–1850)
Philadelphia, Pa.
Bibl. 3

Peter S. Broshey
(c. 1829–1831)
Philadelphia, Pa.
Bibl. 3

Michael Brothe(a)rs
(c. 1772–1773)
Philadelphia, Pa.
Bibl. 3, 23, 36, 44

T. Brothers (c. 1830–1835)
Philadelphia, Pa.
Bibl. 3

George Brougham
(w. 1774)

Maryland
Bibl. 38

Brower & Rusher
(c. 1837–1842)
New York, N.Y.
*Bibl. 23, 25, 28, 29, 35, 36,
44, 83, 91, 114, 124, 138*

B & R

B. D. Brower & Son
(c. 1850)
Albany, N.Y.
Bibl. 23, 124

J. H. Brower
(c. 1848–1849)
Albany, N.Y.
Bibl. 20, 124

S. & B. Brower
(c. 1810–1850)
Albany, N.Y.
Bibl. 23, 25, 29, 36, 44, 114

S & B BROWER

S. Douglas Brower
Troy, N. Y. (c. 1832–1836)
New York, N.Y. (c. 1834)
Albany, N.Y. (c. 1837–1850)
Brower & Rusher
Hall, Hewson & Co.
Hall, Brower & Co.
(c. 1836–1842)
Hall & Hewson
(c. 1842–1847)
Hall, Hewson & Brower
(c. 1847–1850)
Hall and Brower
(c. 1852–1854)
*Bibl. 20, 23, 25, 28, 36, 44,
91, 114, 124*

Walter S. Brower
(c. 1850–1898)
Albany, N.Y.
Bibl. 23, 29, 44

Brown
(See Crosby & Brown; Davis & Brown; Leavenworth, Brown & Co.; Packard & Brown; Shreve, Brown & Co.; Watson & Brown)

Brown & Anderson
(c. 1850–1871)
Wilmington, N.C.
Thomas William Brown
William S. Anderson
Bibl. 21

Brown & Dart
Location unknown
Bibl. 89

Brown(e) & Houlton
(See Houlton & Brown[e])

Brown(e) & Kirby
(c. 1840–1857)
New Haven, Conn.
Bibl. 24, 25, 44, 91, 92, 114, 143

BROWN & KIRBY

Brown & Mann (c. 1805)
Connecticut
Bibl. 28, 91

Brown & Stout
New York, N.Y.
(c. 1809–1811)
Philadelphia, Pa. (c. 1811)
Bibl. 3, 46, 135

Brown & Ward
(c. 1896–1904)
New York, N.Y.
William A. Brown
Frederick T. Ward
Bibl. 114, 127, 157

A. Brown & Co. (1860)
Providence, R.I.
Bibl. 108

A. M. Brown (1875)
Brownville, Me.
Bibl. 105

Alexander Brown
(c. 1840–1847)
Philadelphia, Pa.
Bibl. 3, 23, 36, 44

Chancey Brown
(c. 1845)
Philadelphia, Pa.
Bibl. 3

Charles Brown
(c. 1829–1833)
Philadelphia, Pa.
Bibl. 3

Charles C. Brown
(b. 1827–d. 1871)
Rochester, N.Y.
(c. 1849–1850)
Bibl. 20, 41, 44, 124

D. Brown (c. 1811)
Philadelphia, Pa.
Bibl. 15, 23, 25, 28, 29, 36, 44, 114

D BROWN

E. Brown
(See John Eden Brown)

Ebenezer Brown
(c. 1773–1816)
Boston, Mass.
Bibl. 23, 28, 36, 44

Edward Brown
(c. 1816–1830)
Baltimore, Md.
(c. 1807–1808)
Liberty, Va (c. 1817)
Lynchburg, Va. (c. 1824)
Bibl. 19, 54, 91, 110

BROWN   E BROWN

Edwin F. Brown (1875)
Brunswick, Me.
Bibl. 105

Elnathan C. Brown
(18th century)
Westerly, R.I.
Bibl. 28, 44, 56, 110

Francis Brown
(c. 1837–1844)
New York, N.Y.
Moore & Brown (?)
Jared L. Moore & Co.
Bibl. 15, 124, 135, 138

George Brown (c. 1830)
Barnesville, Ohio
Bibl. 34

George C. Brown
(1834–1835)
New Orleans, La.
Bibl. 141

Henry Brown (Henry Brown Guest) (c. 1777)
Philadelphia, Pa.
Bibl. 3, 23, 36, 44

Henry S. Brown (b. 1833)
New York, N.Y.
Syracuse, N.Y.
(c. 1851–1852)
Utica, N.Y. (c. 1853–1860)
Bibl. 18, 20, 23, 91, 114, 124, 158

Henry T. Brown & Co.
(1878–1880)
Providence, R.I.
Successor to Gorham Co. & Brown (1856–1878)
Became Tilden-Thurber & Co. (1880–present)
Bibl. 127

Isaac C. Brown (c. 1844)
Philadelphia, Pa.
Bibl. 3, 23

J. A. Brown & Co. (1860)
Providence, R.I.
Bibl. 108

James Brown
(c. 1785)
Philadelphia, Pa.
Bibl. 3, 23, 36, 44

James Brown (w. 1792)
Baltimore, Md.
Bibl. 38

James Brown (c. 1800)
Detroit, Mich.
Bibl. 58

I B

James Brown
(c. 1772–1808)
Fredericksburg, Va.
Bibl. 19

Jesse Brown
  (c. 1813–1817)
Baltimore, Md. (w. 1819)
Philadelphia, Pa.
Bibl. 3, 23, 36, 38, 44

John Brown
  (c. 1785–1824)
Philadelphia, Pa.
Baltimore, Md. (1799) (?)
*Bibl. 3, 23, 25, 28, 29, 36,
  38, 44*

J. B

John Brown (c. 1777)
Port Royal, Va.
Bibl. 19

John Eden Brown
  (w. 1810–1816)
Baltimore, Md.
Bibl. 38, 151

John J. Brown
  (c. 1848–1852)
Utica, N.Y.
Bailey & Brothers
  (c. 1846–1852)
Bibl. 18, 20, 124, 158

L. Brown (c. 1838)
Rochester, N.Y.
Bibl. 20, 41, 44

L. S. F. Brown (c. 1872)
Wilmington, N.C.
T. W. Brown & Sons
Bibl. 21

Lester Brown (c. 1843)
Cazenovia, N.Y.
Clark & Brown
Bibl. 20, 124

Levi Brown (c. 1866)
Detroit, Mich.
Chauncey S. Payne
Bibl. 58

Liberty Brown(e)
  (c. 1801–1819)
Baltimore, Md.
Philadelphia, Pa.
Houlton & Brown (c. 1799)
Browne & Seale
  (c. 1810–1811)

*Bibl. 3, 15, 23, 25, 36, 39,
  44, 91, 114*

M. S. Brown & Co.
  (c. 1835)
Shepherdstown, Va.
Bibl. 19

Martin S. Brown
Winchester, Va. (c. 1827)
Shepherdstown, Va.
  (c. 1829–1838)
Bibl. 19

Philip Brown (c. 1841)
Philadelphia, Pa.
Bibl. 3

R. Brown & Son (c. 1830)
Baltimore, Md.
Bibl. 24

R. J. Brown & Son
  (c. 1833)
Boston, Mass.
Bibl. 25, 44

Robert Brown (c. 1774)
Savannah, Ga.
Pinkerd & Brown
Bibl. 17

Robert Brown
  (c. 1827–1831)
Baltimore, Md.
*Bibl. 15, 23, 24, 29, 36, 38,
  114*

R BROWN

Robert Brown & Son
  (1833–?)
Baltimore, Md.
Bibl. 29, 38, 114

R BROWN & SON

Robert Johnson Brown
  (c. 1813)
Boston, Mass.
Bibl. 25, 44, 91

ROBERT J. BROWN

S. Brown (c. 1815–1834)
New York, N.Y.
Bibl. 15, 28, 44, 54, 95

S BROWN   S BROWN

S. D. Brown (1834)
Albany, N.Y.
Bibl. 44

Samuel C. Brown
  (c. 1820–1850)
New York, N.Y.
*Bibl. 15, 23, 24, 25, 29, 36,
  44, 91, 114, 124, 138*

S BROWN

Seth E. Brown
  (b. 1821–d. 1884)
Concord, N.H.; Mass.
  (c. 1844–1864)
*Bibl. 15, 44, 91, 107, 114,
  125*

Seth E Brown

T. J. Brown (c. 1835)
Location unknown
Bibl. 28   T. J. BROWN

T. W. Brown & Sons
  (c. 1872)
Wilmington, N.C.
Thomas William Brown
L. S. F. Brown
E. F. Story
Bibl. 21, 124

Theodore G. Brown
  (after 1825)
New York, N.Y.
Bibl. 23, 124

**Theodore G. Brown &
  Son** (c. 1840)
New York, N.Y.
Bibl. 23

Thomas Brown
(c. 1827–1835)
New York, N.Y.
Bibl. 15, 138

Thomas G. Brown & Sons
(c. 1881–1915)
New York, N.Y.
Successor to
Taylor & Hinsdale
(1807–1817)
Taylor, Baldwin & Co.
(1817–1840)
Baldwin & Co.
(c. 1840–1869)
Thomas G. Brown
(1869–1881)
Bibl. 114, 127, 135, 144, 157

Thomas William Brown
(b. 1803–d. 1872)
Wilmington, N.C.
Brown & Anderson
(c. 1850–1871)
T. W. Brown & Sons
(c. 1872)
Bibl. 21, 124

William Brown
(c. 1810–1852)
Baltimore, Md.
Bibl. 15, 25, 44, 114

| WM BROWN |

William Brown
(c. 1845–1849)
Albany, N.Y.
Bibl. 23, 25, 28, 44, 54, 114, 124

| W. BROWN |

William Brown
(c. 1823–1847)
Philadelphia, Pa.
Bibl. 3, 91

William H. Brown
(c. 1848–1849)
Philadelphia, Pa.
Bibl. 3

William S. Brown
(c. 1849–1850)
Philadelphia, Pa.
Bibl. 3

Browne & Seale
(c. 1810–1811)
Philadelphia, Pa.
Liberty Brown(e)
William Seal(e) (Jr.)
Bibl. 3, 15, 23, 24, 25, 28, 36, 39, 44, 72, 91, 114

Browne, Jennings & Lauter (c. 1915–1922)
Newark, N.J.
(See Reeves & Browne)
Bibl. 127, 157

Hiram Brownson
(c. 1841–1842)
Troy, N.Y.
Bibl. 20, 124

Robert Bruce
(c. 1772–1774)
Williamsburg, Va.
Bibl. 19

Thaddeus Bruder
(c. 1837)
Philadelphia, Pa.
Bibl. 3

Charles Oliver Bruff
(b. 1731–d. 1787)
Elizabeth, N.J.
(c. 1760–1765)
New York, N.Y.
(c. 1765–1776)
Nova Scotia (c. 1783–1787)
Bibl. 3, 15, 23, 24, 25, 28, 29, 44, 46, 50, 54, 91, 95, 102, 104, 114, 118, 119, 124, 138

| C.O.B |

| Charles O Bruff |
| Chas O Bruff |

James Bruff (d. 1780)
Elizabeth, N.J.
(c. 1748–1765)
New York, N.Y. (c. 1766)
Bibl. 46, 54

Joseph Bruff | I B |
(b.c. 1730–1785)
Easton, Md. (w. 1750–1785)
Bibl. 3, 15, 24, 25, 29, 44, 91, 114

| I. BRUFF |

Joseph Bruff II
(b.c. 1770–d. 1803)
Easton, Md. (w. 1790–1800)
Chestertown, Md.
(w. 1800–1803)
Bibl. 29, 38, 91

| I. BRUFF |

Joseph Bruff (c. 1767)
Philadelphia, Pa.
Bibl. 23, 28, 36

Thomas Bruff III
(b. 1760–d. 1803)
Easton, Md. (c. 1785–1791)
Chestertown, Md.
(c. 1791–1803)
Bibl. 25, 29, 44, 91, 102, 114

| T. BRUFF | | T BRUFF |

―――― **Bruleman** (c. 1760)
Philadelphia, Pa.
Bibl. 3

Paul Bruneau (c. 1819)
Philadelphia, Pa.
Bibl. 3

Bruno & Virgins
(c. 1840–1849)
Columbus, Ga.
Macon, Ga.
―――― Bruno
Samuel Stanley Virgin(s)
Bibl. 17

George Bruns
(b. 1839–d. 1920)
Columbia, S.C.
(c. 1855–1914)
Bibl. 5

Isaac Brunson (c. 1800)
Detroit, Mich.
Bibl. 58   I B

Edward Brush (c. 1774)
New York, N.Y.
Bibl. 23, 36, 44

Benjamin Brussetier
(1816–1817)
New Orleans, La.
Bibl. 141

James Bryan
(19th century)
Kentucky (?)
Bibl. 32, 93

JAMES BRYAN

John Bryan (c. 1749)
Williamsburg, Va.
Bibl. 19, 153

Phil(l)ip Bryan
(c. 1802–1803)
Philadelphia, Pa.
Bibl. 3, 12, 23, 24, 25, 29, 44

BRYAN

Butler Bryant
(c. 1838–1848)
Frankfort, Ky.
Louisville, Ky.
Bibl. 32, 93

F. S. Bryant (1861)
Kennebunkport, Me.
Bibl. 105

Irena Brynner (Bryner)
(c. 1949–1960)
New York, N.Y.
Bibl. 117, 156

Chas. B. Bryon Co.
(c. 1909–1915)
New York, N.Y.
Successor to Bryon & Vail
Co.
Bibl. 127, 157

**Edward (Edmund) A.
Bryson** (c. 1841–1848)
Louisville, Ky.
Bibl. 32, 93

Charles W. Buard
(c. 1849)
Philadelphia, Pa.
Bibl. 3

Stanton Bube (c. 1805)
Providence, R. I.
George C. Clark
Bibl. 28

Peter Buche(z)
(c. 1795–1797)
New York, N.Y.
Bibl. 23, 36, 44, 124, 138

John B. Buchey
(c. 1818–1819)
Philadelphia, Pa.
Bibl. 3

Buchez
(See Buche)

I. R. Buchoz
(See Lewis R. Buchoz)

Lewis R. Buchoz (c. 1835)
New York, N.Y.
Bibl. 23, 36, 44, 124

Azariah Buck
(c. 1847–1850)
Rochester, N.Y.
Bibl. 20, 41, 44, 124

Solomon Buck
(c. 1827–1828)
Glens Falls, N.Y.
Bibl. 20, 124

Daniel Buckins
Daniel Buckius
(See Bockius)

**Buckley (Buckhey) &
Anderson** (c. 1804)
Philadelphia, Pa.
J. B. Buckley
———— Anderson
Bibl. 3, 23, 36, 44

Henry Peat Buckley
(1839–1903)
New York, N.Y.
New Orleans, La.
Bibl. 141

H.P. BUCKLEY

J. B. Buckley (c. 1807)
Philadelphia, Pa.
Buckley & Anderson
*Bibl. 3, 23, 24, 25, 36, 44,
114*

BUCKLEY

Samuel Buckley (c. 1811)
Philadelphia, Pa.
Bibl. 3

George Buckman
(w. 1802)
Baltimore, Md.
Bibl. 38

Samuel Bucknell (c. 1825)
Philadelphia, Pa.
Bibl. 3

Buddinott
(See Boudinot)

Daniel Buddy (c. 1769)
Philadelphia, Pa.
Bibl. 3, 23, 36, 44

Buel & Greenleaf
(c. 1798)
New Haven, Conn.
Abel Buel(l)
William Greenleaf
Bibl. 23, 25, 36, 44, 143

Buel & Mix (c. 1783)
New Haven, Conn.
Abel Buel
———— Mix
Bibl. 23, 28, 36, 44, 110, 143

Abel Buel(l)
(b. 1742–d. 1825)
New Haven, Conn.
(c. 1783, c. 1798)
Hartford, Conn.
Killingworth, Conn.
Buel & Mix (c. 1783)
Buel & Greenleaf (c. 1798)
Ebenezer Chittenden

*Bibl. 2, 15, 16, 23, 24, 25,
28, 29, 36, 44, 47, 54, 61,
92, 94, 102, 110, 114, 143*

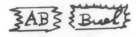

Charles I. Buel (c. 1846)
Saratoga Springs, N.Y.
Schenectady, N.Y.
Bibl. 20, 124

D. H. Buel
(c. 1763?–1825?)
Hartford, Conn.
Bibl. 23, 36, 44, 91

John Buel
(b. 1744–d. 1783)
Derby, Conn.
New Haven, Conn.
*Bibl. 16, 23, 28, 36, 44, 110,
143*

Samuel Buel(l) [S B]
(b. 1742–d. 1819)
Middletown, Conn.
(c. 1777)
Hartford, Conn. (c. 1780)
*Bibl. 15, 16, 23, 24, 25, 28,
29, 44, 61, 91, 92, 110,
114*

William Buel
Rupert, Vt. (c. 1787–1790)
Fair Haven, Vt.
(c. 1790–1796)
Bibl. 54, 110

Lewis Buichle
(c. 1798–1802)
Baltimore, Md.
Bibl. 25, 29, 38, 44, 114

Bull & Morrison (c. 1780)
Hartford, Conn.
Caleb Bull
Norman Morrison
Bibl. 23, 36, 44, 110

Caleb Bull
(b. 1746–d. 1797)
Hartford, Conn.
Bull & Morrison (c. 1780)
Bibl. 16, 23, 28, 36, 44, 110

Epaphras Bull (c. 1813)
Boston, Mass.
Bibl. 23, 36, 44, 110

G. W. Bull (c. 1840)
Farmington, Conn.
*Bibl. 23, 25, 29, 36, 44, 92,
114*

[G. W. BULL]

Martin Bull
(b. 1744–d. 1825)
Farmington, Conn.
Thomas Lee
*Bibl. 16, 23, 28, 36, 44, 92,
110*

Bulles (Bolles) & Childs
(c. 1840)
Hartford, Conn.
Bibl. 25, 44, 114

[BULLES & CHILDS
HARTFORD]

Leola Bullivant
(c. 1914–1921)
St. Louis, Mo.
Bibl. 155

John Buly (c. 1778)
Philadelphia, Pa.
Bibl. 3, 44

Bumm & Shepper
(c. 1818–1823)
Philadelphia, Pa.
Peter Bumm (?)
John D. Shepper
*Bibl. 3, 4, 23, 25, 28, 36, 44,
114*

[BUMM &
SHEPPER]

John S. Bumm
(c. 1837–1850)
Philadelphia, Pa.
Bibl. 3

Peter Bumm
(c. 1814–1833)
Philadelphia, Pa.
Whartenby and Bumm
(c. 1816–1818) (?)
Bumm & Shepper
(c. 1818–1823) (?)
Bibl. 3, 23, 36, 44, 91, 102

[P BUMM]

——— Bunce
Hartford, Conn.
Bradley & Bunce
(c. 1830–1835)
Bibl. 16, 23, 36, 44

H. Bunce (c. 1801)
Augusta, Ga.
Bibl. 17

Benjamin Bunker [BB]
(b. 1751–d. 1842)
Nantucket Island, Mass.
Providence, R.I.
*Bibl. 12, 15, 23, 25, 28, 36,
44, 110, 114*

Francis Bunnell (c. 1850)
Syracuse, N.Y.
Bibl. 20, 124

Daniel Bunting (c. 1844)
Philadelphia, Pa.
Bibl. 3

A. F. Burbank (c. 1845)
Worcester, Mass.
Bibl. 25, 44, 114 [A. F. B.]

[A. F. BURBANK]

Albert Burd
(c. 1823–1824)
Philadelphia, Pa.
Bibl. 3

Charles Burd (c. 1850)
Philadelphia, Pa.
Bibl. 3

E. D. Burd (1875)
Belfast, Me.
Bibl. 105

William Burd
(See William Byrd)

Burdick & Burritt
(c. 1816–1819)
Ithaca, N.Y.
William P. Burdick
Joseph Burritt
Bibl. 20, 124

William P. Burdick
(c. 1815)
Ithaca, N.Y.
Burdick & Burritt
(c. 1816–1819)
Bibl. 20, 91, 124

William S. Burdick
(c. 1810–1814)
New Haven, Conn.
Ufford & Burdick
(c. 1812–c. 1814)
*Bibl. 16, 23, 28, 36, 44, 92,
110, 143*

**George Burdock
(Bordick)**
(c. 1790–1811)
Philadelphia, Pa.
Bibl. 3, 23, 36, 44

Nicholas Burdock
(c. 1797)
Philadelphia, Pa.
*Bibl. 3, 23, 25, 28, 29, 36,
44, 72, 114*

J. P. Burgalic (c. 1799)
New York, N.Y.
Bibl. 23, 36, 44, 124, 138

Frederick Burge (c. 1766)
Bound Brook, N.J.
Bibl. 54

Burger & Prichard
(c. 1776)
New York, N.Y.
Bibl. 35, 83, 91, 124

David I. Burger
(c. 1805–1835)
New York, N.Y.
*Bibl. 15, 23, 24, 25, 29, 36,
44, 91, 114, 124, 138*

John Burger
(c. 1786–1808)
New York, N.Y.
*Bibl. 4, 15, 23, 24, 25, 28,
29, 35, 36, 39, 44, 72, 83,
91, 95, 102, 114, 116, 118,
124, 138*

Joseph Burger
(c. 1830–1831)
Philadelphia, Pa.
New York, N.Y.
(c. 1834–1839)
Bibl. 3, 124, 138

Thomas Burger (c. 1805)
New York, N.Y.
*Bibl. 15, 23, 24, 25, 35, 36,
44, 83, 91, 114, 124, 138*

Thomas & John Burger
(c. 1805)
New York, N.Y.
Bibl. 15, 25, 91, 114, 124

T. B   BURGER

H. F. Burgess (1860)
Fairfield, Me.
Bibl. 105

Leonard G. Burgess
(c. 1831–1850)
Albany, N.Y.
Bibl. 20, 124, 138

Frederick Burgi
(c. 1766–1776)
Bound Brook, N.J.
Hurtin & Burgi
Bibl. 46

**Robert Burham
(Burnham)** (c. 1790)
New York, N.Y.
Bibl. 23, 36, 44, 124

Charles Burk (c. 1848)
Philadelphia, Pa.
Bibl. 3

——— Burke (c. 1790)
Location unknown
Bibl. 24   BURKE

E. K. Burke (c. 1842)
St. Louis, Mo.
Bibl. 54

Edmund K. Burke
(c. 1841)
Louisville, Ky.
Bibl. 32, 93

**Samuel Burkelow
(Burkloe)**
(c. 1790–1813)
Philadelphia, Pa.
Bibl. 3, 23, 36, 44

Thomas F. Burkhand
(c. 1837–1843)
Philadelphia, Pa.
Bibl. 3

Trubert Burkhart
(c. 1839–1846)
Philadelphia, Pa.
Bibl. 3

Burkloe
(See Burkelow)

John Burn (c. 1823–1824)
Philadelphia, Pa.
Bibl. 3

Daniel Burnap
(b. 1760–d. 1838)
Coventry, Conn.
East Windsor, Conn.
*Bibl. 16, 23, 28, 36, 44, 92,
102, 110*

Ela Burnap
(b. 1784–d. 1856)
Boston, Mass. (c. 1810)
New York (c. 1817)
Hartford, Conn. (c. 1813)
Eatonton, Ga. (c. 1821)
Rochester, N.Y.
(c. 1827–1844)
*Bibl. 15, 17, 20, 25, 28, 41,
44, 92, 110, 114, 124*

E Burnap

**Burnet(t) & Rider
(Ryder)** (c. 1795)
Philadelphia, Pa.
Samuel Burnet
Bibl. 23, 24, 25, 29, 36, 114

B.R̄

Aaron Lee Burnet
(c. 1820)
Charleston, S. C.
Bibl. 5

Samuel Burnet (c. 1796)
Newark, N.J.
Philadelphia, Pa.
Burnet(t) & Rider (Ryder)
(c. 1795)
Bibl. 23, 36, 44

Smith Burnet
(b. 1770–d. 1830)
Newark, N.J. (c. 1793–1830)
Bibl. 16, 54

Burnett
(See also Rice & Burnett)

B. L. Burnett
Milledgeville, Ga.
(c. 1847–1848)
Macon, Ga. (c. 1847–1857)
Lexington, Ky. (c. 1857)
C. K. Wentworth & Co.
(c. 1847)
Bibl. 17, 32, 54, 68, 93

Charles A. Burnett
(b. 1760–d. 1849)
Georgetown, D.C.
(c. 1785–1849)
Alexandria, Va.
*Bibl. 15, 19, 23, 24, 25, 28,
29, 36, 44, 46, 54, 91, 95,
104, 114, 116*

C A B   C A BURNETT

Lawrence Burney (Birnie)
(c. 1774–1779)
Philadelphia, Pa.
Bibl. 3

Charles E. Burnham
Utica, N.Y. (c. 1853–1854)
Binghamton, N.Y. (c. 1857)
Bibl. 18, 20, 124

E. B. Burnham (c. 1821)
Salisbury, N.C.
Elliott & Burnham
Bibl. 21

John Burnham
(b. 1792–d. 1870)
Brattleboro, Vt. (1844)
Bibl. 54, 110

P. B. Burnham (c. 1856)
Greenville, S.C.
P. B. Burnham & Co.
Bibl. 5

P. B. Burnham & Co.
(c. 1860)
Greenville, S.C.
P. B. Burnham
Bibl. 89

Robert Burnham
(See Robert Burham)

(Miss) Burns (c. 1810)
Washington, Ga.
Bibl. 17

(Mr.) Burns (c. 1837–1854)
Greenville, S.C.
Isaac H. Benedict
Bibl. 5

Andrew Burns (c. 1796)
Louisville, Ga.
Bibl. 17

Anthony Burns (c. 1785)
Philadelphia, Pa.
Bibl. 3, 23, 36, 44

Hugh Burns
(c. 1809, d. 1812)
Philadelphia, Pa.
Bibl. 3

James Burns
(See James Byrne)

James Burns (c. 1810)
Philadelphia, Pa.
Bibl. 23, 36, 44

John H. Burns
(c. 1834–1841)
New York, N.Y.
Bibl. 15, 23, 36, 44

Andrew Burot
(c. 1819–1827)
Baltimore, Md.
Bibl. 4, 23, 28, 36, 38, 44

Burr & Lee (c. 1815)
Providence, R.I.
Samuel W. Lee
Ezekiel Burr
*Bibl. 23, 25, 36, 41, 48, 91,
110*

Aaron C. Burr   A. C. BURR
(1830–1846)
New York, N.Y.
*Bibl. 15, 20, 24, 25, 28, 36,
41, 44, 91, 114, 124, 138*

Alexander Jay Burr
(b. 1810–d. 1838)
Rochester, N.Y.
(c. 1832–1838)
Bibl. 20, 41, 44, 124

C. A. Burr & Co.
(before 1863)
Rochester, N.Y.
Cornelius A. Burr
John T. Fox
*Bibl. 15, 20, 23, 36, 41, 44,
91, 114, 124*

C. A. BURR & CO.

Christopher Burr
(b. 1787–d. 1825)
Providence, R.I. (c. 1800)
Jabez Gorham
George C. (G.) Clark
*Bibl. 15, 23, 25, 28, 29, 36,
44, 56, 91, 110, 114*

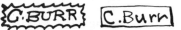

Cornelius A. Burr
(b. 1816–d. 1863)
Rochester, N.Y.
(c. 1838–1850)

Brooklyn, N.Y. (before 1863)
C. A. Burr & Co.
   (before 1863)
Bibl. 20, 25, 41, 44, 91, 124

E. & W. Burr (c. 1793)
Providence, R.I.
Ezekiel Burr
William Burr
Bibl. 36, 44, 91, 110

Ezekiel Burr
   (b. 1765–d. 1846)
Providence, R.I.
E. & W. Burr (c. 1793)
Burr & Lee (c. 1815)
*Bibl. 23, 24, 25, 29, 36, 44,
   54, 56, 91, 94, 110, 114*

Ezekiel & William Burr
   (c. 1793)
Providence, R.I.
Bibl. 23, 91, 110

Nathaniel Burr
   (b. 1698–d. 1784)
Fairfield, Conn.
*Bibl. 24, 25, 44, 61, 92, 94,
   110, 114*

William Burr
   (b. 1772–d. 1810)
Providence, R.I. (c. 1792)
E. & W. Burr (c. 1793)
*Bibl. 15, 23, 25, 28, 36, 44,
   55, 56, 110, 114*

John Burrage (w. 1769)
Annapolis, Md.
Bibl. 38

Burrell
(See Burrill)

—— **Burrill**
Augusta, Ga.
Huntington & Burrill
   (c. 1817–1819)
Bibl. 17

Burrill & Beebe (c. 1836)
New York, N.Y.
George Burrill
Bibl. 15, 124

George Burrill (c. 1837)
New York, N.Y.
Burrill & Beebe (c. 1836)
Bibl. 15, 124, 138

Joseph Burrill (c. 1823)
Boston, Mass.
Bibl. 23, 28, 36, 44, 110

Samuel Burrill (Burrell)
   (c. 1704–d. 1740)
Boston, Mass.
*Bibl. 4, 15, 23, 24, 25, 28,
   29, 36, 44, 50, 80, 91, 110,
   114*

Samuel Burrill Jr.
   (c. 1829)
Boston, Mass.
Bibl. 23, 36, 44

Theophilus Burrill
   (c. 1717–1739,
   d. 1739)
New London, Conn.
Boston, Mass.
Bibl. 16, 23, 28, 36, 44, 110

J. Burritt & Son
   (c. 1838–1862)
Ithaca, N.Y.
Joseph Curtiss Burritt
Bibl. 20, 124

Joseph Burritt (b. 1795)
Ithaca, N.Y.
Burdick & Burritt
   (c. 1816–1819)
Bibl. 20, 124

Joseph Curtiss Burritt
   (b. 1817–d. 1889)
Ithaca, N.Y.
J. Burritt & Son
   (c. 1838–1862)
Bibl. 20, 124

Bardon Burrow
   (c. 1829–1833)
Norfolk, Va.
Bibl. 19

William Burrows
   (c. 1829–1837)
Philadelphia, Pa.
Bibl. 3, 23, 36, 44

Benjamin Burt
   (b. 1729–d. 1805)
Boston, Mass.
*Bibl. 2, 15, 23, 24, 25, 28,
   29, 36, 44, 50, 54, 91, 94,
   102, 110, 114, 116, 118,
   139, 151*

John Burt
   (b. 1691–d. 1745)
Boston, Mass.
*Bibl. 2, 4, 15, 23, 24, 25, 28,
   29, 44, 50, 54, 91, 94, 102,
   110, 114, 118, 119, 139,
   151*

M. Burt (c. 1860)
Cleveland, Ohio
Bibl. 89, 114

M BURT CLEVE'D O

Samuel Burt
   (b. 1724–d. 1754)
Boston, Mass.

*Bibl. 2, 15, 23, 24, 25, 28,
29, 36, 44, 54, 91, 102,
110, 114, 119, 139*

William Burt
(b. 1726–d. 1752)
Boston, Mass.
*Bibl. 2, 4, 23, 24, 25, 28, 29,
36, 39, 44, 54, 104, 110,
114, 119*

Jacob Burton (c. 1839)
Philadelphia, Pa.
Bibl. 3, 23, 36

Burtt
(See Durgin & Burtt)

Burwell & Winship
(c. 1855)
Norfolk, Va.
F. W. Burwell
———— Winship
Bibl. 19

F. W. Burwell
(c. 1846–1855)
Norfolk, Va.
Burwell & Winship (c. 1855)
Bibl. 15, 19, 114

F. W. BURWELL

Fitch Burwell
(c. 1841–1843)
Norfolk, Va. (c. 1843–1844)
Portsmouth, Va.
J. M. Freeman & Co.
(c. 1843–1844)
Bibl. 19

M. Busches (c. 1810)
Philadelphia, Pa.
Bibl. 3

Francis A. Bush (b. 1834)
Utica, N.Y. (c. 1852–1857)
Bibl. 18, 24, 158

George Bush G. Bush
(c. 1812–1837)
Eaton, Pa.
Bibl. 15, 44, 91, 114

John H. Bush (b. 1830)
Utica, N.Y. (c. 1848–1859)
Bibl. 18, 20, 124, 158

Philip Bush Jr.
(b. 1765–d. 1807)
Winchester, Va. (c. 1787)
Frankfort, Ky. (?)
Bibl. 19, 32, 93

John Bushea
(c. 1808–1809)
Philadelphia, Pa.
Bibl. 3

Phineas Bushnell
(b. 1741–d. 1836)
Guilford, Conn.
Saybrook, Conn.
*Bibl. 16, 23, 28, 36, 44, 91,
92, 110*

**Francis Bushwry
(Busshwry)**
(c. 1798–1799)
Philadelphia, Pa.
Bibl. 3

Bussarec
(See Bos[s]ardet)

Benjamin Bussey B B
(b. 1757–d. 1842)
Dedham, Mass.
*Bibl. 2, 23, 24, 25, 28, 29,
36, 44, 110, 114*

Thomas D. Bussey
(b. 1773–d. 1804)
Baltimore, Md.
(w. 1792–1804)
*Bibl. 15, 23, 25, 28, 36, 38,
44, 114*

T.D.Bussey

Busshwry
(See Bushwry)

Jason Buswell (c. 1839)
Portsmouth, N.H.
Bibl. 23, 36, 44, 110, 124

Isaac Butaud
(c. 1813–1818)
Philadelphia, Pa.
Bibl. 3

Butler & DeBerard
(c. 1807–1815)
Utica, N.Y.
Nathaniel Butler
Charles J. J. DeBerard
Bibl. 18, 20, 124

Butler & Keim (c. 1843)
Philadelphia, Pa.
William H. Butler (?)
Alexander Keim
Bibl. 3, 23

Butler & Little
(c. 1759–1765)
Portland, Me.
John Butler
Paul Little
Bibl. 23, 36, 44, 110

Butler & McCart(h)y
(c. 1850)
Philadelphia, Pa.
*Bibl. 4, 15, 23, 25, 28, 44,
91, 114*

BUTLER & M'CARTY

Butler & Osborn
(c. 1805–1807)
Utica, N.Y.
Nathaniel Butler
John Osborn
Bibl. 18, 20, 124

Butler, Wise & Co.
(c. 1842)
Philadelphia, Pa.
Bibl. 3, 23, 25, 44, 114

B W & Co

Butler, Wise & Keim
(c. 1850)
Philadelphia, Pa.
William H. Butler
George K. Wise
Alexander Keim
Bibl. 3, 23

Charles Paxton Butler
(b. 1765–d. 1858)
Charleston, S.C.
Bibl. 5, 25, 44, 54, 114

C P B

Courtland Butler
(c. 1843–1845)
Philadelphia, Pa.
Bibl. 3

Franklin Butler
(c. 1846–1850)
Philadelphia, Pa.
Bibl. 3

Henry W. Butler
(c. 1833–1850)
Philadelphia, Pa.
Bibl. 3, 17, 23, 36, 44

James Butler
(c. 1713–1776)
Boston, Mass.
*Bibl. 23, 24, 25, 28, 29, 36,
44, 94, 102, 110, 114*

J BUTLER

I B

James F. Butler (c. 1850)
Utica, N.Y.
Bibl. 18, 20, 124, 158

John Butler
(b. 1734–d. 1827)
Portland, Me.
Butler & Little
(c. 1759–1765)
*Bibl. 15, 23, 28, 36, 44, 91,
110*

J. BUTLER

IB

Lewis A. Butler (c. 1850)
Binghamton, N.Y.
Bibl. 20, 124

N. H. Butler (c. 1837)
Philadelphia, Pa.
Bibl. 3, 23, 36, 44

Nathaniel Butler
(b. 1760–d. 1829)
Savannah, Ga.
(c. 1790–1797)
Utica, N.Y.
Butler & Osborn
(c. 1805–1807)
Butler & DeBerard
(c. 1807–1815)
Truman Smith (c. 1815)
*Bibl. 17, 18, 20, 23, 28, 36,
44, 91, 124, 158*

N BUTLER

Thomas R. Butler
(c. 1820–1822)
Philadelphia, Pa.
Bibl. 3

William H. Butler
(c. 1842–1843)
Philadelphia, Pa.
Butler & Keim (c. 1843) (?)
Butler, Wise & Keim
(c. 1850)
Bibl. 3, 23

C. Butman (1875)
Cherryfield, Me.
Bibl. 105

Henry Buttercase
(c. 1853–?)
Utica, N.Y.
Bibl. 18

Buttre
(See Adams & Buttre)

J. L. Buzell (c. 1750)
Location unknown
Bibl. 28, 29, 44

J. L. BUZELL

Columbus Buzzel
(c. 1837)
Philadelphia, Pa.
Bibl. 3

———— Bwistrand (c. 1844)
New York, N.Y.
Van Ness & Bwistrand
Bibl. 23

William Byrd (Burd)
(b. 1774–d. 1813)
Augusta, Ga. (c. 1796)
Charleston, S. C. (c. 1802)
Savannah, Ga. (?)
Bibl. 5, 17, 44

W B

James Byrne (Burns)
Philadelphia, Pa. (c. 1784)
New York State
(c. 1789–1797)
Elizabeth, N.J. (c. 1799)
James Byrne & Co. (c. 1799)
*Bibl. 3, 15, 23, 24, 25, 28,
29, 35, 36, 39, 44, 46, 54,
91, 95, 114, 124, 138*

J. Byrne

JByrne

James Byrne & Co.
(c. 1799)
Elizabeth, N.J.
Bibl. 46, 91

John Byrne (c. 1835–1846)
Lexington, Ky.
Bibl. 54, 68, 93

Thomas Byrnes
(c. 1766–1798)
Wilmington, Del.
Woodcock & Byrnes
(c. 1793)
*Bibl. 25, 30, 39, 44, 91, 95,
114*

T BYRNES

C

C
(See Frederick H. Clark, J.
H. Clark, L. H. Cohen,
John A. Coles)

C. & B.
(See Chapman & Barden)

C & C
(See Colton & Collins)

C. & H. Co.
(See Chapin & Hollister Co.)

C & P
(See Clark & Pelletreau,
Cleveland & Post, Curry &
Preston)

C A B
(See Charles A. Burnett)

C A V
(See Clarence A. Vanderbilt)

C A W & Co.
(See C. A. Wetherell & Co.)

C B
(See Caleb Beal, Clement
Beecher, Charles Brewer,
C. Brigden)

C. B. & H.
(See Codding Bros. &
Heilborn)

C C
(See Charles Candell,
Charles Carpenter,
Christian Cornelius, Cellini
Craft)

C. C. & Co. (c. 1810–1830)
Location unknown
Bibl. 89

C C & D
(See Charters, Cann &
Dunn)

C C & S
(See Curtis, Candee & Stiles)

C C S
(See Charles C. Shaver)

C E E
(See Charles Edward Evard)

C G
(See Caesar Ghiselin)

C H
(See Charles Hall, Charles
Hequenbourg, Christopher
Hughes)

C-I
(See Clement Jackson)

C K
(See Cornelius Kierstede)

C K & S
(See C. Klank & Sons)

C L
(See Charles Leach)

C M R
(See Chas. M. Robbins)

C O B
(See Charles Oliver Bruff)

C P A
(See Charles Platt Adriance)

C P B
(See Charles Paxton Butler)

C R
(See Cristopher Robert,
Currier & Roby)

C R R
(See C. Ray Randall & Co.)

C S
(See Caleb Shields)

C. S.
(See Concord Silversmiths,
Ltd.)

C S Co.
(See Chicago Silver Co.)

C S C
(See Central Sterling Co.)

C U G F
(See Colin V. G. Forbes)

C V B
(See Cornelius Vander
Burgh)

C W
(See Captain Charles
Whiting, Christian
Wiltburger Jr., Christian
Charles Lewis Wittich)

Charles Cable
(c. 1816–1818)
Philadelphia, Pa.
Bibl. 3

Jean Cabos
(b. 1757, c. 1804–1806)
Charleston, S.C.
Bibl. 19

**Felix Ferjeux Cachot
(Cashot)**
(c. 1813–1839)
Bardstown, Ky.
Bibl. 32, 68, 93

Jay Cadwell (c. 1850)
Philadelphia, Pa.
Bibl. 3

Cady & Backus (Bachus)
(c. 1792–1796)
New York, N.Y.
Samuel Cady
Delucine Backus
Bibl. 23, 28, 36, 44, 124, 138

Samuel Cady
New York, N.Y.
Cady & Backus
(c. 1792–1796)
Bibl. 23, 28, 36, 44, 124, 138

Michael Cagger
(c. 1832–1838)
Albany, N.Y.
Finch & Cagger
(c. 1832–1838)
Bibl. 20, 124

Abraham Cahn (c. 1850)
Philadelphia, Pa.
Bibl. 3

————— **Caijol** (w. 1795)
Baltimore, Md.
Bibl. 38

Cain & Clements (c. 1817)
Petersburg, Va.
Claiborn W. Cain
Sampson Clements
Bibl. 19

Claiborn W. Cain
(c. 1817–1824)
New York, N.Y. (c. 1831)
Petersburg, Va.
(c. 1817–1824)
Cain & Clements (c. 1817)
Bibl. 19, 138

Michael Cain
(c. 1831–1832)
Albany, N.Y.
Bibl. 20, 124

John Cairns (c. 1827)
Rochester, N.Y.
Bibl. 20, 41, 44, 124

Oliver Calame
Charles Town, Va. (c. 1821)
Frederick Town, Md.
(c. 1819)
Harpers Ferry, Va. (c. 1820)
Bibl. 19, 38

Calder & Co. (c. 1830)
Albany, N.Y.
Troy, N.Y.
Bibl. 23, 28, 36, 44

Alexander Calder
(b. 1898–d. 1976)
Roxbury, Conn.
Bibl. 89, 117

Andrew Calderwood
(c. 1800–1822)
Philadelphia, Pa.
Bibl. 3

Caldwell
(See Zadek & Caldwell)

E. Caldwell (c. 1800)
New York, N.Y.
Bibl. 23, 36, 44, 124

J. E. Caldwell & Co.
(1848–present)
Philadelphia, Pa.
James E. Caldwell
George Banks
Bibl. 3, 15, 44, 78, 122, 127, 135

J. S. Caldwell (1843–1844)
New Orleans, La,
Bibl. 141

James E. Caldwell
(d. 1881)
Philadelphia, Pa. (c. 1832)
Bennett & Caldwell
(c. 1843–1848)
J. E. Caldwell & Co.
(c. 1848–present)
Filley, Mead & Caldwell
(c. 1850) (?)
Bibl. 3, 15, 44, 91, 102, 116, 124, 127

Samuel Caldwell (c. 1825)
Philadelphia, Pa
Bibl. 3

George R. Calhoun
(1830–1860)
Nashville, Tenn.
Bibl. 54, 89

William H. Calhoun
(1839–1860)
Nashville, Tenn.
Bibl. 54, 89

V. D. P. Call (1860)
Milton Plantation, Me.
Bibl. 105

Theresa Callahan
(1973–1980)
St. Louis, Mo.
Bibl. 155

Benjamin Callender
(c. 1784)
Boston, Mass.
Bibl. 28

Thomas G. Calvert
(c. 1815–1850)
Lexington, Ky.
Bibl. 54, 68, 93

Joseph Camain
(See Camoia)

**Alexander Cameron
(Camman) (Cammon)**
(c. 1813–1834)
Albany, N.Y.
Bibl. 4, 20, 23, 24, 25, 28, 29, 36, 114, 124

| A C |

Samuel Cameron
(c. 1828–1830)
Philadelphia, Pa.
Bibl. 3

**Alexander Camman or
Cammon**
(See Alexander Cameron)

William Cammer
(c. 1839–1842)
Philadelphia, Pa.
Bibl. 3

Cammon
(See Camman)

**Joseph Camoia (Camain)
(Camoin)**
(w. 1803–1806)
Baltimore, Md.
Bibl. 38

————— **Camoin** (c. 1797)
Philadelphia, Pa.
Bibl. 3, 23, 28, 36, 44

Camp & Dubbs (1838)
New Orleans, La.
Bibl. 141

Elias Camp (c. 1825–1827)
Bridgeport, Conn.
George Kippen (c. 1827)
Bibl. 23, 24, 25, 36, 44, 92

Campbell-Metcalf Silver Co. (c. 1892–1898)
Providence, R.I.
Bibl. 114, 127, 157

Campbell & Donigan
(1853–1855)
Nashville, Tenn.
John Campbell
George W. Donigan
Bibl. 54, 89

Campbell & Meredith
(c. 1850)
Winchester, Va.
Thomas Boyle Campbell
James Meredith
Bibl. 19

| CAMPBELL | J. MEREDITH |

Campbell & Polk
(c. 1850–1858)
Winchester, Va.
Thomas Boyle Campbell
Robert I. W. Polk
Bibl. 19

| CAMPBELL | POLK |

Campbell & Prior
(c. 1834–1836)
Fayetteville, N.C.
John Campbell
Warren Prior
Bibl. 21, 25, 91

Alexander Campbell
(b. 1775) (c. 1793–1798)
Fayetteville, N.C.
Philadelphia, Pa.
(c. 1798–1799)
Bibl. 3, 21

Alexander H. Campbell
Marion, Va. (c. 1849)
Brooklyn, N.Y. (c. 1850)
Bibl. 19, 124

Andrew Campbell
(d. 1854)
Baltimore, Md.
(c. 1835–1854)
R. & A. Campbell
Bibl. 15, 23, 91

Andrew Campbell
(c. 1829–1842)
Philadelphia, Pa.
Bibl. 3

Archibald Campbell
(w. 1827–1837)
Baltimore, Md.
Bibl. 38

C. Campbell (c. 1827)
Greenville, S.C.
Bibl. 5

Charles Campbell
(c. 1794–1803)
Philadelphia, Pa.
Bibl. 3

Christopher Campbell
(c. 1808–1812)
New York, N.Y.
Bibl. 5, 15, 23, 25, 29, 36, 44, 114, 124

| CAMPBELL |

Isaac Campbell
(c. 1813–1824)
Philadelphia, Pa.
Bibl. 3

J. Campbell (c. 1835)
Cheraw, S. C.
Bibl. 5

James Campbell (c. 1817)
Steubenville, Ohio
Bibl. 34

John Campbell
(c. 1828–1831)
Philadelphia, Pa.
Bibl. 3

John Campbell (b. 1803)
Fayetteville, N.C.
(c. 1834–1836)
Cheraw, S.C.
(1836–?)
Nashville, Tenn. (1836–?)

Selph & Campbell
(c. 1827–1829)
Campbell & Prior
(c. 1834–1836)
Campbell & Donigan
(1853–1855)
Bibl. 21, 25, 44, 91, 114

John W. Campbell
(c. 1814–1819)
New York, N.Y.
Bibl. 15, 23, 36, 44, 124, 138

R. & A. Campbell
(c. 1835–1854) R. & A.C.
Baltimore, Md.
Robert Campbell
Andrew Campbell
Bibl. 4, 15, 23, 24, 25, 28, 29, 44, 91, 114

R & A CAMPBELL

Robert Campbell | R.C |
(b. 1799–d. 1872)
Baltimore, Md.
(w. 1819–1835)
Richards & Campbell
(c. 1819)
R. & A. Campbell
(c. 1835–1854)
Bibl. 4, 23, 24, 25, 28, 29, 36, 44, 91

Robert E. Campbell
(c. 1818–1830)
Ravenna, Ohio
Cincinnati, Ohio
Bibl. 34, 152

| T CAMPBELL |

Thomas Campbell
(c. 1770)
New York, N.Y.
Bibl. 23, 24, 29, 36, 44

Thomas Campbell
(c. 1800–1833)
New York, N.Y. (c. 1800)
Philadelphia, Pa.
(c. 1828–1833)
Bibl. 3, 25, 91, 114, 124, 138

Thomas Boyle Campbell
(b. 1796–d. 1858)
Winchester, Va.
Campbell & Polk
(c. 1850–1858)

Campbell & Meredith
(c. 1850)
Bibl. 19

W(illiam) Campbell
(c. 1765)
Carlisle, Pa.
Philadelphia, Pa.
Bibl. 3, 23, 28, 36, 44

William L. Campbell
(b. 1759–d. 1815)
Winchester, Va.
(c. 1785–1816)
Bibl. 19

CAMPBELL

Cann & Dunn
(See Charters, Cann &
Dunn)

**Anton (Antonio)
Canavillo (Candevalo)**
(c. 1819–1839)
New York, N.Y.
Bibl. 15, 23, 36, 44, 124, 138

S. Canavillo (c. 1825)
New York, N.Y.
Bibl. 23, 36, 44

John H. Canby (c. 1797)
Alexandria, Va.
Bibl. 19

Candee & McEwan
(c. 1858)
Edgefield, S.C.
Bibl. 5

L. B. Candee & Co.
(c. 1830)
Woodbury, Conn.
Lewis Burton Candee
Bibl. 24, 44, 91, 92, 114

L B CANDEE & CO

Lewis Burton Candee
(b. 1806–d. 1861)
Woodbury, Conn. (c. 1825)
Curtis(s) & Candee

(c. 1826–1831)
L. B. Candee & Co.
(c. 1830)
Curtis(s), Candee & Stiles
(c. 1831–1835)
*Bibl. 16, 23, 25, 28, 36, 44,
91, 92, 114*

Charles Candell
(c. 1795–1800)
New York, N.Y.
*Bibl. 23, 24, 25, 29, 36, 44,
54, 114, 124, 138*

Anton Candevalo
(See Canavillo)

Canfield & Brother
(c. 1830)
Baltimore, Md.
Ira B. Canfield
William B. Canfield
Bibl. 23, 36, 44, 95

Canfield Bro. & Co.
(c. 1850)
Baltimore, Md.
Ira B. Canfield
William B. Canfield
Bibl. 4, 28

Canfield & Foot(e)
(c. 1795–1799)
Middletown, Conn.
Samuel Canfield
William Foote
Bibl. 16, 23, 28, 36, 44, 91

Canfield & Hall
(c. 1790–1805)
Middletown, Conn.
Samuel Canfield
*Bibl. 24, 25, 44, 61, 91, 110,
114*

Ira B. Canfield (c. 1834)
Baltimore, Md.
North Haddam, Conn.
Bibl. 83, 91, 95

L. Canfield (c. 1849)
Binghamton, N.Y.
Bibl. 20, 124

L CANFIELD

Lewis Canfield (c. 1845)
Rochester, N.Y.
Bibl. 20, 124

Samuel Canfield
(c. 1780–1807)
Middletown, Conn.
Canfield & Hall
(c. 1790–1805)
Canfield & Foote
(c. 1795–1799)
*Bibl. 16, 23, 24, 25, 28, 29,
36, 44, 91, 92, 94, 110,
114, 124*

CANFIELD

William B. Canfield
Baltimore, Md.
Canfield & Brother (c. 1830)
Canfield Bro. & Co.
(c. 1850)
Bibl. 4, 23, 28, 36, 44, 91, 95

William Canfield
(c. 1843–1846)
Troy, N.Y.
Bibl. 20, 91, 124

Cann
(See Kidney, Cann &
Johnson)

John Cann
(1834–1850)
New York, N.Y.
Dunn & Cann
(c. 1834–1838)
Charters, Cann & Dunn
(c. 1850)
*Bibl. 4, 15, 23, 28, 36, 44,
114, 124, 135, 138*

George Cannon (Canon)
(b. 1767–d. 1835)
Warwick, R.I. (c. 1800)
Nantucket Island, Mass.
(c. 1825–1835)
*Bibl. 12, 15, 24, 25, 44, 110,
114*

G C   G CANNON

G CANON

William Cannon (c. 1738)
Philadelphia, Pa.
Bibl. 3

James Canoll
(c. 1839–1845)
Albany, N.Y.
Bibl. 20, 124

John W. H. Canoll
(c. 1824–1848)
Albany, N.Y.
Bibl. 20, 91, 124

G. Canon
(See G. Cannon)

Godfrey Cant (c. 1796)
New York, N.Y.
Bibl. 23, 28, 36, 44, 124, 138

Canterbury Silversmiths, Inc. (c. 1950)
Brooklyn, N.Y.
Bibl. 127

John Porter Capelle
(c. 1848–1879)
Wilmington, Del.
St. Louis, Mo.
Bibl. 24, 25, 44, 54, 114, 134

CAPELLE

J. P. CAPELLE

Marcus Eugene Capelle
(c. 1875–1879)
St. Louis, Mo.
Bibl. 54

Michael Capper
(c. 1798–1800)
Philadelphia, Pa.
Bibl. 3

George Washington Cappuck (c. 1825)
Mt. Holly, N.J.
Bibl. 54

Captain's Well
(See H. G. Hudson)

Pierce Caralin
(c. 1804–1808)
New York, N.Y.
Bibl. 23, 28, 36, 44, 124

Theodorus (Theodore) Carbin (Karbin)
(c. 1758–1759)
Philadelphia, Pa.
Bibl. 3, 23, 36, 44

Carbon
(See L. F. Dunn)

Joseph Carels
(c. 1817–1818)
Philadelphia, Pa.
Bibl. 3

Carence Crafters
(early 1900s)
Chicago, Ill.
Bibl. 98, 120

Carey & Anthony
(See Anthony & Carey)

Henry A. Cargil (c. 1838)
Nashville, Tenn.
Bibl. 54

—— **Cargill**
Location unknown
Bibl. 28

Michael Cario
(c. 1728–1748)
New York, N.Y. (c. 1728)
Philadelphia, Pa. (c. 1734)
Bibl. 3, 23, 28, 44, 124

William Cario Sr. & Jr.
(b. 1734–d. 1809)
Boston, Mass.
New York, N.Y. (c. 1742)
Portsmouth, N.H. (c. 1763)
(before 1748)
Newmarket, N.H. (c. 1790)
Newfields, N.H. (c. 1809)
Bibl. 15, 23, 24, 25, 29, 36, 44, 70, 91, 94, 110, 114, 124, 149

W CARIO   W CARIO

W. CARIO

W. Cario

—— **Cariolle** (c. 1822)
New Orleans, La.
Bibl. 23, 36, 44, 141

Hugh Carland (c. 1840)
Macon, Ga.
Bibl. 17

Carleton & Co. (c. 1800)
Location unknown
Bibl. 28, 29

CARLETON & CO.

Carleton & Kimball
(c. 1820)
New York, N.Y.
Bibl. 15, 44, 114, 124

CARLETON & KIMBALL

George Carleton
(c. 1810–1820)
New York, N.Y.
Bibl. 15, 24, 25, 44, 114, 124

CARLETON

Abraham Carlisle (Carlile)
(c. 1780–1794)
Philadelphia, Pa.
Bibl. 3, 15, 23, 24, 25, 29, 36, 44, 54, 68, 81, 91, 114

A. Carlisle

A.C.

David Carlson (c. 1927)
Gardner, Mass.
Bibl. 144, 157

John Carman
Philadelphia, Pa. (c. 1771)
New York, N.Y.
Kingston, N.Y.
(c. 1774–1776)
Bibl. 20, 23, 24, 25, 36, 44, 114, 124

 I C

Samuel Carman
(b. 1784, c. 1807–1815)
New York, N.Y.
Bibl. 15, 23, 36, 44, 124, 138

J. Carmichael (c. 1840)
Owego, N.Y.
Bibl. 20, 124

John Carnan
(c. 1771–1777)
Baltimore, Md.
(c. 1773–1774)
Philadelphia, Pa.
Christopher Hughes & Co.
(c. 1773–1774)
Bibl. 3, 28, 38

Nicholas Caron (1718)
New York, N.Y.
Bibl. 44, 124

Carondolet
(See Wm. Lawler,
Carondolet & Marion)

Benjamin R. Carpenter
(c. 1850)
Syracuse, N.Y.
Bibl. 20, 124

Charles Carpenter
Norwich, Conn. (c. 1790)
Boston, Mass. (c. 1807)
*Bibl. 15, 25, 28, 44, 91, 92,
110, 114*

| C C |

Joseph Carpenter
(b. 1747–d. 1804)
Norwich, Conn. (c. 1775)
Canterbury, Conn. (c. 1797)
*Bibl. 15, 16, 23, 24, 25, 28,
36, 44, 61, 78, 91, 92, 94,
110, 114*

| I. C. | | I C |

Lumen Carpenter
(c. 1845–1847)
Oswego, N.Y.
Bibl. 20, 124

Carr
(See Steele & Carr)

B. D. Carr (c. 1845–1846)
Philadelphia, Pa.
Bibl. 3

D. S. Carr & Co. (1860)
Providence, R.I.
Bibl. 108

David S. Carr
(c. 1841–1845)
Troy, N.Y.
Bibl. 20, 124

Frank Carr (1875)
Hallowell, Me.
Bibl. 105

L. & D. S. Carr (1875)
Providence, R.I.
Bibl. 108

Lyman Carr (1861)
Woodstock, Me.
Bibl. 105

Thomas Carr Jr. (c. 1835)
Philadelphia, Pa.
Bibl. 3

Daniel Carrel(l)
Philadelphia, Pa.
(c. 1790, c. 1804–1806)
Charleston, S.C.
(c. 1790–1801)
John & Daniel Carrel(l)
(c. 1785)
*Bibl. 3, 5, 23, 36, 44, 54,
104, 114, 118*

John Carrel(l)
(c. 1790–1794)
Philadelphia, Pa.
John & Daniel Carrel(l)
(c. 1785)
Bibl. 3, 114

John & Daniel Carrel(l)
(c. 1785)
Philadelphia, Pa.
*Bibl. 3, 23, 24, 25, 29, 36,
44, 114*

| CARREL |

| CARRELL |

Peter Carribec (Carribee)
(c. 1745–1796)
Philadelphia, Pa.
Bibl. 3, 23, 36, 44

Peter Carribee
(See Peter Carribec)

J. Carrigan Jr.
(c. 1830–1835)
Philadelphia, Pa.
Bibl. 3

Jacob Carrigan
(c. 1825–1829)
Philadelphia, Pa.
Bibl. 3

Daniel Noble Carrington
(b. 1758–d. 1834)
Danbury, Conn. (c. 1793)
Eli Mygatt
Najah Taylor
Bibl. 28, 110

William Carrington
(c. 1830)
New York, N.Y.
Charleston, S.C.
Carrington, Thomas & Co.
W. Carrington & Co.
James Eyland & Co.
Bibl. 5, 28, 44, 54, 91, 114

| W CARRINGTON |

James Carrol(l)
New York, N.Y. (c. 1825)
Albany, N.Y. (c. 1834)
Bibl. 4, 23, 28, 36, 44, 124

John Carroll (c. 1825)
New York, N.Y.
Bibl. 15, 124, 138

Thomas Carroll
(1820–1860)
Youngstown, Ohio
Bibl. 89

Trumbell Carroll
(1820–1860)
Youngstown, Ohio
Bibl. 89

John Carrow
 (c. 1839–1884)
Philadelphia, Pa.
Dubosq & Carrow
 (c. 1839–1843)
Dubosq, Carrow & Co.
 (c. 1844–1850)
Bibl. 3

John Carrows (c. 1837)
Philadelphia, Pa.
Bibl. 3

Carson & Hall
 (c. 1810–1818)
Albany, N.Y.
Thomas Carson
Green Hall
*Bibl. 4, 15, 20, 23, 25, 28,
 36, 44, 91, 114, 124*

CARSON & HALL

T. C & H

Allen Carson (c. 1849)
Philadelphia, Pa.
Bibl. 3, 23

David Carson
 (c. 1842–1850)
Albany, N.Y.
Bibl. 20, 23, 28, 44, 124

Thomas Carson
 (c. 1810–1850)
Albany, N.Y.
Carson & Hall
 (c. 1810–1818)
*Bibl. 20, 23, 25, 28, 36, 44,
 91, 114, 124*

Thomas H. Carson
 (c. 1838–1843)
Albany, N.Y.
Bibl. 20, 91, 124

Joseph Sayre Cart
 (b. 1767–d. 1822)
Charleston, S.C. (c. 1792)
Augusta, Ga. (c. 1802)
Bibl. 5, 17, 44

CART

Vernal Cart (c. 1797–1829)
Charleston, S.C.
Bibl. 54

Carter & Morrell
Gonzales, Tex.
Bibl. 54

Carter Brothers (1875)
Poland, Me.
Bibl. 105

C. W. Carter (c. 1840)
Location unknown
Bibl. 89

George M. Carter (c. 1839)
Philadelphia, Pa.
Bibl. 3

J. H. Carter
Location unknown
Bibl. 89, 91

Jacob Carter
 (c. 1806–1808)
Philadelphia, Pa.
Bibl. 3

Thomas Carter
 (c. 1823–1824)
Philadelphia, Pa.
Bibl. 3

William Carter
 (c. 1683, d. 1738)
Philadelphia, Pa.
Bibl. 3

William Carter
 (c. 1844–1847)
Philadelphia, Pa.
Bibl. 3

David N. Carvalho
 (b. 1787–d. 1860)
Charleston, S.C.
 (c. 1815–1822)
Baltimore, Md. (c. 1828)
Philadelphia, Pa.
Bibl. 5

D. N. Carvalks (c. 1846)
Philadelphia, Pa.
Bibl. 3

Carvel Hall
(See Chas. C. Briddell, Inc.,
 Towle Silversmiths)

Franklin L. Carver
 (c. 1818)
Philadelphia, Pa.
Bibl. 3

G. Carver (c. 1797)
Philadelphia, Pa.
Bibl. 3

Jacob Carver
 (c. 1785–1833)
Philadelphia, Pa.
Bibl. 3

Samuel Carver (c. 1814)
Philadelphia, Pa.
Bibl. 3

I. H. Cary & Co.
Boston, Mass.
Isaac H. Cary
Bibl. 15, 44, 91, 110

I H CARY & CO.

Lewis Cary
 (b. 1798–d. 1834)
Boston, Mass.
 (c. 1815–1820)
*Bibl. 2, 4, 15, 23, 25, 28, 29,
 36, 44, 91, 110, 114*

George Case (c. 1779)
East Hartford, Conn.
Bibl. 16, 23, 28, 36, 44, 110

Philemon N. Case
 (d. 1852)
Hamilton, N.Y.
 (c. 1849–1852)
Bibl. 20, 124

Gideon Casey
(b. 1726–d. 1786)
Newport, R.I.
South Kingston, R.I.
Samuel Casey (c. 1753)
Bibl. 2, 15, 23, 24, 25, 28,
29, 36, 44, 54, 56, 91, 94,
110, 114, 119

G. CASEY　　G. C.

Samuel Casey
(b. 1724–d. 1780)
Newport, R. I.
(c. 1753)
South Kingston, R.I.
(c. 1753)
Boston, Mass.
Little Rest, R.I.
Gideon Casey (c. 1753)
Bibl. 2, 15, 24, 25, 28, 29,
36, 44, 54, 91, 94, 102,
110, 114, 116, 119, 135,
151

 SC S. CASEY

S.C.

R. Cashell (w. 1811)
Baltimore, Md.
Bibl. 38

R. H. Cashell (c. 1819)
Winchester, Va.
Bibl. 19

Randall H. Cashell
(c. 1807–1811)
Philadelphia, Pa.
Bibl. 3, 44

Felix Ferjeux Cashot
(See Cachot)

B. W. Caskell
Philadelphia, Pa.
Bibl. 54

Randall Caskell
Philadelphia, Pa.
Bibl. 54

Samuel Caskell
(19th century)
Louisville, Ky.
Bibl. 32, 54

William Cassaday
(Cassiday) (Cassedy)
Philadelphia, Pa.
(c. 1846–1850)
Bibl. 3, 91

Abraham Cassal (c. 1840)
Philadelphia, Pa.
Bibl. 3

Cassedy
(See also Cassaday)

Andrew Cassedy (c. 1840)
Philadelphia, Pa.
Bibl. 3, 23, 36, 44

William Cassiday
(See Cassaday)

Stephen Castan (c. 1818)
Philadelphia, Pa.
Bibl. 3　　S C & Co

Stephen Castan & Co.
(c. 1819)
Philadelphia, Pa.
Bibl. 3, 15, 25, 44, 114

J. M. Castens (c. 1810)
Washington, Ga.
Bibl. 17

Castle & Morrell
(c. 1840–1844)
Buffalo, N.Y.
Daniel B. Castle
Joseph Morrell
Bibl. 20, 91, 124

Daniel B. Castle
(c. 1837–1848)
Buffalo, N.Y.
Castle & Morrell
(c. 1840–1844)
Bibl. 20, 91, 124

Francoise Caston (c. 1804)
New York, N.Y.
Bibl. 23, 28, 36, 44

Francis B. Caswell (1860)
Bridgton, Me.
Bibl. 105

John H. Caswell (1875)
Bridgton, Me.
Bibl. 105

Samuel Caswell (d. 1878)
Louisville, Ky.
(c. 1838–1850)
Bibl. 32, 68, 93

John Catlett (d. 1811)
South Carolina (c. 1766)
Augusta, Ga. (c. 1790)
Bibl. 17

Charles Catlin (c. 1841)
Athens, Ga.
Bibl. 17, 114

Charles Catlin
Athens, Ga. (c. 1842)
Augusta, Ga. (c. 1845–1860)
Bibl. 17

C CATLIN

J. & W. Catlin (c. 1823)
Augusta, Ga.
Joel Catlin
Willys Catlin
Bibl. 17

Joel Catlin (c. 1822–1829)
Augusta, Ga.
J. & W. Catlin (c. 1823)
Bibl. 17

Willys Catlin (c. 1823)
Augusta, Ga.
J. & W. Catlin
Bibl. 17

W. CATLIN

John Cauchais (c. 1816)
Philadelphia, Pa.
Bibl. 3, 124, 138

B. Caulette (c. 1828–1833)
Philadelphia, Pa.
Bibl. 3

Richard Cauthorn III
(b. 1743–d. 1790)
Ephesus Springs, Va.
Bibl. 19

Joseph Cave
(c. 1837–1847)
Philadelphia, Pa.
Bibl. 3

Nich (Nicholas) Cavenaugh
(c. 1829–1833)
Philadelphia, Pa.
Bibl. 3

Antoine Cayon
(w. 1800–1801)
Baltimore, Md.
Bibl. 38

Peter Cazelle
Baltimore, Md. (w. 1803)
Bibl. 38

Peter Cazelles (1815–1825)
Cincinnati, Ohio
Bibl. 34, 90, 152

Charles Cecil
(c. 1808–1809)
Philadelphia, Pa.
Bibl. 3

Cellar Shops
(See Raymond Brenner, Inc.)

John Cellers (c. 1814)
Chillicothe, Ohio
Bibl. 34

Cellini Craft, Inc.
(1934–1957)
Chicago, Ill.
Became Randahl Company
(1957). Moved to Skokie,
Ill. Patterns and Designs
bought by Reed & Barton
(1965)
Bibl. 98, 127, 144

Cellini Shop
(1914–present)
Chicago, Ill.
Became Division of Randahl
Company (1969)
Bibl. 98

Jacobi Cembuhler
(See Jacob Sandbuhler)

Central Sterling Co.
(c. 1909–1914)
Brooklyn, N.Y.

Became Weber-Wagner Co.
(c. 1915)
Weber-Wagner & Benson
Co. (c. 1915–1927)
A. L. Wagner Mfg. Co., Inc.
(c. 1927–1931)
A. L. Wagner & Son, Inc.
(c. 1931–1950)
J. Wagner & Son, Inc.
(c. 1950–1967)
Bibl. 131, 127, 157

Cerneau & Co.
(c. 1811–1820)
New York, N.Y.
Bibl. 23, 36, 124

John Cerneau
(c. 1823)
New York, N.Y.
Bibl. 23, 36, 44

Joseph Cerneau
(c. 1807–1848)
New York, N.Y.
Bibl. 23, 36, 44, 124, 138

George Certier
(c. 1845–1850)
Philadelphia, Pa.
Bibl. 3

Chace & Cutter (1870)
Providence, R.I.
Bibl. 108

Barnabas Chace (1875)
Providence, R.I.
Bibl. 108

E. Chadron
(See E. Chaudron)

Samuel Chadwick Jr.
(c. 1839)
Buffalo, N.Y.
Bibl. 20, 124

Thomas Chadwick
(c. 1809–1825)
Philadelphia, Pa.
Bibl. 3, 23, 44

**Thomas Chadwick &
Heims** (c. 1815)
Albany, N.Y.
Bibl. 25, 114

T C & H

Chaffee
(See Root & Chaffee)

James Chalmers, Sr.
(c. 1749–1780)   I C
Annapolis, Md.
Baltimore, Md. (1766–1768)
Bibl. 25, 28, 29, 38, 44, 114

John Chalmers
(b.c. 1750–d.c. 1819,
c. 1770–c. 1791)
Annapolis, Md.
Bibl. 25, 29, 38, 44   I C

Chamberlain
(See Smith & Chamberlain)

Charles Chamberlain
(c. 1833–1839)
Philadelphia, Pa.
Bibl. 3

Lewis Chamberlain
Elkton, Md. (1824)
Philadelphia, Pa.
(c. 1829–1842)
Bibl. 3, 38

Wilson Chamberlain
(c. 1839)
Providence, R.I. (c. 1824)
Portsmouth, N.H. (c. 1839)
New York, N.Y.
(c. 1828–1836)
Bibl. 23, 36, 44, 125, 138

Lewis Chamberlin
(c. 1831–1840)
Philadelphia, Pa.
Bibl. 3

Thomas Champagne
(b. 1796)
New Orleans, La.
Bibl. 141

John Champlin   I C
(b. 1745–d. 1800)
New London, Conn.
(c. 1768–1800)
*Bibl. 15, 16, 23, 24, 25, 28,
36, 44, 61, 92, 110, 114*

Lewis C. Champney
(c. 1845–c. 1850)
Troy, N.Y.
Fisher & Champney

(c. 1846–1847)
Bibl. 20, 91, 124

W. & G. Chance
Charleston, S. C.
James Eyland & Co.
(c. 1820–1827)
Bibl. 89

William Chanceaulone
(b. 1785, w. 1801)
Baltimore, Md.
Bibl. 38

Chandlee & Holloway
(1818–1823)
Baltimore, Md.
Benjamin Chandlee
Robert Holloway
Bibl. 38

Benjamin Chandlee
(d. 1745)
Wilmington, Del.
(c. 1710–1745)
Philadelphia, Pa.
Bibl. 3, 38

Benjamin Chandlee
(c. 1763)
Chester County, Pa.
Bibl. 3

Benjamin Chandlee
(1814–1823)
Baltimore, Md.
Chandlee & Holloway
Bibl. 3, 38

(Goldsmith) Chandlee
(d. 1821)
Winchester, Va. (c. 1775)
Bibl. 19

Chandler & Darrow
(c. 1843–1861)
New York, N.Y.
Bibl. 35, 124, 138

James Chandler (c. 1831)
Schenectady and Troy, N.Y.
James Chandler & Co.
Bibl. 20, 124

James Chandler & Co.
(c. 1831)
Troy, N.Y.
Bibl. 20, 124

John Chandler (w. 1774)
Maryland
Bibl. 38

Stephen Chandler
(c. 1812–1823)
New York, N.Y.
Hemstead & Chandler
Bibl. 15, 23, 24, 25, 36, 44, 114, 124, 138

| CHANDLER |

William Chandless
(c. 1836–1839)
New York, N.Y.
Bibl. 4, 15, 23, 28, 44, 124, 138

Claudius Chap
(See Claudius Chat)

H. Chapel (c. 1845–1846)
Louisville, Ky.
Bibl. 32

Chapell & Roberts
(c. 1850)
Hartford, Conn.
Hiram F. Chapell
L. D. Roberts
Bibl. 23

Henry Chapell (c. 1848)
St. Louis, Mo.
Bibl. 54

Hiram F. Chapell
(c. 1845–1850)
Hartford, Conn.
Chapell & Roberts (c. 1850)
Bibl. 23

Chapin & Hollister Co.
(c. 1915–1922)
Providence, R.I.
Bibl. 127   C. & H. Co.

Aaron Chapin
(b. 1753–d. 1838)
Hartford, Conn.
Bibl. 16, 23, 28, 36, 44, 110

Alexander Chapin
(c. 1846)
Hartford, Conn.
Bibl. 23, 36, 44

E. Chapin (c. 1850)
Perry, N.Y.
Bibl. 20, 124

Edwin G. Chapin (c. 1836)
Buffalo and Little Falls, N.Y.
Bibl. 20, 124

Otis Chapin (c. 1820)
Morrisville, N.Y.
Bibl. 20, 110, 124

S. Chapin (c. 1850–1851)
New York State
Northhampton, Ma.
Bibl. 15, 44, 81, 114

| S. CHAPIN |

S. & A. Chapin (c. 1834)
South Hadley, Mass.
Bibl. 84

Chapman & Barden
(c. 1915)
Successor to Barden, Blake
& Co.
Attleboro, Mass.
Bibl. 127, 157   **C. & B.**

Alonzo Chapman
(c. 1835–1836)
Troy, N.Y.
Bibl. 20, 124

Charles Chapman
(c. 1838–1839)
Troy, N.Y.
Bibl. 20, 124

David W. Chapman
(c. 1834–1841)
Rochester, N.Y.
Bibl. 20, 41, 44, 124

Henry Chapman (b. 1744)
Charleston, S.C. (c. 1774)
Bibl. 5, 28

William Chapman
(c. 1849)
Charleston, S.C.
Bibl. 5

Lewis Charles (c. 1837)
Philadelphia, Pa.
Bibl. 3

J. F. Charpentier
(1852–1853)
New Orleans, La.
Bibl. 141

Charter Company
Trademarks used on sterling
reproductions of early
colonial silver made in
Barbour Silver Co. plant
(c. 1930–1933)
Made by Wallingford
(c. 1933–1942)
Bibl. 127

Charters, Cann & Dunn
(c. 1850)
New York, N.Y.
James Charters
John Cann
David Dunn
*Bibl. 4, 25, 28, 29, 44, 114,
124, 135*

James Charters
(c. 1844–1850)
New York, N.Y.
Charters, Cann & Dunn
(c. 1850)
Bibl. 4, 23, 28, 44, 124, 135

Chase
(See Max H. Storch, Moffatt
& Chase)

Chase & Easton (c. 1837)
Brooklyn, N.Y.
Bibl. 23, 36, 44, 124

Chase & Vaughn
(c. 1842–1844)
Buffalo, N.Y.
Thomas B. Chase
George C. Vaughn
Bibl. 20, 124

F. H. Chase (1875)
Fort Fairfield, Me.
Bibl. 105

George E. Chase (1875)
Providence, R.I.
Bibl. 108

George W. Chase
Utica, N.Y. (c. 1842–1844)
Troy, N.Y. (c. 1845–1847)
Bibl. 18, 20, 23, 124, 158

Hiram Chase (1860–1875)
Belfast, Me.
Bibl. 105

John or Joseph D. Chase
(c. 1820–1851)
New York, N.Y.
Bibl. 23, 36, 44, 91, 124

Thomas B. Chase
(c. 1839–1848)
Buffalo, N.Y.
Chase & Vaughn
Bibl. 20, 124

Chasley (1764)
Boston, Mass.
Bibl. 44, 110

André O. Chastant
(1805–1827)
New Orleans, La.
Bibl. 23, 141

Claudius Chat (Chap)
(c. 1793–1798)
Philadelphia, Pa.
Bibl. 3, 23, 36, 91

Easton Chat (1793)
Philadelphia, Pa.
Bibl. 44

Le Sieur Chat (c. 1790)
New York, N.Y.
Bibl. 28, 44

Chatham
(See John Brock)

John Chattellier (c. 1915)
Newark, N.J.
Bibl. 127, 157

Chaudron (c. 1798)
Philadelphia, Pa.
Bibl. 54

Chaudron & Co. (c. 1810)
Philadelphia, Pa.
Bibl. 25, 28, 46

Chaudron(s) & Rasch
(c. 1798–1820)
Philadelphia, Pa.
Simon Chaudron
Anthony Rasch
*Bibl. 3, 15, 23, 24, 25, 28,
36, 39, 44, 54, 72, 91, 104,
114, 122, 148*

Edward Chaudron
(Chadron) (c. 1816)
Philadelphia, Pa.
Bibl. 3

J. Chaudron (c. 1798)
Philadelphia, Pa.
Bibl. 3

P. Chaudron (c. 1797)
Philadelphia, Pa.
Bibl. 3

Simon Chaudron
(c. 1798–1814)
Philadelphia, Pa.
Chaudron & Rasch
*Bibl. 3, 15, 23, 36, 44, 54,
116, 122, 148*

S(imon) Chaudron(s) &
Co. (c. 1807–1811) S C & Co
Philadelphia, Pa.
*Bibl. 3, 23, 24, 25, 36, 44,
148*

Deruisseau Chaulotte
(w. 1801)
Baltimore, Md.
Bibl. 38

Frederick Chaulotte
(w. 1802)
Baltimore, Md.
Bibl. 38

Charles Chaysenholder
(c. 1814)
Philadelphia, Pa.
Bibl. 3

Cheadell & Co.
(c. 1827–1850)

Auburn, N.Y.
Bibl. 20, 114, 124

John Hatch Cheadell
    (b. 1806–d. 1875)
Auburn, N.Y.
    (c. 1827–1850)
Bibl. 20, 114, 124

Cheavins & Hyde
    (c. 1810)
New York State
Bibl. 46, 91

Chedell & Allen (c. 1844)
Buffalo, N.Y.
Philo Allen
Charles H. Chedell
Bibl. 20, 124

Charles H. Chedell
    (c. 1844)
Buffalo, N.Y.
Chedell & Allen
Bibl. 20, 124

John Hatch Chedell
    (b. 1806–d. 1875)
Auburn, N.Y. (c. 1827)
Bibl. 25, 44

| CHEDELL |

Chelius (c. 1840)
Location unknown
Bibl. 28

Daniel Chene (c. 1786)
New York, N.Y.
*Bibl. 4, 23, 28, 36, 44, 124,
    138*

James Cherry (c. 1824)
Philadelphia, Pa.
Bibl. 3, 23, 36

James Cherry
    (c. 1849–1850)
Philadelphia, Pa.
Bibl. 3, 44

Chevalier & Tanguay
    (c. 1816–1819)
Philadelphia, Pa.
Clement E. Chevalier
——— Tanguay (Tanguy)
Bibl. 3, 23, 36, 44

Clement E. Chevalier
    (c. 1816–1833)

Philadelphia, Pa.
Chevalier & Tanguay
    (c. 1816–1819)
Bibl. 3, 23, 36, 39, 44

Chicago Art Silver Shop
    (1912–1918)
Chicago, Ill.
Edmund Boker (b. 1886)
Ernest Gould
    (b. 1884–d. 1954)
Art Silver Shop
    (1918–1934)
Art Metal Studios
    (1934–c. 1977)
Bibl. 98, 127

**Chicago Monogram
    Studios** (c. 1922–1948)
Chicago, Ill.
Successor to Chicago
    Monogram Jewelry Works
Bibl. 127   *Silvergrams*

Chicago Silver Co.
    (1923–1945)
Chicago, Ill.
Became Gustafson Craft
    (1945–1964)
Bibl. 98, 104, 127, 144

Daniel R. Child (1875)
Providence, R.I.
Bibl. 108

Henry T. Child
    (c. 1840–1842)
Philadelphia, Pa.
Bibl. 3

John Child (c. 1813–1848)
Philadelphia, Pa.
Bibl. 3, 91

S. T. & T. T. Child
    (c. 1848–1850)
Philadelphia, Pa.
Samuel T. Child
Thomas T. Child
Bibl. 3

Samuel T. Child
    (c. 1843–1848)
Philadelphia, Pa.
S. T. & T. T. Child
    (c. 1848–1850)
Bibl. 3

Thomas T. Child (c. 1845)
Philadelphia, Pa.
S. T. & T. T. Child
    (c. 1848–1850)
Bibl. 3

Childs
(See Bulles & Childs)

Childs & Chamberlain
    (c. 1852–1861)
Milledgeville, Ga.
Otis Childs
    (b. 1811–d. 1899)
Asaph King Childs
Bibl. 17, 91

Asaph King Childs
    (b. 1820–d. 1902)
Athens, Ga.
O. & A. K. Childs
    (c. 1847–1861)
Childs & Chamberlain
    (c. 1852–1861)
Bibl. 17, 114

Ezekiel Childs
    (c. 1830–1835)
Philadelphia, Pa.
Bibl. 3

George K. Childs
    (c. 1828–1850)
Philadelphia, Pa.
*Bibl. 3, 4, 15, 23, 25, 28, 36,
    44, 95, 114*

| G.K. CHILDS |

James U. Childs (1875)
Farmington, Me.
Bibl. 105

O. & A. K. Childs
    (c. 1847–1861)
Athens, Ga.
Otis Childs
    (b. 1811–d. 1899)
Asaph King Childs
Bibl. 17, 91

| O & A K CHILDS |

Otis Childs
    (b. 1811–d. 1899)
Milledgeville, Ga.
    (c. 1836–1845)
Athens, Ga. (c. 1846–1861)
Newton, Mass. (c. 1872)

O. & A. K. Childs
(c. 1847–1861)
Childs & Chamberlain
(c. 1852–1861)
Bibl. 17, 114

Peter Chitrey
(See Peter Chitry)

Edward Chitry
(c. 1827–1832)
New York, N.Y.
Bibl. 15, 124, 138

F. Chitry (c. 1840)
Owego, N.Y.
Bibl. 20, 124

**Peter Chitry (Chitrey)
(Chittery)**
(c. 1815–1834)
New York, N.Y.
Philadelphia, Pa.
*Bibl. 3, 4, 15, 24, 28, 29, 30,
36, 39, 44, 79, 114, 124,
138*

| P. CHITRY |

Beriah Chittenden
(b. 1751–d. 1827)
New Haven, Conn. (c. 1787)
Milford, Conn.
Salisbury, Conn. | B C |
Kinderbrook, N.Y.
Middlebury, Ohio
*Bibl. 16, 23, 34, 36, 44, 61,
92, 94, 110, 124, 143*

Ebenezer Chittenden
(b. 1726–d. 1812)
Madison, Conn. | E C |
New Haven, Conn.
(c. 1747–1765)   (E C)
East Guilford, Conn.
Abel Buel(1)
*Bibl. 15, 16, 23, 24, 25, 28,
29, 36, 44, 61, 91, 92, 94,
110, 114, 116, 122, 143*

| E. CHITTENDEN |

Peter Chittery
(See Peter Chitry)

Chitty & Forbes
(c. 1800s)
New York, N.Y.
Bibl. 74

Robert W. Choate
(c. 1829–1837)
Philadelphia, Pa.
Bibl. 3

Stephen D. Choate
(c. 1841–c. 1852)
Louisville, Ky.
Bibl. 32, 68, 90, 93

John B. Chollot
(c. 1816–1819)
Philadelphia, Pa.
Bibl. 3

Christensen
Location unknown
Bibl. 15, 114 | CHRISTENSEN |

George W. Christian
(c. 1850)
Utica, N.Y.
Bibl. 18, 20, 124, 158

Nathan M. Christian
(c. 1840–1851)
Utica, N.Y.
Tanner & Cooley
(c. 1840–1842)
Bibl. 18, 20, 124, 158

William N. Christian
(c. 1846–1847)
Utica, N.Y.
Bibl. 18, 20, 124, 158

——— Christofle
Cincinnati, Ohio
Bibl. 34, 152

Thomas Christy (c. 1794)
Lexington, Ky.
Bibl. 32, 68, 93, 133

William Chrystler
(c. 1828–1835)
Philadelphia, Pa.
Bibl. 3

E. Chubbuck & Son
(c. 1850)
Lockport, N.Y.
Bibl. 20, 114, 124

Samuel W. Chubbuck
(b. 1799–d. 1875)
Utica, N.Y.

Morrisville, N.Y.
Storrs & Chubbuck
(c. 1847–c. 1849)
Bibl. 18, 20, 124, 158

Charles L. Chur
(c. 1837)
Staunton, Va.
Bibl. 19

Church & Metcalf
(c. 1842)
Providence, R.I.
Bibl. 23

Church & Rogers
(c. 1825–1836)
Hartford, Conn.
Joseph Church
Joseph Rogers
William Rogers
*Bibl. 23, 24, 25, 28, 36, 44,
91, 92, 110, 114, 157*

| CHURCH & ROGERS |

C. C. Church
(c. 1819–1830)
Batavia, N.Y.
Bibl. 20, 124

John Church
(b. 1756–d. 1806)
Savannah, Ga.
Philadelphia, Pa.
Bibl. 17

Joseph Church
(b. 1794–d. 1876)
Hartford, Conn.
New Haven, Conn.
Church & Rogers
(c. 1825–1828)
*Bibl. 15, 16, 23, 25, 28, 36,
91, 92, 110, 114, 121*

Ralph Church
(c. 1832–1848)
Buffalo, N.Y.
Bibl. 20, 23, 36, 44, 124

Churchill & Treadwell
(c. 1805–1813)
Boston, Mass.
Jesse Churchill
Isaac Treadwell

Bibl. 4, 24, 25, 28, 29, 36, 44, 110, 114, 135

CHURCHILL & TREADWELL

Jesse Churchill
(c. 1773–1819)
Boston, Mass.
Churchill & Treadwell
(c. 1805–1813)
Bibl. 2, 4, 15, 23, 24, 25, 28, 29, 36, 44, 110, 114

CHURCHILL

I. CHURCHILL

Charles Churchwell
(c. 1781)
Philadelphia, Pa.
Bibl. 3, 23, 36, 44

Citra
(See Silver by Citra)

Andrew S. Clackner
(c. 1847–c. 1850)
Rochester, N Y
Bibl. 20, 124

John S. Clackner
Troy, N.Y. (c. 1833–1837)
Rochester, N.Y.
(c. 1838–1848)
Bibl. 20, 124

Claland
(See Cleland)

Clapp
(See Palmer & Clapp)

Clapp & Riker
(c. 1802–1808)
New York, N.Y.
Philip Clapp
Peter Riker
Bibl. 4, 15, 23, 28, 36, 44, 124, 138

A. L. Clapp (c. 1802)
New York, N.Y.
Bibl. 25, 44, 114, 124

A. L. CLAPP

Philip Clapp
(c. 1802–1819)
New York, N.Y.
Clapp & Riker
(c. 1802–1808)
Bibl. 15, 23, 36, 44, 124, 138

(Widow) Philip Clapp
(c. 1825–1826)
New York, N.Y.
Bibl. 15, 124, 138

Joseph Clarico (d. 1828)
Norfolk, Va. (c. 1813–1828)
Bibl. 19, 21

J CLARICO   I. CLARICO

Clark
(See Reeve & Clark, Yates & Clark)

——— **Clark** (c. 1837)
Circleville, Ohio
Bibl. 34

Clark & Anthony
(c. 1790)
Providence, R.I.
Bibl. 23, 24, 25, 28, 29, 36, 44, 91, 124

CLARK & ANTHONY

Clark & Brother (c. 1825)
Norwalk, Conn.
Bibl. 24, 25, 36, 44, 92, 114

Clark & Brown (c. 1843)
Cazenovia, N.Y.
Norwalk, Conn.
Lester Brown
Jehiel Clark Jr.
Bibl. 20, 24, 25, 36, 44, 124

Clark & Coit (c. 1820)
Norwich, Conn.
——— Clark
Thomas Chester Coit
Bibl. 23, 36, 44, 92, 110

Clark & Hartley
(c. 1839–1841)
Philadelphia, Pa.
——— Clark
Samuel Hartley
Bibl. 3

Clark & Noon
(c. 1915–1922)
Newark, N.J.
Successor to W. F. Cory & Bro.
Bibl. 127

Clark & Pelletreau
(c. 1819)
New York, N.Y.
Curtis H. Clark
Maltby Pelletreau
Bibl. 15, 25, 124, 138

Clark & Turner
(c. 1820–1823)
Cheraw, N.C.
Fayetteville, N.C.
Wadesboro, N.C.
Charles Clark
Franklin Turner
Bibl. 21

Clark, Pelletreau & Upson (c. 1819–1823)
Charleston, S.C.
Curtis (H.) Clark
Gregory Clark Jr. (c. 1822)
——— Upson
Pelletreau (?)
Bibl. 5, 25, 44, 114, 124, 138

C P & U

Clark, Rackett & Co.
(1840–1852)
Augusta, Ga.
Francis C. Clark
Horace Clark
George Rackett
Bibl. 17, 89

C R & Co

CLARK R. & CO

CLARK RACKETT & CO

Alexander C. Clark
(c. 1850)
Syracuse, N.Y.
Bibl. 20, 124

Andrew Clark (b. 1723)
New York, N.Y. (c. 1744)
Fredericksburg, Va.
*Bibl. 3, 19, 23, 44, 36, 91,
124*

Benjamin W. Clark
  (c. 1791–1848)
Philadelphia, Pa.
Bibl. 3

Benjamin & Ellis Clark
  (c. 1811–1840)
Philadelphia, Pa.
Bibl. 3

C. & G. Clark (c. 1833)
Boston, Mass.
Bibl. 23, 28, 44

Charles Clark (c. 1798)
New Haven, Conn.
Boston, Mass.
Bibl. 23, 28, 36, 44

Charles Clark
  (c. 1809–1814)
Philadelphia, Pa.
Ephraim & Charles Clark
  (c. 1806–1811)
Bibl. 3

Charles Clark (c. 1821)
Fayetteville, N.C.
Clark & Turner
  (c. 1820–1823)
Bibl. 21

Curtis (H.) Clark (c. 1817)
New York, N.Y.
Clark & Pelletreau
Clark, Pelletreau & Upson
Bibl. 23, 36, 44, 124, 138

Edward Clark
  (c. 1809–1814)
Philadelphia, Pa.
Bibl. 3

Elias Clark (c. 1802)
Philadelphia, Pa.
Bibl. 3

Ellis Clark (c. 1816–1848)
Philadelphia, Pa.
Bibl. 3

Ephraim Clark (d. 1822)
Philadelphia, Pa.
  (c. 1780–1811)
Ephraim & Charles Clark
  (c. 1806–1811)
Bibl. 3

Ephraim & Charles Clark
  (c. 1806–1811)
Philadelphia, Pa.
Bibl. 3

F. Clark & Co. (c. 1822)
Augusta, Ga.
Francis C. Clark
Bibl. 17

F. & H. Clark
  (c. 1830–1840)
Augusta, Ga.
Francis C. Clark
Horace Clark
Bibl. 17

F. H. Clark & Co.
  (c. 1840–1860)
Memphis, Tenn.
*Bibl. 15, 25, 44, 54, 91, 114,
159*

F. H. CLARK & CO

Francis C. Clark
  (c. 1816–1860)
Augusta, Ga.
F. Clark & Co.
  (c. 1822)
F. & H. Clark
  (c. 1830–1840)
Clark, Rackett & Co.
  (1840–1852)
Bibl. 17, 89

Frederick Clark (c. 1827)
Rochester, N.Y.
Bibl. 20, 41, 124

Frederick H. Clark
  (c. 1915–1922)
Newark, N.J.
Bibl. 127, 157

⬦C⬦ STERLING

Gabriel Duval Clark
  (b. 1813–d. 1896)
Baltimore, Md.
  (w. 1830–1896)
Foxcroft & Clark
  (1831–1839)

*Bibl. 23, 24, 25, 38, 44, 91,
114, 127*

G. D. CLARK

George Clark
  (c. 1842–1843)
Philadelphia, Pa.
Bibl. 3, 91

George C. (G.) Clark
  (c. 1813–1824)
Providence, R.I.
Christopher Burr
Henry (G.) (B.) Mumford
  (c. 1813)
Jabez Gorham
William Hadwen
  (c. 1816–1828)
*Bibl. 23, 24, 25, 28, 29, 36,
44, 56, 91, 114*

G. C. CLARK

George D. Clark (c. 1826)
Baltimore, Md.
Bibl. 23, 24, 29, 44

G. D. CLARK

George R. Clark
  (c. 1827–1846)
Auburn, N.Y. (c. 1827)
Rome, N.Y.
Utica, N.Y.
Jenkin(s) & Clark (c. 1827)
Bibl. 18, 20, 124, 158

Gregory Clark Jr.
  (c. 1822)
Charleston, S. C.
Clark, Pelletreau & Upson
  (c. 1823)
Bibl. 5

Henry Clark
  (c. 1813–1824)
Philadelphia, Pa.
Bibl. 3, 23, 36, 44

Horace Clark (c. 1854)
Augusta, Ga.
F. & H. Clark
  (c. 1830–1840)
Clark, Rackett & Co.
  (c. 1840–1852)
Bibl. 17, 110

Horatio Clark
(c. 1795–1806)
Bennington, Vt.
Hunt & Clark
(c. 1795–1803)
Bibl. 54, 110

Humphrey Clark
(c. 1798–c. 1819)
Auburn, N.Y.
Manlius, N.Y.
Onondaga, N.Y.
Troy, N.Y.
Bibl. 20, 124

I. & H. Clark (c. 1821)
Portsmouth, N.H.
*Bibl. 2, 24, 25, 28, 29, 36,
44, 114*

I. & H. CLARK

I. (J.) Clark (c. 1754)
Boston, Mass.
Salem, Mass.
*Bibl. 2, 15, 23, 24, 25, 28,
29, 36, 44, 54, 56, 72, 110,
114*

I·C

I. CLARK

CLARK   I.C.

J. Clark
(See I. Clark)

J. A. Clark (c. 1835–1850)
Batavia, N.Y.
Bibl. 20, 124

J. H. Clark (c. 1812–1815)
Portsmouth, N.H.
New York, N.Y. Ⓒ
*Bibl. 15, 23, 24, 25, 29, 36,
44, 124*

J. H. CLARK

James Clark (1860)
Pembroke, Me.
Bibl. 105

Jehiel Clark (c. 1808)
Pompey, N.Y.
Bibl. 20, 91, 124

Jehiel Clark Jr. (c. 1843)
Cazenovia, N.Y.
Clark & Brown
Bibl. 20, 124

Jesse Clark (c. 1809–1814)
Philadelphia, Pa.
Bibl. 3

John Clark (c. 1837–1840)
Philadelphia, Pa.
Bibl. 3

John J. Clark
Cambridge, Md.
(c. 1833–?)
Portsmouth, Va.
(c. 1842–1845)
Bibl. 19

John L. Clark
(c. 1837–1838)
Utica, N.Y.
Bibl. 18, 20, 124

John L. Clark
Laurens, S. C.
(c. 1856)
Hodges Depot, S. C.
(c. 1857–?)
Bibl. 5

Jonas C. Clark
(c. 1837–1841)
Watertown, N.Y.
(c. 1836–1837)
Utica, N.Y. (c. 1839–1840)
Albany, N.Y.
L. W. & J. C. Clark
(c. 1836–1837)
Bibl. 20, 124, 158

Joseph Clark
(c. 1791–1817)
Danbury, Conn.
Newburgh, N.Y.
Died in Alabama in 1821.
*Bibl. 15, 16, 20, 24, 25, 28,
29, 36, 44, 91, 92, 110,
114, 124*

J C   CLARK   I C

Joseph Clark
(b. 1814–d. 1872)
Portsmouth, N.H.
(c. 1834–1864)
Bibl. 28, 91, 110, 125

Joseph R. Clark
(c. 1849–1860)
Brookville, Ind.
Bibl. 133

L. W. & J. C. Clark
Watertown, N.Y.
(c. 1836–1837)
Utica, N.Y. (c. 1837)
Lewis W. Clark
Jonas C. Clark
Bibl. 20, 124

Levi Clark
(b. 1801–d. 1875)
Norwalk, Conn.
*Bibl. 15, 16, 24, 25, 28, 29,
36, 44, 61, 91, 92, 110,
114*

CLARK

Lewis W. Clark
(c. 1832–1838)
Utica, N.Y. (c. 1837)
Watertown, N.Y.
(c. 1836–1837)
Charles J. J. DeBerard
L. W. & J. C. Clark
(c. 1836–1837)
*Bibl. 15, 18, 20, 25, 44, 114,
124, 158*

L. W. CLARK

Metcalf B. Clark (c. 1835)
Boston, Mass.
Bibl. 23, 28, 36, 44

Patrick F. Clark
(c. 1842–1843)
Philadelphia, Pa.
Bibl. 3, 23

Peter G. Clark
(b. 1793–d. 1860)
New Haven, Conn. (c. 1810)
*Bibl. 16, 23, 28, 36, 44, 91,
92, 110, 143*

Philip Clark
(c. 1837–1843)
Albany, N.Y.
Bibl. 20, 124

R. D. Clark (1860)
Houlton, Me.
Bibl. 105

Richard Clark (c. 1765)
Philadelphia, Pa.
May & Clark
Bibl. 3

Richard Clark (c. 1795)
New York, N.Y.
Bibl. 23, 36, 44, 124, 138

Samuel Clark
(b. 1659–d. 1705)
Boston, Mass.
Bibl. 4, 15, 23, 28, 36, 44, 102

Thomas Clark
(b. 1725–d. 1781)
Boston, Mass.
(c. 1764)
Bibl. 15, 23, 24, 25, 28, 29, 44, 110, 114

Thomas W. Clark
(c. 1830–1850)
Philadelphia, Pa.
Bibl. 3

William Clark
(b. 1750–d. 1798)
New Milford, Conn.
Bibl. 16, 23, 24, 25, 28, 29, 36, 44, 91, 92, 110, 114

William Clark
(c. 1831–1833)
Philadelphia, Pa.
Bibl. 3

William Barton Clark
(c. 1817–c. 1834)
Utica, N.Y.
Barton & Clark
Bibl. 18, 20, 124, 158

Clarke & Hutchinson
(c. 1813)
Philadelphia, Pa.
Bibl. 3

Ambrose Clarke
(b. 1757–d. 1810,
w. 1783–c. 1790)
Baltimore, Md.
(c. 1783–1784)
Philadelphia, Pa.
Bigger & Clarke
(c. 1783–1784)
Bibl. 3, 38

James Clarke
(b. 1714–d. 1802)
Newport, R.I. (1734)
Bibl. 44, 110

Jonathan Clarke
(b. 1705–d. 1770)
Newport, R.I. (c. 1734)
Providence, R.I. (c. 1755)
Bibl. 2, 23, 24, 25, 29, 36, 44, 54, 56, 69, 72, 80, 91, 94, 102, 104, 110, 114

Claude & French
(c. 1783–1785)
Annapolis, Md.
Abraham Claude
James Ormsby French
Bibl. 38

Claude & Jacob (Jacob & Claude) (c. 1772–1774)
Annapolis, Md.
Abraham Claude
Charles Jacob
Bibl. 38

Abraham Claude
(c. 1750–1800)
Annapolis, Md.
Claude & Jacob
(c. 1772–1774)
Claude & French
(c. 1783–1785)
Bibl. 38

Chat Claude
(See Claudius Chat)

Clausen & Maull
(c. 1830–1833)
Philadelphia, Pa.
———— Clausen
Joseph E. Maull (?)
Bibl. 3

Clayland
(See Cleland)

Barns Clayton (c. 1850)
Philadelphia, Pa.
Bibl. 3

Elias B. Clayton
(c. 1848–1850)
Philadelphia, Pa.
Bibl. 3

Richard Clayton
(b. 1811–d. 1878)
Cincinnati, Ohio
(1834–1859)
Bibl. 34, 90, 91, 114, 152

Clealand
(See Cleland)

William Cleaveland
(See William Cleveland)

Cleaves & Kimball
(1860)
Biddeford, Me.
Bibl. 105

John Clein (c. 1830–1833)
Philadelphia, Pa.
Bibl. 3

John Cleland (Clealand) (Claland) (Clayland)
(c. 1745–c. 1770)
Edenton, N.C.
Bibl. 21

Clement & Broom
(See Broom & Clement)

James W. Clement
(c. 1833–1850)
Philadelphia, Pa.
Broom & Clement
(c. 1837)(?)
Bibl. 3

Clements & Ashburn
(c. 1847)
Philadelphia, Pa.
James Clements
James C. Ashburn
Bibl. 3

James Clements
(c. 1847)
Philadelphia, Pa.
Clements & Ashburn
Bibl. 3

Sampson Clements
(c. 1817)
Petersburg, Va.
Cain & Clements
Bibl. 19

Isaac Clemmons
(c. 1775)
Boston, Mass.
Bibl. 28, 110

Benjamin Clench
(c. 1813–?)
Albany, N.Y.
Truax & Clench
Bibl. 20, 124

Cleveland & Post
(c. 1799? or 1816?)
Norwich, Conn.
William Cleveland
Samuel Post
*Bibl. 23, 24, 25, 28, 29, 36,
39, 44, 91, 92, 110*

Aaron Cleveland
(b. 1782–d. 1843)
Norwich, Conn.
(c. 1820)
*Bibl. 23, 24, 25, 28, 29, 36,
44, 92, 110, 114*

Benjamin Cleveland
(c. 1760)
Norwich, Conn.
Bibl. 24, 29, 36

Benjamin Cleveland
(b. 1767–d. 1837,
c. 1790–1830)
Newark, N.J.
*Bibl. 15, 23, 25, 44, 46, 54,
91, 95, 114, 135*

**William Cleveland
(Cleaveland)**
(b. 1770–d. 1837)
Norwich, Conn.
(c. 1791, c. 1816)
New London, Conn.
(c. 1792–?)
Putnam, Ohio (c. 1808)
Salem, Mass. (c. 1812)
Worthington, Mass.
Zanesville, Ohio
Trott & Cleveland
(c. 1792–?)
Cleveland & Post (c. 1816)
*Bibl. 15, 16, 23, 24, 28, 29,
34, 36, 44, 61, 91, 92, 94,
110, 114, 124*

Josiah Clift
(b. 1818–d. 1893)
Portsmouth, Va. (c. 1833)
Easton, Md. (c. 1834)
Centerville, Md. (c. 1834)
Norfolk, Va. (c. 1842)
Baltimore, Md.
(c. 1846–1852)
Lynchburg, Va.
(c. 1857–1862)
Silverthorn & Clift
(c. 1857–c. 1860)
Bibl. 19, 54

Cline & Curtz
(c. 1819–1822)
Philadelphia, Pa.
Bibl. 3

Benjamin Cline
(c. 1858–1859)
Utica, N.Y.
Bibl. 18, 124, 158

C. & P. Cline
(c. 1842–1847)
Philadelphia, Pa.
Charles Cline (?)
Philip Cline (?)
Bibl. 3

Charles Cline
(c. 1829–1850)

Philadelphia, Pa.
C. & P. Cline
(c. 1842–1847) (?)
Bibl. 3, 23, 36, 44

Charles Cline Jr.
(c. 1849)
Philadelphia, Pa.
Bibl. 3

J. Cline (c. 1857–1865)
Utica, N.Y.
W. & J. Cline
(c. 1857–1860)
Bibl. 18, 124, 158

Philip Cline
(c. 1819–1847?)
Philadelphia, Pa.
C. & P. Cline
(c. 1842–1847) (?)
Bibl. 3

W. & J. Cline
(c. 1857–1860)
Utica, N.Y.
Walter Cline
J. Cline
Bibl. 18, 124, 158

Walter Cline (b. 1825)
Utica, N.Y. (c. 1857–1861)
W. & J. Cline
(c. 1857–1860)
Bibl. 18, 124, 158

Thomas B. Cloutman
(c. 1837)
Buffalo, N.Y.
Bibl. 20, 124

John (Jan) Cluet (c. 1725)
Albany, N.Y.
Kingston, N.Y.
Van Sanford & Cluet
Bibl. 25, 44, 91, 114, 124

Matthew Cluff
Norfolk, Va. (c. 1803–1816)
Elizabeth City, N.C.
(c. 1817–1819)
Ott & Cluff (c. 1803–1806)
Bibl. 19, 95

Isaac D. Cluster (c. 1850)
St. Louis, Mo.
Bibl. 24, 25, 44, 114

I. D. CLUSTER

Abraham L. Coan
(c. 1833–1841)
Mobile, Ala.
Bibl. 148

A. L. COAN, MOBILE

C. E. Coan (Coen) & Co.
(c. 1810)
New York, N.Y.
Bibl. 24, 25, 44, 114, 124

C. COAN & CO

D. B. Coan
(See D. B. Coen)

Charles Coan
(c. 1814–?)
Cooperstown, N.Y.
Ernst & Coan
Bibl. 20, 124

Isaac Coates
(c. 1835–1839)
Philadelphia, Pa.
Bibl. 3

William Coates
(c. 1835–1839)
Buffalo, N.Y.
Bibl. 20, 90, 124

Coats & Boyd (c. 1831)
Philadelphia, Pa.
A. W. Coats (?)
Ezekiel C. Boyd (?)
Bibl. 3

A. W. Coats (c. 1831–1837)
Philadelphia, Pa.
Coats & Boyd (c. 1831) (?)
Bibl. 3

Cobb, Gould & Co.
(1874–1880)
Attleboro, Mass.
Became Watson & Newell
(1880–1886)
Watson, Newell & Co.
(1886–1895)
Watson, Newell Co.

(1895–1919)
Watson Company
(1919–1955)
Wallace Silversmiths
(1955–present)
Bibl. 127, 135

Ephraim Cobb
(b. 1708–d. 1775)
Boston, Mass. (c. 1729)
Plymouth, Mass. (c. 1735)
*Bibl. 2, 4, 15, 23, 24, 25, 28,
29, 44, 72, 91, 94, 110,
114*

E C   E COBB

George Cobham (c. 1834)
New York, N.Y.
Bibl. 15, 124, 138

John Coburn   J. C
(b. 1725–d. 1803)
Boston, Mass. (c. 1750)
*Bibl. 2, 4, 15, 23, 24, 25, 29,
36, 44, 50, 54, 69, 70, 72,
91, 94, 102, 104, 110, 114,
149*

J. COBURN

William D. Cochran
Albany, N.Y. (1830–1836)
Troy, N.Y. (c. 1832–1833)
Schenectady, N.Y. (c. 1841)
Bibl. 20, 124

Cochrane (c. 1820)
Location unknown
Bibl. 24

COCHRANE

George Cockman
(c. 1818–1822)
Philadelphia, Pa.
Bibl. 3

James Cockrell
(c. 1843–1850)
Philadelphia, Pa.
Bibl. 3

Herbert Cockshaw, Jr.
(1936–1937)
New York, N.Y.
Howard & Cockshaw
(1904–1915)
Herbert Cockshaw
(1915–1936)
Bibl. 127, 157

Codding Bros. & Heilborn
(1879–1918)
North Attleboro, Mass.
Bibl. 114, 127, 157

C. B. & H.
STERLING.

D. D. Codding   STERLING.
(c. 1896–1904)   D. D. C.
North Attleboro, Mass.
Bibl. 127, 157

John Coddington
(b. 1690–d. 1743)
Newport, R. I.
*Bibl. 2, 15, 23, 24, 25, 28,
29, 36, 44, 56, 94, 114*

Willard Codman (c. 1839)
Boston, Mass.
Bibl. 23, 36, 44

John Codner
(c. 1754–1782)
Boston, Mass.
Bibl. 28, 44, 110

Coe & Upton (c. 1840)
New York, N.Y.
—— Coe
—— Upton
H. L. Sawyer
*Bibl. 23, 24, 25, 28, 29, 36,
44, 114, 124*

COE & UPTON

H. H. Coe (c. 1840)
Location unknown
Bibl. 24, 124

L. P. Coe (c. 1850–1867)
Mohawk, N.Y.
Bibl. 15, 44, 91, 114, 124

L. P. COE

C. Coen
(See C. E. Coan)

Daniel Bloom Coen
(Coan) (c. 1787–1805)
New York, N.Y.

Bibl. 4, 23, 24, 25, 28, 29, 35, 36, 44, 54, 91, 114, 124, 135, 138

Erastus K. Coffin
(c. 1840–1884)
Salem, Ind.
Bibl. 133

William Coffman
(c. 1839–1850)
Philadelphia, Pa.
Bibl. 3, 23, 36, 44

George Cogswell
(c. 1834–1835)
Albany, N.Y.
Bibl. 20, 124

H. Co(g)gswell (c. 1760)
Boston, Mass.
Bibl. 23, 24, 28, 29, 36, 110

H. COGSWELL

H COGGSWELL

Henry Cogswell
(c. 1846–1853)
Salem, Mass.
Bibl. 25, 44, 114

H. COGSWELL

Cohen & Levy (w. 1819)
Baltimore, Md.
Bibl. 38

Cohen & Rosenberger
(c. 1915–c. 1943)
New York, N.Y.
Successor to Baldwin, Ford
& Co.
(c. 1896–1904)
Ford & Carpenter
(1904–1915)
Bibl. 127

Cohen & Stevens (c. 1808)
Petersburg, Va.
Thomas Cohen
Robert Stevens
Bibl. 19

Albert Cohen (1836–1852)
St. Louis, Mo.
Bibl. 54

Barrow A. Cohen
(c. 1825)
New York, N.Y.
Bibl. 15, 23, 36, 44, 138

Julius Cohen
(1955–c. 1965)
New York, N.Y.
Bibl. 126

L. H. Cohen
(c. 1896–c. 1910)
New York, N.Y.
Became L. H. Cohen Co.
(c. 1910–1922)
Bibl. 127, 157

M. A. Cohen
(c. 1840–1843)
Philadelphia, Pa.
Bibl. 3

Thomas Cohen
Petersburg, Va. (c. 1808)
Lynchburg, Va.
(c. 1809 1814)
Chillicothe, Ohio
(c. 1814–?)
Cohen & Stevens (c. 1808)
Bibl. 19, 25, 34, 44, 54, 114

T COHEN

Thomas Cohen
(1836–1852)
St. Louis, Mo.
Bibl. 89

William Cohen
(c. 1833–1838)
Alexandria, Va.
District of Columbia
Bibl. 19, 23, 36, 44, 54

J. J. Cohn (c. 1896)
New York, N.Y.
Bibl. 127

Louis Coignard (c. 1805)
New York, N.Y.
Bibl. 23, 36, 44, 124, 138

Coit & Mansfield
(c. 1816–1819)
Norwich, Conn.

C & M

Thomas Chester Coit
Elisha Hyde Mansfield
Bibl. 16, 23, 24, 25, 28, 29, 36, 44, 92, 110

Edward Coit (d. 1839)
Norwich, Conn. (c. 1825)
Bibl. 23, 24, 25, 29, 36, 44, 61, 91, 92, 110, 114

E. COIT

Thomas Chester Coit
(b. 1791–d. 1841)
Norwich, Conn.
(c. 1812–1820)
Natchez, Miss.
Coit & Mansfield
(c. 1816–1819)
Clark & Coit (c. 1820)
Bibl. 16, 23, 24, 25, 28, 29, 36, 44, 92, 110, 114

T.C.C.

John Coke
(b. 1704–d. 1767)
Williamsburg, Va.
(c. 1724–1760)
Bibl. 19, 153

Samuel Coke (d. 1773)
Williamsburg, Va.
(c. 1760–1773)
Bibl. 19, 153

George Colden
(c. 1832–1833)
New York, N.Y.
Bibl. 15, 124, 138

Cole & Van Court
(c. 1850)
New York, N.Y.
Bibl. 23, 124

Albert Cole
(See Albert Coles)

Charles C. Cole (1875)
Norway, Me.
Bibl. 105

Ebenezer Cole
  (c. 1818–1826)
New York State
Benjamin B. Wood
Bibl. 15, 23, 25, 36, 44, 54,
  91, 114, 124, 138

Horace Cole (1875)
Norway, Me.
Bibl. 105

Jacob Cole (c. 1785)
Philadelphia, Pa.
Bibl. 3, 23, 36, 44

John Cole (c. 1686)
Boston, Mass.
Bibl. 23, 28, 36, 44, 110

John A. Cole
  (c. 1841–1859)
New York, N.Y.
Bibl. 23, 91, 121, 124, 138

William Groat Cole
  (b. 1815–d. 1898)
Utica, N.Y. (c. 1843–1850)
Bibl. 18, 20, 124, 158

Coleman
(See Decker & Coleman)

Alvan Coleman
  (c. 1847–1849)
Troy, N.Y.
Bibl. 20, 124

Benjamin Coleman (Jr.)
  (c. 1785–d. 1820)
Burlington, N.J.
Sag Harbor, N.Y. (c. 1802)
Bibl. 15, 20, 23, 24, 25, 29,
  36, 44, 91, 114, 124

| B COLEMAN |

C. C. Coleman (c. 1835)
Burlington, N.J.
Bibl. 23, 25, 36, 44, 114

| C C COLEMAN |

James Coleman (c. 1833)
Philadelphia, Pa.
Bibl. 3

John Coleman (c. 1814)
New York, N.Y.
Bibl. 23, 36, 44, 124

John Coleman (c. 1848)
Philadelphia, Pa.
Bibl. 3

John F. Coleman (c. 1850)
Philadelphia, Pa.
Bibl. 3

Joseph Coleman
  (b. 1839–d. 1900)
Massillon, Ohio
Bibl. 34, 124

Nathaniel Coleman
  (b. 1765–d. 1842)
Burlington, N.J.
Bibl. 15, 23, 24, 25, 28, 29,
  36, 39, 44, 46, 54, 91, 95,
  114

| N. COLEMAN | | N. C |

Samuel Coleman
  (b. 1761–d. 1842)
Burlington, N.J. (c. 1805)
Trenton, N.J.
Bibl. 15, 23, 24, 25, 29, 36,
  44, 46, 54, 91, 104, 114

| S. COLEMAN |

William Coleman
  (w. 1783–1793?)
Baltimore, Md.
Bibl. 38, 44

Coles & Reynolds
  (c. 1873)
New York, N.Y.
Became George W. Shiebler
  & Co.
Bibl. 127

Albert Coles (Cole)
  (c. 1835–1849)
New York, N.Y.
  (c. 1851–1875)
Bibl. 4, 15, 23, 24, 25, 28,
  29, 35, 44, 88, 89, 91, 104,
  114, 124, 138

Albert Coles & Co.
  (c. 1851–1875)
New York, N.Y.
Bibl. 15, 124

John A. Coles (c. 1850)
New York, N.Y.
Bibl. 28, 29, 44

| C |

Lambert Colette
(Collette)
  (c. 1835–1848)
Buffalo, N.Y.
Bibl. 20, 23, 36, 44, 124

Samuel Coley
New York, N.Y.
Bibl. 89

Simeon Coley (c. 1766)
New York, N.Y.
William & Simeon Coley
Bibl. 23, 24, 25, 28, 36, 44,
  124, 138

William & Simeon Coley
  (c. 1766)
New York, N.Y.
Bibl. 15, 25, 44, 114, 124,
  138

William Coley (w. 1766)
New York, N.Y.
Rupert, Vt.
Van Voorhis & Coley
  (c. 1786)
Bibl. 4, 15, 23, 24, 25, 28,
  29, 36, 44, 54, 95, 110,
  114, 124, 135, 138

William Coley II
  (1801–1815)
New York, N.Y.
Bibl. 124

Thomas Colgan
(c. 1760–1771)
New York, N.Y.
Bibl. 25, 35, 114, 124

J. B. Collet (c. 1805)
New York, N.Y.
Bibl. 23, 36, 44, 124

Collette
(See Colette)

Peleg Collings
(1836–1850)
Cincinnati, Ohio
May be same man as Peleg
Collins
Bibl. 54

Francis Collingwood
(c. 1817–1845)
Elmira, N.Y.
Bibl. 20, 124

Collins
(See Colton & Collins, Hazen
& Collins, Shipp &
Collins)

Arnold Collins
(c. 1690–1735,
d. 1735)
Newport, R.I.
*Bibl. 2, 15, 23, 24, 25, 28,
29, 36, 44, 50, 56, 110,
114*

Blakely Collins
(c. 1846–c. 1850)
Troy, N.Y.
Bibl. 20, 124

F. Collins (c. 1862–1865)
Attica and Washington, Ind.
Bibl. 133

F. COLLINS

H. M. Collins (c. 1853)
Chattanooga, Tenn.
Bibl. 54

Patrick Collins
(c. 1839–1844)
Albany, N.Y.
Bibl. 20, 124

Peleg Collins
(b. 1799)
Cincinnati, Ohio
(1820–1850)
(See Peleg Collings)
Bibl. 34, 90, 152

Selden Collins Jr.
(b. 1819–d. 1885)
Utica, N.Y.
James Murdock & Co.
Murdock & Andrews
(c. 1838–1849)
Murdock & Collins
(c. 1849–1850)
*Bibl. 18, 24, 25, 44, 91, 114,
124, 158*

S. COLLINS

W. A. Collins
(c. 1840–1841)
Troy, N.Y.
Bibl. 20, 124

Warren Collins (1875)
Readford, Me.
Bibl. 105

William & L. Collins
(c. 1831–1835)
New York, N.Y.
Colton & Collins
(c. 1825–1835)
Bibl. 15, 23, 36, 44, 124, 138

David W. Collom
(c. 1846–1850)
Philadelphia, Pa.
Bibl. 3

John Colnenn
(c. 1825–1833)
Philadelphia, Pa.
Bibl. 3

John Colner (c. 1818)
New York, N.Y.
Bibl. 23, 36, 44, 124

John Colonel
(c. 1804–1822)
Philadelphia, Pa.
Bibl. 3, 23, 36, 44

Abraham Colser
(c. 1845–1846)
Albany, N.Y.
Bibl. 20, 23, 124

Colton & Baldwin
(c. 1819–1822)
Philadelphia, Pa.
Bibl. 3, 23, 36, 44

Colton & Collins
(c. 1825–1835)
New York, N.Y.
Levi Colton
Williams & L. Collins
*Bibl. 15, 23, 25, 36, 44, 114,
124, 138*

Demas Colton Jr.
(c. 1826–1829)
New York, N.Y.
*Bibl. 15, 25, 44, 114, 124,
138*

D. COLTON JR.

Levi Colton (c. 1825)
New York, N.Y.
Colton & Collins
(c. 1825–1835)
Bibl. 15, 23, 36, 44, 124, 138

Noah Colton (c. 1770)
Rhode Island
Bibl. 54

Oren Colton
(c. 1818–1822)
Philadelphia, Pa.
Bibl. 13, 44

**Columbian Souvenir Mfg.
Co.** (c. 1893)
Chicago, Ill.
Louis Burger
Bibl. 130

Colwell & Lawrence
(c. 1850)
Albany, N.Y.
Bibl. 4, 23, 28, 44, 124

William Commel
(c. 1837)
Philadelphia, Pa.
Bibl. 3

Commonwealth
(See International-
Commonwealth)

Community
(See Oneida)

William Compton
(c. 1844–1846)
Rochester, N.Y.
Bibl. 20, 124

Concord Silversmiths,
Ltd. (1939–c. 1945)
Concord, N.H.
Successor to Concord Silver
Co. (1925–1939)
Became Ellmore Silver Co.
(c. 1945)
Dies purchased by Crown
Silver Co. (1960)
Bibl. 127, 147

A. Conery (c. 1838–1854)
Frankfort, Ky.
Bibl. 32, 93

John Coney
(b. 1655–d. 1722)
Boston, Mass.
Bibl. 2, 7, 15, 23, 24, 25, 28,
29, 36, 44, 50, 54, 91, 94,
102, 104, 110, 114, 116,
118, 119, 139, 142, 143,
151

T. Conlyn (c. 1845)
Philadelphia, Pa.
Bibl. 15, 25, 44, 114

T. CONLYN

John Connell
(c. 1831–1833)
Philadelphia, Pa.
Bibl. 3

M. Connell (c. 1800)
Philadelphia, Pa. (?)
Bibl. 28, 29, 44, 72

M: CONNELL

Patrick Connelly
(c. 1834–1836)

Albany, N.Y.
Bibl. 20

William Conner
(See William J. Connor)

James Conning
(b. 1813–d. 1872)
New York, N.Y. (c. 1840)
Mobile, Ala. (c. 1842–1872)
Bibl. 24, 25, 28, 29, 44, 54,
95, 104, 114, 124, 148

J CONNING

William A. Conning
(b. 1834)
Mobile, Ala. (c. 1850)
Bibl. 54, 148

Patrick Connolly
(c. 1837–1848)
Buffalo, N.Y.
Bibl. 20, 124

Connor & Stickles
(c. 1837)
New York, N.Y.
Bibl. 15, 124, 138

John H. Connor
(c. 1833–1838)
New York, N.Y.
Eoff & Conner
(c. 1833–1835)
Bibl. 15, 23, 24, 25, 28, 36,
44, 114, 122, 124, 135, 138

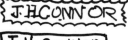

John W. Connor (1836)
Norwalk, Conn.
Bibl. 29, 44, 92

William J. Connor
(Conner) (c. 1855)
Charleston, S.C.
Bibl. 5

G. Conrad Jr.
(c. 1830)
Philadelphia, Pa.
Bibl. 3

George Conrad
(c. 1839–1843)
Philadelphia, Pa.
Bibl. 3

George Oliver Conrad
(b. 1823–d. 1907,
c. 1846–1854)
Charlottesville, Va.
Harrisonburg, Va.
Luray, Va.
Bear & Conrad
(c. 1846–1851)
Bibl. 19

Godfrey Conrad
(c. 1831–1848)
Philadelphia, Pa.
Bibl. 3

Osborn Conrad
(c. 1841–1851)
Philadelphia, Pa.
Bibl. 3, 91

Robert Conway (w. 1794)
Baltimore, Md.
Bibl. 38

Thomas A. Conway
(d. 1871)
Baltimore, Md. (1819–1824)
Cincinnati, Ohio
(c. 1825–1848)
Bibl. 34, 38, 90, 152

Joseph Conyers (c. 1700)
Boston, Mass.
Bibl. 23, 28, 36, 44, 50, 110

I. C

Richard Conyers
(c. 1688–1708,
d. 1708)
Boston, Mass.
Bibl. 15, 23, 25, 28, 29, 36,
44, 94, 102, 110, 114, 116,
118

Cook
(See Morgan & Cook)

Cook & Co. (c. 1797–1805)
New York, N.Y.

John Cook
Bibl. 23, 36, 44, 138

Cook & Co. (c. 1849)
Syracuse, N.Y.
Bibl. 20, 25, 125

Cook & Simpson (c. 1866)
Boonesville, Mo.
Bibl. 134

COOK & SIMPSON

Cook & Stillwell
(c. 1847–1859)
Rochester, N.Y.
Erastus Cook
Mortimer F. Stillwell
Bibl. 20, 41, 124

A. H. Cook (c. 1838–1840)
Hudson, N.Y.
Bibl. 20, 91, 124

Benjamin Ely Cook
(b. 1803–d. 1900)
Amherst, Mass.
(c. 1827–1833)
Northampton, Mass.
(c. 1827–1833)
Troy, N.Y.
Storrs & Cook
(c. 1827–1833)
B. E. Cook (c. 1833–1885)
B. E. Cook & Son (c. 1885)
*Bibl. 15, 20, 25, 44, 84, 110,
114, 124*

B. E. COOK
NORTHAMPTON

Charles L. Cook
(c. 1843–1850)
Philadelphia, Pa.
Bibl. 3

Erastus Cook
(b. 1793–d. 1864)
Rochester, N.Y.
(c. 1815–1859)
Madison, Wis.
(c. 1859–1864)
Ezra B. Booth
Cook & Stillwell
(c. 1847–1859)
*Bibl. 20, 25, 41, 44, 91, 114,
124*

F. B. Cook (c. 1820)
Location unknown
Bibl. 24

F. B. COOK

G. E. Cook & Co. (c. 1860)
Clarksville, Tenn.
Bibl. 54, 159

G. W. Cook (1843–1866)
Boonesville, Mo.
Bibl. 89

COOK-BOONVILLE—

H. Cook (c. 1810)
Location unknown
Bibl. 24

H. T. COOK

H. T. Cook (c. 1840)
Toledo, Oh.
Syracuse, N.Y.
Bibl. 89

Harry Cook (c. 1815–1817)
Poughkeepsie, N.Y.
Adriance & Cook
(c. 1814–1815)
Bibl. 20, 91

J. Cook (c. 1820)
Portland, Mo. (?)
Bibl. 28, 72

J. COOK

John Cook
New York, N.Y. (c. 1795)
Boston, Mass. (c. 1813)
Cook & Co. (c. 1797–1805)
*Bibl. 23, 24, 25, 29, 36, 44,
110, 114*

I COOK   J. COOK

COOK

Joseph Cook(e)
(c. 1785–1795)
Philadelphia, Pa.
Bibl. 25, 36

William G. Cook
(w. 1817–1824)
Baltimore, Md.
Bibl. 38

Cooke & Co. (c. 1785)
Philadelphia, Pa.
Bibl. 3, 23, 36, 44

Cooke & Son
(c. 1833–1838)
Petersburg, Va.
William Cooke
William A. Cooke
Bibl. 19

Cooke & White (c. 1833)
Norfolk, Va.
William A. Cooke
Andrew White
Bibl. 19, 91

COOKE & WHITE

D. C. Cooke
Charleston, S.C.
New York, N.Y.
Pelletreau, Bennett & Cooke
Bennett, Cooke & Co.
Pelletreau, Bennett & Co.
Bibl. 5, 91

Daniel S. Cooke (1875)
Providence, R.I.
Bibl. 108

John Cooke (c. 1804)
New York, N.Y.
Bibl. 28

John B. Cooke
(c. 1838–1843)
Petersburg, Va.
Bibl. 15, 19, 44, 114

J. B. COOKE   J. B. COOKE

Joseph Cooke
(c. 1785–1796)
Philadelphia, Pa.
*Bibl. 3, 4, 15, 23, 28, 44,
102, 114*

William Cooke
Petersburg, Va.
Cooke & Son
(c. 1833–1838)
Bibl. 19, 89

William A. Cooke
Petersburg, Va.
(c. 1826–1834)
Norfolk, Va. (c. 1834)
Cooke & White (c. 1833)
William A. Cooke & Co.
(c. 1833)
Cooke & Son
(c. 1833–1838)
Bibl. 19

W. A. COOKE

William A. Cooke & Co.
(c. 1833–1834)
Norfolk, Va.
Bibl. 19

Henry P. Cooley
Troy, N.Y. (c. 1842–1842)
Cooperstown, N.Y.
(c. 1843–1846)
Bibl. 20, 124

Oliver B. Cooley
(b. 1809–d. 1844)
Utica, N.Y.
Storrs & Cooley
(c. 1831–1839)
Tanner & Cooley
(c. 1840–1842)
Bibl. 18, 20, 25, 44, 91, 114, 124, 158

| O. B Cooley |

| COOLEY |

J. H. Coolidge (1875)
Portland, Me.
Bibl. 105

Joseph Coolidge Jr.
(b. 1747–d. 1821)
Boston, Mass.
Bibl. 2, 15, 23, 24, 25, 28, 29, 36, 44, 110, 114

| Coolidge |

| JC |

Jeremiah (Jerry) Coon
(c. 1846)
Cleveland, Ohio
Bibl. 54

John W. Coon (Coom)
(c. 1840–1846)
Cleveland, Ohio
Bibl. 23, 34

——— **Cooper** (c. 1816)
Philadelphia, Pa.
Bibl. 3, 23, 36, 44

Cooper & Fisher (c. 1850)
New York, N.Y.
Bibl. 24, 25, 44, 122, 124

COOPER & FISHER
131 AMITY ST. N.Y.

Cooper & Gaither
(c. 1855)
Greenville, S.C.
Joseph Cooper
J. W. Gaither
Bibl. 5

Cooper & Yongue
(c. 1852)
Columbia, S.C.
Joseph Cooper
Robert A. Yongue
Bibl. 5, 44

| COOPER & YONGUE |

Archibald Cooper
Louisville, Ky.
(c. 1838–1848)
Frankfort, Ky. (c. 1842)
William & Archibald Cooper
(c. 1838–1844)
Bibl. 32, 68, 90

B. Cooper (c. 1814)
New York, N.Y.
Bibl. 36, 44, 124

B. & J. Cooper
(c. 1810–1830)
New York, N.Y.
Bibl. 23, 25, 28, 36, 44, 114

| B & J. COOPER |

Cornelius Cooper (1860)
Providence, R.I.
Bibl. 108

David Cooper
(c. 1829–1833)
Philadelphia, Pa.
Bibl. 3

Francis W. Cooper
(c. 1840–1851)
New York, N.Y.
Bibl. 4, 15, 23, 25, 28, 44, 114, 124, 138

| F. W. COOPER |

| F.W.C. | | FWC NY |

G. Cooper (c. 1800)
Location unknown
Bibl. 28, 29

| G. COOPER |

John Cooper (c. 1814)
New York, N.Y.
Bibl. 23, 36, 44

Joseph Cooper (c. 1770)
New York, N.Y.
Bibl. 23, 36, 44, 124

Joseph Cooper
Columbia, S.C.
(c. 1843–1854,
c. 1856–1860)
Greenville, S.C. (c. 1855)
Cooper & Yongue
Cooper & Gaither
Bibl. 5

Joseph B. Cooper
(c. 1842–1846)
Philadelphia, Pa.
Bibl. 3

Robert H. Cooper
(c. 1850)
Philadelphia, Pa.
Bibl. 3

Samuel B. Cooper
(c. 1840)
Philadelphia, Pa.
Bibl. 3

Thomas Cooper (1875)
Providence, R.I.
Bibl. 108

W. & A. Cooper
(See William & Archibald
Cooper)

William Cooper
Louisville, Ky.
(c. 1838–1844)
Frankfort, Ky. (c. 1842)

William & Archibald Cooper
(c. 1838–1844)
Bibl. 32, 90, 93

William Cooper (c. 1844)
Philadelphia, Pa.
Bibl. 3, 23

**William & Archibald
Cooper (W. & A.
Cooper)**
Louisville, Ky.
(c. 1838–1844)
Frankfort, Ky. (c. 1842)
Bibl. 32, 54, 68, 90, 93

John Cope (c. 1792)
Richmond, Va.
Bibl. 19, 112

Elizabeth Copeland
(c. 1916)
Boston, Mass.
Detroit, Mich.
Bibl. 104, 120

John Copeland (d. 1773)
Edenton, N.C. (c. 1769)
Bibl. 21

Robert Copeland
(w. 1796)
Baltimore, Md.
Bibl. 38

Robert Copeland (c. 1850)
New York, N.Y.
Bibl. 23

Joseph Copp
(b. 1732–d. 1813)
New London, Conn.
(c. 1757–1776)
*Bibl. 15, 16, 24, 25, 28, 36,
44, 61, 92, 94, 110, 114*

N. P. Copp (c. 1827)
Georgetown, Ohio
Bibl. 34

Nathaniel P. Copp
Troy N.Y. (c. 1832–1835)
Albany, N.Y. (c. 1844–1845)
*Bibl. 4, 20, 23, 28, 36, 44,
124*

Frederick Coppock
Palmyra, N.Y. (c. 1830)
Buffalo, N.Y. (c. 1830)
W. R. & F. Coppock
(c. 1830)
Bibl. 20, 124

George F. Coppock
(c. 1847–1848)
Utica, N.Y.
Bibl. 18, 20, 124, 158

W. R. & F. Coppock
(c. 1830)
Palmyra, N.Y.
William R. Coppock
Frederick Coppock
Bibl. 20, 124

William R. Coppock
(c. 1831)
Palmyra, N.Y.
W. R. & F. Coppock
(c. 1830)
Bibl. 20, 124

**George Washington
Coppuck**
(b. 1804–d. 1882)
Mt. Holly, N.J.
Bibl. 46

John Copson (c. 1720)
Philadelphia, Pa.
Bibl. 3

Corbett
Location unknown
Bibl. 15

CORBETT

Jesse Corbett
Keene, N.H.
Bibl. 15, 44, 91, 125

John Corbett (c. 1800)
Whitingham, Vt.
Bibl. 54, 91, 110

J. CORBETT

John Corby (c. 1806)
Philadelphia, Pa.
Bibl. 3

Presley Cordell
(c. 1799–1837)
Leesburg, Va.
Bibl. 19

William B. Cordell
Warrenton, Va.
(c. 1814–1820)
Charles Town, Va.
(c. 1810–?)
Frankland & Cordell
(c. 1822) (?)
Bibl. 19

Ferdinand Corew
(c. 1837)
Philadelphia, Pa.
Bibl. 3

William Corey
(c. 1828–1833)
Philadelphia, Pa.
Bibl. 3

Arthur Corgee
(c. 1823–1824)
Philadelphia, Pa.
Bibl. 3

John Cork (c. 1837–1850)
Philadelphia, Pa.
Bibl. 3

William Corky (c. 1811)
New York, N.Y.
Bibl. 23, 36

William Corley (1811)
New York, N.Y.
Bibl. 44, 124, 138

Cornelius Cornelison
(c. 1712)
New York, N.Y.
Bibl. 4, 23, 28, 36, 44, 138

Christian Cornelius
   (c. 1810–1819)
Philadelphia, Pa.
Bibl. 3, 15, 23, 24, 25, 29,
   36, 44, 114

| C. CORNELIUS |

Walter Cornell
   (b. 1729–d. 1800)
Providence, R.I.
   (c. 1780–1800)
Bibl. 15, 23, 24, 25, 29, 36,
   44, 56, 91, 110, 114

| CORNELL |

| W. CORNELL |

Edward Corner (w. 1811)
Easton, Md.
Bibl. 38

Nathaniel Cornwell
(Corwell)
   (b. 1776–d. 1837)
Hudson, N.Y.
   (c. 1816–1817)
Danbury, Conn.
Bibl. 20, 24, 44, 91, 92, 110,
   124

| N. CORWELL |

Josiah Corrin
   (c. 1823–1824)
Philadelphia, Pa.
Bibl. 3, 23, 36, 44

Jacques W. Cortelyou
   (b. 1781–d. 1822)
New Brunswick, N.J.
   (c. 1805)
Bibl. 15, 25, 44, 46, 54, 114

| J. W. CORTELYOU |

Edward Corvazier
   (c. 1846)
Philadelphia, Pa.
Bibl. 3

N. Corwell
(See Cornwell)

W. F. Cory & Bro.
   (c. 1896–1915)
Newark, N.J.
Became Clark & Noon
   (c. 1915–1922)
Bibl. 114, 127, 157

Y **STERLING.**

Coryton & Lynn
   (c. 1795–1796)
Alexandria, Va.
Josiah Coryton
Adam Lynn
Bibl. 19

Josiah Coryton
   (c. 1795–1797)
Alexandria, Va.
Coryton & Lynn
   (c. 1795–1796)
Bibl. 19, 91

Cosby & Hopkins
   (c. 1846–1847)
Petersburg, Va.
Cosby, Hopkins & Co.
   (c. 1846–1847)
Thomas E. Cosby
Thomas R. Hopkins
Bibl. 19

T. E. Cosby & Co.
   (c. 1841–1846)
Petersburg, Va.
Thomas E. Cosby
Bibl. 19, 91

Thomas E. Cosby
   (c. 1815–1858)
Petersburg, Va.
T. E. Cosby & Co.
   (c. 1841–c. 1846)
Cosby & Hopkins
   (c. 1846–1847)
Cosby, Hopkins & Co.
   (c. 1846–1847)
Bibl. 19, 91

R. Costello (1875)
Portland, Me.
Bibl. 105

Ezekiel Costen
   (c. 1845–1850)
Philadelphia, Pa.
Bibl. 3

Abel Cottey (c. 1712)
Philadelphia, Pa.
Bibl. 3

S. Cottle Co.
   (1865–c. 1920)
New York, N.Y.
Bibl. 114, 127, 157

Cotton
(See Hayes & Cotton)

Pierre Coudrain
   (1768–1779)
New Orleans, La.
Bibl. 141

Alexis Coulon
   (1853–1869)
New Orleans, La.
Bibl. 141

Hilaire Courcelle
   (c. 1822)
New Orleans, La.
Bibl. 23, 36, 44

Pierre Louis Couret
   (w. 1805)
Baltimore, Md.
Bibl. 38

James Alexander
Courtonne
   (b. 1720–d. 1793)
Charleston, S.C.
   (c. 1751–1784)
Philadelphia, Pa. (?)
Bibl. 5, 54

William Courts (w. 1829)
Baltimore, Md.
Bibl. 38

Emile Couvertie
   (1838–1867)
New Orleans, La.
Bibl. 141

L. Couvertie (Louis
Couvertie) (c. 1822)
New Orleans, La.
Bibl. 15, 23, 24, 25, 29, 44,
   114

| L'COUVERTIE |

John B. Couvertier
    (w. 1810–1812)
Baltimore, Md.
Bibl. 38

Couzens
(See Cozens)

Covell & Higgins (c. 1850)
Syracuse, N.Y.
William W. Covell
George E. Higgins
Bibl. 20, 124

J. W. Covell (1860)
Bangor, Me.
Bibl. 105

William W. Covell
    (c. 1850)
Syracuse, N.Y.
Covell & Higgins
Bibl. 20, 124

John Coverley
    (b. 1730–d. 1800)
Boston, Mass. (c. 1766)
Bibl. 15, 25, 44, 88

Thomas Coverly
    (b. 1750–d. 1800)
Newburyport, Mass.
Newport, R. I.
*Bibl. 15, 23, 25, 28, 29, 36,
    44, 50, 56, 110, 114, 118*

William Cowan
    (b. 1779–d. 1831)
Fredericksburg, Va. (c. 1803)
Richmond, Va.
    (c. 1803–1831)
McCay & Cowan
    (c. 1805–1807)
Bibl. 19, 91, 124

**William D. Cowan
    (Cowen)**
    (c. 1808–1814)
Philadelphia, Pa.
*Bibl. 3, 15, 23, 24, 25, 29,
    36, 44, 114*

Charles Cowdrick
    (c. 1833–1839)
Philadelphia, Pa.
Bibl. 3

Charles H. Cowdrick
    (c. 1840–1850)
Philadelphia, Pa.
Bibl. 3

John Cowell (b. 1707)
    (c. 1728)
Boston, Mass.
Bibl. 70, 102, 110

Robert Cowell (c. 1777)
Philadelphia, Pa.
Bibl. 3

William Cowell
    (b. 1682–d. 1736)
Boston, Mass.
*Bibl. 2, 15, 23, 24, 25, 28,
    29, 36, 39, 44, 54, 91, 94,
    102, 110, 114, 116, 119,
    135, 139, 151*

William Cowell Jr.
    (b. 1713–d. 1761)
Boston, Mass.
*Bibl. 2, 15, 23, 25, 28, 36,
    44, 69, 91, 94, 102, 110,
    114, 119, 135, 151*

William D. Cowen
(See William D. Cowan)

Cowles & Albertson
    (c. 1849–1858)
Cleveland, Ohio
Royal Cowles
Joseph P. Albertson
Bibl. 54, 114

Ralph Cowles
    (c. 1840–1850)
Cleveland, Ohio
Bibl. 23, 24, 25, 29, 34, 44

Royal Cowles
    (c. 1849–1858)
Cleveland, Ohio
Cowles & Albertson
Bibl. 54

C. J. Cowperthwait
    (c. 1846–1849)
Philadelphia, Pa.
Bibl. 3

Albion Cox (d. 1795)
Philadelphia, Pa.
Bibl. 3

Benjamin Cox
    (c. 1809–1813)
Philadelphia, Pa.
Bibl. 3, 91

J. & I. Cox (c. 1817–1853)
New York, N.Y.
John & James Cox
*Bibl. 15, 24, 25, 28, 29, 44,
    91, 114, 124, 138*

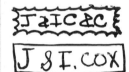

J. & J. Cox & Clark
    (c. 1831–1833)
New York, N.Y.
John & James Cox
────── Clark
*Bibl. 15, 25, 44, 114, 124,
    138*

John Cox (c. 1818)
Philadelphia, Pa.
Ward & Cox
Bibl. 3, 23, 36, 44

John & James Cox
(See J. & I. Cox)

William Cox
(c. 1825–1837)
Fredericksburg, Va.
Bibl. 19

Coywell Specialty Co.
(c. 1915–1922)
New York, N.Y.
Bibl. 127, 157

J. B. Cozens (Couzens)
(c. 1823–1829)
Philadelphia, Pa.
Bibl. 3

**Jacob B. Cozens
(Couzens)**(c. 1818)
Philadelphia, Pa.
Bibl. 3

**Josiah B. Cozens
(Couzens)**
(c. 1819–1824)
Philadelphia, Pa.
Bibl. 3

Jared Crab (c. 1823)
Elkton, Ky.
Bibl. 32, 54, 68, 93

Stephen Crafts (c. 1815)
New York, N.Y.
Bibl. 15, 23, 36, 44, 124, 138

James Craig (d. 1794)
Williamsburg, Va.
(c. 1746–1774)
Bibl. 19, 23, 36, 153

Gardner Cram
(1875)
Brunswick, Me.
Bibl. 105

Richard Cram
(c. 1845–1848)
Rochester, N.Y.
Bibl. 20, 124

**Benjamin Crandall
(Crandell)** (c. 1824)
Providence, R.I.
Bibl. 23, 28, 36, 44, 110

Benjamin Crandall
(c. 1839)
Portsmouth, N.H.
Bibl. 23, 36

Benjamin F. Crane
(c. 1842–1861)
St. Louis, Mo.
Benjamin F. Crane & Co.
Bibl. 54, 134

BENJ F CRANE

Benjamin F. Crane & Co.
(c. 1842–1861)
St. Louis, Mo.
Benjamin F. Crane
Prince H. Jones
Bibl. 54

Silas Crane (c. 1840–1870)
Covington, Ind.
Lemp & Crane
(c. 1864–1870)
Bibl. 133

Stephen M. Crane
(c. 1813)
New York, N.Y.
Bibl. 23, 36, 44, 124, 138

Samuel Cranston
(b. 1659–d. 1727)
Newport, R. I.
Bibl. 23, 28, 36, 44, 110

V. Craup (c. 1816)
Philadelphia, Pa.
Bibl. 3

Alfred Craven (c. 1843)
Philadelphia, Pa.
Bibl. 3

Alfred Craven (c. 1851)
York, S. C.
Bibl. 5

Margret Craver
(c. 1935–1949)
New York, N.Y.
Bibl. 89, 117

Crawford (c. 1815)
New York State
Bibl. 54

John Crawford
(c. 1815–1835,
c. 1837–1843)
New York, N.Y.
(c. 1815–1835)
Philadelphia, Pa.
(c. 1837–1843)
*Bibl. 3, 4, 15, 23, 25, 28, 29,
35, 44, 54, 83, 114, 124,
138*

C. Crawley (c. 1829–1833)
Philadelphia, Pa.
Bibl. 3

Edmond Crawley
(c. 1817–1824)
Philadelphia, Pa.
Bibl. 3

Edmund T. Crawley
(c. 1824)
Philadelphia, Pa.
Bibl. 3

John Crawley
(See John Crowley)

George Creamer (c. 1850)
Poughkeepsie, N.Y.
Bibl. 20, 124

Credon
(See Claudius Redon)

V. Crepu (c. 1820–1822)
Philadelphia, Pa.
Bibl. 3

Victor Crepu (c. 1830)
Augusta, Ga.
S. A. Saltonstall
Bibl. 17

James Creswell
(c. 1795–1799)
Philadelphia, Pa.
Bibl. 3

S. J. Creswell (c. 1840)
Philadelphia, Pa.
Bibl. 3

Benjamin Creuse (c. 1772)
Philadelphia, Pa.
Bibl. 3

John T. Crew
    (c. 1830–1850)
Albany, N.Y.
Bibl. 20, 23, 28, 44, 124

Peter Crider (c. 1845)
Philadelphia, Pa.
Bibl. 3

Jacob K. Crisher
    (c. 1840–1850)
Terre Haute, Ind.
Bibl. 133

Elnathan F. Crissey
    (c. 1847)
Rochester, N.Y.
Dunning & Crissey
Bibl. 20, 124

Charles Crittenden
Canfield, Ohio (c. 1816)
Cleveland, Ohio (c. 1820)
Talmadge, Ohio (c. 1830)
Bibl. 34

Newton E. Crittenden
Leroy, N.Y. (c. 1824)
Cleveland, Ohio
    (c. 1826–1872)
*Bibl. 15, 20, 23, 25, 34, 36,
    44, 54, 89, 91, 95, 114,
    124*

N. E. CRITTENDEN

John G. Crocker
    (c. 1832–1834)
Utica, N.Y.
Bibl. 18, 20, 124, 158

William Crocker (c. 1837)
Philadelphia, Pa.
Bibl. 3

**Frederick Crocks (Crox)
    (Croix) (Crooks)**
    (c. 1835–1850)
Philadelphia, Pa.
Bibl. 3

Croix
(See Crocks)

Barclay Croker (c. 1808)
Petersburg, Va.
Bibl. 19

William S. Croker
    (c. 1839)
Harpers Ferry, Va.
Bibl. 19

——— **Cromwell** (c. 1844)
Poughkeepsie, N.Y.
Van Vliet & Cromwell
Bibl. 20

Henry Crone (c. 1780)
Lancaster, Pa.
Bibl. 23, 36, 44, 112

T. Cronsberry (c. 1848)
Location unknown
Bibl. 3

J. M. Crooker (1860–1875)
Waterville, Me.
Bibl. 105

Crooks
(See Crocks)

Crosby & Brown
    (c. 1849–1850)
Boston, Mass.
Samuel T. Crosby
——— Brown
Bibl. 23, 91

C. A. W. Crosby (c. 1850)
Location unknown
Bibl. 89

Charles Crosby
    (c. 1835–1836)
Angelica, N.Y.
Bibl. 20, 124

Jonathan Crosby
    (b. 1743, c. 1796)
Boston, Mass.
*Bibl. 4, 23, 24, 25, 28, 29,
    36, 44, 110, 114*

Ransom Crosby (c. 1840)
New York, N.Y.
Higbie & Crosby
Bibl. 124, 138

Samuel T. Crosby
    (c. 1849–1850)
Boston, Mass.
Crosby & Brown
    (c. 1849–1850)
Brackett, Crosby & Brown
    (c. 1850)
Bibl. 23, 28, 44, 91, 114

——— **Cross** (c. 1695)
Boston, Mass.
Bibl. 4, 28

Charles W. Cross (1860)
Sangeville, Me.
Bibl. 105

William Cross
    (b. 1658, c. 1695)
Boston, Mass.
*Bibl. 15, 24, 25, 29, 44, 102,
    110, 114*

W.C.

W.C.

Alexander Crouckeshanks
    (c. 1768)
Boston, Mass.
Bibl. 28, 44, 110

Victoire Crouss (c. 1817)
Philadelphia, Pa.
Bibl. 3

George Crow (c. 1788)
New Castle County, Del.
Bibl. 30

Thomas Crow
    (c. 1770–1782)
Wilmington, Del.
Bibl. 3

David B. Crowell
    (c. 1849–1850)
Philadelphia, Pa.
Bibl. 3

Crowley & Farr
    (c. 1823–1825)
Philadelphia, Pa.
John Crowley
John C. Farr (?)
Bibl. 3, 54

E. Crowley (c. 1833)
Philadelphia, Pa.
Somers & Crowley
 (c. 1828–1833) (?)
Johnson & Crowley
 (c. 1830–1833)
Bibl. 3

John Crowley (Crawley)
 (c. 1803–1825)
Philadelphia, Pa.
Crowley & Farr
 (c. 1823–1825)
Bibl. 3, 54

Crown Silver Inc.
 (c. 1955–1960)
New York, N.Y.
Bibl. 127

Henry Crown
 (b. 1731)
Maryland (w. 1774)
Bibl. 38

Crox
(See Crocks)

Henry Crump (c. 1848)
Philadelphia, Pa.
Bibl. 3

Thomas Crumpton
 (c. 1823–1824)
Philadelphia, Pa.
Bibl. 3

William Crumpton
 (c. 1811–1822)
Philadelphia, Pa.
Bibl. 3

John Cullen
 (c. 1840–1845)
Leesburg, Va.
Bibl. 19

Hugh Cullin (c. 1844)
Louisa Court House, Va.
Bibl. 19

H. C. Culman   H.C.
 (c. 1909–1917)
Honolulu, Hawaii
Bibl. 127

David B. Cumming(s)
 (c. 1811)

Philadelphia, Pa.
Bibl. 3, 4, 23, 28, 36, 44

George Cummings
 (c. 1843)
Hartford, Conn.
Bibl. 23

Henry Cummings
 (c. 1849–1850)
Philadelphia, Pa.
Bibl. 3

John Cummings (c. 1837
Philadelphia, Pa.
Bibl. 3

John B. Cummings
 (c. 1841–1850)
Philadelphia, Pa.
Bibl. 3

William Cummings
 (c. 1841–1850)
Philadelphia, Pa.
Bibl. 3

A. J. Cunningham
Charleston, S. C.
 (c. 1830–1835)
New York, N.Y.
Bibl. 5, 138

Robert Cunningham
 (c. 1844–1845)
Louisville, Ky.
Bibl. 32

T. D. Curbier (c. 1800)
Philadelphia, Pa. (?)
Bibl. 89   T. D. CURBIER

Jule F. Cure
 (c. 1839–1840)
Philadelphia, Pa.
Bibl. 3

Lewis Cure (c. 1811–1819)
Philadelphia, Pa.
Bibl. 3

I. B. Curran & Co.
 (c. 1839)
Ithaca, N.Y.
I. B. Curran
Bibl. 20, 25

I. B. Curran
 (c. 1835–1839)
Ithaca, N.Y.
I. B. Curran & Co. (c. 1839)
Bibl. 20, 25, 124   I B CURRAN

James Curran
 (c. 1843–1850)
Philadelphia, Pa.
Bibl. 3

Currier & Roby
 (c. 1900–1940)
New York, N.Y.
Became division of Elgin
 Silversmith Co., Inc.
 (c. 1940–1976)
Bibl. 127, 157

Currier & Trott
 (c. 1823–1857)
Boston, Mass. (1875–1880)
John Proctor Trott
*Bibl. 23, 24, 25, 29, 33, 44,
 91, 114*

Currier & Trott

A. S. Currier
Location unknown
Bibl. 15, 44

A. S. Currier

Edmund M. Currier
 (b. 1793–d. 1853)
Salem, Mass. (c. 1837–1853)
*Bibl. 25, 44, 54, 91, 102,
 110, 114, 125*

Thomas D. Currier
 (1860–1875)
Waldenboro, Me.
Bibl. 105

James W. Currin
 (c. 1843–1850)
Philadelphia, Pa.
Owens & Currin
 (c. 1846–1850)
Bibl. 3

Joseph Currin (c. 1829)
Philadelphia, Pa.
Bibl. 23, 36, 44

Curry & Preston
(c. 1825–1831)
Philadelphia, Pa.
Newburgh, N. Y.
John Curry
Stephen L. Preston
*Bibl. 3, 15, 23, 24, 25, 29,
36, 44, 114*

John Curry (c. 1825–1850)
Philadelphia, Pa.
Newburgh, N. Y.
Curry & Preston
(c. 1825–1831)
*Bibl. 3, 4, 15, 20, 23, 24, 25,
28, 29, 36, 44, 91, 114*

J CURRY

Curtis(s) & Candee
(c. 1826–1831)
Woodbury, Conn.
Lewis Burton Candee
Daniel Curtis(s)
Bibl. 16, 23, 36, 44

Curtis & Dunning
(c. 1828)
Woodbury, Conn.
Lemuel Curtis (?)
Joseph N, Dunning
*Bibl. 23, 24, 25, 29, 36, 44,
110, 114*

CURTIS & DUNNING

CURTIS & DUNNING

Curtis(s) & Stiles (c. 1835)
Woodbury, Conn.
Daniel Curtis(s)
Benjamin Stiles
*Bibl. 15, 16, 23, 24, 25, 36,
44, 92, 114*

CURTISS & STILES

Curtis(s), Candee & Stiles
(c. 1831–1835)
Woodbury, Conn.
Daniel Curtis(s)
Lewis Burton Candee
Benjamin Stiles

*Bibl. 15, 16, 23, 24, 25, 28,
29, 36, 44, 91, 92, 114*

CURTISS CANDEE & STILES

C C & S

D. Curtis (c. 1820)
Lexington, Ky.
Bibl. 32, 44, 68

Daniel Curtis (c. 1816)
Fredericksburg, Va.
Bibl. 19, 44

Daniel Curtis(s)
(b. 1801–d. 1878)
Woodbury, Conn.
Curtis(s) & Candee
(c. 1826–1831)
Curtis(s), Candee & Stiles
(c. 1831–1835)
Curtis(s) & Stiles (c. 1835)
*Bibl. 16, 19, 23, 28, 36, 91,
110, 114*

Francis Curtis (c. 1845)
Woodbury, Conn.
Bibl. 23, 92

F CURTIS & CO

H. H. Curtis & Co.
(c. 1890–1915)
North Attleboro, Mass.
Bibl. 114, 127, 157

Joel Curtis
(b. 1786–d. 1844)
Wolcott, Conn.
(c. 1810–1825)
Cairo, N.Y.
*Bibl. 16, 23, 28, 36, 44, 110,
124*

Lewis Curtis
(b. 1774–d. 1845)
Farmington, Conn.
St. Charles, Mo. (c. 1820)
Hazel Green, Wis. (c. 1845)
*Bibl. 16, 23, 25, 28, 29, 36,
44, 91, 92, 110, 114, 124*

L. CURTIS

Solomon Curtis
(c. 1793, d. 1793)
Philadelphia, Pa.
Bibl. 3

Thomas Curtis
(c. 1831–1837)
New York, N.Y.
Bibl. 15, 23, 36, 44, 124, 138

Daniel Curtiss
(See Daniel Curtis)

Isaac Cushman (c. 1823)
Boston, Mass.
Bibl. 23, 36, 44, 110

R. J. Cushman (1875)
Boothbay, Me.
Bibl. 105

Simon Cushman (1861)
Bath, Me.
Bibl. 105

William Cushman (1860)
Portland, Me.
Bibl. 105

Isaac D. Custer
(c. 1847–1854)
St. Louis, Mo.
Bibl. 54   I D CUSTER

**Cutler, Silliman, Ward &
Co.** (c. 1767)
New Haven, Conn.
Richard Cutler
Hezekiah Silliman
Ambrose Ward
Bibl. 16, 28, 36, 44, 143

A. Cutler
(b. 1808–d. 1894)
Boston, Mass.
(c. 1820–1852)
*Bibl. 15, 23, 24, 25, 28, 29,
36, 44, 54, 91, 110, 114*
A. CUTLER   A CUTLER

Eben Cutler
(c. 1820–1846)
New Haven, Conn.
Boston, Mass.
*Bibl. 23, 24, 25, 29, 36, 44,
92, 110, 114, 143*

E CUTLER

John N. Cutler
(c. 1829–1850)
Albany, N.Y.
Bibl. 20, 23, 28, 44, 124

Richard Cutler
(b. 1736–d. 1810)
New Haven, Conn. (c. 1760)
Cutler, Silliman, Ward & Co.
(c. 1767)
Richard Cutler & Sons
(c. 1800–1810)
Bibl. 16, 23, 28, 36, 44, 92,
94, 110, 143

Richard Cutler Jr.
(b. 1774–d. 1811)
New Haven, Conn.
(c. 1800–1810)
Richard Cutler & Sons
Bibl. 16, 23, 28, 44, 110, 143

Richard Cutler & Sons
(c. 1800–1810)
New Haven, Conn.
Richard Cutler
Richard Cutler Jr.
William Cutler
Bibl. 16, 23, 36, 44, 110, 143

William Cutler
(b. 1785–d. 1817)
New Haven, Conn.
(c. 1800–1810)
Connecticut
Richard Cutler & Sons
(c. 1800–1810)
Bibl. 16, 23, 28, 44, 110, 143

William Cutler (c. 1823)
Portland, Me.
Bibl. 23, 36, 44, 105

Abraham Cuyler (c. 1740)
Albany, N.Y.
Bibl. 54, 124 **A C**

Jacob Cuyler (b. 1741)
Albany, N.Y. (c. 1765)
Bibl. 54, 124 **I C**

Stanislas Czekayski
(c. 1822–1824)
Philadelphia, Pa.
Bibl. 3

D

D
(See Biggins-Rodgers Co.,
Dawson Company
Manufacturers, Dodge,
Inc., Wm. B. Durgin Co.,
Gold Recovery & Refining
Corp.)

D & B
(See Downing & Baldwin)

D & Co.
(See DeForest & Co.)

D. & H.
(See Dominick & Haff)

D & P
(See Downing & Phelps)

D & W
(See Davis & Watson)

D B
(See Drobenare Bros. Inc.,
Duncan Beard, Daniel
Boyer)

D B & A D
(See Bayley & Douglas)

D B H & Co.
(See D. B. Hindman & Co.)

D C F
(See Daniel C. Fueter)

D D
(See Daniel Deshon, Douglas
Donaldson, Daniel Dupuy)

D. D. C.
(See D. D. Codding)

D D D
(See Dupuy & Sons)

D F
(See Daniel C. Fueter)

D G
(See David Greenleaf Jr.)

D H
(See David Hall, Daniel
Henchman)

D J
(See Daniel Jackson, David
Jesse)

D M
(See David Moseley, David
Mygatt)

D N
(See D. Nagin Mfg. Corp.,
Daniel Neall, David
Northee)

D P
(See Daniel Parker)

D R
(See Daniel Rogers, Daniel
Russell)

D R C
(See Damaks Refining Co.)

D S
(See Dorst Co., David Smith,
Daniel Syng)

D T
(See David Tyler)

D T G
(See D. T. Goodhue)

D V
(See Daniel Van Voorhis,
David Vinton)

D V V
(See Daniel Van Voorhis)

D Y
(See Daniel You)

Willson Dabrall
(See Wilson Dalziel)

Louis H. Dadin
(c. 1849–1852)
Charleston, S.C.
Bibl. 5, 124

SPOONS

A spoon can be dated from the shape. The method of construction has also changed through the years. Prior to 1800 most spoons looked as if they were made from two pieces: a bowl, and a straight piece that formed the handle. After 1800 spoons were usually made from one piece of silver. The design of the bowl changed from fig-shaped to elliptical, then to the narrow oval shape used today. The early spoon had a large bowl if compared to a twentieth-century spoon. The early handle was straight, but by 1730 the tip was bent down, and about 1830 the tip was turned upward. Each spoon was cut out of a sheet of silver and then hand-hammered. From 1850 to the present most spoons have had handles with the upturned tip. A few patterns are authentic copies and even the tilt of the handle has been copied. Designs were engraved, chased (raised), or applied. After 1830 most spoons were cast with the raised designs in the mold. The designers of the 1920s often made spoons and other flatware in very new shapes with unusual bowl shapes, flat straight handles, and decorations that were applied.

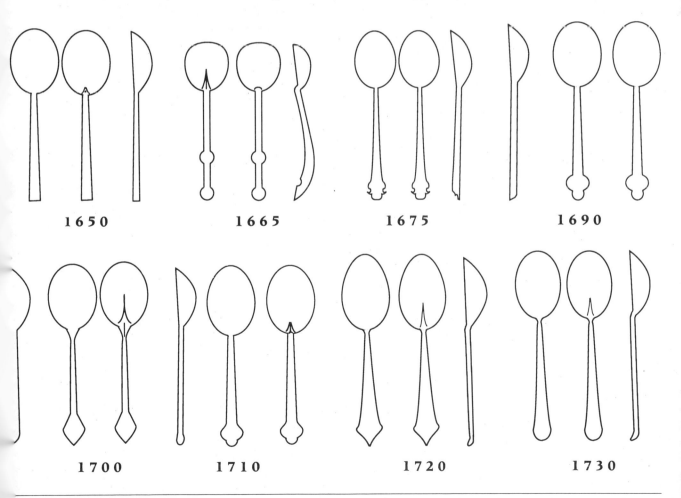

1650 1665 1675 1690

1700 1710 1720 1730

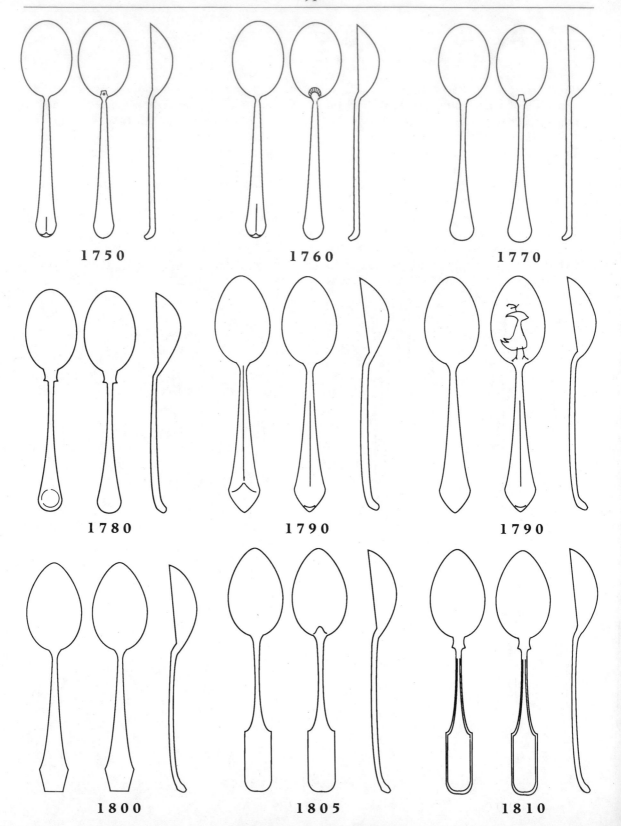

1750

1760

1770

1780

1790

1790

1800

1805

1810

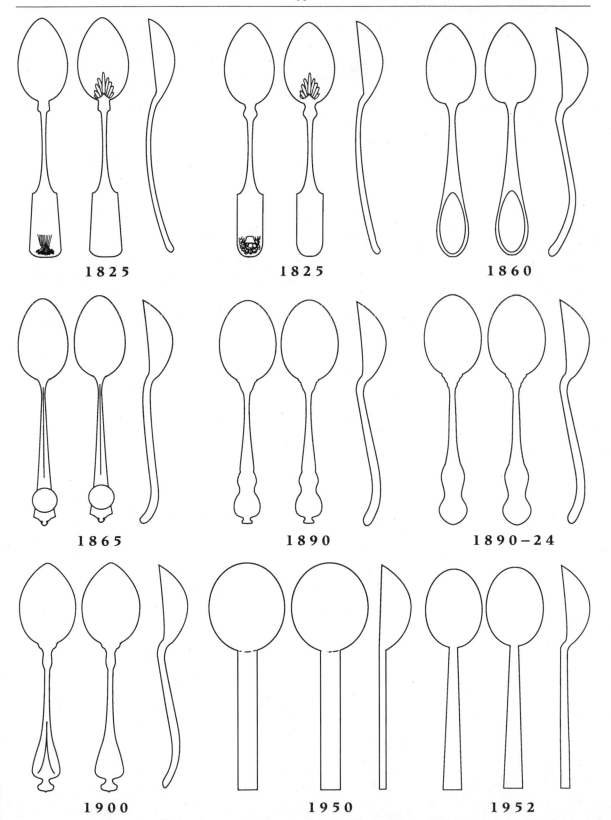

1825

1825

1860

1865

1890

1890–24

1900

1950

1952

Thomas Daft (c. 1775)
Philadelphia, Pa.
Bibl. 3

Henry Dagget
(b. 1741–d. 1830)
New Haven, Conn.
Isaac Beers (c. 1800)
Bibl. 16, 23, 28, 36, 44, 110, 143

Daggett & Blair (c. 1821)
St. Louis, Mo.
John C. Daggett
Daniel Blair
Bibl. 54, 134

John C. Daggett
St. Louis, Mo.
(c. 1817–1821)
Massachusetts
Daggett & Blair (c. 1821)
Bibl. 54

Henry Dagon
(c. 1847–1850)
Philadelphia, Pa.
Bibl. 3

Jean Dagorret
(1830–1850)
New Orleans, La.
Bibl. 141

John Dallon (c. 1791)
Philadelphia, Pa.
Bibl. 3, 23, 36, 44

Dally & Halsey
(c. 1787–1789)
New York, N.Y.
Philip Dally
Jabez Halsey
Bibl. 23, 28, 36, 44, 91, 124, 138

Philip Dally
(c. 1779–1789)
New York, N.Y.
Dally & Halsey
(c. 1787–1789)
Bibl. 23, 24, 25, 35, 36, 44, 54, 91, 114, 124, 138

John Dalton (c. 1790)
Philadelphia, Pa.
Bibl. 3

Wilson Dalziel (Willson Dabrall)
(b. 1749–d. 1781)
Georgetown, S.C.
(c. 1774–1781)
Bibl. 5, 28

Damaks Refining Co.
(c. 1950)
New York, N.Y.
Bibl. 127

Dana & Maynard (c. 1841)
Utica, N.Y.
——— Dana
Thomas Maynard
Bibl. 18, 124

Daniel D. Dana (1860)
Warren, R.I.
Bibl. 108

E. B. Dana & Co. (c. 1832)
Elmira, N.Y.
Bibl. 20, 124

Peyton Dana
(b. 1795–d. 1849)
Providence, R. I.
(c. 1803–1820)
Bibl. 15, 25, 28, 44, 80, 91, 110, 114

George Dane
(c. 1797–1826)
London, England
Macon, Ga.
Bibl. 17

Thomas Dane
(b. 1726–d. 1796)
Boston, Mass. (c. 1745)
Bibl. 15, 23, 24, 25, 28, 29, 36, 44, 54, 69, 78, 94, 102, 104, 110, 114

Anthony D'Angen (Dangen) (Dangin)
(See Antoine Danjen)

George C. Daniel (c. 1829)
Elizabeth City, N.C.
Halifax, Nova Scotia
Bibl. 21

James H. Daniel
(c. 1830–1850)
Philadelphia, Pa.
Bibl. 3

Joshua Daniel
(c. 1830–1850)
Philadelphia, Pa.
Bibl. 3

Perry O. Daniel (c. 1830)
Boston, Mass.
Bibl. 29, 44

PERRY O. DANIEL

Charles W. Daniels
(c. 1836–1838)
Troy, N.Y.
Bibl. 20, 23, 36, 44, 124

G. L. Daniels
(c. 1840–1843)
Rome, N.Y.
Bibl. 20, 124

Danjean
(See next entry)

Antoine Danjen (D'Angen) (Dangin) (Danjean) (Anthony Dangen)
(b. 1781–d. 1827)
St. Louis, Mo.
Bibl. 54, 122, 134   A D

Simon Danou (1849)
New Orleans, La.
Bibl. 141

Danul
(See Daniel)

John Darby (c. 1801–1831)
Charleston, S.C.
Bibl. 5, 25, 44, 114   DARBY

J. DARBY

William Darby
(c. 1790–1797)
Charleston, S.C.
Bibl. 5, 44

John Dargee
(c. 1810–1815)
New York, N.Y.
Bibl. 23, 36, 44, 138

John Darragh (c. 1785)
Philadelphia, Pa.
Bibl. 3

Frederick Darrigrand
(b. 1826)
Utica, N.Y. (c. 1854–1865)
Bibl. 18, 158

David Darrow (c. 1825)
New York, N.Y.
Bibl. 24, 44, 124

Edmund Darrow
(c. 1843–1861)
New York, N.Y.
*Bibl. 15, 35, 44, 83, 114,
124, 138*

John F. Darrow (c. 1818)
Catskill, N.Y.
Bibl. 15, 20, 25, 44, 114, 124

Victoire Daubayson
(c. 1820–1822)
Philadelphia, Pa.
Bibl. 3, 23, 36, 44

Simon Dauce
(c. 1798–1819)
Philadelphia, Pa.
Bibl. 3, 23, 36, 44

Simon Dauci
(c. 1823–1833)
Philadelphia, Pa.
Bibl. 3

E. J. Daumont & Co.
(c. 1820)
Lexington, Ky.
Bibl. 32, 93

Edmund J. Daumont
Louisville, Ky.
E. J. Daumont & Co.
(c. 1820)
James I. Lemon & Co.
(c. 1859–1861)
Bibl. 32, 93

Peter Daumont
(c. 1840–1867)
Louisville, Ky.
Cincinnati, Oh. (c. 1840)
Indianapolis, Ind.
Richard Ewing Smith
(c. 1821–1849)
Bibl. 32, 90, 93, 133, 138

Jules D'Autel
Augusta, Ga. (c. 1841)
Athens, Ga. (c. 1845)

Davane, Davanne
(See Daverne)

John Davenport
(b. 1753–d. 1842)
Portsmouth, N.H. (c. 1773)
Bibl. 54, 110, 125

Jonathan Davenport
(d. 1801)
Baltimore, Md.
(c. 1789–1793)
Philadelphia, Pa.
(c. 1793–1796)
*Bibl. 15, 29, 38, 44, 54, 91,
114*

Robert Davenport
(c. 1806–1822)

Philadelphia, Pa.
Barrington & Davenport
(c. 1806–1807)
Bibl. 3, 23, 36, 44

Samuel Davenport
(b. 1720–d. 1793)
Milton, Mass.
Bibl. 23, 28, 36, 44, 110

**John Daverne (Davane)
(Davanne)**
Baltimore, Md.
(c. 1766–1801)
Bibl. 5, 23, 28, 36, 38, 44

David & Dupuy
(c. 1792–1805)
Philadelphia, Pa.
John David
John David (Jr.)
Daniel Dupuy
Bibl. 23, 36, 44, 91

Henry David (c. 1849)
New York, N.Y.
Bibl. 23, 124, 138

John David
(b. 1736–d. 1793,
c. 1763–1777)
Philadelphia, Pa.
New York, N.Y.
David & Dupuy
(c. 1792–1805)
*Bibl. 2, 3, 15, 23, 24, 25, 28,
29, 30, 36, 39, 44, 50, 54,
81, 91, 95, 102, 104, 114,
118, 119, 139*

John David (Jr.) (d. 1805)
Philadelphia, Pa.
(c. 1792–1805)
David & Dupuy
*Bibl. 3, 4, 15, 23, 24, 25, 29,
36, 44, 81, 91, 95, 114*

Lewis A. David
  (c. 1823–1840)
Philadelphia, Pa.
Bibl. 3, 4, 23, 36, 44

Marquis David
  (c. 1855–1859)
Charleston, S.C.
L Epstein (?)
Bibl. 5

Peter David
  (b. 1691–d. 1755)
Philadelphia, Pa. (c. 1738)
*Bibl. 2, 3, 15, 23, 24, 25, 28,
  29, 36, 39, 81, 91, 95, 114,
  124*

**Barzillai (Brazillai)
  Davidson**
(See Barzillai Davison)

Charles Davidson
(See Charles Davison)

Samuel Davidson
  (c. 1774)
Baltimore, Md.
Bibl. 38

Adam Davie
(See Davy)

Davies & Battel
  (1844–1850)
Utica, N.Y.
Thomas Davies
William A. Davies
Albert T. Battel(s)
Bibl. 18, 20, 124, 158

Davies & Taylor
  (c. 1851–1852)
Utica, N.Y.
Thomas Davies
William S. Taylor
Bibl. 18, 124

B. F. & T. M. Davies
  (c. 1858–1879)
Utica, N.Y.
Benjamin F. & Thomas M.
  Davies
Edward N. Sanford
Bibl. 18, 124

Benjamin F. Davies
  (b. 1830)
Utica, N.Y.
Thomas Davies & Sons
  (c. 1856–1858)
B. F. & T. M. Davies
  (1858–1879)
Bibl. 18, 20, 124, 158

Thomas Davies
  (b. 1801)
Utica, N.Y.
Storrs & Davies
  (c. 1829–1830)
Leach & Davies
  (c. 1835–1840)
Davies & Battel
  (c. 1844–1850)
Davies & Taylor
  (c. 1851–1852)
Thomas Davies & Sons
  (c. 1856–1858)
Bibl. 18, 20, 124

Thomas Davies & Sons
  (c. 1856–1858)
Utica, N.Y.
Thomas Davies
Thomas M. Davies
Benjamin F. Davies
Bibl. 18, 124

Thomas M. Davies
  (b. 1833–d. 1882)
Utica, N.Y.
Thomas Davies & Sons
  (c. 1856–1858)
B. F. & T. M. Davies
  (1858–1879)
Bibl. 18, 124, 158

William A. Davies
  (b. 1828)
Utica, N.Y.
Davies & Battel
  (c. 1844–1850)
Bibl. 18, 20, 158

Davis
(See Mosher & Davis)

Davis & Babbitt (c. 1815)
Providence, R.I.
Samuel Davis (?)
C. Babbitt (?)
Bibl. 23, 28, 36, 44, 110

Davis & Brown
  (c. 1802–1820)
Boston, Mass.
*Bibl. 15, 23, 24, 25, 29, 44,
  78, 91, 110, 114*

DAVIS & BROWN

Davis & Galt
  (1888–c. 1922)
Philadelphia, Pa.
Bibl. 114, 127, 135, 157

Davis & Watson (c. 1815)
Boston, Mass.
Samuel Davis
Edward E. Watson
*Bibl. 15, 23, 24, 25, 29, 36,
  44, 110*

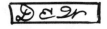

Davis, Baxter & Co.
  (1860)
Portland, Me.
Bibl. 105

Davis, Palmer & Co.
  (c. 1841–1846)
Boston, Mass.
*Bibl. 2, 15, 23, 24, 25, 28,
  29, 44, 91, 114*

Davis Palmer & Co.

Davis Palmer & Co.

Davis, Watson & Co.
  (c. 1820)
Boston, Mass.
Samuel Davis
Edward E. Watson
Bartlett M. Bramhill
Bibl. 25, 28, 29, 91, 114

DAVIS WATSON & CO.

A. Davis Co. (c. 1904)
Chicago, Ill.
Successor to M. C.
  Eppenstein & Co.
  (c. 1894–1904)
Bibl. 127

Aaron Davis
  (c. 1811–1818)
Philadelphia, Pa.
New York, N.Y.
  (c. 1831–1832)
Bibl. 3, 138

Caleb Davis
  (b. 1769–d. 1834)
Woodstock, Va.
  (c. 1792)
Clarksburg, Va.
  (c. 1824)
Bibl. 19

Charles Percy Davis
  (1858–c. 1928)
St. Louis, Mo.
Bibl. 155

E. L. Davis (1875)
Cherryfield, Me.
Bibl. 105

Edward Davis
  (d. 1781) (c. 1770)
Newburyport, Mass.
*Bibl. 2, 15, 23, 24, 25, 28,
  29, 44, 50, 54, 72, 91, 110,
  114*

Elias Davis
  (b. 1782–d. 1856)
Boston, Mass.
  (c. 1805–1825)
Newburyport, R.I. (c. 1775)
*Bibl. 15, 23, 25, 36, 44, 110,
  114*

George Davis
  (c. 1832–1836)
Albany, N.Y.
Bibl. 20, 124

John Davis (c. 1818)
Philadelphia, Pa.
Bibl. 3

John Wheelwright Davis
  (b. 1800)
Newburyport, Mass.
Moulton & Davis
  (c. 1824–1830)
Bibl. 15, 23, 25, 36, 44, 110

Joshua George Davis
  (c. 1796–1840)
Boston, Mass.
*Bibl. 4, 15, 23, 24, 25, 28,
  29, 36, 44, 72, 110, 114*

Richard Davis (c. 1837)
Philadelphia, Pa.
Bibl. 3

Riley A. Davis (c. 1850)
New Bern, N.C.
Bibl. 22

Sampson Davis
  (b. 1772–d. 1806)
Woodstock, Vt.
  (c. 1790–1806)
Bibl. 54

Samuel Davis
  (c. 1801–1842)
Boston, Mass.
  (2 different men)
Plymouth, Mass.
Providence, R.I.
Davis & Babbitt (c. 1815) (?)
Davis & Watson (c. 1815)
Davis, Watson & Co.
  (c. 1820)
*Bibl. 23, 24, 25, 28, 29, 44,
  91, 110, 114*

Samuel B. Davis
  (c. 1837–1850)
Philadelphia, Pa.
Bibl. 3

T. F. Davis (1861)
Farmington, Me.
Bibl. 105

T. W. Davis (c. 1857)
Greenville, S.C.
Bibl. 5

Thomas Aspinwall Davis
  (c. 1824–1830)
Boston, Mass.
*Bibl. 4, 15, 23, 24, 25, 28,
  29, 36, 44, 91, 110, 114*

W. M. Davis (c. 1825)
Morrisville, N.Y.
Bibl. 20, 124

William Davis
Boston, Mass. (c. 1823)
Philadelphia, Pa. (c. 1843)
Bibl. 3, 23, 28, 36, 110

**Barzillai (Brazillai)
  Davison (Davidson)**
  (b. 1740–d. 1828)
Norwich, Conn.
Bibl. 16, 23, 28, 44, 110, 138

Charles Davison
  (c. 1803–1806)
Norwich, Conn.
Norfolk, Va.
*Bibl. 19, 23, 24, 25, 29, 36,
  44, 91, 92, 110, 114*

Clement Davison
  (c. 1819–1838)
New York, N.Y.
*Bibl. 15, 28, 44, 114, 124,
  138*

I. Davison
(See I. Davisson)

Jesse G. Davison
  (c. 1849–1850)
Richmond, Va.
Bibl. 19

John G. Davison
   (c. 1842–1843)
Utica, N.Y.
Bibl. 18, 20, 124, 158

Peter I. Davison
   (b. 1786–d. 1873)
Sherburne, N.Y.
   (c. 1815–1860)
Bibl. 20, 124

I. Davisson (Davison)
   (1849–1850)
Bloomington, Ind.
Bibl. 133

DAVISON

Adam Davy (Davie)
   (c. 1795–1798)
Philadelphia, Pa.
Bibl. 3, 23, 28, 36, 44

Dawco
(See Dawson Company
   Manufacturers)

Dawe & McIver
   (c. 1785)
Alexandria, Va.
Philip Dawe
Colin (?) McIver
Bibl. 19, 54

Philip Dawe
   (c. 1771–1806)
Alexandria, Va. (c. 1785)
Dumfries, Va.
Dawe & McIver (c. 1785)
Bibl. 19

Robert Dawes
   (b. 1767)
Boston, Mass.
Bibl. 2, 54, 119

Simon Dawes
   (c. 1829–1833)
Philadelphia, Pa.
Bibl. 3

William Dawes
   (b. 1719–d. 1802)
Boston, Mass.
Bibl. 23, 28, 36, 44, 110

Henry Dawkins
   (c. 1754–1776)
New York, N.Y.
Philadelphia, Pa.
Bibl. 3, 28, 124

R. Daws (c. 1800)
Location unknown
Bibl. 28, 29, 44, 110

**Dawson Company
Manufacturers**
   (c. 1925–present)
Cleveland, Ohio
Bibl. 127

John Dawson (c. 1767)
New York, N.Y.
Bibl. 23, 28, 36, 44, 124, 138

Jonas (James) Dawson
   (c. 1813–1824)
Philadelphia, Pa.
Bibl. 3

William Dawson
   (c. 1793–1797)
Philadelphia, Pa.
New York, N.Y. (c. 1797)
Bibl. 3, 23, 36, 44

Day
(See Eolles & Day)

Day, Clark & Co.
   (c. 1895–1935)
Newark, N.J.
New York, N.Y.
Bibl. 114, 127, 157

George Day (c. 1794–1806)
Charleston, S. C.
John Lowe (?)
Bibl. 5

Israel Day (c. 1807)
Baltimore, Md.
Bibl. 38

John Day
Philadelphia, Pa. (?)
   (c. 1815–1820)
Boston, Mass.
   (c. 1820–1825)
Bibl. 15, 25, 44, 114

Sidney B. Day
   (c. 1847–c. 1850)
Macon, Ga.
Bibl. 17

**Sidney B. Day and E.
   Maussenet** (c. 1846)
Macon, Ga.
Bibl. 89

E. L. Deacon Jewelry Co.
   (c. 1909)
Denver, Colo.   E. L. D.
Became Eugene L. Deacon,
   Los Angeles, Calif.
   (c. 1915)
Bibl. 127, 157

Edward Deacon
   (c. 1836–1838)
New York, N.Y.
Bibl. 15, 124, 138

Samuel R. Deacon
   (c. 1823–1824)
Philadelphia, Pa.
Bibl. 3

Thomas Deaderick
   (b. 1765–d. 1831)
Winchester, Va.
Nashville, Tenn.
Bibl. 19, 54

Reuben Dean
   (b. 1759–d.1811)
Windsor, Vt.
Bibl. 54, 110

E. S. Deane (1875)
Augusta, Me.
Bibl. 105

James Deane (b. 1726)
New York, N.Y. (c. 1760)
Bibl. 23, 36, 44, 124

D. Deardorff (c. 1840)
Dayton, Ohio
Bibl. 34

David Deas (c. 1829–1833)
Philadelphia, Pa.
Bibl. 3, 23, 36, 44

Philip Deas (c. 1837)
Philadelphia, Pa.
Bibl. 3

N. De Benneville
(c. 1820–1822)
Philadelphia, Pa.
Bibl. 3

**Charles J. J. DeBerard
(DeBerad)**
(c. 1807–1834)
Utica, N.Y. (c. 1807–1815)
Onondaga, N.Y. (c. 1819)
Butler & DeBerard
(c. 1807–1815)
Lewis W. Clark
(c. 1832–1838)
Bibl. 18, 20, 124, 158

Abraham DeBour
(c. 1805)
Philadelphia, Pa.
Bibl. 3

John Debrot (c. 1819)
Philadelphia, Pa.
Bibl. 3

Michael Samuel Debruhl
(c. 1798–1806)
Charleston, S.C.
Abbeville, S.C. (?)
Mary Matilda Dunseth
(c. 1804)
Bibl. 5

Debutante
(See Mandalian Mfg. Co.)

Joseph Decatrell
(c. 1816–1822)
Philadelphia, Pa.
Bibl. 3

Decker & Coleman
(c. 1847–1849)
Troy, N.Y.
Bibl. 20, 124

James Decker
(c. 1830–1848)
New York, N.Y. (c. 1830)
Troy, N.Y.
*Bibl. 20, 23, 24, 25, 36, 44,
114, 124*

J. DECKER

Leonard Decker
(c. 1845–1849)
Troy, N.Y.
Bibl. 20, 124

DeForest & Co.
(c. 1827–1828)
New York, N.Y.
Bibl. 15, 25, 44, 114, 124

D & C°

DeForest & Fowler
(c. 1827–1828)
New York, N.Y.
—————— DeForest
Gilbert Fowler (?)
Bibl. 15, 124, 138

**William C. Defrees
(Defriez)**
(c. 1848–1881)
St. Louis, Mo.
Kentucky
Bibl. 54, 93

WILLIAM C. DEFREES

W C Defriez

Michael Deganny
(c. 1819)
Baltimore, Md.
Bibl. 38

Godfrey DeGilse (c. 1837)
Columbus, Ga.
Bibl. 17

I. N. Deitsch
(c. 1904–1920)
New York, N.Y.
Bibl. 127, 157

Dekra
(See Argentum Silver
Company)

Philip H. Delachaux
(c. 1820–1822)
Philadelphia, Pa.
Bibl. 3

William DeLacy
Norfolk, Va. (c. 1815)
New York, N.Y.
(c. 1824–1825)
Bibl. 19, 138

Andrew Delagrow
(c. 1795)
Philadelphia, Pa.
Bibl. 3, 23, 36, 44

Emanuel De La Motta
(b. 1761–d. 1821)
Savannah, Ga. (c. 1784)
Bibl. 17

Jebez Delano
(b. 1763–d. 1848)
New Bedford, Mass.
(c. 1784)
*Bibl. 15, 23, 25, 28, 36, 44,
110, 114*

I DELANO

I:D

Charles Delaplace
(c. 1795–c. 1800)
Augusta, Ga.
Bibl. 17

John Delarue (Delaroux)
(c. 1882)
New Orleans, La.
*Bibl. 23, 24, 25, 36, 44, 54,
114*

Jean Delauney (c. 1805)
New York, N.Y.
Bibl. 23, 36, 44, 124, 138

John Delauney (c. 1816)
Philadelphia, Pa.
Bibl. 3

Delaware Silver Co.
(c. 1895–1900)
Location Unknown
Bibl. 127

DELAWARE SILVER CO.

Stephen Deleane (b. 1786)
Baltimore, Md. (c. 1803)
Bibl. 38

**Delleker & Richardson
　(Richardson &
　Delleker)** (c. 1819)
Philadelphia, Pa.
Samuel Delleker
John Richardson
Bibl. 3

Samuel Delleker
　(c. 1819–1825)
Philadelphia, Pa.
Delleker & Richardson
　(c. 1819)
Young & Delleker
　(c. 1823–1824)
Bibl. 3

**Nicolas Delonguemare
　(Jr.)** (d. 1711)
Charleston, S.C.
　(1699–1711)
Bibl. 5, 102

Francis Deloste
　(c. 1812–1851)
Baltimore, Md.
Suire & Deloste
　(c. 1822–1826)
Bibl. 38

William L. DeMatteo
　(c. 1970–present)
Alexandria, Va.
(One of the founders of
　Hand & Hammer)
Bibl. 127

deM

Andrew Demilt (c. 1805)
New York, N.Y.
*Bibl. 15, 23, 24, 25, 29, 44,
　89, 95, 114, 124*

DEMILT

**Thomas & Benjamin
　Demilt** (c. 1810)
New York, N.Y.
Bibl. 28, 46, 91, 124, 138

DEMILT

John Demmock (c. 1798)
Boston, Mass.
Bibl. 23, 28, 36, 44, 110

Jean Demorsy (c. 1822)
New Orleans, La.
Bibl. 23, 36, 44

John Demort (c. 1810)
New York, N.Y.
Bibl. 23, 36, 44, 124

Lucien Demort (c. 1810)
New York, N.Y.
Bibl. 23, 36, 44, 124, 138

D. C. Denham
　(c. 1820–1825)
New York, N.Y.
Bibl. 15, 44, 91, 114, 124

John Denham (c. 1848)
Philadelphia, Pa.
Bibl. 3

John DeNise (c. 1698)
Philadelphia, Pa.
Bibl. 29, 33, 44, 114

John Denise (Johan Nys)
　(c. 1798)
New York, N.Y.
*Bibl. 24, 25, 29, 33, 44, 102,
　124*

John & Tunis Denise
Kingston, R.I. (c. 1770)
New York, N.Y. (c. 1798)
*Bibl. 4, 23, 24, 25, 28, 29,
　35, 36, 44, 83, 95, 124*

J & T D

Ruth Israel Denison
　(1925–1978)
St. Louis, Mo.
Bibl. 155

T. Denison (c. 1790)
New York, N.Y.
Bibl. 28, 29, 44, 72, 124

T DENISON　　T DENISON

Henry Dennery (c. 1819)
New York, N.Y.
Bibl. 15, 124, 138

John Denning
　(c. 1833–1835)
Philadelphia, Pa.
Bibl. 3

Dennis & Fitch
　(c. 1835–1839)
Troy, N.Y.
*Bibl. 15, 20, 23, 25, 36, 44,
　114, 124*

DENNIS & FITCH

Augustus Dennis
　(c. 1831–1833)
Troy, N.Y.
Bibl. 20, 124

Ebenezer Dennis
　(b. 1753–d. 1785)
Hartford, Conn.
*Bibl. 16, 23, 28, 36, 44, 92,
　110*

George Dennis Jr.
　(b. 1753, c. 1770)
Norwich, Conn.
Bibl. 16, 23, 28, 36, 44, 110

Johannis Dennis
(See Johannis Nys)

Stephen A. Dennis
　(c. 1839–1845)
Troy, N.Y.
Bibl. 20, 124

De Noys
(See Johannis Nys)

Conway Dentz (c. 1850)
Philadelphia, Pa.
Bibl. 3

Denver
(See George Bell Co.)

**De Parisien
De Perrizang**
(See Parisien)

De Peyser
(See De Pryster)

L. DePoorter
  (c. 1829–1830)
Charleston, S.C.
Bibl. 5

William De Pryster (De Peyser) (c. 1733)
New York, N.Y.
Bibl. 4, 23, 28, 36, 44, 124

Derby Silver Co.
  (1873–1898)
Derby, Conn.
Became International Silver
  (1898)
Bibl. 127, 135, 157

DeRiemer & Mead
  (c. 1830–1831)
Ithaca, N.Y.
Cornelius Brouwer DeRiemer
Edward Edmund Mead (?)
Bibl. 20, 23, 28, 36, 44, 124

C. B. DeRiemer & Co.
  (c. 1831–1833)
Auburn, N.Y.
Bibl. 20, 124

Cornelius Brouwer DeRiemer
  (b. 1804–d. 1872)
Auburn, N.Y. (c. 1840)
Ithaca, N.Y.
DeRiemer & Mead
  (c. 1830–1831)
Bibl. 20, 23, 36, 44, 124

Jacob Roome DeRiemer
  (b. 1805–d. 1863)
New York, N.Y. (c. 1830)
Bibl. 23, 36, 44, 124

Peter DeRiemer
  (b. 1738–d. 1814)
New York, N.Y.
  (c. 1763–1796)
*Bibl. 4, 23, 24, 25, 28, 29,
  35, 36, 54, 91, 95, 102,
  114, 116, 119, 124, 138*

Jose de Rivera (b. 1904)
New York, N.Y.
Bibl. 89, 117

John Derr (c. 1825–1848)
Philadelphia, Pa.
Bibl. 3

Francis Deschamps
  (c. 1846–1849)
Philadelphia, Pa.
Bibl. 3

Louis Descuret (Desuret) (Desueret)
Philadelphia, Pa.
  (c. 1799–1811)
Blondell & Descuret
  (c. 1798–1799)
Bibl. 3, 23, 36, 44

Daniel Deshon
  (b. 1698–d. 1781)
New London, Conn.
*Bibl. 15, 16, 23, 24, 25, 28,
  29, 36, 44, 61, 92, 94, 114*

Pierre-Jean Desnoyers
  (b. 1772–d. 1846)
  (c. 1790–1835)
Gallipolis, Ohio (c. 1790)
Detroit, Mich. (c. 1796)
Pittsburgh, Pa.
Jean-Baptiste Piquette
  (c. 1803–1805)
Bibl. 58

Desquet & Tanguy
  (c. 1805)
Philadelphia, Pa.
Bibl. 3, 23, 36, 44

Desueret, Desuret
(See Descuret)

Charles de Temple
  (b. 1929)
New York, N.Y.
Bibl. 117

Jacob Deterle (Deterly)
  (b. 1786–d. 1848)
Cincinnati, Ohio
  (c. 1812–1833)
Woodruff & Deterly
Bibl. 34, 90, 91

Deterly
(See Deterle)

G. Deuconer (c. 1817)
Philadelphia, Pa.
Bibl. 3

Augustus Deuschler
  (b. 1822)
Utica, N.Y.
  (c. 1858–1859)
Bibl. 18, 125, 158

(Monsieur) Joseph De Vacht (c. 1790)
Gallipolis, Ohio
Bibl. 34

J. & M. Develin (Devlin)
  (c. 1848–1850)
Philadelphia, Pa.
Bibl. 3

John Deverell | Deverell |
  (c. 1764–1813)
Boston, Mass.
*Bibl. 23, 24, 25, 28, 29, 36,
  44, 110, 114*

James Devine
  (c. 1848–1849)
Philadelphia, Pa.
Bibl. 3

Charles Devit(t)
  (c. 1844–1846)
Philadelphia, Pa.
Bibl. 3, 23

Devlin (See Develin)

Daniel DeWald
  (c. 1823–1827)
Canton, Ohio
Bibl. 34

Dwight Dewey (c. 1840)
Ravenna, Ohio
Bibl. 34

Francis Dewing (c. 1716)
Boston, Mass.
Bibl. 28, 110

Abram Henry Dewitt
  (c. 1847)
Columbus, Ga.
Bibl. 17

Garrit Dewitt
Sparta, Ga. (c. 1823–1827)
Bibl. 17

Zachariah De Witt
 (c. 1821)
Hamilton, Ohio
Bibl. 34

Benjamin Dexter (c. 1830)
New Bedford, Mass.
Bibl. 54, 91, 110, 114

John Dexter
 (b. 1735–d. 1800)
Dedham, Mass.
Marlboro, Mass.
Bibl. 23, 28, 36, 44, 110

Minerva Dexter (b. 1785)
Middletown, Conn.
 (c. 1810)
Bibl. 16, 28, 110

W. W. Dexter
 (c. 1843–1846)
Earlville, N.Y.
Bibl. 20, 124

John Dey (c. 1846)
Philadelphia, Pa.
Bibl. 3

E(lias) De Young & Co.
 (c. 1836–c. 1839)
Louisville, Ky.
Bibl. 32, 54, 93

Michael De Young
 (c. 1816–1836)
Baltimore, Md.
Bibl. 25, 29, 38, 44, 114

**Diaz Silversmiths &
 Goldsmiths**
 (present)
Tucson, Az.
Bibl. 146

Dibble & Jacks (c. 1842)
Savannah, Ga.
Oscar J. H. Dibble
Pulaski Jacks
Bibl. 17

Henry E. Dibble
 (c. 1847)
Columbus, Ga.
Bibl. 17

Oscar J. H. Dibble
 (c. 1835–1849)
Savannah, Ga. (c. 1842)
Columbus, Ga. (c. 1845)
Dibble & Jacks (c. 1842)
Bibl. 17

O J H DIBBLE

H. Dickerson & Co.
 (c. 1815)
Philadelphia, Pa.
Bibl. 23, 36, 44

John Dickerson
 (b. 1755–d. 1828)
Philadelphia, Pa. (c. 1778)
Morristown, N.J.
 (c. 1778–1796)
*Bibl. 3, 4, 23, 28, 36, 44, 46,
54*

Dickinson & Hannum
 (c. 1843)
Syracuse, N.Y.
Pliny Dickinson
John Hannum
Bibl. 20, 84, 124

Dickinson & Henry
 (c. 1793)
Philadelphia, Pa.
Bibl. 39

**Dickinson (Dickson)
 (Dixon) & Robeson
 (Robinson)**
Philadelphia, Pa.
 (c. 1796–1797)
D. L. Dickinson (Dickson)
 (Dixon)
——— Robeson
Bibl. 3, 23, 36, 44

Anson Dickinson (c. 1800)
Litchfield, Conn.
New York, N.Y.
Bibl. 28, 124

Charles Dickinson
 (c. 1812)
Zanesville, Ohio
Bibl. 34

**D. L. Dickinson (Dickson)
 (Dixon)**
Philadelphia, Pa.
 (c. 1796–1797)
Portsmouth, Va. (c. 1806)
Dickinson & Robeson
 (c. 1796–1797)
Bibl. 19

G. W. Dickinson
Location unknown
Bibl. 89

John Dickinson
 (c. 1822–1825)
Philadelphia, Pa.
Bibl. 3

Jonathan Dickinson
 (c. 1794–1796)
Philadelphia, Pa.
Bibl. 3, 23, 36, 44

P. Dickinson & Co.
 (c. 1837–1843)
Syracuse, N.Y.
Bibl. 20, 91, 124

Pliny Dickinson
 (c. 1828–1847)
Syracuse, N.Y.
Dickinson & Hannum
 (c. 1843)
Bibl. 20, 84, 91, 124

Richard Dickinson
 (c. 1768)
Mt. Holly, N.J.
Bibl. 3

**Sarah B. Dickinson
 (Wood)** (c. 1896)
Niagara Falls, N.Y.
Same mark as that used by
 Thomas V. Dickinson
Bibl. 114, 127

Thomas V. Dickinson
  (c. 1891)
Buffalo, N.Y.
Same mark as that used by
  Sarah B. Dickinson
Bibl. 127

William Dickinson
  (c. 1843–1845)
Philadelphia, Pa.
Bibl. 3

Dickson
(See D. L. Dickinson)

Dickson, White & Co.
  (c. 1837)
Philadelphia, Pa.
Bibl. 3, 54

Henry Dickson
  (b. 1774–d. 1854)
Paintsville, Ky.
Bibl. 32, 54, 68, 93

Pierre & Jacques Didier
  (c. 1821)
St. Louis, Mo.
Bibl. 54

Philip Diehr
  (c. 1840–1850)
Philadelphia, Pa.
Bibl. 3

Gerhard Diercks (d. 1886)
Columbia, S.C.
  (c. 1855–1880)
Bibl. 5

Bernard Gregory Dietz
  (c. 1848)
Cleveland, Ohio
Bibl. 34, 54

Francois Dieudonné
  (d. 1738)
New Orleans, La.
  (1725–1738)
Bibl. 141

Dikeman
(See Wetmore & Dikeman)

Aaron Dikeman
  (c. 1824–1855)
New York, N.Y.
St. Louis, Mo.

*Bibl. 15, 25, 44, 54, 114,
  124, 134, 138*

| A. DIKEMAN |

Burr Dikeman
  (c. 1845–1855)
St. Louis, Mo.
Bibl. 54

Henry A. Dikeman
  (c. 1845–1855)
St. Louis, Mo.
Bib. 54

Rene Dikeman
  (c. 1845–1855)
St. Louis, Mo.
Bibl. 54

R. M. Dill (1875)
Freeport, Me.
Bibl. 105

D. Dilling (c. 1760)
Location unknown
Bibl. 28

D DILLING

Dillon & Hovel
  (1856–1857)
New Orleans, La.
Bibl. 141

Dwight Dillon
  (1943–1959)
St. Louis, Mo.
Bibl. 155

Edward Dillon
  (1852–1866)
New Orleans, La.
Bibl. 141

Richard Dimes Company
  (c. 1908–1955)
South Boston, Mass.
Became King Silver
  Company (1955)
Rogers, Lunt & Bowlen
  (Lunt Silversmiths)
  (c. 1957)
Tools, dies, and flatware
  patterns bought by
  Manchester Silver
  Company (c. 1956)
Bibl. 127, 147

John Dimmock (c. 1801)
New York, N.Y.
Bibl. 23, 36, 44, 124, 138

Dimond & Gurnee
  (c. 1831–1832)
New York, N.Y.
Bibl. 15, 124, 138

Isaac M. Dimond
  (c. 1828–1838)
New York, N.Y.
*Bibl. 15, 23, 36, 44, 91, 124,
  138*

Otto F. Dingeldein
  (c. 1936–1980)
St. Louis, Mo.
Bibl. 155

James Dinwiddie
  (b. 1820–d. 1885)
Lynchburg, Va.
  (c. 1840–1868)
Bibl. 19, 54

| JAMES DINWIDDIE |

G. (C.) E. Disbrow
  (c. 1825)
New York, N.Y.
*Bibl. 24, 25, 44, 110, 114,
  124*

| G E DISBROW |

Dix
(See Woodbury, Dix, &
  Hartwell)

Joseph Dix (c. 1769)
Philadelphia, Pa.
Bibl. 3

Dixon
(See D. L. Dickinson)

A. Dixon (c. 1800)
Location unknown
Bibl. 28

Harry S. Dixon
　(1890–1967)
San Francisco, Calif.
Bibl. 140

Isaac Dixon (c. 1843–1850)
Philadelphia, Pa.
Bibl. 3, 15, 25, 44, 91, 114

Basil Dixwell
　(b. 1711–d. 1746)
Boston, Mass.
*Bibl. 2, 15, 23, 28, 36, 44,
　110*

John Dixwell
　(b. 1680–d. 1725)
Boston, Mass.
*Bibl. 2, 4, 10, 15, 23, 24, 25,
　28, 29, 36, 44, 69, 70, 91,
　94, 102, 110, 114, 116,
　118, 119, 143, 151*

A. W. Doane (1875)
Bangor, Me.
Bibl. 105

John Doane
　(b. 1733–d. 1767)
Boston, Mass.
Bibl. 15, 28, 110　

Joshua Doane
　(c. 1720–1753,
　d. 1753)
Providence, R.I.
*Bibl. 15, 23, 24, 25, 28, 29,
　36, 44, 56, 94, 110, 114*

Alexander M. Dobbie
Utica, N.Y. (c. 1844–1849)
Troy, N.Y. (c. 1845–1846)
Bibl. 18, 20, 23, 124, 158

Adam Dobbs
New York, N.Y. (c. 1788)

Philadelphia, Pa. (c. 1813)
Bibl. 28, 36, 44

Frederick Dobleman
　(c. 1813–1818)
Philadelphia, Pa.
Bibl. 3, 23, 36, 44

F. F. G. Doblenar (c. 1810)
Philadelphia, Pa.
Bibl. 23, 36

Thomas Dodd
　(b. 1787–d. 1824)
Hartford, Conn.
Goodwin & Dodd
Bibl. 89, 110

Dodge
(See Longley & Dodge)

Dodge, Inc.
　(c. 1940–present)
Los Angeles, Calif.
Bibl. 127

Abraham Dodge Jr.
　(c. 1825)
Ithaca, N.Y.
Munger & Dodge
　(c. 1824–1825)
Bibl. 20, 124

Benjamin Dodge (c. 1836)
Boston, Mass.
Bibl. 23, 36, 44

D. M. Dodge (1835)
Lowell, Mass.
Bibl. 106

Daniel H. Dodge
　(c. 1816–1824)
Philadelphia, Pa.
Wood & Dodge
　(c. 1816–1817)
Bibl. 3

E. Dodge (c. 1828–1833)
Philadelphia, Pa.
Bibl. 3

E. S. Dodge (c. 1845–1850)
Batavia, N.Y.
Bibl. 20, 124

Ezekiel Dodge
　(c. 1792–1793)

New York, N.Y.
*Bibl. 15, 23, 25, 36, 44, 114,
　124*

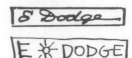

Ezra W. Dodge
　(c. 1766–1798)
New London, Conn.
Bibl. 16, 23, 28, 36, 44, 110

Ezra W. Dodge
　(c. 1821)
Wheeling, Va.
Bibl. 19

John Dodge　
New York, N.Y.
　(c. 1790–1817)
Catskill, N.Y.
　(c. 1818–1819)
*Bibl. 15, 20, 23, 24, 25, 29,
　36, 44, 91, 114, 124, 138*

Nehemiah Dodge
　(c. 1790–1824)
Providence, R.I.
Pitman & Dodge (c. 1790)
*Bibl. 15, 23, 24, 25, 28, 29,
　36, 39, 44, 54, 56, 91, 94,
　110, 114*

S. M. Dodge (c. 1840)
New York State (?)
Bibl. 89

Seril Dodge
　(b. 1757–d. 1802)
Providence, R.I.
　(c. 1784–1796)
*Bibl. 23, 24, 25, 28, 29, 36,
　39, 44, 56, 91, 94, 110,
　114*

William Waldo Dodge, Jr.
(b. 1895–d. 1971)
Asheville, N. C.
Bibl. 127

Joseph Doerflinger
(c. 1845–1850)
Richmond, Va.
Bibl. 19

Bonnie Doerr
(c. 1972–1980)
St. Louis, Mo.
Bibl. 155

Philip Doflein
(c. 1845–1850)
Philadelphia, Pa.
Bibl. 3

Victor Dohet
(c. 1790–1817)
Savannah, Ga.
Bibl. 17

Godfried Dold
(c. 1852–1896)
Louisville, Ky.
Madison, Ind.
Brooks & Dold   G. DOLD
Bibl. 133

Daniel N. Dole
(b. 1775–d. 1814)
Portsmouth, N.H. (c. 1805)
Newburyport, Mass.
(c. 1811)
*Bibl. 15, 24, 25, 28, 29, 89,
91, 114*

D N DOLE

Ebenezer Gore Dole
(b. 1805–d. 1885)
Hallowell, Me.
Bibl. 28, 29, 44, 91, 110

E G DOLE

Daniel Doler (c. 1765)
Boston, Mass.
Bibl. 23, 28, 36, 44, 110

Dolfinger & Hudson
(See Hudson & Dolfinger)

Jacob Dolfinger
(b. 1820–d. 1892)
Louisville, Ky.
(c. 1848–1861)
Hudson & Dolfinger
(c. 1855–1858)
Hirshbuhl & Dolfinger
(c. 1859–1861)
Bibl. 32, 54, 93

J. Doll (c. 1820–1830)
New York, N.Y.
Bibl. 15, 25, 44, 91, 114

J. DOLL

W. H. Doll (c. 1845–1850)
New York, N.Y.
Bibl. 15, 44, 114

Dominick & Haff Inc.
(1889–1928)
New York, N.Y.   **D. & H.**
Newark, N.J.
Successor to Wm. Gale &
Son
Gale & North (1860–1868)
Gale, North & Dominick
(1860–1870)
Dominick & Haff
(1872–1889)
Became Reed & Barton
(1928)
Bibl. 120, 127, 135, 147, 157

Bernhardus Dominick
(c. 1775)
Philadelphia, Pa.
Bibl. 3

Frederick Dominick
(c. 1768–1777)
Philadelphia, Pa.
Bibl. 3

Nathaniel Dominy
(b. 1764–d. 1809)
Easthampton, N.Y. (c. 1804)
Bibl. 20, 124

Gothard Domuth
(c. 1734?)
Savannah, Ga.
Bibl. 17

Alexander Don
(c. 1815–1817)
Albany, N.Y.
Bibl. 20, 124

Joseph Donald (c. 1828)
Buffalo, N.Y.
Bibl. 20, 124

Douglas Donaldson
(b. 1882–d. 1972)
California
Bibl. 120, 140

Đ Đ

Stephen Donaldson
(1760–1790)
Leesburg, Va.
Bibl. 89

**John W. Donalon
(Donaldson)** (c. 1823)
Boston, Mass.
Bibl. 23, 36, 44, 110

Abel Done (c. 1818–1819)
Philadelphia, Pa.
Bibl. 3

Donleavy
(See Dunlevy)

A. Donnaud (c. 1816)
Philadelphia, Pa.
Bibl. 3

D. C. Donnell (1861)
Bath, Me.
Bibl. 105

Charles Donnelly
(c. 1847–1879)
Philadelphia, Pa.
Bibl. 3, 23, 91

William Donovan
(c. 1784–1785)
Philadelphia, Pa.
Bibl. 3, 23, 28, 29, 36, 44

W DONOVAN

C. Dontremei (c. 1805)
Philadelphia, Pa.
Bibl. 3, 23, 36, 44

G. Dontremei
(Same as C. Dontremei)

Amos Doolittle
  (b. 1754–d. 1832)
New Haven, Conn.
New Hampshire
*Bibl. 15, 16, 23, 24, 25, 28,
  29, 36, 44, 61, 91, 94, 110,
  114, 135, 143*

Enos Doolittle
  (b. 1751–1806)
Hartford, Conn. (c. 1781)
Bibl. 16, 23, 28, 36, 44, 110

John Doran (1829–1931)
Cincinnati, Ohio
*Bibl. 23, 34, 36, 44, 54, 90,
  152*

A. M. Doret (c. 1831)
Charleston, S.C.
Bibl. 5

Joseph Dorflinger
  (c. 1837)
Philadelphia, Pa.
Bibl. 3

Peter Dorgy
  (c. 1816–1817)
Philadelphia, Pa.
Bibl. 3, 23, 36, 44

George Dorie (c. 1845)
Philadelphia, Pa.
Bibl. 3, 23

**Dorling Company of
  America, Inc.**
  (c. 1949)
Jenkintown, Pa.
Bibl. 127

C. W. Dorn (c. 1847–1848)
Philadelphia, Pa.
Bibl. 3

Samuel Dorrance
  (b. 1778–d. 1815)
Providence, R.I.
  (c. 1795–1800)
Pitman & Dorrance
*Bibl. 15, 44, 94, 110, 114,
  135*

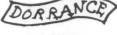

Dorsey
(See Garrow & Dorsey)

Henry C. Dorsey
  (c. 1845–1846)
Louisville, Ky.
Bibl. 32, 54, 68, 93

John Dorsey
  (c. 1793–1794)
Philadelphia, Pa.
Bibl. 3, 36

Joshua Dorsey
  (c. 1793–1804)
Philadelphia, Pa.
*Bibl. 3, 4, 15, 23, 24, 25, 29,
  39, 54, 91, 95, 114*

| I DORSEY |

Samuel Dorsey (c. 1804)
Philadelphia, Pa.
Bibl. 3, 23, 36, 44

Simon Dorsey
  (c. 1820–1822)
Philadelphia, Pa.
Bibl. 3, 23, 36, 44

Joshua Dorson (c. 1802)
Philadelphia, Pa.
Bibl. 23, 36

Dorst Co. (1896–c. 1940)
Cincinnati, Ohio
Possibly successor to Jonas,
  Dorst & Co.
Became Dorst Jewelry Co.
  (c. 1940–present)
Bibl. 127, 157   Ⓢ

Dorwig
(See Dowig)

Leonore Doskow, Inc.
  (1934–present)
New York, N.Y.
Montrose, N.Y.
Bibl. 127

LEONORE DOSKOW
HANDMADE STERLING

Michael Doster
  (c. 1831–1850)
Philadelphia, Pa.
Bibl. 3, 23, 36, 44

George Doty (c. 1835)
Buffalo, N.Y.
Bibl. 20, 114, 124

John F. Doty
  (c. 1813–1823)
Albany, N.Y.
Bibl. 20, 124

John W. Doty
  (c. 1844)
Rochester, N.Y.
Bibl. 20, 124

William Gaylord Doud
  (b. 1820–d. 1841,
  c. 1839–1841)
Middletown, Conn.
Utica, N.Y. (1841)
Tanner & Cooley
  (c. 1840–1842)
Stephens & Doud
  (c. 1841–?)
Bibl. 18, 20, 124, 158

E. Doughty
Location unknown
Bibl. 89

Alexander Douglas
  (c. 1792)
New York, N.Y.
Bibl. 23, 36, 44, 124

Cantwell Douglas
(See Douglass)

Henry Douglas
  (c. 1837–1838)
New York, N.Y.
Bibl. 15, 124

James W. Douglas
  (c. 1791)

Philadelphia, Pa.
Bibl. 29, 44

Robert Douglas
(b. 1740–d. 1776)
New London, Conn.
(c. 1766)
*Bibl. 16, 23, 24, 25, 28, 36,
44, 61, 92, 110, 114*

Douglass & Heckman
(c. 1837)
Philadelphia, Pa.
Bibl. 3, 23, 36, 44

**Cantwell Douglass
(Douglas)**
(c. 1772–1807)
Savannah, Ga.
Baltimore, Md.
Bibl. 17, 23, 28, 36, 38, 44

James Douglass
(c. 1800–1802)
New York, N.Y.
Bibl. 23, 36, 124, 138

**Jeremott William
Douglass**
(c. 1790–1793)
Philadelphia, Pa.
*Bibl. 3, 23, 24, 25, 36, 44,
114*

John Douglass
(c. 1840–1842)
Philadelphia, Pa.
Bibl. 3, 23, 36, 44

John D. Douglass
(c. 1833)
Utica, N.Y.
Bingham, Ball & Co.
(?–1833)
Bibl. 18, 20, 124

James Doull
(c. 1823–1849)
Philadelphia, Pa.
Bibl. 3

Doumouet
(See John Baptiste
Dumoutet)

Gille (Cule) Doutiemer
(c. 1791)
Philadelphia, Pa.
Bibl. 3, 23, 36, 44

Henrick Douty (c. 1774)
Philadelphia, Pa.
Bibl. 3

Joseph Dover
(c. 1820–1822)
Philadelphia, Pa.
Bibl. 3

Burrows Dowdney
(c. 1768–1771)
Philadelphia, Pa.
Bibl. 3

William Dowdney
(c. 1773–?)
Alexandria, Va.
Bibl. 19, 54

George G. Dowell
(c. 1843–1847)
Philadelphia, Pa.
Dunlevy & Dowell
(c. 1843–1846)
Bibl. 3, 23

Christopher Dowig
(See George Christopher
Dowig)

**George Christopher
Dowig (Dorwig)
(Drewrey) (Drewry)**
(b. 1724–d. 1807)
Philadelphia, Pa.
(c. 1765–1773)
Baltimore, Md.
(c. 1773–1795)
*Bibl. 3, 4, 23, 24, 25, 28, 29,
36, 38, 44, 54*

 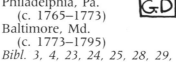

J. Downes (c. 1770)
Philadelphia, Pa.
Bibl. 23, 24, 28, 29, 36, 44

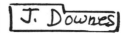

David Downie (c. 1817)
Augusta, Ga.
Bibl. 17

Downing & Baldwin
(1835–1860)
New York, N.Y.
*Bibl. 15, 25, 44, 93, 114,
124, 138*

Downing & Phelps
Newark, N.J. (c. 1815)
New York, N.Y. (c. 1825)
George R. Downing
Silas Phelps
*Bibl. 15, 24, 25, 28, 29, 36,
44, 46, 54, 124*

DOWNING & PHELPS

D & P

George R. Downing
(c. 1810–1825)
Newark, N.J. (c. 1815)
New York, N.Y. (c. 1825)
Downing & Phelps
*Bibl. 25, 28, 29, 36, 44, 46,
54, 91, 114, 124, 138*

G R D

Samuel P. Downing
(c. 1817)
Canandaigua, N.Y.
Bibl. 20, 124

John Draper (c. 1844)
Cincinnati, Ohio
Bibl. 34, 152

Joseph Draper
(b. 1800–d. 1864)
Wilmington, Del.
(c. 1816–1832)
Cincinnati, Ohio
(1832–1856)
Hopkinsville, Ky.

*Bibl. 15, 24, 25, 30, 32, 44,
54, 90, 91, 93, 114*

J DRAPER

J. Dray (c. 1846)
Portsmouth, Va.
Bibl. 19

R. Dreden (c. 1839)
Philadelphia, Pa.
Bibl. 3

Dreer & Hayes
(c. 1842–1850)
Philadelphia, Pa.
Ferdinand J. Dreer
George Hayes
Bibl. 3

Ferdinand J. Dreer
(c. 1837–1850)
Philadelphia, Pa.
Annin & Dreer
(c. 1837–1841)
Dreer & Hayes
(c. 1842–1850)
Bibl. 3

Dreicer & Co., Inc.
(1910–1923)
New York, N.Y.
Bibl. 126

Albina H. Dresser (1875)
Bluehill, Me.
Bibl. 105

C. A. Drew (1875)
Lewiston, Me.
Bibl. 105

Mary L. Lischer Drewes
(1933–c. 1980)
St. Louis, Mo.
Bibl. 155

George Drewr(e)y
(See George Christopher
Dowig)

Dreyfous & Bro.
(c. 1820–1822)
Philadelphia, Pa.
Bibl. 3

Dreyfous Fils Aime
(c. 1819)
Philadelphia, Pa.
Bibl. 3

Joseph Dreyfous
(c. 1825)
Philadelphia, Pa.
Bibl. 3

Simon (Simeon) Dreyfous
Philadelphia, Pa.
(c. 1825–1837)
New York, N.Y.
(c. 1838–1850)
Bibl. 3, 138

John Drinker
(c. 1835–1838)
New York, N. Y.
Bibl. 15, 23, 36, 44, 124, 138

Major William C. Driver
(d. 1874) (1861–1870)
New Orleans, La.
Bibl. 141

Drobenare Bros. Inc.
(c. 1960–1973)
New York, N.Y.
Bibl. 127

M. A. Dropsie
(c. 1842–1849)
Philadelphia, Pa.
Bibl. 3

Dross
(See Droz)

Benjamin Drown(e)
(b. 1759–d. 1793)
Portsmouth, N.H.
*Bibl. 23, 25, 36, 44, 91, 94,
110, 114, 125*

B DROWNE

Samuel Drown(e)
(b. 1749–d. 1815)
Portsmouth, N.H.
*Bibl. 15, 23, 24, 25, 28, 29,
36, 39, 44, 72, 91, 94, 110,
114, 125*

**Thomas Pickering
Drown(e)**
(b. 1782–d. 1849)
Boston, Mass.
(c. 1790–1816)
Newbury, Mass.
Portsmouth, N.H.
*Bibl. 14, 23, 28, 29, 36, 91,
110, 114, 125*

T P DROWN

Shem Drowne
(b. 1683–d. 1774)
Boston, Mass.
Bibl. 23, 28, 29, 36, 44, 72

(S.D)   (S.D)

Droz & Son
(c. 1806–1814)
Philadelphia, Pa.
Bibl. 3

Charles A. Droz (Dross)
(c. 1811–1841)
Philadelphia, Pa.
Bibl. 3

Hannah Droz (Dross)
(c. 1842–1850)
Philadelphia, Pa.
Bibl. 3

**Hymbert (Lambert) Droz
(Dross)** (c. 1793–1811)
Philadelphia, Pa.
Bibl. 3

John Droz (c. 1824)
Cincinnati, Ohio
Bibl. 34, 152

Arnold Druding
(c. 1843–1850)
Philadelphia, Pa.
Bibl. 3

Francis Druding
(c. 1847–1850)
Philadelphia, Pa.
Bibl. 3

Antoine Drumont
(c. 1808–1810)
New York, N.Y.
Bibl. 23, 36, 44, 124, 138

Arnold Drunnin
(c. 1837)
Philadelphia, Pa.
Bibl. 3

William Drysdale
(c. 1816–1850)
Philadelphia, Pa.
Bibl. 3

William Drysdale Jr.
(c. 1842–1845)
Philadelphia, Pa.
Bibl. 3

Du Barry
(See Napier)

Edward Dubasee
(c. 1847–1850)
Philadelphia, Pa.
Bibl. 3

Dubois & Co. (c. 1803)
Philadelphia, Pa.
New York, N.Y.
(c. 1849–1850)
Bibl. 3, 23, 36, 44, 138

Abraham Dubois
(b. 1777–d. 1807)
Philadelphia, Pa.
(c. 1777–1802)
New York, N.Y. (c. 1803)
*Bibl. 3, 4, 15, 23, 24, 25, 28,
29, 36, 39, 44, 54, 114,
116, 124, 142*

Abraham Dubois Sr. & Jr.
(c. 1785–1807)
Philadelphia, Pa.
*Bibl. 3, 15, 23, 36, 91, 95,
102, 151*

B. T. Dubois (c. 1830)
Philadelphia, Pa. (?)
Bibl. 89

Francis Dubois
(c. 1831–1833)
Philadelphia, Pa.
Bibl. 3

George Dubois (c. 1841)
Philadelphia, Pa.
Bibl. 3

Henry Dubois
(c. 1825–1833)
Philadelphia, Pa.
Bibl. 3

James Dubois
(c. 1827–1831)
Albany, N.Y.
Bibl. 20, 124

John Dubois
(c. 1831–1833)
Philadelphia, Pa.
Bibl. 3

Joseph Dubois
(c. 1790–1797)
New York, N.Y.
*Bibl. 4, 15, 23, 24, 25, 28,
29, 30, 35, 36, 44, 72, 91,
114, 124, 138*

| J DUBOIS | I DUBOIS |

Peter Dubois
(c. 1841–1843)
Philadelphia, Pa.
Bibl. 3

Philo Dubois
(c. 1842–1848)
Buffalo, N.Y.
*Bibl. 15, 20, 25, 44, 91, 114,
124*

P. DUBOIS BUFFALO

Thomas Dubois (c. 1849)
Philadelphia, Pa.
Bibl. 3

Tunis D. Dubois
(c. 1797–1799)
New York, N.Y.
*Bibl. 15, 23, 24, 25, 28, 29,
35, 36, 44, 72, 83, 91, 95,
114, 124, 138*

| T. D. D. | T. D. DUBOIS |

———— Dubosq
(c. 1829–1830)
Philadelphia, Pa.
Bibl. 3

Dubosq & Baton
(c. 1835–1841)
Philadelphia, Pa.
Bibl. 3

Dubosq & Carrow
(c. 1839–1843)
Philadelphia, Pa.
George Dubosq (?)
John Carrow
Bibl. 3

Dubosq & Jardella
(c. 1833)
Philadelphia, Pa.
Bibl. 3

Dubosq & Scheer
(c. 1849–1850)
Philadelphia, Pa.
———— Dubosq
John C. Scheer (?)
Bibl. 3

Dubosq, Baton & Co.
(c. 1839–1840)
Philadelphia, Pa.
Bibl. 3

Dubosq, Carrow & Co.
(c. 1844–1850)
Philadelphia, Pa.
George Dubosq (?)
John Carrow
Bibl. 3, 93

Francis P. Dubosq
(c. 1837–1850)
Philadelphia, Pa.
Bibl. 3

George Dubosq
(c. 1839–1850)
Philadelphia, Pa.
Dubosq & Carrow
(c. 1839–1843) (?)
Dubosq, Carrow & Co.
(c. 1844–1850) (?)
Bibl. 3

H. & W. Dubosq (Dubusq)
(c. 1846–1850)
Philadelphia, Pa.
New York, N.Y.
Bibl. 3, 23, 138

Henry Dubosq Jr.
(c. 1818–1850)
Philadelphia, Pa.
Bibl. 3

Peter Dubosq
(c. 1835–1850)
Philadelphia, Pa.
Bibl. 3

Philip L. Dubosq
(c. 1837–1850)
Philadelphia, Pa.
Bibl. 3

Theodore Dubosq
(c. 1829–1850)
Philadelphia, Pa.
Bibl. 3

William Dubosq
(c. 1835–1837)
Philadelphia, Pa.
Bibl. 3

William A. Dubosq
(c. 1839)
Philadelphia, Pa.
Bibl. 3

Duche & Donnand
(c. 1820–1822)
Philadelphia, Pa.
Bibl. 3, 23, 36, 44

Benne R. Duché
(See Rene Rock Duché)

Rene Rock (Roche) Duché (Duchi)
New York, N.Y.
(1795–1811)
Philadelphia, Pa.
(1823–1824)
Bibl. 3, 15, 23, 28, 36, 44, 124, 138

A. L. Ducomman
(c. 1795–1798)
Philadelphia, Pa.
Bibl. 3

Henry Ducommun
(c. 1818–1850)
Philadelphia, Pa.
Bibl. 3

Henry Ducommun Jr. & Co. (c. 1843–1844)
Philadelphia, Pa.
Bibl. 3

Lewis Ducray (c. 1771)
Philadelphia, Pa.
Bibl. 3

——— Dudley (c. 1784)
Philadelphia, Pa.
Bibl. 3

Benjamin Dudley
(c. 1768)
Birmington, Ga.
Savannah, Ga.
Bibl. 17, 23, 36, 44

Joseph Dudley (1860)
Providence, R.I.
Bibl. 108

L. R. Dudley (1860)
Newport, Me.
Bibl. 105

George Duff (c. 1837)
Philadelphia, Pa.
Bibl. 3

George C. Duff (c. 1846)
New Bern, N.C.
New York, N.Y. (c. 1840)
Bibl. 22, 124, 138

——— Duffee (c. 1785)
Location unknown
Bibl. 28

DUFFEE

James Duffel
(b. 1761–d. 1835)
Georgetown, S.C.
(c. 1790–1800)
New York, N.Y. (c. 1801)
Fredericksburg, Va.
(c. 1802–1807)
Lynchberg, Va.

⬭ J D ⬭

(c. 1810–1828)
Bibl. 15, 29, 36, 44, 54, 114, 124, 138

I Duffel		J. DUFFEL

I Duffel

George Hurd Duffey
(b. 1800–d. 1855)
Alexandria, Va.
Bibl. 19, 54

John Duffey
(c. 1790–1809)
Alexandria, Va.
Bibl. 19, 54

Major George Nelson Duffey
(b. 1820–d. 1896)
Alexandria, Va.
Bibl. 19, 54

Edward Duffield
(c. 1756–1775,
d. 1803)
Philadelphia, Pa.
Bibl. 3, 28, 102

Duhme (c. 1839)
Cincinnati, Ohio
Bibl. 54, 90, 91

Duhme & Co.
(c. 1842–1896)
Cincinnati, Ohio
Bibl. 24, 25, 44, 54, 90, 91, 93, 114

⊣ DUHME ⊢

John Dulty Sr. (c. 1807)
Zanesville, Ohio
Bibl. 34

Anthony Dumesnil(l)
(d. 1833)
Lexington, Ky.
(c. 1818–1833)
Bibl. 32, 44, 93

Jeremiah Dummer (Dunner)
(b. 1645–d. 1718)
Boston, Mass.

Bibl. 2, 8, 15, 23, 24, 25, 28, 29, 36, 44, 54, 91, 102, 110, 114, 116, 118, 119, 135, 142, 143, 151

P. Dumont (c. 1844–1846)
Louisville, Ky.
Bibl. 32

Dumontot, Dumorte
(See Dumoutet)

Joseph Dumourier
(c. 1814–1816)
Philadelphia, Pa.
Bibl. 3, 23, 36, 44

Elizabeth Dumoutet
(c. 1817–1822)
Philadelphia, Pa.
Bibl. 3

John Baptiste Dumoutet
(Doumoutet)
(Dumontot) (Dumorte)
(Dymotit) (Doumouet)
(b. 1761–d. 1813)
Philadelphia, Pa.
(c. 1793–c. 1813)
Charleston, S.C.
Bibl. 3, 5, 15, 23, 24, 25, 28, 29, 36, 39, 44, 46, 54, 91, 114

Dunbar & Bangs (c. 1850)
Worcester, Mass.
Bibl. 15, 25, 44, 89

DUNBAR & BANGS
WORCESTER
FINE

John Dunbar (c. 1796)
Baltimore, Md.
Bibl. 38

Rufus Davenport Dunbar
(b. 1807–d. 1869)
Worcester, Mass.
Bibl. 15, 44, 91, 110, 114, 135

R. D. DUNBAR

William Henry Duncan
(c. 1850)
Shelby County, Ky.
Springfield, Ky.
Washington County, Ky.
Bibl. 32, 54, 68, 93

Pratt Dundas (c. 1837)
Philadelphia, Pa.
Bibl. 3, 23, 36, 44

Dungeon Rock
(See H. M. Hill & Co.)

R Dunham
Location unknown
Bibl. 28, 29   R DUNHAM

George Dunkerley
(c. 1844–1847)
Philadelphia, Pa.
Bibl. 3

Joseph Dunkerly (c. 1787)
Boston, Mass.
Bibl. 23, 28, 36, 44

Dunlevy
(See Shaw & Dunlevy)

Dunkirk
(See Gold Recovery & Refining Corp.)

Dunkirk Silversmiths, Inc.
(c. 1945–1950)
Meriden, Conn.
Successor to Gold Recovery & Refining Corp.
Bibl. 127

Dunkirk

Robert Dunlev(e)y
(c. 1787)
Philadelphia, Pa.
Bibl. 28

Robert Dunlev(e)y
(Donleavy)
(c. 1830–1837)
Philadelphia, Pa.
Bibl. 3, 4, 23, 36, 44

Dunlevy & Dowell
(c. 1843–1846)
Philadelphia, Pa.
Robert Dunlevy Jr.
George G. Dowell
Bibl. 3, 23

Dunlevy & Wise
(c. 1847–1850)
Philadelphia, Pa.
Robert Dunlevy Jr.
George K. Wise (?)
Bibl. 3, 23

Robert Dunlevy Jr.
(Donleavy)
(c. 1839–1850)
Philadelphia, Pa.
Dunlevy & Dowell
(c. 1843–1846) (?)
Dunlevy & Wise
(c. 1847–1850)
Bibl. 3, 23

James Dunlop (c. 1784)
Bennington, Vt.
Bibl. 54, 110

Dunn
(See Kidney & Dunn)

Dunn & Cann
(c. 1834–1838)
New York, N.Y.
David Dunn
John Cann
Bibl. 15, 44, 114, 124, 138

Dunn & Son
(c. 1787–1791)
New York, N.Y.
Bibl. 23, 36, 44, 91, 124

A. A. Dunn (1860)
Ellsworth, Me.
Bibl. 105

Cary Dunn (d. 1798)
Underhill, Vt. (c. 1765)
Morristown, N.J. (c. 1778)
Newark, N.J. (c. 1782)
New York, N.Y.

Bibl. 4, 15, 23, 24, 25, 28,
29, 30, 35, 36, 46, 54, 83,
91, 95, 102, 114, 124, 138

C DUNN

David Dunn
(c. 1834–1850)
New York, N.Y.
Dunn & Cann
(c. 1834–1838)
Charters, Cann & Dunn
(c. 1850)
Bibl. 15, 23, 36, 44, 124,
135, 138

G. F. Dunn (1860)
Ellsworth, Me.
Bibl. 105

James Dunn (1860–1875)
Presque Isle, Me.
Bibl. 105

John Dunn (c. 1823–1824)
Philadelphia, Pa.
Bibl. 3

L. F. Dunn (c. 1883)
Niagara Falls, N.Y.
Bibl. 127

CARBON

Jeremiah Dunner
(See Dummer)

Dunning
(See also Curtis & Dunning)

—— **Dunning** (c. 1839)
Penn Yan, N.Y.
Ayers & Dunning
Bibl. 20

Dunning & Crissey
(c. 1847)
Rochester, N.Y.
Elnathan F. Crissey
Julius N. Dunning
Bibl. 20, 124

Julius N. Dunning
(c. 1847)
Rochester, N.Y.
Dunning & Crissey
Bibl. 20, 124

Dennis Dunscomb
(b. 1741)
New York, N.Y. (c. 1765)
Bibl. 23, 36, 44, 124

Mary Matilda Dunseth
(c. 1804)
Charleston, S.C.
Michael Samuel Debruhl
(c. 1798–1806)
Bibl. 5

Augustine Dunyon (1860)
Portland, Me.
Bibl. 105

H. Duon (c. 1819)
Baltimore, Md.
Not a silversmith but a lace
maker.
Bibl. 23, 36, 38, 44

John Baptiste Duplat
(c. 1809–1820)
Charleston, S.C.
Bibl. 5

Rose Duplat (c. 1806)
Charleston, S.C.
Bibl. 5

Dupuy & Sons
(See Daniel Dupuy & Sons)

Andrew Dupuy (d. 1743)
Charleston, S.C.
Bibl. 5, 54

Bernard Dupuy
(c. 1828–1844)
Raleigh, N.C.
Bibl. 21, 25, 44, 114

B. DUPUY

Daniel Dupuy
(b. 1719–d. 1807)
New York, N.Y. (c. 1719)
Reading, Pa. (c. 1777)
Philadelphia, Pa.
(c. 1784–1790)

Daniel Dupuy & Sons
(c. 1784)
David & Dupuy
(c. 1792–1805)
Bibl. 3, 4, 15, 23, 24, 25, 28,
29, 36, 39, 44, 54, 81, 91,
95, 114

Daniel Dupuy Jr.
(b. 1753–d. 1826)
Philadelphia, Pa.
(c. 1782–1813)
John & Daniel Dupuy Jr.
(c. 1783–1785)
Bibl. 3, 15, 23, 25, 28, 36,
44, 91, 95, 114, 116

D. DuPuY

Daniel Dupuy & Sons
(c. 1784)
Philadelphia, Pa.
Daniel Dupuy
John Dupuy
Bibl. 23, 24, 25, 29, 36, 44,
91, 114

John Dupuy
(b. 1747–d. 1838)
Reading, Pa. (c. 1777)
Philadelphia, Pa. (c. 1784)
John & Daniel Dupuy Jr.
(c. 1783–1785)
Daniel Dupuy & Sons
(c. 1784)
Bibl. 3, 36, 44, 91

John & Daniel Dupuy Jr.
(c. 1783–1785)
Philadelphia, Pa.
Bibl. 3, 15, 23, 36, 44, 91

Odean Dupuy (c. 1735)
Philadelphia, Pa.
Bibl. 3

Cyrus Durand
(b. 1787–d. 1868)
Newark, N.J.
Bibl. 28

John Durand
(See Durandeau)

Louis Durand (c. 1834)
New York, N.Y.
Bibl. 15, 91, 124

John Durandeau
(Durand)
(c. 1833–1836)
New York, N.Y.
Belloni & Durandeau
(c. 1835–1836)
Bibl. 15, 23, 36, 44, 124, 138

Ferdinand Durcy
(b. 1777–d. 1851)
New Orleans, La
(1834–1835)
Bibl. 141

Elihu Durfee (c. 1828)
Palmyra, N.Y.
Bibl. 20, 124

Durgin & Burtt
(c. 1859–1863)
St. Louis, Mo.
Freeman A. Durgin
——— Burtt
Bibl. 54, 155   DURGIN & BURTT

Freeman A. Durgin
(c. 1859–1911)
St. Louis, Mo.
Durgin & Burtt
Bibl. 54, 134, 155

Wm. B. Durgin Co.
(c. 1853–1906)
Concord, N.H.
Became Gorham Co.
(c. 1906); moved to
Providence, R.I. (1931)
*Bibl. 114, 120, 127, 135, 144,
147, 152, 157*

William B. Durgin
(b. 1833–d. 1905)
Concord, N.H.
(c. 1856–1905)
*Bibl. 24, 25, 44, 91, 114,
116, 122, 125, 135*

WM B DURGIN

Dusenberry (c. 1800)
Location unknown
Bibl. 28   DUSENBERRY

William C. Dusenberry
(c. 1819–1835)
New York, N.Y.
*Bibl. 15, 24, 25, 44, 79, 91,
114, 124, 138*

W. C. DUSENBERRY

Pierre Eugene Du
Simitiere
(c. 1776, d. 1784)
Philadelphia, Pa.
Bibl. 3

Hannah Duston
(See Kimball & Son)

Dutens (Duteus) &
Harper
(c. 1755–1756)
Philadelphia, Pa.
Charles J. Dutens
David Harper
Bibl. 3, 23, 36, 44

Charles J. Dutens
(Duteus)
Philadelphia, Pa.
(c. 1751–1757)
New York, N.Y. (c. 1751)
Dutens & Harper
(c. 1755–1756)
Bibl. 3, 23, 36, 44

——— Duvalier (c. 1800)
Location unknown
Bibl. 28, 29, 44

DUVALIER

Daniel Duyckinck
(c. 1790–1800)
New York, N.Y.
*Bibl. 23, 25, 28, 36, 44, 114,
124, 138*

D. DUYCKINCK

Timothy Dwight
(b. 1654–d. 1691)
Boston, Mass.
*Bibl. 2, 4, 25, 29, 36, 44, 54,
66, 102, 110, 114, 116, 119*

William Dye
Fayetteville, N.C.
Bibl. 21

A. S. Dygert (c. 1830)
Location unknown
Bibl. 24

A. S. DYGERT

Dymotit
(See Dumoutet)

E

E
(See Ellmore Silver Co., Inc.,
Strong & Elder Co.)

E & H
(See Eoff & Howell)

E & P
(See Eoff & Phyfe)

E & S
(See Easton & Sanford, Eoff
& Shepherd)

E A
(See Ebenezer Austin)

E A Co.
(See E. A. Bliss Co.)

E A M C O
(See Electrolytic Art Metal
Co.)

E B
(See Eleazer Baker, Everadus
Bogardus, Elias Boudinot,
Ephraim Brasher, Ezekiel
Burr)

E B & Co.
(See Erastus Barton & Co.,
E. Benjamin & Co.)

E B C
(See Empire Silver Co. Inc.)

E C
(See Elias Camp, Ebenezer
    Chittenden, Ephraim
    Cobb, Elizabeth Copeland)

E F
(See Ebenezer Frothingham)

E G
(See Eliakim Garretson)

E H
(See Eliphaz Hart, Eliakim
    Hitchcock)

E. H. E.
(See Edwards, Horton &
    Edwards)

E. J. T. Co.
(See E. J. Towle Mfg. Co.)

E. L. D.
(See E. L. Deacon Jewelry Co.)

E L S C O
(See Elgin Silversmith Co.,
    Inc.)

E M
(See Edmund Milne)

E M E
(See Edgar M. Eoff)

E P
(See Edward Pear, Elias
    Pelletreau, Edward
    Putman)

E P L
(See Edward P. Lescare)

E R
(See Enos Reeves)

E S
(See Edward Sandell)

E. S. C. O.
(See Eagle Silver Co.)

E S C O
(See Elgin Silversmith Co.,
    Inc.)

E S D P
(See Porter)

E W
(See Edward Webb, Edward
    White, Edward Winslow)

E-Z O P E
(See Scharling & Co.)

Eagle Silver Co.
    (c. 1922–1953)
Providence, R. I.
Bibl. 127

                   E . S . C . O .

Eagles & Morris (c. 1799)
New York, N.Y.
Bibl. 23, 36, 44, 124, 138

Samuel Eakins (c. 1837)
Philadelphia, Pa.
Bibl. 3

Joseph E. Ealer
St. Louis, Mo.
    (1838–1842)
New Orleans, La.
    (1845–1870)
Bibl. 54, 141, 155

Joshua Eames (d. 1722)
Boston, Mass. (c. 1700)
Bibl. 23, 28, 36, 44, 110

Alfred Earnshaw
    (c. 1846–1849)
Troy, N.Y.
Bibl. 20, 124

George Easley (c. 1838)
Lexington, Ky.
Bibl. 32, 68, 93

Easman
(See Benjamin Eastman)

Easterling Company
    (1944–1974)
Chicago, Ill.
Pattern rights & sterling
    inventory sold to
    Westerling Co. (1974)
Bibl. 127

**Benjamin Eastman
(Easman)**
    (c. 1777–1790)
Pasquotank County, N.C.
Bibl. 21

Moses Eastman
    (b. 1794–d. 1850)
Concord, N.H.
Savannah, Ga. (1828–1850)
J. Penfield & Co.
    (c. 1820–1828)
Bibl. 17, 91, 125

M EASTMAN

Seth Eastman
    (b. 1801–d. 1885)
Concord, N.H.
    (c. 1828–1849)
*Bibl. 15, 25, 44, 91, 94, 114,
    125, 135*

Easton
(See Chase & Easton)

Easton & Sanford
    (c. 1830–1838)
Nantucket Island, Mass.
James Easton
Frederick C. Sanford
*Bibl. 12, 23, 24, 25, 28, 29,
    36, 44, 114*

                   E & S

         Easton & Sanford

James Easton (2d)
    (b. 1807–d. 1903)
Nantucket, Mass.
Easton & Sanford
    (c. 1830–1838)
*Bibl. 12, 23, 24, 25, 28, 36,
    44, 110, 114*

J.EASTON

NANTUCKET

J. EASTON 2nd

PURE COIN

Nathaniel Easton
(c. 1780–1815)
Nantucket Island, Mass.
Bibl. 12, 23, 24, 25, 36, 44,
110, 114

Thomas Eastwick
(c. 1743)
Boston, Mass.
Bibl. 23, 36, 44, 110

Eastwood-Park Company
(c. 1909–1922)
Newark, N.J.
Bibl. 127, 157

(Captain) James B. Eaton
(d. 1829)
Boston, Mass. (c. 1805)
Macon, Ga.
Charleston, S.C.
(c. 1829) (?)
Bibl. 5, 15, 17, 25, 91, 110

| J. B. EATON |

Timothy Eaton
(c. 1793–1794)
Philadelphia, Pa.
Bibl. 3, 15, 23, 25, 36, 44,
114

| T EATON |

W. Eaves & A. Falize
(c. 1842)
Lexington, Ky.
Bibl. 32, 93

W. T. Eaves (c. 1845–1848)
Lexington, Ky.
St. Louis, Mo.
Bibl. 32, 54, 90, 93, 155

Eayas
(See Thomas Stevens Eayres)

Eayers
(See Thomas Stevens Eayres)

Thomas Stevens Eayres
(Eayas) (Eayers)
(b. 1760–d. c. 1813)
Boston, Mass. (c. 1785)
Worcester, Mass.
(c. 1791–1793)

Bibl. 15, 23, 24, 28, 29, 36,
44, 69, 94, 114, 119

| T.E | | EAYRES |

John Eberman Jr.
(c. 1771–1772)
Lancaster, Pa.
Bibl. 3, 112

D. Eccleston (c. 1805)
Lancaster, Pa.
Bibl. 3

John Eckart
(c. 1848–1850)
Camden, N.J.
Bibl. 3

Alexander Perry Eckel
(b. 1821–d. 1906,
c. 1845)
Greensboro, N.C.
Front Royal, Va. (?)
Jefferson County, Tenn. (?)
Bibl. 22

Andrew Eckel
(c. 1837–1840)
Philadelphia, Pa.
Bibl. 3

David Eckerman (c. 1819)
Philadelphia, Pa.
Bibl. 3

Valentine Eckert (c. 1839)
Philadelphia, Pa.
Bibl. 3

Eckfeldt & Ackley
(c. 1896–1935)
Newark, N.J.
Bibl. 127

Adam Eckfeldt
(c. 1800–1850)
Philadelphia, Pa.
Bibl. 3

Charles Eckfeldt
(c. 1839–1843)
Philadelphia, Pa.
Bibl. 3

Jacob Eckfield
(c. 1783, d. 1818)
Philadelphia, Pa.
Bibl. 3

John Eckart (c. 1845)
Philadelphia, Pa.
Bibl. 3

Lewis Ecuyer
(b. 1829, c. 1851–1854)
Utica, N.Y.
Bibl. 18, 124, 158

Eddy & Barrows (c. 1832)
Tollard, Conn.
———— Eddy
James Madison Barrows (?)
Bibl. 28

John Edgar (c. 1807)
New York, N.Y.
Bibl. 23, 36, 44, 124, 138

Charles Edler
(c. 1844–1846)
Philadelphia, Pa.
Bibl. 3

J. C. Edler (c. 1841)
Philadelphia, Pa.
Bibl. 3

Claude Edmechat
New York, N.Y. (c. 1790)
Philadelphia, Pa.
(c. 1793–1798)
Bibl. 23, 28, 36, 44, 124, 138

T. Edmond (c. 1800)
Location unknown
Bibl. 24

William Edmond (c. 1848)
Philadelphia, Pa.
Bibl. 3

H. L. Edmons (1875)
Pawtucket, R.I.
Bibl. 108

Edmunds & Wiggins
(1875)
Bangor, Me.
Bibl. 105

Benjamin F. Edmunds
Boston, Mass.
(c. 1857)
Manchester, N.H.
(c. 1850–1856)
Bibl. 15, 44, 114

Oliver Edson
(c. 1804–1810)
Ballston Spa, N.Y.
Bibl. 20, 124

Edwards & Allen
(See Allen & Edwards)

**Edwards, Horton &
Edwards** (c. 1850)
Chicago, Ill.
Bibl. 127

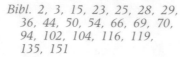

Abraham Edwards
(c. 1763)
Ashby, Mass.
Bibl. 28, 44

Andrew Edwards
(c. 1763–1798)
Boston, Mass.
Bibl. 4, 23, 28, 36, 44, 110

Calvin Edwards
(b. 1698, c. 1710)
Ashby, Mass.
Bibl. 23, 28, 36, 44, 110

Gage D. Edwards
(c. 1827–1836)
Athens, Ga.
Bibl. 17

J. T. & E. M. Edwards
(1852–1864)
Chicago, Ill.
Bibl. 98

J.T. & E.M.E.

John Edwards
(b. 1671–d. 1746)
Annapolis, Md.
(c. 1735)
Bucks County, Pa.
Boston, Mass.

*Bibl. 2, 3, 15, 23, 25, 28, 29,
36, 44, 50, 54, 66, 69, 70,
94, 102, 104, 116, 119,
135, 151*

Joseph Edwards Sr.
(b. 1707–d. 1777)
Boston, Mass.
Bibl. 23, 24, 29, 36, 44

Joseph Edwards Jr.   I E
(b. 1737–d. 1783)
Boston, Mass.
*Bibl. 2, 15, 23, 25, 28, 29,
36, 44, 54, 69, 91, 94, 102,
110, 114, 116, 119, 135*

I Edwards

Peter Edwards (c. 1850)
Philadelphia, Pa.
Bibl. 3

S. P. Edwards (1875)
Otisville, Me.
Bibl. 105

Samuel Edwards
(b. 1705–d. 1762,
c. 1729)
Boston, Mass.
Natick, Mass.
*Bibl. 2, 15, 23, 24, 25, 28,
29, 36, 39, 49, 54, 66, 69,
91, 94, 104, 110, 114, 118,
119*

Thomas Edwards
(b. 1702–d. 1755)
Boston, Mass. (c. 1725)
New York, N.Y. (c. 1731)
*Bibl. 2, 4, 15, 23, 24, 25, 28,
36, 44, 70, 91, 94, 110,
114, 116, 118, 119, 124,
139*

Robert Egan (c. 1772)
Williamsburg, Va.
Bibl. 19

Jacob Ege
(b. 1754–d. 1795)
Richmond, Va.
Bibl. 19

James L. Ege & Co.
(c. 1832)
Fredericksburg, Va.
Bibl. 19

Edward Egg
(c. 1860–1880)
Columbia, S.C.
Bibl. 5

Edward Elder (c. 1812)
Lexington, Ky.
Bibl. 32, 93

William Elder (c. 1841)
Philadelphia, Pa.
Bibl. 3

Elderkin & Staniford
(c. 1790–1792)
Windham, Conn.
Alfred Elderkin
John Staniford
Bibl. 23, 36, 44, 91, 110

Alfred Elderkin
(b. 1759–d. 1833)
Windham, Conn.
(c. 1790–1792)
Killingsworth, Conn.
Red Hook, N.Y.
Elderkin & Staniford
(c. 1790–1792)
*Bibl. 15, 16, 23, 25, 28, 36,
44, 91, 92, 110, 114*

Elisha Elderkin
(b. 1753–d. 1822)
Killingworth, Conn.
New Haven, Conn.
*Bibl. 16, 23, 28, 36, 49, 110,
143*

Electrolytic Art Metal Co.
(c. 1915–1920)
Trenton, N.J.   [EAMCO]
Bibl. 127, 157

Eleder (-Hickok) Co.
(1918–c. 1931)
Newark, N.J.
Successor to Lebkuecher &
   Co. (c. 1896–1915)
F. A. Lester (c. 1915)
Merged Matthews Company,
   became Hickok-Matthews
   Company (c. 1931)
Bibl. 127

Jacob H. Eler
(c. 1829–1833)
Philadelphia, Pa.
Bibl. 3

Wm. R. Elfers Co., Inc.
(c. 1931)
New York, N.Y.   W(E)R
Bibl. 127   wЕʀ

Jeremiah Elfreth Jr.   [J E]
(c. 1723–1765)
Philadelphia, Pa.   [J E]
(c. 1752)
Bibl. 25, 44, 54, 81, 95, 114,
118, 119   [I E]

Elgin Silversmith Co., Inc.
(1946–present)
New York, N.Y.   [EL·SIL·Co]
Successor to Ludwig &
   Redlich (1890–1895)
Redlich & Co. Inc.   [ESCO]
   (c. 1895–1946)
Bibl. 127, 146

H. P. Elias (c. 1840)
Location unknown
Bibl. 89

James Elleman (1860)
Providence, R.I.
Bibl. 108

Peter Elleson (c. 1796)
New York, N.Y.
Bibl. 28

Joseph Ellicott (c. 1778)
Bucks County, Pa.
Bibl. 3

George Elliot(t)
(c. 1810–1852)
Wilmington, Del.
Bibl. 25, 30, 44, 114

[G. ELLIOT]

H. Elliot (19th century)
Location unknown
Bibl. 15, 28, 44, 114

[H ELLIOT]

——— Elliott
(c. 1818–1822)
Philadelphia, Pa.
Bibl. 3

Elliott & Burnham
(c. 1821)
Salisbury, N.C.
Zebulon Elliott
E. B. Burnham
Bibl. 21, 91

B. R. Elliott (1870)
Farmington, Me.
Bibl. 105

Benjamin P. Elliott
(c. 1843–1850)
Philadelphia, Pa.
Bibl. 3

James Elliott (c. 1804)
Philadelphia, Pa.
Bibl. 3

James Elliott
(b. 1773–d. 1865)
Winnsboro, S.C.
(c. 1807)
Bibl. 5, 44

[J. E]

John Aaron Elliott
(b. 1788–d. 1857)
Sharon, Conn. (c. 1815)
Michigan   [A E]
New York State
Bibl. 15, 16, 23, 25, 28, 36,
92, 110, 114, 124

Joseph Elliott (c. 1768)
New Castle County, Del.
Bibl. 3, 23, 30, 36, 44

Zebulon Elliott
New York, N.Y.
(c. 1814–1821)
Salisbury, N.C. (c. 1821)
Elliott & Burnham (c. 1821)
Bibl. 22, 91, 124, 138

Benjamin Ellis
(c. 1829–1833)
Philadelphia, Pa.
Bibl. 3

George Ellis (c. 1850)
Philadelphia, Pa.
Bibl. 3

Hugh Ellis (c. 1810–1825)
Philadelphia, Pa.
Bibl. 3

Lewis W. Ellis (c. 1837)
Philadelphia, Pa.
Bibl. 3, 23, 36, 44

Samuel (S. O.) Ellis
(c. 1839–1847)
Philadelphia, Pa.
Bibl. 3

Elliston & Raworth
(c. 1802)
Nashville, Tenn.
Bibl. 54

Joseph Thorp Elliston
(1798–1856)
Nashville, Tenn.
Bibl. 54, 89

Peter Elliston (Ellison)
(c. 1791–1800)
New York, N.Y.
Bibl. 23, 24, 25, 36, 44, 91,
95, 114, 124, 138

[ELLISTON]

Ellmore Silver Co., Inc.
   (c. 1935–1960)
Meriden, Conn.
Merged Concern
   Silversmiths, Ltd., G. H.
   French & Co., and F. M.
   Whiting Co.
Bibl. 127

David Ellsworth
   (b. 1742–d. 1821)
Windsor, Conn.
   (c. 1772–1792)
Bibl. 16, 23, 28, 36, 44, 110

Thomas Elmes (c. 1841)
Philadelphia, Pa.
Bibl. 3

Ormond Elsbre (d. 1801)
Augusta, Ga.
Bibl. 17

Hermann Elson
   (c. 1843–1848)
Philadelphia, Pa.
Bibl. 3

Julius Elson
   (c. 1842–1844)
Philadelphia, Pa.
Bibl. 3

Francis Eltheridge
   (c. 1749)
Annapolis, Md.
Bibl. 38

A. D. Elton (c. 1841–1845)
Geneva, N.Y.
Hall & Elton
Bibl. 20, 124

Thomas Eltonhead
   (c. 1835)
Baltimore, Md.
Bibl. 23, 36, 44

William D. Eltonhead
   (c. 1849–1850)
Philadelphia, Pa.
Bibl. 3

William Elvins
   (c. 1796–1808)
Baltimore, Md.
Bibl. 38

Effingham Embree
   (c. 1785–1794)
New York, N.Y.
*Bibl. 28, 29, 44, 91, 124,
   135, 138*

| EMBREE |

Albert Emerick
   (c. 1847–1850)
Philadelphia, Pa.
Bibl. 3, 23

Augustus Emerick
   (c. 1825–1829)
Philadelphia, Pa.
Bibl. 3

Thomas P. Emerson
   (c. 1855–1871)
Lafayette, Ind.
Bibl. 133   **T.P. EMERSON**

Emery & Co. (c. 1798)
Boston, Mass.
New York, N.Y.
Stephen Emery
Salem, Mass. (?)
*Bibl. 23, 28, 36, 44, 110,
   118, 119*

James Emery (1860–1875)
Bucksport, Me.
Bibl. 105

Stephen Emery | S E |
   (b. 1725–d. 1801)
Salem, Mass.
Boston, Mass.
Emery & Co. (c. 1798)
*Bibl. 4, 15, 23, 24, 25, 28,
   29, 36, 39, 54, 72, 91, 94,
   110, 114*

| S Emery | | S. EMERY |

    (S E)

(Emery)   (Emery)

Thomas Knox Emery
   (b. 1781–d. 1815)
Boston, Mass.
New York, N.Y. | T E |
*Bibl. 4, 15, 23, 24, 25, 28,
   29, 36, 44, 54, 72, 91, 110,
   114*

 | T. K. E |

W. L. Emery & Son (1875)
Sanford, Me.
Bibl. 105

D. Emmons
Location unknown
Bibl. 89   **D. EMMONS**

L. Emmons (c. 1850)
Location unknown
Bibl. 15, 91, 114

| L. EMMONS |

Samuel Emmons
   (c. 1831–1833)
Philadelphia, Pa.
Bibl. 3

Thomas Emond
   (c. 1802–1819)
Petersburg, Va.
Bibl. 19, 91 | T. EMOND |

Thomas Emond
   (c. 1806–1821)
Raleigh, N.C.
Bibl. 21

Empire Art Silver
(See E. & J. Bass)

Empire Silver Co. Inc.
   (1946–present)
Brooklyn, N.Y.
Bibl. 146

Theobald Endt (c. 1742)
Philadelphia, Pa.
Bibl. 3

Samuel Engard
(c. 1837–1842)
Philadelphia, Pa.
Bibl. 3

George England (c. 1800)
New York, N.Y.
Bibl. 4, 23, 36, 124

James England (d. 1830)
Charleston, S.C.
(c. 1801–1806)
Baltimore, Md.
(c. 1807–1830)
Bibl. 5, 38

William England (c. 1717)
Philadelphia, Pa.
Bibl. 3, 4, 23, 28, 36, 44

Englander (c. 1865)
New Orleans, La.
Bibl. 141

C. W. Englebert (c. 1839)
Philadelphia, Pa.
Bibl. 3

Charles M. Englehart
(c. 1839–1850)
Philadelphia, Pa.
Bibl. 3

M. Englehart (c. 1837)
Philadelphia, Pa.
Bibl. 3

John English
(c. 1819–1828)
Philadelphia, Pa.
Bibl. 3

J. Enno & Hale (c. 1830)
Bangor, Me.
Probably Fennod Hale
Bibl. 89, 91

J. ENNO & HALE

—— **Ensign** (c. 1800)
Location unknown
Bibl. 28, 29, 44

ENSIGN

Charles Ensign
(c. 1842–1850)
Troy, N.Y.
Bibl. 20, 124

John Ent
(c. 1763–1794,
d. 1794)
Philadelphia, Pa.
Bibl. 3

Eoff & Connor
(c. 1833–1835)
New York, N.Y.
Garret Eoff
John H. Connor
Bibl. 15, 23, 24, 25, 28, 36,
44, 91, 114, 124, 135, 138

J. H. CONNOR & G. EOFF

J H CONNOR & G EOFF

Eoff & Howell   E & H
(c. 1805–1810)
New York, N.Y.
Garret Eoff
Paul Howell
Bibl. 15, 23, 24, 25, 28, 29,
36, 44, 54, 91, 114, 124,
135, 138

EOFF & HOWELL

Eoff & Moore (c. 1835)
New York, N.Y.
Garret Eoff
John C. Moore
Bibl. 15, 23, 24, 25, 36, 44,
91, 114, 124, 135, 138

G. EOFF   J. C. MOORE

Eoff & Phyfe   E & P
(c. 1844–1850)
New York, N.Y.
Garret Eoff
William Phyfe
Bibl. 4, 15, 23, 24, 25, 29,
35, 91, 114, 124, 135, 138

Eoff & Shepherd (c. 1850)
New York, N.Y.
Garret Eoff (?)
—— Shepherd
Bibl. 15, 25, 28, 29, 44, 114,
122, 124, 135

E & S

Edgar M. Eoff
(b. 1785–d. 1858)
New York, N.Y. (c. 1850)
Bibl. 15, 23, 24, 25, 44, 114,
124

E. M. E.

Garret (Garritt) Eoff
(b. 1779–d. 1845)
New York, N.Y.
Eoff & Howell
(c. 1805–1810)
Eoff & Connor
(c. 1833–1835)
Eoff & Moore (c. 1835)
Eoff & Phyfe (c. 1844–1850)
Eoff & Shepherd
(c. 1850) (?)
Bibl. 4, 23, 24, 25, 28, 29,
35, 36, 39, 54, 79, 91, 114,
122, 124, 135

G. EOFF   G. Eoff

Mortimer E. Eoff
(c. 1850)
New York, N.Y.
Bibl. 23, 25, 124

Eolles (Bolles) & Day
(c. 1825)
Hartford, Conn.
Bibl. 24, 25, 44

EOLLES & DAY
HARTFORD

EOLLES & DAY
HARTFORD

John Eppelsheimer
(c. 1845)
Philadelphia, Pa.
Bibl. 3

M. C. Eppenstein & Co.
(c. 1894–1904)
Chicago, Ill.
Became A. Davis Co.
(c. 1904)
Bibl. 127

Ashman Epps (c. 1848)
Philadelphia, Pa.
Bibl. 3

Ellery Epps (c. 1808)
Boston, Mass.
Bibl. 23, 28, 36, 44, 110

William Epps (1866–1880)
New Orleans, La.
Bibl. 141

Equer & Aquimac
  (c. 1816)
New York, N.Y.
Bibl. 23, 36, 44, 124, 138

John Erens (c. 1845–1846)
Louisville, Ky.
Bibl. 32, 93

Ernst & Coan (c. 1814)
Cooperstown, N.Y.
John Frederick Ernst Jr. (?)
Charles Coan
Bibl. 20, 124

Henry B. Ernst
  (c. 1830–1836,
  c. 1844–1845)
Cooperstown, N.Y.
Bibl. 20, 124

John Frederick Ernst Jr.
  (c. 1808–d. 1830)
Cooperstown, N.Y.
Ernst & Coan (c. 1814) (?)
Bibl. 20, 124

John Ervan (Erwin)
  (c. 1815)
New York, N.Y.
Bibl. 15, 23

Andrew Erwin (c. 1837)
Philadelphia, Pa.
Bibl. 3, 23, 36, 44

Henry Erwin
  (c. 1795–1842)
Philadelphia, Pa.
John McMullen (c. 1796)
*Bibl. 3, 15, 23, 24, 29, 36,
  39, 44, 54, 114*

**Henry Erwin & John
  McMullen (McMullin)**
Philadelphia, Pa. (c. 1796)
Bibl. 54, 91

James Erwin
Baltimore, Md. (c. 1809)
New York, N.Y. (c. 1815)
Bibl. 44, 124

John Erwin (c. 1809–1819)
Baltimore, Md.
New York, N.Y.
*Bibl. 15, 24, 28, 29, 36, 38,
  91, 114, 124*

John Erwin (c. 1816)
Philadelphia, Pa.
Lownes & Erwin
Bibl. 3

Thomas M. Erwin
  (d. 1889)
Louisville, Ky.
  (c. 1845–1846)
Bibl. 32

William C. Erwin (c. 1850)
Rochester, N.Y.
Bibl. 20, 124

Jacob Esler (c. 1829–1833)
Philadelphia, Pa.
Bibl. 3

Benjamin Essex (1860)
Warwick, R.I.
Bibl. 108

Charles Esslinger
  (c. 1840–1848)
Buffalo, N.Y.
Bibl. 20, 124

Robert Estep
  (c. 1812–1818)
Paris, Ohio
Bibl. 34

Esterle Sons
Louisville, Ky.
Bibl. 54, 93

Jacob R. Esterle
  (b. 1814–d. 1868)
Louisville, Ky.
  (c. 1832–1868)
Bibl. 32, 54, 93

Hayacinth Esteva
  (c. 1804–1808)
New York, N.Y.
Bibl. 23, 36, 124, 138

**George Eter (Etter)
  (Ettris)** (1833–1850)
Philadelphia, Pa.
Bibl. 3

John E. Ethridge
  (d. 1894,
  c. 1838–1848)
Louisville, Ky.
Bibl. 32, 54

Ettenheimer (c. 1850)
Ohio (?)
Rochester, N.Y.
Bibl. 89, 91

Ettenheimer

B. Etter (c. 1780)
Location unknown
Bibl. 28, 29, 44

G. Etter
(See G. Eter)

Benjamin Etting (c. 1769)
New York, N.Y.
Bibl. 2, 4, 23, 36, 124

G. Ettris
(See G. Eter)

Eubank & Jeffries
(See Jeffries & Eubank)

James Eubank (c. 1815)
Glasgow, Ky.
Joseph Eubank
Joseph Eubank, Jr.
Bibl. 32, 93

Joseph Eubank
Glasgow, Ky. (c. 1808)
James Eubank
  (c. 1815–1834)
Joseph Eubank, Jr.
  (c. 1815–1834)
William M. Savage
  (before c. 1815)
Bibl. 32, 54, 68, 93

Joseph Eubank, Jr.
(c. 1815–c. 1841)
Glasgow, Ky.
James Eubank
(c. 1815–1834)
Joseph Eubank
(c. 1815–1834)
Jeffries & Eubank (c. 1834)
Bibl. 93

Evans & Allen
(c. 1850)
Binghamton, N.Y.
Bibl. 20, 124

Evans & Anderson
(c. 1864–1866)
Newark, N.J.
Succeeded by Horace B.
Anderson
Bibl. 127

EVANS & ANDERSON

Evans & Cook
(See Theo. Evans & Co.)

Evans & Manning
(c. 1850)
New York, N.Y.
Bibl. 89, 124

EVANS & MANNING

Evans Case Co.
(c. 1920–present)
North Attleboro, Mass.
Division of Hilsingor Corp.,
Plainville, Mass.
Bibl. 127

Alfred J. Evans
(c. 1831–1854)
Binghamton, N.Y.
H. & A. J. Evans
(c. 1836–1841)
Bibl. 20, 114, 124

A J EVANS

David Evans
Philadelphia, Pa.
(before 1773)
Baltimore, Md.
(c. 1773–1795)
Bibl. 3, 38

Edwin T. Evans
(c. 1836–1841)
Binghamton, N.Y.
Bibl. 20, 124

H. & A. J. Evans
Binghamton, N.Y.
(c. 1836–1841)
Horatio Evans
Alfred J. Evans
Bibl. 20, 124

Henry Evans
(c. 1835–1862)
Newark, N.J.
Bibl. 23, 24, 25, 28, 29, 44,
91, 114, 124, 135

HENRY EVANS

Horatio Evans (c. 1841)
Binghamton, N.Y.
H. & A. J. Evans
(c. 1836–1841)
Bibl. 20, 124

James Evans (c. 1821)
Chenango Point, N.Y.
Bibl. 20, 124

John Evans (c. 1816–1830)
New York, N.Y.
Bibl. 4, 23, 24, 28, 29, 36,
44, 78, 124

EVANS

Oliver Evans (c. 1833)
Philadelphia, Pa.
Bibl. 3

R. C. Evans (c. 1811)
Norwich, N.Y.
Bibl. 20, 54, 124

Robert Evans
(c. 1768, d. 1812)
Boston, Mass.
Bibl. 4, 15, 23, 24, 25, 28,
29, 44, 54, 72, 91, 94, 110,
114, 135, 139

Roger Evans (c. 1815)
Waterford, N.Y.
Bibl. 20, 124

Theo. Evans & Co.
(c. 1855–1865)
New York, N.Y.
Theodore Evans
John Cook
Became Evans & Cook
(c. 1865–1870)
George W. Shiebler & Co.
(c. 1870–1915)
Bibl. 127, 157

T. EVANS & CO.

Thomas Evans & Sons
(b. 1834)
Binghamton, N.Y.
Bibl. 20, 124

W. R. Evans (c. 1850)
Covington, Ky.
Bibl. 32, 54, 89, 93

W. R. EVANS

William M. Evans
(c. 1813–1848)
Philadelphia, Pa.
Bibl. 3, 90

C. E. Evard & Brother
(c. 1849–?)
Staunton, Va.
Charles Eugene Evard
Charles Edward Evard
Bibl. 19

Charles A. Evard
(c. 1847–1849)
Lynchburg, Va.
Bibl. 19

Charles C. Evard (c. 1837)
Philadelphia, Pa.
Bibl. 3

Charles Edward Evard
(b. 1825–d. 1906)
Leesburg, Va.
(c. 1846–1867)
Staunton, Va.
(c. 1849–1850)
C. E. Evard & Brother
(c. 1849–?)
Bibl. 19,54

Charles Eugene Evard
(d. 1857)
Philadelphia, Pa. (c. 1837)
Lynchburg, Va.
(c. 1846–1867)
Winchester, Va.
(c. 1842, c. 1848)
Staunton, Va.
(c. 1849–?)
C. E. Evard & Brother
(c. 1849–?)
Bibl. 19, 54

EVER DRY
(See Weidlich Bros. Mfg.
Co.)

Cornelius Everest
(c. 1847–1850)
Philadelphia, Pa.
Bibl. 3

Jesse Everite (Everitt)
(c. 1811–c. 1819)
New York, N.Y.
Bibl. 3, 15, 36, 44, 124, 138

**John Evertsen (Evertson)
(Eversten)**
(c. 1813–1822)
Albany, N.Y.
Bibl. 4, 20, 23, 36, 44, 124

Evolution
(See Napier)

John Ewan
(b. 1786–d. 1852)
Charleston, S.C.
(c. 1823–1852)
P. Mood & Co.
(c. 1823–1834)
Mood & Ewan (c. 1824)
*Bibl. 5, 15, 23, 25, 28, 29,
36, 39, 44, 54, 91, 95, 114,
138*

J.EWAN   **J.EWAN**

JOHN EVAN

William H. Ewan
(c. 1849–1859)
Charleston, S.C.
Bibl. 5, 15, 25, 44, 54, 114

Wm H. Ewan

John Ewet (c. 1832)
New York, N.Y.
Bibl. 15, 124, 138

John Ewing
(b. 1755–d. 1799)
Lancaster, Pa.
(c. 1778–1798)
Bibl. 3, 54, 112

Warren B. Ewing
(c. 1840–1876)
Shelbyville, Ky.
Sharrard and Ewing
(c. 1840)
Bibl. 32, 44, 68, 93

Eyland & Hayden
(c. 1832–1835)
Charleston, S.C.
James Eyland
Nathaniel Hayden
Bibl. 5

James Eyland
(b. 1795–d. 1835)
Charleston, S.C.
(c. 1819–1835)
James Eyland & Co.
(c. 1820–1827)
Eyland & Hayden
(c. 1832–1835)
Bibl. 5, 25, 44, 54, 91, 114

J EYLAND

James Eyland & Co.
(c. 1820–1827)
Charleston, S.C.
James Eyland
W. & G. Chance
William Carrington
Bibl. 5, 44, 91

J EYLAND & CO.

Matthias Eyre (c. 1775)
Philadelphia, Pa.
Bibl. 3

Simon Eytinge
(c. 1829–1831)
Philadelphia, Pa.
Bibl. 3

F

F
(See LeRoy W. Fairchild &
Co., Michael C. Fina Co.,
Inc., French & Franklin,
Ferd. Fuchs & Bros.)

F & B
(See Foster & Bailey,
Theodore W. Foster &
Bro. Co.)

F & C
(See Federal Silver
Company)

F & G
(See Fletcher & Gardiner)

F. & H.
(See Farrington &
Hunnewell)

F & M
(See Frost & Mumford)

F Co
(See Fessenden & Company)

F C
(See Ford & Carpenter)

F E & CO
(See Federal Silver
Company)

F J
(See Fairchild & Johnson)

F M
(See Franklin Mint, Fried,
Mills & Co., Inc.,
Frederick Marquand)

F M A
(See Francis M. Ackley)

F M B
(See Fred M. Birch Co., Inc.)

F. N. & Co.
(See Fishel, Nessler & Co.)

F R
(See Francis Richardson,
   Francis Richardson II)

F. S. & Co.
(See Frederick S. Hoffman)

F S B & Co.
(See F. S. Blackman & Co.)

F S G
(See Friedman Silver Co.,
   Inc.)

F S S
(See Fortunoff Silver Sales of
   Westbury, Inc.)

F W C
(See Francis W. Cooper)

Faber & Hoover
   (c. 1837)
Philadelphia, Pa.
William Faber
   (c. 1828–1850)
Joseph E. Hoover
   (c. 1837–1841)
Bibl. 3, 4, 23, 28, 36, 44

Christian Friedrich Faber
   (b. 1814–d. 1873)
   (1846–1873)
New Orleans, La.
Bibl. 141

Otto G. Faber
   (c. 1895–1915)
Baltimore, Md.
Bibl. 127, 157

W. Faber & Sons
Philadelphia, Pa.
Bibl. 89, 91

William Faber
   (c. 1828–1850)
Philadelphia, Pa.
Faber & Hoover (c. 1837)
Bibl. 3, 4, 23, 28, 36, 44

William Faber
   (1868–1881)
New Orleans, La.
Bibl. 141

H. Fabian
Chester, S.C. (c. 1853)
Lancaster, S.C. (c. 1853)
Bibl. 5

Augustus P. Faff (c. 1837)
Philadelphia, Pa.
Bibl. 3

George M. Fagaler
   (c. 1808)
Philadelphia, Pa.
Bibl. 23, 36, 44

B. Fagan (c. 1845)
Cassville, Ga.
Bibl. 17

George M. Fagley
   (c. 1806)
Philadelphia, Pa.
Bibl. 3

Fairchild & Johnson
   (1898–1919)
New York, N.Y.
Successor to LeRoy Fairchild
   & Co. (1889–1898)
Became Fairchild & Co.
   (c. 1919–1922)
Bibl. 127, 135

Fairchild & Taylor
   (c. 1838)
Wheeling, Va.
Artemas O. Fairchild
————— Taylor
Bibl. 19

Artemas O. Fairchild
   (c. 1839–1851)
Wheeling, Va.
Fairchild & Taylor (c. 1838)
Bibl. 1

Caleb Fairchild
   (c. 1830–1831)
Waterloo, N.Y.
Bibl. 20, 122, 124

James L. Fairchild
   (c. 1824–1838)
New York, N.Y.
Bibl. 15, 23, 36, 44, 138

Joseph Fairchild
   (c. 1824–1837)
New Haven, Conn.
*Bibl. 5, 16, 23, 25, 28, 36,
   44, 92, 110, 114, 124, 143*

LeRoy W. Fairchild & Co.
   (1867–1873)
New York, N.Y.
Successor to LeRoy W.
   Fairchild (1843–1867)
Became L. W. Fairchild
   (1873–1886)
L. W. Fairchild & Sons
   (1886–1889)
LeRoy Fairchild & Co.
   (1889–1898)
Fairchild & Johnson
   (1898–1919)
Fairchild & Company
   (c. 1919–1922)
Bibl. 114, 127, 135, 139, 157

Robert Fairchild
   (b. 1738–d. 1794)
Durham, Conn. (c. 1739)
Stratford, Conn. (c. 1747)
New Haven, Conn. (c. 1772)
New York, N.Y.
   (c. 1780–1794)
*Bibl. 15, 16, 17, 25, 29, 36,
   44, 54, 91, 92, 94, 102,
   110, 114, 116, 124, 143,
   151*

Fairman, Draper & Co.
   (c. 1823–1825)
Philadelphia, Pa.
Gideon Fairman
————— Draper
Bibl. 3

Gideon Fairman
   (b. 1774–d. 1827,
   c. 1800–1822)
New London, Conn.

Albany, N.Y.
Philadelphia, Pa.
(c. 1823–1825)
Fairman, Draper & Co.
(c. 1823–1825)
Murray, Draper, Fairman &
Co.(?)
Bibl. 3, 28, 44, 110, 124

George Gustavus Fakes
(c. 1807)
Baltimore, Md.
Bibl. 38

I. John Fales
(b. 1780–d. 1857)
Bristol & Newport, R.I.
Bibl. 15, 44, 91, 110, 114

I·FALES

C. O. Faller (c. 1885–1895)
LaPorte, Ind.
Successor to John Faller &
Son
Bibl. 133

John Faller
(c. 1854–1885)
John Faller & Son
(c. 1866–1885)
New York, N.Y.
LaPorte, Ind.
Became C. O. Faller
Bibl. 133

J. FALLER LAPORTE

Charles Faris
(b. 1764–d. 1800)
Annapolis, Md.
(c. 1785–1800)
*Bibl. 15, 23, 24, 25, 28, 29,
36, 38, 44, 114*

Cs Faris

Chas Faris

Chas Faris

Hyram Faris
(b. 1769–d. 1800)
Annapolis, Md.
(c. 1790–1800)
Bibl. 15, 38

William Faris
(b. 1728–d. 1804)
Annapolis, Md.
(c. 1760–1780)
*Bibl. 15, 19, 22, 25, 29, 38,
39, 44, 54, 102, 104*

William Faris Jr. (b. 1762)
Annapolis, Md. (c. 1782)
Norfolk, Va. (c. 1786)
Havana, Cuba
(c. 1792–1794)
Edenton, N.C.
(c. 1798–1803)
Bibl. 15, 19, 38

Charles Farley
(b. 1791–d. 1877)
Portland, Me.
(c. 1828–1830)
Ipswich, Mass.
Wyer & Farley
(c. 1828–1830)
*Bibl. 15, 23, 24, 25, 28, 36,
44, 91, 94, 105, 110, 114*

C FARLEY   FARLEY

Farnam & Ward
(c. 1810, c. 1816)
Norwich, Conn. (c. 1810)
Boston, Mass. (c. 1816)
Rufus Farnam
——— Ward
*Bibl. 23, 24, 25, 28, 29, 36,
44, 91, 110, 122*

FARNAM & WARD

C. H. Farnam
Location unknown
Bibl. 28, 29

C H FARNAM

Henry Farnam
(b. 1773–d. 1833)
Boston, Mass.
*Bibl. 4, 15, 3, 24, 25, 28, 29,
36, 44, 54, 91, 110, 114*

H. Farnam

Rufus Farnam
(b. 1771, c. 1799–1833)
Boston, Mass.
(c. 1799–1830)
Hanover, N.H. (c. 1833)
Norwich, Conn. (c. 1810)
Farnam & Ward
(c. 1810, c. 1816)
*Bibl. 15, 23, 24, 25, 28, 29,
36, 44, 54, 72, 91, 94, 110,
114, 125*

R. FARNAM   R. F.

Rufus & Henry Farnam
(c. 1800–1807)
Boston, Mass.
Hanover, N.H.
*Bibl. 2, 15, 25, 28, 29, 36,
44, 91, 110, 114*

R. & H. FARNAM

Thomas Farnam
(c. 1825–1836)
Boston, Mass.
*Bibl. 24, 25, 28, 29, 36, 44,
110, 114*

Th FARNAM

Farnham & Owen
(c. 1810–1830)
Location unknown
Bibl. 29, 44, 114

FARNHAM & OWEN

Samuel H. Farnham
(b. 1813)
Oxford, N.Y. (c. 1840–1845)
Bibl. 20

J. C. Farnsworth
Location unknown
Bibl. 28

J. C. Farnsworth

Farnum (See also Farnam)

J. C. Farnum (1875)
Bethel, Me.
Bibl. 105

Farr
(See Crowley & Farr)

Farr & Co. (c. 1837–1850)
Philadelphia, Pa.
Bibl. 3, 91

Farr & Gilbert
(c. 1813–1814)
Manlius, N.Y.
Joseph Farr
——— Gilbert
Bibl. 20, 124

Bela Farr (c. 1829)
Norwich, N.Y.
Bibl. 20, 124

John Farr (c. 1834)
Utica, N.Y.
Bibl. 20, 124, 158

John C. Farr (c. 1812)
Boston, Mass.
Bibl. 23, 24, 29, 36, 39, 91,
110

J C FARR

JOHN C FARR

John C. Farr
(c. 1824–1840)
Philadelphia, Pa.
Crowley & Farr
Bibl. 3, 25, 44, 54, 91, 110,
114

JOHN C FARR

J.C.FARR

John S. Farr
Norwich, N.Y.
(c. 1834–1837)
Elmira, N.Y. (c. 1849)
Bibl. 20, 114

Joseph Farr
(c. 1775–d. 1845)
Manlius, N.Y.
(c. 1813–1845)
Farr & Gilbert
(c. 1813–1814)
Bibl. 20, 124

Farrington & Co. (1875)
Providence, R.I.
Bibl. 108

Farrington & Hunnewell
Boston, Mass. (1835–1885)
John Farrington
George W. Hunnewell
Bibl. 4, 23, 24, 25, 28, 29,
36, 44, 91, 114, 127

FARRINGTON & HUNNEWELL

F & H

B. S. Farrington
(1860–1875)
Cumberland, Md.
Bibl. 108

John Farrington (c. 1833)
Boston, Mass.
Farrington & Hunnewell
Bibl. 3, 4, 28, 44

John H. Fasbender
Charleston, S.C.
(before 1804)
Richmond, Va.
(c. 1804–c. 1819)
Bibl. 19

Fassett & Follet
(c. 1793–1795)
Bennington, Vt.
——— Fassett
Timothy Follet
Bibl. 54, 110

Fatman Brothers (c. 1843)
Philadelphia, Pa.
Bibl. 3

Fatton & Co.
(c. 1840–1841)
Philadelphia, Pa.
Bibl. 3

Frederick Fatton
(c. 1830–1839)
Philadelphia, Pa.
Bibl. 3

John W. Faulkner
(c. 1835)
New York, N.Y.
Bibl. 24, 25, 44, 114, 124

F. J. Favor (1875)
Providence, R.I.
Bibl. 108

John James Favre
(c. 1797)
Philadelphia, Pa.
Bibl. 3

Fay & Fisher (c. 1841)
Troy, N.Y.
Henry C. Fay
George Fisher
Bibl. 20, 124

George H. Fay (b. 1830)
Utica, N.Y. (c. 1853–1857)
Bibl. 18, 124, 158

Henry C. Fay
(c. 1842–1843)
Troy, N.Y.
Albany, N.Y. (c. 1850)
Fay & Fisher (c. 1841)
Bibl. 20, 124

August Feckhart
(c. 1849–1850)
Rochester, N.Y.
Bibl. 20, 41, 44, 124

Federal Silver Company
(c. 1920–1961)
New York, N.Y.
Bibl. 127

Michael Feeley (1875)
Providence, R.I.
Bibl. 108

W. J. Feeley Co.
(c. 1875–1937)
Providence, R.I.
Bibl. 114, 127

Judy McCreary Felch
(c. 1977–1980)
St. Louis, Mo.
Bibl. 155

Albert Feldenheimer
(c. 1891–1896)
Portland, Ore.
Became A. & C.
  Feldenheimer
  (c. 1896–1904)
Bibl. 127

Fellette
(See Fillette)

Fellows & Green (c. 1825)
Portland, Ma. (1834)
Bibl. 28, 29, 44, 91, 105

FELLOWS & GREEN

Fellows & Storm
(c. 1839–1844)
Albany, N.Y.
New York, N.Y.
Abraham Fellows
Abraham G. Storm
*Bibl. 23, 24, 25, 29, 36, 44,
  114, 124, 138*

FELLOWS & STORM

Fellows, Cargill & Co.
(c. 1835–1841)
New York, N.Y.
Bibl. 21, 93, 124, 138

Abraham Fellows
(b. 1786–d. 1851)
Troy, N.Y.
  (c. 1810–1819,
  c. 1829–1835,
  c. 1844–1850)
Newport, R.I. (c. 1826)
New York, N.Y.
  (c. 1837–1838)
Albany, N.Y. (c. 1841–1844)
Buffalo, N.Y. (c. 1851)
Fellows & Storm
  (c. 1839–1844)
*Bibl. 15, 20, 24, 25, 28, 29,
  36, 44, 56, 91, 114, 124,
  138*

FELLOWS

Frank H. Fellows (1860)
Livermore, Md.
Bibl. 105

I. W. & J. K. Fellows
(c. 1834)
Lowell, Mass.
Ignatius W. Fellows
James K. Fellows
Bibl. 15, 25, 44, 114

I. W. & J. K. FELLOWS

Ignatius W. Fellows
(See I. W. & J. K. Fellows)

J. Fellows & Co.
(c. 1810–1813)
Troy, N.Y.
James Fellows
Bibl. 20, 124

J. C. Fellows
(c. 1844–1847)
Albany, N.Y.
Bibl. 20, 124

James Fellows (c. 1810)
Troy, N.Y.
J. Fellows & Co.
  (c. 1810–1813)
Bibl. 20, 91, 124

James K. Fellows
(c. 1832–1834)
Lowell, Mass.
I. W. & J. K. Fellows
  (c. 1834)
Bibl. 15, 25, 44, 114

J. K. FELLOWS

John F. Fellows (c. 1824)
Portsmouth, N.H.
Werner (Warner) & Fellows
Bibl. 23, 36, 91, 125

Louis Strite Fellows
(c. 1845)
New York State
Bibl. 21, 91, 138

Philip M. Fellows
(c. 1839–1841)
Troy, N.Y.
Bibl. 20, 124

J. S. Felt (c. 1825)
Portland, Me.
Bibl. 14, 25, 28, 105, 114

J. S. FELT

Robert Felton
(c. 1683)
Philadelphia, Pa.
Bibl. 3

Alexander Fenlester
(c. 1807)
Baltimore, Md.
Bibl. 38

Jason Fenn (c. 1820)
Lancaster, Ohio
Bibl. 34

Fenniman Co.
(c. 1915–1922)
New York, N.Y.
Bibl. 127, 157

Fenno & Hale (c. 1840)
Bangor, Me.
Bibl. 25, 44, 91, 105, 114

FENNO & HALE

James Fenno (c. 1825)
Lowell, Mass.
Bibl. 28, 29, 44, 89, 110

J. Fenno

Charles Edward Ferguson
(b. 1752)
Williamsburg, Va.
  (c. 1778–1781)
Richmond, Va. (c. 1782)
Bibl. 19

Elijah Ferguson
(c. 1833–1850)
New Bern, N.C.
Bibl. 21

George Ferguson
(c. 1820–1822)
Philadelphia, Pa.
Bibl. 3

John Ferguson
(c. 1801–1810)
Philadelphia, Pa.
Moore & Ferguson
  (c. 1801–1805)
Bibl. 3, 23, 36, 39, 44, 91

Louis Ferit (Ferret)
(c. 1819–1825)

Philadelphia, Pa.
Bibl. 3

Mathew Fernbach
(c. 1819)
Norfolk, Va.
Bibl. 19

Ebenezar Ferran
(1817–1902)
Manchester, N.H.
Bibl. 107

Henry Ferrenbach
(b. 1826–d. 1854)
New Orleans, La.
(1850–1854)
Bibl. 141

Ferret
(See Ferit)

John F. Ferrette (c. 1821)
Charleston, S.C.
Bibl. 5

Lewis Ferrey (c. 1837)
Philadelphia, Pa.
Bibl. 3

Jean Ferrier (1816–1854)
New Orleans, La.
Bibl. 23, 38, 44

Ferris & McElwee
(c. 1813)
Philadelphia, Pa.
Benjamin Ferris (?)
James McElwee
Bibl. 3

Benjamin Ferris
Philadelphia, Pa.
(c. 1802–1811)
Ferris & McElwee
(c. 1813) (?)
Albany, N.Y. (c. 1816)
New York, N.Y.
Waterford, N.Y. (c. 1811)
Bibl. 3, 15, 20, 21, 23, 28, 36, 124, 134

Edward B. Ferris
(c. 1846–1848)
Philadelphia, Pa.
Bibl. 3, 91

R. Ferris (c. 1850)
Location unknown
Bibl. 44

[R. FERRIS]

Ziba Ferris
(b. 1786–d. 1875)
Wilmington, Del.
(c. 1810–1860)
Bibl. 25, 30, 44, 91, 114

[ZIBA FERRIS]

William Ferriss (c. 1813)
Glens Falls, N.Y.
Buffalo, N.Y. (c. 1836–1839)
Bibl. 20, 124

Jacob (J. W.) Fertig
(c. 1810–1811)
Philadelphia, Pa.
Bibl. 3

Fessenden & Company
(1860–1922)
Providence, R.I.
Successor to Wm. P.
Fessenden & Co.
(1858–1860)
Bibl. 115, 127, 147, 157

Fessenden Brothers
(1875)
Providence, R.I.
Bibl. 108

William Fessenden
(1860)
Newport and Providence,
R.I.
Bibl. 23, 24, 44, 91, 108

[FESSENDEN]

John Fessler Sr.
(b. 1757–d. 1820,
c. 1785–1820)
Frederick, Md.
Lancaster, Pa.
Bibl. 38

John Fessler Jr.
(c. 1800–1820)
Frederick, Md.
Bibl. 38

Fest & Bro. (c. 1850)
Philadelphia, Pa.
Bibl. 3

Alfred Fest (c. 1850)
Philadelphia, Pa.
Bibl. 3

Edwy Fest (c. 1842–1850)
Philadelphia, Pa.
Bibl. 3

Peter Feurt
(b. 1703–d. 1737)
Boston, Mass.
(c. 1727–1732)
New York, N.Y.
Bibl. 2, 25, 28, 29, 44, 69, 94, 110, 114, 124, 138

Joseph Feytel (1851–1870)
New Orleans, La.
Bibl. 141

J.N. FEYTEL

NEW ORLEANS

Godfrey Ficher
(c. 1811–1813)
Philadelphia, Pa.
Bibl. 3

James B. Fidler (c. 1850)
Philadelphia, Pa.
Bibl. 3

Field
(See Henderson, Field &
Co.)

———— **Field** (c. 1817)
Auburn, N.Y.
Bibl. 20

Field & Halliwell
(c. 1806–1813)
Poughkeepsie, N.Y.
John Field
George Halliwell
Bibl. 20, 124

Field & Monger
(c. 1805–1806)
Poughkeepsie, N.Y.
John Field
Benjamin Monger
Bibl. 20, 124

Charles Field
(c. 1835–1850)
Philadelphia, Pa.
Bibl. 3

David E. Field
(c. 1840–1848)
Cleveland, Ohio
Bibl. 34, 54

George Field (c. 1840)
Philadelphia, Pa.
Bibl. 3

John Field (d. 1821)
Poughkeepsie, N.Y.
(c. 1799–1806)
Field & Monger
(c. 1805–1806)
Field & Halliwell
(c. 1806–1813)
Bibl. 20, 124

John H. Field (c. 1811)
Batavia, N.Y.
Bibl. 20, 124, 138

Josiah M. Field (1875)
Newport, R.I.
Bibl. 105

L. S. Field (1875)
Newport, R.I.
Bibl. 105

Marshall Field & Co.
(1881–present)
Chicago, Ill.
Successor to
Farwell, Field & Company
(1864–1865)
Field, Palmer & Leiter
(1865–1866)
Field, Leiter & Company
(1866–1881)
Bibl. 127

Marshall Field &
Company Craft Shop
(c. 1904–1950)
Chicago, Ill.
Bibl. 98, 120, 144

Peter Field
Hudson, N.Y. (c. 1785)
Albany, N.Y. (c. 1795–1800)
Bibl. 20, 124, 138

Peter Field (Jr.)
New York, N.Y.
(c. 1805–1837)
Newburgh, N.Y.
(c. 1807–1810)
Bibl. 15, 20, 25, 44, 95, 114, 124, 138

P. FIELD JR

Peter W. Field
May be Peter Field Jr.
Bibl. 89

Samuel Field(s)
(c. 1816–1829)
Philadelphia, Pa.
Steel & Field (c. 1814–1825)
Henderson, Field & Co.
(c. 1816)
Bibl. 3, 23, 36, 44

George Fielding
New York, N.Y.
(c. 1731–1750)
Albany, N.Y. (c. 1765)
Bibl. 4, 15, 23, 25, 28, 29, 35, 36, 44, 54, 72, 114, 124, 138

GF

John S. Fifield
(18th century)
Westerly, R.I.
Dover, N.H. (c. 1859–1865)
Bibl. 28, 44, 125

File
(See Pheil)

Francis Fillette (Fellette)
(b. 1791–d. 1838)
Charleston, S.C.
(w. 1807–1838)

—— Pineau
Bibl. 5

Filley, Mead & Caldwell
(c. 1850)
Philadelphia, Pa.
—— Filley
John O. Mead
James E. Caldwell (?)
Bibl. 3, 135

Fillkwik Co.
(c. 1920–1936)
Attleboro, Mass.
Became Shields, Inc.
(1936–1939)
Rex Products Corporation,
New Rochelle, N.Y. (1939)
Bibl. 127

Fillkwik

Michael C. Fina Co., Inc.
(1935–present)
New York, N.Y.
Bibl. 127

Finch & Cagger
(c. 1832–1838)
Albany, N.Y.
Hiram Finch
Michael Cagger
Bibl. 20, 124

Hiram Finch
(c. 1829–1840)
Albany, N.Y.
Finch & Cagger
(c. 1832–1838)
Bibl. 4, 20, 23, 28, 36, 44, 124

Peter Finch (c. 1826)
Georgetown, S.C.
John Hawkins
Bibl. 5

William C. Finck Co.
(c. 1896–1915)
Elizabeth, N.J.
Bibl. 114, 127, 157

925 1000 STERLING

The Rev. James Findley
(c. 1810)
Zanesville, Ohio
Bibl. 34

Fine Arts Sterling Company (1944–1979)
Philadelphia, Pa.
  (1944–1972)
Morgantown, Pa.
  (1972–1977)
Jenkintown, Pa.
  (1977–1979)
Bibl. 127, 146

Samuel Finefield
Troy, N.Y. (c. 1834–1835)
Buffalo, N.Y. (c. 1835–1836)
New York, N.Y. (?) (c. 1835)
Bibl. 20, 23, 124

Samuel Finewall (c. 1835)
New York, N.Y.
Bibl. 36, 44

——— **Finlayson** (c. 1782)
Charleston, S.C.
Bibl. 5, 44, 54

Henry Finlayson (d. 1788)
Savannah, Ga. (c. 1775)
Bibl. 17, 28

Francis Finncy (c. 1844)
Philadelphia, Pa.
Bibl. 3, 23

John Finney (c. 1754)
Charlestown, Md.
Bibl. 38

John P. Fireng (Firing)
Burlington, N.J.
  (c. 1810–1830)
Philadelphia, Pa.
  (c. 1823–1833)
Bibl. 3, 23, 24, 25, 28, 29,
  36, 44, 114

| J. P. FIRENG |

Jean B. Fischesser
  (c. 1857)
Walhalla, S.C.
Bibl. 5

Isaac Fish Jr.
  (c. 1843–1850)
Utica, N.Y.
Bibl. 18, 20, 114, 124, 158

Willson Fish (c. 1838)
Rochester, N.Y.
Bibl. 20, 124

Fishel, Nessler & Co.
  (c. 1886–1937)
New York, N.Y.
Bibl. 127, 157

Fisher
(See Cooper & Fisher)

Fisher & Champney
  (c. 1846–1847)
Troy, N. Y.
George Fisher
Lewis C. Champney
Bibl. 20, 124

Fisher Silversmiths, Inc.
  (c. 1936–present)
Jersey City, N.J.
New York, N.Y.
Successor to M. Fred Hirsch
  Co.
Bibl. 127

George Fisher
  (c. 1837–1846)
Troy, N.Y.
Fay & Fisher (c. 1841)
George Fisher & Co.
  (c. 1842–1844)
Fisher & Champney
  (c. 1846–1847)
Bibl. 20, 124

George Fisher & Co.
  (c. 1842–1844)
Troy, N.Y.
Bibl. 20, 124

Henry Fisher
  (c. 1849–1850)
Philadelphia, Pa.
Bibl. 3

James Fisher
  (c. 1821–1832)
New York, N.Y.
Bibl. 15, 23, 36, 44, 124

John Fisher (c. 1790)
York, Pa.
Bibl. 3

John P. Fisher
  (c. 1820–1822)
Philadelphia, Pa.
Bibl. 3

Martin Fisher
  (c. 1793–1799)
Philadelphia, Pa.
Bibl. 3

Robert Y. Fisher
  (c. 1824)
Philadelphia, Pa.
Bibl. 3

Thomas A. Fisher
  (b. 1765)
Philadelphia, Pa. (c. 1797)
Baltimore, Md. (c. 1803)
Easton, Md. (c. 1803–1807)
Bibl. 3, 15, 23, 24, 25, 28,
  29, 36, 38, 44, 91, 114

| T. FISHER | | T Fisher |
| T.Fisher | | T. Fisher |
| T.Fisher |

William Fisher
  (c. 1841–1845)
Charleston, Va.
Bibl. 19

R. Fiske (19th century)
Location unknown
Bibl. 89

| R. Fiske |

Amon Fister (c. 1794)
Philadelphia, Pa.
Bibl. 3

Fitch & Hobart
  (c. 1811–1813)
New Haven, Conn.
New Bern, N.C.
Joshua Hobart
Allen Fitch
Bibl. 21, 23, 28, 36, 44, 92,
  110, 143

Fitch
(See Dennis & Fitch)

Allen Fitch
    (b. 1785–d. 1839)
New Haven, Conn.
    (c. 1808–?)
New Bern, N.C.
    (c. 1811–c. 1826)
Fitch & Hobart
    (c. 1811–1813)
Bibl. 16, 21, 23, 28, 36, 44,
    110, 143

David Fitch (c. 1835)
Philadelphia, Pa.
Bibl. 3

Dennis M. Fitch
    (c. 1840–1850)
Troy, N.Y.
Not New Haven, Conn.
Bibl. 20, 23, 24, 25, 36, 44,
    91, 114, 124

    D M FITCH

James Fitch (d. 1826)
Auburn, N.Y.
    (c. 1816–1821)
Graves & Fitch
    (c. 1816–1821)
Bibl. 20, 25, 114, 124

John Fitch
    (b. 1743–d. 1798)
Trenton, N.J. (c. 1769–1776)
New York, N.Y. (c. 1782)
East Windsor, Conn.
East Hartford, N.J.   J F
Kentucky
Bibl. 3, 23, 24, 25, 29, 36,
    44, 46, 54, 61, 93, 94, 102,
    110, 124

    J. FITCH

William Fitch (c. 1831)
Batavia, N.Y.
Keyes & Fitch
Bibl. 20, 124

John Fite
    (b. 1783–d. 1818)
Baltimore, Md.
    (c. 1807–1818)
Bibl. 15, 24, 25, 29, 38, 44,
    114

    I. FITE   J F

Enoch Fithian
    (c. 1771–1776)
Greenwich, N.J.
Bibl. 46, 54

James Fitzer (c. 1849)
Camden, N.J.
Bibl. 3

Francis Fitzgerald (1860)
Lewiston, Me.
Bibl. 105

**George (G. K.) R.
    Fitzgerald**
    (c. 1841–1848)
Philadelphia, Pa.
Bibl. 3, 23

James Fitzgerald
    (c. 1841–1846)
Philadelphia, Pa.
Bibl. 3, 23

R. Fitzgerald & Co.
    (c. 1827)
Plattsburg, N.Y.
Bibl. 20, 124

George W. Flach
    (b. 1818–d. 1877)
Charleston, S.C.
    (c. 1840–1870)
Bibl. 5

Josiah Flagg   J. F
    (c. 1713–1765)
Boston, Mass.
Bibl. 4, 23, 25, 28, 36, 44,
    114

Josiah Flagg Jr. (b. 1738)
Boston, Mass. (c. 1810)
Bibl. 28, 44, 110

S. Flagg (c. 1825)
Location unknown
Bibl. 15, 44, 114

    S FLAGG

Edward Flaig (c. 1830)
Danville, Ky.
Bibl. 32, 93

James Flanagan (c. 1833)
Philadelphia, Pa.
Bibl. 3

Henry Flatcher (c. 1818)
Lexington, Ky.
(probably Henry Fletcher)
Bibl. 54

Paul Flato (c. 1939)
New York, N.Y.
Hollywood, Calif.
Bibl. 117

George Fleegal
    (c. 1819–1824)
Philadelphia, Pa.
Bibl. 3

Flere & Harris (c. 1767)
Charleston, S.C.
Thomas Flere
Charles Harris
Bibl. 44

Thomas Flere (c. 1767)
Charleston, S.C.
Flere & Harris (c. 1767)
Bibl. 5

L. H. Flersheim (c. 1839)
Buffalo, N.Y.
Bibl. 20, 124

Fletcher & Bennett
(See Bennett & Fletcher)

Fletcher & Gardiner
Boston, Mass. (c. 1810)
Philadelphia, Pa.
    (c. 1815–1822)
Charles Fletcher
Thomas Fletcher
Baldwin Gardiner
Sidney Gardiner
Bibl. 3, 4, 15, 23, 24, 25, 28,
    29, 36, 39, 44, 54, 91, 95,
    102, 104, 110, 114, 116,
    122, 149

    F. & G.

Fletcher, Bennett & Co.
(See Bennett & Fletcher)

C. & G. Fletcher
    (c. 1819–1824)
Philadelphia, Pa.
Bibl. 3

Charles Fletcher
(c. 1810–1833)
Philadelphia, Pa.
Fletcher & Gardiner
(c. 1810)
Bibl. 3, 23, 36, 44, 114

Francis C. Fletcher
(c. 1833–1834)
Troy, N.Y.
Bibl. 20, 124

George Fletcher
(c. 1821–1831)
Philadelphia, Pa.
Bibl. 3

Henry Fletcher
Lexington, Ky.
(c. 1818–1830)
Louisville, Ky.
Bennett & Fletcher
(1830–1894)
Bibl. 32, 54, 68, 93

James (Santiago) Fletcher
(d. 1809)
New Orleans, La.
Bibl. 141

Leonard Fletcher (c. 1819)
Philadelphia, Pa.
Bibl. 3

Samuel Fletcher (c. 1804)
Philadelphia, Pa.
Bibl. 3

T. Fletcher & T. Bailey
(c. 1830)
Philadelphia, Pa.
Bibl. 54

Thomas Fletcher
(b. 1787–d. 1866)
Boston, Mass. (c. 1810)
Philadelphia, Pa.
(c. 1813–1830)
Bennett & Fletcher
Fletcher & Gardiner
*Bibl. 3, 15, 23, 24, 25, 28,
29, 36, 39, 44, 72, 91, 95,
102, 104, 110, 114, 116,
122, 149, 151*

⬭ T FLETCHER   ▭ T. F.

T. FLETCHER   PHILAD.

John Flexion (c. 1837)
Philadelphia, Pa.
Bibl. 3

Daniel Fling
(c. 1809–1822)
Philadelphia, Pa.
Bibl. 3

George Fling
(c. 1749)
Philadelphia, Pa.
Bibl. 23, 28, 36, 44

F. P. Flint (c. 1816–1823)
Nashville, Tenn.
Richmond & Flint
Bibl. 89

James Flood
(c. 1839–1850)
Philadelphia, Pa.
Bibl. 3

William Flood (c. 1837)
Philadelphia, Pa.
Bibl. 3

Simon Flootron (c. 1838)
St. Louis, Mo.
Bibl. 54, 155

William Floto (c. 1849)
Philadelphia, Pa.
Bibl. 3

Lewis Flott(e)
(c. 1814–1818)
Baltimore, Md.
Bibl. 23, 28, 36, 38, 44

John Flot(t)ard & Co.
(c. 1793)
Flot(t)ard (c. 1793)
Charleston, S.C.
Bibl. 5

——— Flot(t)ard
(c. 1793)
Charleston, S.C.
John Flot(t)ard & Co.
Bibl. 5

Jacob Flournoy (b. 1663)
Williamsburg, Va.
(c. 1700–1712)
Bibl. 19, 153

Henry Flower
(c. 1753–1755)
Philadelphia, Pa.
Bibl. 3

Joseph Flower (c. 1844)
Philadelphia, Pa.
Bibl. 3, 23

J. Flowers (c. 1853–1855)
Nashville, Tenn.
Bibl. 54

E. D. Flye (1875)
Freedom, Me.
Bibl. 105

Charles Fobes (c. 1850)
Philadelphia, Pa.
Bibl. 3

Jacob Fogle
(b. 1803–d. 1867)
Milledgeville, Ga.
(c. 1825–1837)
Columbus, Ga. (1837–1841)
Foster & Fogle
(c. 1835–1837)
Bibl. 17

A. Fogliata (c. 1903–1907)
Chicago, Ill.
Bibl. 89

George Foley (c. 1823)
Canton, Ohio
Bibl. 34

William Folkrod
(c. 1849–1850)
Philadelphia, Pa.
Bibl. 3

Timothy Follet
(b. 1754–d. 1803)
Bennington, Vt.
(c. 1784–1801)
Fassett & Follet
(c. 1793–1795)
Bibl. 54, 116

Alexander A. Folloppe
(c. 1808–1810)
Boston, Mass.
New York, N.Y.
*Bibl. 23, 36, 44, 110, 124,
138*

John Folsom
(b. 1756–d. 1839)
Albany, N.Y. (c. 1781)
Bibl. 20, 23, 28, 36, 44, 91, 124

Folwell & Haines (c. 1844)
Philadelphia, Pa.
John T. Folwell (?)
Imlah Haines (?)
Bibl. 3

Folwell, Shadforth & Co.
(c. 1791)
Richmond, Va.
Petersburg, Va.
—————— Folwell
Whitaker Shadforth
Bibl. 19

Godfrey G. Folwell
(c. 1832–1845)
Philadelphia, Pa.
Bibl. 3

John T. Folwell
(c. 1847–1850)
Philadelphia, Pa.
Folwell & Haines
(c. 1844) (?)
Bibl. 3

Samuel Folwell
(c. 1788–1793)
Philadelphia, Pa.
Bibl. 3

Louis H. Fontenay
(c. 1840)
Charleston, S.C.
Bibl. 5

William Foote (Foot)
(b. 1772, c. 1797)
Middletown, Conn.
(c. 1795–1799)
East Haddam, Conn.
(c. 1796–1799?)
Colchester, Conn.
Glastonbury, Conn.
Michigan
Canfield & Foote
(c. 1795–1799)
Bibl. 16, 23, 28, 36, 44, 110

Abraham Gerritze Forbes
(c. 1769–1795)
New York, N.Y.

Bibl. 15, 16, 23, 24, 25, 28, 29, 35, 36, 44, 91, 114, 124, 135, 138

Benjamin G. Forbes
(c. 1817–1837)
New York, N.Y.
Fordham & Forbes
(c. 1826–1828)
Bibl. 4, 15, 23, 28, 36, 44, 124, 135, 138

B. G. Forbes

C. & I. W. Forbes
(c. 1810–1825)
New York, N.Y.
Colin & John W. Forbes
(not Garret Forbes)
Bibl. 15, 23, 25, 36, 44, 91, 114, 124, 135, 138

C & I W FORBES

Colin & John W. Forbes
(c. 1825)
New York, N.Y.
C. & I. W. Forbes
Bibl. 15, 23, 25, 36, 44, 124

Colin Van Gilder Forbes
(c. 1808–1839)
New York, N.Y.
Bibl. 4, 15, 23, 25, 28, 29, 36, 44, 91, 95, 114, 124, 135, 138

C FORBES   C V G F

Colin V. G. Forbes & Son
(c. 1826–1838)
New York, N.Y.
Bibl. 15, 23, 24, 25, 29, 36, 44, 91, 114, 116, 124, 135, 138

FORBES & SON
FORBES & SON

Garret Forbes
(b. 1785–d. 1851)
New York, N.Y. (c. 1808)
Bibl. 4, 15, 23, 25, 28, 29, 35, 36, 44, 83, 91, 95, 114, 124, 135, 138

G. FORBES

J. W. Forbes & Co.
(c. 1819)
New York, N.Y.
John W. Forbes
Bibl. 15, 91, 134, 138

John Wesley or Wolfe Forbes
(b. 1781–d. 1864)
New York, N.Y.
(c. 1808–1838)
J. W. Forbes & Co. (c. 1819)
Bibl. 2, 4, 15, 23, 24, 25, 28, 29, 30, 35, 39, 54, 83, 91, 95, 102, 104, 116, 122, 124, 135, 151

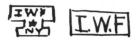

I.W. FORBES

L. Forbes & Co.
(c. 1840–1865)
St. Louis, Mo.
Leonard Forbes
Bibl. 54, 91, 134, 155

L. FORBES & CO.

William Garret Forbes
(b. 1751–1840)
New York, N.Y.
(w. 1773–1830)
Bibl. 4, 15, 23, 24, 25, 28, 29, 30, 35, 36, 39, 44, 50, 54, 83, 91, 95, 104, 114, 116, 122, 124, 135, 138

Jabez W. Force
(c. 1819–1839)
New York, N.Y.
Wood & Force `J W FORCE`
(c. 1839–1841)
Bibl. 15, 23, 24, 25, 29, 36, 44, 114, 124, 138

`FORCE`

S. Forcheimer (1851)
New Orleans, La.
Bibl. 141

—————— **Ford** (c. 1879)
New Haven, Conn.
Bibl. 2

Ford & Brother (c. 1847)
Oswego, N.Y.
Bibl. 20   `FORD & BROTHER`

Ford & Carpenter
(c. 1904–1915)
New York, N.Y.
Successor to Baldwin, Ford & Co.
Became Cohen & Rosenberger
Bibl. 127

Asa R. Ford (c. 1827)
Sackets Harbor, N.Y.
Bibl. 20, 124

George H. Ford
New Haven, Conn.
Benjamin & Ford
(c. 1828–1874?)
Bibl. 28

James M. Ford
(19th century)
Location unknown
Bibl. 28

Samuel Ford
Philadelphia, Pa. (c. 1797)
Baltimore, Md.
(c. 1802–1803)   `S F`
Bibl. 3, 4, 23, 24, 25, 28, 36, 38, 44, 114

William Ford (c. 1848)
Philadelphia, Pa.
Bibl. 3

William Forde
(c. 1820–1828)

Philadelphia, Pa.
Bibl. 3

Fordham & Forbes
(c. 1826–1828)
New York, N.Y.
Merrit Fordham
Benjamin G. Forbes
Bibl. 15, 124, 138

Merrit Fordham
(c. 1827–1833)
New York, N.Y.
Fordham & Forbes
(c. 1826–1828)
Bibl. 15, 124, 138

Alexander Forest (c. 1802)
Baltimore, Md.
Bibl. 23, 36, 44

Formality
(See Silver Counselors of Home Decorators, Inc.)

Benoni B. Forman
Albany, N.Y.
(c. 1813–1815, c. 1834–1846)
Troy, N.Y. (c. 1846 1848)
Bibl. 20, 23, 28, 36, 44, 91, 114, 124   `B. B. FORMAN`

Alexander (Alex) Forrest
(c. 1802–1803)
Baltimore, Md.
Bibl. 4, 28, 38, 44

Christian Forrey (c. 1773)
Lancaster, Pa.
Bibl. 3

J. Silas Fors
(c. 1839–1851)
Wheeling, Va.
Bibl. 19

Orlando C. Forsyth
(c. 1810)
New York, N.Y.
(c. 1835–1837)
Bibl. 24, 91, 95, 124

George H. Forsythe
(c. 1843–1848)
Louisville, Ky.
Bibl. 32, 54, 68, 93

Anthony Fortune
(c. 1767)
Philadelphia, Pa.
Bibl. 3, 23, 36, 44

Fortunoff Silver Sales of Westbury, Inc.
(1922–present)
Westbury, N.Y.
Bibl. 141

R. K. or J. M. ? Foss
Boston, Mass.
Lincoln & Foss (c. 1850)
Haddock, Lincoln & Foss
(c. 1850–1865)
Bibl. 91, 114

Foster
(See Phillips & Foster)

Foster & Bailey
(1878–1898)
Providence, R.I.
Theodore W. Foster
Samuel H. Bailey
Successor to White & Foster
(c. 1873–1878)
White, Foster & Co.
(c. 1878)
Became Theodore W. Foster & Bros. Co.
(1898–c. 1951)
Bibl. 114, 127   **F. & B.**

Foster & Fogle
(c. 1835–1837)
Milledgeville, Ga.
(c. 1835–1837)
Columbus, Ga.
W. Foster
Jacob Fogle
Bibl. 17

Foster & Purple
(c. 1844–1845)
Columbus, Ga.
W. Foster
Samuel B. Purple
Bibl. 17, 91

Foster & Richards
(c. 1815)   `J. F.`
New York, N.Y.
John Foster   `T. RICHARDS`
Thomas Richards
Bibl. 24, 25, 44, 91, 124

Foster & Ward (c. 1840)
Columbus, Ga.
W. Foster
———— Ward
Bibl. 17

Abraham Foster (b. 1728)
Philadelphia, Pa.
(c. 1800–1816)
Boston, Mass.
*Bibl. 3, 23, 28, 36, 39, 44,
110*

Andrew Foster (1875)
Machias, Me.
Bibl. 105

Carl Foster (c. 1831–1833)
Philadelphia, Pa.
Bibl. 3

Chandler Foster
(c. 1832–1840)
Albany, N.Y.
Bibl. 20, 124

Elliott K. Foster
(c. 1829–1843)
Indianapolis, Inc.
Bibl. 133   FOSTER

E.K. FOSTER

George B. Foster
(b. 1810–d. 1881)
Boston, Mass. (c. 1840)
Salem, Mass. (c. 1837–1840)
*Bibl. 23, 25, 28, 36, 44, 72,
91, 114*

GEORGE B FOSTER

G FOSTER

Henry Foster (c. 1841)
New York, N.Y. (c. 1838)
Savannah, Ga.
Bibl. 17, 138

Hiram Foster
(c. 1817–1818)
Philadelphia, Pa.
Bibl. 3, 23, 36

Jeremiah Foster
(b. 1791–d. 1823)
Hopkinsville, Ky.
Bibl. 32, 54, 68, 93

John Foster
New York (c. 1811–1817)
Winchester, Va.
(c. 1817–c. 1825)
Woodstock, Va. (c. 1825)
Martinsburg, Va.
(c. 1827–1835)
Foster & Richards (c. 1815)
Phillips & Foster (c. 1817)
*Bibl. 15, 19, 23, 24, 25, 29,
36, 44, 91, 114, 124, 138*

J. FOSTER

John A. Foster (1860)
Machias, Me.
Bibl. 105

Joseph Foster
(b. 1760–d. 1839)
Boston, Mass.
(c. 1789, 1798–1839)
*Bibl. 2, 4, 15, 23, 24, 25, 28,
36, 44, 54, 72, 80, 91, 94,
102, 110, 114, 116, 138,
151*

FOSTER   I. FOSTER

**Nathaniel & Thomas
Foster** (c. 1820–1860)
Newburyport, Mass.
*Bibl. 14, 15, 23, 25, 28, 36,
44, 91, 110, 114*

N &T. FOSTER

Samuel Foster
(c. 1676–1702)
Boston, Mass.
Bibl. 23, 28, 36, 44, 110

**Theodore W. Foster &
Bro. Co.**
(c. 1898–1951)
Providence, R.I.
Successor to White & Foster
(c. 1873–1878)
White, Foster & Co.
(c. 1878)
Foster & Bailey
(c. 1878–1898)
Bibl. 120, 127, 157

F. & B.

Thomas Foster
(b. 1799–d. 1887)
Newburyport, Mass.
(c. 1823)
*Bibl. 15, 24, 25, 28, 29, 36,
44, 91, 110, 114*

T. FOSTER

W. Foster (c. 1835–1845)
Columbus, Ga.
Foster & Fogle
(c. 1835–1837)
Foster & Ward (c. 1840)
Foster & Purple
(c. 1844–1845)
Bibl. 17

W. K. Foster (1861)
Bangor, Me.
Bibl. 105

Louis Fouche (1822)
New Orleans, La.
Bibl. 141

———— **Fournier** (c. 1796)
Philadelphia, Pa.
Bibl. 3

Fourniquet & Wheatley
(c. 1815)
New York, N.Y.
Louis Fourniquet
Frederick G. Wheatley
*Bibl. 15, 23, 36, 44, 91, 124,
138*

**Louis (Lewis)
Fourn(i)(e)quet**
(d. 1825)
New York, N.Y.
(c. 1795–1823)
Fourniquet & Wheatley
*Bibl. 15, 23, 24, 25, 28, 29,
35, 36, 44, 54, 72, 91, 114,
124, 138*

Fowle & Kirkland
(c. 1828–1833)
Northampton, Mass.
Nathaniel Fowle
Samuel W. Kirkland
Bibl. 84, 91

Nathaniel Fowle
(b. 1748–d. 1817)
Northampton, Mass.
(c. 1819–1820,
c. 1833–1850)
Fowle & Kirkland
(c. 1828–1833)
Bibl. 84, 91, 110

Gilbert Fowler
(c. 1825–1830)
New York, N.Y.
DeForest & Fowler (?)
Bibl. 15, 23, 36, 44, 124, 138

Wells Fowler (c. 1855)
Clarksville, Tenn.
Bibl. 54

Andrew W. Fox (c. 1843)
Hartford, Conn.
Bibl. 23

Asa Fox
Buffalo, N.Y. (c. 1811)
Leroy, N.Y. (c. 1815)
Bibl. 20, 124

DeForest Fox
(c. 1846–c. 1850)
Troy, N.Y.
Bibl. 20, 124

John Fox (c. 1809)
Philadelphia, Pa.
Bibl. 3

John T. Fox
(c. 1841–c. 1850)
Rochester, N.Y.
Brooklyn, N.Y. (?)
C. A. Burr & Co. (c. 1863)
Bibl. 20, 41, 124

Foxcroft & Clark
(c. 1831–1839)
Baltimore, Md.
James A. Foxcroft
Gabriel D. Clark
Bibl. 83

James A. Foxcroft
(c. 1822–1839)
Baltimore, Md.
Foxcroft & Clark
(c. 1831–1839)
Bibl. 38

G. F. Foy & Co. (c. 1850)
Location unknown
Bibl. 89   G. F. FOY & CO.

Thomas Fradgley (c. 1797)
New York, N.Y.
Bibl. 23, 36, 44, 124, 138

J. F. Fradley & Co.
(c. 1867–1936)
New York, N.Y.
Bibl. 114, 127, 157

TRADE MARK

Basil Francis
(c. 1766–1768)
Baltimore, Md.
Bibl. 3, 38

Edward Francis
(c. 1828–1837)
Leesburg, Va.
Bibl. 15, 19, 114   E. FRANCIS

Julius C. Francis
(b. 1785–d. 1858)
Middletown, Conn.
Hughes & Francis
(c. 1807–1809)
Bibl. 16, 23, 28, 36, 44, 110

Justus Francis (c. 1850)
Hartford, Conn.
Bibl. 23

Nathaniel Francis
(c. 1805–1828)
New York, N.Y.
*Bibl. 15, 23, 24, 25, 28, 29,
30, 35, 36, 44, 91, 114,
124, 138*   N.FRANCIS

N. FRANCIS

FRANCIS

Thomas Francis
(c. 1841–1848)
Philadelphia, Pa.
Bibl. 3

George Franciscus Sr.
(c. 1776–1791,
d. 1791)
Baltimore, Md.
*Bibl. 15, 23, 25, 29, 36, 38,
44, 114*

G. FRANCISCUS

George Franciscus Jr.
Baltimore, Md.
(c. 1810–1818)
Lancaster, Pa.
(c. 1819–1840)
Bibl. 15, 25, 28, 38, 44, 112

G. FRANCISCUS

Aug. C. Frank Co., Inc.
(1894–present)
Philadelphia, Pa.
Medal division transferred to
Medallic Art Company
(1972)
Bibl. 127

Jacob Frank(s)
(c. 1785–1794)
Philadelphia, Pa.
Bibl. 3, 24, 25, 36, 44, 114

J·FRANK

Frankland & Cordell
(c. 1822)
Warrenton, Va.
—— Frankland
William B. Cordell (?)
Bibl. 19

The Franklin Mint
(1963–present)
Franklin Center, Pa.
Bibl. 127

J. & S. Franks (c. 1850)
Philadelphia, Pa.
Bibl. 3

Jacob Franks
(c. 1845–1849)
Philadelphia, Pa.
Bibl. 3

William Franks (c. 1839)
Philadelphia, Pa.
Bibl. 3, 36, 44

William Fran(c)ks
(c. 1839–1840)
Philadelphia, Pa.
Bibl. 3, 23

Frantz & Opitz
(1880–1897)
New Orleans, La.
Bibl. 141

Frantz Brothers & Co.
(1898–1902)
New Orleans, La.
Bibl. 141

FRANTZ BROS. & CO.

William Frantz & Co.
(1903–1919)
New Orleans, La.
Bibl. 141

William Fraser (c. 1738)
Philadelphia, Pa.
Bibl. 3, 23, 28, 36, 44

William Fraser
(c. 1825–1833)
Philadelphia, Pa.
Bibl. 3

Alexander Frazer
(Frazier)
Paris, Ky. (c. 1799)
Lexington, Ky.
(c. 1803–1810)
Phillips & Frazer (c. 1799)
Bibl. 32, 54, 68, 93

H. N. Frazer (c. 1839)
Vienna, N.Y.
Bibl. 20, 124

Robert Frazer (Frazier)
(b. 1759–d. 1851)
Paris, Ky. (c. 1799)
Lexington, Ky.
(c. 1799–1851)
Phillips & Frazer (c. 1799)
Bibl. 32, 54, 68, 93

Robert Frazer Jr.
(c. 1838–1851)
Lexington, Ky.

Bibl. 32, 93

ROBERT FRAZER JR

A. Frazier
(See A. Frazer)

R. Frazier
(See R. Frazer)

Samuel Frazier
(c. 1822–1824)
Baltimore, Md.
Bibl. 38

William Frazier (c. 1824)
Philadelphia, Pa.
Bibl. 3

Frear & Halliwell
(c. 1813–1816)
Poughkeepsie, N.Y.
John B. Frear (?)
George Halliwell
Bibl. 20, 124

John B. Frear (d. 1821)
Poughkeepsie, N.Y.
(c. 1816–1821)
Frear & Halliwell (?)
(c. 1813–1816)
Bibl. 20, 124

Daniel Frederick
(c. 1847–1850)
Philadelphia, Pa.
Bibl. 3

John H. Frederick
(c. 1823–1850)
Philadelphia, Pa.
Bibl. 3

K. L. Frederick (c. 1835)
Philadelphia, Pa.
Bibl. 3

William N. Frederick
(1965–present)
Chicago, Ill.
Bibl. 98

Daniel Fredericks
(c. 1841)
Philadelphia, Pa.
Bibl. 3

Fredline
(See Friedlein)

Noel Freeborn
(c. 1849–1865)
Rhode Island
Bibl. 28, 29, 44, 91, 110

Noel Freeborn (1860)
Wickford, R.I.
Bibl. 108

Freeman & Pollard
(c. 1832–1834)
Norfolk, Va.
Joseph M. Freeman
Lewis R. Pollard
Bibl. 19, 91

FREEMAN & POLLARD

Freeman & Wallin
(c. 1839–1840)
Philadelphia, Pa.
William Freeman
Robert Wallin
Bibl. 15, 25, 44, 91, 114

FREEMAN & WALLIN

J. M. Freeman(s) & Co.
(c. 1843–1844)
Norfolk, Va.
Joseph M. Freeman (?)
Fitch Burwell
Bibl. 19, 28, 29, 44, 91

J. M. FREEMAN & CO

J. M. FREEMAN & CO.

Joel N. Freeman (c. 1860)
Augusta, Ga.
Bibl. 17, 114

J. N. FREEMAN

Joseph M. Freeman
(b. 1806–d. 1882)
Norfolk, Va. (c. 1831–1856)
Freeman & Pollard
(c. 1832–1834)
J. M. Freeman & Co.
(c. 1843–1844) (?)
Bibl. 15, 19, 24, 91

FREEMAN

J. M. FREEMAN

L. Freeman (c. 1830–1860)
Crown Point, Ind.
Valparaiso, Ind.
Bibl. 133   L. FREEMAN

N. A. Freeman (c. 1850)
Richmond, Va.
Bibl. 89, 124

N. A. FREEMAN

Thomas W. Freeman
(d. 1853)
Augusta, Ga. (c. 1841)
Bibl. 17, 91

William Freeman
(c. 1839–1840)
Philadelphia, Pa.
Freeman & Wallin
Bibl. 3, 23, 36, 44

Freemans
(See J. M. Freeman & Co.)

Robert Freeston
(c. 1818–1833)
Philadelphia, Pa.
Bibl. 3

Meyer Freide (c. 1848)
St. Louis, Mo.
Bibl. 64

Freidline
(See Friedlein)

French & Franklin
(c. 1896)
North Attleboro, Mass.
Bibl. 127

G. H. French & Co.
(1920–c. 1939)
North Attleboro, Mass.
Became Ellmore Silver
Company, Inc.
(c. 1939–1960)
Bibl. 127

James Ormsby French
(c. 1771)
Annapolis, Md.
(c. 1783–1785)
Baltimore, Md.

Claude & French
(c. 1783–1785)
Bibl. 38

Matthew French
(c. 1814–1823)
Baltimore, Md.
Bibl. 38

Natalie E. Freund
(1950–1965)
St. Louis, Mo.
Bibl. 155

C. R. Fricke (c. 1820)
Philadelphia, Pa. (?)
Bibl. 89

C. R. Fricke

Fried, Mills & Co., Inc.
(c. 1915–1935)
Newark, N.J.
Bibl. 127, 157

Henry Friedeberg
(c. 1849–1850)
Philadelphia, Pa.
Bibl. 3

Clemens Friedel
(1872–1963)
San Antonio, Tex.
Providence, R.I. (worked for
Gorham 1901–1907)
Los Angeles, Calif. (1908)
Pasadena, Calif. (1909)
Bibl. 120, 140, 144

John L. Friedlein
(c. 1835–1850)
Philadelphia, Pa.
Bibl. 3

Friedman Silver Co., Inc.
(1908–1960)
Brooklyn, N.Y.
Became Gorham (1960)
Bibl. 127, 146

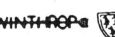

J. Fries (c. 1850)
Location unknown
Bibl. 15, 24, 44, 79

J. & P. Fries (c. 1837)
Philadelphia, Pa.
Bibl. 3

John Fries (c. 1830–1850)
Philadelphia, Pa.
Bibl. 3, 114

P. Fries (c. 1837)
Philadelphia, Pa.
Bibl. 3

James Frith (Frinth)
(c. 1840–1850)
Philadelphia, Pa.
Bibl. 3, 23, 36, 44

C. Fritz (c. 1848–1850)
Philadelphia, Pa.
Bibl. 3

Henry Fritz (b. 1829)
(1860)
New Orleans, La.
Bibl. 141

Benjamin C. Frobisher
(b. 1792–d. 1862)
Boston, Mass. (c. 1834)
Stodder & Frobisher
(c. 1816–1825) (?)
*Bibl. 4, 15, 23, 24, 25, 28,
29, 36, 44, 91, 110, 114*

B. C. Frobisher

FROBISHER

James Frodsham (c. 1845)
St. Louis, Mo.
Bibl. 54, 155

Charles Froeligh
(c. 1857–c. 1860)
Utica, N.Y.
Bibl. 18, 124, 158

Frost & Mum(n)ford
(c. 1810)
Providence, R.I.
William R. Frost
Henry (G.) (B.) Mumford (?)
*Bibl. 23, 24, 25, 28, 29, 36,
44, 110, 114*

B. F. Frost (1875)
Providence, R.I.
Bibl. 108

Chester Frost & Co.
(1875–1895)
Chicago, Ill.
Bibl. 89

S. P. Frost (1860)
Rockland, Me.
Bibl. 105

**Ebenezer Frothingham
(Frotheringham)**
(b. 1756–d. 1814)
Boston, Mass.
Bibl. 23, 28, 36, 44, 54, 110

 E F

C. Fry (c. 1837–1858)
Canton, Ohio
Bibl. 34

N. L. Fry (c. 1844–1848)
Philadelphia, Pa.
Titlow & Fry (c. 1844–1847)
Bibl. 3, 23

John W. Fryer
(c. 1784–1813)
Albany, N.Y.
Balch & Fryer (c. 1784)
*Bibl. 20, 23, 28, 36, 44, 122,
124*

Peter Fryer
Albany, N.Y. (c. 1824–1825)
Norwich, N.Y.
(c. 1828–1830,
1838–1840)
Bibl. 20, 124

Fuchs & Beiderhase
(1891–c. 1896)
New York, N.Y.
Became Alvin Mfg. Co.
Bibl. 114, 127, 157

Ferd. Fuchs & Bros.
(1884–c. 1922)
New York, N.Y.
Ferdinand & Rudolph Fuchs
Bibl. 114, 127, 157

Daniel Christian Fueter
(d. 1785)
New York, N.Y.
(c. 1754–1805)

*Bibl. 4, 15, 24, 25, 28, 29,
36, 44, 54, 95, 104, 114,
116, 118, 119, 124, 135,
138, 151*

David Fueter (c. 1789)
New York, N.Y.
Bibl. 4, 28, 44, 102

Lewis Fueter
(c. 1770–1775)
New York, N.Y.
*Bibl. 4, 15, 23, 24, 25, 29,
35, 36, 44, 54, 91, 95, 102,
114, 116, 124, 135, 138*

L. FUETER

FUETER

Alexander Fuller (c. 1811)
New York, N.Y.
Bibl. 23, 36, 44, 124, 138

Asa C. Fuller
(c. 1834–?)
Utica, N.Y.
Hawley, Fuller & Co.
Bibl. 18, 20, 124, 158

David Fuller
(c. 1854–1855)
Utica, N.Y.
Bibl. 18, 124, 158

F. A. Fuller (c. 1850)
Jamestown, N.Y.
Bibl. 20, 124

George W. Fuller
(c. 1829–1844)
Lewisburg, Va.
(c. 1829–1832)
Staunton, Va.
Bibl. 19

David C. Fulton
(c. 1838–1841)
Louisville, Ky.
Bibl. 32, 54, 93

James C. Fulton
(c. 1838–1861)
Louisville, Ky.
Bibl. 32, 91, 93

Thomas G. Funston
(c. 1850)
Philadelphia, Pa.
Bibl. 3, 23

———— **Furer** (c. 1759)
New York, N.Y.
Bibl. 28

Lewis Furis (c. 1810)
New York, N.Y.
Bibl. 24, 44, 124

Furis

Philip H. Furman
(c. 1821–1842)
Schenectady, N.Y.
Bibl. 20, 91, 124

Charles Furnace
(c. 1837–1838)
Albany, N.Y.
Bibl. 20, 124

Roger Fursden (Fursdon)
(c. 1784)
Charleston, S.C.
Bibl. 5, 44

Moritz Furste (b. 1782)
Philadelphia, Pa.
(c. 1807–1833)
Bibl. 3, 102

Peter Furt (d. 1737)
New York, N.Y.
(c. 1720–1727)
Boston, Mass.
(c. 1727–1737)
Bibl. 23, 36

John W. Fury (c. 1850)
Philadelphia, Pa.
Bibl. 3

Fuselli & Hilburn
(c. 1866–1873)
Bowling Green, Ky.
Peter Fuselli
Jonas Jacob Hilburn
Bibl. 54, 93

Fuselli & McGoodwin
(c. 1873–1885)
Bowling Green, Ky.
Peter Fuselli

I. D. McGoodwin
Bibl. 54, 93

Fuselli & Valenti
(late 19th century)
Bowling Green, Ky.
Peter Fuselli
Philip Valenti
Bibl. 54, 93

Peter Fuselli
(c. 1850–1880)
Bowling Green, Ky.
Fuselli & Valenti
Fuselli & Hilburn
(c. 1866–1873)
Fuselli & McGoodwin
(c. 1873–1885)
Bibl. 54, 93

Fuselli
(See also McLure & Fusselli)

G

G
(See George Bell Co., F. S.
Gilbert, Frances M.
Glessner, Goldman
Silversmiths Co., A. T.
Gunner Mfg. Co.)

G & D
(See Goodwin & Dodd)

G & H
(See Gale & Hayden)

G & M
(See Gale & Mosely)

G & S
(See Gale & Stickler)

G & W
(See Grosjean & Woodward)

G. Mfg. Co.
(See Ginnell Mfg. Co.)

G A
(See George Aiken)

G B
(See George Bardick,
Geradus Boyce)

G B O
(See Gerrit Onclebagh)

G C
(See George Cannon, Gideon
Casey)

G D
(See George Dowig, George
Drewry)

G E H
(See Geo. E. Homer)

G F
(See George Fielding)

G G
(See Greenberry Griffith)

G H
(See George Hanners Jr.,
George A. Henckel & Co.)

G H F
(See G. H. French & Co.)

G J
(See Goodnow & Jenks)

G L
(See Gabriel Lewyn)

G R
(See George Ridout, George
W. Riggs)

G R D
(See George R. Downing)

G S
(See Gould Silver Co.,
George Sharp, Godfrey
Shiving, George Stephens)

G S A
(See Godinger Silver Art Co.,
Ltd.)

G T
(See George Tyler)

Joseph Gaddy (c. 1772)
Halifax, N.C.
Bibl. 21

Henry L. Gadeken
(c. 1845–1850)
Philadelphia, Pa.
Bibl. 3

Gaely
(See Geley)

John Gaffney
(c. 1827–1829)
Charleston, S.C.
Bibl. 5

J. Gafkins (c. 1832)
Providence, R.I.
Bibl. 23, 36, 44

W. B. Gainey (c. 1859)
Pendleton, S.C.
Bibl. 5

Greenbury Gaither
(c. 1822–1834)
Washington, D.C.
Bibl. 23, 25, 36, 44, 72, 114

J. W. Gaither
(c. 1843–1855)
Greenville, S.C.
Cooper & Gaither
Bibl. 5

John Gaither (c. 1811)
Alexandria, Va.
Griffith & Gaither
(c. 1809–1811) (?)
Bibl. 19, 91

———— **Galbard**
(19th century)
Philadelphia, Pa. (?)
Bibl. 89

| Galbard |

Patrick Galbraith
(**Gilbraith**)
Philadelphia, Pa.
(c. 1794–1817)
Bibl. 3

Gale & Hayden (c. 1848)
New York, N.Y.
Charleston, S. C.
William Gale

—— Hayden
*Bibl. 4, 15, 23, 24, 25, 28,
29, 44, 104, 114, 138*

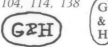

Gale & Moseley
(c. 1828–1833)
New York, N.Y.
William Gale
Joseph Moseley   G&M
*Bibl. 5, 23, 24, 25, 28, 29,
36, 44, 91, 104, 114, 124,
135, 138*

Gale & Stickler (c. 1823)
New York, N.Y.
William Gale
John Stickler | G & S |
*Bibl. 23, 24, 25, 29, 36, 44,
114, 124, 135, 138*

Gale & Willis
(c. 1860–1862)
New York, N.Y.
William Gale
—— Willis
*Bibl. 23, 24, 25, 28, 36, 44,
91, 104, 114, 116, 124,
135, 138*

| GALE & WILLIS |

Gale, Wood & Hughes
(c. 1833–1845)
New York, N.Y.
William Gale
Jacob Wood | G. W & H |
Jasper W. Hughes
*Bibl. 4, 15, 23, 24, 25, 28,
29, 36, 44, 91, 114, 124,
135, 138*

J. L. & O. W. Gale
(c. 1826)
New York, N.Y.
John L. Gale
O. W. Gale
Bibl. 15, 124, 138

John L. Gale
(c. 1816–1837) | J. GALE |
New York, N.Y.
Heyer & Gale | J. L. G. |
(c. 1800–1807)
J. L. & O. W. Gale
(c. 1826)

*Bibl. 4, 15, 23, 28, 29, 36,
44, 114, 124, 138*

| J. L. GALE |

John S. Gale (c. 1825)
New York, N.Y.
Bibl. 15, 23, 36, 39, 124, 138

| J. GALE |

Joseph Gale
(c. 1788–1799)
Fayetteville, N.C.
Lord & Gale (c. 1792)
Bibl. 21

O. W. Gale
New York, N.Y.
J. L. & O. W. Gale (c. 1826)
Bibl. 15

William Gale
(b. 1799–d. 1867) | W. G. |
New York, N.Y.
Gale & Stickler (c. 1823)
Gale & Moseley
(c. 1828–1833) | W G |
Gale, Wood & Hughes
(c. 1833–1844)
Gale & Hayden (c. 1848)
Gale & Willis
(c. 1860–1862)
*Bibl. 4, 15, 23, 25, 28, 29,
35, 36, 44, 54, 91, 104,
114, 116, 122, 124, 135,
138*

William Gale Jr.
(b. 1825, c. 1844–1850)
New York, N.Y.
*Bibl. 23, 25, 29, 36, 44, 91,
116, 124, 135, 138*

| WM. GALE JR. |

William Gale & Son   W. G.
(c. 1850–1870)
New York, N.Y.   G & S
*Bibl. 24, 25, 28, 29, 35, 36,
39, 44, 78, 83*

W. GALE & SON | W. G & S |

Gallard & Co.
(c. 1811–1822)
Philadelphia, Pa.
Peter Gallard (?)
Bibl. 3

Peter Gallard (Gillard)
(c. 1807–1811)
Philadelphia, Pa.
Gallard & Co.
(c. 1811–1822) (?)
Bibl. 3, 91

C. Gallome (c. 1819)
Baltimore, Md.
Bibl. 38

**Christopher Gallup
(Gallop) (Gullup)**
(b. 1764–d. 1849)
North Groton (Ledyard),
Conn.
*Bibl. 16, 23, 28, 36, 44, 92,
110*

Galt & Bro., Inc.
(1934–present)
Washington, D. C.
Successor to
James Galt (1802–1847)
M. W. Galt & Bro.,
(1847–1879)
M. W. Galt, Bro. & Co.
(1879–1892)
Galt & Bro. (1892–1934)
Bibl. 127, 130

James Galt
(b. 1741–d. 1800)
Richmond, Va.
(c. 1766–1771)
Bibl. 19

James Galt (d. 1847)
Alexandria, Va.
(1802–1847)
Bibl. 19, 135, 153

Peter Galt
(b. 1777–d. 1830)
Baltimore, Md.
(c. 1800–1825)
Bibl. 38

Samuel Galt
(b. 1700–d. 1761)
Mill Creek, Va. (c. 1738)
Hampton, Va.
(c. 1749–1751)
Williamsburg, Va.
(c. 1751–1759)
Bibl. 19, 23, 36, 44, 153

Stirling Galt
(c. 1802–1830)
Baltimore, Md.
Bibl. 38

William Galt (b. 1723)
Yorktown, Va. (c. 1751)
Alexandria, Va. (c. 1791)
Williamsburg, Va.
Bibl. 19

J. A. Galtz (c. 1855)
Nashville, Tenn.
Bibl. 54

Charles Gamble
(c. 1847–1849)
Philadelphia, Pa.
Bibl. 3

James Gamble & Son
(c. 1852)
Gamble & Son
Charleston, S.C.
James Gamble
Richard J. Gamble
Bibl. 5

Richard J. Gamble
(c. 1849–1852)
Charleston, S.C.
James Gamble & Son
Gamble & Son
Bibl. 5

Hugh Ganley
(c. 1842–1847)
Utica, N.Y.
Bibl. 18, 20, 124, 158

Aaron Gannet
(c. 1842–1844)
Troy, N.Y.
Bibl. 20, 124

Albert J. Gannon
(c. 1906–1914)
Philadelphia, Penn.
Bibl. 127, 157

John Gard (c. 1849–1850)
Philadelphia, Pa.
Bibl. 3, 23

Garden Silversmiths
(c. 1966–present)
Hollis, N. Y.
Successor to Arrowsmith
Silver Corp.

Own dies of Apollo and
Bernard Rice's Sons
Bibl. 127, 146

Francis Garden (c. 1745)
Boston, Mass.
Bibl. 28, 94, 110

B. Gardiner & Co.
(c. 1840)
New York, N.Y.
Bibl. 23, 24, 25, 29, 36, 44, 83, 91, 114, 124, 135, 138

| B. G. & Co |
| B GARDINER & CO |

Baldwin Gardiner
Philadelphia, Pa.
(c. 1814–1817)
New York, N.Y.
(c. 1827–1838)
Fletcher & Gardiner
(c. 1815–1822)
Bibl. 3, 4, 15, 23, 24, 28, 29, 35, 44, 54, 83, 91, 102, 104, 114, 116, 122, 124, 138

| B GARDINER | B. G |

J. & A. Gardiner
(c. 1853–1861)
St. Louis, Mo.
Bibl. 54, 91, 155

John Gardiner (Gardner)
Boston, Mass. (?) | I G |
(c. 1730–1776)
New London, Conn.
(c. 1734–1776)
Bibl. 2, 15, 16, 23, 24, 25, 28, 29, 36, 44, 61, 69, 91, 92, 110, 114, 119

| J. GARDINER |
| J: GARDINER |

Sidney Gardiner (Gardner)
Boston, Mass. (before 1810)
Philadelphia, Pa.
(c. 1810–1825)
Fletcher & Gardiner

Bibl. 3, 23, 28, 36, 44, 91, 95, 102, 110, 116, 122, 149, 151

Barzillai Gardner
(b. 1778)
Charlotte, N.C.
(c. 1807–?)
McBride & Gardner
(c. 1807)
Bibl. 22

Benjamin F. Gardner
(c. 1817)
Nantucket Island, Mass.
Bibl. 12, 44, 110

George Gardner
(c. 1841–1842)
Philadelphia, Pa.
Bibl. 3

John Gardner
(See John Gardiner)

Samuel Gardner
(c. 1826–1840)
Syracuse, N.Y.
Bibl. 20, 124

Sidney Gardner
(See Sidney Gardiner)

William W. Gardner
(c. 1858–1859)
Utica, N.Y.
Bibl. 18, 124, 158

Garland & Menard
(c. 1828–1829)
Macon, Ga.
John R. Garland
Alexander Menard
Bibl. 17

John R. Garland
Greenville, S.C.
(c. 1826–1828)
Macon, Ga. (c. 1828–1829)
Greensboro, N.C. (c. 1843)
Charlotte, N.C.
Garland & Menard
(c. 1828–1829)
Rockwell & Garland
(c. 1829)
Bibl. 5, 17, 21

William Garland (c. 1850)
New York, N.Y.?
Bibl. 15, 44, 91, 114

| W GARLAND |

Shavelier Garllow
(c. 1813)
Philadelphia, Pa.
Bibl. 3, 23, 36

Garner & Stewart
(c. 1850)
Lexington, Ky.
Eli C. Garner Sr.
George W. Stewart
Bibl. 32, 54

Garner & Winchester
(c. 1842–1862)
Lexington, Ky.
Eli C. Garner Sr.
Daniel F. Winchester
Bibl. 32, 54, 93, 104

Edwin T. Garner
(c. 1842–1843)
Utica, N.Y.
Bibl. 18, 20, 124, 158

Eli C. Garner (Sr.?)
(b. 1817–d. 1878)
Lexington, Ky.
(c. 1838–1864)
Garner & Winchester
(c. 1842–1862)
Garner & Stewart (c. 1850)
Bibl. 32, 54, 68, 93, 104

G. G. Garner (c. 1808)
Fincastle, Va.
Bibl. 19

George Garner (c. 1850)
Lexington, Ky.
Bibl. 32, 93

John Garner (d. 1832)
Cincinnati, Ohio
(1829–1832)
*Bibl. 23, 34, 36, 44, 54, 90,
152*

—— **Garnsey**
Location unknown
Bibl. 28

Amos Garnsey (1875)
Sanford, Me.
Bibl. 105

David Garnsey (c. 1810)
Frankfort, Ky.
Bibl. 32, 54, 68, 93

S. Garre (c. 1825)
New York, N.Y.
Bibl. 24, 25, 44, 114, 124

| S G | | S GARRE |

Anthony Garren (Gerren)
(c. 1811–1814)
Philadelphia, Pa.
Bibl. 3, 23, 36, 44

Philip Garret(t)
(b. 1780–d. 1851)
Philadelphia, Pa.
(c. 1801–1835)
*Bibl. 3, 15, 23, 24, 25, 28,
29, 36, 39, 44, 46*

| P. GARRETT |

Philip Garret(t) & Son
(c. 1828–1835)
Philadelphia, Pa.
Philip Garret(t)
(b. 1780–d. 1851)
Bibl. 3, 91, 114

Eliakim Garretson
(b. 1762–1827)
Wilmington, Del.
(c. 1785–1800)
Bibl. 25, 30, 44, 114

| E. GARRETSON | | E G |

Garrett & Hartley
(c. 1837)
Philadelphia, Pa.
—— Garrett
Samuel Hartley
Bibl. 3, 23

Garrett & Haydock
(c. 1837–1840)
Philadelphia, Pa.
Bibl. 3

Everard Garrett
(c. 1760–c. 1777)
Chowan County, N.C.
Bibl. 21

Thomas C. Garrett
(c. 1829–1840)
Philadelphia, Pa.
Bibl. 3, 24, 25, 44, 114

| T C GARRETT |

Thomas C. Garrett & Co.
(c. 1841–1850)
Philadelphia, Pa.
Bibl. 3, 23, 29, 36, 44

| T. C. GARRETT & CO. |

Jacob J. Garrigues
(c. 1837)
Philadelphia, Pa.
Bibl. 3

—— **Garrington**
(19th century)
Location unknown
Bibl. 54

John Garrison
(c. 1825–1826)
New York, N.Y.
Bibl. 15, 23, 36, 44, 124, 138

Joseph Garrison
(c. 1836–1838)
New York, N.Y.
Bibl. 15, 124, 138

A. Garroch (c. 1850)
Location unknown
Bibl. 15, 44, 114

| A GARROCH |

Garrow & Dorsey
(c. 1800)
Baltimore, Md.
Philadelphia, Pa.
Bibl. 3, 23, 36, 44

William Garton (c. 1753)
Annapolis, Md.
Bibl. 38

—— **Gaskins**
Location unknown
Bibl. 21

James Gaskins
(c. 1804–1830)
Norfolk, Va.

Portsmouth, Va.
Bibl. 15, 19, 25, 28, 29, 39,
44, 72, 91, 114

W. W. Gaskins (c. 1806)
Norfolk, Va.
Bibl. 23, 24, 25, 29, 36, 44,
114

| W W G |

G. Gast (1868–1870)
New Orleans, La.
Bibl. 141

Gates
(See Goetes)

James Gates (c. 1815)
Chillicothe, Ohio
Bibl. 34

Benjamin Gatfield
(c. 1826)
New York, N.Y.
Bibl. 15, 124, 138

Gatham
(See William Gethen)

G. Gatther (c. 1825)
(probably Greenbury
Gaither)
Bibl. 24

| G. GATTHER |

Peter Gaudechaud
(Goudchaud)
(Gudichaud)
(Godichew)
Philadelphia, Pa.
(c. 1814–1833)
Bibl. 3

Gaultier
(See Gottier)

Gotleib Gause
(c. 1840–1841)
Philadelphia, Pa.
Bibl. 3

J. B. Gaushier (c. 1835)
Philadelphia, Pa.
Bibl. 3

Benjamin Gautier
Norfolk, Va. (c. 1812–1815)
New York, N.Y. (1809)
Bibl. 19, 138

Nicholas Gautier
Norfolk, Va. (c. 1768–?)
Portsmouth, Va.
(c. 1776–1778)
Bibl. 19

Gavett
(See Ward & Govett)

William P. Gaw
(c. 1816–1822)
Philadelphia, Pa.
Widdifield & Gaw
(c. 1820–1822)
Bibl. 3

Charles Gay (c. 1779)
Baltimore, Md.
Bibl. 23, 36, 44, 110

Charles H. Gay (c. 1837)
Athens, Ga.
Bibl. 17

Nathaniel Gay
(b. 1643–d. 1713)
Boston, Mass.
Bibl. 23, 28, 36, 44

S. Gayhart (c. 1846–1849)
Camden, N.J.
Bibl. 3

—— **Gaylord**
(c. 1822–?)
Batavia, N.Y.
Sargent & Gaylord
Bibl. 20

S. Gazlay (c. 1850)
Location unknown

Bibl. 15, 44, 114

S. GAZLAY

Gealey
(See Geley)

Gebelein Silversmiths,
Inc. (1945–present)
Boston, Mass.
Now a retail store in East
Arlington, Vt.
George Gebelein
(1909–1945)
Bibl. 120, 127, 144

STERLING   GEBELEIN   BOSTON

George Gebelein
(1878–1945)
Boston, Mass.
Became Gebelein
Silversmiths, Inc.
(1945–present)
Bibl. 120

GEBELEIN

Charles Geddes (c. 1778)
New York State
Bibl. 3, 124, 138

James Geddes
(See James Geddy)

James Geddy (Geddes)
(b. 1731–d. 1807)
Petersburg, Va.
(c. 1783–1807)
Williamsburg, Va.
James Geddy & Sons
(c. 1790)
Bibl. 15, 19, 25, 44, 114,
118, 153

| I. G |
(I G)
| J G |

James Geddy Jr.
(c. 1789–1803)
Petersburg, Va.
James Geddy & Sons
(c. 1790)
Bibl. 19, 102

James Geddy & Sons
(c. 1790)
Petersburg, Va.
James Geddy
James Geddy Jr.
William Waddill Geddy
Bibl. 19

William Waddill Geddy
  (c. 1790–1811)
Petersburg, Va.
James Geddy & Sons
  (c. 1790)
Bibl. 19

| W W G |

Joseph Gee (c. 1788)
Philadelphia, Pa.
*Bibl. 3, 4, 23, 25, 28, 36, 44,
  72, 102, 114*

| G E E |

Nicholas Geffroy
  (b. 1761–d. 1839)
Newport, R. I.
*Bibl. 24, 25, 28, 29, 36, 44,
  54, 56, 72, 91, 94, 110,
  114, 124, 138*

| N.GEFFROY |

| GEFFROY | | N.GEFFROY |

John G. Gehring
  (c. 1827–1831)
Baltimore, Md.
Bibl. 38

**John Ulrich
  Geissendanner**
  (c. 1737)
Charleston, S.C.
Bibl. 54

Geissler & Delang
  (c. 1869)
Evansville, Ind.
Bibl. 133

GEISSLER & DELANG

Philip L. Geissler & Co.
  (c. 1857–1881)
Evansville, Ind.
Bibl. 133

P.L. GEISSLER & CO.

**Peter Geley (Gealey)
  (Geyley) (Gaely)
  (Gilley)** (d. 1815)
Philadelphia, Pa.
  (c. 1793–1814)
Bibl. 3, 23, 28, 36, 44

Gelston & Co. (c. 1837)
New York, N.Y.
George S. Gelston
*Bibl. 4, 23, 24, 25, 28, 35,
  36, 44, 83, 114, 124, 135*

| GELSTON & CO |

Gelston & Gould
  (c. 1816–1820)
Baltimore, Md.
Hugh Gelston
James Gould
Bibl. 23, 36, 38, 44

Gelston & Treadwell
  (c. 1836)
New York, N.Y.
George S. Gelston
——— Treadwell
*Bibl. 23, 25, 28, 35, 36, 44,
  83*

Gelston, Ladd & Co.
  (c. 1840)
New York, N.Y.
George S. Gelston
——— Ladd
*Bibl. 23, 24, 25, 28, 29, 36,
  44, 91, 114, 124, 135, 138*

| GELSTON LADD&CO |

George P. Gelston
Boston, Mass.
Walcott & Gelston
  (c. 1820–1830)
Bibl. 28

George S. Gelston
  (c. 1833)
New York, N.Y. | GELSTON |
Gelston & Treadwell
  (c. 1836)
Gelston & Co. (c. 1837)
Gelston, Ladd & Co.
  (c. 1840)
*Bibl. 4, 23, 24, 28, 29, 36,
  44, 91, 114, 124, 135, 138*

| G. S. GELSTON |

Henry Gelston (c. 1828)
Boston, Mass.
Bibl. 28, 124, 135

Hugh Gelston
  (b. 1794–d. 1873)

Baltimore, Md. | GELSTON |
Gelston & Gould
Welles & Co.
  (c. 1816–1820)
*Bibl. 25, 28, 29, 38, 44, 91,
  110, 114*

| H U.   GELSTON |

Maltby Gelston (d. 1828)
Boston, Mass.
Walcott & Gelston
Bibl. 28, 91

Welles Gelston
(See Welles & Gelston)

Gem Silver Co.
(See Wilcox-Roth Co.)

Gems 'N' Silver Inc.
  (c. 1984)
Barrington, Mass.
Bibl. 146

W. T. & T. V. Gendar
  (c. 1850)
New York, N.Y.
Bibl. 15, 44, 138

| W. T. & T. V. GENDAR |

Gennet & James
  (c. 1849–1866)
Richmond, Va.
Charles Gennet Jr.
Joseph H. James
Bibl. 19, 91

| GENNET & JAMES |

A. Gennet (c. 1850)
Binghamton, N.Y.
Bibl. 20, 124

Charles Gennet Jr.
  (b. 1807–d. 1887)
Richmond, Va.
  (c. 1837–c. 1866)
Gennet & James
  (c. 1849–1866)
Bibl. 19, 91

| C. GENNET |

| C. GENNET JR. |

W. Gennett (c. 1850–?)
Watertown, N.Y.
Bibl. 20, 124

Genova Silver Co., Inc.
(c. 1950)
New York, N.Y.
Bibl. 127

Arthur R. Geoffroy
(c. 1896–1904)
New York, N.Y.
Bibl. 114, 127, 157

Georgeon (Gorgeon) &
Philipe (c. 1794)
Philadelphia, Pa.
Bernard Georgeon
———— Philipe
Bibl. 3, 23, 36

Bernard Georgeon
(c. 1795–1798)
Philadelphia, Pa.
Georgeon & Philipe
Bibl. 3, 28, 36, 44

Isaac Gere
(b. 1771–d. 1812)
Northampton, Mass.
(c. 1793)
Bibl. 84, 110

Gerg
(See Gery)

Geriung
(See Guerin)

Michael Germain
(b. 1752–d. 1806)
Savannah, Ga.
Bibl. 17

John German
(See John D. Germon)

Joseph German (c. 1819)
Baltimore, Md.
Bibl. 23, 36, 38

George E. Germer
(1868–1936)
New York, N.Y.
Boston, Mass.
Providence, R.I.
Bibl. 111, 120

Greenberry D. Germon
(c. 1813–1833)
Philadelphia, Pa.
Bibl. 3, 4, 23, 28, 36

John D. Germon | I. G. |
(German)
(c. 1785–1825)
Philadelphia, Pa.
Bibl. 3, 4, 15, 23, 24, 25, 28,
29, 36, 39, 44, 91, 95, 114,
116, 151 | Germon |

William Gernon
(1843–1844)
New Orleans, La.
Bibl. 141

Francis Gero (c. 1818)
Philadelphia, Pa.
Bibl. 3, 23, 36

Gerren
(See Garren)

Gerrish & Pearson
(c. 1800)
New York, N.Y.
Bibl. 24, 25, 44, 114

Andrew Gerrish
(b. 1784–d. 1835)
Portsmouth, N.H.
(1800–1810)
Bibl. 15, 44, 110, 114, 125

| A. GERRISH. |

Timothy Gerrish
(b. 1753–d. 1813)
Portsmouth, N.H.
Bibl. 15, 23, 24, 25, 28, 29,
36, 44, 91, 110, 114

Frederick Gerstaecker
(c. 1828)
Cincinnati, Ohio
Bibl. 3, 152

Herman Gery (Gerg)
(c. 1848–1850)
Philadelphia, Pa.
Bibl. 3

Christian Gessler
(c. 1841–1850)
Philadelphia, Pa.
Bibl. 3

Getham
(See William Gethen)

John Ward Gethen
(c. 1811–1814)   I W G
Philadelphia, Pa.
Bibl. 3, 15, 19, 23, 36, 44,
91, 114

William Gethen (Getham)
(Gatham)
(c. 1797–1808)
Philadelphia, Pa.
Bibl. 3, 23, 24, 25, 29, 44,
91, 114 | W GETHEN |

James Getty (c. 1772)
(perhaps James Geddy)
Williamsburg, Va.
Bibl. 23, 36, 44

Peter Getz | P Getz |
(b. 1764–d. 1809)
Lancaster, Pa.
(c. 1782–1792)
Bibl. 3, 23, 24, 25, 29, 36,
39, 44, 91, 110, 114, 118

Geyley
(See Geley)

Caesar Ghiselin (Gisling)
(Griselm)
(b. 1670–d. 1734)
Philadelphia, Pa.
(c. 1700–1715)
Annapolis, Md.
(c. 1715–1728)
Bibl. 3, 23, 24, 25, 28, 29,
36, 38, 44, 54, 81, 95, 114,
116, 118, 119

William Ghiselin (Gisling)
(c. 1782?)
Philadelphia, Pa.
(c. 1751–1762)
*Bibl. 3, 15, 23, 24, 25, 28,
29, 36, 39, 44, 81, 91, 114*

Thomas Gibbons
(c. 1750–1752)
Philadelphia, Pa.
Bibl. 3

Daniel Gibbs (c. 1716)
Boston, Mass.
Bibl. 23, 28, 36, 44, 110

Eli M. Gibbs
(c. 1820–1829)
Norwich, N.Y.
Bibl. 20, 124

**Eliza Gibbs (widow of
John)** (c. 1798)
Providence, R.I.
Bibl. 25

J. N. Gibbs (1830)
Medford, Mass.
Bibl. 106

James Gibbs (c. 1847)
Philadelphia, Pa.
Bibl. 3

John Gibbs
(b. 1751–d. 1797)
Providence, R.I.
*Bibl. 15, 23, 24, 25, 28, 29,
36, 44, 54, 56, 91, 110,
114*

John Firron Gibbs
(b. 1784)
Providence, R.I. (c. 1803)
Bibl. 23, 36, 44, 91, 110

William Giberson
(c. 1823–1825)
Philadelphia, Pa.
Bibl. 3

Gibney & Reade (c. 1847)
New York, N.Y.
Michael Gibney
—— Reade
Bibl. 23, 124

Michael Gibney
(c. 1836–1851)
New York, N.Y.
Gibney & Reade
*Bibl. 15, 23, 25, 28, 44, 114,
124, 127, 138*

Gibson
(See Morgan & Gibson)

Luther R. Gibson
(c. 1851)
Norfolk, Va.
Bibl. 19

Peter Gibson (c. 1702)
Yorktown, Va.
Bibl. 19

Thomas Gibson
Philadelphia, Pa.
(c. 1797–1800)
Charleston, S.C.
James Jack(s) & Co.
Bibl. 5

William Gibson
(c. 1845–1849)
Philadelphia, Pa.
Bibl. 3, 23, 24, 25, 44, 114

Samuel Gideon (c. 1770)
Rhode Island
Bibl. 54

**John Ulrich
Giessendanner**
(c. 1737)
Charleston, S.C.
Bibl. 5, 44

Adelheid E. Giessow
(1929–present)
St. Louis, Mo.
Bibl. 155

Giffing & Sweeney
(c. 1809–1814)
Geneva, N.Y.

William Giffing Jr.
John Sweeney
Bibl. 20, 124

Christopher Giffing
(c. 1815–1835)
New York, N.Y.
*Bibl. 15, 25, 28, 29, 36, 44,
91, 114, 124, 138*

William Giffing Jr.
(c. 1809–1814)
Geneva, N.Y.
Giffing & Sweeney
Bibl. 20, 124

Clifton C. Gifford
(c. 1850)
Rochester, N.Y.
Bibl. 20, 124

Ellis Gifford
(c. 1849–1867)
Fall River, Mass.
Bibl. 15, 25, 44, 91, 110, 114

S. K. Gifford (c. 1836)
Camden, S.C.
Bibl. 5

C. Gigon & Bros. (c. 1839)
Philadelphia, Pa.
Bibl. 3

Gustavus Gigon
(c. 1845–1847)
Philadelphia, Pa.
Bibl. 3

Z. & G. Gigon
(c. 1842–1850)
Philadelphia, Pa.
Bibl. 3

Gilbert
(See also G. W. Shiebler &
Co.)

—— **Gilbert**
(c. 1813–1814)
Manlius, N.Y.
Farr & Gilbert
Bibl. 20

Gilbert & Cunningham
(c. 1839–1840)
New York, N.Y.
*Bibl. 4, 15, 23, 28, 36, 44,
114, 124, 138*

Charles Gilbert
(c. 1835–1837)
Philadelphia, Pa.
Bibl. 3

F. S. Gilbert   STERLING **G**
(c. 1904–1915)
North Attleboro, Mass.
Bibl. 127, 157

Henry Gilbert (c. 1850)
Mt. Morris, N.Y.
Bibl. 20, 124

John Gilbert
(c. 1828–1833)
Philadelphia, Pa.
Bibl. 3

Philo B. Gilbert
(c. 1839–1844)
New York, N.Y.
Bibl. 15, 23, 124

Samuel Gilbert   S G
(b. 1775–d. 1850)
Hebron, Conn. (c. 1798)
*Bibl. 2, 16, 23, 24, 25, 28,
29, 36, 44, 92, 102, 110,
114*

William W. Gilbert
(b. 1746–d. 1818)
New York, N.Y.
(c. 1770–1788)
*Bibl. 4, 15, 23, 24, 25, 28,
29, 35, 36, 44, 54, 83, 91,
104, 114, 124, 138*

WG

W Gilbert   GILBERT

Gilbraith
(See Galbraith)

Edward Giles (c. 1841)
Philadelphia, Pa.
Bibl. 3

Caleb Gill   GILL
(b. 1774–d. 1855)
Hingham, Mass.
*Bibl. 23, 24, 25, 28, 29, 36,
44, 110, 114*

John Gill (b. 1798)
New Bern, N.C.
(c. 1814–c. 1843)
Bibl. 21

Leavitt Gill
(b. 1789–d. 1854)
Hingham, Mass.
(c. 1810–1840)
Bibl. 28, 36, 44, 91, 110

Gillard
(See Gallard)

John Gillaspie (Gillispie)
(c. 1845–1846)
Louisville, Ky.
Bibl. 32, 54, 68, 93

Samuel Gillespie
(c. 1848–1849)
Louisville, Ky.
Bibl. 32, 93

A. B. Gillett
(c. 1850–1880)
Warren, Ohio
Adrian, Mich.
Bloomington, Ill.
Indianapolis, Ind.
Bibl. 133

A.B. GILLETT

Joab Gillett
(c. 1810–1833)
Cazenovia, N.Y.
Bibl. 20, 91, 95, 124

Gilley
(See Geley)

Gillispie
(See Gillaspie)

Benjamin Clark Gilman
(b. 1763–d. 1835)
Exeter, N.H.
*Bibl. 15, 25, 28, 44, 54, 91,
102, 110, 114, 125*

B C G

J. E. Gilman (1860)
Portland, Me.
Bibl. 105

John Ward Gilman   I W G
(b. 1774–d. 1823)
Exeter, N.H. (c. 1792)
*Bibl. 15, 24, 25, 28, 29, 36,
44, 91, 94, 110, 114, 125*

Gilpin & Taylor
(c. 1837–1842)
Philadelphia, Pa.
Bibl. 3

Joseph S. Gilpin
Maysville, Ky.
Bibl. 54, 93

Vincent C. Gilpin
(c. 1837–1843)
Philadelphia, Pa.
Bibl. 3

Ginnell Mfg. Co.
(c. 1915–1922)
Booklyn, N.Y.
Bibl. 127, 157   **G. MFG. CO.**

John B. Ginochio
(c. 1837–1854)
New York, N.Y.
*Bibl. 15, 22, 25, 44, 91, 114,
124, 138*   J B GINOCHIO

**Jean-Baptiste Francois
(John B. F.) Giquel**
(b. 1777–d. 1847)
New Orleans, La.
(1810–1832)
Bibl. 23, 36, 44, 141

Francis Girard (c. 1817)
Philadelphia, Pa.
Bibl. 3, 23, 36, 44

Henry Giraud (Girrad)
(c. 1805)
New York, N.Y.
Bibl. 23, 36, 44, 124, 138

William F. Gird
(c. 1799–1806)
Alexandria, Va.
Bibl. 19

Girrad
(See Giraud)

Stephen Girreaun
(c. 1785)
Philadelphia, Pa.
Bibl. 3, 23, 36, 44

Gisling
(See Ghiselin)

John Gistner
(c. 1794–1796)
Philadelphia, Pa.
Bibl. 3

Thomas Giude (b. 1751)
New York, N.Y. (c. 1774)
Bibl. 28

A. Givan (c. 1849)
Albany, N.Y.
May be G. A. Given
Bibl. 23, 28, 44

G. A. Given (c. 1848–1849)
Albany, N.Y.
Bibl. 20, 124

Glass & Baird (c. 1804)
Raleigh, N.C.
David Glass
David Baird
Bibl. 21

David Glass
(c. 1803–c. 1856)
Raleigh, N.C.
Glass & Baird (c. 1804)
Bibl. 21

Thomas Glass
(c. 1771–1801)
Raleigh, N.C.
Hanover, Va.
Norfolk, Va.
Bibl. 19, 21

Glaze & Radcliff(e)
(c. 1848–1851)
Columbia, S.C.
William Glaze
Thomas W. Radcliffe
Bibl. 5, 44

| GLAZE & RADCLIFF |

William Glaze
(c. 1838–1882)
Columbia, S.C.
Veal & Glaze (c. 1838–1841)

Glaze & Radcliffe
(c. 1848–1851)
Bibl. 5

Gleason & Hovey
(c. 1846–1848)
Rome, N.Y.
F. A. Gleason
J. S. Hovey
Bibl. 20, 124

F. A. Gleason (c. 1848)
Rome, N.Y.
Gleason & Hovey
(c. 1846–1848)
Bibl. 20, 124

R. Gleason & Sons
(1907–1946)
Dorchester, Mass.
Bibl. 135

John W. Gleaves (c. 1850)
Philadelphia, Pa.
Bibl. 3

Herman W. Glendenning
(c. 1920–1971)
Gardner, Mass.
Bibl. 127

Glendenning Sterling
Handwrought

George Glenford (c. 1848)
Philadelphia, Pa.
Bibl. 3

William Glenn (c. 1811)
Philadelphia, Pa.
Bibl. 3

W. H. Glenny & Co.
(c. 1840–1898)
Rochester, N.Y.
Bibl. 127

W. H. Glenny, Sons & Co.
(1840–c. 1898)
Buffalo, N.Y.
Bibl. 127

Frances M. Glessner
(b. 1848–d. 1922)
Chicago, Ill. (c. 1904–1915)
Bibl. 98, 115, 120, 127, 144

Joseph Glidden
(b. 1707–d. 1780)
Boston, Mass.
Bibl. 23, 36, 44, 110

Globe Art Mfg. Co.
(c. 1915–1922)
Newark, N.J.
Bibl. 127, 157

Globe Silver Co.
(c. 1957–1961)
New York, N.Y.
Bibl. 127

Edwin Glover
(c. 1843–1869)
Fayetteville, N.C.
Bibl. 21

Christian Gobrecht
(Gobright)
(c. 1819–1844)
Philadelphia, Pa.
Bibl. 3

Gobright
(See Gobrecht)

────── **Goddard** (c. 1810)
Location unknown
Bibl. 24   (GODDARD)

Benjamin Goddard III
Worcester, Mass.
Bibl. 89, 91

| Benj Goddard |

D. Goddard & Co.
(c. 1845–1850)
Daniel Goddard
(b. 1796–d. 1884)
Worcester, Mass.
Bibl. 15, 25, 91, 110, 114

| D. Goddard & C° |

D. Goddard & Son
(c. 1845)
Daniel Goddard
(b. 1796–d. 1884)
Worcester, Mass.
Bibl. 23, 24, 25, 29, 44

| D. GODDARD & SON |

L. D. Goddard (1840)
Worcester, Mass.
Bibl. 106

Luther Goddard & Son
(c. 1830)
Worcester, Mass.
Bibl. 89, 110

L GODDARD & SON

Nicholas Goddard
(b. 1773–d. 1823)
Rutland, Vt. (c. 1807–1810)
Lord & Goddard
(c. 1797–1810)
Bibl. 54, 91, 110

M. T. Godfrey (c. 1845)
Cambridge, Mass.
Bibl. 23

Godichew
(See Gaudechaud)

**Godinger Silver Art Co.,
Ltd.** (1974–present)
New York, N.Y.
Bibl. 127, 146

Godley & Johnson
(See Johnson & Godley)

Richard Godley
Albany, N. Y.
Johnson & Godley
(c. 1843–1849)
Bibl. 20, 124

Jacob Godschalk (c. 1771)
Philadelphia, Pa.
Bibl. 3

Philip Goelet
(b. 1701–d. 1748)
New York, N.Y. (c. 1731)
*Bibl. 2, 4, 15, 23, 24, 25, 28,
30, 36, 39, 44, 54, 91, 95,
114, 124, 138, 151*

Peter Goetes (Gates)
(c. 1813–1844)
Bardstown, Ky.
Bibl. 32, 54, 68, 93

**Gladys Gertrude Skelly
Goetz**
(c. 1937–1960)
St. Louis, Mo.
Bibl. 155

Charles Goff (1875)
Auburn, Me.
Bibl. 105

Jeremiah Goforth
(c. 1700)
Philadelphia, Pa.
Bibl. 3, 23, 36, 44

**Gold Recovery &
Refining Corp.**
(c. 1940–1945)
New York, N.Y.
Became Dunkirk
Silversmiths, Meriden,
Conn.
Bibl. 127

Golden Wheel
(See Reibling-Lewis, Inc.)

Goldman Silversmiths Co.
(c. 1940–1945)
New York, N.Y.
Bibl. 127

Alexander Goldman
(c. 1920–1930)
New York, N.Y.
Bibl. 127

J. Goldsbrough & Co.
(1895)
Biddeford, Me.
Bibl. 105

M. T. Goldsmith
(c. 1864–1909)
Brooklyn, N.Y.
Bibl. 127

BRITANNIA ARTISTIC SILVER

Thomas Goldsmith
(b. 1823–d. 1885)
Troy, N.Y. (c. 1842–1850)
Bibl. 20

B. Goldstone (c. 1839)
Philadelphia, Pa.
Bibl. 3

Joseph Goldthwaite
(b. 1706–d. 1780)
Boston, Mass.
*Bibl. 2, 15, 23, 24, 25, 28,
29, 36, 44, 70, 94, 104,
110, 114*

James L. Goman
(c. 1847–1848)
Utica, N.Y.
Bibl. 18, 20, 124, 158

John Gombach (c. 1802)
Philadelphia, Pa.
Bibl. 3, 23, 36, 44

Jeremiah Gomph
(1855–c. 1865)
Albany, N.Y. (1855–1862)
Utica, N.Y. (1862–c. 1865)
Bibl. 127

Gontler
(1838–1842)
New Orleans, La.
Bibl. 41

Gooch & Hequembourg
(c. 1845)
St. Louis, Mo.
Bibl. 54, 155

George F. Good (1860)
Saco, Me.
Bibl. 105

Goodby Mfg. Co. (c. 1931)
San Francisco, Calif.
Bibl. 127

Henry Gooddy (c. 1767)
Philadelphia, Pa.
Bibl. 3

L. Goode (c. 1835)
Location unknown
Bibl. 24, 28

L. GOODE

Goodfellow & Son
(c. 1799)
Philadelphia, Pa.
Bibl. 3

William Goodfellow
(c. 1793–1818)
Philadelphia, Pa.
Bibl. 3

A. E. Goodhue
(c. 1950–1957)
Quincy, Mass.
Bibl. 127

Daniel T. Goodhue
(c. 1840)
Boston, Mass.
Bibl. 15, 25, 44, 91, 110

D T GOODHUE	D T G

John Goodhue
(c. 1822–1855)
Salem, Mass.
Bibl. 15, 23, 24, 25, 28, 29, 36, 44, 91, 110, 114

J. GOODHUE

Henry Gooding
(c. 1820–1854)
Boston, Mass.
Bibl. 4, 15, 23, 24, 25, 28, 29, 36, 44, 91, 110, 114

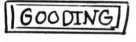

GOODING

Joseph Gooding
(c. 1861)
Boston, Mass.
Bibl. 23, 25, 36, 44

Josiah Gooding
(c. 1841–1859)
Boston, Mass.
Bibl. 15, 25, 28, 29, 44, 114

Josiah Gooding

Goodnow & Jenks
(1893–1905)
Boston, Mass.
Successor to Kennard & Jenks
Bibl. 114, 127, 157

Goodnow & Smith (1840)
Bucksport, Me.
Bibl. 105

—— **Goodrich** (c. 1850)
Philadelphia, Pa
Smith & Goodrich
Bibl. 3

C. W. Goodrich
(c. 1816–1866)
New Orleans, La.
Hyde & Goodrich
Bibl. 54

Erastus H. Goodrich
(c. 1837–1848)
Buffalo, N.Y.
Bibl. 20, 124

Goodwill Mfg. Co.
(c. 1927)
Providence, R.I.
Bibl. 127

Goodwin & Dodd
(1811–1812)
Hartford, Conn.
Horace Goodwin
Thomas Dodd
Bibl. 16, 23, 25, 28, 36, 44, 91, 92, 110, 114

G & D

Allyn Goodwin
(b. 1797–d. 1869)
Hartford, Conn.
H. & A. Goodwin
Bibl. 16, 23, 28, 36, 44, 91, 110

Benjamin Goodwin
(b. 1732–d. 1792)
Boston, Mass.
Easton, Mass.
Bibl. 15, 23, 25, 28, 29, 36, 44, 110, 114

B Goodwin

H. & A. Goodwin
(1821–1825)
Hartford, Conn. | GOODWIN |
Horace & Allyn Goodwin
Bibl. 16, 23, 24, 25, 28, 29, 36, 44, 61, 91, 92, 110, 114

Homer Goodwin (c. 1857)
Cleveland, Ohio
Bibl. 65

Horace Goodwin
(b. 1787–d. 1864)
Hartford, Conn.
(c. 1811–1852)
New Britain, Conn.
Vermont
Goodwin & Dodd
H. & A. Goodwin
Bibl. 16, 23, 28, 36, 44, 91, 92, 94, 110

Ralph Goodwin
(b. 1793–d. 1866)
Hartford, Conn.
Bibl. 16, 23, 28, 36, 44, 110

Samuel Goodwin
(c. 1820–1822)
Philadelphia, Pa.
Bibl. 3

Daniel Gookin (b. 1682)
Boston, Mass. (c. 1696)
Bibl. 54, 102, 110, 119

Gordon & Co. (c. 1849)
Boston, Mass.
Bibl. 4, 23, 28, 44

A. & J. Gordon (c. 1798)
New York, N.Y.
Alexander S. Gordon
James Gordon
Bibl. 4, 23, 28, 36, 44, 124

Alexander S. Gordon
(c. 1795–1803)
New York, N.Y.
A. & J. Gordon (c. 1798)
Bibl. 15, 23, 24, 25, 29, 35, 36, 44, 54, 102, 114, 124, 138

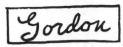

Andrew Gordon (c. 1796)
New York, N.Y.
Bibl. 28, 44

GORDON

G. C. Gordon (c. 1845)
Edgefield, S.C.
Bibl. 5

George Gordon
(c. 1795–1840)
Newburgh, N.Y.
New York, N.Y.
*Bibl. 20, 23, 24, 25, 29, 36,
44, 78, 91, 114, 124, 138*

G Gordon

George Gordon
(c. 1847–1850)
Philadelphia, Pa.
Bibl. 3

George Clinton Gordon
(pre-1840–c. 1847)
Augusta, Ga.
Bibl. 17

James Gordon
(c. 1795–1798)
New York, N.Y.
A. & J. Gordon (c. 1798)
Bibl. 15, 23, 36, 44, 124, 138

James Gordon (c. 1813)
Savannah, Ga.
Bibl. 17

James Samuel Gordon
(c. 1769–1771)
Philadelphia, Pa.
Bibl. 3, 23, 28, 36, 44

John Gore (c. 1832–1835)
New York, N.Y.
Bibl. 15, 124

Gorgeon
(See Georgeon)

GORHAM CHRONOLOGY
Gorham & Beebe
(c. 1825–1831) ?
Gorham & Webster
(1831–1837)
Gorham, Webster & Price
(1837–1841)
J. Gorham & Son
(1841–1850)
Gorham & Thurber
(1850–1852)
Gorham & Co.
(1852–1865)
Gorham Manufacturing Co.
(1865–1961)
Gorham Corporation
(1961–present)

Gorham & Beebe
(c. 1825–1831) ?
Providence, R.I.
Jabez Gorham
Stanton Beebe
Bibl. 25

Gorham & Co.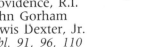
(1852–1865)
Providence, R.I.
John Gorham
Lewis Dexter, Jr.
Bibl. 91, 96, 110

Gorham & Co.

Gorham & Thurber
(1850–1852)
Providence, R.I.
John Gorham
Gorham Thurber
Bibl. 23, 24, 25, 44, 96, 135

Gorham & Thurber

Gorham & Webster
(1831–1837)
Providence, R.I.
Jabez Gorham
Henry Webster
*Bibl. 15, 23, 24, 25, 28, 29,
36, 44, 56, 91, 96, 135*

Gorham & Webster

Gorham Co. and Brown
(1856–1878)
Providence, R.I.
Became Henry T. Brown &
Co.
Bibl. 127

Gorham Corp.
(1961–present)
Providence, R.I.
(Div. of Textron Corp. after
1967)
Bibl. 96, 104, 114, 135, 151

**Gorham Manufacturing
Co.** (1865–1961)
Providence, R.I.
Acquired the following
companies:
Silversmiths Company
(Whiting Manufacturing
Co., William B. Kerr
Company, and William B.
Durgin Company)—1924;
Alvin Silver Co.—1928;
McChesney Co.—1931;
Quaker Silver Co.—1959;
Friedman Silver
Co.—1960; Graff,
Washbourne &
Dunn—1961
Bibl. 85, 91, 96, 135

STERLING

MARK	YEAR	MARK	YEAR
A.	1868	M.	1880
B.	1869	N.	1881
C.	1870	O.	1882
D.	1871	P.	1883
E.	1872	Q.	1884
F.	1873	☁	1885
G.	1874	▣	1886
H.	1875	✿	1887
		⊛	1888
I.	1876	❂	1889
J.	1877	✾	1890
K.	1878	▦	1891
L.	1879	⚘	1892

MARK	YEAR	MARK	YEAR
	1893		1924
	1894		1925
	1895		1926
	1896		1927
	1897		1928
	1898		1929
	1899		1930
	1900		1931
	1901		1932
	1902		1933
	1903		
	1904		
	1905		
	1906		
	1907		
	1908		
	1909		
	1910		1941
	1911		
	1912		
	1913		
	1914		
	1915		
	1916		1951
	1917		
	1918		
	1919		
	1920		
	1921		
	1922		
	1923		

Year marks were discontinued in 1933 and resumed in January 1941 on sterling hollow-ware except lower-priced items.

A square frame indicates the decade of the 1940s. The numeral indicates the year of the decade.

A pentagon indicates the decade of the 1950s with the numeral indicating the year of the decade.

A hexagon indicates the decade of the 60s; a heptagon was used for the 70s; and an octagon for the 80s.

Gorham, Webster & Price
(1837–1841)
Providence, R.I.
Jabez Gorham
Henry L. Webster
William G. Price
Bibl. 15, 25, 44, 91, 96, 135

| Gorham Webster & Price |

J. (Jabez) Gorham & Son
(1841–1850)
Providence, R.I.
Jabez Gorham
John Gorham
Henry Owen Gorham
Bibl. 15, 23, 24, 25, 28, 29, 44, 91, 96, 110, 135

| J Gorham & Son |

| J.G. & Son |

Jabez Gorham
(b. 1792–d. 1869)
Providence, R.I.
(1813–1847)
George C. G. Clark
William Hadwen
Christopher Burr
Henry Mumford | J GORHAM |
Gorham & Beebe
Gorham & Webster
Gorham, Webster & Price
J. Gorham & Son
Bibl. 15, 23, 24, 25, 28, 36, 44, 96

John Gorham (c. 1814)
New Haven, Conn.
Bibl. 16, 23, 28, 36, 92

John Gorham
(b. 1820–d. 1898)
Providence, R.I.
(1841–1878)
J. Gorham & Son
Gorham & Thurber
Gorham & Co.
Gorham Mfg. Co.
Bibl. 15, 23, 28, 44, 96, 114, 116, 122, 135, 143

Jonathan Gorham
(c. 1816)
Nantucket Island, Mass.
Bibl. 12

Miles Gorham
(b. 1757–d. 1847)
New Haven, Conn.
Bibl. 16, 23, 24, 25, 28, 29, 36, 44, 61, 69, 91, 92, 94, 110, 114, 143

| M G | | M GORHAM |

Richard Gorham
(b. 1775–d. 1841)
New Haven, Conn.
Shethear & Gorham
(c. 1806–1808)
Bibl. 16, 23, 28, 36, 44, 92, 116, 143

William Gorrie (c. 1816)
Charleston, S.C.
Bibl. 5

John Goshea (Gosher)
(c. 1824–1833)
Philadelphia, Pa.
Bibl. 3

Gott
(See George Ott)

Francis Gottier (Gaultier)
(d. 1784)
Charleston, S.C.
(c. 1741–1783)
Bibl. 5, 44, 54

Gottschalk & Bolland
(c. 1848)
St. Louis, Mo.
Bibl. 54, 155

Goudchaud
(See Gaudechaud)

Jesse W. Gouge & Co.
(c. 1828)
Philadelphia, Pa.
Bibl. 3

James Gough
(c. 1769–1795)
New York, N.Y.

Bibl. 23, 24, 25, 28, 36, 39,
44, 114, 124, 138

Mel Gouiran
Location unknown
Bibl. 22

Michael Gouiran
(Gowran)
(c. 1820–1833)
Philadelphia, Pa.
Bibl. 3

Gould & Ward (c. 1850)
Baltimore, Md.
James Gould
William H. Ward
Bibl. 24, 25, 36, 38, 44, 114

GOULD & WARD

Gould Silver Co.
Charleston, S.C.
Bibl. 146

Gould, Stowell & Ward
(c. 1855–1858)
Baltimore, Md.
James Gould
A. Stowell Jr.
William H. Ward
Bibl. 23, 36, 38, 44, 102

Edwin F. Gould
Utica, N.Y. (c. 1842–1844)
Cortland, N.Y.
(c. 1846–1847)
Bibl. 18, 20, 124, 158

Ezra B. Gould (c. 1841)
Rochester, N.Y.
Bibl. 20, 124

James Gould
(b. 1795–d. 1874)
Baltimore, Md.
Boston, Mass.
Gelston & Gould
(c. 1816–1820)
Gould, Stowell & Ward
(c. 1855–1858)
Gould & Ward (c. 1850)
Bibl. 23, 24, 25, 29, 36, 38,
44, 110

J. GOULD

John Gould
(c. 1831–1850)
New York, N.Y.
Philadelphia, Pa.
Bibl. 3, 15, 23, 36, 44, 124,
138

L. C. Gould (1860)
Camden, Me.
Bibl. 105

Govert
(See James Govett)

Govett (Gavett)
(See Ward & Govett)

George Govett
(c. 1811–1850)
Philadelphia, Pa.
Bibl. 3

James Govett (Govert)
(c. 1802–1813)
Philadelphia, Pa.
Bibl. 3, 23, 44

John & William Gowdey
(c. 1757–1795)
Charleston, S. C.
Bibl. 44

Thomas Gowdey (Gowdy)
(c. 1853–1855)
Nashville, Tenn.
Bibl. 54

William Gowdey (d. 1798)
Charleston, S.C.
(c. 1757–1795)
John & William Gowdey
Bibl. 5, 25, 54, 114

William Gowen
(b. 1749–d. 1803)
Medford, Mass. (c. 1777)
Charlestown, Mass.
Bibl. 23, 24, 25, 28, 29, 36,
44, 94, 110, 114, 151

W GOWEN   W G

Gowran
(See Gouiran)

Graf & Neimann (c. 1900)
Pittsburgh, Pa.
Bibl. 127

Graff, Washbourne &
Dunn (1899–1961)
New York, N.Y.
Successor to Wood &
Hughes
Became Gorham Corp.
(1961)
Bibl. 127, 144, 147

Gragg & Thayer
(c. 1808–1809)
Troy, N.Y.
Hugh Gragg
Amos Thayer (?)
Bibl. 20

Hugh Gragg
(c. 1808–1809)
Troy, N.Y.
Gragg & Thayer
Bibl. 20

Graham
(See Oliver & Graham)

———— **Graham** (c. 1803)
Portsmouth, Va.
Bibl. 19

Dr. Christopher
Columbus Graham
(b. 1787)
Springfield, Ky. (c. 1812)
Bibl. 20, 32, 54

Daniel Graham (b. 1764)
West Suffield, Conn.
(c. 1789)
Bibl. 16, 28, 36, 44

John Graham
(c. 1837–1840)
Philadelphia, Pa.
Bibl. 3

Mitchell Graham (c. 1837)
Philadelphia, Pa.
Bibl. 3

Samuel Graham
  (c. 1825)
Philadelphia, Pa.
Bibl. 3

William Graham (c. 1733)
Philadelphia, Pa.
Bibl. 3

Christian Grammer
  (c. 1800)
Baltimore, Md.
Bibl. 38

Granat Bros. Inc.
  (c. 1929–present)
San Francisco, Calif.
Bibl. 127

Granat

Misse Grandmaison
  (1822–1827)
New Orleans, La.
Bibl. 141

Grant & Smith
(See Smith & Grant)

Israel Boone Grant
  (c. 1817–1820)
St. Louis, Mo.
Bibl. 54

James Grant (c. 1789)
Albany, N.Y.
Bibl. 20

John Grant
  (b.1793–d 1817)
Savannah, Ga.
Bibl. 17

Thomas Grant
  (b. 1731–d. 1804)
Marblehead, Mass.
Bibl. 15, 23, 24, 25, 28, 29, 36, 44, 72

| T GRANT |

William Grant (Jr.)
  (b. 1766–d. 1809)
Marblehead, Mass.
Bibl. 3, 4, 23, 24, 25, 28, 29, 36, 44

| W Grant |

| W G | (W G)

William Grant (c. 1808)
Lexington, Ky.
Smith & Grant
Bibl. 32

Gerard Graval (c. 1807)
Philadelphia, Pa.
Bibl. 3

Louisa M. Gravelle
  (c. 1820–1830)
Philadelphia, Pa.
Bibl. 3

Rene L. Gravelle
  (c. 1811–1831)
Philadelphia, Pa.
Lefevre & Gravelle
  (c. 1811)
Bibl. 3, 23, 36, 44

Gerrit Graverat (c. 1772)
Detroit, Mich.
Bibl. 58

Graves & Fitch
  (c. 1816–1821)
Auburn, N.Y.
Samuel Graves (?)
James Fitch
Bibl. 20, 25

Graves & Nichols
  (c. 1809–1816)
Cooperstown, N.Y.
Bibl. 20

Graves & Thompson
  (c. 1844)
Winchester, Va.
George B. Graves
William Thompson
Bibl. 19

George B. Graves (c. 1840)
Winchester, Va.
Graves & Thompson
  (c. 1844)
John L. Albert (c. 1827)
Bibl. 19

George W. Graves
  (c. 1848)

Winchester, Va.
Bibl. 19

Jesse Graves
  (c. 1804–1847)
Cooperstown, N.Y.
Bibl. 20

Samuel Graves
Auburn, N.Y.
  (c. 1816–1823)
Batavia, N.Y. (c. 1824)
Graves & Fitch
  (c. 1816–1821) (?)
Bibl. 20

Thomas Graves
  (c. 1828–1830)
Cincinnati, Ohio
Bibl. 23, 44, 152

Nicholas Gravier
  (c. 1822)
New Orleans, La.
Bibl. 23, 36, 44

Gray & Libby (c. 1850)
Location unknown
Bibl. 28

Charles Gray (b. 1749)
Maryland (c. 1774)
Bibl. 28, 38

———— **Gray** (c. 1850)
Cleveland, Ohio
Bibl. 65

G. Gray (c. 1839)
Portsmouth, N.H.
Bibl. 23, 24, 25, 28, 29, 36, 44

| G. GRAY |

Henry A. Gray (c. 1854)
Edgefield, S.C.
Bibl. 5

Jeremiah Gray (1860)
Richmond, Me.
Bibl. 105

John Gray
  (b. 1692–d. 1720)
New London, Conn.
Boston, Mass.

Bibl. 4, 16, 23, 24, 25, 28, 29, 36, 44, 50, 70

John Gray (c. 1811)
Philadelphia, Pa.
Bibl. 3

R. B. Gray & Company
(1855–1872)
San Francisco, Calif.
Bibl. 127

Robert Gray
(b. 1792–d. 1850)
Portsmouth, N.H (c. 1830)
Bibl. 15, 23, 24, 25, 28, 29, 36, 44, 91, 110, 114, 125

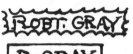

Samuel Gray
(b. 1684–d. 1713)
New London, Conn.
Boston, Mass.
Bibl. 15, 16, 23, 24, 25, 28, 29, 36, 44, 54, 61, 92, 94, 110, 114

Thomas Gray
(c. 1818–1820)
Lexington, Ky.
Bibl. 32, 54, 68, 93

William Gray
(b. 1772–d. 1803)
Charleston, S.C. (c. 1800)
Bibl. 5

William H. Gray
(c. 1845–1846)
Philadelphia, Pa.
Bibl. 3

A. W. Greeley
(1875–1890)
Ellsworth, Me.
Bibl. 105

Green
(See Fellows & Green,
Lincoln & Green, Whitaker
& Green[e])

—————— **Green** (c. 1843)
Hartford, Conn.
Bibl. 23

Bartholomew Green
(b. 1697–d. 1738)
Boston, Mass.
Bibl. 15, 28, 110, 114

B: GREEN

Benjamin Green(e)
(b. 1712–d. 1776)
Boston, Mass.
Bibl. 15, 24, 28, 29, 36, 94, 110, 114

B: GREEN

Edward Green (c. 1826)
Fairfax, Va.
Bibl. 19

G. Green (1840)
Clinton, Mass.
Bibl. 106

Glover Green (c. 1844)
Philadelphia, Pa.
Bibl. 3

James Green
(c. 1797–1798)
Albany, N.Y.
Bibl. 20, 124

James Green (c. 1764)
Savannah, Ga.
New York, N.Y. (c. 1805)
Bibl. 23, 36, 44, 124, 138

John Green
(c. 1794–1796)
Philadelphia, Pa.
Bibl. 3

John N. Green
(c. 1830–1842)
Baltimore, Md.
Bibl. 38

Josiah B. Green
(c. 1847–1850)
Leesburg, Va.
Bibl. 19

Rufus Green(e)
(b. 1707–d. 1777)
Boston, Mass.
Bibl. 2, 4, 15, 23, 24, 25, 28, 29, 36, 44, 54, 69, 70, 94, 110, 114, 119

William Greenawalt
Halifax, N.C.
Bibl. 21

Gaither Greenburg
(c. 1820)
Washington, D.C.
May be Greenberg Gaither.
Bibl. 44

William C. Greence & Co.
(1875)
Providence, R.I.
Bibl. 108

Greene & Bros.
(c. 1835–1837)
Philadelphia, Pa.
New York, N.Y.
(c. 1839–1840)
Bibl. 3, 138

William Greene
(c. 1837–1841)
Philadelphia, Pa.
Bibl. 3, 124

William Greene & Co.
(c. 1815)
Providence, R.I.
Bibl. 23, 28, 36, 44

Max Greener
(19th century)
Shelbyville, Ky.
Bibl. 32, 54, 93

Greenleaf & Crosby
(1867–c. 1920)
Jacksonville, Fla.
Bibl. 126

Benjamin Greenleaf
(b. 1756?–d. 1780)
Newburyport, Mass.
(c. 1756)
Bibl. 15, 110

David Greenleaf
(b. 1737–d. 1800)
Hartford, Conn.
Norwich, Conn.
Boston, Mass.
*Bibl. 15, 16, 23, 24, 25, 29,
36, 44, 91, 92, 110, 114*

D Greenleaf

GREENLEAF

David Greenleaf Jr.
(b. 1765–d. 1835)
Hartford, Conn.
Frederick Oakes
*Bibl. 15, 16, 23, 25, 28, 29,
36, 44, 61, 91, 92, 94, 110,
114*

GREENLEAF

D. GREENLEAF

D.G

George Greenleaf
(b. 1790–d. 1850)
Newburyport, Conn.
Bibl. 54, 110

G Greenleaf

Joseph Greenleaf
(d. 1798)
New London, Conn.
(c. 1778–1798)
Bibl. 15, 16, 23, 28, 44, 110

Daniel Greenough
(b. 1685/6–d. 1746)
Newcastle, N.H.
(c. 1710–1714)
Portsmouth, N.H.
*Bibl. 28, 54, 102, 110, 119,
125, 135*

Charles F. Greenwood
(b. 1858–d. 1904)
Norfolk, Va.
C. F. Greenwood & Bro.
(c. 1851)
Bibl. 19

C. F. GREENWOOD

C. F. Greenwood & Bro.
(c. 1851)
Norfolk, Va.
Charles F. Greenwood
Frederick Greenwood
Bibl. 19

John Greer (d. 1774)
Carlisle, Pa.
Bibl. 3

Peter Greffin (c. 1801)
Philadelphia, Pa.
Bibl. 3, 23, 36, 44

—— **Gregg**
(b. 1751–d. 1820)
Savannah, Ga.
Bibl. 17

Gregg & Hayden
(See Hayden & Gregg)

Gregg, Hayden & Co.
(See Hayden, Gregg & Co.)

**Gregg, Hayden &
Whilden**
(See Hayden & Whilden)

Jacob Gregg
(b. 1766–d. 1832)
Alexandria, Va.
Bibl. 19

William Gregg
(b. 1800–d. 1867)
Lexington, Ky.
(c. 1818–1821)
Petersburg, Va.
(c. 1821–1824)
Columbia, S.C.
(c. 1824–1831)
Charleston, S. C.
(c. 1838–1855)
Hayden & Gregg
(c. 1832–1846)
Hayden, Gregg & Co.
(c. 1846–1852)

*Bibl. 5, 19, 32, 44, 54, 91,
93, 133*

W. GREGG

Gregor & Co. (1858–1961)
New Orleans, La.
Bibl. 141

Gregor & Wilson
(1856–1858)
New Orleans, La.
Bibl. 141

GREGOR & WILSON

George W. Gregor
(1856–1861)
New Orleans, La.
Bibl. 141

Gregory (c. 1825)
Location unknown
Bibl. 15, 114

Gregory

**Gregory & Bontecou
(Bonticou)**
(c. 1802–1805)
New Haven, Conn.
Augusta, Ga.
Levi Gregory
Roswell Bontecou
(Bonticou)
Bibl. 17

Gregory & Shuber
(c. 1837)
Philadelphia, Pa.
James Gregory
—— Shuber
Bibl. 3

F. L. Gregory (1886)
Niagara Falls, N.Y.
Bibl. 127

James Gregory (c. 1837)
Philadelphia, Pa.
Gregory & Shuber
Bibl. 3

Levi Gregory
(c. 1802–1805)
Augusta, Ga.
Gregory & Bontecou
(Bonticou)
Bibl. 17

George W. Greiner
(d. 1891)
Waynesboro, Va.
(c. 1837–1843)
Bibl. 19

Isaiah Grendle (1860)
Eastport, Me.
Bibl. 105

Charles W. Greshoff
(1888–1898)
Baltimore, Md.
Bibl. 127

Francis A. Greshoff
(1864–1885)
Baltimore, Md.
Became Francis A. Greshoff
& Son (1887–1894)
Bibl. 127

Michael Gretter
(b. 1785–d. 1868)
Richmond, Va.
(c. 1806–c. 1813)
Lynchburg, Va. (c. 1814)
Baltimore, Md.
Bibl. 19, 95

ML. GRETTER

Griffee
(See George F. Griffith)

Griffen & Hoyt
(c. 1819–1832)
New York, N.Y.
Peter Griffen
Walter B. Hoyt
*Bibl. 15, 23, 24, 25, 29, 36,
44, 91, 114*

GRIFFEN & HOYT

Griffen & Son
(c. 1832–1837)
Albany, N.Y. (c. 1832)
New York, N.Y.
Peter Griffen
William Griffen
Bibl. 15, 25, 44, 91, 114, 124

GRIFFEN & SON

C. B. Griffen (Griffin)
Troy, N.Y. (c. 1827–1829)
Little Falls, N.Y.
(c. 1833–1834)
G. M. & C. B. Griffen
(c. 1827–1829)
Bibl. 20, 124

G. M. & C. B. Griffen
(c. 1827–1829)
Troy, N.Y.
George M. Griffen
C. B. Griffen
Bibl. 20, 124

George M. Griffen
Troy, N.Y. (c. 1827–1829)
Athens, Ga. (c. 1839)
Savannah, Ga.
(c. 1839–1855)
G. M. & C. B. Griffen
(c. 1827–1829)
Bibl. 17, 20, 124

Isaiah Griffen
(c. 1802–1823)
Hudson, N.Y.
Bibl. 20, 124

John Griffen
Staunton, Va.
(c. 1773–1794)
Germantown, N.C.
(c. 1794–1803)
Bibl. 21

Peter Griffen
(c. 1815–1840)
Albany, N.Y. (c. 1832)
New York, N.Y.
(c. 1819–1832)
Griffen & Hoyt
(c. 1819–1832)
Griffen & Son
(c. 1832–1837)

*Bibl. 15, 23, 24, 25, 36, 44,
91, 114, 124*

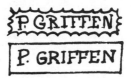

David Griffeth
(b. 1735–d. 1779)
Portsmouth, N.H. (c. 1763)
*Bibl. 25, 54, 94, 102, 110,
125*

**Nathaniel Griffeth
(Griffith)**
(b. 1740–d. 1771)
Portsmouth, N.H.
Bibl. 54, 110, 125

Samuel Griffeth
(b. 1729–d. 1773)
Portsmouth, N.H.
(c. 1757–?)
Bibl. 54, 110, 125

Griffin
(See C. B. Griffen)

Edward Griffin
(c. 1828–?)
Utica, N.Y.
Bibl. 18, 20, 158

George Griffin
(c. 1841–1852)
Louisville, Ky.
Bibl. 32, 54, 60, 93

Isaiah Griffin (c. 1802)
Location unknown
Bibl. 28

John Griffin
Staunton, Va. (before 1794
and after 1803)
Germantown, N.C.
(c. 1794–1803)
Bibl. 19

Griffing
(See Giffing)

Edward Griffing (c. 1831)
Oswego, N.Y.
Aspinwall & Griffing
Bibl. 20, 124

Griffith & Gaither
(c. 1809–?)
Alexandria, Va.
C. Greenberry Griffith
John Gaither(?)
Bibl. 19

David Grif(f)ith (c. 1798)
Boston, Mass.
Bibl. 23, 28, 36

**C. Greenberry Griffith
(Greenberry Griffith)**
(b. 1787–d. 1848)
Baltimore, Md.
(c. 1816–1818)
Washington, D.C. (c. 1830)
Alexandria, Va.
Griffith & Gaither
Riggs & Griffith
(c. 1816–1818) (?)
Bibl. 15, 19, 38

       (G. G)

Edward Griffith (d. 1805)
Savannah, Ga.
(c. 1785–1786)
Augusta, Ga. (c. 1801–1802)
Thompson & Griffith
(c. 1785–1786)
Bibl. 17

Edward Griffith (c. 1847)
Albany, N.Y.
Bibl. 20

**George F. Griffith
(Griffee)**
(c. 1841–1850)
Philadelphia, Pa.
Bibl. 3

Greenberry Griffith
(See C. Greenberry Griffith)

Henry Griffith
(c. 1816–1818)
Baltimore, Md.
Riggs & Griffith (?)
Bibl. 15, 38

L. Griffith (c. 1842–1843)
Philadelphia, Pa.
Bibl. 3

Samuel Griffith (c. 1847)
Philadelphia, Pa.
Bibl. 3

James Griffiths (c. 1836)
Glens Falls, N.Y.
Bibl. 20, 124

John Griffiths (c. 1855)
Greenville, S. C.
Bibl. 5

Griffon
(See A. L. Silberstein)

Griffon Cutlery Works
(1915–present)
Springville, N.Y.
Successor to A. L. Silberstein
(c. 1904–1915)
Bibl. 127

C. Grifing (c. 1825)
New York, N.Y.
Bibl. 23

William Grigg (d. 1797)
Albany, N.Y. (c. 1770–1778)
*Bibl. 4, 15, 20, 23, 24, 25,
28, 29, 30, 35, 36, 44, 54,
91, 95, 114, 124*

Benjamin(e) Grignon
(17th century)
Charleston, S.C.
Bibl. 5

Benjamin(e) Grignon
(c. 1685)
Boston, Mass.
Oxford, Mass.
Bibl. 2, 23, 28, 36, 44, 110

René Grignon (d. 1715)
Oxford, Mass.
(c. 1691, c. 1699)
Boston, Mass. (c. 1696)
Norwich, Mass. (c. 1708)
*Bibl. 2, 15, 16, 23, 24, 25,
28, 29, 36, 69, 94, 110,
114, 119*

John Paul Grimke
(b. 1713–d. 1791)
Charleston, S.C.
(c. 1740–1772)
Bibl. 5, 23, 36, 44, 54, 102

D. C. Grimwood (1860)
Providence, R.I.
Bibl. 108

George Griscom (c. 1791)
Philadelphia, Pa.
Bibl. 3, 23, 36, 44

Caesar Griselm
(See Cesar Ghiselin)

A. B. Griswold & Co.
(1865–1924)
New Orleans, La.
Became A. B. Griswold &
Co., Ltd. (1906–1924)
Bibl. 141

A.B.GRISWOLD&C⁰ N.O.H.

**Arther Breeze Griswold
& Co.** (1866)
New Orleans, La.
Bibl. 54

Chaucey D. Griswold
(c. 1838–1839)
Troy, N.Y.
Bibl. 20, 124

Francis A. Griswold
(c. 1838–1839)
Louisville, Ky.
Bibl. 32, 93

Gaylord Griswold
(b. 1807)
Utica, N.Y. (c. 1831)
B. F. Brooks & Co.
(c. 1829–1831)
Bibl. 18, 20, 124, 158

Gilbert Griswold
(c. 1810–1825)
Middletown, Conn.
Portland, Me.
*Bibl. 16, 23, 28, 36, 44, 105,
110*

H. A. Griswold (c. 1850)
Whitehall, N.Y.
Bibl. 20, 124

J. Griswold (c. 1805)
Salem, N.Y.
Bibl. 20

Joab Griswold
　(c. 1832–1835)
Buffalo, N.Y.
Utica, N.Y.
Brooks & Griswold (c. 1832)
Bibl. 18, 20, 124, 158

William Griswold
　(c. 1820)
Portland, Me.
Middletown, Conn. (?)
Bibl. 15, 23, 24, 25, 29, 44,
　91, 92, 105, 110, 114

W. GRISWOLD

Jacob Marius Groen
　(Morrisgreen)   I·M
　(d. 1750)
New York, N.Y. (c. 1701)
Bibl. 44, 119, 124, 138

J. R. Groff (c. 1841–1850)
Philadelphia, Pa.
Bibl. 3, 23

Ed. Groneberg
　(c. 1855–1856)
Baltimore, Md.
Bibl. 127

J. L. Gropengiesser
　(c. 1841–1850)
Philadelphia, Pa.
Bibl. 3

Grosjean
(See also Woodward &
　Grosjean)

Grosjean & Woodward
　(c. 1840–1853)
New York, N.Y.
Charles Grosjean   G & W
Eli Woodward
Bibl. 127

Francis J. Gross
　(c. 1841–1850)
Philadelphia, Pa.
Bibl. 3

William Grout (c. 1816)
Philadelphia, Pa.
Bibl. 3

George Gruber (c. 1840)
Berryville, Va.
Bibl. 19

Gudichaud
(See Gaudechaud)

Victor A. Gue (b. 1800)
Charleston, S. C.
　(c. 1831–1835)
Bibl. 5

Auguste Guelberth
　(c. 1836–1848)
St. Louis, Mo.
Bibl. 54, 89, 155

A. GUELBERTH
- St. Louis -

Dominick Guercy
　(c. 1795–1798)
New York, N.Y.
Bibl. 23, 36, 44, 124, 138

Anthony Guerin (Gurine)
　(Geriung) (Gurnine)
　(Guirna)
Philadelphia, Pa.
　(c. 1791–1814)
Bibl. 3, 23, 28, 36, 44

Isaac Guernsey
　(b. 1741–d. 1767)
Northampton, Mass.
　(c. 1765–1767)
Bibl. 84, 110

Theodore Guesnard
　(b. 1790–d. 1863)
　(Guesmard)
Philadelphia, Pa.
　(c. 1818–1822)
Mobile, Ala. (1852)
Bibl. 3, 148

Henry Brown Guest
(See Henry Brown)

E. Guey (c. 1820)
Location unknown
Bibl. 24

E GUEY

Lewis Guienot
　(1870–1877)
Baltimore, Md.
Bibl. 127

James S. Guignard
Columbia, S.C.
Radcliffe & Guignard
　(c. 1856–1858)
Bibl. 5

W. Guilbalt (1895)
Biddeford, Me.
Bibl. 105

Guild
(See Wm. N. Boynton)
Mark registered by Boynton
　(1882). Also used by
　U. S. Jewelers' Guild until
　c. 1904; by J. H. Purdy &
　Co. (c. 1896–1924) and
　by other Guild members.

John Guild (Guile)
　(c. 1818–1825)
Philadelphia, Pa.
Bibl. 3

Noah Gullle (c. 1701)
Boston, Mass.
Bibl. 23, 28, 36, 44, 72, 110

Guimarin & Brelet
　(c. 1824)
Augusta, Ga.
John Guimarin
Francis Brelet
Bibl. 17

John Guimarin
　(c. 1815–1847)
Augusta, Ga.
Guimarin & Brelet (c. 1824)
Brelet, Wearer & Co.
　(c. 1825)   J. GUIMARIN
Bibl. 17

Frederick Edward
　Guinand (Guinaud)
Baltimore, Md.
　(c. 1814–1827)
Bibl. 15, 25, 38, 44, 90, 114

F E. GUINAND

Joseph Guingan
(c. 1837–1838)
Albany, N.Y.
Bibl. 20, 124

Jacob Guinguigner
(b. 1795–d. 1853)
New York, N.Y.
(c. 1836–1838)
Utica, N.Y.
(c. 1840–1853?)
Bibl. 18, 20, 124, 138, 158

————— **Guion**
New York, N.Y.
Howe & Guion
(c. 1839–1840)
Bibl. 15, 24, 91

Rence Guiot (b. 1793)
Baltimore, Md. (c. 1803)
Bibl. 38

Guirna
(See Guerin)

Calvin Guiteau
(c. 1828–1845)
Watertown, N.Y.
Nashville, Tenn.
Bibl. 20, 91, 124, 159

Nathan Gulick
(b. 1777–d. 1826)
(c. 1818–1826)
Maysville, Ky.
Easton, Pa.
New Jersey
Bibl. 32, 93

Nathan & Elizabeth Gulick (c. 1818–1826)
Maysville, Ky.
Bibl. 32 N. & E. G.

Gullup
(See Gallup)

Henry Guluger (c. 1817)
St. Louis, Mo.
Bibl. 54

Gump's (1861–present)
San Francisco, Calif.
Bibl. 126

————— **Gunn**
New York, N.Y.

Gunn & Mitchell
(c. 1832)
Bibl. 15

Gunn & Mitchell (c. 1832)
New York, N.Y.
Henry Mitchell
(c. 1837–1841) (?)
————— Gunn
Bibl. 15, 124

Enos Gunn
(b. 1770–d. 1813)
Waterbury, Conn. (c. 1792)
*Bibl. 16, 23, 24, 25, 28, 29,
36, 44, 92, 110, 114*

ENOS GUNN E. GUNN

A. T. Gunner Mfg. Co.
(1920–present)
Attleboro, Mass.
Bibl. 127

O. T. Guptil (1861)
Cornish, Me.
Bibl. 105

John P. Gurau
(c. 1797–1819)
Savannah, Ga.
Bibl. 17

Gurine
(See Guerin)

William Gurley W. G
(b. 1764–d. 1844)
Norwich, Conn. (c. 1804)
*Bibl. 16, 23, 24, 25, 28, 29,
36, 44, 92, 110, 114*

The Rev. William Gurley
(c. 1810–1812)
Zanesville, Ohio
Bibl. 34

Gurnee & Co. (c. 1835)
New York, N.Y.
Benjamin Gurnee
Bibl. 23, 25, 36, 44, 91

Gurnee & Stephen
(See B. & S. Gurnee)

B. & S. Gurnee
(c. 1833–1837)
New York, N.Y.

Benjamin Gurnee
Stephen Gurnee
*Bibl. 4, 15, 23, 28, 36, 44,
124, 138*

Benjamin Gurnee
(c. 1824–1840)
New York, N.Y.
Benjamin Gurnee & Co.
(c. 1826–1828)
Gurnee & Co. (c. 1835)
Gurnee & Stephen
B. & S. Gurnee
*Bibl. 15, 23, 25, 36, 44, 91,
114, 124, 138*

Ⓖ GURNEE

Benjamin Gurnee & Co.
(c. 1826–1828)
New York, N.Y.
Bibl. 15, 124, 138

Daniel Gurnee (c. 1850)
New York, N.Y.
Bibl. 23, 124, 138

Stephen Gurnee
New York, N.Y.
B. & S. Gurnee
Bibl. 4, 23, 28, 36, 44, 124

Gurnine
(See Guerin)

Gustafson Craft
(1945–1964)
Chicago, Ill.
Successor to Chicago Silver
Company
Bibl. 98

Guthre & Jefferis
(c. 1840)
Wilmington, Del.
James Guthre
Emmor Jefferis
Bibl. 25, 44, 114

James Guthre
(b. 1796–d. 1877)
Wilmington, Del.
Philadelphia, Pa.
Guthre & Jefferis (c. 1840)
Bibl. 15, 25, 30, 44, 91, 114

J. GUTHRE

Philip Ranard Guyeon & Yver (c. 1796)
Philadelphia, Pa.
Bibl. 3

Benjamin Guyer (c. 1848)
Philadelphia, Pa.
Bibl. 3

Gwinn & McCloy (1875)
Providence, R.I.
Bibl. 108

John Gyles
(b. 1781–d. 1822)
Charleston, S.C.
(c. 1808–1822)
Bibl. 5

F. J. R. Gyllenberg
(1906–1927)
Boston, Mass.
Bibl. 144

H

H
(See Hayden Mfg. Co., M. Fred Hirsch Co., Inc., Hirsch & Oppenheimer)

H & H
(See Hall & Hewson)

H & M
(See Hall & Merriman, Hays & Myers)

H & N
(See Hyde & Nevins)

H & N J
(See William B. Heyer)

H. & S.
(See Hart & Smith, Hayward & Sweet, Holbrook & Simmons, Hotchkiss & Schreuder, A. B. Schreuder)

H & W
(See Hart & Wilcox)

H Mfg. Co.
(See Holbrook Mfg. Co.)

H A
(See Henry Andrews)

H A & Co
(See Horton & Angell)

H B
(See Henry Bailey, Henry Biershing, Hendrik Boelen)

H. C.
(See H. C. Culman)

H. F. B. & Co.
(See H. F. Barrows & Co.)

H G
(See Harrison & Groeschel)

H L
(See Howard Sterling Co., Henry Loring)

H L P
(See Helen Porter Philbrick)

H M
(See Hayes & McFarland)

H O
(See Harvey & Otis, Hirsch & Oppenheimer)

H P
(See Henry Peterson, Henry Pitkin, Henry Pratt, Henry Pursell)

H S
(See Hartford Sterling Company, Heer-Schofield Co., Hezekiah Silliman)

H. S. B. & Co.
(See Hibbard, Spencer, Bartlett & Co.)

H W
(See Henry Westermeyer, Henry White)

James A. Haas
(c. 1846–1849)
Philadelphia, Pa.
Bibl. 3

N. Haas (c. 1846–1850)
Philadelphia, Pa.
Bibl. 3

Joseph Hacker
(c. 1831–1850)
Philadelphia, Pa.
Bibl. 3

William Hacker
(c. 1848–1849)
Philadelphia, Pa.
Bibl. 3

Charles Hackett
(c. 1790–1806)
Easton, Md.
Bibl. 38

William Hackle
(c. 1763–1772)
Baltimore, Md.
Bibl. 3, 23, 28, 29, 36, 38, 44

William Hadder
(c. 1837)
Philadelphia, Pa.
Bibl. 3

Haddock & Andrews
(c. 1838–1847)
Boston, Mass.
Henry Haddock
Henry Andrews
Bibl. 4, 23, 28, 36, 44

Haddock, Lincoln & Foss
(c. 1850–1865)
Boston, Mass.
Henry Haddock
A. L. Lincoln
———— Foss
Bibl. 28, 44, 114, 122

HADDOCK, LINCOLN & FOSS

Henry Haddock
(c. 1836–1850)
Boston, Mass.
Haddock & Andrews
(c. 1838–1847)

Haddock, Lincoln & Foss
(c. 1850–1865)
Bibl. 4, 23, 28, 36, 44

**William Hadwen
(Hadwin)**
(b. 1791–d. 1862,
c. 1816–1828)
Nantucket Island, Mass.
Providence, R.I.
George C. (G.) Clark
Jabez Gorham
*Bibl. 12, 23, 24, 25, 28, 36,
44, 110, 114*

Haes
(See George Hays)

John Hafline (d. 1804)
Philadelphia, Pa.
(c. 1785–1803)
Bibl. 3

Elias Hager (c. 1841–1844)
Rochester, N.Y.
Bibl. 20, 41, 44, 124

Wolfgung Haggan
(c. 1752)
Reading, Pa.
Bibl. 44

**J. H. Haggenmacher &
Co.** (c. 1836)
Philadelphia, Pa.
Bibl. 3, 23, 36, 44

John Hague
(c. 1831–1835)
New York, N.Y.
Bibl. 15, 124

C. G. Hahn (c. 1798)
Philadelphia, Pa.
Bibl. 3

Haight & Leach (c. 1850)
Auburn, N.Y.
John W. Haight
Leonard D. Leach
Bibl. 20, 91, 124

Haight & Leonard
(c. 1847)
Newburgh, N.Y.
Nelson Haight
D. Gillis Leonard
Bibl. 20, 91, 124

Haight & Sterling
(c. 1841–1843)
Newburgh, N.Y.
Nelson Haight
———— Sterling
Bibl. 20, 91, 124

John W. Haight
(c. 1838–1850)
Auburn, N.Y.
Haight & Leach (c. 1850)
Bibl. 20, 91, 114, 124

Nelson Haight
(c. 1839–1852)
Newburgh, N.Y.
Haight & Sterling
(c. 1841–1843)
Haight & Leonard (c. 1847)
*Bibl. 15, 20, 25, 44, 91, 114,
124*

**Holme Haike (Haikes)
(Hakes)**
Paris, Ky. (c. 1840)
Bibl. 32, 54, 68

Moses Haine (c. 1775)
Philadelphia, Pa.
Bibl. 3

Abraham Haines (c. 1801)
New York, N.Y.
Bibl. 23, 36, 44, 124, 138

Imlah Haines
(c. 1829–1833)
Philadelphia, Pa.
Folwell & Haines
(c. 1844) (?)
Bibl. 3

Joshua J. Hair (c. 1848)
Louisville, Ky.
Bibl. 32, 93

Hakes
(See Haike)

Hale
(See J. Enno & Hale)

Charles Hale (1875)
Bangor, Me.
Bibl. 105

J. J. Hale
Kentucky
Bibl. 54

J. R. Hale (c. 1840–1850)
Location unknown
Bibl. 15, 44, 114

| J. R. HALE |

Henry Halewood (c. 1788)
Richmond, Va.
Bibl. 19

Haley & Haley (c. 1850)
Paris, Ky.
P. Haley
G. W. Haley
Bibl. 32, 93

G. W. Haley (c. 1850)
Paris, Ky.
Haley & Haley
Bibl. 32

P. Haley (c. 1850)
Paris, Ky.
Haley & Haley
Bibl. 32, 93

William Halfpenny
(c. 1835)
Philadelphia, Pa.
Bibl. 3

Hall & Bennet (c. 1840?)
New York State
Bibl. 89 | HALL & BENNET |

Hall & Bliss
(c. 1816–1818)
Albany, N.Y.
Bibl. 15, 20, 44, 91, 114, 124

Hall & Brower
(c. 1852–1854)
Albany, N.Y.
Green Hall
S. Douglas Brower
*Bibl. 4, 20, 23, 28, 36, 44,
124*

Hall & Elton (c. 1841)
Geneva, N.Y.
Abraham B. Hall
A. D. Elton
Bibl. 20, 25, 44, 91, 114, 124

Hall & Hewson
  (c. 1842–1847)
Albany, N.Y.
Green Hall   H & H
John D. Hewson
S. Douglas Brower
*Bibl. 4, 20, 23, 24, 28, 29,
  36, 91, 124*

Hall & Merriman
New Haven, Conn. (c. 1825)
Albany, N.Y.
Bibl. 24, 25, 29, 44, 114

H & M

Hall (Hull) & Sanger
  (c. 1840?)
Location unknown
Bibl. 28, 89

Hall & Sanger

Hall & Snow (c. 1835)
Cleveland, Ohio
Ransom E. Hall
William H. Snow
Bibl. 54, 65, 89

Hall Bros. & Co.
  (c. 1910–1915)
Pittsburgh, Penn.
Bibl. 127

H.B. & Co.

Hall, Brower & Co.
  (c. 1836–1842)
Albany, N.Y.
Green Hall
S. Douglas Brower
John D. Hewson
Bibl. 23, 36, 44, 124

Hall, Hewson & Brower
  (c. 1847–1850)
Albany, N.Y.
Green Hall
John D. Hewson
S. Douglas Brower
*Bibl. 4, 15, 20, 23, 28,
  44, 91, 114, 124*

Hall, Hewson & Co.
  (c. 1836–1842)
Albany, N.Y.
Green Hall
John D. Hewson
S. Douglas Brower
Thomas V. Z. Merrifield
Bibl. 4, 20, 28, 91, 124

**Hall, Hewson &
  Merrifield** (c. 1840)
Albany, N.Y.
Green Hall
John D. Hewson
Thomas V. Z. Merrifield
*Bibl. 4, 23, 28, 36, 44, 91,
  124*

A. B. Hall
Location unknown
(May be Abraham H. Hall)
Bibl. 28

Abijah Hall
Albany, N.Y. (c. 1813)
New York, N.Y.
  (c. 1830–1835)
*Bibl. 20, 23, 28, 36, 44, 124,
  138*

Abraham B. Hall
  (c. 1806–1839)
Geneva, N.Y.
Hall & Elton (c. 1841)
Bibl. 20, 44, 114, 124

Asa Hall (b. 1760–d. 1819)
Washington, Ga.
  (c. 1811–1819)
Raynham, Mass.
Bibl. 17, 20, 110

C. Hall (c. 1815)
Ovid, N.Y.
Bibl. 20, 124

Charles Hall
  (b. 1742–d. 1783)
Lancaster, Pa.
  (c. 1755–1780)
*Bibl. 3, 15, 23, 36, 44, 46,
  54, 62, 91, 95, 112, 114,
  116*

C Hall   C H

D. G. Hall (1860–1875)
Lewiston, Me.
Bibl. 105

David Hall (d. 1779)
Philadelphia, Pa.
  (c. 1760–1777)
Burlington, N.J.
  (c. 1777–1778)
*Bibl. 3, 15, 23, 24, 25, 28,
  29, 36, 39, 44, 46, 54, 81,
  91, 112, 114*

Drew Hall (c. 1789–1805)
New York, N.Y.
*Bibl. 4, 23, 28, 36, 44, 124,
  138*

George Hall
  (c. 1823–1842)
Philadelphia, Pa.
Bibl. 3

George W. Hall (c. 1840)
Newburgh, N.Y.
Ayers & Hall (c. 1800) (?)
Bibl. 20, 124

Green Hall
  (b. 1782–d. 1863)
New York, N.Y.
Albany, N.Y. (c. 1810–1827)
Carson & Hall
  (c. 1810–1818)
Hall & Brower
  (c. 1852–1854)
Hall, Brower & Co.
  (c. 1836–1842)
Hall, Hewson & Merrifield
  (c. 1840)
Hall & Hewson
  (c. 1842–1847)
Hall, Hewson & Brower
  (c. 1847–1850)
Hall, Hewson & Co.
  (c. 1836–1842)
*Bibl. 20, 23, 28, 36, 44, 91,
  114, 124, 138*

Ivory Hall
  (b. 1795–d. 1880)
Concord, N.H. (c. 1801)
Bibl. 23, 36, 44, 91, 125

J. & A. B. Hall (c. 1813)
Geneva, N.Y.
Bibl. 20, 91, 124

J. R. Hall (1835)
Lowell, Mass.
Bibl. 106

John Hall (c. 1804–1840)
Philadelphia, Pa.
Bibl. 3

John Hall (c. 1848)
Louisville, Ky.
Bibl. 32

Joseph Hall (c. 1781)
Albany, N.Y.
*Bibl. 15, 20, 23, 24, 25, 28,
    29, 36, 44, 91, 114, 124*

I. Hall	J Hall

Peter Hall (c. 1818–1824)
Philadelphia, Pa.
Bibl. 3

R. G. Hall (1860)
Lewiston, Me.
Bibl. 105

Ransom E. Hall
    (c. 1829–1836)
Cleveland, Ohio (c. 1835)
Detroit, Mich.
Geneva, N.Y.
Hall & Snow (c. 1835)
Bibl. 20, 54, 65, 124

S. B. Hall (c. 1837–1850)
Nicholasville, Ky.
Clayton, Ind.
Became S. B. Hall & Son
    (c. 1850–1860)
Bibl. 133

**Alonzo Corwin Hallack
(Halleck)**
Paris, Ky. (c. 1840–1853)
L. Matthews (c. 1852)
Bibl. 32, 93

A C HALLACK

John Hallam
    (c. 1752–1800)
New London, Conn.
*Bibl. 16, 23, 28, 36, 44, 92,
    102, 110*

Halleck
(See Hallack)

—— **Haller (Hiller)**
    (c. 1837)
Circleville, Ohio
Bibl. 34

Elias H. Halliday
    (c. 1828–1833)
Philadelphia, Pa.
Bibl. 3

Hiram Halliday
    (c. 1834–1844)
Albany, N.Y.
Bibl. 20, 124

James H. Halliday
    (c. 1841–1843)
Philadelphia, Pa.
Bibl. 3, 23

George Halliwell
    (c. 1813–1817)
New York, N.Y.
    (c. 1804–1805)
Poughkeepsie, N.Y.
Field & Halliwell
    (c. 1806–1813)
Frear & Halliwell
    (c. 1813–1816)
Bibl. 20, 124, 138

**Hallmark Silversmiths,
Inc.** (c. 1917–1954)
New York, N.Y.
Became Hunt-Hallmark Co.
    (1954)
Bibl. 127   **HALLMARK**

Charles Halsel (c. 1839)
Philadelphia, Pa.
Bibl. 3

Jabez Halsey
    (b. 1762–d. 1820)
New York, N.Y.
    (c. 1787–1796)
Dally & Halsey
    (c. 1787–1789)
*Bibl. 15, 23, 24, 28, 29, 30,
    35, 36, 44, 71, 78, 95, 114,
    124, 138*

I. HALSEY	HALSEY

Halstead & Son (c. 1799)
New York, N.Y.
Bibl. 23, 36, 44, 124, 138

**Benjamin Halsted
(Halstead)**
New York State
    (c. 1764–1766,
    1786–1806)
Elizabeth, N.J.
    (c. 1766–?)
Philadelphia, Pa.
    (c. 1783–1785)
Benjamin & Matthias Halsted
    (c. 1766–1769)
*Bibl. 3, 4, 23, 24, 25, 28, 29,
    30, 36, 44, 46, 54, 91, 95,
    114, 122, 124, 138*

**Benjamin & Matthias
Halsted** (c. 1766–1769)
Elizabeth, N.J.
Bibl. 46

Joseph Halstrick
    (b. 1815–d. 1886)
Boston, Mass.
Stanwood & Halstrick
    (c. 1850)
Bibl. 4, 23, 44

William S. Halstrick
Location unknown
Bibl. 28

George Ham
    (b. 1767–d. 1832)
Portsmouth, N.H. (c. 1810)
Bibl. 23, 28, 36, 44, 110, 125

William Hamelin
    (b. 1772)
Middletown, Conn.
    (c. 1791)
Bibl. 39

Hamersly
(See Hammersley)

Hamill & Co.
    (c. 1817–1819)
New York, N.Y.
James Hamill
Bibl. 15, 23, 36, 44, 124, 138

James Hamill
New York, N.Y.
  (c. 1810–1816)
Portsmouth, Ohio (c. 1820)
Hamill & Co. (c. 1817–1819)
Bibl. 15, 23, 24, 25, 28, 29,
  34, 36, 44, 114, 124, 138

Hamilton & Adams
  (c. 1837–1842)
Elmira, N.Y.
Daniel S. Hamilton
H. B. Adams (?)
Bibl. 20, 124

Hamilton & Diesinger
  (c. 1895–1899)
Philadelphia, Pa.
Successor to Hamilton &
  Davis (c. 1880–1895)
Became M. F. Hamilton &
  Son (c. 1899–1909)
Bibl. 114, 127, 157

Hamilton & Hamilton, Jr.
  (c. 1896–1915)
Providence, R.I.
Bibl. 114, 157

Hamilton Mfg. Co.
  (c. 1895)
Chicago, Ill.
Bibl. 127   **HAMILTON MFG. CO.**

Hamilton Silver Mfg. Co.
  (c. 1912)
New York, N.Y.
Became T. N. Benedict Mfg.
  Co.
Bibl. 127

HAMILTON SILVER MFG. CO.
   New York

Charles Hamilton
  (c. 1761)
Poughkeepsie, N.Y.
Bibl. 54, 124

Daniel S. Hamilton
  (c. 1848)
Elmira, N.Y.
Hamilton & Adams
  (c. 1837–1842)
Bibl. 20, 124

James Hamilton (c. 1766)
Annapolis, Md.
Bibl. 23, 28, 36, 44

James Hamilton
  (c. 1776–1781)
Fredericksburg, Va.
Bibl. 19

James Hamilton (c. 1848)
Philadelphia, Pa.
Bibl. 3

John Hamilton (c. 1798)
New York, N.Y.
Bibl. 23, 36, 44, 110, 124,
  138

R. J. Hamilton
  (c. 1837–1846)
Philadelphia, Pa.
Bibl. 3

Samuel Hamilton
  (c. 1837)
Philadelphia, Pa.
Bibl. 3

Cyrus Hamlin
  (b. 1810–d. 1900)
Portland, Me. (w. 1831)
Bibl. 23, 28, 36, 44, 105

William Hamlin
  (b. 1772–d. 1869?)
Middletown, Conn.
Providence, R.I.
Bibl. 15, 16, 23, 24, 25, 28,
  29, 36, 44, 56, 91, 92, 102,
  110, 114

Crosby Hamman
  (Hammond)
  (c. 1823–1825)
Philadelphia, Pa.
Bibl. 3

Peter Hamman
  (Hammond) (c. 1817)
Philadelphia, Pa.
Bibl. 3

Thomas Hammersley
  (Hammersly)
  (Hamersly)
  (b. 1727–d. 1781)
New York, N.Y. (c. 1756)
Bibl. 15, 23, 24, 29, 30, 35,
  36, 44, 72, 91, 95, 102,
  104, 114, 124, 138

Hammersmith & Field
  (c. 1899–1915)
San Francisco, Calif.
John A. Hammersmith
Hampton S. Field
Bibl. 127

Richard Hammett
  (c. 1844–1845)
Troy, N.Y.
Bibl. 20, 124

Hammond & Philbrick
  (1853–1854)
New Orleans, La.
Bibl. 141

Crosby Hammond
(See Hamman)

Eleazer Hammond
  (c. 1837–1838)
Troy, N.Y.
Bibl. 20, 124

Peter Hammond
(See Hamman)

Seneca Hammond
  (c. 1804–?)
Utica, N.Y.
Osborn & Hammond
Bibl. 20, 124, 158

William St. Leger Hamot
 (d. 1851)
New Orleans, La.
 (1827–1844)
Bibl. 141

Hampshire House
(See Murrary L. Schacter &
Co.)

Hampshire Silver Co.
 (c. 1950–1960)
New York, N.Y.
Bibl. 127

Hampton & Palmer
 (c. 1830–1832)
Salisbury, N.C.
James Brandon Hampton
John C. Palmer
Bibl. 21

Henry Hampton (c. 1835)
Richmond, Va.
Bibl. 19

James Brandon Hampton
 (c. 1801–1832)
Salisbury, N.C.
Hampton & Palmer
 (c. 1830–1832)
Bibl. 21

Matthias Wm. Hanck
 (1911–1955)
Chicago, Ill.
Bibl. 98

John Hancock
 (b. 1732–d. 1784)
Talbot County, Md.
Boston, Mass.
Charlestown, Mass.
Providence, R.I.
*Bibl. 2, 15, 23, 24, 28, 29,
 36, 38, 44, 56, 72, 102,
 110, 114*

Robert Hancock
 (c. 1793–1794)
Philadelphia, Pa.
Bibl. 3

Hand & Hammer
 (1979–present)
Alexandria, Va.
Bibl. 127

J. Hand (c. 1837)
Philadelphia, Pa.
Bibl. 3

Joseph S. K. Hand
 (c. 1833–1850)
Philadelphia, Pa.
Spencer & Hand (c. 1843)
Bibl. 3

L. R. Handerson (1830)
Worcester, Mass.
Bibl. 106

John Handle
 (c. 1839–1848)
Philadelphia, Pa.
Bibl. 3, 23, 36, 44

A. Hanford (c. 1820–1830)
Peekskill, N.Y.
Bibl. 15, 44, 91, 114, 124

Abraham Hanis (c. 1840)
Charleston, S.C.
Bibl. 5

Benjamin Hanks
 (b. 1755–d. 1824)
Windham, Conn.
 (c. 1777–1779)
Litchfield, Conn. (c. 1783)
Ashford, Conn. (c. 1790)
*Bibl. 16, 23, 28, 36, 44, 92,
 110*

Hanle & Debler, Inc.
 (1933–1935)
New York, N.Y.
Became
A. H. Hanle, Inc.
 (1935–1971)
The Kirk Corporation (1971)
Bibl. 127

C. A. Hanna
Location unknown
Bibl. 89

George Hannah (c. 1720)
Boston, Mass.
Bibl. 70

William W. Hannah
 (c. 1840–1850)
Albany, N.Y.
Hudson, N.Y.
*Bibl. 15, 20, 23, 25, 28, 29,
 36, 44, 114, 124*

W W HANNAH

George Hanners
 (b. 1696–d. 1740)
Boston, Mass.
*Bibl. 2, 15, 23, 24, 28, 29,
 36, 44, 50, 54, 72, 94, 102,
 110, 114, 139, 151*

George Hanners Jr.
 (b. 1721–d. 1760)
Boston, Mass.
*Bibl. 2, 15, 23, 28, 29, 44,
 54, 110, 114*

John Hannum
 (c. 1837–1849)
Northampton, Mass.
Syracuse, N.Y.
Dickinson & Hannum
 (c. 1843)
Bibl. 20, 84, 124

Hano & Co. (c. 1848)
Philadelphia, Pa.
Bibl. 3

L. Hano (c. 1849)
Philadelphia, Pa.
Bibl. 3

Hanover & Bickford
 (1875)
Lewiston, Me.
Bibl. 105

Hamlet Hansbrough
 (c. 1800–1839)
Lexington, Ky.
Bibl. 32, 93

James Hansell
 (c. 1816–1850)
Philadelphia, Pa.

Valley Forge, Pa.
Bibl. 3, 25, 44, 114

Robert Hansell (c. 1823)
Boston, Mass.
Bibl. 23, 28, 36, 44, 110

**Benjamin Hanson
(Hansen)**
(c. 1822–1840)
Albany, N.Y.
Bibl. 20, 91, 124

Pierre Harache (c. 1691)
Williamsburg, Va.
Bibl. 23, 36, 44

Harbottle & Smith
(c. 1850)
Auburn, N.Y.
George Harbottle
Charles A. Smith
Bibl. 20, 124

George Harbottle (c. 1850)
Auburn, N.Y.
Harbottle & Smith
Bibl. 20, 124

W. Hardeman (1838)
Lexington, Ky.
Bibl. 54

James Harden
(c. 1818–1824)
Philadelphia, Pa.
Bibl. 3

C. H. Harding (c. 1850)
Location unknown
Bibl. 28   C. H. HARDING

N. & C. Harding (c. 1830)
New York, N.Y.
Bibl. 36

Newell Harding
(b. 1796–d. 1862)
Boston, Mass.
Haverhill, Mass.
*Bibl. 4, 15, 23, 24, 25, 28,
29, 36, 44, 72, 91, 110,
114*

Newell Harding & Co.
(c. 1830–1860)
Boston, Mass.
*Bibl. 23, 24, 25, 28, 36, 39,
44, 91, 94, 102, 114, 122*

Freeman M. Hardison
(1860)
S. Berwick, Me.
Bibl. 105

Jacob N. Hardman
(c. 1845–1849)
Louisville, Ky.
Bibl. 32, 93

William Hardman
(c. 1838–1840)
Lexington, Ky.
Bibl. 32, 68, 93

W HARDMAN

Hardwood
(See John Harwood)

J. H. Hardy (c. 1820)
Lexington, Ky.
Bibl. 32, 54, 93

Stephen Hardy   S.H.
(b. 1781–d. 1843)
Boston, Mass.
Portsmouth, N.H.
*Bibl. 23, 24, 28, 29, 36, 44,
91, 94, 110, 114, 125*

William Harker (c. 1850)
Philadelphia, Pa.
Bibl. 3

Willis Harker (c. 1845)
Philadelphia, Pa.
Bibl. 3

James Harkins
(c. 1840–1847)
Philadelphia, Pa.
Bibl. 3

Harland & Blair
(1830–1833)
New Orleans La.
Henry Harland
Daniel Blair
Bibl. 141

Henry Harland
(b. 1787–d. 1841)
Norwich, Conn.
(1805–1841)
New Orleans, La.
(1815–1832)
Harland & Blair
Bibl. 141

Thomas Harland
(b. 1735–d. 1807)
Norwich, Conn.
*Bibl. 16, 23, 24, 25, 28, 29,
36, 44, 54, 92, 94, 102,
110, 114, 135, 138, 143*

HARLAND

Thomas Harland Jr.
(c. 1781–1806)
Norwich, Conn.
*Bibl. 16, 23, 28, 36, 44, 92,
110, 135*

William Harlow (1860)
Portland, Me.
Bibl. 105

Alexander Harman
(c. 1835)
Philadelphia, Pa.
Bibl. 3

George A. Harman (1875)
Portland, Me.
Bibl. 105

Reuben Harmon
(b. 1750–d. 1806)
Rupert, Vt.
New York, N.Y. (?)
Van Voorhis & Coley
(c. 1786)
Bibl. 28, 54, 124

Thomas W. Harpel
(c. 1813)
Philadelphia, Pa.
Bibl. 23, 36, 44

Alexander Harper
(c. 1819)
Philadelphia, Pa.
Bibl. 3, 23, 36, 44

Benjamin Harper
(c. 1843)
Philadelphia, Pa.
Bibl. 3

David Harper
(c. 1755–1756)
Philadelphia, Pa.
Dutens & Harper
Bibl. 3, 23, 36, 44

George W. Harper
(c. 1832–1835)
New York, N.Y.
Bibl. 15, 23, 124, 138

John M. Harper
(c. 1841–1850)
Philadelphia, Pa.
Bibl. 3

Thomas Harper
(c. 1773–1782)
Charleston, S.C.
Bibl. 5, 54

Thomas E. Harper
(c. 1847–1850)
Philadelphia, Pa.
Bibl. 3

Thomas W. Harper
Philadelphia, Pa.
(c. 1813–1817)
New York, N.Y.
(c. 1825–1835)
*Bibl. 3, 15, 23, 36, 44, 124,
138*

William W. Harpur
(c. 1839–1850)
Philadelphia, Pa.
Bibl. 3

Francis Harrall
(c. 1828–1830)
Philadelphia, Pa.
Bibl. 3

**Marquand Harriman &
Co.**
(See Marquand, Harriman &
Co.)

Samuel Harrington
(c. 1842–c. 1845)
Amherst, Mass.
Prevear & Harrington
(c. 1841–1842)
Bibl. 84, 91

William Harrington
(c. 1849–1850)
Philadelphia, Pa.
Bibl. 3

Harris & Co.
(c. 1771–1777)
Charleston, S.C.
Charles Harris
James Mortimer Harris
Bibl. 5

Harris & Co. (c. 1850)
New York, N.Y.
George Harris
Bibl. 23, 124

Harris & Hoyt
Kentucky
Bibl. 54, 93

Harris & Kendrick
(c. 1831–1832)
Louisville, Ky.
John C. Harris (?)
William Kendrick
Bibl. 32, 54, 68, 91

Harris & Schafer Co., Inc.
(1880–1938)
Washington, D.C.
Bibl. 127, 157

Harris & Stanwood
(c. 1835)
Boston, Mass.
William Harris
Henry B. Stanwood
*Bibl. 23, 24, 29, 36, 44, 91,
114, 151*

HARRIS & STANWOOD

Harris, Stanwood & Co.
(c. 1845)
Boston, Mass.
———— Harris
———— Stanwood
Bibl. 4, 15, 25, 28

HARRIS, STANWOOD & CO.

Harris & Wilcox
Albany, N.Y. (c. 1844)
Troy, N.Y. (c. 1847–1850)
Heman J. Harris
Alanson D. Wilcox
*Bibl. 4, 20, 25, 28, 29, 91,
114, 124*

HARRIS & WILCOX

Charles Harris
(c. 1767–1798)
Charleston, S.C.
Flere & Harris (c. 1767)
Harris & Co. (c. 1771–1777)
Bibl. 5, 44, 102

Edward Harris (c. 1848)
Philadelphia, Pa.
Bibl. 3, 23

Frederick Harris
(1834–1835)
New Orleans, La.
Bibl. 141

George Harris
New York, N.Y.
(c. 1802, c. 1850)
Pittsburgh, Pa. (c. 1815)
Harris & Co. (N.Y.) (c. 1850)
Bibl. 23, 26, 44, 124, 138

Heman Harris (c. 1820)
Albany, N.Y.
Troy, N.Y. (c. 1833–1847)
Harris, & Wilcox
Bibl. 20, 23, 36, 44, 124

James Mortimer Harris
(c. 1771–1782)
Charleston, S.C.
Harris & Co. (S.C.)
(c. 1767–1798)
Bibl. 5

John C. Harris
(c. 1831–1836)
Louisville, Ky.

Harris & Kendrick
(c. 1831–1832) (?)
Bibl. 32, 93

R. Harris & Co.
(c. 1874–present)
Washington, D.C.
Bibl. 127

Thomas Harris
(c. 1818–1822)
Philadelphia, Pa.
Bibl. 3

Thomas B. Harris
(c. 1871)
New Orleans, La.
Bibl. 127

Harrison & Groeschel
(c. 1896–1904)
New York, N.Y.
Bibl. 114, 127, 157

Harry & Bear (c. 1842)
Harrisonburg, Va.
Jehu W. Bear
Bibl. 19

Jacob Harsen
Detroit, Mich. (c. 1760)
Bibl. 52

Hart & Bliss
(c. 1803–1804)
Middletown, Conn.
Judah Hart
Jonathan Bliss
Bibl. 16, 23, 28, 36, 44, 110

Hart & Brewer
(c. 1800–1803)
Middletown, Conn.
Judah Hart
Charles Brewer
*Bibl. 16, 23, 24, 25, 28, 36,
92, 110, 114*

Hart & Smith
(c. 1814–1816)
Baltimore, Md.
William Hart
John Smith
*Bibl. 15, 24, 25, 28, 29, 38,
44, 114*

HART & SMITH H & S

Hart & Wilcox (Willcox)
Norwich, Conn.
(c. 1805–1807)
Judah Hart
Alvan Wilcox
*Bibl. 16, 23, 24, 25, 28, 29,
36, 44, 91, 92, 94, 110,
114*

HART & WILCOX H & W

Eliphaz Hart
(b. 1789–d. 1866)
New Britain, Conn.
Norwich, Conn.
*Bibl. 15, 16, 23, 24, 25, 28,
29, 36, 44, 91, 92, 110,
114*

E HART E H

John Hart (c. 1776)
Philadelphia, Pa.
Bibl. 3, 23, 36, 44

John I. (J.) Hart
(c. 1820–1826)
New York, N.Y.
Bibl. 15, 23, 36, 44

Jonathan Hart (c. 1815)
Canandaigua, N.Y.
Bibl. 25, 114

Judah Hart (1777–1824)
Berlin, Conn. (c. 1803)
Middletown, Conn.
(c. 1803–1804)
Norwich, Conn.
(c. 1805–1807)
Griswald, Md. (c. 1816)
Brownsville, Ohio (c. 1822)
Hart & Brewer
(c. 1800–1803)
Hart & Bliss (c. 1803–1804)
Hart & Wilcox
(c. 1805–1807)
*Bibl. 15, 16, 23, 24, 25, 28,
29, 36, 44, 61, 91, 92, 94,
110, 114*

Walter Hart
(c. 1849–1850)
Philadelphia, Pa.
Bibl. 3, 23

William Hart W. HART
(c. 1810–1824)
Philadelphia, Pa.
Baltimore, Md.
(c. 1814–1816)
Hart & Smith
(c. 1814–1816)
*Bibl. 3, 15, 23, 24, 29, 36,
38, 44, 91, 114*

Hartford
(See also Bulles & Childs)

**Hartford Sterling
Company** (1900–1924)
Philadelphia, Pa.
Successor to Tennant Co.
Bibl. 127, 157

George Hartford (c. 1794)
Philadelphia, Pa.
Bibl. 3, 23, 36, 44

Hartin & Bargi (c. 1766)
Bound Brook, N.J.
Bibl. 23, 36

Harting & Koesning
(c. 1850)
Kentucky
Bibl. 54, 93, 114

Jeremiah Hartley
(c. 1837–1850)
Philadelphia, Pa.
Bibl. 3

Samuel Hartley
Philadelphia, Pa.
(c. 1818–1825,
c. 1837–1850)
New York, N.Y.
(c. 1827–1828)
Albany, N.Y. (c. 1828–1838)
Garrett & Hartley (c. 1837)
Clark & Hartley
(c. 1839–1841)
*Bibl. 3, 15, 20, 23, 36, 44,
124, 138*

Thomas Hartley
(c. 1827–1828)
New York, N.Y.
Bibl. 15, 124, 138

Philip Hartman
(c. 1813–1814)
Philadelphia, Pa.
Bibl. 3, 23, 36, 44

Esther Hartshorn
(b. 1923)
Springfield, Mass.
Bibl. 117

Jonathan Hartt
(c. 1810–1815)
Canandaigua, N.Y.
Bibl. 20, 124

Hartwell
(See Woodbury, Dix, &
Hartwell)

Samuel S. Hartwell
(c. 1842)
Philadelphia, Pa.
Bibl. 3

Harvey & Otis
(c. 1896–present)
Providence, R.I.
Bibl. 127

H-O

Lewis Harvey
(See Harvey Lewis)

John Harward (c. 1816)
Philadelphia, Pa.
Bibl. 44

Harwell
(See Randle & Harwell)

———— Harwood
Location unknown
Bibl. 28, 29

HAR
WOOD

Benjamin Harwood
(c. 1819)
Philadelphia, Pa.
Bibl. 3

John Harwood
(Hardwood)
Philadelphia, Pa.
Robinson & Harwood
(c. 1814–1822)
Bibl. 3, 23, 36

Alexander R. Hascy
(c. 1831–1850)
Albany, N.Y.
*Bibl. 15, 20, 25, 28, 44, 114,
124*

HASCY

Nelson Hascy
(c. 1843–1849)
Albany, N.Y.
Bibl. 20, 23, 28, 44, 124

N. HASCY

Samuel Hascy
(c. 1819–1829)
Albany, N.Y.
Samuel Hascy & Son
(c. 1829–1831)
Bibl. 20, 124

Samuel Hascy & Son
(c. 1829–1831)
Albany, N.Y.
Bibl. 20, 124

Haselton & Co.
Portsmouth, N.H.
Bibl. 15, 44, 114

Haselton & Co.

Ira Haselton
(b. 1797–d. 1869)
Portsmouth, N.H.
(1821–1825)
Bibl. 25, 44, 110, 114

George W. Haselwood
(c. 1848)
Philadelphia, Pa.
Bibl. 3

William Haselwood
(c. 1848–1850)
Philadelphia, Pa.
Bibl. 3

Alexander Hasey
(See Alexander R. Hascy)

Barnabas Haskell (c. 1833)
Boston, Mass.
Bibl. 4, 23, 28, 36, 44

Henry C. Haskell
(c. 1896–1915)
New York, N.Y.
Bibl. 114, 127

Thomas M. Haskell
(1860–1875)
New Gloucester, Me.
Bibl. 105

V. W. Haskell (c. 1850)
Orleans, Mass.
Bibl. 15, 44, 91, 114

V. W. HASKELL

William F. Haskell (1860)
Foxcroft, Me.
Bibl. 105

Haskin & Martin (c. 1830)
Location unknown
Bibl. 24

James Hasle (c. 1748)
Maryland (c. 1774)
Bibl. 38

Charles Hassan
(See Charles Hassell)

Moses Hassan (Hessen)
(c. 1848–1852)
Louisville, Ky.
Bibl. 32, 93

John Hasselbring
(c. 1890–1955)
Brooklyn, N.Y.
Became Crown Silver Inc.
Bibl. 127, 157

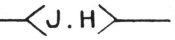

Charles Hassell (Hassan)
(c. 1837–1842)
Philadelphia, Pa.
Bibl. 3

John Hastier
(b. 1691–d. 1771)
New York, N.Y.
*Bibl. 2, 4, 15, 23, 24, 25, 28,
29, 30, 35, 36, 44, 54, 83,
95, 119, 124, 138, 139*

Marguerite Hastier
(c. 1771)
New York, N.Y.

M H

Bibl. 15, 23, 24, 25, 28, 29, 36, 39, 44, 104, 114, 124, 138

Hasting
(See Bolles [Holles] & Hasting)

B. B. Hastings
(c. 1830–1846)
Cleveland, Ohio
Bibl. 15, 23, 24, 25, 28, 34, 36, 44, 54, 114

HASTINGS   HASTINGS

D. B. Hastings
Boston, Mass.
Bibl. 79

H. Hastings (c. 1815)
New York, N.Y.
Ohio(?)
Bibl. 24, 25, 34, 44, 91, 114

H HASTINGS

Hasty & Snow (1860)
Portland, Me.
Bibl. 105

Hatch & Cross (1860)
Portland, Me.
Bibl. 105

B. B. Hatch (c. 1836–1840)
Cleveland, Ohio
Bibl. 34

Israel (I. A.) Hatch
(c. 1844–1845)
Philadelphia, Pa.
Bibl. 3

John Hatch (c. 1831)
Portsmouth, Ohio
Bibl. 34

W. H. H. Hatch (1875)
Portland, Me.
Bibl. 105

Haterick
(See James Hattrick)

James L. Hathway
(c. 1842)
Norfolk, Va.
Bibl. 19

Hattrick & Shannon
(c. 1844)
Philadelphia, Pa.
James Hattrick
Robert Shannon
Bibl. 3

Hattrick & Smith
(c. 1837)
Philadelphia, Pa.
James Hattrick
———— Smith
Bibl. 3

**James (J.R.) Hattrick
(Haterick)**
Philadelphia, Pa.
(c. 1839–1850)
Hattrick & Smith (c. 1837)
Hattrick & Shannon
(c. 1844)
Bibl. 3

Samuel Haugh
(See Samuel Hough)

John Haushall
(c. 1816–1817)
Philadelphia, Pa.
Bibl. 3

Henry Hausmann
(b. 1845–d. 1878)
New Orleans, La.
Bibl. 141

H.H. NEW ORLEANS

T. Hausmann & Son
(1890–1893)
New Orleans, La.
Became T. Hausmann &
Sons (1894–1906)
T. Hausmann & Sons Ltd.
(1906–1917)
T. Hausmann's Inc.
(c. 1918–present)
Bibl. 141

HAUSMANN & SON

T. Hausmann & Sons
(1894–1906)
New Orleans, La.
Successor to T. Hausmann &
Son (1890–1893)
Became T. Hausmann &
Sons, Ltd. (1906–1917)
T. Hausmann's, Inc.
(1918–present)
Bibl. 141

Theresa Hausmann
(1881–1889)
New Orleans, La.
Bibl. 141

Thomas Havens (1860)
Portland, Me.
Bibl. 105

William Haverstick
(b. 1756–d. 1823)
Lancaster, Pa.
(c. 1781–1798)
Philadelphia, Pa.

W H

Bibl. 3, 23, 24, 25, 36, 44, 91, 102, 112, 114

Havone Corporation
(c. 1915)
New York, N.Y.
Patents and trademarks
taken over by
Elgin-American Mfg. Co.
Bibl. 127, 157

HAVONE

Hawes & Co. (c. 1850)
Location unknown
Bibl. 24

Otis Hawkes (1860)
Providence, R.I.
Bibl. 108

Thomas Hawkes (1875)
Providence, R.I.
Bibl. 108

James Hawkins (c. 1841)
Philadelphia, Pa.
Bibl. 3

John Hawkins (c. 1826)
Georgetown, S.C.
Peter Finch
Bibl. 5

Hawley
(See Tracy & Hawley)

Hawley, Fuller & Co.
  (c. 1850)
Utica, N.Y.
Horace H. Hawley
Asa C. Fuller
Bibl. 18, 124

Hawley & Leach
  (c. 1853–1856)
Utica, N.Y.
Horace H. Hawley
Almon Leach
George Leach
Bibl. 18, 91, 124, 158

H. H. Hawley & Co.
  (c. 1850)
Utica, N.Y.
Horace H. Hawley
Bibl. 18, 124

Horace H. Hawley
  (b. 1818)
Utica, N.Y. (c. 1837–1856)
H. H. Hawley & Co.
  (c. 1850)
Hawley, Fuller & Co.
  (c. 1850)
Hawley & Leach
  (c. 1853–1856)
Bibl. 18, 91, 124, 158

John Dean Hawley
  (b. 1821–d. 1913)
Syracuse, N.Y.
  (c. 1844–1851)
Cazenovia, N.Y.
Willard & Hawley
  (c. 1844–1851)
Bibl. 20, 91, 124

Noah Hawley
  (c. 1810–1816)
New York, N.Y.
Bibl. 23, 24, 36, 44, 124

O. A. Hawley
  (c. 1850–?)
Cazenovia, N.Y.
Bibl. 20, 124

T. S. Hawley (c. 1837)
Canajoharie, N.Y.
Bibl. 20, 124

John Haws (c. 1837)
Philadelphia, Pa.
Bibl. 3, 23, 36, 44

Hawthorne Mfg. Co.
  (before 1904)
New York, N.Y.
Bibl. 127, 157

John Hay (c. 1830–1850?)
New York State (?)
Bibl. 89

Hayden, Brothers & Co.
  (c. 1852–1855)
Charleston, S.C.
Nathaniel Hayden
Bibl. 5, 44

HAYDEN BROTHER & CO.

Hayden & Gregg (Gregg & Hayden)
  (c. 1832–1846)
New York, N.Y.
Charleston, S.C.
Nathaniel Hayden
William Gregg
Bibl. 23, 24, 25, 28, 29, 36, 44, 54, 89, 114

| HAYDEN & GREGG |
| Gregg & Hayden |

Hayden, Gregg & Co. (Gregg, Hayden & Co.)
  (c. 1846–1852)
Charleston, S.C.
H. Sidney Hayden
Nathaniel Hayden
William Gregg
Bibl. 5, 24, 25, 44, 91, 93, 124

| GREGG, HAYDEN & CO. |

Hayden & Whilden
  (c. 1855–1863)
Charleston, S.C.
H. Sidney Hayden (?)
William G. Whilden (?)
Bibl. 5

HAYDEN & WHILDEN

Hayden Mfg. Co.
  (c. 1893–1909)
Newark, N.J.
Became G. W. Parks Co.,
  Inc. (c. 1909–1922)
Bibl. 114, 127, 157

H. Sidney Hayden
Charleston, S.C.
Hayden, Gregg & Co.
  (c. 1846–1852)
Hayden & Whilden
  (c. 1855–1863) (?)
Bibl. 5, 44, 54

J. Hayden (c. 1840)
Columbus, Ga.
Bibl. 17   J. HAYDEN

Jesse Hayden
  (c. 1811–1845)
Martinsburg, Va.
Bibl. 19

Nathaniel Hayden
  (b. 1805–d. 1875)
Charleston, S.C.
  (c. 1832–1843)
Eyland & Hayden
Hayden & Gregg
  (c. 1832–1846)
Hayden, Gregg & Co.
  (c. 1846–1852)
Hayden, Brothers & Co.
  (c. 1852–1855)
Bibl. 5, 44, 114

| N. HAYDEN |

William H. Hayden
  (d. 1853)
Martinsburg, Va.
  (c. 1845–1851)
Bibl. 19

William W. Hayden Co.
  (c. 1904–1909)
Newark, N.J.
Bibl. 127, 157

Eden Haydock
(c. 1839–1850)
Philadelphia, Pa.
Bibl. 3

James B. Haydock
(c. 1846–1849)
Location unknown
Bibl. 3

Thomas O. Haydock
(c. 1850)
Philadelphia, Pa.
Bibl. 3

Hayes & Adriance
(c. 1816–1826)
Poughkeepsie, N.Y.
Peter P. Hayes
John Adriance
Bibl. 15, 20, 25, 44, 91, 95, 114, 124

Hayes & Cotton (c. 1831)
Newark, N.J.
Bibl. 23, 28, 36, 44

Hayes & McFarland
(c. 1885)
Mt. Vernon, N.Y.
Merged Mauser
   Manufacturing Company
   and Roger Williams Silver
   Company, became Mt.
   Vernon Silversmiths
   Company (1903)
Became Gorham (1913?)
Bibl. 127, 157

C. B. Hayes & Co.
(c. 1845)
Poughkeepsie, N.Y.
Bibl. 20, 124

Edmund M. Hayes
(c. 1842–1843)
Poughkeepsie, N.Y.
Bibl. 20, 124

George Hayes
(c. 1842–1850)
Philadelphia, Pa.
Dreer & Hayes
Bibl. 3

Peter P. Hayes
(b. 1788–d. 1842)
Poughkeepsie, N.Y.
Hayes & Adriance
(c. 1816–1826)
Bibl. 15, 20, 25, 44, 91, 95, 114, 124

P. P. HAYES

Peter P. Hayes & Son
(c. 1841–1842)
Poughkeepsie, N.Y.
Bibl. 20, 91, 124

W. Hayes (c. 1780)
Connecticut (?)
Bibl. 28, 29, 44, 92, 110

W. Hayes   W H

O. A. Hayford (1860)
Canton, Me.
Bibl. 105

D. Haynes & Son
(c. 1842–1845)
Troy, N.Y.
David Haynes (?)
Bibl. 20, 124

David Haynes
(c. 1835–c. 1850)
Troy, N.Y.
D. Haynes & Son
(c. 1842–1845) (?)
Bibl. 20, 124

Isaac Haynes (1875)
Oldtown, Me.
Bibl. 105

J. R. Haynes (1848–1859)
Cincinnati, Ohio
Bibl. 54, 90, 127

Lafayette Haynes
(c. 1836–1837)
Troy, N.Y.
Bibl. 20, 124

Hays & Myers (c. 1770)
New York, N.Y.
Andrew Hays
Myer Myers
Bibl. 2, 15, 23, 24, 25, 28, 29, 35, 36, 44, 83, 102, 114

H & H   HAYS & MYERS

Andrew Hays
(c. 1769–1770)
New York, N.Y.
Hays & Myers (c. 1770)
Bibl. 4, 15, 23, 28, 36, 44, 91, 124

George Hays (Haes)
(b. 1819)
Utica, N.Y. (c. 1849–1859)
Bibl. 18, 124

Hayward & Sweet
(c. 1887–1904)
Attleboro, Mass.
(See Walter E. Hayward Co., Inc.)
Bibl. 114, 127, 135, 157

H. ★ S.   H. & S.
H. & S.   STERLING.

**Walter E. Hayward Co.,
Inc.** (c. 1904–present)
Attleboro, Mass.
Successor to Thompson,
   Hayward & Co.
   (1851–1855)
C. E. Hayward Co.
   (1855–1887)
Hayward & Sweet
   (1887–c. 1904)
Bibl. 127, 135   HAYWARD

Hayward

William A. Hayward
(1860)
Providence, R.I.
Bibl. 108

Hazen & Collins
(1843–1847)
Cincinnati, Ohio
N. L. Hazen
——— Collins
Bibl. 54, 90, 91

Nathan L. Hazen
(b. 1809–d. 1851)
Troy, N.Y. (c. 1829–1830)
Cincinnati, Ohio
(1831–1851)
Hazen & Collins
(1843–1847)
*Bibl. 20, 24, 54, 90, 91, 114,
124*

Joseph Head (c. 1798)
Philadelphia, Pa.
Bibl. 3, 23, 25, 36, 44, 114

Nelson Head (1874–1884)
Leesburg, Va.
Bibl. 89

William Headington
(c. 1806–1807)
Frankfort, Ky.
Bibl. 32, 93

William Headman
(c. 1828–1850)
Philadelphia, Pa.
Bibl. 3

John S. Heald (c. 1810)
Baltimore, Md.
Pittsburgh, Pa.
Ball & Heald (c. 1811–1812)
Bibl. 24, 25, 38, 44, 91, 114

| J. S. HEALD |

**William Healey (Heyley)
(Helly)** (c. 1785–1799)
Philadelphia, Pa.
Bibl. 3

Samuel Healy (d. 1773)
Boston, Mass.
Bibl. 28, 36, 38, 110

R. Hearn
Location unknown
Bibl. 28

| R. HEARN |

Samuel Heasley
(c. 1847–1852)
Winchester, Ky.
Bibl. 32, 54

John Heath (c. 1760–1763)
New York, N.Y.

*Bibl. 4, 15, 23, 24, 25, 28,
29, 35, 36, 44, 54, 91, 95,
102, 104, 114, 116, 124,
138, 151*

Ralph Heath
(c. 1807–1815)
Cambridge, Ohio
Chillicothe, Ohio
Bibl. 34, 44

Willard B. Heath
(1860–1875)
Bangor, Me.
Bibl. 105

John J. Hebard
(c. 1831–1832)
Poughkeepsie, N.Y.
Bibl. 20, 124

Hebbard & Co. (c. 1850)
New York, N.Y.
Bibl. 23

Henry Hebberd
(c. 1847–1851)
New York, N.Y.
Bibl. 4, 23, 28, 44

| HEBBERD |

Benjamin Hebrank
(c. 1812)
Zanesville, Ohio
Bibl. 34

John David Hechstetter
(c. 1796)
Philadelphia, Pa.
Bibl. 3

Lewis (Ludwig) Heck
(b. 1755–d. 1817)
Lancaster, Pa.
*Bibl. 3, 23, 24, 25, 29, 36,
44, 50, 54, 95, 104, 112,
114*

| L H |

Heckman
(See Douglass & Heckman)

Archimedes Heckman
(c. 1839–1840)
Philadelphia, Pa.
Bibl. 17

John Hector (c. 1774)
Charleston, S.C.
Bibl. 5, 44

Hedden & Heydorn
(c. 1810)
New Jersey
Bibl. 46

Richard B. Hedden
(c. 1824–1826)
New York, N.Y.
Bibl. 15, 124, 138

George Hedge(s) (Hedger)
Waterford, N.Y.
(c. 1819–1848)
Buffalo, N.Y. (c. 1828–1848)
*Bibl. 15, 20, 28, 44, 95, 114,
124, 151*

| HEDGES |

Daniel (David) Hedges Jr.
(b. 1779–d. 1856)
Easthampton, N.Y.
*Bibl. 20, 23, 24, 25, 29, 36,
44, 91, 114, 124*

| HEDGES |

Heer Bros. Co., Inc.
(c. 1927–1928)
Baltimore, Md.
Bibl. 127

Heer-Schofield Co.
(c. 1905–1928)
Baltimore, Md.
Successor to Baltimore
Silversmiths Mfg. Co.
Became Frank M. Schofield
Co. (c. 1928–1930)
Schofield Co. (c. 1930–1967)
Stieff Co. (1967)
Bibl. 127

Heeren Bros. & Co.
(c. 1887–1900)
Pittsburgh, Pa.
Bibl. 127

A. Judson Heffron
(c. 1859–1860)
Utica, N.Y.
Bibl. 18, 158

James Hegeman
(c. 1829–c. 1850)
Troy, N.Y.
Bibl. 20, 124

John Heilig (Helig)
(c. 1801–1850)
Philadelphia, Pa.
Bibl. 3

Gottlieb Heimberg
(c. 1842–1847)
St. Louis, Mo.
Bibl. 54, 155

Daniel Heineman
(c. 1837)
Philadelphia, Pa.
Bibl. 3

George Heineman
(c. 1847–1849)
Philadelphia, Pa.
Bibl. 3

L. C. (L. G.) Heineman
(c. 1849–1850)
Philadelphia, Pa.
Bibl. 3

Paul Heinrich (1870–1880)
New Orleans, La.
Bibl. 141

Heintz Art Metal Shop
(c. 1906–1929)
Buffalo, N.Y.
Became Heintz Bros. Mfg.
Bibl. 89, 120, 127

Heirloom
(See Oneida)

Frederick Heisley
(c. 1786–1816)
Fredericktown, Md.
Bibl. 38

James P. Heiss
(c. 1849–1850)
Philadelphia, Pa.
Bibl. 3

Henry Helge(r)fort
(c. 1849)
Philadelphia, Pa.
Bibl. 3, 23

Helig
(See Heilig)

Jacob Heller
(c. 1837–1850)
Philadelphia, Pa.
Bibl. 3

John Heller
(c. 1837)
Philadelphia, Pa.
Bibl. 3

Helly
(See Healey)

Christian Helm
(c. 1802–1804)
Philadelphia, Pa.
Bibl. 3

Thomas Helm
(c. 1835–1850)
Philadelphia, Pa.
Bibl. 3

Nathaniel Helme
(c. 1761–1789)
South Kingston, R.I.
Bibl. 24, 25, 28, 29, 44, 56, 91, 102, 110, 114

Henry Helwich (Helvich)
(c. 1815–1817)
New York, N.Y.
Bibl. 15, 124, 138

George Hemburgh
(c. 1845)
St. Louis, Mo.
Bibl. 54, 155

Thomas Heming (c. 1764)
New York (?), N.Y.
Bibl. 28

Alexander Hemphill
(c. 1741)
Philadelphia, Pa.
Bibl 3, 23

Thomas J. Hemphill
(c. 1836–1841)
Philadelphia, Pa.
Bibl. 3

Daniel Booth Hempsted
(b. 1784–d. 1852)
Eatonton, Ga. (1821)
New London, Conn.
Daniel B. Hempsted & Co.
(c. 1821) (?)
Bibl. 44, 91, 92, 94, 110, 114, 138

Daniel B. Hempsted & Co. (c. 1821)
Eatonton, Ga.
Daniel B. Hempsted
Nathaniel Saltonstall
Bibl. 17

E. Hempsted (c. 1820)
Location unknown
Bibl. 28, 110

Hemstead & Chandler
(c. 1811–c. 1815)
New York, N.Y.
—— Hemstead
Stephen Chandler
Bibl. 23, 36, 44, 124, 138

Daniel Henchman
(b. 1730–d. 1775)
Boston, Mass.
Bibl. 2, 15, 23, 24, 25, 28, 29, 36, 44, 54, 69, 91, 94, 102, 110, 114, 116, 119, 135, 139

George A. Henckel & Co.
(c. 1909–1940)
New York, N.Y.
Became Currier & Roby
(c. 1940)
Bibl. 127, 157

Henderson & Lossing
  (c. 1835)
Poughkeepsie, N.Y.
Adam Henderson (?)
Benson John Lossing
Bibl. 20, 124

A. A. Henderson
  (c. 1835–1837)
Philadelphia, Pa.
Bibl. 3, 15, 24, 25, 44, 114

Adam Henderson
  (c. 1846)
Poughkeepsie, N.Y.
Henderson & Lossing
  (c. 1835) (?)
Bibl. 20, 25, 44

Henderson Field & Co.
  (c. 1816)
Philadelphia, Pa.
Bibl. 23

Henderson, Field & Co.
  (c. 1816)
Philadelphia, Pa.
Stephen Henderson
Samuel Field
Bibl. 3

Logan Henderson
  (c. 1767)
Charleston, S.C.
Oliphant & Henderson
  (c. 1767)
Bibl. 5

Stephen Henderson
  (c. 1803–1816)
Philadelphia, Pa.
Henderson, Field & Co.
  (c. 1816)
Bibl. 3

William Henderson
  (c. 1770)
Appoquinimink, Del.
New Castle, Del.
Bibl. 3

John Hendrick
  (c. 1835–1836)
Albany, N.Y.
Bibl. 20, 124

Ahasuerus Hendricks
  (d. 1727)
New York, N.Y.
  (c. 1678–1698)
*Bibl. 2, 4, 15, 23, 24, 25, 28,
  29, 30, 36, 44, 54, 95, 102,
  114, 116, 119, 124, 138*

John Hendricks (c. 1848)
Philadelphia, Pa.
Bibl. 3, 23

Hendrickse
(See Hendricks)

William Hendrickson
  (c. 1848–1850)
Philadelphia, Pa.
Bibl. 3, 23

**Hennegan, Bates &
  Company**
  (c. 1857–1930)
Wheeling, W. Va.
  (1857–1874)
Baltimore, Md.
  (1874–c. 1930)
Bibl. 127

HENNEGAN, BATES & CO.

John A. Henneman
  (b. 1835–d. 1889)
Chester, Pa. (c. 1854)
Spartanburg, S.C.
  (c. 1859–1889)
Norfolk, Va.
Bibl. 5

Henry
(See Dickinson & Henry)

——— **Henry** (c. 1793)
Philadelphia, Pa.
Dickinson & Henry
Bibl. 3

Felix Henry (c. 1815)
New York, N.Y.
*Bibl. 15, 23, 36, 44, 114,
  124, 138*

John Henry (1867–1880)
New Orleans, La.
Bibl. 141

Samuel Hensley
  (c. 1829–1833)
Mt. Sterling, Ky.
Bibl. 32, 54, 68, 93

Hephaestus, Ltd.
  (1969–c. 1980)
St. Louis, Mo.
Matt A. Meis
John Baltrushunas
Bibl. 155

Frederick Hepton
  (c. 1785)
Philadelphia, Pa.
Bibl. 3

Charles Hequembourg, Jr.
  (b. 1788–d. 1875)
New Haven, Conn.
  (1809–1822)
Albany, N.Y. (1822–1826)
New York, N.Y.
  (c. 1827–1830)
Paterson, N.J.
  (c. 1830–1835)
Buffalo, N.Y.
  (c. 1835–1842)
St. Louis, Mo.
  (c. 1843–1851, c. 1857)
George William
  Hequembourg
Theodore Hequembourg
*Bibl. 15, 16, 20, 23, 24, 25,
  28, 36, 44, 61, 89, 92, 94,
  110, 114, 124, 134, 138,
  143, 155*

**George William
  Hequembourg**
  (b. 1821–d. 1854)
St. Louis, Mo. (1848–1854)
Charles Hequembourg, Jr.
Theodore Hequembourg
Bibl. 89, 155

Theodore Hequembourg
  (b. 1815–d. 1888)
St. Louis, Mo. (1842–1857)
George William
  Hequembourg
Charles Hequembourg, Jr.
*Bibl. 20, 54, 89, 124, 134,
  155*

A. Herbel (c. 1821–1853)
St. Louis, Mo.
Bibl. 54, 155

Lawrence Herbert
(c. 1748–1751)
Philadelphia, Pa.
Bibl. 3, 28

Matthew Herbert
(b. 1710–d. 1746)
Saint Marys County, Md.
(c. 1732–1746)
Bibl. 38

Timothy B. Herbert
(c. 1824–1829)
New York, N.Y.
*Bibl. 15, 23, 36, 44, 91, 124,
138*

**Widow of Timothy
Herbert** (c. 1831–1832)
New York, N.Y.
Bibl. 15

Herbst & Wassall
(c. 1904–1931)
Newark, N.J.
Bibl. 127, 157

Francis Herils (Herrils)
(c. 1804–1833)
Philadelphia, Pa.
Bibl. 3, 23, 36, 44

Charles Heringer
(c. 1844–1850)
Philadelphia, Pa.
Bibl. 3

John C. Heringer
(c. 1849–1850)
Philadelphia, Pa.
Bibl. 3

F. A. Hermann Co.
(c. 1908–1978)
Melrose Highlands, Mass.
Bibl. 127

Silvercryst

Erskine Heron
(c. 1762–1765)
Charleston, S.C.
Bibl 5, 54

Isaac Heron
Philadelphia, Pa. (c. 1763)
Bound Brook, N.J. (c. 1764)
Middlesex City, N.J.
(c. 1764)
New York, N.Y.
(c. 1766–1780)
*Bibl. 3, 23, 28, 36, 44, 46,
54, 124, 138*

Isaac Heroy
(c. 1813–1815)
Newburgh, N.Y.
Troy, N.Y.
(c. 1823–1824)
Reeve & Heroy
Bibl. 20, 124

Herrils
(See Herils)

William Herrington
(c. 1850)
Syracuse, N.Y.
Philadelphia, Pa.
Bibl. 3, 20, 124

L. Hertz (1855)
New Orleans, La.
Bibl. 141

C. Hervey (1860–1875)
Belfast, Me.
Bibl. 105

Stephen Hesler (c. 1801)
Baltimore, Md.
Bibl. 38

Hess & Culbertson
(1883–present)
St. Louis, Mo.
Bibl. 155

Hessen
(See Moses Hassan)

Jacob Hester (c. 1823)
Philadelphia, Pa.
Bibl. 3

John M. Hetzel (c. 1795)
Newton, N.J.
Bibl. 46, 54

John Heughan (c. 1772)
Schenectady, N.Y.
Bibl. 28

William Heurtin
(b. 1703–d. 1765)
Newark, N.J.
New York, N.Y.
*Bibl. 4, 23, 24, 25, 34, 44,
46, 54, 114, 124, 138*

Archill Hevitt (Huet)
(c. 1804)
Baltimore, Md.
Bibl. 38

Abram Hewes (b. 1827)
Boston, Mass. (c. 1823)
Bibl. 28, 124, 158

Joel F. Hewes (c. 1908)
Boston, Mass.(?)
Bibl. 144

Joel F. Hewes

C. W. Hewit
(c. 1850–?)
Utica, N.Y.
Bibl. 18, 20

Abraham Hews Jr.
(b. 1797–d. 1867)
Boston, Mass.
(c. 1823–1850)
*Bibl. 23, 24, 25, 28, 29, 36,
44, 91, 110, 114*

A HEWS JR

John D. Hewson (d. 1852)
Albany, N.Y. (c. 1815–1817)
Hall, Hewson & Co.
Hall, Brower & Co.
(c. 1836–1842)
Hall, Hewson & Merrifield
(c. 1840)
Hall & Hewson
(c. 1842–1847)
Hall, Hewson & Brower
(c. 1847–1850)
Bibl. 20, 23, 28, 36, 44, 124

William Hewson
(c. 1818–1822)
Albany, N.Y.
Bibl. 20, 124

Charles Heyde
(c. 1839–1840)
Philadelphia, Pa.
Bibl. 3

Charles W. Heydon
(c. 1841–1845)
Portsmouth, Va.
Bibl. 19

Heydorn
(See Hedden & Heydorn)

Heydorn & Imlay
(c. 1810)
Hartford, Conn.
C. Heydorn
R. Imlay
Bibl. 24, 25, 44, 46, 61, 91, 92, 94

Heyer & Gale
(c. 1800–1807)
New York, N.Y.
William B. Heyer
John L. Gale
Bibl. 23, 24, 25, 30, 35, 36, 44, 114, 124, 135, 138

W B Heyer   J Gale

William Braisted Heyer
(c. 1798–1828)
New York, N.Y.
Heyer & Gale
(c. 1800–1807)
Bibl. 4, 15, 23, 24, 28, 29, 30, 35, 36, 39, 44, 74, 83, 95, 114, 116, 122, 124, 135, 138, 151

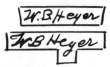

Widow of William B. Heyer (c. 1831–1832)
New York, N.Y.
Bibl. 15

Heyley
(See Healey)

Oscar Heyman & Co.
(c. 1912)
New York, N.Y.
Bibl. 126

Moses Hiams (b. 1751)
Philadelphia, Pa. (c. 1775)
Bibl. 28

Hibbard, Spencer, Bartlett & Co.
(c. 1884–1906)
Chicago, Ill.
Bibl. 127

Andrew Hibben
(c. 1764, d. 1784)
Charleston, S.C.
Bibl. 5

John Hickman
Louisville, Ky. (1832–1850)
Taylorsville, Ky.
(c. 1850–1862)
Bibl. 32, 54, 68, 91, 93

Hickok-Matthews Company
(c. 1931–present)
Montville, N.J.
Merged Eleder-Hickok Company and Matthews Co. (c. 1931)
Bibl. 127, 146

George W. Hickok & Co.
(c. 1892)
Santa Fe, N.M.
Bibl. 127

Hicks Silver Co.
(See A. R. Justice Co.)

Joseph Hicks
(c. 1798–1823)
Harrisonburg, Va.
Bibl. 19

Higbie & Crosby
New York, N.Y.
(c. 1825–1831)
Ransom Crosby
Bibl. 23, 24, 25, 29, 36, 44, 110, 114

HIGBIE & CROSBY

Thomas Higginbotham
(c. 1829–1830)
Augusta, Ga.
Sparta, Ga.
Bibl. 17

Higgins, Marchand & Co.
(c. 1867)
Philadelphia, Pa.
Bibl. 127

Abraham Higgins
(c. 1738–1763)
Eastham, Mass.
Bibl. 28, 110

George E. Higgins
(c. 1850)
Syracuse, N.Y.
Covell & Higgins
Bibl. 20, 124

Samuel Higginson
(c. 1771–1775)
Annapolis, Md. (c. 1774)
St. Marys County, Md.
Whetcroft & Higginson
(c. 1774)
Bibl. 38

Christian Hight
(c. 1819–1822)
Philadelphia, Pa.
Bibl. 3

Hi-Grade Silver Co., Inc.
(c. 1927)
New York, N.Y.
Bibl. 127

CREAMERS

Creamers were very small in the eighteenth century. They slowly increased in size and by 1825 were as large as the early eighteenth-century teapots. The most famous creamer shape is the Queen Anne (1755), with three small feet. The shape has been copied ever since its introduction. Tea sets were made with matching teapot, creamer, and sugar bowl. When the teapot became bulbous with a footed base about 1825 the creamer had the same design characteristics. Victorian creamers often had overall flower decorations or exotic animal feet. Curved lines swirled over the Art Nouveau creamer, sharp angular panels were favored by the Art Deco designers.

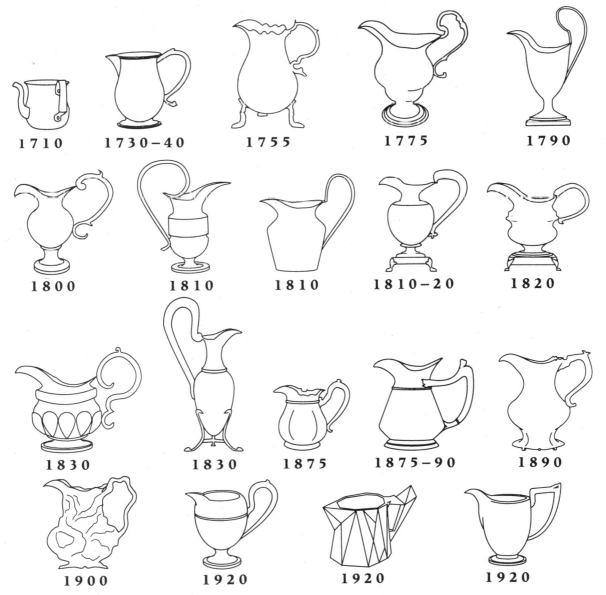

1710   1730-40   1755   1775   1790

1800   1810   1810   1810-20   1820

1830   1830   1875   1875-90   1890

1900   1920   1920   1920

Jonas Jacob Hilburn
  (c. 1857–1877)
Bowling Green, Ky.
Fuselli & Hilburn
  (1866–1873)
Bibl. 54, 93

Hildeburn & Bros.
  (c. 1849–1850)
Philadelphia, Pa.
Bibl. 3

Hildeburn & Watson
(See Watson & Hildeburn)

Samuel Hildeburn
  (c. 1810–1837)
Philadelphia, Pa.
Bibl. 3, 36, 44, 54, 91

(HILDEBURN)

Woolworth Hildeburn
  (c. 1816–1819)
Philadelphia, Pa.
Bibl. 3

—— **Hill** (c. 1782)
(May have been Richard
  Hill)
Petersburg, Va.
Hill & Waddill
Bibl. 19

Hill & Johnson (c. 1849)
Richmond, Va.
John Hill
W. M. Johnson
Bibl. 19

Hill & Waddill
  (c. 1780–1782)
Petersburg, Va.
Noel Waddill
Bibl. 19, 23, 36, 44

Alvin M. Hill (1874–1909)
New Orleans, La.
Bibl. 141

A.M.HILL

Arundel Hill (c. 1829)
Steubenville, Ohio
Bibl. 34

Benjamin Hill
  (c. 1687–?)
Boston, Mass.
Bibl. 54

Charles F. Hill
  (c. 1816–1852)
Canandaigua, N.Y.
Hartford, Conn.
Bibl. 20, 91, 95, 114, 124

E. Hill (c. 1821–1844)
Cincinnati, Ohio
Bibl. 34, 90, 152

E. H. Hill
  (b. 1814–d. 1873)
Kentucky (?)
Bibl. 54, 90, 93

F. F. Hill (1875)
Portland, Me.
Bibl. 105

H. M. Hill & Co.
  (c. 1891–1914)
Lynn, Mass.
Bibl. 28, 29, 127, 157

Hugh Hill
Norfolk, Va. (before 1770)
Williamsburg, Va.
  (after 1770)
Bibl. 19

James Hill (c. 1770)
Boston, Mass.
Bibl. 15, 23, 25, 36, 44, 110, 114

[J. HILL]

John Hill (c. 1818–1850)
Richmond, Va.
Hill & Johnson (c. 1849)
Bibl. 19

Nobel Spencer A. Hill
  (c. 1795)
Bennington, Vt.
Bibl. 54, 110

Warren F. Hill (1860)
Gray, Me.
Bibl. 105

William F. Hill
  (c. 1815–1817)

New York, N.Y.
Bibl. 15, 25, 44, 114, 124, 138

[W. F. Hill]

Thomas Hilldrup
  (c. 1795, d. 1804)
Hartford, Conn.
Bibl. 16, 23, 28, 36, 44, 110

Hillebrand & Co.
  (c. 1855)
Nashville, Tenn.
Bibl. 54

—— **Hiller**
(See Haller)

Benjamin Hiller
  (b. 1687–d. 1745)
Boston, Mass. (until 1745)
Bibl. 2, 15, 24, 28, 29, 33, 36, 44, 69, 94, 110, 114, 118, 119

Joseph Hiller
  (b. 1721–d. 1758)
Boston, Mass.
Charlestown, Mass.
Bibl. 23, 28, 36, 44, 102, 110

Major Joseph Hiller
  (c. 1748–1814)
Salem, Mass.
Bibl. 28

Christopher Hilliard
  (b. 1802–d. 1871)
Hagerstown, Md.
Bibl. 38

George W. Hilliard
  (c. 1823)
Fayetteville, N.C.
Bibl. 21

William Hilliard
  (c. 1801–1810)
Fayetteville, N.C.
Bibl. 21

C. F. Hills (c. 1850)
Hartford, Conn.
Bibl. 23

Frederick Hillworth
(c. 1844–1849)
Philadelphia, Pa.
Bibl. 3

Philip Hillyartiner
(c. 1844)
Philadelphia, Pa
Bibl. 3

William Hilton (c. 1814)
Philadelphia, Pa.
Bibl. 3, 23, 36, 44, 54

Adolphe Himmel   A.H.
(b. 1825–d. 1877)   N.O.
New Orleans, La.
Bibl. 127, 141

A.H. NEW ORLEANS

Camilla G. Hinchman
(c. 1972–1980)
St. Louis, Mo.
Bibl. 155

Richard Hinckley
(c. 1839–1841)
Philadelphia, Pa.
Bibl. 3

Robert H. Hinckley
(c. 1839–1841)
Philadelphia, Pa.
Bibl. 3, 91

John Hind (d. 1775)
Philadelphia Pa.
Bibl. 3, 23, 36, 44

**D. B. Hindman & Co.
(Hinman)**
(c. 1833–1837)
Philadelphia, Pa.
Bibl. 3, 15, 25, 44, 91, 114

Robert Hines
(c. 1848–1850)
Philadelphia, Pa.
Bibl. 3

Benjamin Hinkin
(c. 1837)

Philadelphia, Pa.
Bibl. 3

Benjamin Hinkle
(c. 1840–1850)
Philadelphia, Pa.
Thirion & Hinkle (c. 1850)
Bibl. 3

John P. Hinkle (c. 1824)
Philadelphia, Pa.
Bibl. 3

Hinman
(See Hindman)

Hinsdale & Atkin
(c. 1830–1838)
New York, N.Y.
Horace Hinsdale
John H. Atkin
*Bibl. 15, 24, 25, 44, 91, 114,
124, 135, 138*

HINSDALE & ATKIN

Hinsdale & Taylor
(See Taylor & Hinsdale)

E. Hinsdale & Co.
(before 1810)
Newark, N.J.
Epaphras Hinsdale
John Taylor
Bibl. 46, 124, 138

**Epaphras (Epahras)
Hinsdale**
(b. 1769–d. 1810)
Newark, N.J. (?–1810)
New York, N.Y.
E. Hinsdale & Co.
(before 1810)
*Bibl. 23, 24, 28, 29, 36, 44,
46, 54, 91, 124, 138*

HINSDALE

Horace Seymour Hinsdale
(b. 1782–d. 1858)
Newark, N.J. (c. 1815–1842)
New York, N.Y.
(c. 1815, c. 1830–1838)
Taylor & Hinsdale
(1807–1817)
Palmer & Hinsdale (c. 1815)
Hinsdale & Atkin
(c. 1830–1838)

*Bibl. 15, 23, 25, 28, 44, 91,
102, 114, 124, 135, 138*

William M. Hinton
(b. 1830)
Paris, Ky.
(c. 1844–1847, c. 1854)
Shelbyville, Ky.
(c. 1847–1854)
Bibl. 32, 54, 68, 93

Hirsch & Oppenheimer
(c. 1904–1927)
Chicago, Ill.
Bibl. 127, 157

M. Fred Hirsch Co., Inc.
(c. 1920–1945)
Jersey City, N.J.
Became Fisher Silversmiths,
Inc. (c. 1945)
Bibl. 127

Hirshbuhl & Dolfinger
(c. 1859–1861)
Louisville, Ky.
Joseph J. Hirshbuhl
Jacob Dolfinger
Bibl. 32, 93

Elisha F. Hirst (Hurst)
(c. 1850–1881)
Hirst & Co.
Richmond, Ind.
Bibl. 133

Daniel Hitchborn
(c. 1752–1828)
Boston, Mass.
Bibl. 23, 36, 44

Eliakim Hitchborn
(See Hitchcock)

Samuel Hitchborn
(c. 1780–1828)
Boston, Mass.
Bibl. 36, 44, 79, 110

Hitchcock
(See Sigourney & Hitchcock)

Eliakim Hitchcock   E H
  (Hitchborn)
  (b. 1726–d. 1788)
Cheshire, Conn.
New Haven, Conn.
Bibl. 15, 16, 23, 24, 25, 28,
  29, 36, 44, 54, 61, 91, 92,
  94, 110, 114, 143

John G. Hiter
  (c. 1813–1819)
Lexington, Ky.
Ayres & Hiter (c. 1813)
Bibl. 32, 54, 93

Hoard & Hoes
  (1859–1862)
Chicago, Ill.
Successor to S. Hoard & Co.
  (1852–1855)
Hoard & Avery (1856–1858)
Became James H. Hoes &
  Co. (1862–1863)
Matson & Hoes (1864–1867)
N. Matson & Co.
  (1867–1888)
Spaulding & Co.
  (1889–1929)
Spaulding-Gorham Co.
  (1929–1943)
Spaulding & Company
  (1943–present)
Bibl. 98, 127

HOARD & HOES

Joshua Hobart(h)
  (c. 1811–1813)
New Haven, Conn.
New Bern, N.C.
Fitch & Hobart
  (c. 1811–1813)
Bibl. 16, 21, 23, 24, 25, 28,
  29, 36, 44, 92, 110, 114,
  143   J. HOBART

Nathan Hobbs
  (b. 1792–d. 1868)
Boston, Mass.
Bibl. 4, 15, 23, 24, 25, 28,
  29, 36, 44, 91, 110, 114

N HOBBS   HOBBS

Joseph Hocker
  (c. 1829–1833)
Philadelphia, Pa.
Bibl. 3

Willis Hocker
  (c. 1846–1849)
Philadelphia, Pa.
Bibl. 3

Hocknell
(See Steele & Hocknell)

James Hodge (c. 1853)
Columbia, Tenn.
Bibl. 54

John Hodge   J HODGE
  (c. 1775–1800)
Hadley, Mass.
Bibl. 3, 23, 24, 29, 36, 44,
  114

T. Hodgman
Location unknown
Bibl. 28

William Hodgson (c. 1785)
Philadelphia, Pa.
Bibl. 3

Daniel Hodkins
  (c. 1840–1841)
Albany, N.Y.
Bibl. 20, 124

——— Hodsdon
Location unknown
Bibl. 28

R. S. Hodsdon (1875)
Kenduskeag, Me.
Bibl. 105

Theodore Hoefer (1870)
New Orleans, La.
Bibl. 141

Edward Hoell (1830–1873)
New Bern, N.C.
Greenville, N.C.
  (c. 1830–1847)
Pitt County, N.C. (c. 1873)
Washington, N.C.
Bibl. 21

James H. Hoes & Co.
  (1862–1863)
Chicago, Ill.
Successor to Hoard & Hoes
  (1859–1862)
(See Hoard & Hoes)
Bibl. 98

Augustus E. Hofer
  (c. 1841–1843)
Albany, N.Y.
Bibl. 20, 124

George Frederick Hoff
  (b. 1810)
Lancaster, Pa.
Bibl. 3

George W. Hoff
  (c. 1850)
Auburn, N.Y.
Hyde & Hoff
Bibl. 20, 124

John Hoff
  (c. 1776, d. 1818)
Lancaster, Pa.
Bibl. 3

Hoffman Manufacturing
  Co. (c. 1927)
Newark, N.J.
Bibl. 127

Christian Frederick
  Hoffman (b. 1786)
New York, N.Y.
  (c. 1819–1820)
Philadelphia, Pa.
  (1820–1849)
Bard & Hoffman (Bird &
  Hoffman) (c. 1837)
Bibl. 3, 23, 36, 44, 124, 138

Frederick S. Hoffman
  (c. 1896)
Brooklyn, N.Y.
Became Webster Brother &
  Co.
A. A. Webster & Co.
Clarence B. Webster
  (c. 1904)
Bibl. 114, 127, 157

James M. Hoffman
  (c. 1804–1820)
Philadelphia, Pa.
Bibl. 23, 24, 25, 29, 36, 44,
  114

J. M. HOFFMAN

John H. Hoffman
(c. 1848–1850)
Philadelphia, Pa.
Bibl. 3

Max Hoffman
(c. 1848–1851)
Newark, N.J.
Bibl. 127

Henry Hoffner (c. 1791)
Philadelphia, Pa.
Bibl. 3

John Hoffner (c. 1818)
Philadelphia, Pa.
Bibl. 3

Hogan & Wade (c. 1850)
Cleveland, Ohio
Bibl. 89

**Augustus F. Hoguet
(Hognet)**
Philadelphia, Pa.
(c. 1814–1833)
Bibl. 3

Holbrook & Simmons
(c. 1896)
New York, N.Y.
Successor to Holbrook, Dagg
& Co.
Became Holbrook &
Thornton
Thornton & Co. (c. 1896)
Bibl. 127

H. & S.

Holbrook Mfg. Co.
(1905–1916)
Attleboro, Mass.
Bibl. 127

**Holbrook, Whiting &
Albee** (c. 1878)
North Attleboro, Mass.
Became F. M. Whiting & Co.
(1878–1891)
F. M. Whiting (1891–1895)
F. M. Whiting Co.
(1895–1896)
Frank M. Whiting & Co.
(1896–1940)
Became division of Ellmore
Silver Co.
(c. 1940–1960)
Out of business in 1960
Bibl. 127

Holden & Boning
(c. 1843)
Philadelphia, Pa.
Eli Holden
William Boning
Bibl. 3, 91

Eli Holden (c. 1843–1850)
Philadelphia, Pa.
Holden & Boning (c. 1843)
Bibl. 3

A. A. Holdredge (c. 1841)
Glens Falls, N.Y.
Bibl. 20, 124

Julius Holister
(See Julius Hollister)

Littleton Holland
(b. 1770–d. 1847)
Baltimore, Md.
(c. 1800–1847)
*Bibl. 15, 23, 24, 25, 28, 29,
36, 38, 39, 44, 54, 78, 80,
91, 95, 114, 122*

Nelson Holland
(c. 1827–1828)
Northampton, Mass.
Phelps & Holland
Bibl. 84

Holles (Bolles) & Hasting
(c. 1840)
Location unknown
Bibl. 89

A. Hollinger (c. 1839)
Philadelphia, Pa.
Bibl. 3

John Hollingshead
(c. 1768)
Philadelphia, Pa.
Bibl. 3, 23, 36, 44

Morgan Hollingshead
(c. 1775)
Moorestown, N.J.
Bibl. 3

William Hollingshead
(c. 1754–1785)
Philadelphia, Pa.
*Bibl. 3, 15, 23, 24, 25, 28,
29, 36, 44, 54, 81, 91, 95,
102, 114, 151*

Jacob Hollinshead
(c. 1768–1772)
Salem, N.J.
Bibl. 3

Joseph Hollinshead
(c. 1740–1765)
Burlington, N.J.
Bibl. 46, 54

Hollister (1820)
Greenfield, Mass.
Bibl. 106

Julius Hollister (Holister)
(b. 1818–d. 1905)
Hartford, Conn. (c. 1845)
Greenfield, Mass.
Oswego, N.Y. (c. 1846)
Seymour & Hollister
Bibl. 15, 20, 23, 25, 44, 114

Robert Holloway (c. 1822)
Baltimore, Md.
Bibl. 38, 114

D. Holman
Baltimore, Md.
Munroe & Holman
(c. 1826–1829)
Bibl. 38

Holmes
(See Rand & Crane)

Holmes & Edwards
(1882–1898)
Bridgeport, Conn.
Became International Silver
    Company (1898); moved
    to Meriden (1931)
Bibl. 127

Holmes & Rowan
(c. 1847–1850)
Philadelphia, Pa.
Bibl. 3

A. C. Holmes (1875)
Buckfield, Me.
Bibl. 105

Adrian B. Holmes
(c. 1801–1849)
New York, N.Y.
*Bibl. 15, 23, 24, 25, 29, 36,
    44, 91, 114, 124, 138*

A. HOLMES

George H. Holmes
(c. 1840–1850)
Philadelphia, Pa.
Bibl. 3

Israel Holmes
(b. 1768–d. 1802)
Greenwich, Conn.
Waterbury, Conn.
Bibl. 16, 23, 28, 36, 44, 143

J. Holmes (c. 1816)
New York, N.Y.
Bibl. 23, 36, 44

J. Holmes (c. 1842)
Philadelphia, Pa.
Bibl. 3

William Holmes (c. 1801)
New York, N.Y.
Bibl. 23, 36, 44, 124

William Holmes
(Boston)
(See William Homes)

E. Holsey (c. 1820)
Philadelphia, Pa.
Bibl. 24, 25, 44, 114

E HOLSEY

Holsted
(See Myers and Holsted)

David Holt Jr.
(c. 1831–1833)
Harpers Ferry, Va.
Bibl. 19

G. W. Holt
(See G. W. Hoff)

David Holton (c. 1804)
Baltimore, Md.
Bibl. 23, 28, 36, 44

John Holton
(See Houlton)

Jacob Holtzbaum
(c. 1790–1793)
Fredericktown, Md.
Koontz & Holtzbaum
    (c. 1793)
Bibl. 38

Frederick Holyland
(1865–1881)
New Orleans, La.
Bibl. 141

Edward Holyoke
(c. 1817–1825)
Boston, Mass.
*Bibl. 23, 24, 25, 28, 36, 44,
    110, 114*

HOLYOKE

Charles Holzaphel
(c. 1846)
New York, N.Y.
Bibl. 23, 124, 138

Geo. E. Homer
(1875–present)
Boston, Mass.
Bibl. 114, 127, 157

William Homes (Holmes)
(b. 1717–d. 1783)
Boston, Mass.
*Bibl. 2, 15, 23, 24, 25, 28,
    29, 36, 39, 44, 50, 54, 91,
    94, 102, 110, 114*

HOMES   HOMES

**William Homes Jr.
(Holmes)**
(b. 1742–d. 1825)
Boston, Mass.
*Bibl. 2, 15, 23, 24, 25, 28,
    29, 36, 44, 91, 94, 110,
    114, 151*

W H   HOMES

Samuel D. Honeyman
(c. 1841)
Charleston, Va.
Bibl. 19

Hood & Tobey
(c. 1848–1849)
Albany, N.Y.
*Bibl. 15, 20, 23, 24, 25, 28,
    29, 44, 114, 124*

HOOD & TOBEY

Benjamin L. Hood
(c. 1841–1844)
Buffalo, N.Y.
Rochester, N.Y.
Bibl. 20, 124

Harry O. Hood
(c. 1842–1844)
Buffalo, N.Y.
Rochester, N.Y.
Bibl. 20, 124

Jacob Hood (c. 1825)
Philadelphia, Pa.
Bibl. 3

Frederick Hoofman
(c. 1819)
New York, N.Y.
Bibl. 15

Hooker & Morgan
(c. 1813)
Pine Plains, N.Y.
Bibl. 20, 124

William Hooker
(c. 1813–1814)
Philadelphia, Pa.
Bibl. 3

William Hookey
(b. 1733–d. 1812)
Newport, R.I.
Bibl. 6, 23, 28, 44, 91, 110

Jacob Hoop
(c. 1823–1824)
Philadelphia, Pa.
Bibl. 3

William W. Hooper
(c. 1832–1833)
Macon, Ga.
Milledgeville, Ga.
Bibl. 17

Henry Hoover
(c. 1816–c. 1822)
Philadelphia, Pa.
Bibl. 3, 23, 36, 44

Joseph E. Hoover
(c. 1837–1841)
Philadelphia, Pa.
Faber & Hoover (c. 1837)
Bibl. 3, 23, 36, 44

Constantine Hope
(c. 1807–1809)
Savannah, Ga.
Bibl. 17, 91   HOPE

Hopewell Silver Company
(c. 1913–1918)
Taunton, Mass.
Division of Reed & Barton
Bibl. 127   HOPEWELL SILVER CO.

Hopkins & Briele
(c. 1879–1886)
Baltimore, Md.
Bibl. 127

Henry Hopkins
(c. 1831–1833)
Philadelphia, Pa.
Bibl. 3

James E. Hopkins
(c. 1828–1830)
Westfield, N.Y.
Bibl. 20, 124

Jesse Hopkins
(b. 1766–d. 1836)
Waterbury, Conn.
Bibl. 16, 23, 28, 36, 44, 110

Joseph W. Hopkins
(b. 1730–d. 1801)
Waterbury, Conn.
Bibl. 16, 23, 24, 25, 28, 36, 44, 61, 91, 92, 94, 110, 114   HOPKINS

Joshua Hopkins (1875)
New Sharon, Me.
Bibl. 105

Lawrence Hopkins
(c. 1836–1837)
New York, N.Y.
Bibl. 15, 138

Robert Hopkins (c. 1833)
Philadelphia, Pa.
Bibl. 3, 124

Stephen Hopkins Jr.
(b. 1721–d. 1796)   S. H
Waterbury, Conn.
Bibl. 16, 23, 24, 25, 28, 44, 91, 92, 110, 114

Thomas R. Hopkins
(d. 1869)
Petersburg, Va.
Cosby & Hopkins
(c. 1846–1847)
Bibl. 19

Henry Hopkis (b. 1801)
New Orleans, La. (1820)
Bibl. 141

Benjamin C. Hopper
(c. 1844–1850)
Philadelphia, Pa.
Bibl. 3

Joseph (J. M.) Hopper
(c. 1816–1841)
Philadelphia, Pa.
Bibl. 3

Samuel M. Hopper
(c. 1835–1850)
Philadelphia, Pa.
Bibl. 3, 23, 36, 44, 91, 114

Hugh Horah
(b. 1760–d. 1822)
Salisbury, N.C.
Wilkinson & Horah
(c. 1820–1821)
Bibl. 21

James Horah
(b. 1826–d. 1864)
Salisbury, N.C. (c. 1849)
Bibl. 21

William Henry Horah
(b. 1788–d. 1863)
Salisbury, N.C.
Bibl. 21

Horn & Kneass
(c. 1811–1837)
Philadelphia, Pa.
Henry Horn
William Kneass
Bibl. 3

Edwin B. Horn
(c. 1843–1865)
Boston, Mass.
Bibl. 23, 28, 44, 91

Henry Horn
(c. 1809–1840)
Philadelphia, Pa.
Bolton & Horn (c. 1808)
Horn & Kneass
(c. 1811–1837)
Bibl. 3

George Horner (c. 1848)
Camden, N.J.
Bibl. 3

Horton & Angell
(1870–present)
Attleboro, Mass.
Now called Horton Angell
Bibl. 127, 157

Horton & Rikeman
(c. 1850–1856)
Savannah, Ga.
H. P. Horton
———— Rikeman
Bibl. 17, 89
HORTON & RIKEMAN

Horton Brothers (1861)
Biddeford, Me.
Bibl. 105

H. P. Horton
(c. 1850)
Savannah, Ga.
Horton & Rikeman
(c. 1850–1856)
Bibl. 17

H P HORTON

Henry V. Horton (c. 1848)
Louisville, Ky.
Bibl. 32, 90, 93

Harley Hosford (c. 1820)
New York, N.Y.
*Bibl. 23, 24, 25, 36, 44, 114,
124, 138*

HOSFORD

Samuel Hoskins (c. 1835)
Philadelphia, Pa.
Bibl. 3

Hotchkiss & Co.
(c. 1847–1848)
Buffalo, N.Y.
John W. Hotchkiss
Bibl. 20, 124

Hotchkiss & Norton
(See also Norton &
Hotchkiss)
(c. 1841–1842)
Palmyra, N.Y.
David Hotchkiss
Benjamin R. Norton
Bibl. 20, 124

**Hotchkiss & Schreuder
(Schroeder)**
Syracuse, N.Y.   **H & S**
(c. 1850–1871)
David Hotchkiss
Andrew B. Schreuder
*Bibl. 20, 24, 28, 29, 91, 114,
124, 127*

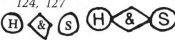

David Hotchkiss
(c. 1840–1855)
Palmyra, N.Y. (c. 1840)
Syracuse, N.Y.
(c. 1847–1855)
Hotchkiss & Norton
(c. 1841–1842)
Norton & Hotchkiss
(c. 1849–c. 1850)
Hotchkiss & Schreuder
(c. 1850–1871)
*Bibl. 15, 20, 25, 49, 91, 114,
124*

D. HOTCHKISS

Hezekiah Hotchkiss
(b. 1729–d. 1761)
New Haven, Conn.
*Bibl. 16, 23, 28, 36, 44, 110,
143*

John W. Hotchkiss
Rochester, N.Y. (c. 1850)
Buffalo, N.Y. (c. 1847)
Hotchkiss & Co.
(c. 1847–1848)
Bibl. 20, 124

William Hotchkiss
(b. 1744, w. 1775)
Maryland
Bibl. 38

Frederick Houck
(c. 1834–1839)
Harpers Ferry, Va.
Bibl. 19

John E. S. Hough
(c. 1846–1852)
Leesburg, Va.
Bibl. 19

Samuel Hough (Haugh)
(b. 1675–1717)
Boston, Mass.
*Bibl. 2, 15, 23, 24, 25, 28,
29, 44, 54, 110, 114*

S H

Houlton
(See John Holton)

**Houlton & Brown(e)
(Brown & Houlton)**
(c. 1794–1798)
Baltimore, Md.
John Houlton
Liberty Brown(e)
Bibl. 15, 35, 38, 39, 44, 114

HOULTON
& BROWNE

Houlton, Otto & Falk
(c. 1797)
Philadelphia, Pa.
John Houlton
——— Otto
——— Falk
Bibl. 25, 44, 114

John Houlton (Holton)
(c. 1794–1801)
Baltimore, Md.
(c. 1794–1798)
Philadelphia, Pa.

Houlton, Otto & Falk
Houlton & Brown(e)
(c. 1794–1798)
*Bibl. 3, 4, 15, 23, 24, 28, 29,
36, 38, 44*

HOULTON

A. House (c. 1850)
Location unknown
Bibl. 15, 44, 114   A. HOUSE

**Weddell (Wenddell)
House** (c. 1845)
(See P. M. Weddell)
Cleveland, Ohio
Not a silversmith but a
hotel.
Bibl. 23, 89

George Smith Houston
(c. 1802–c. 1808)
Augusta, Ga.
George Smith Houston &
Co.
Bibl. 17

**George Smith Houston &
Co.** (c. 1802–1808)
Augusta, Ga.
George Smith Houston
Bibl. 17

Henry Houston (d. 1799)
Philadelphia, Pa.
Bibl. 3

J. C. Houston
Fayetteville, N.C.
Beasley & Houston
(c. 1886–c. 1890)
Bibl. 21

Jacob Houtzell
(c. 1801–1808)
Philadelphia, Pa.
Bibl. 3, 23, 36, 44

Cyrus Hovey (1830)
Lowell, Mass.
Bibl. 106

J. R. Hovey (c. 1817)
Norwich, N.Y.
Bibl. 20, 124

J. S. Hovey (c. 1848)
Rome, N.Y.
Gleason & Hovey

(c. 1846–1848)
Bibl. 20, 124

Hovy (c. 1800)   HOVY
Location unknown
Bibl. 24, 28

David How (b. 1745)
Castine, Me.
Boston, Mass. (w. 1805)
Bibl. 23, 28, 36, 44

William How (Howe)
(c. 1842–1846)
Philadelphia, Pa.
Bibl. 3, 23

Howard & Co.
(c. 1866–1922)
New York, N.Y.
*Bibl. 35, 54, 78, 83, 114,
127, 157*   HOWARD & CO.

HOWARD & CO.
HOWARD & CO.
1903
STERLING.
NEW YORK.

Howard & Cockshaw Co.
(c. 1904–1915)
New York, N.Y.
Became Herbert Cockshaw
(1915–1936)
Herbert Cockshaw, Jr.
(1936–1937)
Bibl. 127, 157

Howard Sterling Co.
(1891–1901)
Providence, R.I.
Successor to Sterling Co.
(1886–1891)
Bibl. 114, 127, 130, 135, 157

TRADE MARK
1776

**Abram (Abraham)
Howard** (c. 1810)
Salem, Mass.
Bibl. 23, 28, 36, 44, 110

John Howard
(c. 1819–1822)
Philadelphia, Pa.
New York, N.Y. (1824)

*Bibl. 3, 15, 23, 36, 44, 114,
124, 138*

N. Howard (c. 1850–1855)
Location unknown
Bibl. 15, 44, 114

Thomas Howard
(c. 1620)
Jamestown, Va.
Not Philadelphia, Pa.
Bibl. 23, 36, 44

Thomas Howard
(c. 1775–1791)
Philadelphia, Pa.
Bibl. 3

William Howard
(b. c. 1720,
w. 1749–1775?)
Pickawaxon, Md.
Bibl. 38

William Howard
(c. 1800–1823)
Boston, Mass.
Bibl. 23, 28, 36, 44, 110

Nathaniel Howcott
(c. 1828)
Edenton, N.C.
Bibl. 21

Howe & Guion
(c. 1839–1840)
New York, N.Y.
George C. Howe
——— Guion
Bibl. 15, 24, 91, 124, 138

HOWE & GUION

George C. Howe
(c. 1810–1843)
New York, N.Y.
Howe & Guion
(c. 1839–1840)

George C. Howe & Co.
(c. 1837–1838)
Stebbins & Howe
(c. 1830–1832) (?)
*Bibl. 15, 23, 24, 25, 29, 35,
36, 44, 83, 91, 95, 114,
124, 138*

GEORGE C. HOWE
GEO. C. HOWE

George C. Howe & Co.
(c. 1837–1838)
New York, N.Y.
*Bibl. 15, 23, 25, 36, 44, 114,
124, 138*

GEO. C. HOWE & CO.

Otis Howe
(b. 1788–d. 1825)
Sackets Harbor, N.Y.
(c. 1816–1817)
Boston, Mass.
Portsmouth, N.H.
Albany, N.Y.
Watertown, N.Y.
Putney & Howe
(c. 1816–1817)
*Bibl. 20, 28, 36, 44, 110,
124, 125*

William Howe
(See How)

Howell & Arnold
(c. 1797–1798)
Albany, N.Y.
Silas White Howell
——— Arnold
Bibl. 20, 23, 36, 44, 46, 124

Howell & Hall
(c. 1801)
Albany, N.Y.
Silas White Howell
——— Hall
Bibl. 20, 124

Benjamin H. Howell(s)
(c. 1837–1848)
Buffalo, N.Y.
Bibl. 20

Benoni H. Howell(s)
(c. 1835–1848)
Buffalo, N.Y.   HOWELL
Newburgh, N.Y.
Bibl. 15, 20, 44, 91, 114, 124

C. (S.) (G.) W. Howell
(c. 1790)
Location unknown
Bibl. 28, 29, 36

G W Howell

James Howell
(c. 1800–1813)
Philadelphia, Pa.
James Howell & Co.
(c. 1802–1810)
*Bibl. 2, 3, 4, 15, 23, 24, 25,
28, 29, 36, 39, 44, 54, 72,
91, 114*

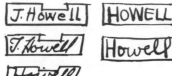

James Howell & Co.
(c. 1802–1810)
Philadelphia, Pa.
Bibl. 24, 25, 39, 79, 91, 114

John Howell
(c. 1776–1794)
Augusta, Ga.
Bibl. 17

John Howell
(b. 1785–d. 1815)
Savannah, Ga. (c. 1806)
Bibl. 17

Paul Howell
(c. 1810–1812)
New York, N.Y.
Eoff & Howell
(c. 1805–1810)
*Bibl. 15, 23, 24, 25, 29, 36,
44, 91, 114, 124, 135, 138*

P Howell

P. HOWELL

S. Howell (c. 1800)
Philadelphia, Pa.
(Could be James Howell's
mark)
Bibl. 15

S Howell

Silas White Howell
(b. 1770, c. 1793–1801)
New Brunswick, N.J.
Albany, N.Y.
Howell & Arnold
(c. 1797–1798)
Howell & Hall (c. 1801)
*Bibl. 20, 23, 25, 29, 36, 44,
46, 54, 91, 114, 124*

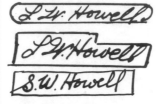

William Howell (c. 1841)
Philadelphia, Pa.
Bibl. 3, 23

Howland & Hayden
(c. 1860–1875)
Bath, Me.
Bibl. 105

J. T. Howland (1861)
Bath, Me.
Bibl. 105

John (J. L.) Howland
New York, N.Y.
(c. 1837–1838)
Philadelphia, Pa.
(c. 1828–1833)
Bibl. 3, 138

Hoyt & Kippen (c. 1830)
Albany, N.Y.
George Kippen
George B. Hoyt
Bibl. 25, 114, 124

Hoyt
(See Harris & Hoyt, Whitney
& Hoyt)

F. Hoyt & Co.
(c. 1850–1851)
Sumter, S.C.
Freeman Hoyt
Charles T. Mason
Bibl. 5

Freeman Hoyt
(b. 1805–d. 1869)
Sumter, S.C. (c. 1831–1869)
F. Hoyt & Co.
(c. 1850–1851)
Bibl. 5

George A. Hoyt
(c. 1822–1844)
Albany, N.Y.
George A. Hoyt & Co.
(c. 1829–1833)
George A. Hoyt & Son
(c. 1845–1846)
Bibl. 20, 114, 124

George A. Hoyt & Co.
(c. 1829–1833)
Albany, N.Y.
Bibl. 20, 124

George A. Hoyt & Son
(c. 1845–1846)
Albany, N.Y.
Bibl. 20, 23, 36, 124

George B. Hoyt
(c. 1827–1850)
Albany, N.Y. (c. 1830–1842)
Middletown, Conn.
Troy, N.Y. (?)
Hoyt & Kippen (c. 1830)
Boyd & Hoyt (c. 1830–1842)
*Bibl. 20, 23, 24, 25, 28, 29,
44, 92, 114, 124*

GEO B HOYT

Henry Hoyt
(b. 1801–d. 1836)
Albany, N.Y. (1829–1836)
Bibl. 20, 91, 124

Henry E. Hoyt (b. 1791)
New York, N.Y.
(1812–1852)
*Bibl. 23, 24, 25, 29, 36, 44,
91, 114, 124, 138*

H E HOYT

HENRY HOYT

James A. Hoyt
(c. 1838–c. 1850)
Troy, N.Y.
Bibl. 20, 124

Jonathan Perkins Hoyt
(b. 1805, c. 1847–1871)
Clarksville, Ga. (1847–1849)
Laurens, S.C. (1852–1871)
Bibl. 5, 17

S. Hoyt & Co. (c. 1842)
New York, N.Y.
Seymour Hoyt
Bibl. 23, 24. 25, 91, 114, 124

| S. HOYT & CO. |

Seymour Hoyt
(c. 1817–1850)
New York, N.Y.
S. Hoyt & Co. (c. 1842)
Bibl. 15, 23, 24, 25, 29, 36, 44, 91, 114, 126, 138

| S HOYT. PEARL ST |

| S.HOYT |

Walter B. Hoyt
(c. 1819–1832)
New York, N.Y.
Griffen & Hoyt
Bibl. 15, 124, 138

William Hubbal(l)
(c. 1834)
Washington, D.C.
Bibl. 23, 36, 44

Addison T. Hubbard
(c. 1870)
Cleveland, Ohio
Bibl. 65

James E. Hubbard (1875)
Providence, R.I.
Bibl. 108

Robert B. Hubbard (1875)
Providence, R.I.
Bibl. 108

John Hubbs
(c. 1830–1837)
Philadelphia, Pa.
Bibl. 3

Henry Huber Jr.
(c. 1818–1824)
Philadelphia, Pa.
Bibl. 3

John L. Hubert (c. 1848)
Philadelphia, Pa.
Bibl. 3

Lafayette Hubert
(c. 1846–1850)
Philadelphia, Pa.
Bibl. 3

Samuel Huckel
(c. 1818–1829)
Philadelphia, Pa.
Bibl. 3

Henry Huddy
(c. 1843–1844)
Philadelphia, Pa.
Bibl. 3

William M. Huddy
(c. 1835)
Philadelphia, Pa.
Bibl. 3

**Hudson & Dolfinger
(Dolfinger & Hudson)**
(c. 1855–1858)
Louisville, Ky.
Henry Hudson
Jacob Dolfinger
Bibl. 54, 91, 93

H. G. Hudson
(c. 1891–1904)
Amesbury, Mass.
Bibl. 127, 157

Henry Hudson (d. 1888)
Louisville, Ky.
(c. 1841–1856)
Hudson & Dolfinger
(c. 1855–1858)
Bibl. 32, 54, 68, 91, 93

J. B. Hudson
(1866–present)
Minneapolis, Minn.
Division of Dayton Hudson

Jewelers
Bibl. 127   JBH

Jonathan Hudson
(b. 1834)
Geneva, N.Y.
Bibl. 20, 114, 124

William Huertin (d. 1771
New York, N.Y. (c. 1731)
Bibl. 15, 28, 29, 114, 124

| W H | | W H |

James Hues (c. 1808)
Wilmington, N.C.
Bibl. 21

Huet
(See Hevitt)

Major Joseph Hufty
(b. 1806–d. 1861)
New Orleans, La.
Bibl. 141

Christopher Huges & Co.
(See Christopher Hughes &
Co.)

Joseph Huggins (c. 1837)
Philadelphia, Pa.
Bibl. 3

Hughes & Bliss
(c. 1806)
Middletown, Conn.
Edmund Hughes
Jonathan Bliss
Bibl. 16, 23, 28, 36, 44, 110

Hughes & Francis
(c. 1807–1809)
Middletown, Conn.
Edmund Hug(h)es
Julius C. Francis
Bibl. 16, 23, 28, 36, 44, 110

Hughes & Hall
(c. 1840–1850)
Middletown, Conn.
Bibl. 15, 24, 44, 114

| HUGHES & HALL |

Charles Hughes (c. 1849)
Philadelphia, Pa.
Bibl. 3, 23

Christopher Hughes   `C. H`
   (b. 1744–d. 1824)
Baltimore, Md.   `C H`
   (c. 1771–1790)
Christopher Hughes & Co.
   (c. 1773–1774)
Bibl. 3, 24, 25, 29, 38, 44,
   114, 118

Christopher Hughes
   (Huges) & Co.
Baltimore, Md.
   (c. 1773–1774)
Christopher Hughes
John Carnan
Bibl. 4, 23, 28, 36, 38

Edmund Hughes
   (b. 1781–d. 1851)
Hampton, Conn. (c. 1804)
Middletown, Conn.
   (c. 1806–1809)
Ward & Hughes (c. 1806)
Hughes & Bliss (c. 1806)
Hughes & Francis
   (c. 1807–1809)
Bibl. 15, 16, 23, 25, 28, 36,
   44, 91, 92, 94, 110, 114

`E. HUGHES`

George W. Hughes
   (c. 1829–1833)
Philadelphia, Pa.
Bibl. 3

Henry Hughes (b. 1756)
Baltimore, Md.
   (c. 1774–1781)
Bibl. 23, 28, 36, 38, 44

J. Hughes (c. 1798)
Middletown, Conn.
Bibl. 23, 24, 36

`J HUGHES`

Jasper W. Hughes
   (c. 1827–1840)
New York, N.Y.
Gale, Wood & Hughes
   (c. 1833–1844)
Wood & Hughes
Bibl. 15, 91, 114, 124, 135,
   138

Jeremiah Hughes
   (b. 1783–d. 1848)
Annapolis, Md.
   (c. 1805–1820)
Bibl. 25, 29, 38, 44, 114

`J. HUGHES`

William Hughes   `W. H`
   (b. 1744–d. 1791)
Baltimore, Md.
   (c. 1785–1791)
Bibl. 25, 29, 38, 44, 114

John Hughs (c. 1768)
Norfolk, Va.
Bibl. 19

Tubehill Hughs (c. 1768)
Norfolk, Va.
Bibl. 19

Charles T. Huguenail
   (c. 1799)
Philadelphia, Pa.
Bibl. 3

C. A. Huguenin
Philadelphia, Pa.
   (c. 1820–1825)
Mobile, Ala. (c. 1856–1867)
Bibl. 3, 148

Charles Frederick
   Huguenin
Philadelphia, Pa.
   (c. 1797–1802)
Fayetteville, N.C.
Halifax, N.C.
Bibl. 3, 21

Davis L. Hugunin
   (c. 1830–1833)
Philadelphia, Pa.
Bibl. 3

Philip Hulbeart (d. 1764)
Philadelphia, Pa.
   (c. 1750–1764)
Bibl. 3, 15, 23, 25, 36, 44,
   81, 91, 114, 116

Daniel S. Hulett   `D·H`
   (c. 1833–1849)
Schenectady, N.Y.
Bibl. 20, 124

Alexander Huling
   (c. 1837)
Philadelphia, Pa.
Bibl. 3

Hull & Sanderson
   (c. 1652–1683)
Boston, Mass.
John Hull
Robert Sanderson
Bibl. 4, 23, 24, 25, 28, 29,
   36, 44, 54, 104, 110, 114,
   116, 142

Hull & Sanger
(See Hall & Sanger)

Hull & Smith
   (c. 1815–1816)
Batavia, N.Y.
William Hull
—— Smith
Bibl. 20, 124

Benjamin Hull
   (b. 1649–d. 1678)
Boston, Mass.
Bibl. 54, 119

John Hull
   (b. 1624–d. 1683)
Boston, Mass.
Hull & Sanderson
Bibl. 9, 15, 23, 24, 25, 28,
   29, 36, 44, 94, 102, 104,
   110, 114, 116, 119, 135,
   151

William Hull (c. 1816)
Batavia, N.Y.
Hull & Smith
   (c. 1815–1816)
Bibl. 20, 124

Hull-House Shops
   (c. 1898–1940)
Chicago, Ill.
Bibl. 98

August (Augustus)
   Humbert (d. 1823)
New York, N.Y.
   (c. 1818–1819)
Bibl. 15, 23, 36, 44, 124, 138

Widow of August Humbert
(c. 1824–1826)
New York, N.Y.
Bibl. 15, 138

Michael Humble
Louisville, Ky.
Bibl. 54, 93

David Humphrey(s)
(c. 1789–1793)
Lexington, Ky.
Bibl. 32, 54, 84, 93

Richard Humphrey(s)
(b. 1749–d. 1832)
Wilmington, Del.
(c. 1771–1796)
Philadelphia, Pa.
*Bibl. 3, 15, 23, 24, 25, 28,
29, 30, 36, 39, 44, 54, 81,
102, 114, 116, 118, 119,
151*

Joshua Humphreys
(b. 1743–d. 1823,
c. 1775–1785)
Lexington, Ky.
Richmond, Va.
Bibl. 19, 32

Thomas B. Humphreys
(c. 1809–1850)
Philadelphia, Pa.
(1809–1814)
Baltimore, Md.
(w. 1829–1835)
Louisa Court House, Va.
(1831–1836)
Richmond, Va. (1831–1850)
Thomas B. Humphreys &
Son (c. 1849)
*Bibl. 3, 4, 19, 23, 28, 36, 38,
44*

**Thomas B. Humphreys &
Son** (c. 1849)
Richmond, Va.
Thomas B. Humphreys
Thomas F. Humphreys
Bibl. 15, 19, 44, 114

T. B. Humphreys & Son

Thomas F. Humphreys
(c. 1849–1869)
Richmond, Va.
Thomas B. Humphreys &
Son (c. 1849)
Bibl. 19

Bouman Hunlock
(c. 1752)
Philadelphia, Pa.
Bibl. 3, 23, 36, 44

George W. Hunnewell
(c. 1836)
Boston, Mass.
Farrington & Hunnewell
Bibl. 23, 36, 44, 91

James B. Hunnicutt, Jr.
(c. 1839–1866)
Richmond, Ind.
Bibl. 133

Walter Hunold
(c. 1903–c. 1925)
Providence, R.I.
Nussbaum & Hunold
(c. 1920)
Bibl. 127

Smith Hunsicker
(c. 1832–c. 1835)
Shepherdstown, Va.
Bibl. 19

Hunt & Clark
(c. 1795–1803)
Bennington, Vt.
Jonathan Hunt
Horatio Clark
Bibl. 54, 110

Hunt & Owens (1875)
Providence, R.I.
Bibl. 108

Edmund Hunt (c. 1700s)
Philadelphia, Pa.
Bibl. 54

Edward Hunt
(c. 1717–1718)
Philadelphia, Pa.
Bibl. 3, 4, 23, 28, 36, 44

George J. Hunt (c. 1905)
Boston, Mass.
Bibl. 127

H. B. Hunt
Location unknown
Bibl. 89

H. B. Hunt

J. D. Hunt (1860)
Bangor, Me.
Bibl. 105

John T. Hunt
(c. 1819–1840)
Lynchburg, Va.
Bibl. 19, 54

Jonathan Hunt
(b. 1771–d. 1843)
Bennington, Vt.
(c. 1795–1803)
Hunt & Clark
Bibl. 54, 110

William Hunt (c. 1819)
Boston, Mass. (?)
Bibl. 44

William Hunt
(c. 1819–1822)
Philadelphia, Pa.
Bibl. 3, 23, 36, 44

William I. Hunt
(c. 1815–1816)
Albany, N.Y.
Bibl. 20, 124

Wm. E. Hunt Co. (c. 1927)
Providence, R.I.
Bibl. 127

Hunter & Pearse
  (c. 1831–1832)
New York, N.Y.
William H. Hunter
Hart Pearse
Bibl. 15, 124, 138

Daniel Hunter (c. 1785)
Newport, R.I.
Bibl. 28

George Hunter (b. 1741)
Portsmouth, N.H. (c. 1761)
Bibl. 54, 110, 125

John Hunter
  (c. 1835–1847)
Albany, N.Y.
New York, N.Y.
Bibl. 20, 24, 124, 138

William H. Hunter
  (c. 1832–1833)
New York, N.Y.
Hunter & Pearse
  (c. 1831–1832)
Bibl. 15, 124, 138

Huntington & Burrill
  (c. 1817–1819)
Augusta, Ga.
Burrill
Bibl. 17

Huntington & Lynch
  (c. 1834)
Hillsboro, N.C.
John Huntington
Lemuel Lynch
Bibl. 21

Huntington & Packard
  (c. 1811)
Springfield, Mass.
Jonathan Packard
Richard Huntington
Bibl. 11, 91, 110

Huntington & Wynne
  (c. 1827–1828)
Salisbury, N.C.
John Huntington
Robert Wynne
Bibl. 21

Asa Huntington
  (b. 1792–d. 1857)
Rochester, N.Y.

  (c. 1821–1822)
Pittsford, N.Y.
  (c. 1853–1857)
Bibl. 20, 41, 124

John Huntington
  (d. 1855)
Oxford, N.C. (c. 1824)
Salisbury, N.C.
  (c. 1827–1828)
Charlotte, N.C.
  (c. 1828–1832)
Hillsboro, N.C. (c. 1834)
William & John Huntington
  (c. 1824)
Huntington & Wynne
  (c. 1827–1828)
Trotter & Huntington
  (c. 1828–1832)
Huntington & Lynch
  (c. 1834)
Bibl. 21

M. P. Huntington & Co.
  (c. 1819)
Milton, N.C.
Martin Palmer Huntington
William Huntington
Bibl. 21

**Martin Palmer
  Huntington**
  (c. 1815–1832)
Milton, N.C. (c. 1819)
Hillsboro, N.C.
M. P. Huntington & Co.
  (c. 1819)
Bibl. 21

Phil(ip) Huntington
  (b. 1770–d. 1825)
Norwich, Conn.
*Bibl. 16, 23, 24, 25, 28, 29,
  36, 44, 92, 110, 114*

Richard Huntington
  (b. 1786–d. 1855)
Springfield, Mass.
  (c. 1811–1823)
Utica, N.Y. (c. 1823–1855)
Huntington & Packard

*Bibl. 18, 20, 24, 25, 41, 44,
  91, 110, 114, 124, 158*

Huntington

Roswell Huntington
  (b. 1763–d. 1836,
  c. 1784)
Norwich, Conn.
Hillsboro, N.C.
*Bibl. 16, 21, 23, 28, 36, 44,
  92, 110*

S. Huntington (c. 1850)
Portland, Me.
*Bibl. 24, 25, 28, 44, 91, 105,
  114*

S HUNTINGTON

William Huntington
  (b. 1792–d. 1874)
Hillsboro, N.C.
  (c. 1815–1824)
Milton, N.C. (c. 1819)
Oxford, N.C. (c. 1824)
William Huntington & Co.
  (c. 1816–1820)
M. P. Huntington & Co.
  (c. 1819)
William & John Huntington
  (c. 1824)
Bibl. 21

**William Huntington &
  Co.** (c. 1816–1820)
Hillsboro, N.C.
William Huntington
John Van Hook Jr.
Bibl. 21

**William & John
  Huntington** (c. 1824)
Oxford, N.C.
William Huntington
John Huntington
Bibl. 21

Jacob Hupp
  (c. 1828–1833)
Philadelphia, Pa.
Bibl. 3

John H. Huquenele
  (c. 1839–1842)
Philadelphia, Pa.
Bibl. 3

Benjamin Hurd
(b. 1739–d. 1781)
Boston, Mass.
Roxbury, Mass.
*Bibl 15, 23, 24, 25, 27, 28, ,
29, 36, 44, 91, 94, 110,
114, 135*

Isaac Hurd (c. 1754)
Boston, Mass.
Bibl. 23, 36

Jacob Hurd
(b. 1702–d. 1758)
Boston, Mass.
*Bibl. 15, 23, 24, 27, 28, 29,
36, 44, 54, 91, 94, 102,
104, 110, 114, 116, 118,
119, 135, 139, 142, 151*

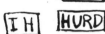

Nathaniel Hurd
(b. 1729–d. 1777)
Boston, Mass.
*Bibl. 15, 23, 24, 25, 27, 28,
29, 36, 44, 91, 102, 110,
114, 135*

Philip Hurlbeart (d. 1764)
Philadelphia, Pa. (c. 1761)
Bibl. 24, 28, 29

Hurly Silver Co.
(1890–1894)
Scriba, N.Y.

Successor to John Hurly
Silver Co. (1890)
Became Benedict Silver Co.
(1894)
Bibl. 127

Hurm & Co. (c. 1796)
Charleston, S.C.
Bibl. 5

P. Hurm (c. 1797)
Charleston, S.C.
Bibl. 5

E. Hurst
(See E. Hirst)

Henry Hurst
(b. 1665–d. 1717)
Boston, Mass.
*Bibl. 2, 15, 23, 24, 25, 28,
29, 36, 44, 69, 110, 114,
116, 119*

John Hurt (Hurtt)
(c. 1839–1842)
Philadelphia, Pa.
Bibl. 3

Hurtin & Burgi
(c. 1766–1776)
Bound Brook, N.J.
William Hurtin
Frederick Burgi
Bibl. 28, 44, 46

Christian Hurtin
(c. 1792–1793)
Goshen, N.Y.
Bibl. 20, 124

Joshua Hurtin
(b. 1738–d. 1780)
Newark, N.J.
Bibl. 46, 54

William Hurtin
(c. 1766–1776)
Bound Brook, N.J.
Hurtin & Burgi
Bibl. 46, 54, 124

William Hurtin Jr.
(c. 1776)
Newark, N.J.
New York State
Bibl. 46, 138

Hurtt (See Hurt)

John Husband
(c. 1795–1796)
Philadelphia, Pa.
Bibl. 3, 23, 28, 36, 44

Stephen Hussey
(c. 1818–1830)
Easton, Md.
Bibl. 24, 25, 29, 38, 44, 114

James Huston (c. 1799)
Baltimore, Md.
Bibl. 28, 36, 38, 44

William Huston
(c. 1767–1771)
Philadelphia, Pa.
Bibl. 3

Jacob Hutchins (c. 1774)
New York, N.Y.
*Bibl. 23, 24, 25, 29, 36, 44,
114, 124*

Nicholas Hutchins
(b. 1777–d. 1845)
Baltimore, Md.
(c. 1810–1830)
*Bibl. 24, 25, 29, 38, 44, 91,
114*

Hutchinson
(See Clarke & Hutchinson)

Charles Hutchinson
(c. 1847)
Warrenton, Va.
Bibl. 19

J. Hutchinson
(c. 1820–1850)
Location unknown
Bibl. 28, 72

J. H. Hutchinson & Co.
(c. 1891–1915)
Portsmouth, N.H.
Bibl. 127, 157

Old Constitution.

James Hutchinson
(c. 1823–1832)
Martinsburg, Va.
Bibl. 19

John Hutchinson
(c. 1820–1821)
Fredericksburg, Va.
Bibl. 19, 138

Samuel Hutchinson
(c. 1828–1839)
Philadelphia, Pa.
Bibl. 3, 15, 25, 44, 91

| S. HUTCHINSON |

Thomas Hutchinson
(c. 1773)
Lancaster, Pa.
Bibl. 3, 112

Thomas Hutchinson
(c. 1816–1824, d. 1820)
Philadelphia, Pa.
Bibl. 3

William Hutchinson
(d. 1832)
New Orleans, La. (1832)
Bibl. 141

John Hutt (c. 1774)
New York, N.Y.
Bibl. 28, 124

Hutton
(See Jones & Hutton)

George Hutton
(b. 1729–d. 1806)
Albany, N.Y.
Isaac & George Hutton
(c. 1799–1815)
*Bibl. 20, 23, 24, 28, 36, 44,
91, 124*

Isaac Hutton
(b. 1766–d. 1855)
Albany, N.Y. (c. 1790–1815)
Isaac & George Hutton
(c. '799–1815)
*Bibl. 15, 20, 23, 24, 25, 28,
29, 30, 36, 39, 44, 54, 72,
91, 95, 104, 114, 116, 119,
122, 124*

| HUTTON |

Isaac & George Hutton
(c. 1799–1815)
Albany, N.Y.
*Bibl. 20, 23, 36, 44, 91, 122,
124*

**John Strangeways
Hutton**
(b. 1684–d. 1792)
New York, N.Y. (c. 1720)
Philadelphia, Pa.
*Bibl. 3, 4, 23, 24, 25, 28, 29,
30, 35, 36, 44, 83, 114,
124*

Samuel Hutton (c. 1850)
Philadelphia, Pa.
Bibl. 3, 23

George Huyler
(c. 1819–1833)
New York, N.Y.
*Bibl. 15, 25, 44, 114, 124,
138*

| HUYLER |

Francis Hycorn
(w. 1822, d. 1834)
Baltimore, Md.
Bibl. 38

Hyde
(See Cheavins & Hyde)

———— **Hyde** (c. 1730?)
Newport, R.I.
Bibl. 28, 44, 110

| HYDE |

Hyde & Goodrich
(c. 1816–1866)
New Orleans, La.
James N. Hyde
C. W. Goodrich
*Bibl. 23, 24, 25, 28, 29, 36,
44, 91, 104, 114*

| HYDE & GOODRICH |

Hyde & Hoff (c. 1850)
Auburn, N.Y.
James Hyde
George W. Hoff
Bibl. 20, 124

Hyde & Nevins
(c. 1798–1819)
New York, N.Y.
J. N. Hyde
Rufus Nevins
*Bibl. 15, 23, 24, 25, 28, 29,
36, 44, 91, 114, 124, 138*

| H & N |

| Hyde & Nevins |

| HYDE & NEWINS |

Charles L. Hyde (c. 1842)
Philadelphia, Pa.
Bibl. 3

J. N. Hyde
New York, N.Y.
Hyde & Nevins
(c. 1798–1819)
*Bibl. 15, 23, 24, 25, 28, 29,
36, 44, 138*

James Hyde (c. 1850)
Auburn, N.Y.
Hyde & Hoff
Bibl. 20, 91, 124

James N. Hyde (c. 1816)
New Orleans, La.
Hyde & Goodrich
(c. 1816–1866)
Bibl. 54, 114

Hyman & Co.
(c. 1845–1846)
Richmond, Va.
Lewis Hyman
Bibl. 19

H. Hyman (c. 1818–1819)
Philadelphia, Pa.
Bibl. 3

Henry W. Hyman
Lexington, Ky. (c. 1800)
Richmond, Va.
(c. 1845–1846)
*Bibl. 15, 19, 25, 32, 44, 54,
68, 89, 93, 114, 138*

| H HYMAN RHD |

| H.HYMAN R.N.D |

Lewis Hyman
(c. 1845–1846)

Richmond, Va.
Hyman & Co.
Bibl. 19

William Hymas
(c. 1818–1822)
Philadelphia, Pa.
Bibl. 3

Thomas Hynes
(c. 1822–1827,
c. 1847–1853)
Baltimore, Md.
May be father and son.
Bibl. 38

I

I & P T
(See John & Peter Targee)

I A
(See John Adam, John
Allen, Allen & Edwards,
Jeronimus Alstyne, Isaac
Anthony, Joseph Anthony
Jr., Josiah Austin, John
Avery)

I B
(See John Bailey, James
Barret, John Benjamin,
John Bering, Jurian
Blanck, Jacob Boelen,
Jacob Boelen II, Joseph
Bruff, Isaac Brunson, John
Burger, John Burt, James
Butler, John Butler)

I B L
(See John Burt Lyng)

I C
(See John Carman, Joseph
Carpenter, James
Chalmers, John Chalmers,
John Champlin, Jonathan
Clarke, John Coburn,
John Coddington, John
Coney, I. Clark, Joseph
Clark, Jacob Cuyler)

I D
(See Jonathan Davenport,
John David, John David
Jr., John Dixwell,
Jeremiah Dummer)

I D M
(See John David Miller)

I E
(See John Edwards, Joseph
Edwards, Allen &
Edwards, Jeremiah
Elfreth Jr.)

I G
(See John Gardiner, James
Geddy, John D. Germon,
Joseph Goldwaithe, John
Gray)

I G L
(See Jacob Gerrit Lansing
Jr., Jacob Gerritse
Lansing)

I H
(See Jacob Hurd, John
Strangeways Hutton)

I H L
(See Josiah H. Lownes)

I H M
(See John H. Merkler)

I H R
(See John H. Russel)

I I
(See Jacob Jennings)

I I S
(See John J. Staples Jr.)

I J
(See John Jenkins)

I K
(See Joseph Keeler, Jesse
Kip)

I L
(See John Lampey, Jeffrey
Lang, John I. Leacock,
John Le Roux, John
Lynch, John Lyng)

I L T
(See John Letelier)

I M
(See Jacob Marius Groen,
John McMullin, Jacob
Mohler, John Moulinar,
Joseph M. Moulton III,
John Murdoch)

I N
(See Joseph Newkirke,
Joseph Noyes, Johannis
Nys)

I.N.D.
(See I. N. Deitsch)

I N R
(See Joseph & Nathaniel
Richardson)

I O
(See Jonathan Otis)

I P
(See James Patterson, John
Patterson, John Pearson,
Jacob Perkins, Isaac
Peronneau, John Potwine,
Job Prince)

I R
(See Jonathan Reed, John
Reynolds, Joseph
Richardson Sr., Joseph
Richardson Jr., Joseph
Rogers, John Ross, John
Royalston)

I R & S
(See Isaac Reed & Son)

I S
(See Jonathan Sarrazin, Joel
Sayre, Jonas Schindler,
John Sheppard, I. Smith,
Joseph Smith, I. Stuart,
John Syng)

I T
(See John Targee, Jacob Ten
Eyck, John Touzell,
Joseph Toy, Jonathan
Trott Jr., James Turner)

I V
(See J. Vanderhan, John
    Vernon)

I V S
(See Jacobus Van Der
    Spiegel, Johannes Van Der
    Spiegel, John Van
    Steenbergh Jr., John
    Stuart)

I W
(See Isaiah Wagster, Joseph
    Warner, John Wendover)

I W F
(See John W. Forbes)

I W G
(See John W. Gethen, John
    Ward Gilman)

Henry Iagol(e)
    (b. 1716–d. 1761)
New York, N.Y.
Bibl. 23, 36, 124

Ideal Silver Company
    (c. 1905–1906)
Portland, Conn.
Bibl. 127

G. P. H. Illig (Ilig)
    (c. 1836)
Louisville, Ky.
Bibl. 32, 54, 68

David Smith Ilsley
    (b. 1801–d. 1827)
Portland, Me.
    (c. 1824)
Bibl. 28, 110

Imlay
(See Heydorn & Imlay)

Inaugural
(See Silver Counselors of
    Home Decorators, Inc.)

John Inch
    (b. 1720–d. 1763)
Annapolis, Md.
    (c. 1741–1763)
Bibl. 25, 29, 38, 44, 118

Jeremiah Inches (1860)
Smithfield, R.I.

Bibl. 108

Charles Inglehart (c. 1840)
Philadelphia, Pa.
Bibl. 3

Henry Ingraham
    (c. 1829–1833)
Philadelphia, Pa.
Bibl. 3

Joseph Holt Ingraham
    (b. 1752–d. 1841)
Portland, Me. (c. 1785)
Bibl. 23, 36, 44, 105, 110

Charles W. Ingram
    (c. 1835–1846)
Philadelphia, Pa.
Bibl. 3

James Ingram
Albany, N.Y. (c. 1837–1842)
Troy, N.Y. (c. 1843–1850)
Bibl. 20, 124

Benjamin Inman
    (c. 1814–1819)
Philadelphia, Pa.
Bibl. 3, 23, 36, 44

J. T. Inman & Co.
    (1892–1964)
Attleboro, Mass.
James McNerney, owner
    (1892–1944)
Roy W. Inman, owner
    (1944–1964)
Became Whiting & Davis Co.
    (1964)
Bibl. 114, 127, 157

 STERLING.

INMAN STERLING

**International-
    Commonwealth Silver
    Co.** (c. 1915–1922)
New York, N.Y.
Successor to International
    Silver Deposit Works
Bibl. 127, 157

International Silver Co.
    (1898–present)
Meriden, Conn.
Consolidation including,
    among others,
Derby Silver Co.
Holmes & Edwards Silver
    Co.
La Pierre Mfg. Co.
Maltby, Stevens & Curtiss
Meriden Britannia Co.
Rogers & Bro.
Rogers & Hamilton Co.
Simpson, Hall, Miller & Co.
Watrous Mfg. Co.
E. G. Webster & Bro.
E. G. Webster & Son
Webster Mfg. Co.
Wilcox & Evertsen
Manufacture of sterling
    discontinued in 1976
After 1981 various divisions
    sold to different
    companies, including
    American Silver Co.,
    Wallace International
    Silversmiths, and Oneida,
    Ltd., Silversmiths
*Bibl. 121, 127, 135, 146, 147,
    152, 157*

 INTERNATIONAL SILVER COMPANY

INTERNATIONAL  STERLING

INTERNATIONAL  STERLING

INTERNATIONAL  STERLING

INTERNATIONAL STERLING

William Ireland
    (before 1803)
Charleston, S.C.
Bibl. 5

Matt Irion
    (c. 1872–1929)
Louisville, Ky.
Bibl. 32, 93

Sayres Irons (1860)
Providence, R.I.
Bibl. 108

David Irving
  (c. 1848–1850)
Philadelphia, Pa.
Bibl. 3

Mason T. Irwin
  (c. 1838–1839)
Louisville, Ky.
Bibl. 32, 93

Thomas M. Irwin
  (c. 1832–1850)
Louisville, Ky.
Bibl. 54, 68

Michael Isaac(k)s (c. 1765)
New York, N.Y.
Bibl. 23, 36, 44, 124

Isabel
(See Ysabelle)

Lester Isadore
  (c. 1820–1863)
Rochester, N.Y.
Bibl. 54, 124

LESTER ISADORE

Isbell & Co.
Cincinnati, Ohio
Bibl. 34, 152

B. Ivers (c. 1800)
Location unknown
Bibl. 28, 29, 44, 89

B·Ivers

David Ives
Location unknown
Bibl. 28

L. Ives
Location unknown
Bibl. 28

John Izabell (c. 1818)
Lexington, Ky.
Bibl. 32, 54, 93

J

J & A S
(See J. & A. Simmons)

J & B
(See Johnson & Ball)

J & R
(See Johnson & Reat,
  Johnson & Riley)

J & T D
(See John & Tunis Denise)

J A
(See John Adams, Jeronimus
  Alstyne, Joseph Anthony
  Jr., Joseph Anthony &
  Son, John Avery)

J A & J A
(See Joseph Anthony & Son)

J B
(See James Barret, John
  Bedford, James Black,
  John Black, John Boyce,
  John Brown)

J C
(See John Chattellier, Joseph
  Clark, Jonathan Clarke,
  John Coburn, Joseph
  Coolidge, Jonathan
  Crosby)

J C B & Co.
(See J. C. Blackman & Co.)

J C M
(See John C. Moore)

J D
(See John David, John
  David Jr., John Denise,
  James Duffel)

J E
(See Jeremiah Elfreth Jr.,
  James Elliott)

J E T
(See E. J. Towle Mfg. Co.)

J F
(See John Fitch, John Fite,
  Josiah Flagg, Foster &
  Richards)

J G
(See John Gardiner, James
  Geddy, John Gibbs, James
  Gough)

J H
(See John Heath, John
  Husband)

J.H.
(See John Hasselbring)

J H C
(See John H. Connor)

J I
(See John Inch)

J J S
(See John J. Staples Jr.)

J K
(See James Kendall)

J K C
(See Jack Kellmer Co.)

J L
(See J. Lamson, John Burt
  Lyng)

J L G
(See John L. Gale)

J L W
(See John L. Westervelt)

J M
(See J. Merchant, Joseph
  Moulton, Joseph M.
  Moulton III, Joseph
  Moulton IV)

J Mc F
(See John McFarlane)

J P
(See J. N. Provenzano)

J. P. P.
(See Petterson Studio)

J P T
(See John Proctor Trott)

J P T & Son
(See John P. Trott & Son)

J P W
(See Joseph P. Warner)

J R
(See Joseph Richardson Sr.,
  Joseph Richardson Jr.,
  John Royalston, Joseph
  Russell)

J R S C
(See J. Rogers Silver Co.,
  Inc.)

J S
(See Joseph Shoemaker,
  John Staniford)

J S & Co.
(See Joseph Seymour & Co.)

J S B
(See John Stiles Bird)

J T R
(See Joseph T. Rice)

J W
(See John Waite, John
  Walraven, John
  Wanamaker, James Ward,
  John Wendover, Joseph
  Wyatt)

J W B
(See Joseph W. Boyd)

J W F
(See John W. Faulkner)

J W P
(See John W. Phillips)

Jaccard & Co.
  (c. 1830–1860)
St. Louis, Mo.   JACCARD & CO
D. C. Jaccard
Bibl. 24, 25, 29, 44, 54, 89,
  91, 114, 134, 155

D. C. Jaccard
  (c. 1830–1860)
St. Louis, Mo.

Jaccard & Co.
Bibl. 54, 91, 134, 155

Eugene Jaccard (c. 1837)
St. Louis, Mo.
E. Jaccard & Co.
Bibl. 54, 91, 134, 155

E. (Eugene) Jaccard & Co.
  (c. 1852–1871)
St. Louis, Mo.
Eugene Jaccard
Bibl. 54, 91, 134, 155

Louis Jaccard (Jackard)
  (c. 1829–1860)
St. Louis, Mo.
Bibl. 54, 89, 91, 134, 155

L. Jaccard

James Jack(s) (d. 1822)
Charleston, S.C.
  (c. 1784–1797)
Philadelphia, Pa.
  (c. 1797–1800)
Charleston, S.C.
  (c. 1800–1822)
James Jack(s) & Co.
  (c. 1797–1800)
Bibl. 3, 5, 23, 36, 44

James Jack(s) & Co.
  (c. 1797–1800)
Philadelphia, Pa.
James Jacks
Thomas Gibson
Bibl. 5

Jackard
(See Louis Jaccard)

Richard D. Jackman
  (c. 1822)
Wellsburg, Va.
Bibl. 19

James Jacks
(See James Jack)

Pulaski Jacks (c. 1842)
Savannah, Ga.
Dibble & Jacks
Bibl. 17

William Jacks
  (c. 1798–1800)
Philadelphia, Pa.
Bibl. 3, 23, 36, 44

Jackson & McConky
  (c. 1808–1809)
Savannah, Ga.
William Jackson
David Marion McConky
Bibl. 17

Jackson
(See Zahm & Jackson)

A. Jackson (c. 1840)
Norwalk, Conn.
Bibl. 25, 44, 92, 114

Charles Jackson (c. 1816)
Schenectady, N.Y.
Bibl. 20, 124

Clement Jackson
  (b. 1741–d. 1777)
Portsmouth, N.H. (c. 1762)
Bibl. 54, 110, 125

Daniel Jackson
  (c. 1782–1790)
New York, N.Y.
Bibl. 15, 23, 24, 25, 29, 36,
  44, 91, 114, 124

Ephraim Jackson
  (c. 1813–1817)
Philadelphia, Pa.
Bibl. 3

George Jackson (c. 1827)
Baltimore, Md.
Bibl. 38

James Jackson (b. 1756)
Maryland (c. 1775)
Bibl. 23, 28, 38, 44

James Jackson
Troy, N.Y. (c. 1840–1842)
Syracuse, N.Y. (c. 1850)
Bibl. 20, 124

John Jackson (c. 1726)
Nantucket Island, Mass.
  (b. 1730–d. 1872)
Bibl. 12, 91, 110

John Jackson (c. 1731)
New York, N.Y.

*Bibl. 4, 23, 25, 28, 29, 35,
36, 44, 54, 83, 95, 124,
138*

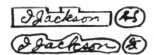

Joseph Jackson (d. 1831)
Baltimore, Md.
  (c. 1803–1813)
Richmond, Va.
  (c. 1815–1818)
*Bibl. 19, 23, 24, 28, 29, 36,
38, 44, 91, 114*

Low Jackson (d. 1753)
Nansemond County, Va.
Bibl. 54

Richard Jackson
  (c. 1804–1812)
East Springfield, Ohio
Bibl. 34

Robert Jackson (c. 1752)
Fredericksburg, Va.
Bibl. 19

Thomas Jackson
  (c. 1837–1849)
Philadelphia, Pa.
Bibl. 3

William Jackson
  (c. 1808–1809)
Savannah, Ga.
Jackson & McConky
Bibl. 17

Jacob & Claude
(See Claude & Jacob)

Celestin Jacob (c. 1840)
Philadelphia, Pa.
Myers & Jacob (?)
Bibl. 3

Charles Jacob
Annapolis, Md.
  (c. 1772–1777)
Port Tobacco, Md.
  (c. 1778)
Claude & Jacob
  (c. 1772–1774)
Bibl. 38

George W. Jacob(s)
  (b. 1775–d. 1846)
Baltimore, Md.
  (c. 1802–1831)
Philadelphia, Pa.
  (c. 1836–1846)
*Bibl. 3, 4, 23, 24, 28, 29, 36,
38, 44, 91*

Lewis Jacob (1860)
Providence, R.I.
Bibl. 108

Moses Jacob(s) (b. 1753)
Philadelphia, Pa. (c. 1775)
Bibl. 3, 23, 28, 36, 44

Jacobi & Jenkins
  (c. 1894–1908)
Baltimore, Md.
William F. Jacobi
Talbot Jenkins
Bibl. 89, 157

A. Jacobi (1879–1890)
Baltimore, Md.
See Jenkins & Jenkins
Bibl. 89

William F. Jacobi
Baltimore, Md.
Jacobi & Jenkins
  (c. 1894–1908)
Bibl. 89

A. Jacobs (c. 1800)
New York, N.Y.
Bibl. 28

A. Jacobs & Co. (c. 1820)
Philadelphia, Pa.
Abel Jacobs
Bibl. 24, 25, 44, 114

Abel Jacobs (c. 1816)
Philadelphia, Pa. (c. 1820)
Baltimore, Md. (?)
A. Jacobs & Co.
  (c. 1820) (?)
*Bibl. 15, 23, 24, 25, 29, 36,
44, 114*

D. Jacobs (c. 1852)
Charleston, S.C.
Bibl. 5

George Jacobs
(See George W. Jacob)

John M. Jacobs
  (c. 1839–1844)
Warrenton, Va.
Bibl. 19

M. Jacobs (1866–1867)
New Orleans, La.
Bibl. 141

Moses Jacobs
(See Moses Jacob)

Rufus Jacoby
  (c. 1980–present)
Silver Spring, Md.
Bibl. 127

JACOBY HANDMADE STERLING

Henry W. Jacot
  (c. 1841–1850)
Philadelphia, Pa.
Bibl. 3

Julius Jacot
  (c. 1848–1850)
Philadelphia, Pa.
Bonsall & Jacot
  (c. 1849)
Bibl. 3

James
(See Musgrave & James)

Charles James (1860)
Pembroke, Me.
Bibl. 105

Jacob S. James (c. 1837)
Philadelphia, Pa.
Bibl. 3

Joseph H. James (c. 1849)
Richmond, Va.
Gennet & James
  (c. 1849–1866)
Bibl. 19, 91

L. S. James (1860–1875)
Gardiner, Me.
Bibl. 105

John D. Jameson
(c. 1823)
Trenton, N.J.
Kentucky
Bibl. 32, 93

Jean Baptiste Jamin
(c. 1796)
Baltimore, Md.
Bibl. 38

Jacques Joseph Jamme
(b. 1793, c. 1816)
Charleston, S.C.
Bibl. 5

Jange (c. 1825)
Location unknown
Bibl. 24
•JANGE•

Joshua Janney (c. 1791)
Alexandria, Va.
Bibl. 19, 54

August William Jansen
(b. 1835–d. 1898)
New Orleans, La.
C. Kuchler & Co.
Bibl. 141

January & Nutman
(c. 1818)
Lexington, Ky.
Andrew McConnell January
John C. Nutman
Bibl. 32, 54, 98

**Andrew McConnell
January**
(b. 1794–d. 1877)
Lexington, Ky.
(c. 1812–1818)
January & Nutman (c. 1818)
Bibl. 32, 54, 93

Lewis Janvier (January)
(d. 1748)
Charleston, S.C.
(c. 1734–1748)
Bibl. 5, 23, 36, 44, 54, 119

Daniel Jaques
(b. 1785–d. 1818)
Charleston, S.C.
(c. 1813–1818)
Bibl. 5

—— **Jardella** (c. 1833)
Philadelphia, Pa.
Dubosq & Jardella
Bibl. 3

Robert R. Jarvie
(c. 1865–1940)
Chicago, Ill.
Jarvie Shop (1904–1920)
Bibl. 98, 115, 120, 144

Munson Jarvis
(b. 1742–d. 1825)
New Brunswick, Canada
Stamford, Conn.
*Bibl. 2, 15, 16, 23, 24, 25,
28, 29, 36, 44, 61, 91, 92,
94, 102, 110, 114*

M J   M I

Henry J. Javain (d. 1838)
Charleston, S.C.
(c. 1835–1838)
Bibl. 5, 25, 44, 114

JAVAIN

David Jaworski
(1975–present)
St. Louis, Mo.
Bibl. 155

Harmon Jaynes (1875)
Bowdoinham, Me.
Bibl. 105

Thomas Jeanes
(c. 1835–1837)
Philadelphia, Pa.
Bibl. 3

John Jeangu (c. 1804)
Philadelphia, Pa.
Bibl. 3

L. F. Jeanmarie
(c. 1853)
Winchester, Tenn.
Bibl. 54

Theophilus H. Jeanneret
(c. 1818)
Philadelphia, Pa.
Bibl. 3

Jeannert
(See also Sleeper &
Jeannert)

—— **Jeannert** (c. 1850)
Philadelphia, Pa.
Sleeper & Jeannert
Bibl. 3

David H. Jefferies
(c. 1846–1850)
Philadelphia, Pa.
Bibl. 3

E. Jefferies (c. 1837–1839)
Philadelphia, Pa.
Bibl. 3

Emmor Jefferis
(b. 1804–d. 1892)
Wilmington, Del.
Guthre & Jefferis (c. 1840)
Bibl. 25, 30, 44, 114
E. JEFFERIS

Ephraim Jefferson
(b. 1788–d. 1844)
Smyrna, Del. (c. 1810)
Bibl. 25, 30, 44, 114
E. JEFFERSON

Samuel Jeffreys
(c. 1771–1778)
Philadelphia, Pa.
Bibl. 3

**Jeffries & Eubank
(Eubank & Jeffries)**
(c. 1834)
Glasgow, Ky.
James Jeffries
Joseph Eubank Jr.
Bibl. 36, 54, 68, 93

James Jeffries
(c. 1820–1860)
Glasgow, Ky.
Jeffries & Eubank
(c. 1834)
Bibl. 32, 54, 93

Smith Jeffries
(c. 1825–1835)
Winchester, Ky.
Bibl. 32, 54, 68, 93

Jenckes & Co.
(c. 1798–1800)

Providence, R.I.
John C. Jenckes
Bibl. 23, 36, 44, 110

John Jenckes & Co.
   (c. 1800–1852)
Providence, R.I.
John C. Jenckes
Bibl. 25, 110, 114

John C. Jenckes
   (b. 1776–d. 1852)
Providence, R.I. (c. 1795)
Jenckes & Co.
John Jenckes & Co.
*Bibl. 15, 23, 24, 25, 28, 29,
   36, 56*

J C JENCKES

J JENCKES

Jenkin(s) & Clark
   (c. 1827)
Auburn, N.Y.
Benjamin R. Jenkins (?)
George R. Clark
Bibl. 20, 124

Jenkins & Jenkins
   (1908–c. 1915)
Baltimore, Md.
Successor to A. Jacobi
   (1879–1890)
Jacobi & Co. (1890–1894)
Jacobi & Jenkins
   (1894–1908)
Dies purchased by Schofield
   Company, Inc. (c. 1915)
Bibl. 23, 89, 127

Benjamin R. Jenkins
   (c. 1827)
Auburn, N.Y.
Jenkin(s) & Clark
Bibl. 20, 24, 89, 124

B. R. Jenkins

Edward J. Jenkins
   (c. 1843–1850)
Philadelphia, Pa.
Bibl. 3

**Harman (Herman?)
   Jenkins** (c. 1817–1823)
Albany, N.Y.
I. & H. Jenkins
   (c. 1815–1816)
Bibl. 20, 24, 91, 124

I. & H. Jenkins
   (c. 1815–1816)
Albany, N.Y.
(Not Baltimore, Md.)
Ira Jenkins
Harman Jenkins
*Bibl. 15, 20, 25, 44, 91, 114,
   124*

I & H Jenkins

Ira Jenkins (c. 1813)
Albany, N.Y.
I. & H. Jenkins
   (c. 1815–1816)
Bibl. 20, 91, 124

Isaac Jenkins (1860–1875)
Bassalboro, Me.
Bibl. 105

James Jenkins (c. 1794)
Philadelphia, Pa.
Bibl. 3

John Jenkins   I J
   (b. 1777–d. 1796)
Philadelphia, Pa.
*Bibl. 3, 23, 24, 25, 28, 36,
   39, 44, 95, 114*

John Jenkins
   (c. 1844–1848)
Philadelphia, Pa.
Bibl. 3

Josias Jenkins (b. 1794)
Baltimore, Md. (c. 1811)
Bibl. 38

Martin J. Jenkins
   (c. 1847–1848)
Troy, N.Y.
Bibl. 20, 124

Talbot Jenkins
Baltimore, Md.
Jacobi & Jenkins
   (c. 1894–1908)
Bibl. 89

Lewis E. Jenks
   (c. 1875–1885)
Boston, Mass.
Bibl. 127

B. Jenner (c. 1846)
Philadelphia, Pa.
Bibl. 3

Jenning(s) & Lander
   (c. 1848–1851)
New York, N.Y.
*Bibl. 15, 25, 44, 91, 114,
   124, 138*

JENNING & LANDER

Jennings & Lauter
   (c. 1922)
New York, N.Y.
Successor to Reeves &
   Sillcocks (c. 1896–1904)
Reeves & Browne
   (c. 1904–1915)
Browne, Jennings & Lauter
   (c. 1915–1922)
Bibl. 127

Jennings Bros. Co. (1907)
Bridgeport, Conn.
Bibl. 89

Jacob Jennings
   (b. 1729–d. 1817)
Norwalk, Conn. (c. 1763)
*Bibl. 16, 23, 24, 25, 28, 36,
   44, 61, 92, 94, 110, 114*

Jacob Jennings Jr.
   (b. 1779)
Norwalk, Conn. (c. 1810)
Bibl. 16, 23, 28, 36, 44, 110

O. S. Jennings
   (1860–1861)
New Orleans, La.
Bibl. 141

Thomas Jennings
   (c. 1837)
Philadelphia, Pa.
Bibl. 3

Chauncey Jerome
   (c. 1846–1849)
Philadelphia, Pa.
Bibl. 3

Michael Jerry (b. 1937)
Syracuse, N.Y.
Bibl. 89, 156

David Jesse (Jess)
(b. 1670–d. 1705)
Boston, Mass. (c. 1695)
Bibl. 2, 15, 23, 24, 25, 28, 29, 36, 44, 70, 110, 114, 116, 119

S. C. & J. S. Jett
(1857–1859)
St. Louis, Mo.
Bibl. 155

Steven C. Jett
(c. 1848–1860)
St. Louis, Mo.
Bibl. 54, 91, 104, 134, 155

| S. C. JETT |

Charles E. Jeuneret
(c. 1817)
St. Louis, Mo.
Bibl. 54

The Jewelers' Crown Guild (1892–c. 1904)
Rockford, Ill.
Bibl. 127

William H. Jewett (1875)
Bridgton, Me.
Bibl. 105

John Job (c. 1819)
Philadelphia, Pa.
Bibl. 3

John M. Johannes
(b. 1799–d. 1883)
Baltimore, Md.
(c. 1828–1850)
Webb & Johannes
Bibl. 23, 36, 38, 44

—— **John** (c. 1760)
Location unknown
Bibl. 36 | JOHN |

Johnsohn
Location unknown
Bibl. 15 | JOHNSOHN |

Johnson
(See Kidney, Cann &
Johnson)

—— **Johnson** (c. 1810)
Burton, Ohio
Bibl. 34

Johnson & Ball
(c. 1785–1790)
Baltimore, Md.
William Ball, Jr.
Israel H. Johnson (?)
Bibl. 23, 25, 29, 36, 38, 44, 91, 114

Johnson & Crowley
(c. 1830–1833)
Philadelphia, Pa.
—— Johnson
E. Crowley
Bibl. 3

**Johnson & Godley
(Godley & Johnson)**
(c. 1843–1850)
Albany, N.Y.
Samuel Johnson
Richard Godley
Bibl. 4, 20, 23, 28, 44, 114, 124, 127

Johnson & Lewis
(c. 1837–1842)
Philadelphia, Pa.
—— Johnson
John M. Lewis (?)
Bibl. 3

Johnson & Reat
(c. 1810–1815)
Baltimore, Md.
Portland, Me. (?)
Richmond, Va.
Reuben Johnson
James Reat
Bibl. 15, 19, 23, 24, 25, 28, 29, 36, 38, 105, 114, 122

| JOHNSON & REAT |

Johnson & Riley (c. 1786)
Baltimore, Md.
Israel H. Johnson (?)
—— Riley
Bibl. 24, 25, 29, 38, 44, 114

Alonzo W. Johnson
(c. 1831–1838)
Albany, N.Y.
C. & A. W. Johnson
Bibl. 20

B. Johnson (c. 1840)
Richmond, Va.
Bibl. 19

C. & A. W. Johnson
(c. 1831–1838)
Albany, N.Y.
Chauncey Johnson
Alonzo W. Johnson
Bibl. 20, 91, 124

Chauncey Johnson
(c. 1824–1831,
c. 1838–1841)
Albany, N.Y.
C. & A. W. Johnson
(c. 1831–1838)
Bibl. 15, 20, 23, 25, 28, 36, 44, 72, 91, 114, 124

| C. JOHNSON |

D. A. Johnson (c. 1855)
Nashville, Tenn.
Bibl. 54

Daniel B. Johnson
(b. 1817)
Utica, N.Y. (c. 1834–1858)
Bibl. 18, 20, 124, 158

E. J. Johnson (c. 1842)
Macon, Ga.
Bibl. 88

E. S. Johnson & Co.
(c. 1896–1922)
New York, N.Y.
Bibl. 114, 127, 157

Edward Johnson (b. 1754)
Maryland (c. 1774)
Bibl. 38

Elisha Johnson (c. 1841)
Greensboro, N.C.
Bibl. 21

Israel H. Johnson
Baltimore, Md.
(c. 1786–1790)
Easton, Md. (c. 1793)
Johnson & Ball
(c. 1785–1790) (?)
Johnson & Riley
(c. 1786) (?)
Bibl. 38

J. Johnson (c. 1827)
Weedsport, N.Y.
Bibl. 20, 124

James R. Johnson
(b. 1808–d. 1855)
Fredericksburg, Va.
(c. 1829)
Norfolk, Va.
(c. 1829–1838,
c. 1851–1852)
Richmond, Va. (c. 1832)
Clarksburg, Va.
(c. 1840–1846)
Bibl. 19

John Johnson (c. 1815)
Pittsburgh, Pa.
Bibl. 23, 36, 44

Maycock W. Johnson
(c. 1815)
Albany, N.Y.
*Bibl. 4, 20, 23, 24, 25, 28,
29, 36, 44, 91, 114, 124*

N. B. Johnson (c. 1838)
Watertown, N.Y.
Bibl. 20, 124

Reuben Johnson
(b. 1782–d. 1820)
Richmond, Va.
Johnson & Reat
(c. 1810–1815)
Bibl. 19

**Robert Johnson
(Johnston)**
(c. 1823–1850)
Philadelphia, Pa.
Bibl. 3

Samuel Johnson   S. J
(b. 1726–d. 1796)
New York, N.Y.
(c. 1780–1796)
*Bibl. 4, 23, 24, 25, 28, 29,
35, 36, 44, 54, 83, 91, 95,
114, 124, 138*

JOHNSON

Samuel Johnson
Winchester, Va.
(c. 1827–1829)
Harpers Ferry, Va. (c. 1830)
Bibl. 19

Samuel Johnson (c. 1834)
Albany, N.Y.
Johnson & Godley
Bibl. 20

**Samuel (Simeon) W.
Johnson**
(c. 1836–1844)
Louisville, Ky.
Bibl. 32, 133

W. M. Johnson (c. 1849)
Richmond, Va.
Hill & Johnson
Bibl. 19

William Johnson (c. 1799)
Boston, Mass.
Bibl. 28, 118

William Johnson (c. 1829)
Charlottesville, Va.
Bibl. 19

William E. Johnson
(c. 1841)
Philadelphia, Pa.
Bibl. 3

A. Johnston (c. 1830)
Philadelphia, Pa.
Bibl. 24, 25, 44, 91, 114

A JOHNSTON

Edmund J. Johnston
(c. 1845–1870?)

Macon, Ga.
W. B. Johnston & Bro.
(c. 1845–1849)
Bibl. 17

J. H. Johnston & Co.
(1844–c. 1915)
New York, N.Y.   **C. B. M. C.**
Bibl. 127, 157   **C. P. F.**

James Johnston
(c. 1812–1843)
Louisville, Ky.
Bibl. 32, 54, 68, 93

Robert Johnston
(See Robert Johnson)

W. B. Johnston & Brother
(c. 1845–1849)
Macon, Ga.
William Blackstone Johnston
Edmund J. Johnston
Bibl. 17

William Johnston
(c. 1826–1827)
Winchester, Va. (c. 1827)
Woodstock, Va.
Meredith & Johnston
(c. 1827)
Bibl. 19

**William B. Johnston &
Co.** (c. 1839–1842)
Macon, Ga.
William Blackstone Johnston
Bibl. 17

**William Blackstone
Johnston**
Macon, Ga.
William B. Johnston & Co.
(c. 1839–1842)
W. B. Johnston & Bro.
(c. 1845–1849)   Wᵐ B Johnston
Bibl. 17, 104

Johonnot & Tuells
(c. 1809)
Windsor, Vt.
William B. Johonnot
Bibl. 54, 91, 110

William B. Johonnot
(b. 1766–d. 1849)
Middletown, Conn.
(c. 1787)

Windsor, Vt.
(c. 1792, c. 1809)
Johonnot & Tuells (c. 1809)
*Bibl. 16, 23, 24, 25, 28, 36,
44, 54, 91, 92, 110, 114*

John Jolineth
(b. 1792–d. 1869)
Philadelphia, Pa.
(1817–1836)
Bibl. 3, 90

John Jolivet
(c. 1829–1850)
Philadelphia, Pa.
Bibl. 3

Joseph Jonas (c. 1817)
Philadelphia, Pa.
Bibl. 3

Joseph Jonas
(c. 1817–1824)
Cincinnati, Ohio
Bibl. 34, 152

Francis Jonckheere
(c. 1807–1824)
Baltimore, Md.
Bibl. 38

Jones
(See Newland & Jones,
Ward & Jones)

Jones & Hutton
(c. 1840–1862?)
Wilmington, Del.
Philip Jones (?)
———— Hutton
Bibl. 25, 30, 44, 114

Jones & Hutton   P. Jones

Jones & Peirce
Boston, Mass. (c. 1810)
John B. Jones
Bibl. 15, 44, 110, 114

JONES & PEIRCE

Jones & Ward (c. 1809)
Boston, Mass.
Richard Ward
John B. Jones

*Bibl. 15, 23, 24, 25, 28, 36,
44, 91, 110, 114, 157*

JONES & WARD

Jones & Wood (c. 1846)
Syracuse, N.Y.
J. F. Jones (?)
———— Wood
Bibl. 20, 124

Jones & Woodland Co.
(c. 1896–present)
Newark, N.J.
Became division of Krementz
& Co. (1977)
Bibl. 127, 146

Jones, Ball & Co.
(c. 1852–1854)
Boston, Mass.
John B. Jones
S. S. Ball
*Bibl. 15, 23, 25, 28, 36, 44,
91, 114, 116, 122, 157*

JONES, BALL & CO.

Jones, Ball & Poor
(c. 1846–c. 1852)
Boston, Mass.
John B. Jones
S. S. Ball
*Bibl. 15, 23, 24, 25, 28, 36,
44, 72, 91, 104, 114, 116,
122, 135, 157*

JONES, BALL & POOR

Jones, Low(s) & Ball
(c. 1839)
Boston, Mass.
John B. Jones
John J. Low
———— Ball
*Bibl. 15, 24, 25, 28, 44, 72,
91, 114, 135, 157*

JONES LOWS & BALL
JONES LOW & BALL

**Jones, Shreve, Brown &
Co.** (c. 1854)
Boston, Mass.

John B. Jones
Benjamin Shreve
———— Brown
(See Benjamin Shreve)
Bibl. 15, 114, 122, 157

Albert Jones
Greenfield, Mass.
(c. 1827–1828)
Bibl. 15, 44, 91, 110

A. JONES

C. H. Jones & Co.
(c. 1854)
Georgetown, S.C.
Bibl. 5

Caleb Jones
(b. 1797–1827)
Plattsburg, N.Y. (c. 1818)
Burlington, Vt.
Bibl. 20, 110, 124

Christopher Jones
(c. 1847)
St. Louis, Mo.
Bibl. 54, 138, 155

Daniel Jones (d. 1822)
Wellsburg, Va. (c. 1821)
Bibl. 17

E. Jones (c. 1820)
Baltimore, Md.
Bibl. 23, 36

Elisha Jones
(c. 1827–1833)
New York, N.Y.
*Bibl. 15, 25, 44, 114, 124,
138*

E. JONES

G. B. Jones (c. 1815)
Rogersville, Tenn.
Bibl. 89

G. W. Jones (c. 1838)
Savannah, Ga.
Bibl. 17

George B. Jones
(b. 1815–d. 1875)
Boston, Mass.
Bibl. 23, 28, 36, 44, 91, 104

George W. Jones
(c. 1840–1841)
Philadelphia, Pa.
Bibl. 3

**Griffith (William) G.
Jones** (c. 1824–1827)
Baltimore, Md.
Bibl. 38

H. Jones (c. 1816)
Painesville, Ohio
Bibl. 34

Harlow Jones (c. 1811)
Canandaigua, N.Y.
Swift & Jones (c. 1810) (?)
Bibl. 20, 124

Isaac Jones (d. 1805)
Charleston, S.C. (c. 1800)
Bibl. 5

J. F. Jones (c. 1850)
Syracuse, N.Y.
Jones & Wood (c. 1846) (?)
Bibl. 20, 124

J. Walter Jones
(c. 1842–1845)
Troy, N.Y.
Bibl. 20, 124

Jacob Jones
(c. 1817–1818)
Baltimore, Md.
Bibl. 38

James Jones (d. 1815)
Philadelphia, Pa.
Bibl. 3, 15, 23, 36, 44

| J. JONES 57 MARKET ST. |

James M. Jones
(c. 1825–1850)
Savannah, Ga.
Spear & Jones (c. 1841)
Bibl. 17

John Jones (d. 1768)
Philadelphia, Pa. (c. 1750)
Bibl. 3, 23

John Jones (c. 1784)
Staunton, Va.
Bibl. 3, 19, 23

John B. Jones
(b. 1782–d. 1854)
Boston, Mass.
Jones & Ward (c. 1809)
Jones & Pierce (c. 1810)
Baldwin & Jones (c. 1813)
John B. Jones & Co.
(c. 1838)
Jones, Low(s) & Ball
(c. 1839) | J JONES |
Low(s), Ball & Co.
(1840–c. 1846)
Jones, Ball & Poor
(c. 1846–c. 1852)
Jones, Ball & Co.
(c. 1852–c. 1854)
Jones, Shreve, Brown & Co.
(c. 1854)
*Bibl. 4, 15, 23, 24, 25, 28,
29, 36, 44, 54, 78, 91, 94,
110, 114* | J. B. JONES |

John B. Jones & Co.
(c. 1838)
Boston, Mass.
John B. Jones
S. S. Ball
*Bibl. 15, 25, 28, 44, 110,
114, 151*

| J B JONES & CO |

John W. Jones & Son
(19th century)
Mt. Sterling, Ky.
Bibl. 32, 54

Levi Jones (c. 1845–1846)
Philadelphia, Pa.
Bibl. 3

Philip Jones (c. 1843)
Wilmington, Del.
Jones & Hutton | P. JONES |
(c. 1840–1862?)
Bibl. 25, 44

Prince H. Jones
(c. 1842–1861)
St. Louis, Mo.
Benjamin F. Crane & Co.
Bibl. 54, 155

Robert E. Jones
(c. 1837–1838)
Utica, N.Y.
Bibl. 18, 20, 158

Rowland Jones
(c. 1837–1838)
Utica, N.Y.
Bibl. 18, 20, 124, 158

Samuel G. Jones
(c. 1799–1829)
Baltimore, Md.
(c. 1799–1815)
Philadelphia, Pa.
(c. 1804–1814)
Patton & Jones
(c. 1799–1815)
Bibl. 38

Samuel S. Jones (c. 1844)
Philadelphia, Pa.
Bibl. 3

Samuel W. Jones
(c. 1792–1802?)
Augusta, Ga.
Bibl. 17

Thomas L. Jones (c. 1850)
Location unknown
Bibl. 15, 44, 114

| THOS. L. JONES |

William Jones
(b. 1694–d. 1730)
Marblehead, Mass. (c. 1715)
*Bibl. 2, 15, 23, 25, 28, 36,
44, 66, 69, 91, 94, 110,
114*

William Jones
(c. 1820–1823)
New York, N.Y.
Boyce & Jones
(c. 1825–1830) (?)
Bibl. 23, 36, 124, 138

William E. Jones (b. 1826)
Rochester, N.Y. (c. 1847)
Bibl. 20, 41, 44, 124

William G. Jones (c. 1837)
Philadelphia, Pa.
Bibl. 3

William H. Jones
(c. 1837–1841)
Charleston, S.C.
Bibl. 5

William Talbot Jones
(c. 1796?)
Savannah, Ga.
Bibl. 17

Peter Jordan (c. 1823)
Philadelphia, Pa.
Bibl. 23, 36, 44

R. Jordan (c. 1819)
Richmond, Va.
Bibl. 19

Samuel Jordan (c. 1807)
Baltimore, Md.
Bibl. 38

Peter Joubert (Jubart)
(c. 1807–1830)
Philadelphia, Pa.
Bibl. 3, 23, 36, 44

Peter Jourdan
(c. 1823–1824)
Philadelphia, Pa.
Bibl. 3

Michael Journot
(c. 1809–1810)
Philadelphia, Pa.
Bibl. 3

Thomas E. Joyce
(c. 1820–1825)
Philadelphia, Pa.
Bibl. 3

Jubart
(See Joubert)

—— **Judah** (c. 1774)
New York, N.Y.
Bibl. 28, 36, 44, 124, 138

Benjamin Judd (c. 1812)
Burton, Ohio
Bibl. 34

Judson & Lawrence
(c. 1803)
Stillwater, N.Y.
Bibl. 20, 124

C. H. Judson (c. 1846)
Syracuse, N.Y.
Bibl. 20, 124

Hiram Judson | H. JUDSON |
(c. 1824–1854)
Syracuse, N.Y.
Bibl. 15, 20, 25, 44, 114, 124

Thomas W. Judson
(c. 1850)
Syracuse, N.Y.
Bibl. 20, 124

Juergens & Andersen
(1857–1895)
Chicago, Ill.
Successor to Juergens & Son
(1854–1857)
Succeeded by Juergens &
Andersen Company
(1893–present)
Bibl. 98

**Juergens & Andersen
Company** (1893–present)
Chicago, Ill.
Successor to Juergens & Son
(1854–1857)
Juergens & Andersen
(1857–1895)
Bibl. 98

Cadmus Julian (c. 1840)
Philadelphia, Pa.
Bibl. 3

The Julmat (c. 1910)
Chicago, Ill.
Bibl. 98

A. R. Justice (Justus) Co.
(c. 1881–1936)
Philadelphia, Pa.
Bibl. 127

HICKS SILVER CO.

RIVERTON SILVER CO.

Joseph J. Justice
(c. 1844–1848)
Philadelphia, Pa.
Bibl. 3

Swan Justice (Justis)
(c. 1818–1819)

Richmond, Va. | S JUSTIS |
Bibl. 19

Justis & Armiger
(c. 1891–1893)
Baltimore, Md.
Succeeded by James R.
Armiger (1893)
Bibl. 127

K

K
(See Keystone Silver Co.,
Kent Silversmiths, Wm.
Knoll & Co., J. B. & S. M.
Knowles Co., Gustave F.
Kolb, Koonz Mfg. Co.,
Peter L. Krider Co.)

K & D
(See Kidney & Dunn)

K & K
(See Kraus, Kragel & Co.)

K & McD
(See Ketcham & McDougall)

K. & R.
(See Kimbell & Restaurick)

K & S
(See Kirk & Smith)

K B
(See Krider & Biddle)

K C & J
(See Kidney, Cann &
Johnson)

K E
(See Koechin & Englehardt)

K J
(See Kraus & Jantzen)

K L
(See Knight Leverett)

K S
(See Keystone Silver Co.)

J. Kadmus (c. 1839)
St. Louis, Mo.
Bibl. 54, 155

William Kahmer
(c. 1843–1850)
Philadelphia, Pa.
Bibl. 3

H. Q. Kakle
(c. 1838–1848)
St. Louis, Mo.
Bibl. 54, 155

Rufus G. Kallock (1860)
Ashland, Me.
Bibl. 105

The Kalo Shop
(1900–1970)
Chicago, Ill.
Bibl. 98, 120, 127, 144

HANDWROUGHT
AT
THE KALO SHOPS
CHICAGO
AND
NEW YORK

**William Kanapauge
(Kannapaux)**
Charleston, S.C.
(c. 1809–1819)
Bibl. 5

———— **Kanot** (c. 1781)
Alexandria, Va.
Bibl. 54

Karbin
(See Carbin)

J. N. Karl (c. 1810)
Philadelphia, Pa.
Bibl. 3

E. M. Karmel & Co.
(c. 1915–1922)
Brooklyn, N.Y.
Bibl. 127, 157

A. L. Karn (c. 1809–1810)
Philadelphia, Pa.
Bibl. 3

C. Karner (Karrar)
(c. 1809–1811)

Philadelphia, Pa.
Bibl. 3

P. Karsner & Co. (c. 1821)
Kingston, Tenn.
Bibl. 89

J. Katz & Co.
(c. 1901–1904)
Baltimore, Md.
Bibl. 127

Eugene Katzenstein
(b. 1825)
New Orleans, La.
(1852–1880)
Bibl. 141

Am(os) Kay (c. 1725)
Boston, Mass.
Bibl. 23, 28, 29, 36, 44, 110

A K

Kayser
(See Lohse & Kayser)

B. Kayton (c. 1847)
Fredericksburg, Va.
Bibl. 19

W. W. Keach (1860)
Providence, R.I.
Bibl. 108

John W. Kean
(c. 1837–1850)
Philadelphia, Pa.
Bibl. 3

———— **Keating**
(c. 1840–1843)
Philadelphia, Pa.
Warner & Keating
Bibl. 3

Lambert Keatting Jr.
(c. 1831–1843)
Philadelphia, Pa.
Bibl. 3

J. Kedzie & Co.
(c. 1847–1848)
Rochester, N.Y.
John Kedzie
Bibl. 20, 41, 44, 114, 124

J. KEDZIE&CO

John Kedzie
(b. 1809–d. 1889)
Rochester, N.Y.
(c. 1838–1868)
(not Philadelphia, Pa.)
J. Kedzie & Co.
(c. 1847–1848)
Bibl. 20, 25, 41, 44, 114, 124

J KEDZIE

John Keel (c. 1835–1837)
Philadelphia, Pa.
Bibl. 3

A. Keeler (c. 1800)
New London, Conn.
Norwalk, Conn.
Bibl. 23, 24, 36, 110

KEELER

Joseph Keeler
(b. 1786–d. 1824)
Norwalk, Conn. (c. 1810)
*Bibl. 15, 16, 23, 24, 25, 28,
29, 36, 44, 89, 91, 92, 110,
114*

I.K KEELER

KEELER

KEELER IK

**Thad(d)eus Keeler
(Keller)**
New York, N.Y.
(c. 1805–1813)
Boston, Mass. (c. 1823?)
*Bibl. 15, 23, 24, 25, 28, 29,
35, 36, 44, 54, 83, 89, 91,
114, 124, 138*

T. KEELER T. K

C. F. Kees & Co.
(c. 1904–1909)
New York, N.Y.
Successor to Henry I. Leibe
Mfg. Co.
Became Archibald-Klement
Co.
Bibl. 127, 157

George Keesee
(c. 1831–1846)
Richmond, Va.
Bibl. 19

G. KEESEE

G. H. Keeve
(c. 1848–1849)
Louisville, Ky.
Bibl. 32, 93

Joseph Keiff
(c. 1828–1833)
Philadelphia, Pa.
Bibl. 3, 23, 36, 44

Alexander Keim
(c. 1841–1850)
Philadelphia, Pa.
Butler & Keim (c. 1843)
Butler, Wise & Keim
(c. 1850)
Bibl. 3, 23

John Keim (c. 1777)
Reading, Pa.
Bibl. 3

T. & W. Keith (c. 1805)
New York, N.Y.
Bibl. 23, 29, 36, 44

Timothy Keith
(b. 1774–d. 1806)
Boston, Mass.
(c. 1800–1805)
Bibl. 25, 28, 91, 110, 114

T. Keith   T. KEITH

Timothy & William Keith
(c. 1829)
Worcester, Mass.
*Bibl. 23, 25, 36, 44, 91, 94,
110, 114*

T & W KEITH

Grael Keley (Kelley)
(c. 1823)
Boston, Mass.
Bibl. 23, 28, 36, 44

Keller & Hoerner
(1861–1865)
New Orleans, La.
Bibl. 141

Charles Keller (c. 1841)
Philadelphia, Pa.
Bibl. 3

George Keller (c. 1846)
Philadelphia, Pa.
Bibl. 3

Thaddeus Keller
(See Thadeus Keeler)

Kelley & McBean
(c. 1900)
New York, N.Y.
Bibl. 127

David Kelley
(c. 1806–1816)
Philadelphia, Pa.
Bibl. 3, 91

E. G. & J. S. Kelley
(c. 1820–1842)
Nantucket, Mass.
Providence, R.I.
Edward G. Kelley
James S. Kelley
Bibl. 23, 28, 36, 44

E & J. Kelley

Edward G. Kelley
(b. 1818)
Nantucket Island, Mass.
(c. 1840)
E. G. & J. S. Kelley
(c. 1820–1842)
H. A. & E. G. Kelley
Bibl. 12

Grael Kelley
(See Grael Keley)

H. A. & E. G. Kelley
(before 1842)
Nantucket, Mass.
Henry A. Kelley
Edward G. Kelley
Bibl. 44

H. A. & E. G. Kelley

Henry A. Kelley
(c. 1815–1869)
Nantucket Island, Mass.
H. A. & E. G. Kelley
Bibl. 12, 44

H A KELLEY

James S. Kelley
(b. 1820–d. 1900)
Nantucket Island, Mass.
(c. 1838–1856)
New Bedford, Mass. (1856)
E. G. & J. S. Kelley
(c. 1820–1842)
Bibl. 12, 44

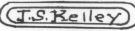

Royal T. Kelley
(c. 1835–1836)
Buffalo, N.Y.
Bibl. 20, 124

John V. Kellinger
(c. 1837)
Philadelphia, Pa.
Bibl. 3

Jack Kellmer Co.
(c. 1937–present)
Philadelphia, Pa.
Bibl. 89, 127

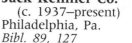

Allen Kell(e)y
(c. 1810–1825)
Nantucket Island, Mass.
Providence, R.I.
Bibl. 12, 23, 28, 36, 44

Robert Kelly
(c. 1843–1844)
Philadelphia, Pa.
Bibl. 3

Thomas Kelvey
(c. 1817–1831)
Cincinnati, Ohio
West Union, Ohio
Bibl. 34, 152

Kenab
(See Charles Kendal)

**Charles Kendal(l)
(Kendle) (Kindle)
(Kenab)**
New York, N.Y.
(c. 1780–1797)
*Bibl. 15, 23, 25, 28, 36, 44,
114, 124, 138*

C. KENDALL

James Kendall
  (b. 1768–d. 1808)
  (c. 1790–1800)
Wilmington, Del.
Philadelphia, Pa.
Bibl. 15, 25, 30, 44, 91, 114

| J. KENDALL | J. K |

Sullivan Kendall
  (b. 1787–d. 1853)
Hallowell, Me.
Bibl. 15, 44, 91, 110, 114

| S KENDALL |

Kendle
(See Kendal)

Kendrick
(See also Hendricks)

William Kendrick
  (b. 1810–d. 1880)
Louisville, Ky.
  (c. 1824–1880)
Harris & Kendrick
  (c. 1831–1832)
Lemon & Kendrick
  (c. 1831–1842)
E. C. Beard & Co.
  (c. 1831–1852)
*Bibl. 23, 24, 25, 29, 32, 36,
  44, 54, 68, 89, 91, 93, 114*

| W KENDRICK | W. KENDRICK LOUISVILLE |

Kennard & Jenks
  (c. 1875–1880)
Boston, Mass.
Purchased by Gorham Mfg.
  Co.
Bibl. 127

Kennedy
(See Morgan & Kennedy)

Hugh Kennedy
  (c. 1837–1850)
Philadelphia, Pa.
Bibl. 3, 91

John Kennedy
  (b. 1823, c. 1839)
Charleston, S.C.
Bibl. 5

Matthew Kennedy
  (c. 1825)
Philadelphia, Pa.
Bibl. 23, 36, 44

Nathan Kennedy (c. 1825)
Philadelphia, Pa.
Bibl. 3

Patrick Kennedy
  (c. 1795–1801)
Philadelphia, Pa.
Bibl. 3

Kenney
(See Kinney)

Anwyl Kenrick (c. 1775)
Maryland
Bibl. 36, 44

William Kensell (c. 1835)
Philadelphia, Pa.
Bibl. 3

Kent
(See Yates & Kent)

Kent & Stanley Co., Ltd.
  (1888–1898)
Providence, R.I.
E. F. Kent
S. W. Stanley
Successor to Wm. H.
  Robinson & Co.
Became Bassett Jewelry
  Company
Bibl. 114, 127, 157

STERLING.

Kent Silversmiths
  (1936–present)
New York, N.Y.
Bibl. 127, 146

Luke Kent (c. 1817–1841)
Cincinnati, Ohio
Bibl. 34, 90, 152

Thomas Kent
Cincinnati, Ohio
  (c. 1821–1844)
Nashville, Tenn. (c. 1855)
Bibl. 34, 54, 90, 152

Samuel Keplinger
  (b. 1770–d. 1849)
Baltimore, Md.
  (c. 1812–1849?)
Bibl. 25, 29, 38, 44, 114

| S KEPLINGER |

William Keplinger
  (c. 1829–1831)
Baltimore, Md.
Bibl. 38

Alexander Kerr (d. 1738)
Williamsburg, Va. (c. 1734)
Bibl. 19, 153

| A K |

William B. Kerr & Co.
  (c. 1855–1906)
Newark, N.J.
Became Gorham
Bibl. 111, 120, 127, 131, 157

Robert M. Kerrison
  (c. 1842–1850)
Philadelphia, Pa.
Bibl. 3

Kersey & Pearce
  (c. 1845–1850)
Richmond, Va.
Edward Kersey
Hamett A. Pearce
Bibl. 19

Edward Kersey
  (c. 1845–1878)
Richmond, Va.
Kersey & Pearce | E. KERSEY |
  (c. 1845–1850)
Bibl. 19

Robert Kersey (c. 1793)
Easton, Md.
Bibl. 38

John Kershaw
 (c. 1789–1791)
Charleston, S.C.
Bibl. 5

John Kessler Jr.
 (c. 1806–1807)
Philadelphia, Pa.
Bibl. 3

Susan Kessler
 (c. 1976–1980)
Hephaestus, Ltd.
St. Louis, Mo.
Bibl. 155

H. Kessner & Company
 (c. 1927)
New York, N.Y.
Bibl. 127

Ketcham & McDougall
 (1875–present)
New York, N.Y.
Successor to Prime &
 Roshore (1832–1834)
Roshore & Prime
 (1834–1848)
Prime & Roshore & Co.
 (1848–1850)
Roshore & Wood
 (1850–1853)
Roshore & Ketcham
 (1853–1854)
Ketcham & Brother
 (1854–1857)
Ketcham Bro. & Co.
 (1857–1875)
Bibl. 127

James Ketcham
(See James Ketcham)

Joseph Ketcham
 (c. 1815–1826)
New York, N.Y.
Bibl. 15, 124

James Ketcham
 (Ketcham)
 (c. 1807–1849)
New York, N.Y.
Utica, N.Y.
*Bibl. 18, 20, 23, 24, 25, 36,
 44, 91, 114, 124, 138, 158*

L. A. Ketchum & Co.
 (c. 1840–1842)
Buffalo, N.Y.
Lewis A. Ketchum
Bibl. 20, 124

Lewis A. Ketchum
 (c. 1837–1840)
Buffalo, N.Y.
L. A. Ketchum & Co.
 (c. 1840–1842)
Bibl. 20, 124

Thomas Kettel(l)
 (b. 1760–d. 1850)
Charlestown, Mass.
 (c. 1784)
*Bibl. 23, 25, 28, 29, 36, 44,
 94, 110, 114*

T. K.	T + K

George Kew (c. 1840)
Philadelphia, Pa.
Bibl. 3

Key & Sons (c. 1850)
Philadelphia, Pa.
F. C. Key
Bibl. 3

F. C. Key (c. 1848–1850)
Camden, N.J.
Philadelphia, Pa.
Key & Sons (c. 1850)
Bibl. 3

Keyes & Fitch (c. 1831)
Batavia, N.Y.
S. C. Keyes
William Fitch
Bibl. 20, 124

Keyes & Stocking
 (c. 1831)
Batavia, N.Y.
S. C. Keyes
Reuben Stocking
Bibl. 20, 124

S. C. Keyes (c. 1830–1834)
Batavia, N.Y.
Keyes & Fitch (c. 1831)
Keyes & Stocking (c. 1831)
Bibl. 20, 24, 124

Joseph Keyser
 (c. 1828–1833)

Philadelphia, Pa.
Bibl. 3

William Keyser (c. 1850)
Philadelphia, Pa.
Bibl. 3, 23

Keystone Silver Co.
 (1914–present)
Philadelphia, Pa.
Bibl. 127, 146

Keystoneware
(See Keystone Silver Co.)

John Keywood (c. 1851)
Wheeling, Va.
Bibl. 19

Robert Keyworth
 (c. 1830–1833)
Washington, D.C.
*Bibl. 23, 24, 25, 29, 36, 44,
 91, 114*

R. KEYWORTH

P. Kibbe
Location unknown
Bibl. 54, 114

Hubert Kidel (1826–1844)
New Orleans, La.
Bibl. 141

Kidney, Cann & Johnson
 (c. 1850–1853)
New York, N.Y.
*Bibl. 4, 23, 24, 25, 28, 29,
 44, 54, 114, 124*

K. C. & J.

Kidney & Dunn (c. 1844)
New York, N.Y.
*Bibl. 23, 24, 25, 29, 44, 114,
 124*

Cornelius Kierstede
(Kierstead) (Kiestede)
(b. 1674–d. 1757,
c. 1702–1729)
New Haven, Conn.
New York, N.Y.
*Bibl. 2, 4, 15, 16, 23, 25, 28,
29, 36, 44, 54, 61, 92, 94,
95, 102, 104, 110, 114,
116, 118, 119, 124, 138,
143, 151*

John Killingsworth
(c. 1812)
Raleigh, N.C.
Bibl. 21

Kimball
(See Carleton & Kimball)

Kimball & Restaurick
(c. 1904)
Boston, Mass.
Bibl. 127, 157   **K. & R.**

Kimball & Son
(1840–c. 1927)
Haverhill, Mass.
Bibl. 127, 157

John Kimball (c. 1785)
Boston, Mass.
Bibl. 28 | J. KIMBALL |

Kimball
(See Woodford & Kimball)

Lewis A. Kimball
(c. 1837–1842)
Buffalo, N.Y.
Boston, Mass.
Bibl. 15, 25, 44, 91, 114, 124

| L. KIMBALL |

O. Kimball (c. 1842–1843)
Elmira, N.Y.
Yates & Kimball
Bibl. 20, 124

William H. Kimberly
(b. 1780–d. 1821,

c. 1805–1821)
Baltimore, Md.
New York, N.Y.
*Bibl. 15, 23, 24, 25, 29, 36,
38, 44, 95, 114, 124, 138*

| W. K | | Kimberly |

KIMBERLY

William H. Kimberly
(c. 1842)
St. Louis, Mo.
Bibl. 54, 155

Jane Kind
(b. 1624–d. 1710)
Boston, Mass.
Bibl. 28

S. Kind & Son
(1872–c. 1922)
Philadelphia, Pa.
Bibl. 127, 157   **S. K. & S.**

Kindle
(See Kendal)

—— King (c. 1817)
Warren, Ohio
Bibl. 34

King Silver Co.
(c. 1955–1957)
Boston, Mass.
Became Lunt Silversmiths
Bibl. 127

Ernest King (c. 1854)
New Orleans, La.
Bibl. 141

G. W. King (c. 1790)
Location unknown
Bibl. 24 | G. W. KING |

George King
(c. 1834–1844)
New York, N.Y.
Bibl. 15, 23, 91, 124, 138

Gilbert King (c. 1845)
Rochester, N.Y.
Bibl. 20, 124

Henry King (c. 1830)
Troy, N.Y.
Bibl. 20, 124

Henry S. King (1875)
Newport, Me.
Bibl. 105

John King (c. 1817–1819)
Philadelphia, Pa.
Bibl. 3

Joseph King
(c. 1770–1807)
Middletown, Conn.
Bibl. 16, 23, 28, 36, 44, 110

R. King (c. 1820)
Philadelphia, Pa. (?)
Bibl. 15, 44, 114 | R KING |

Solomon King (c. 1808)
Baltimore, Md.
Wheeling, Va.
Bibl. 19

Thomas King (c. 1840)
Leesburg, Va.
Bibl. 19

Thomas R. King
(c. 1819–1831)
Baltimore, Md.
Bibl. 25, 29, 38, 44, 114

| T R KING |

Walter King (c. 1817)
Warren, Ohio
Bibl. 34, 88

William King
(c. 1806–1816)
Philadelphia, Pa.
Bibl. 3

William King (c. 1838)
Charleston, S.C.
Bibl. 5

King's Enamel &
Silverware, Inc.
(c. 1931)
New York, N.Y.
Bibl. 127

John Kingston
(c. 1775–1795)
New York, N.Y.
*Bibl. 4, 23, 28, 36, 44, 91,
124, 138*

James Kinkead
  (c. 1765–1774)
Christiana, Del.
Philadelphia, Pa.
Bibl. 3

A. Kinley (c. 1841)
Philadelphia, Pa.
Bibl. 3, 23

Kinne
(See Thomas Kinney)

Thomas Kinne Jr.
  (c. 1836)
Cortland, N.Y.
Bibl. 20, 124

Thomas Kinney (Kenney) (Kinne)
  (b. 1785–d. 1824?)
Norwich, Conn.
  (c. 1785–1824)
Cortland, N.Y.
Bibl. 16, 23, 24, 25, 28, 36, 44, 61, 91, 92, 110, 114

William & Jesse Kinsel
  (c. 1837–1839)
Philadelphia, Pa.
Bibl. 3

Kinsey
(See Scovil & Kinsey)

David I. Kinsey
  (b. 1819–d. 1871)
Cincinnati, Ohio
  (1840–1871)
E. & D. Kinsey
  (1844–1861)
Bibl. 15, 23, 24, 25, 29, 34, 44, 54, 90, 91, 114, 152

⟨DAVID KINSEY⟩

DAVID KINSEY

D. KINSEY

E. & D. Kinsey
  (1844–1861)
Newport, Ky.   E & D KINSEY
Cincinnati, Ohio
Edward Kinsey

David I. Kinsey
Bibl. 15, 23, 24, 25, 29, 32, 44, 54, 89, 90, 91, 93, 114

Edmund Kinsey (c. 1845)
Jamaica, N.Y.
Bibl. 20, 124

Edward Kinsey
  (b. 1810–d. 1865)
Newport, Ky.
Cincinnati, Ohio
  (1834–1861)   E. KINSEY
E. & D. Kinsey
  (1844–1861)
Bibl. 32, 34, 54, 72, 90, 91, 93, 114, 152

F. Kinsey
Cincinnati, Ohio (c. 1837)
Bibl. 34

John Kinzie
  (c. 1804, d. 1828)
Chicago, Ill.
Detroit, Mich.
St. Joseph, Mich.
Maumee, Ohio
Bibl. 58

Benjamin Kip (c. 1702)
New York, N.Y.
Bibl. 4, 23, 28, 36, 44

Jesse Kip
  (b. 1660–d. 1722)
Newtown, N.Y.   I K
New York, N.Y.
Bibl. 25, 54, 95, 102, 104, 114, 124, 138, 139, 151

William Kip
  (c. 1825–1850)
Kinderhook, N.Y.
Bibl. 20

R. M. Kipp (c. 1833)
Wheeling, Va.
Stocking & Kipp
Bibl. 19

George Kippen
  (b. 1790–d. 1845)
Bridgeport, Conn. (c. 1827)
Albany, N.Y. (c. 1830)
Middletown, Conn.
Hoyt & Kippen (c. 1830)

Elias Camp (c. 1825–1827)
Bibl. 15, 16, 23, 24, 25, 28, 29, 36, 44, 61, 91, 92, 94, 110, 114, 124   G. KIPPEN

G. Kippen & Hoyt
(See Hoyt & Kippen)

Kirby
(See Brown(e) & Kirby)

H. A. Kirby Co.
  (c. 1905–1920)
Providence, R.I.
Successor to Kirby, Mowry
  & Co. (c. 1886–1905)
Bibl. 127

William Kirby (c. 1783)
New York, N.Y.
Bibl. 23, 36, 44, 124

J. H. Kirchoff (c. 1805)
Philadelphia, Pa.
Bibl. 3

E. H. Kirckhaff (c. 1803)
Philadelphia, Pa.
Bibl. 3

Kirk Stieff Company
  (1979–present)
Baltimore, Md.
Successor to Stieff Company
  (1904–1979)
Samuel Kirk & Sons, Inc.
  (c. 1925–1979)
(See Samuel Kirk)
Bibl. 4, 15, 23, 24, 25, 28, 29, 36, 39, 44, 54, 72, 86, 91, 104, 114, 116, 118, 122, 131, 135

Year marks used on hollowware:

1901	①	1919	◯
1902	②	1920 or	◠ ◡
1903 to 1916	③ ... ⑯	1921	−
		1922	+
1917 or	⬠ ◇	1923 or	‡ ++
1918	△	1924	#
		1925	◇

Year	Mark	Year	Code
1926 or 1927 or 1928	◇	1953	T
		1954	U
		1955	W
		1956	X
1929 or 1930		1957	Y
		1958	Z
		1959	1
		1960	2
1930	☆	1961	3
1931 or 1932		1962	4
		1963	5
		1964	6
		1965	7
1933 or 1934		1966	8
		1967	9
		1968	10
		1969	11
1935 or 1936		1970	12
		1971	13
1936	A	1972	14
1937	B	1973	15
1938	C	1974	16
1939	D	1975	17
1940	E	1976	18
1941	F	1977	19
1942	G	1978	20
1943	H	1979	21
1944	J	1980	22
1945	K	1981	23
1946	L	1982	24
1947	M	1983	25
1948	N	1984	26
1949	O	1985	27
1950	P	1986	28
1951	R	1987	29
1952	S	1988	30

STIEFF STERLING

STIEFF ROSE

KIRK STIEFF

KIRK ROSE

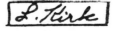

Kirk & Smith
(c. 1818–1823)
Baltimore, Md.
Samuel Kirk
John Smith
Bibl. 15, 23, 24, 25, 28, 36, 38, 44, 86

KIRK & SMITH   K & S

Abdiel Kirk (c. 1835)
Albany, N.Y.
Bibl. 20, 124

Arthur Nevill Kirk
(1881–1958)
Detroit, Mich
Bibl. 120

Charles D. Kirk
(1861–1868)
Baltimore, Md.
Samuel Kirk & Sons
Bibl. 91

Clarence E. Kirk
(1861–1868)
Baltimore, Md.
Samuel Kirk & Sons
Bibl. 91

Henry Child Kirk
(b. 1827–d. 1894)
Baltimore, Md.
Samuel Kirk & Son
(c. 1846–1861, 1868–1870)
Samuel Kirk & Sons
(1861–1868)
Bibl. 89

Henry Child Kirk Jr.
(1870–1924)
Baltimore, Md.
Samuel Kirk & Son
(1870–1896)
Samuel Kirk & Son Co.
(1896–1924)
Bibl. 89

Joshua Kirk
(c. 1848–1849)
Philadelphia, Pa.
Bibl. 3

Robert Sherman Kirk
(b. 1800–d. 1874,
c. 1827–1833)
Baltimore, Md.
Philadelphia, Pa.
Bibl. 3, 38

Samuel Kirk
(b. 1793–d. 1872)
Baltimore, Md. (1821–1846)
Kirk & Smith
Succeeded by Samuel Kirk &
Son
*Bibl. 4, 15, 23, 24, 25, 28,
29, 36, 39, 44, 86, 91, 104,
114, 116, 118, 122, 135*

KIRK

Samuel Kirk & Son
(1846–1861, 1868–1896)
Baltimore, Md.
Company periodically made
slight changes in name:
Samuel Kirk & Sons
(1861–1868)
Samuel Kirk & Son Co.
(1896–1924)
Samuel Kirk & Son Inc.
(1924–1979)
Bibl. 4, 15, 23, 24, 25, 28,

29, 36, 39, 44, 86, 91, 104, 114, 116, 118, 122, 135

```
SK & Son
```

```
S KIRK & SON
```

```
S. Kirk & Sons
```

```
S. Kirk & Son Co.
```

```
S. Kirk & Son Inc.
Sterling
```

```
S. Kirk & Son Sterling
```

J. Kirkham (c. 1840)
Location unknown
Bibl. 24

Samuel W. Kirkland
   (c. 1828–1835)
Northampton, Mass.
Fowle & Kirkland
   (c. 1828–1833)
Bibl. 84

E. M. Kirkpatrick
   (c. 1856–1861)
York, S.C.
Bibl. 5

Peter Kirkwood   P K
Chestertown, Md.
   (c. 1790–1795)
Annapolis, Md.
   (c. 1799–1801)
Bibl. 25, 29, 38, 44

Warner Kirthright
   (c. 1802)
Baltimore, Md.
Bibl. 38

Joseph P. Kirtland
   (b. 1770, w. 1796)
Middletown, Conn.
Bibl. 16, 23, 28, 36, 44, 110

Andrew B. Kitchen
   (d. 1840)
Philadelphia, Pa.
Bailey & Kitchen
Bibl. 3, 23, 36, 44, 127

Kitts & Stoy
   (c. 1851–1852)

Louisville, Ky.
John Kitts
David C. Stoy
Bibl. 32, 93

Kitts & Werne
   (c. 1865–1874)
Louisville, Ky.
John Kitts
Joseph Werne
Bibl. 32, 54, 68, 93

John Kitts (c. 1836–1878)
Louisville, Ky.
Scott & Kitts
Smith & Kitts
   (c. 1844–1845)
Kitts & Stoy (c. 1851–1852)
John Kitts & Co.
   (c. 1859–1878)   J. KITTS
Kitts & Werne
   (c. 1865–1874)
Bibl. 25, 32, 44, 54, 68, 93, 114

John Kitts & Co.
   (c. 1859–1878)
Louisville, Ky.
Bibl. 32, 93

Klank Mfg. Co.
   (c. 1892–1894)
Baltimore, Md.
Became Sterling Silver Mfg.
   Co.
Bibl. 127

C. Klank & Sons
   (1895–1911)
Baltimore, Md.
Successor to Klank & Bro.
   (1872–1892)
Conrad Klank & Sons
   (1892)
C. Klank & Sons Mfg. Co.
   (1893–1894)
Became Schofield Co., Inc.
   (c. 1905), but continued
   to be listed under this
   name through 1911
Bibl. 127, 135

William Klank
   (c. 1895–1899)
Baltimore, Md.
Bibl. 127

John Klauer (c. 1842)
St. Louis, Mo.
Bibl. 54, 155

John Klein (c. 1828–1850)
Philadelphia, Pa.
Bibl. 3

John A. Klein
   (c. 1833–1837)
Leesburg, Va.
Bibl. 19

Jacob Kleiser (Kleizer)
   (c. 1822–1824)
Philadelphia, Pa.
Bibl. 3

B. Kline & Co. (c. 1837)
Philadelphia, Pa.
Bartholomew Kline
Bibl. 3, 4, 23, 28, 36, 44

Bartholomew Kline
   (c. 1837–1850)
Philadelphia, Pa.
B. Kline & Co. (c. 1837)
Bibl. 3, 23, 36

F. S. Kline & Co. (c. 1850)
Lyons, N.Y.
Foster S. Kline (?)
Bibl. 20, 124

Foster S. Kline (c. 1850)
Syracuse, N.Y.
F. S. Kline & Co.
   (c. 1850) (?)
Bibl. 20, 124

Peter Kline (c. 1835)
Philadelphia, Pa.
Bibl. 3

Philip Kline
(See Cline)

Joseph Klingle
   (c. 1823–1825)
Philadelphia, Pa.
Bibl. 3

John J. Klink (d. 1900)
Louisville, Ky.
   (c. 1841–1859)
Bibl. 32, 93

John Kloebner
(c. 1845–1850)
Richmond, Va.
Bibl. 19

Bernard T. Kluth (c. 1850)
Louisville, Ky.
Bibl. 32, 93

Knapp & Leslie
(c. 1850–1854)
Mobile, Ala.
Alanson Knapp
Franklin A. Leslie
Bibl. 148   KNAPP & LESLIE

Alanson Knapp (b. 1800)
Mobile, Ala. (c. 1838–1867)
Dunning & Knapp
(c. 1826–1837)
Knapp & Leslie   A. KNAPP
(c. 1850–1854)
Bibl. 148

Jesse Knapp   J KNAPP
(c. 1825–1830)
Boston, Mass.
Bibl. 15, 44, 91, 110

William Knapp
(c. 1764–1768)
Annapolis, Md.
Bibl. 38

Philip Knappe
(c. 1839–1841)
Philadelphia, Pa.
Bibl. 3

Christian Kneass
(c. 1811–1837)
Philadelphia, Pa.
Bibl. 3

William Kneass
(c. 1805–1842)
Philadelphia, Pa.
Horn & Kneass
(c. 1811–1837)
Bibl. 3

Joseph I. Kneeland
(b. 1698–d. 1760)
Boston, Mass.
*Bibl. 2, 4, 15, 23, 24, 25, 28,
29, 36, 44, 60, 110, 114,
119*

John Knepfly
(c. 1845–1880)
New Albany, Ind.
Bibl. 133

J . KNEPFLY

Benjamin Knight (c. 1822)
Painesville, Ohio
Bibl. 34

John W. Knight (c. 1845)
Rochester, N.Y.
Bibl. 20, 124

Mary Catherine Knight
(b. 1876)
The Handicraft Shop
Boston, Mass.
Wellesley Hills, Mass.
Bibl. 89

Philip Knipe
(c. 1829–1833)
Philadelphia, Pa.
Bibl. 3

Julius Knock
(c. 1845–1850)
Philadelphia, Pa.
Bibl. 3

Wm. Knoll & Co.
(c. 1904–1915)
New York, N.Y.
Bibl. 127, 157

Knorr & Baker (c. 1830)
Philadelphia, Pa.
James Knorr
———— Baker
Bibl. 3

James Knorr
(c. 1828–1829)
Philadelphia, Pa.
Knorr & Baker (c. 1830)
Bibl. 3

Knowles & Ladd
(c. 1864–1875)
Providence, R.I.
(See Webster & Knowles)
Bibl. 24, 108, 127

J. B. & S. M. Knowles Co.
(1875–1905)
Providence, R.I.

(See Webster & Knowles)   RED CROSS
Bibl. 114, 127, 157

John Knowles (c. 1784)
Philadelphia, Pa.
Bibl. 3

Ebenezer B. Knowlton
(c. 1848)
Cazenovia, N.Y.
Bibl. 20, 124

Henry Knox (c. 1848)
Louisville, Ky.
Bibl. 32, 93

Augustus Koch (c. 1850)
Philadelphia, Pa.
Bibl. 3

Carl Koch (c. 1846–1848)
Philadelphia, Pa.
Bibl. 3

H. Kock (Koch)
(c. 1838–1845)
St. Louis, Mo.
Bibl. 54, 155

Henry Kocksperger
(c. 1837)
Philadelphia, Pa.
Bibl. 3

Koechin & Englehardt
(c. 1906–1915)
Newark, N.J.
Bibl. 127, 157

Florence Koehler
(b. 1861–d. 1944)
Chicago, Ill.
Bibl. 117, 127

Renard A. Koehnemann
(1946–1967)
Chicago, Ill.
Bibl. 98

Koesning
(See Harting & Koesning)

Gustave F. Kolb
(c. 1917–1921)
New York, N.Y.
Bibl. 127

Peter Kolb (c. 1829–1850)
Philadelphia, Pa.
Bibl. 3

John Kolby (c. 1807–1808)
Philadelphia, Pa.
Bibl. 3

Abraham I. Kolster
(c. 1850)
Syracuse, N.Y.
Bibl. 20, 124

Koontz & Holtzbaum
(c. 1793)
Fredericktown, Md.
Henry Koontz Jr.
Jacob Holtzbaum
Bibl. 38

Henry Koontz Jr.
(c. 1781–c. 1793)
Fredericktown, Md.
Koontz & Holtzbaum
(c. 1793)
Bibl. 38

Koonz Mfg. Co. (c. 1922)
Greenfield, Mass.
Bibl. 127, 157

Henrk Kopke (c. 1850)
New York, N.Y.
Bibl. 23, 124

Louis A. Kotzow (1875)
Providence, R.I.
Bibl. 108

Charles Kraemer (c. 1882)
Baltimore, Md.
Bibl. 127

William Kramer (c. 1848)
Philadelphia, Pa.
Bibl. 3

Kraus & Jantzen
(c. 1904–1922)
New York, N.Y.
Successor to Kraus, Kragel &
Co.
Became Kraus, McKeever &
Adams
Bibl. 127

Kraus, Kragel & Co.
(c. 1896–1904)
New York, N.Y.
Became Kraus & Jantzen
(c. 1904–1922)
Bibl. 114, 127

Kraus, McKeever &
Adams (c. 1922)
New York, N.Y.
Successor to Kraus &
Jantzen (c. 1904–1922)
Bibl. 127

John Samuel Krause
(b. 1782–d. 1813)
Lancaster, Pa.
Bethlehem, Pa. (w. 1805)
Bibl. 3, 23, 36, 44, 91

Peter Krebs (c. 1844)
New York, N.Y.
Bibl. 23, 124, 138

Krider & Biddle
(c. 1860–1870)
Philadelphia, Pa.
Successor to Peter L. Krider
(c. 1850–1870)
Became Peter L. Krider Co.
(c. 1870–1903)
Simons Bros. & Co.
*Bibl. 25, 28, 29, 44, 114,
127, 157*

Peter L. Krider (c. 1850)
Philadelphia, Pa.
Krider & Biddle
*Bibl. 4, 23, 24, 25, 28, 44,
54, 104, 114*

Peter L. Krider Co.
(c. 1870–1903)
Philadelphia, Pa.
Successor to Krider & Biddle
(c. 1860–1870)
Became Simons Bros. & Co.
Bibl. 114, 127, 157

Leonard Krower
(c. 1896–1943)
New Orleans, La.
Became Leonard Krower &
Son, Inc.
(c. 1943–1965)
Bibl. 127, 157

Leonard Krower & Son,
Inc. (c. 1943–1965)
New Orleans, La.
Successor to Leonard Krower
(c. 1896–c. 1943)
Became Gordon Jewelry
Corporation
Bibl. 127, 157

Mary Kruming
(c. 1945–1970)
New York, N.Y.
Bibl. 117

Jacob Kucher (Kuchler)
(c. 1806–1833)
Philadelphia, Pa.
*Bibl. 3, 23, 24, 25, 28, 29,
36, 44, 91, 114*

I. KUCHER

C. Kuchler & Co. (1870)
New Orleans, La.
Christopf Christian Kuchler
Augustus William Jansen
Bibl. 141

Christopf Christian
Kuchler (1852–1870)
New Orleans, La.
C. Kuchler & Co.
Bibl. 15, 25, 44, 114, 141

C. KUCHLER

J. Kuchler
(See J. Kucher)

Kuehler & Janson
(c. 1871)
New Orleans, La.
Bibl. 127

M. H. Kum (c. 1820)
Location unknown
Bibl. 24

William Kumbel
(c. 1780–c. 1789)
New York, N.Y.
Bibl. 23, 36, 44, 124, 138

Henry Kunler (1861–1866)
New Orleans, La.
Bibl. 141

Henry Kunsman
Fredericksburg, Va. (c. 1819)
Richmond, Va. (c. 1820)
Raleigh, N.C. (c. 1823)
Salisbury, N.C. (c. 1823)
Savage & Kunsman
(c. 1823)
Bibl. 19, 21

Frank Kursch & Son Co.
(c. 1904–1915)
Newark, N.J.
Mark identical to
Shoemaker, Pickering &
Co.
Bibl. 127, 157

John Kurtz (c. 1823–1824)
Philadelphia, Pa.
Bibl. 3

———— **Kurtzborn**
(See Bauman & Kurtzborn)

L

L
(See Eleder-Hickok Co.,
Hickok Matthews
Company, Providence
Stock Co., Warwick
Sterling Co.)

L & G
(See Lincoln & Green)

L & W
(See Leonard & Wilson)

L A
(See Oliver Mfg. Co.)

L B
(See Loring Bailey, Luther
Bradley, Lewis Buichle)

L B S
(See Lucas Stoutenburgh Sr.)

L E S C O
(See Levine Silversmith Co.)

L F
(See Lewis Fueter)

L H
(See Lewis Ludwig Heck,
Littleton Holland)

L K
(See Leonard Krower)

L K & S
(See Leonard Krower & Son,
Inc.)

L. S. & Co.
(See Louis Stern Co., Inc.)

L S B
(See Lucas Stoutenburgh)

L. S. P.
(See L. S. Peterson Co.)

L Sterling
(See The Lenau Co.)

L W
(See Lemuel Wells)

L W & Co.
(See Lemuel Wells & Co.)

Francis Labacoone
(before 1773)
Georgetown, S.C.
Bibl. 5

Augustus LaBlanc
(c. 1819)
Philadelphia, Pa.
Bibl. 3

John Lacey (c. 1819–1825)
Philadelphia, Pa.
Bibl. 3

Peter Lachaise
(c. 1794–1808)
New York, N.Y.
Bibl. 23, 36, 44, 124, 138

Henry Lackey
(c. 1808–1811)
Philadelphia, Pa.
Bibl. 3

Ladd
(See Knowles & Ladd)

Horatio H. Ladd (c. 1800)
Manchester, N.H.
H. H. Ladd & Co. (c. 1830)
Bibl. 28, 91, 124

H. H. Ladd & Co.
(c. 1830)
Manchester, N.H.
Bibl. 89, 91, 125

| H. H. LADD & CO. |

William F. Ladd
(c. 1828–1845)
New York, N.Y.
*Bibl. 29, 36, 44, 79, 91, 114,
116, 124*

| WM F. LADD | (WM F. LADD)

Jacob Ladomus
(c. 1843–1850)
Philadelphia, Pa.
Bibl. 3, 15, 25, 44, 114

| J. LADOMUS |

Lewis Ladomus
(c. 1830–1850)
Philadelphia, Pa.
Bibl. 3, 24, 91

John Joseph Lafar
(b. 1781–d. 1849)
Charleston, S.C.
(c. 1805–1849)
Bibl. 5, 25, 44, 114 | LAFAR |

Joseph David Lafar
(b. 1786–d. 1818)
Charleston, S.C. (c. 1816)
Bibl. 5

Peter X. Lafar
(b. 1779–d. 1814)
Charleston, S.C.
(c. 1805–1814)
Bibl. 5, 44 | L'AFAR |

Antoine Laforme (c. 1836)
Boston, Mass.
Bibl. 23, 36, 44

Bernard Laforme (c. 1836)
Boston, Mass.
Bibl. 23, 36

F. J. Laforme
(b. 1823–d. 1893)
Boston, Mass. (c. 1835)
Bibl. 4, 23, 28, 36, 44

Vincent Laforme (c. 1850)
Boston, Mass.
*Bibl. 4, 23, 25, 28, 29, 44,
104, 114*

**Vincent Laforme &
Brother** (c. 1850–1855)
Boston, Mass.
Bibl. 15, 23, 25, 44, 114

V. L. & B

V. L & Bro

Lagazze & Sonnier
(c. 1814–1816)
Philadelphia, Pa.
John Lagazze
Joseph Sonnier
Bibl. 3

John Lagazze
Philadelphia, Pa.
Lagazze & Sonnier
(c. 1814–1816)
Bibl. 3

J. C. La Grange
Charlottesville, Va.
Staunton, Va.
A. Robinson & Co.
(c. 1839–1842)
Bibl. 89

Stephen Lain(e)court
(c. 1800–1805)
New York, N.Y.
Bibl. 23, 36, 44, 124

**Ebenezer Knowlton
Lakeman**
(b. 1799–d. 1857)
Salem, Mass. (c. 1819–1830)
Stevens & Lakeman

(c. 1825)
*Bibl. 15, 23, 25, 28, 29, 36,
39, 44, 91, 110, 114, 124*

E. K. LAKEMAN

John Lalande (Lalarde)
(c. 1844–1850)
Philadelphia, Pa.
Bibl. 3

Benjamin Lamar
(See Benjamin Lemaire)

**Matthias Lamar (Lamer)
(Lemaire) (Lemar)**
(d. 1809)
Philadelphia, Pa.
(c. 1781–1797)
*Bibl. 3, 4, 23, 24, 25, 28, 29,
36, 44, 81, 91, 114*

B.L. ML LAMAR

Anthony Lamb (c. 1760)
New York, N.Y.
Bibl. 28, 124

John Lamb (c. 1756)
New York, N.Y.
Bibl. 28, 124

J. S. Lambard (1860–1875)
Gardiner, Me.
Bibl. 105

John Lambe (c. 1787)
Baltimore, Md.
Bibl. 23

E. J. Lambers (c. 1821)
Philadelphia, Pa.
Bibl. 3, 23

D. Lambertoz (d. 1817)
Wilmington, N.C. (c. 1795)
Savannah, Ga. (c. 1799)
Bibl. 17, 21

Matthias Lamer
(See Matthias Lamar)

Peter Lamesiere (c. 1811)
Philadelphia, Pa.
Bibl. 3, 23, 36, 44

Lewis Lammel
(c. 1843–1850)

Philadelphia, Pa.
Bibl. 3

A. Lamoine
(See A. Lemoine)

Robert Lamont
(c. 1842–1845)
Philadelphia, Pa.
Bard & Lamont
(c. 1841–1845)
Bibl. 3, 23, 91

Pierre Lamothe
St. Marc, Santo Domingo
(c. 1800)
Santiago, Cuba (1803–1809)
New Orleans, La.
(1809–1823)
Pierre Lamothe & Son
*Bibl. 23, 24, 25, 29, 36, 44,
114, 141*

Lamothe

Pierre Lamothe & Son
(c. 1822)
New Orleans, La.
Bibl. 23, 36

Pierre Lamothe & Son

La Motta
(See De La Motta)

Augustus Lamoyne
(c. 1816)
Philadelphia, Pa.
Bibl. 3

John Lampe(y)
Annapolis, Md. (c. 1779)
Baltimore, Md.
(c. 1780–1787)
Bibl. 36, 38, 44   I L

C. H. Lamson (1875)
Portland, Me.
Bibl. 105

John Lamson (c. 1790)
Boston, Mass. (c. 1816)
Baltimore, Md.
Bibl. 28, 29, 36, 44, 91, 110

L. Lamson (c. 1800)
Location unknown
Bibl. 24

L Lamson

**Augustus Lamvine
(Lemvine)**
(c. 1811–1816)
Philadelphia, Pa.
Bibl. 3

Americus Lancaster
(c. 1842–1850)
Philadelphia, Pa.
Bibl. 3

Arman Lancaster (c. 1837)
Philadelphia, Pa.
Bibl. 3

M. Lancaster (c. 1839)
Philadelphia, Pa.
Bibl. 3

Richard Lancaster
(c. 1818–1822)
Philadelphia, Pa.
Rickards & Lancaster
(c. 1817)
Bibl. 3

Tobias D. Lander
(c. 1826–1833)
Newburgh, N.Y.
Bibl. 15, 20, 44, 91, 114, 124

LANDER

Xavier Landsee
(b. 1824–d. 1870)
New Orleans, La.
Bibl. 141

Lane, Bailey & Co.
(c. 1850)
Madison, N.Y.
Bibl. 20, 124

Lane & Bros. (c. 1840)
Clarks Mills, N.Y.
Bibl. 20, 124

Aaron Lane
(b. 1753–d. 1819)
Elizabeth, N.J.
(c. 1775–1780)
*Bibl. 24, 25, 28, 36, 44, 46,
54, 114*

James Lane
(c. 1803–1818)
Philadelphia, Pa.
Bibl. 3

William Lane
(c. 1772–1790)
Nixonton, N.C.
Pasquotank County, N.C.
Bibl. 21

Z. Lane (1875)
Poland, Me.
Bibl. 105

Abraham Lang (c. 1850)
Philadelphia, Pa.
Bibl. 3

Edward Lang
(b. 1742–d. 1830)
Salem, Mass.
*Bibl. 2, 21, 24, 29, 36, 44,
54, 91, 102, 110, 114*

E L   LANG

Jeffrey Lang
(b. 1707–d. 1758)   I L
Salem, Mass.
*Bibl. 2, 15, 23, 24, 25, 28,
29, 44, 54, 70, 91, 94, 102,
110, 114, 151*

I. LANG   LANG

Lewis W. Lang
(c. 1837–1844)
Philadelphia, Pa.
Bibl. 3

Nathaniel Lang
(b. 1736–d. 1826)
Salem, Mass.
Bibl. 15, 25, 44, 91, 110, 114

N. LANG

Richard Lang
(b. 1733–d. 1820)
Salem, Mass.
*Bibl. 2, 15, 23, 24, 29, 36,
44, 91, 110, 114*

R. LANG

William Lange (c. 1844)
New York, N.Y.
*Bibl. 23, 24, 25, 29, 44, 114,
124, 138*

·LANGE·

Joseph Langer (c. 1811)
Philadelphia, Pa.
Bibl. 3, 23, 36, 44

E. P. Langworthy & Son
(c. 1814)
Ballston Spa, N.Y.
Elisha Perkins Langworthy
Bibl. 20, 124

**Elisha Perkins
Langworthy**
(b. 1766–d. 1827)
Ballston Spa, N.Y.
E. P. Langworthy & Son
(c. 1814)
Bibl. 20, 21, 124

Lyman B. Langworthy
(b. 1787–d. 1880)
Ballston Spa, N.Y.
(c. 1808–1814)
Bibl. 20, 124

**William Andrews
Langworthy**
(b. 1790–d. 1868)
Ballston Spa, N.Y. (c. 1822)
Saratoga Springs, N.Y.
Bibl. 20

Gerrit Lansing (b. 1812)
Albany, N.Y. (c. 1838)
Bibl. 20

**Jacob Gerritse (Gerrittze)
Lansing**
(b. 1681–d. 1767)
Albany, N.Y.
Bibl. 29, 54, 114, 119, 124

I●L   I.G.L.

Jacob H. Lansing (c. 1847)
Rochester, N.Y.
Bibl. 20, 124

John (Jacob) Gerrit Lansing Jr.
  (b. 1736–d. 1803)
Albany, N.Y. (c. 1765–1790)
Bibl. 15, 20, 23, 24, 25, 28, 36, 44, 54, 91, 95, 114, 124

Alphonse La Paglia
  (1952–1953)
Meriden, Conn.
Became International Silver
  Company (1953)
Bibl. 127

John B. Laperouse
  (c. 1822)
New Orleans, La.
Bibl. 23, 36, 44

La Pierre Mfg. Co.
  (c. 1888–1929)
Newark, N.J.
New York, N.Y.
Became International Silver
  Company (1929)
Moved to Wallingford,
  Conn.
Bibl. 114, 127, 157

Charles La Place
  (c. 1795–1796)
Wilmington, N.C.
Bibl. 21

—————— **La Pointe** (c. 1795)
Baltimore, Md.
Bibl. 38

Francis Laquain (c. 1794)
Philadelphia, Pa.
Bibl. 3

F. Larchambault (c. 1830)
Location unknown
Bibl. 89

| F. LARCHAMBAULT |

Alexander E. Larer
  (c. 1846–1850)
Philadelphia, Pa.
Bibl. 3

Laret & Brechémin
  (c. 1816–1818)
Philadelphia, Pa.
Michael Laret
Louis Brechémin
Bibl. 3

Michael Laret (Larit)
  (c. 1814–1818)
Philadelphia, Pa.
Laret & Brechémin
Bibl. 3

Eustachio La Rive
  (b. c. 1729)
New Orleans, La.
  (1778–1789)
Bibl. 141

Peter Larousse(bierre)
  (c. 1797)
New York, N.Y.
Bibl. 23, 36, 44

Peter L. LaRousselier (La Roussitur)
Charleston, S.C.
  (c. 1803–1809)
Bibl. 5

Elias Larson (c. 1850)
Rochester, N.Y.
Bibl. 20, 124

William La Rue
  (c. 1847–1849)
Philadelphia, Pa.
Bibl. 3

Larzelere & Moffat
  (c. 1835)
Buffalo, N.Y.
Abraham Larzelere
William Moffat
Bibl. 20, 124

Abraham Larzelere
  (c. 1815–1835)
Buffalo, N.Y.
Larzelere & Moffat (c. 1835)
Bibl. 20, 124

La Secla, Fried & Co.
  (c. 1909–1922)
Newark, N.J.
Bibl. 127, 157

James E. Lasell
  (c. 1844–1846)

Troy, N.Y.
Bibl. 20, 124

Luther R. Lasell (b. 1798)
Lanesborough, Mass.
Troy, N.Y. (1831–1846)
Bibl. 20, 110, 124

Peter Lashing (c. 1805)
New York, N.Y.
Bibl. 24, 36, 44, 124, 138

John Latchow (c. 1829)
Baltimore, Md.
Bibl. 38

James Latham (c. 1795)
Albany, N.Y.
Bibl. 20, 124

Rufus Lathrop
  (b. 1731–d. 1805)
Norwich, Conn.
Bibl. 16, 28, 36, 44, 110

James Latimer
  (c. 1813–1822)
Philadelphia, Pa.
Bibl. 3

| J.E. Latimer |

John B. M. La(e)tourn(e)au (Letourneaux)
  (b. 1796–d. 1853)
Baltimore, Md.
Bibl. 17, 38

John P. Latruite
  (c. 1807–1843)
Washington, D.C.
Baltimore, Md.
Alexandria, Va.
Bibl. 19, 36, 44

A. Latta (c. 1837)
Philadelphia, Pa.
Bibl. 3

Orson Lattimer (c. 1832)
Jefferson, Ohio
Bibl. 34

A. Lauder (c. 1840)
Location unknown
Bibl. 24

| A LAUDER |

George Laval
(c. 1842–1843)
Philadelphia, Pa.
Bibl. 3

Peter Laval (c. 1842)
Philadelphia, Pa.
Bibl. 3

William P. Law
(c. 1837–1850)
Philadelphia, Pa.
Bibl. 3

Lawing & Brewer
(c. 1842–1843)
Charlotte, N.C.
Samuel Lawing
N. Alexander F. Brewer
Bibl. 21

Samuel Lawing
(b. 1807–d. 1865)
Charlotte, N.C.
Lawing & Brewer
(c. 1842–1843)
Bibl. 21

William Lawler
St. Louis, Mo. (c. 1842)
New Orleans, La.
(c. 1846–1854)
San Francisco, Calif.
(c. 1854–1882)
Bibl. 55, 127, 141, 155

**William Lawler,
Carondolet & Marion**
(c. 1842)
St. Louis, Mo.
Bibl. 54, 155

Lawrence
(See Judson & Lawrence)

—————— **Lawrence** (c. 1835)
Philadelphia, Pa.
Bibl. 3

John Lawrence (d. 1798)
Philadelphia, Pa.
Bibl. 3

Joseph Lawrence
(c. 1818–1822)
Philadelphia, Pa.
Bibl. 3

Joseph Lawrence
(c. 1839–1850)
Philadelphia, Pa.
Bibl. 3

Joseph H. Lawrence
(c. 1823–1825)
Philadelphia, Pa.
Bibl. 3

Josiah Lawrence
(c. 1817–1837)
Philadelphia, Pa.
Bibl. 3

Josiah H. Lawrence
(c. 1817–1824)
Philadelphia, Pa.
Bibl. 23, 36, 44

L. U. Lawrence (c. 1812)
Augusta, Ga.
Bibl. 17

Martin M. Lawrence
(c. 1832–1840)
New York, N.Y.
*Bibl. 15, 25, 44, 114, 124,
138*

Robert D. Lawrie
(c. 1840–1850)
Philadelphia, Pa.
Taylor & Lawrie
(c. 1837–1850)
Taylor, Lawrie & Wood
(after 1841)
Bibl. 3, 4, 28

Robert O. Lawrie
(c. 1840)
Philadelphia, Pa.
Bibl. 23, 36, 44

John Lawrison (c. 1791)
Alexandria, Va.
Bibl. 19, 54

John Laws (c. 1818–1830)
Philadelphia, Pa.
Bibl. 3

Er. L. Lawshe
(1850 c. 1885)
Atlanta, Ga.
Bibl. 89

**Er. Lawshe & William A.
Hayes** (1870–1883)
Atlanta, Ga.
Bibl. 89

Alexander Lawson
(c. 1794–1799)
Philadelphia, Pa.
Bibl. 3

Peter Laycock (c. 1750)
Philadelphia, Pa.
Bibl. 44

Moses Lazarus (c. 1830)
Philadelphia, Pa.
Bibl. 3

Francis Lea
(w. 1789, d. 1805)
Fayette County, Ky.
Lexington, Ky.
Bibl. 32, 54, 68, 93

Samuel I. (J.) Lea (Lee)
Baltimore, Md.
(c. 1814–1822)
Bibl. 15, 24, 25, 29, 44, 114

S·I·LEA

⊞ F a

S.J LEE

Leach & Bennett
(c. 1856–1858)
Utica, N.Y.
Almon Leach
L. M. Bennett
Bibl. 18, 124, 158

Leach & Bradley
(c. 1832–1835)
Utica, N.Y.
Ebenezer Leach
Horace S. Bradley
*Bibl. 18, 20, 23, 28, 36, 44,
124, 158*

Leach & Davies
(c. 1835–1840)
Utica, N.Y.
Ebenezer Leach
Thomas Davies
Bibl. 18, 20, 124, 158

Almon Leach (b. 1823)
Utica, N.Y. (c. 1845–1858)
Hawley & Leach
  (c. 1853–1856)
Leach & Bennett
Bibl. 18, 20, 124, 158

Charles Leach
  (b. 1765–d. 1814)
Boston, Mass.
Bibl. 23, 24, 25, 28, 29, 36,
  44, 110, 114

Charles B. Leach
  (c. 1843–1847)
Utica, N.Y.
Bibl. 18, 20, 124, 158

Ebenezer Leach (c. 1797)
Utica, N.Y. (c. 1832–1840)
Leach & Bradley
  (c. 1832–1835)
Leach & Davies
  (c. 1835–1840)
Bibl. 18, 20, 91, 124, 158

George Leach
  (c. 1854–1857)
Utica, N.Y.
Hawley & Leach
  (c. 1853–1856)
Bibl. 18, 91, 124, 158

John Leach (c. 1780)
Boston, Mass.
Bibl. 23, 36, 44, 110

Leonard D. Leach
  (c. 1850)
Auburn, N.Y.
Haight & Leach
Bibl. 20, 91, 124

Nathaniel Leach (c. 1789)
Boston, Mass.
Bibl. 4, 15, 23, 25, 28, 36,
  44, 110, 114

Samuel Leach
  (c. 1741–1780)
Philadelphia, Pa.
Bibl. 3, 23, 24, 28, 29, 36,
  44, 114

John I. Leacock
  (c. 1748–1799)
Philadelphia, Pa.

Bibl. 3, 15, 23, 24, 25, 28,
  29, 30, 36, 39, 44, 54, 81,
  95, 102, 114

Peter Leacock (c. 1750)
Philadelphia, Pa.
Bibl. 36

William League (b. 1798)
Baltimore, Md. (c. 1815)
Bibl. 38

Leavenworth, Brown &
  Co. (c. 1836)
Binghamton, N.Y.
Bibl. 20, 124

T. B. Leavenworth
  (c. 1869)
Detroit, Mich.
Bibl. 127

John Lebeau (c. 1848)
St. Louis, Mo.
Bibl. 54, 155

Christian David Lebey
  (c. 1787–1827)
Savannah, Ga.
McConky & Lebey
  (c. 1811–1812)
Bibl. 17

Lebkeucher & Co.
  (c. 1896–1915)
Newark, N.J.
Arthur E. Lebkeucher
Frances A. Lebkeucher
Charles C. Wientge
Became F. A. Lester
  (c. 1915–1918)
Eleder Co. (c. 1918–1922)
Eleder-Hickok Co.
  (c. 1922–1931)
Hickok-Matthews Company
  (c. 1931–present)
Bibl. 114, 127, 157

Lewis Le Blanc (c. 1818)
Philadelphia, Pa.
Bibl. 3, 23, 36, 44

Lebolt & Co.
  (c. 1899–present)
Chicago, Ill.
Bibl. 89, 98, 127, 144, 157

Lebolt Handmade

Henry Leclere
  (c. 1791–1826)
Savannah, Ga.
Bibl. 17

Joseph J. Leddel (c. 1752)
New York, N.Y.
Bibl. 28, 116

Joseph Ledell (c. 1797)
Philadelphia, Pa.
Bibl. 23, 36, 44, 102

Samuel E. Ledman
  (19th century)
Louisville, Ky.
Bibl. 32, 54, 93

———— **Le Dore** (c. 1797)
Philadelphia, Pa.
Bibl. 3, 23, 36, 44

Lee
(See also Roberts & Lee)

George Lee (c. 1837–1850)
Philadelphia, Pa.
Bibl. 3, 38

John A. Lee
  (c. 1840–1850)
Mansfield, Ohio
Bibl. 34

Samuel I. Lee
(See Samuel I. Lea)

Samuel W. Lee
  (b. 1785–d. 1861,
  c. 1815–1822)
Providence, R.I. (c. 1815)
Rochester, N.Y. (c. 1822)
Burr & Lee (c. 1815)
Scofield & Lee (c. 1822)
Bibl. 15, 20, 23, 24, 25, 29,
  36, 41, 44, 91, 110, 114,
  124

Samuel W. Lee Jr.
  (c. 1849–1850)
Rochester, N.Y.
Bibl. 20, 41, 44, 124

Thomas Lee
  (b. 1717–d. 1806)
Farmington, Conn.
Martin Bull
Bibl. 28, 110

Thomas Lee
(c. 1799–c. 1807)
Savannah, Ga.
Bibl. 17

Gideon H. Leeds
(c. 1841–1842)
Philadelphia, Pa.
Bibl. 3

Howard G. Leeds
(c. 1840)
Philadelphia, Pa.
Bibl. 3

Peter Leevell (c. 1841)
Philadelphia, Pa.
Bibl. 3

Lefevre & Gravelle
(c. 1811)
Philadelphia, Pa.
John Felix Lefevre
Louisa M. Gravelle
Rene L. Gravelle
Bibl. 3, 23, 36, 44

F. Lefevre (c. 1818)
Philadelphia, Pa.
Mobile, Ala. (c. 1850)
Bibl. 3, 23, 36, 44, 148

John Felix Lefevre
(d. 1813)
Philadelphia, Pa.
(c. 1806–1813)
Lefevre & Gravelle (c. 1811)
Bibl. 3, 23, 36, 44

Theodore Lefevre
(c. 1820–1822)
Philadelphia, Pa.
Bibl. 3

Lefferts & Hall
(c. 1818–1822)
Philadelphia, Pa.
Charles Lefferts
———— Hall
Bibl. 3

Charles Lefferts
(c. 1818–1822)
Philadelphia, Pa.
Ovid, N.Y. (c. 1827)
Lefferts & Hall
Bibl. 3, 20, 124

Daniel Legare
(b. 1688–d. 1724)
Boston, Mass.
Bibl. 28, 44, 110

Francis Legare
(b. 1636–d. 1711)
Boston, Mass.
Bibl. 23, 28, 36, 44, 110

Solomon Legare
(b. 1674–1760)
Charleston, S.C.
(c. 1696–1740)
Bibl. 5, 102

Louis Andrew Legay
New York, N.Y. (c. 1836)
Columbus, Ga.
(c. 1842–1845)
Bibl. 17, 138

John F. Legoux
(c. 1797–1811)
Savannah, Ga.
Bibl. 17

John Francis Le Gras
(c. 1796)
Baltimore, Md.
Philippe & Le Gras
Bibl. 38

Nicholas Le Huray
(c. 1809–1831)
Philadelphia, Pa.
Bibl. 3, 15, 44, 91, 114

Nicholas J. Le Huray Jr.
(c. 1821–1846)
Philadelphia, Pa.
Bibl. 3, 15, 25, 44, 91, 114

Theodore Le Huray
(c. 1843–1850)
Philadelphia, Pa.
Bibl. 3

Henry L. Leibe Mfg. Co.
(c. 1904)
Newark, N.J.

Became C. F. Kees & Co.
(c. 1904–1909)
Archibald-Klement Co., Inc.
(c. 1909–1922)
Bibl. 127, 157

**Nathaniel Augustine
Leinbach**
(c. 1850–1860)
Salem, N.C.
Bibl. 21

Traugott Leinbach
(b. 1796–d. 1863)
Salem, N.C. (c. 1821–1860)
Bethlehem, Pa.
Bibl. 21, 91

Karl F. Leinonen
(c. 1901–1932)
Boston, Mass.
Bibl. 127, 144

Joseph Leland (c. 1846)
Philadelphia, Pa.
Bibl. 3

Joseph Lelurge
(c. 1817–1822)
Philadelphia, Pa.
Bibl. 3

Baptiste Lemaire (Lemar)
(c. 1804)
Philadelphia, Pa.
Bibl. 3, 23, 36

**Benjamin Lemaire
(Lemar) (Lamar)**
(d. 1785)
Philadelphia, Pa.
Bibl. 15, 23, 25, 95, 114

**Matthias Lemaire
(Lemar) (Lamer)**
(See Matthias Lamar)

Matthew Le Merre
(c. 1781)
Philadelphia, Pa.
Bibl. 3

Lemist & Tappan
  (c. 1818–1819)
Philadelphia, Pa.
William Lemist
William B. Tappan
Bibl. 3

William Lemist
  (c. 1816–1819)
Philadelphia, Pa.
Lemist & Tappan
  (c. 1818–1819)
Bibl. 3

A. Lemoine (Limone)
  (c. 1810–1817)
Philadelphia, Pa.
Bibl. 3

Lemon & Kendrick
  (c. 1831–1842)
Louisville, Ky.
James Innes Lemon
William Kendrick
Bibl. 32, 54, 68, 91, 93

Lemon & Son (after 1861)
Louisville, Ky.
James Innes Lemon
Bibl. 68, 93

James I. Lemon & Co.
  (c. 1859–1861)
Louisville, Ky.
James Innes Lemon
Edmund J. Daumont
Bibl. 32, 93

James Innes Lemon
  (b. 1804–d. 1869)
Louisville, Ky.
  (c. 1828–1869)
Lexington, Ky.
Lemon & Kendrick
  (c. 1831–1842)
James I. Lemon & Co.
  (c. 1859–1861)
Lemon & Son (after 1861)
Bibl. 32, 54, 68, 93

Lemp & Crane
  (c. 1864–1870)
Silas Crane
Alphonso Lemp
Covington, Ind.
Bibl. 133

Alphonso Lemp
  (c. 1864–1881)

Lemp & Crane
  (c. 1864–1870)
Covington, Ind.
Bibl. 133

Lemvine
(See Lamvine)

The Lenau Co.
  (c. 1896–1904)
Attleboro Falls, Mass.
Bibl. 114, 127, 157

L STERLING.

Peter Lench
  (c. 1805–1809)
New York, N.Y.
Bibl. 23, 36, 138

M. Lendigree (c. 1814)
New York, N.Y.
Bibl. 23, 36, 44, 124

Lendner
(See Lindner)

G. Lenhart (c. 1845)
Bowling Green, Ky.
Bibl. 15, 25, 32, 44, 54, 68, 93, 114

G Lenhart

W. Lenon
(See W. Lenoir)

Raimond Lenoir (c. 1818)
Savannah, Ga.
Bibl. 17

William Lenoir (Lenon)
Philadelphia, Pa.
  (c. 1843–1850)
Bibl. 3

**Andrew Lenormant
  (Lenorment)**
Charleston, S.C.
  (c. 1801–1810)
Bibl. 5

Lenox China, Inc.
  (1906–present)
Lawrenceville, N.J.
Began making sterling silver
  flatware in 1987
Bibl. 89   LENOX STERLING

Lenox Silver Inc. (c. 1950)
New York, N.Y.
Bibl. 127

LENOX

John Lent (c. 1751–1791)
New York, N.Y.
Philadelphia, Pa.
Bibl. 23, 25, 28, 36, 44, 114, 124, 138

J Lent

Lentner
(See Lindner)

George K. Lentz (c. 1825)
Philadelphia, Pa.
Bibl. 3, 15, 44, 114

G. K. LENTZ

Leonard & Rogers
  (c. 1831–1833)
New York, N.Y.
Allen Leonard
Augustus Rogers
Bibl. 15, 124, 138

Leonard & Wilson
  (c. 1847–1850)
Philadelphia, Pa.
Allen Leonard
―――― Wilson
Bibl. 3, 23, 25, 44, 114

L&W

Allen Leonard
  (c. 1827–1840)
New York, N.Y.
Leonard & Rogers
Leonard & Wilson
Bibl. 15, 23, 25, 44, 114, 124, 138

A. LEONARD

Allen Leonard
  (c. 1844–1850)
Philadelphia, Pa.
Bibl. 3, 36

D. Gillis Leonard
(c. 1841–1847)
Newburgh, N.Y.
Haight & Leonard (c. 1847)
Bibl. 20, 124

H. Leonard (c. 1855)
Nashville, Tenn.
Bibl. 54

J. Leonard (c. 1850)
Location unknown
Bibl. 15, 44, 114

J: LEONARD

J. C. Leonard (1875)
Bangor, Me.
Bibl. 105

Jacob Leonard (c. 1828)
Fredericksburg, Va.
Bibl. 19

Samuel T. Leonard
(b. 1786–d. 1848,
c. 1805–1848)
Baltimore, Md.
Chestertown, Md.
Lynch & Leonard
(c. 1805–1840)
Bibl. 24, 25, 29, 38, 114

LEONARD   S. LEONARD

Alexander Le Page
(c. 1818)
Philadelphia, Pa.
Bibl. 3

Edward Leppleman
(c. 1836–1839)
Buffalo, N.Y.
Bibl. 20, 124, 138

Peter Leret (Le Ret)
(c. 1787–1802)
Baltimore, Md.
Carlisle, Pa.
Philadelphia, Pa.
*Bibl. 15, 23, 24, 28, 29, 36,
38, 44, 50, 91, 95, 114*

P. LE RET   P. L.

Bartholomew Le Roux
(b. 1663–d. 1713)
New York, N.Y.
(c. 1689–1713)

*Bibl. 2, 15, 23, 24, 25, 28,
29, 35, 36, 44, 54, 95, 104,
114, 116, 119, 124, 135,
138, 142, 151*

Bartholomew Le Roux II
(b. 1720–d. 1763)
New York, N.Y.
*Bibl. 4, 15, 23, 25, 35, 44,
102, 116, 119, 124, 135,
138*

Charles Le Roux
(b. 1689–d. 1748)
New York, N.Y.
(c. 1713–1745)
*Bibl. 2, 4, 15, 23, 24, 25, 28,
29, 30, 35, 36, 44, 54, 91,
95, 102, 114, 116, 124,
135, 138, 139, 151*

John Le Roux (b. 1695)
Albany, N.Y. (c. 1716–1725)
New York, N.Y.
*Bibl. 4, 15, 20, 23, 24, 25,
28, 29, 30, 36, 44, 54, 114,
124, 135, 138*

Alexander Le Row
(c. 1827)
Fly Creek, N.Y.
Bibl. 20, 124

Abraham Le Roy
(c. 1757, d. 1763)
Lancaster, Pa.
Bibl. 3, 112

John Leroy (c. 1827–1832)
New York, N.Y.
Bibl. 15, 124, 138

**Edward P. Lescare
(Lescure)**
Philadelphia, Pa.
(c. 1822–1850)
*Bibl. 3, 15, 23, 24, 25, 36,
44, 91, 114*

Louis Leschot (d. 1838)
Charlottesville, Va. (c. 1836)
Bibl. 19

Lescure
(See Lescare)

John Lesfauries (c. 1800)
Baltimore, Md.
Bibl. 38

Francis Lesfro (c. 1802)
Baltimore, Md.
Bibl. 38

Joseph Lesher
(c. 1900–1915)
Victor, Colo.
Bibl. 127, 157

REFERENDUM

Leslie & Parry (c. 1803)
Philadelphia, Pa.
Robert Leslie
———— Parry
Bibl. 3

Leslie & Price
(c. 1793–1800)
Philadelphia, Pa.
Robert Leslie
Isaac Price
Abraham Patton
Bibl. 3

Robert Leslie (d. 1804)
Philadelphia, Pa.
(c. 1788–1803)
Baltimore, Md.
(c. 1795–1796)
Leslie & Price
(c. 1793–1800)
Leslie & Parry (c. 1803)
Robert Leslie & Co.
(c. 1795–1796)
Bibl. 3, 38

Robert Leslie & Co.
(c. 1795–1796)
Baltimore, Md.
Robert Leslie
Abraham Patton
Bibl. 38

Lesser & Rheinauer
(c. 1897–1898)
New York, N.Y.
Bibl. 127

William Lesser (c. 1859)
Orangeburg, S.C.
Bibl. 5

F. A. Lester
(See Lebkuecher & Co.)

J. U. Lester (c. 1843–1845)
Oswego, N.Y.
Bibl. 20

Talbot G. Lester
  (c. 1831–1840)
Portsmouth, Va.
Bibl. 19

John (I) Letelier
  (Letellier) (Le Telier)
Philadelphia, Pa.
  (c. 1770–1793)
Wilmington, Del. (c. 1793)
Chester Co., Pa.
  (c. 1795–1798)
Washington, D.C.
  (c. 1800–1810)
Alexandria, Va.
Richmond, Va.
Bibl. 3, 15, 23, 24, 25, 28,
  29, 30, 36, 54, 81, 91, 95,
  114, 122

LeTeLier

I. LETELIER

I LETELLER

Letourneau & Pearson
  (c. 1802–1803)
Savannah, Ga.
John Letourneau
John Pearson
Bibl. 17

John Letourneau
  (d. 1803)
Savannah, Ga.
Letourneau & Pearson
  (c. 1802–1803)
Bibl. 17, 124

Michel Letourneau(x)
  (c. 1797)
Quebec, Canada
New York, N.Y.
Bibl. 17, 23, 36, 44, 124, 138

Letourneaux
(See La[e]tourn[e]au)

Henry Leuba
  (19th century)
Lexington, Ky.
Bibl. 54, 93

George Levely
  (c. 1774–1796)
Baltimore, Md.
Philadelphia, Pa.
Bibl. 3, 23, 36, 38, 44

Knight Leverett   K L
  (b. 1703–d. 1753)
Boston, Mass.
Bibl. 2, 4, 15, 23, 24, 25, 28,
  29, 36, 78, 94, 102, 104,
  110, 114

K Leverett   K LEVERETT

Lewis Levering (c. 1835)
Philadelphia, Pa.
Bibl. 3

Levi & Englander
  (1865–1868)
New Orleans, La.
Bibl. 141

Garretson Levi
  (c. 1840–1843)
Philadelphia, Pa.
Bibl. 3

Isaac Levi (c. 1780)
Philadelphia, Pa.
Bibl. 3

Isaac C. Levi (c. 1880s)
New Orleans, La.
Bibl. 141

Jeremiah Levi (c. 1750)
Pickawaxon, Md.
Bibl. 38

Jonas Levi
(See Jonas Levy)

Levine Silversmith Co.
  (c. 1927–1931)
New York, N.Y.
Bibl. 127   LESCO

William Levis
  (b. 1785–d. 1842)
Philadelphia, Pa.
  (c. 1810–1814)
Bibl. 3, 23, 36, 112

Levitt & Gold   ℄
  (c. 1915–1922)
New York, N.Y.
Possibly became Levitt & Co.
  (c. 1935)
Bibl. 127, 157

Abraham Levy (c. 1813)
Charleston, S.C.
Bibl. 5

Henry A. Levy
  (c. 1841–1850)
Philadelphia, Pa.
Bibl. 3

John I. Levy
  (c. 1818–1822)
Norfolk, Va.
Bibl. 19

Jona(e)s (Joseph) Levy
  (Levi)
Connersville, Ind.
  (c. 1821)   J. LEVY
Cincinnati, Ohio
  (c. 1822–c. 1829)
New York, N.Y. (c. 1838)
Memphis, Tenn.
  (c. 1855–1860)
J. Levy & Co. (c. 1829)
Bibl. 15, 25, 34, 44, 89, 90,
  114, 124, 133, 138, 152

Lewis B. Levy
  (c. 1841–1845)
Philadelphia, Pa.
Bibl. 3

M. Levy & Co.
  (c. 1816–1817)
Philadelphia, Pa.
Bibl. 3

Martin Levy
  (c. 1814–1817)
Philadelphia, Pa.
Bibl. 3

Michael Levy
  (c. 1802–1816)
Philadelphia, Pa.
Bibl. 3

Michael & Isaac Levy
  (c. 1785)
Maryland
Bibl. 38

Chas. J. Leward
(c. 1896–1904)
New York, N.Y.
Bibl. 114, 127, 157

Gabriel Lewin
(See Gabriel Lewyn)

Lewis
(See Sterret & Lewis)

—————— **Lewis** (c. 1796)
Philadelphia, Pa.
Bibl. 3

Lewis & Smith
(c. 1805–1811)
Philadelphia, Pa.
*Bibl. 3, 4, 23, 24, 25, 28, 29,
36, 39, 44, 80, 91, 114,
122*

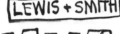

Lewis Bros. (c. 1896–1904)
New York, N.Y.
Bibl. 114, 127, 157

C. C. Lewis (c. 1844–1847)
Staunton, Va.
Bibl. 19

Fred Lewis (1875)
Camden, Me.
Bibl. 105

Frederick H. Lewis
(c. 1850)
Rochester, N.Y.
Bibl. 20, 124

Harvey Lewis (d. 1835)
Philadelphia, Pa.
(c. 1811–1826)
*Bibl. 3, 4, 15, 23, 24, 25, 28,
29, 36, 39, 54, 72, 91, 95,
102, 104, 114, 116, 122,
151*

{H LEWIS} | H. LEWIS |

| HARVEY LEWIS |

Isaac Lewis
(b. 1773–d. 1860)
Huntington, Conn.
Ridgefield, Conn.
*Bibl. 15, 16, 23, 24, 25, 28,
29, 36, 44, 46, 91, 92, 94,
110, 114*

| I LEWIS |

Isaac Lewis (c. 1782)
Newark, N.J.
Bibl. 46, 54

J. H. Lewis (c. 1810)
Albany, N.Y.
Bibl. 25, 44

J. N. Lewis
York, S.C.
J. N. Lewis & Co.
(c. 1854–1856)
Bennett, Lewis & Co.
(c. 1856)
Bibl. 5

(J. N.) Lewis & Co.
(c. 1854–1856)
York, S.C.
J. N. Lewis
Jordan Bennett (?)
D. W. Wilson
Bibl. 5

John M. (I.) Lewis
(c. 1830–1850)
Philadelphia, Pa. | J I LEWIS |
Johnson & Lewis
(c. 1837–1842) (?)
Bibl. 3, 15, 114

John V. Lewis
(1847–1852)
Utica, N.Y.
Bibl. 18, 20, 124, 158

Jonathan Lewis (c. 1797)
Poughkeepsie, N.Y.
Bibl. 20, 124

S. M. Lewis & Co.
(c. 1896–1904)
New York, N.Y.
Bibl. 114, 127, 157

**S. M. L. & CO.
STERLING**

Samuel Lewis (c. 1843)
Washington, D.C.
Bibl. 89

Tunis Lewis (c. 1805)
New York, N.Y.
Bibl. 23, 36, 44, 124, 138

William Lewis (c. 1813)
Batavia, N.Y.
Bibl. 20, 124

Gabriel Lewyn (Lewin)
(c. 1768–1780)
Baltimore, Md. | G L |
*Bibl. 4, 23, 24, 25, 28, 29,
36, 38, 44, 54, 91, 95, 151*

John A. L'Hommedieu
(d. 1867)
Mobile, Ala. (c. 1839–1867)
William T. L'Hommedieu
(c. 1830)
Bibl. 54, 148

| L'Hommedieu |

| J. A. L'Hommedieu |

**John A. & William T.
L'Hommedieu**
Mobile, Ala. (c. 1830)
Bibl. 54, 148 | L'H. Bros |

William T. L'Hommedieu
(c. 1830, d. 1834)
Mobile, Ala.
John A. L'Hommedieu
(c. 1830)
Bibl. 54, 148

**Lhulier (Luhlier) (Lunier)
& Co.** (c. 1846)
Philadelphia, Pa.
Bibl. 3

**Cassimer (Cashmere)
Lhulier (Luhlier)
(Lunier)**
(c. 1825–1850)
Philadelphia, Pa.
Bibl. 3

**Lewis Lhulier (Luhlier)
(Lunier)**
(c. 1829–1849)
Philadelphia, Pa.
Bibl. 3

Jacob G. L. Libby
(c. 1820–1846)
Boston, Mass.
Bibl. 24, 25, 28, 29, 44, 91,
110, 114

J G Libby   Libby

J. G. L. Libby

John Lidden (c. 1850)
St. Louis, Mo.
Bibl. 24, 25, 44, 114, 155

LIDDEN

Liebs Silver Co., Inc.
(c. 1922–1931)
New York, N.Y.
Successor to Liebs Co.
(c. 1915–1922)
Bibl. 127, 157

Lifetime
(See Zell Bros.)

James Lightfoot (b. 1726)
New York, N.Y. (c. 1749)
Bibl. 23, 36, 44, 124

R. L. Lightfoot
(c. 1853)
Jackson, Tenn.

Edward Lilienthal
(1858–1888)
New Orleans, La.
Bibl. 141

Julius Lilienthal
(1853–1867)
New Orleans, La.
Bibl. 141

J. LILIENTHAL

J. H. Lillie (c. 1837)
Elmira, N.Y.
Badger & Lillie
Bibl. 20, 124

John Limeburner
(c. 1790–1791)
Philadelphia, Pa.
Bibl. 3

Limone
(See Lemoine)

C. J. Linbaugh (1875)
Waldenboro, Me.
Bibl. 105

Peter Linch (c. 1805)
New York, N.Y.
Bibl. 23, 36, 44, 124

Lincoln & Foss (c. 1850)
Boston, Mass.
A. L. Lincoln
———— Foss
Bibl. 15, 23, 24, 25, 29, 36,
44, 54, 89, 91, 114, 116

LINCOLN & FOSS

Lincoln & Green
(c. 1790–1810)
Boston, Mass.
Bibl. 24, 25, 28, 29, 44, 91,
110, 114

Lincoln and Reed (Read)
(c. 1835–1846)
Boston, Mass.
Bibl. 15, 23, 24, 25, 28, 29,
36, 44, 89, 91, 114

LINCOLN & READ

A. L. Lincoln
(c. 1820–1850)
Boston, Mass.
(c. 1850–1865)
St. Louis, Mo.
Lincoln & Foss (c. 1850)
Haddock, Lincoln & Foss
(c. 1850–1865)
Bibl. 15, 24, 25, 44, 110,
114, 155

A L Lincoln

Elijah Lincoln
(b. 1794–d. 1861)
Hingham, Mass.
(c. 1818–1833)
Bibl. 15, 23, 25, 28, 29, 36,
94, 110, 114

E. Lincoln

John Lind (Linn)
(c. 1775–1805)
Philadelphia, Pa.
Bibl. 3

Charles Linder (c. 1811)
Geneva, N.Y.
Bibl. 20, 124

George Lindner
(Lendner) (Lentner)
(c. 1837–1850)
Philadelphia, Pa.
Bibl. 3, 23, 36, 44

William Lindsay
(c. 1839–1841)
Portsmouth, Ohio
Bibl. 34

William K. Lindsay
(c. 1839)
Wheeling, Va.
Bibl. 19

Lindsey & Tiffany
(1860–1870)
Providence, R.I.
Bibl. 108

Thomas Lindsey (c. 1799)
Philadelphia, Pa.
Bibl. 3

Clark Lindsley
(c. 1843–1850)
Hartford, Conn.
Bibl. 23, 25, 44, 91, 92, 94,
114
C. LINDSLEY

Ben Linebaugh (c. 1825)
Russellville, Ky.
Bibl. 32, 54

John Linerd (c. 1816)
Philadelphia, Pa.
Bibl. 3

James Lines (c. 1839)
Charleston, S.C.
Bibl. 5

Henry Lingley (c. 1810)
New York, N.Y.
Bibl. 23, 36, 44, 124

James L. Linibaugh
(1830)
New Orleans, La.
Bibl. 141

Link & Angell
(c. 1900–1910)

Newark, N.J.
Successor to Link, Angell &
  Weiss (c. 1893–1900)
Became William Link
  (c. 1910–1915)
Bibl. 127, 157

Link, Angell & Weiss
  (c. 1893–1900)
Newark, N.J.
Successor to Wm. Link Co.
  (1886–1893)
Became Link & Angell
  (c. 1900–1910)
Bibl. 127, 157

Peter Link (c. 1811–1822)
Philadelphia, Pa.
Bibl. 3, 23, 36, 44, 124

William Link
  (c. 1871–c. 1915)
Newark, N.J.
William Link
  (1871–1882; 1886–1893)
Link & Conkling
  (1882–1886)
Link, Angell & Weiss
  (1893–c. 1900)
Link & Angell
  (c. 1900–1910)
Wm. Link Co.
  (c. 1910–c. 1915)
Bibl. 114, 127, 157

William Linker
  (c. 1906–1915)
Philadelphia, Pa.
Bibl. 127, 157

Linn
(See Lind)

Robert Linn (c. 1831)
Pendleton, S.C.
Bibl. 5

—— **Lintot** (c. 1762)
New York, N.Y.
Bibl. 28, 36, 44

Jacques Lipchitz
  (c. 1941–1968)
Hastings-on-Hudson, N.Y.
Bibl. 117

Lipincott
(See Lippincott)

Abraham Lipman
Charleston, S.C.
  (c. 1816–1821)
Columbia, S.C.
  (c. 1822–1830)
Bibl. 5

Joseph Lippincott
  (Lippincott)
Haddonfield, N.J.
  (c. 1768–1788)
Bibl. 46, 54

Robert Lisenbee (c. 1860)
Abbeville, S.C.
Bibl. 5

—— **Lisset** (c. 1819)
Philadelphia, Pa.
Bibl. 3

List & Smith
(See Smith & List)

John List (c. 1837–1850)
Philadelphia, Pa.
Smith & List
Bibl. 3

Archibald Little
  (c. 1839–1840)
Camden, N.J.
Philadelphia, Pa.
Bibl. 3

John Little (c. 1823–1838)
Martinsburg, Va.
Bibl. 19

Paul Little
  (b. 1740–d. 1818)
Windham, Conn.
  (c. 1761–1776)
Portland, Me.
Butler & Little
  (c. 1759–1765)
Bibl. 15, 23, 25, 36, 44, 91,
105, 110, 114

Peter Little
  (b. 1775–d. 1830)
Baltimore, Md.
  (c. 1796–1816)
Bibl. 38

Thomas Little
  (c. 1813–1819)
Philadelphia, Pa.
Bibl. 3

William C. Little
  (b. 1745–d. 1816)
Newbury Port, Mass.
  (c. 1725–1775)
Bibl. 14, 15, 24, 25, 28, 29,
36, 44, 91, 110, 114, 125

William Little
  (c. 1813–1819)
Philadelphia, Pa.
Bibl. 3

A. M. Littlefield (1875)
Sanford, Me.
Bibl. 105

T. Hodgman Littleton
  (after 1800)
Location unknown
Bibl. 28

Henry Livingston
  (c. 1731)
Charleston, S.C.
Bibl. 5

H. Lloyd (c. 1836–1842)
Cooperstown, N.Y.
Bibl. 20, 124

W. A. Lloyd (c. 1810)
Philadelphia, Pa.
Bibl. 54

Paul Lobel (c. 1937–1948)
New York, N.Y.
Bibl. 89, 156

P. H. Lockling & Sons
  (c. 1920–1930)
New York, N.Y.
Bibl. 127

L. or I. Lockward
Location unknown
Bibl. 15, 44, 91   LOCKWARD

—— **Lockwood** (c. 1841)
Newburgh, N.Y.
Pratt & Lockwood
Bibl. 20

Alfred (A.) Lockwood
(c. 1817–1847)
New York, N.Y.
Bibl. 15, 23, 24, 25, 29, 36,
44, 91, 95, 114, 138

ALFRED LOCKWOOD
N. YORK

A. LOCKWOOD

Charles Lockwood
(c. 1817)
New York, N.Y.
Bibl. 15, 124, 138

Frederick Lockwood
(c. 1828–1845)
New York, N.Y.
Bibl. 4, 23, 24, 25, 28, 29,
44, 114, 124, 138

F LOCKWOOD

James Lockwood
(c. 1799–1838)
New York, N.Y.
Bibl. 15, 23, 24, 25, 36, 44,
91, 114, 124, 138

J. LOCKWOOD

LOCKWOOD

Laetitia Locton (c. 1811)
Philadelphia, Pa.
Bibl. 3

Lewis Lodds
(c. 1836–1837)
Buffalo, N.Y.
Bibl. 20, 124

Peter Lodds
(c. 1836–1837)
Buffalo, N.Y.
Bibl. 20, 124

John J. Loew
(c. 1846–1848)
Philadelphia, Pa.
Bibl. 3

Purnel Lofland (d. 1825)
Philadelphia, Pa. (c. 1810)
Bibl. 3, 23, 36, 44

Adam Logan   A. LOGAN
(c. 1803–1823)
New York, N.Y.
Bibl. 23, 24, 25, 29, 36, 44,
114, 124, 138

James Logan (c. 1769)
Philadelphia, Pa.
Bibl. 3, 23, 36, 44

Millie B. Logan
(c. 1871–1908)
Rochester, N.Y.
Bibl. 127, 157

Richard Logan (c. 1837)
Albany, N.Y.
Bibl. 20, 124

Robert Logan (c. 1819)
St. Louis, Mo.
Bibl. 54, 155

Lohse & Kayser
(c. 1831–1835)
Philadelphia, Pa.
Bibl. 3

V. Lollo (c. 1950)   VL
Brooklyn, N.Y.
Bibl. 127

Barthelemy Edouard
Lombard
(c. 1800–1830)   LOMBARD
Charleston, S.C.
Bibl. 5, 25, 44, 114

Asa Lond
(See Asa Loud)

Andrew K. Long
(c. 1837–1844)
Philadelphia, Pa.
Bibl. 3, 23, 36, 44

George W. Long
(c. 1837–1850)
Philadelphia, Pa.
Bibl. 3

N. Long   N LONG
Location unknown
Bibl. 15, 44, 91, 114

Robert Long
(b. 1753, c. 1774)
Maryland
Bibl. 28, 38

Robert M. Long
(c. 1832–1837)
Buffalo, N.Y.
Bibl. 20, 124

Samuel R. Long
(c. 1842–1846)
Philadelphia, Pa.
Bibl. 3

Thomas Long Company
(1946–present)
Boston, Mass.
Bibl. 127

LONGCRAFT

William Long
(c. 1807–1822)
Philadelphia, Pa.
Bibl. 3, 23, 36, 44, 95

Longcraft
(See Thomas Long
Company)

Longley & Dodge
(c. 1810)
Charleston, S.C.
Bibl. 5, 25, 44, 114

Henry Longl(e)y (c. 1810)
New York, N.Y.
Bibl. 23, 24, 25, 29, 36, 44,
114, 124, 138

Loomis and Ralph
(c. 1819–1838)
Frankfort, Ky. (c. 1819)
Bibl. 32, 54, 68, 93

G. Loomis & Co. (c. 1850)
Erie, Pa.
Bibl. 24, 25, 44, 91, 114

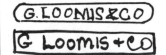

Warham P. Loomis
Louisville, Ky.
Bibl. 54, 91, 93

Worham P. Loomis
  (c. 1819–1854)
Frankfort, Ky.
Bibl. 32, 54, 91

W P Loomis

John Lorange
  (c. 1837–1850)
Philadelphia, Pa.
Bibl. 3

——— **Lord** (c. 1792)
Fayetteville, N.C.
Lord & Gale
Bibl. 21

Lord & Gale (c. 1792)
Fayetteville, N.C.
——— Lord
Joseph Gale
Bibl. 21

Lord & Goddard
  (c. 1797–1807)
Rutland, Vt.
Benjamin Lord
Nicholas Goddard
Bibl. 54, 91, 110

Lord & Smith
  (c. 1824–1829)
New York, N.Y.
Jabez C. Lord
George Smith
Bibl. 15, 36, 44, 124, 138

B. B. Lord & Co.
  (c. 1830–1839)
Athens, Ga.
Benjamin B. Lord
Ebenezer Lord
Joel White
Bibl. 17

Benjamin B. Lord
  (b. 1770–d. 1843)
Pittsfield, Mass. (1796)
Rutland, Vt. (c. 1797–1807)
Athens, Ga. (c. 1831)
Norwich, Conn.
Lord & Goddard
  (c. 1797–1807)
B. B. Lord & Co.
  (c. 1830–1839)

William P. Sage
*Bibl. 15, 17, 23, 24, 25, 36,
  44, 91, 92, 110, 114*

Ebenezer Lord
  (c. 1801–1838)
Athens, Ga.
B. B. Lord & Co.
  (c. 1830–1839)
Bibl. 17, 110

H. Lord & Co.
  (c. 1805)
Savannah, Ga.
Hezekiah Lord
Cornelius Paulding
Isaac Marquand
Bibl. 17

Hezekiah Lord (c. 1805)
Savannah, Ga.
H. Lord & Co.
Bibl. 17

Jabez C. Lord   J. LORD
  (c. 1825–1840)
New York, N.Y.   J. LORD
Lord & Smith
  (c. 1824–1829)
*Bibl. 15, 23, 24, 25, 29, 36,
  44, 114, 124, 138*

James Lord (1860)
Frysburg, Me.
Bibl. 105

Joseph Lord (d. 1795)
Philadelphia, Pa.
Bibl. 3

Joseph Lord (c. 1815)
Philadelphia, Pa.
Bibl. 23, 36, 44

T. Lord (c. 1825)   T. LORD
Location unknown
Bibl. 15, 49, 91, 114

Peter Lorin (c. 1751)
New York, N.Y.
Bibl. 44, 124, 138

Eliphalet (Elijah) Loring
  (b. 1740–d. 1768)
Barnstable, Mass.
Boston, Mass.

Eliphalet Loring Jr. (b. 1765)
*Bibl. 15, 23, 24, 25, 28, 29,
  36, 44, 91, 110, 114*

E. Loring

Henry Loring   HL
  (b. 1773–d. 1818)
Boston, Mass. (c. 1794)
*Bibl. 2, 15, 23, 24, 28, 36,
  110, 114*

Joseph Loring
  (b. 1743–d. 1815,
  c. 1785–1796)
Boston, Mass.
Hull, Mass.
*Bibl. 2, 15, 23, 24, 25, 28,
  29, 36, 39, 44, 54, 91, 94,
  102, 110, 114, 116, 119,
  122, 135, 139*

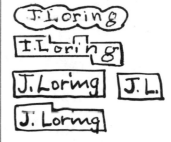

**Lormger (Lorronge)
  (Lorronger)**
(See Lorange)

Benson John Lossing
  (b. 1813–d. 1891)
Poughkeepsie, N.Y.
Henderson & Lossing
  (c. 1835)
Bibl. 2, 20, 28, 124

Benjamin C. Lotier
  (c. 1846–1847)
Philadelphia, Pa.
Bibl. 3, 23

Lott & Schmitt, Inc.
  (c. 1915–1922)
New York, N.Y.
Bibl. 127, 157

Asa Loud (Lond)
  (b. 1765–d. 1823)
Hartford, Conn. (c. 1792)
Bibl. 16, 23, 28, 36, 44

Benjamin Louderback
  (c. 1830–1845)
Philadelphia, Pa.
Bibl. 3

George Loughlin
  (c. 1849–1850)
Philadelphia, Pa.
Bibl. 3

Lawrence Loughlin
  (c. 1848)
Philadelphia, Pa.
Bibl. 3

A. D. Louiset
  (c. 1816–1817)
Philadelphia, Pa.
Bibl. 3

Daniel Love
  (c. 1817–1840)
Liberty, Va. (now Bedford)
Lynchburg, Va.
Bibl. 19

James Love (c. 1832–1836)
Louisville, Ky.
Bibl. 32, 54, 68, 91, 93

John Love (c. 1801–1809)
Charleston, S.C.
Bibl. 5

Lovell & Smith
  (c. 1841–1843)
Philadelphia, Pa.
Bibl. 3

A. E. Lovell (c. 1844–1849)
Philadelphia, Pa.
Bibl. 3

Peter Lovell (c. 1837)
Philadelphia, Pa.
Bibl. 3

Robert Lovett | LOVETT |
  (c. 1818–1838)
New York, N.Y.
Philadelphia, Pa.
Bibl. 3, 15, 25, 44, 114, 124,
  138

Robert Lovett Jr.
  (c. 1840–1850)
Philadelphia, Pa.
Bibl. 3

Low(s), Ball & Co.
  (1840–1846)
Boston, Mass.
John B. Jones
S. S. Ball(?)
John J. Low(?)
Bibl. 2, 15, 23, 25, 28, 36,
  44, 91, 152

LOWS, BALL & COMPANY

Daniel Low & Co., Inc.
  (1867–present)
Salem, Mass.
Bibl. 127, 157

WITCH

Francis Low
  (b. 1806–d. 1855)
Boston, Mass.
John J. Low & Co. (c. 1828)
Bibl. 15, 23, 28, 36, 44

John J. Low & Co.
  (c. 1828)
Boston, Mass.
John J. Low
Francis Low
Bibl. 15, 24, 25, 28, 29, 36,
  44, 54, 91, 94, 114, 154

| J J LOW & CO | | LOW & CO |

John J. (S.) Low
  (b. 1800–d. 1876)
Boston, Mass.
Salem, Mass.
Low(s), Ball & Co.(?)
John J. Low & Co.
Shreve, Crump & Low Co.
Bibl. 23, 25, 28, 36, 44, 91,
  110

| J. J. LOW |

Joseph J. Low
  (c. 1843–1850)
Philadelphia, Pa.
Bibl. 3

Mark Low (c. 1847–1850)
Philadelphia, Pa.
Bibl. 3

Peter Low (c. 1832–1837)
Buffalo, N.Y.
Bibl. 20, 124

Joshua Lowe | I LOWE |
  (c. 1828–1833)
New York, N.Y.
Bibl. 15, 25, 44, 91, 114,
  124, 135

| J. LOWE | I. LOWE

Lowell & Senter
  (c. 1830–1870)
Portland, Me.
Bibl. 25, 28, 44, 91, 105, 114

A. Lowell (c. 1830)
Location unknown
Bibl. 24, 89 | A LOWELL |

Benjamin F. Lowell
  (1946–present)
Malibu Beach, Calif.
Bibl. 127

G. R. Lowell (1875)
Providence, R.I.
Bibl. 108

John Lowell (1860–1875)
Bangor, Me.
Bibl. 105

Lowens
(See Lownes)

Isaac Lower
  (c. 1844–1846)
Philadelphia, Pa.
Bibl. 3

Jacob Lower
  (c. 1833–1850)
Philadelphia, Pa.
Bibl. 3

Joseph Lower | LOWER |
  (c. 1803–1831)
Philadelphia, Pa.
Bibl. 3, 23, 24, 25, 29, 36,
  44, 114

Theodore O. Lower
  (c. 1844)
Philadelphia, Pa.
Bibl. 3

William Lower
  (c. 1837–1848)
Philadelphia, Pa.
Bibl. 3

F. N. Lown
Location unknown
Bibl. 89

Isaac Lowner (c. 1844)
Philadelphia, Pa.
Bibl. 23

Jacob Lowner (c. 1833)
Philadelphia, Pa.
Bibl. 23, 36, 44

William Lowner (c. 1837)
Philadelphia, Pa.
Bibl. 23, 36, 44

Lownes & Erwin (c. 1816)
Philadelphia, Pa.
Joseph Lownes
John Erwin
Bibl. 3, 23, 36, 44, 91, 95

Caleb Lownes (c. 1779)
Philadelphia, Pa.
Bibl. 3

David Lownes (d. 1810)
Philadelphia, Pa.
  (c. 1785–1807)
Bibl. 3

Edward Lownes
  (b. 1792–d. 1834)
Philadelphia, Pa.
  (c. 1806–1833)
*Bibl. 3, 4, 15, 23, 24, 25, 28,
  29, 36, 39, 44, 91, 104,
  114, 122*

Hyatt Lownes (c. 1792)
Hagerstown, Md.
Bibl. 38

J. & J. H. Lownes
  (c. 1816–1819)
Philadelphia, Pa.
Joseph Lownes
Josiah H. Lownes
Bibl. 3, 4, 23, 28, 36, 44, 91

Joseph Lownes
  (b. 1758–d. 1820)

Philadelphia, Pa.
Lownes & Erwin (c. 1816)
J. & J. H. Lownes
  (c. 1816–1819)
*Bibl. 3, 4, 15, 23, 24, 25, 28,
  29, 36, 39, 44, 54, 81, 91,
  95, 102, 104, 114, 116,
  119, 122*

Joseph & Josiah Lownes
(See J. & J. H. Lownes)

Josiah H. Lownes   I H L
  (d. 1822)
Philadelphia, Pa.   J H L
  (c. 1820–1822)
J. & J. H. Lownes
  (c. 1816–1819)
*Bibl. 3, 23, 24, 25, 29, 36,
  44, 114, 116*

J. J. Lowrey
  (c. 1840–1844)
Pendleton, S.C.
Bibl. 5

R. B. Lowrie
  (c. 1847–1849)
Philadelphia, Pa.
Bibl. 3, 23

Salvador Lowry (c. 1824)
Baltimore, Md.
Bibl. 38

Adrian Loyer
  (d. 1781)
Savannah, Ga.
  (c. 1756–1760)
Bibl. 17, 23, 36, 44

Ivory Lucas (c. 1732–1748)
New London, Conn.
Oglestown (New Castle),
  Del.
Bibl. 2

James Lucet
  (c. 1802–1805)
New York, N.Y.
Bibl. 23, 36, 44, 124, 138

John P. Lucke (c. 1849)
Philadelphia, Pa.
Bibl. 3

Mrs. Luckey
  (c. 1830–1840)
Pittsburgh, Pa.
Bibl. 127

Ludwig & Redlich
  (c. 1890–1895)
Adolph Ludwig
Became Redlich & Co.
  (c. 1895)
Bibl. 127

John Ludwig
  (c. 1790–1791)
Philadelphia, Pa.
Bibl. 3

Luhlier
(See Lhulier)

G. W. Lukens (c. 1830)
Philadelphia, Pa.
Bibl. 39

G. W. LUKENS

Isaiah Lukens
  (b. 1779–d. 1846)
Philadelphia, Pa.
  (c. 1823–1831)
Bibl. 3, 91

J. Lukens (c. 1837)
Philadelphia, Pa.
Bibl. 3

William Lukens (c. 1847)
Philadelphia, Pa.
Bibl. 3

J. Lukey (c. 1830–1840)
Pittsburgh, Pa.
Bibl. 15, 44, 114   J. LUKEY

Lullaby
(See Alvin Corporation)

Lambert Luls (Lulis)
  (c. 1804)
New York, N.Y.
Bibl. 23, 36, 44, 124, 138

C. Lumsden & Co.
  (c. 1834)
Petersburg, Va.
Susanna E. Nichols
Charles Lumsden
Bibl. 19

Charles Lumsden
Petersburg, Va. (c. 1834)
Richmond, Va.
C. Lumsden & Co. (c. 1834)
Bibl. 19

CHAS. LUMSDEN

Thomas Lumsden
(c. 1801–1806)
Norfolk, Va.
Bibl. 19

Lund & Antz (1853–1855)
New Orleans, La.
Bibl. 141

Lunier
(See Lhulier)

John M. Lunquest
(c. 1835–1846)
Charleston, S.C.
Edgefield, S.C.
Bibl. 5

Lunt Silversmiths
(Trade name used since
1935)
Greenfield, Mass.
(See Rogers, Lunt & Bowlen
Co.)
Bibl. 127, 135, 147

"Treasure" Solid Silver

LUNT STERLING

Charles Lupp
(b. 1788–d. 1825)
New Brunswick, N.J.
(c. 1810–1825)
Bibl. 46, 54

Henry Lupp
(b. 1760–d. 1800)
New Brunswick, N.J.
(c. 1783–1800)
Bibl. 24, 25, 44, 46, 54

H Lupp

Henry Lupp
(c. 1790–1845)
New Brunswick, N.J.
Bibl. 54, 95

John Lupp
(b. 1734–d. 1805)
New Brunswick, N.J.
(c. 1782–1805)
Bibl. 46, 54, 95

**Lawrence (Lewis) (Louis)
K. Lupp(e)**
(b. 1783)
New Brunswick, N.J.
(c. 1804–1806)
*Bibl. 15, 24, 25, 44, 46, 54,
91, 114*

L. LUPP

 L. Lupp   L. Luppe

Peter Lupp (d. 1807)
New Brunswick, N.J.
(c. 1760–1807)
*Bibl. 15, 24, 39, 44, 46, 54,
91, 95, 114*

P.L.   PL

Samuel Vickers Lupp
(b. 1789–d. 1809)
New Brunswick, N.J.
(c. 1809)
Bibl. 25, 44, 46, 54, 114

S V LUPP

William Lupp
(b. 1766–d. 1845)
New Brunswick, N.J.
(c. 1790–1845)
Bibl. 46, 54

L. Luppe
(See L. Lupp)

Benjamin Lusada
(c. 1797)
New York, N.Y.
Bibl. 23, 36, 138

John G. Luscomb
Boston, Mass.
(c. 1813–1823)
Salem, Mass. (1846–1865)
*Bibl. 4, 23, 28, 36, 44, 91,
110*

John Lussaur (c. 1791)
New York, N.Y.
Bibl. 23, 36, 44, 124, 138

Luther & Co. (1873)
Providence, R.I.
Bibl. 108

Benjamin Luzerder
(c. 1796)
New York, N.Y.
Bibl. 28, 44, 124

John Lyburn
(c. 1820–1822)
Philadelphia, Pa.
Bibl. 3, 138

John Lycett
(c. 1818–1822)
Philadelphia, Pa.
Bibl. 3, 155

John C. Lycett (c. 1821)
St. Louis, Mo.
Bibl. 54

David Lyell
(b. 1670–d. 1725)
Matawan, N.J.
(c. 1717–1725)
*Bibl. 4, 23, 28, 36, 44, 46,
54, 124*

Lyman
(See Savage & Lyman)

R. Lyman (1840)
Lowell, Mass.
Bibl. 15, 106, 114

R. LYMAN

Lynch & Leonard
(c. 1805–1840)
Baltimore, Md.
Chestertown, Md.
——— Lynch
Samuel T. Leonard
Bibl. 29, 38, 44, 89

LYNCH &
LEONARD   LYNCH &
        LEONARD

F. Lynch
Petersburg, Va.
Bibl. 19

John Lynch   I LYNCH
(b. 1761–d. 1848)
Baltimore, Md.
(c. 1786–1848)

Bibl. 23, 24, 25, 28, 29, 36, 38, 39, 44, 91, 114, 122

John H. Lynch (1875)
Bangor, Me.
Bibl. 105

L. George Lynch
(c. 1840)
Hillsboro, N.C.
Bibl. 21

Lemuel Lynch
(b. 1808–d. 1893)
Hillsboro, N.C. (c. 1828)
Greensboro, N.C. (c. 1829)
Concord, N.C. (c. 1834)
Hillsboro, N.C. (c. 1834)
Huntington & Lynch
(c. 1834)
Bibl. 21

Seaborn Lynch
(c. 1840)
Hillsboro, N.C.
Bibl. 21

Thomas M. Lynch
(c. 1840)
Oxford, N.C.
Bibl. 21

William Lyndall
(c. 1844)
Philadelphia, Pa.
Bibl. 3

Thomas Lynde
(b. 1748–d. 1812)
Malden, Mass.
Worcester, Mass.
Bibl. 23, 24, 25, 28, 29, 36, 44, 72, 110, 114

| T LYNDE | T LYNDE |

John Lyng (c. 1734)
Philadelphia, Pa.
Bibl. 23, 28, 36, 44

| I + L |

John Burt Lyng (d. 1785)
New York, N.Y. (c. 1761)
Bibl. 4, 15, 23, 25, 28, 29, 35, 36, 44, 54, 91, 95, 114, 124, 138, 151

Philip Lyng (c. 1778–1785)
Philadelphia, Pa.
Bibl. 3, 23

Adam Lynn
(b. 1775–d. 1836)
Alexandria, Va.
(c. 1795–1835)
Coryton & Lynn
(c. 1795–1796)
Bibl. 15, 19, 25, 29, 44, 91, 114

George Lyon
(c. 1819–1844)
Wilmington, N.C.
Bibl. 21

W. H. Lyon (c. 1891–1920)
Newburgh, N.Y.
Bibl. 127

R. A. Lytle (c. 1825)
Baltimore, Md.
Bibl. 24, 25, 44, 114

| R A LYTLE |

M

M
(See Hickok Matthews
Company, Mueck-Cary
Co., Inc.)

M & D
(See Moulton & Davis)

M & H
(See Moore & Hibbard)

M & R
(See McFee & Reeder)

M B
(See Merriman & Bradley,
Miles Beach)

McA
(See Kraus, McKeever &
Adams)

M F
(See Marshall Field & Co.)

M. F. H. Co.
(See M. Fred Hirsch Co.,
Inc.)

M G
(See Michael Gibney, Miles
Gorham)

M H
(See Marguerite Hastier)

M I
(See Munson Jarvis)

M J
(See Munson Jarvis)

M L
(See Matthias Lamar)

M M
(See Marcus Merriman,
Myer Myers)

M M & Co.
(See Marcus Merriman &
Co.)

M P
(See Matthew Petit)

M P C
(See Pryor Mfg. Co., Inc.)

M R
(See Moody Russel)

M S
(See Moreau Sarrazin)

Mabrid (Malrid) & Co.
New York, N.Y. (c. 1787)
Bibl. 23, 36, 44, 124

George James Macauley
(c. 1802)
Charleston, S.C.
Bibl. 5

**MacFarland
MacFarlane**
(See John McFarlane)

Alexander MacHarey
(c. 1842)
Albany, N.Y.
Bibl. 23

Thomas W. Machen
(c. 1812–1830)
New Bern, N.C.
Bibl. 21

Austin Machon (c. 1759)
Philadelphia, Pa.
Bibl. 3, 23, 36, 44

W. H. Mack (1875)
Eastport, Me.
Bibl. 105

James Mackey
(c. 1816–1818)
Baltimore, Md.
Bibl. 38

John Mackey
(c. 1841–1842)
Philadelphia, Pa.
Bibl. 3, 23

Edward Mackinder
(c. 1839)
St. Louis, Mo.
Bibl. 54, 135

George B. Macomber
(1875)
Thomaston, Me.
Bibl. 105

Horace L. Macomber
(1860–1875)
Castine, Me.
Bibl. 105

S. K. Macomber
(1860–1875)
Rockland, Me.
Bibl. 105

James Madock (c. 1796)
Martinsburg, Va.
Bibl. 19

F. W. Maffit (c. 1846)
Syracuse, N.Y.
Bibl. 20, 124

Thomas M. Maggee
(b. 1828)
New Orleans, La. (c. 1860)
Bibl. 141

Simon M. Magnus
(c. 1849–1850)
Albany, N.Y.
Bibl. 20, 124

Erik Magnussen
(b. 1884–d. 1961)
Denmark
Designer for Gorham Co.
(1925–1929)
Chicago, Ill. (c. 1932)
Los Angeles, Calif.
(1932–1938)
Bibl. 104, 127

Matthew Maher (Mahue)
(c. 1761)
Philadelphia, Pa.
Bibl. 81

Thomas S. Mahin
(b. 1819–d. 1880)
Franklin, Ky.
Bibl. 32, 68, 93

**Wm. P. Mahne Silver
Company** (1946–present)
St. Louis, Mo.
William P. Mahne
John R. Geddis
Bibl. 127

Robert Maholland
(c. 1850)
Philadelphia, Pa.
Bibl. 81

D. J. Mahoney
(c. 1896–1904)
New York, N.Y.
Bibl. 127, 157

M

John Mahony (Mahoney)
(c. 1847–1849)
Utica, N.Y.
Bibl. 18, 124, 158

William A. Mahony
(c. 1837–1849)
Philadelphia, Pa.
Bibl. 3

Mahue
(See Maher)

Peter A. Maille
(c. 1819–1831)
Charleston, S.C.
Bibl. 5

David Main
(b. 1752–d. 1843)
Stonington, Conn. (c. 1773)
Bibl. 16, 23, 28, 36, 44, 110

Thomas Mainwaring
(c. 1664)
New Jersey
Bibl. 23, 36, 44

Jean Claude Mairot
(c. 1822)
New Orleans, La.
Bibl. 23, 36

Majestic Mfg. Co.
(c. 1895–1904)
New York, N.Y.
Bibl. 114, 127, 157

Majestic Silver Co., Inc.
(c. 1930)
New York, N.Y.
Bibl. 127

Francois Paul Malcher
(b. 1751–d. 1810)
Detroit, Mich. (c. 1790)

Gallipolis, Ohio
Bibl. 58, 91

P. M.

John A. Mallory (c. 1839)
Delhi, N.Y.
Bibl. 20, 124

Samuel Mallory (c. 1842)
Catskill, N.Y.
Bibl. 20, 124

Malrid & Co.
(See Mabrid & Co.)

**Maltby, Stevens & Curtiss
Co.** (c. 1890–1896)
Wallingford, Conn.
Elizur Seneca Stevens
Chapman Maltby
John Curtiss
Successor to Maltby, Stevens
& Company (c. 1890)
Became Watrous Mfg. Co.
(1896–1898)
Bibl. 114, 127, 157

Ⓜ STERLING

Manchester Mfg. Co.
(c. 1904–1914)
Providence, R.I.
Successor to W. H.
Manchester & Co.
(1887–1904)
Became Manchester Silver
Co. (c. 1914–1985)
Bibl. 114, 127, 135, 152, 157

Manchester Silver Co.
(c. 1914–1985)
Providence, R.I.
W. H. Manchester & Co.
(1887–1904)
Manchester Mfg. Co.
(c. 1904–1914)
Became J. C. Boardman Co.
(1985)
Bibl. 127, 128, 135, 146, 147

Mandalian & Hawkins
(c. 1922)
North Attleboro, Mass.
Became Mandalian Mfg. Co.
(c. 1922–1935)
Bibl. 127

M & H

Mandalian Mfg. Co.
(c. 1922–1935)
North Attleboro, Mass.
Successor to Mandalian &
Hawkins
Bibl. 127

◇M DEBUTANTE

Henry Mander
(c. 1848–1850)
Philadelphia, Pa.
Bibl. 3, 23

Horace Manley (c. 1836)
Canandaigua, N.Y.
Bibl. 20, 124

James Manley (c. 1790)
Philadelphia, Pa.
Bibl. 3

Matthew Manley (c. 1843)
Philadelphia, Pa.
Bibl. 3

Mann
(See Brown & Mann)

Alexander Mann (b. 1777)
Middletown, Conn.
(c. 1804)
Brewer & Mann
(c. 1803–1805)
Bibl. 16, 23, 28, 36, 44, 91,
92, 110

L. Mannerback (c. 1820)
Reading, Pa.
Bibl. 23, 36

William Mannerback
(c. 1820–1835)
Reading, Pa.
Bibl. 25, 29, 44, 54, 91, 114

W MANNERBACK   READING

Manning
(See Evans & Manning)

Daniel Manning (c. 1823)
Boston, Mass.
Bibl. 28, 36, 44, 110

Ezra L. Manning (b. 1838)
Utica, N.Y.
(c. 1858–c. 1860)

Bibl. 18, 124, 158

John Manning
(c. 1819–1822)
Philadelphia, Pa.
Bibl. 3

Joseph Manning
(c. 1823–1840)
New York, N.Y.
Bibl. 15, 23, 124, 138

Samuel Manning (c. 1823)
Boston, Mass.
Bibl. 23, 36, 44, 110

Elisha Hyde Mansfield
(b. 1795)
Norwich, Conn. (c. 1816)
Coit & Mansfield
(c. 1816–1819)
Bibl. 16, 23, 28, 36, 110

John Mansfield
(b. 1601–d. 1674)
Charlestown, Mass.
(c. 1634)
Boston, Mass. (c. 1650)
Bibl. 2, 23, 28, 36, 44, 102,
110, 116, 119

Samuel A. Mansfield
(c. 1848–1850)
Philadelphia, Pa.
Bibl. 3

Thomas Mansfield
(c. 1804)
Philadelphia, Pa.
Bibl. 3, 23, 36, 44

Warren Mansfield Co.
(c. 1867–1907)
Portland, Me.
Bibl. 127

John Mansure
(c. 1844–1850)
Philadelphia, Pa.
Bibl. 3

Jules Manuel
(c. 1849–1850)
Philadelphia, Pa.
Bibl. 3

Joseph Marand (c. 1804)
Baltimore, Md.
Bibl. 38

Benjamin Marble
  (c. 1840–1850)
Albany, N.Y.
Bibl. 25, 44, 124

Simeon Marble
  (b. 1776–d. 1856)
New Haven, Conn.
Sibley & Marble
  (c. 1801–1806)
*Bibl. 16, 23, 24, 25, 28, 29,
  36, 44, 92, 110, 114, 143*

S MARBLE

Marce
(See Maree)

Marcel Novelty Co.
  (c. 1896–1915)
New York, N.Y.
Bibl. 114, 127, 157

Isaac Marceloe (c. 1735)
Philadelphia, Pa.
Bibl. 3

**Louis Marchalle
  (Marchelle) (Marshall)**
Norfolk, Va.
  (c. 1793–c. 1806)
Bibl. 19

Evariste Marchand
  (c. 1822)
New Orleans, La.
Bibl. 23, 36, 44

Marchelle
(See Marchalle)

Frank W. W. Marchisi
  (b. 1832)
Utica, N.Y. (c. 1855–1860)
Bibl. 18, 124, 158

Joseph Marchisi
  (b. 1802–d. 1874,
  c. 1845–1868)
Chittenango, N.Y.
Utica, N.Y.
Bibl. 18, 20, 124, 158

Marcus
(See Starr & Marcus)

Fred I. Marcy & Co.
  (1878–1896)
Providence, R.I.
Bibl. 114, 127, 157

Henry Maree (Marce)
  (c. 1845–1850)
Philadelphia, Pa.
Bibl. 3

Marie Louise
(See R. Blackinton & Co.)

L. Mario (c. 1825)
Location unknown
Bibl. 13

Marion Mfg. Co. (c. 1886)
Salt Lake City, Utah
Bibl. 127

**Jacob Marius Groen
  (Morrisgreen)**
(See Groen)

Isaac Marks
  (c. 1795–1799)
Philadelphia, Pa.
Bibl. 3

Michael Marmigan
  (c. 1814–1815)
Baltimore, Md.
Bibl. 38

Marquand & Brother
  (c. 1815–1831)
New York, N.Y.
Isaac Marquand
Frederick Marquand
*Bibl. 23, 36, 44, 91, 124,
  135, 138*

Marquand & Co.
  (c. 1834–1839)
New York, N.Y.
Henry Ball
Frederick Marquand
Josiah P. Marquand
Erastus O. Tompkins
*Bibl. 15, 23, 25, 28, 36, 44,
  72, 91, 116, 122, 124, 135,
  138*

Marquand & Paulding
  (c. 1801–1810)
Savannah, Ga.
Isaac Marquand

Cornelius Paulding
Bibl. 17, 138

**Marquand, Harriman &
  Co.** (c. 1809–1812)
New York, N.Y.
Isaac Marquand
Orlando Harriman
Cornelius Paulding
Bibl. 17, 46, 124, 138

**Marquand, Paulding &
  Penfield**
  (c. 1810–1816)
Savannah, Ga.
Isaac Marquand
Cornelius Paulding
Josiah Penfield
Bibl. 17

Frederick Marquand
  (b. 1799–d. 1882)
New York, N.Y. (c. 1815)
Savannah, Ga.
  (c. 1820–1828)   (F.M)
Marquand & Brother
  (c. 1815–1831)
J. Penfield & Co.
  (c. 1820–1828)
Marquand & Co.   F. M.
  (c. 1834–1839)
*Bibl. 15, 17, 23, 24, 25, 28,
  29, 35, 36, 44, 72, 83, 91,
  104, 114, 122, 124, 135,
  138*   F MARQUAND

F. MARQUAND

Isaac Marquand
  (b. 1766–d. 1838)
Fairfield, Conn. (c. 1787)
Edenton, N.C.
  (c. 1791–1796)
Savannah, Ga.
  (c. 1800)
New York, N.Y.
  (1805–1839)
Whiting & Marquand
Marquand & Paulding
  (c. 1801–1810)
H. Lord & Co. (c. 1805)
E. Barton & Co.
Marquand & Brother
Marquand, Harriman & Co.
Marquand, Paulding &
  Penfield
*Bibl. 15, 17, 21, 23, 36, 44,
  91, 110, 124, 138*

Josiah P. Marquand
(c. 1834)
New York, N.Y.
Marquand & Co.
(c. 1834–1839)
Bibl. 15, 124

Marrs & Stewart (c. 1802)
Philadelphia, Pa.
Robert Marrs
———— Stewart
Bibl. 3

Robert Marrs
(c. 1803–1818)
Philadelphia, Pa.
Marrs & Stewart (c. 1802)
Bibl. 3

S. Mars (c. 1770)
Location unknown
Bibl. 28, 29, 44, 72

Marsac (1833)
New Orleans, La.
Bibl. 141

W. B. Marsdon (1860)
Waterville, Me.
Bibl. 105

Benedict Beal Marsh
(b. 1804–d. 1875)
Flemingsburg, Ky.
Paris, Ky.
Richmond, Ky.
Bibl. 32, 68, 93   B B MARSH

Benjamin Marsh   B MARSH
(c. 1840–1850)   ALBANY
Albany, N.Y.
Bibl. 20, 28, 114, 124

Edwin A. Marsh
Buffalo, N.Y. (c. 1832–1840)
Rochester, N.Y.
(c. 1847–1850)
Bibl. 20, 124

Eli P. Marsh (b. 1815)
Utica, N.Y.
(c. 1858–1859)
Bibl. 18, 124

Thomas King Marsh
(b. 1804)

Paris, Ky. (c. 1831–1850)
Bibl. 24, 25, 32, 44, 54, 68

| T K MARSH |

Marshall
(See Spencer & Marshall)

———— **Marshall** (c. 1833)
Philadelphia, Pa.
Bibl. 3

Marshall & Smith
(c. 1837)
Philadelphia, Pa.
Bibl. 3, 91

Marshall & Tempest
(c. 1813–1830)
Philadelphia, Pa. | MARSHALL &
———— Marshall | TEMPEST
Robert Tempest
Bibl. 3, 23, 24, 25, 44, 91, 114

Marshall & White
(c. 1817)
Petersburg, Va.
G. Marshall
Andrew White
Bibl. 19

Marshall Field & Co.
(See Field, Marshall)

Alexander D. Marshall
(c. 1847–1848)
Philadelphia, Pa.
Bibl. 3

Charles Marshall (1875)
Unity, Me.
Bibl. 105

G. Marshall
(c. 1816)
Petersburg, Va.
(c. 1817–   )
Richmond, Va.
Marshall & White
(c. 1817–   )
G. Marshall & Co.
Bibl. 19

John Marshall
(c. 1838–1840)
Troy, N.Y.
Bibl. 20, 124

John C. Marshall (c. 1899)
Louisville, Ky.
(c. 1836–1849)
Bibl. 32, 54, 93

Joseph Marshall
(c. 1818–1850)
Philadelphia, Pa.
Bibl. 3, 4, 23, 28, 36, 44, 91

Louis Marshall
(See Louis Marchalle)

Thomas Henry Marshall
Albany, N.Y. (c. 1832–1836)
Troy, N.Y. (c. 1836)
Rochester, N.Y.
(c. 1838–1852)
Bibl. 15, 20, 23, 25, 36, 41, 44, 114, 124

| T. H. MARSHALL |

Martelé
(See Gorham Manufacturing Co.)

———— **Martin** (c. 1811)
Philadelphia, Pa.
Bibl. 3

A. P. Martin (1861)
Woodstock, Me.
Bibl. 105

Abraham W. Martin
(c. 1835–1840)
New York, N.Y.
Bibl. 15, 23, 36, 44, 124, 138

Ambrose Martin
(c. 1840–1850)
Philadelphia, Pa.
Bibl. 3

E. Martin (c. 1853)
Winchester, Tenn.
Bibl. 54

J. M. Martin (c. 1871)
New Orleans, La.
Bibl. 141

John Martin
(c. 1823–1835)
Philadelphia, Pa.
Bibl. 3

John (J. L.) J. Martin
(c. 1844–1850)
Philadelphia, Pa.
Bibl. 3

Lewis Martin (c. 1811)
Philadelphia, Pa.
Bibl. 3

M. Martin (c. 1790)
Location unknown
Bibl. 24

Patrick Martin
(c. 1820–1850)
Philadelphia, Pa.
Bibl. 3, 44, 114

Peter Martin (c. 1756)
New York, N.Y.
*Bibl. 4, 15, 23, 24, 25, 28,
29, 36, 44, 114, 124, 138*

| P. M. | P MARTIN |

(P. MARTIN)

Peter Martin II (c. 1825)
New York, N.Y.
Bibl. 25, 44, 91, 124

P. MARTIN

Thomas Martin (c. 1764)
Philadelphia, Pa.
Baltimore, Md.
Bibl. 38

Valentine Martin
(c. 1842–1859)
Boston, Mass.
Bibl. 25, 28, 29, 44, 102, 114

| V. MARTIN |

Warner Martin
(c. 1836–1840)
New York, N.Y.
Bibl. 15, 124, 138

Zebedee Martin (c. 1806)
Baltimore, Md.
Bibl. 38

Peter Martinet (c. 1811)
Savannah, Ga.
Bibl. 17

John Martini (c. 1859)
Charleston, S.C.
Bibl. 5

J. Martiniere (c. 1820)
Augusta, Ga.
Morand, Alleoud & Co.
Bibl. 17

Maryland Silver Co.
(c. 1906–1908)
Baltimore, Md.
Bibl. 127

John F. Mascher
(c. 1845–1850)
Philadelphia, Pa.
Bibl. 3

Samuel Masham
(b. 1738, c. 1774)
Maryland
Bibl. 38

Seraphim Masi (c. 1832)
Washington, D.C.
Bibl. 28, 44, 104

Mason
(See also Masson)

Charles T. Mason
(d. 1893)
Sumter, S.C.
(c. 1851–?)
F. Hoyt & Co.
(c. 1850–1851)
Bibl. 5

Henry Mason (1875)
Saco, Me.
Bibl. 105

J. D. Mason (c. 1830)
Philadelphia, Pa.
Bibl. 24, 25, 44, 114

| J D MASON |

John Mason (c. 1890)
New York, N.Y.
Bibl. 127

Levant L. Mason
Rochester, N.Y.
(c. 1847–1850)
Jamestown, N.Y. (c. 1850)
Bibl. 20, 124

Richard Mason
(c. 1814–1824)
Baltimore, Md.
Bibl. 38

Samuel Mason Jr.
(c. 1820–1830)
Philadelphia, Pa.
Bibl. 3

Thomas Mason
(c. 1795–1797)
Alexandria, Va.
Bibl. 19

Charles R. Massey
(c. 1837–1839)
Philadelphia, Pa.
Bibl. 3

**Charles A. Masson
(Mason)**
Philadelphia, Pa.
(c. 1829–1850)
Bibl. 3, 91

Masterman & Son
(c. 1870)
Charleston, S.C.
William Masterman
Bibl. 5

William Masterman
(c. 1852–1870)
Charleston, S.C.
Masterman & Son
(c. 1870)
Bibl. 5

Caleb Maston (1860)
N. Windham, Me.
Bibl. 105

Mather & North
(c. 1827–1829)
New Britain, Conn.
(c. 1827)
New York, N.Y.
(1827–1829)
Thaddeus Mather
Thomas Mather
William B. North (?)
*Bibl. 15, 23, 24, 25, 29, 36,
44, 89, 91, 114, 124, 138*

| MATHER & P. NORTH |

| MATHER & NORTH |

Mather & Pitkin
  (c. 1844–1848)
Buffalo, N.Y.
Theodore Mather
Joseph F. Pitkin
Bibl. 20, 124

Thaddeus Mather
New Britain, Conn.
  (c. 1827)
Columbia, S.C.
New York, N.Y.
  (c. 1827–1829?)
Mather & North
  (c. 1827–1829)
Bibl. 5, 91, 138

Theodore Mather
  (c. 1844–1848)
Buffalo, N.Y.
Mather & Pitkin
Bibl. 20, 124

Thomas Mather (c. 1825)
New York, N.Y.
Mather & North
  (c. 1827–1829)
Bibl. 15, 124, 138

F. Mathew (h. 1825)
Mobile, Ala. (c. 1850)
Bibl. 54

Mathews & Prior (c. 1904)
New York, N.Y.
Bibl. 127, 157

Harriet Mathews
  (b. 1807–d. 1882)
Charlottesville, Va. (c. 1850)
Bibl. 19

Richard Mathews
  (c. 1836–1848)
Charlottesville, Va.
Bibl. 19, 114

Thomas Mathews
  (d. 1852)
Charleston, Va.
  (c. 1810–?)
Bibl. 19

Mathewson & Holbrook
  (1860)
Providence, R.I.
Bibl. 108

Daniel Mathewson (1875)
Burrillville, R.I.
Bibl. 108

Aime Mathey
  (c. 1826–1865)
New York, N.Y.
Aime Mathey & Co.
  (c. 1836)
Bibl. 15, 114, 124, 138

Aime Mathey & Co.
  (c. 1836)
New York, N.Y.
Aime Mathey
Augustus Mathey
Bibl. 15, 124

Augustus Mathey
  (c. 1824–1828)
New York, N.Y.
Aime Mathey & Co.
  (c. 1836)
Bibl. 15, 25, 44, 89, 124, 138

Lewis Mathey
  (c. 1797–1803)
Philadelphia, Pa.
Brandt & Mathey
  (c. 1795–1799)
Bibl. 3

Peter Mathiew
  (c. 1837–1843)
Philadelphia, Pa.
Bibl. 3

White Matlack (c. 1777)
Philadelphia, Pa.
William Matlack (c. 1780)
Bibl. 3

White & William Matlack
  (c. 1780)
Philadelphia, Pa.
Bibl. 3

William Matlack
  (c. 1797)
Philadelphia, Pa.
Bibl. 3

William Matlack
  (c. 1828–1833)

Philadelphia, Pa.
Bibl. 3, 23, 36, 44

Matson & Hoes
  (1864–1867)
Chicago, Ill.
Successor to James H. Hoes
  & Co.
(See N. Matson & Co.)
Bibl. 98

MATSON & HOES
PURE COIN

N. Matson & Co.
  (1867–1888)
Chicago, Ill.
Newell Matson
George E. Johnson
L. J. Norton
W. E. Higby
Successor to Matson & Hoes
  (1864–1867)
Became Spaulding & Co.
  (1888–1929;
  1943–present)
Spaulding-Gorham Co.
  (1929–1943)
Bibl. 98, 127

N. MATSON PURE COIN

Newell Matson
  (b. 1815–d. 1887)
Painesville, Ohio
Owego, N.Y. (c. 1845)
Milwaukee, Wisc.
N. Matson & Co.
*Bibl. 15, 20, 25, 44, 91, 114,
124*

N MATSON

H. E. Matteson (c. 1840)
Location unknown
Bibl. 89

Matthews Company, Inc.
  (c. 1907–1931)
Newark, N.J.
Merged Eleder-Hickok
  Company
Became Hickok-Matthews
  Company
Bibl. 127, 157

L. Matthews (c. 1852)
Paris, Ky.
Alonzo Corwin Hallack
  (c. 1840–1853)
Bibl. 32, 54, 68

Peter Matthews (c. 1845)
Philadelphia, Pa.
Bibl. 3

Charles Matthias (c. 1849)
Philadelphia, Pa.
Bibl. 3

John Maull (c. 1848–1849)
Philadelphia, Pa.
Bibl. 3

Joseph E. Maull
(c. 1830–1837)
Philadelphia, Pa.
Clausen & Maull
(c. 1830–1833) (?)
Bibl. 3

Mauran, Greene & Co.
(1872)
Providence, R.I.
Bibl. 108

J. T. Mauran (1874)
Providence, R.I.
Bibl. 108

———— **Maurel** (c. 1810)
Charleston, S.C.
Maurel & Boudo
Bibl. 5

Maurel & Boudo (c. 1810)
Charleston, S.C.
———— Maurel
Louis Bouldo
Bibl. 5

Frederick Maus
(c. 1782–1793)
Philadelphia, Pa.
Bibl. 3

**Mauser Manufacturing
Company**
(c. 1890–1903)
New York, N.Y.
Successor to Frank Mauser
& Co. (c. 1887–1890)
Merged Hayes & McFarlane
Co. and Roger Willams Co.
Became Mt. Vernon
Company Silversmiths,
Inc. (c. 1903)
Became Gorham Mfg.
Company (c. 1913)
Bibl. 114, 120, 127, 130, 157

E. Maussenet
(c. 1841–1845)
Macon, Ga.
Bibl. 17

John Mautz (c. 1841)
Philadelphia, Pa.
Bibl. 3

D. Maverick (c. 1828)
New York, N.Y.
Bibl. 28, 29

**Peter Rushton (C.)
Maverick**
(c. 1755–1811)
New York, N.Y.
*Bibl. 23, 28, 36, 44, 102,
124, 138*

John Mawdsley
(c. 1846–1847)
Philadelphia, Pa.
Bibl. 3

A. Maxwell (c. 1805–1811)
Philadelphia, Pa.
Bibl. 3

May & Clark (c. 1765)
Philadelphia, Pa.
Samuel May
Richard Clark
Bibl. 3

Frank T. May Co.
(c. 1904–1943)
New York, N.Y.
Rutherford, N.J.
Bibl. 127

Samuel May (c. 1765)
Philadelphia, Pa.
May & Clark
Bibl. 3

Elias Mayer (c. 1831–1833)
Philadelphia, Pa.
Bibl. 3

Gotlieb A. Mayer
(c. 1840–1868)
Norfolk, Va.
Minton & Mayer
(c. 1840–1842)
Bibl. 19

G. MAYER

**Jacob Mayer (Meier)
(Myre) (Myers)**
Cleveland, Ohio
(c. 1830–1846)
Bibl. 23, 34, 54

**Joseph Mayer & Bros.
(Inc.)** (c. 1897–1920)
Seattle, Wash.
Became Joseph Mayer, Inc.
(c. 1920–1945)
Bibl. 127, 147, 152, 157

Joseph Mayer, Inc.
(c. 1920–1945)
Seattle, Wash.
Successor to Joseph Mayer &
Bros., Inc.
(c. 1897–1920)
Became E. J. Towle Mfg. Co.
(c. 1945–present)
Bibl. 127, 147, 152, 157

Maynard & Taylor
(c. 1852–1858)
Utica, N.Y.
Thomas Maynard
William S. Taylor
*Bibl. 18, 20, 91, 114, 124,
158*

R. H. Maynard
(c. 1825–1829)
Black Rock, N.Y.
Buffalo, N.Y.
*Bibl. 15, 20, 25, 44, 91, 114,
124*

R. H. MAYNARD

Thomas Maynard
(d. 1860)
Utica, N.Y. (c. 1841–1859)
Cleveland, Ohio

Maynard & Taylor
(c. 1852–1858)
Dana & Maynard (c. 1841)
Bibl. 18, 91, 124, 158

Mayo & Co.
(c. 1896–1904)
Chicago, Ill.
Bibl. 114, 127, 157

Benjamin J. Mayo
(1860–1902)
Newark, N.J.
Bibl. 135

Joseph B. Mayo
(1868–1896)
Newark, N.J.
Bibl. 127

**Charles Maysenhoelder
(Maysenhaelder)**
Philadelphia, Pa.
(c. 1810–1825)
Bibl. 3, 23, 36, 39, 44

**James Edward
Mazurkewicz**
(b. 1943–?)
Cleveland, Ohio
Bibl. 89, 127

**(Note that *Mc* on
following pages was
sometimes listed as
M'.)**

McAdam, Wilson & Co.
(1876)
Providence, R.I.
Bibl. 108

William McAdams
(c. 1846–1850)
Philadelphia, Pa.
Bibl. 3

James McAllister
(c. 1840–1850)
Philadelphia, Pa.
Bibl. 3

O. S. McAllister (1875)
Burnham, Me.
Bibl. 105

Charles McAuky
(c. 1831–1833)

New York, N.Y.
Bibl. 15

McAuliffe & Hadley
(c. 1918)
Boston, Mass.
Bibl. 144

McBride & Gardner (c. 1807)
Charlotte, N.C.
Andrew McBride
Barzillai Gardner
Bibl. 21

Andrew McBride (c. 1807)
Charlotte, N.C.
McBride & Gardner
Bibl. 21

Henry McBride (c. 1810)
Macklenburg County, N.C.
Bibl. 21

McBryde & Patton
(c. 1819–1822)
Clinton, Ga.
Andrew McBryde
———— Patton
Bibl. 17

Andrew McBryde
Clinton, Ga. (c. 1819–1822)
Monticello, Ga. (c. 1822)
McBryde & Patton
(c. 1819–1822)
Bibl. 17

———— **McBurney** (c. 1855)
Nashville, Tenn.
Bibl. 54

McCabe & Walker
(c. 1805–1806)
Richmond, Va.
William McCabe
James Walker
Bibl. 19

John McCabe (c. 1773)
Baltimore, Md.
Bibl. 3

William McCabe
(c. 1804–1819)
Richmond, Va.
McCabe & Walker
(c. 1805–1806)
Bibl. 19

S. & M. McCain (c. 1824)
Genesee, N.Y.
Bibl. 20, 124

S. McCain (c. 1830)
Batavia, N.Y.
Bibl. 20, 124

John McCalse (c. 1774)
Baltimore, Md.
Bibl. 44

McCall
(See Van Voorhis, Schanck
& McCall)

Daniel McCalvey (c. 1837)
Philadelphia, Pa.
Bibl. 3

Michael McCann
(c. 1839–1845)
Philadelphia, Pa.
Bibl. 3

John McCarter (McCarty)
Philadelphia, Pa.
(c. 1845–1850)
Bibl. 3

Edward McCarty
(c. 1845–1850)
Philadelphia, Pa.
Bibl. 3, 23

Charles McCauley
(c. 1834)
New York, N.Y.
Bibl. 15, 124, 138

James McCauley (c. 1833)
New York, N.Y.
Bibl. 15, 124, 138

John A. McCaulley
(c. 1840)
Lexington, Ky.
Richmond, Ky.
Bibl. 32, 54, 68, 93

McCay & Cowan
(c. 1805–1807)
Richmond, Va.
William McCay
William Cowan
Bibl. 19

William McCay
  (b. 1753–d. 1829)
Richmond, Va.
  (c. 1805–1807)
Petersburg, Va.
  (c. 1811)
McCay & Cowan
  (c. 1805–1807)
Bibl. 19

The McChesney Co.
  (1921–1926)
Newark, N.J.
Became Dominick & Haff
  (1926–1928)
Reed & Burton (1928–1931)
Gorham Company
  (1931–present)
Bibl. 127

William McClain (c. 1848)
Philadelphia, Pa.
Bibl. 3

James McClanan
  (c. 1836–1837)
Buffalo, N.Y.
Myer & McClanan
Bibl. 20, 124

W. S. McClean Jr.
  (c. 1837)
Philadelphia, Pa.
Bibl. 3

Daniel McCleary
  (c. 1837–1841)
Philadelphia, Pa.
Bibl. 3

James McClever
  (c. 1828–1833)
Philadelphia, Pa.
Bibl. 3

John McClinch (c. 1760)
Boston, Mass.
Bibl. 28, 110

F. McCloskey (c. 1850)
Philadelphia, Pa.
Bibl. 3

Samuel McClure (c. 1808)
Fredericksburg, Va.
Bibl. 19

John (I.) C. McClymo(a)n
  (c. 1805–1840)
New York, N.Y.
*Bibl. 4, 15, 23, 24, 25, 28,
  29, 36, 44, 91, 114, 124,
  138*

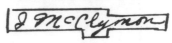

William McClymon
  (c. 1800–1815)
Schenectady, N.Y.
Bibl. 20, 25, 44, 114, 124

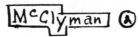

John McCollin
  (c. 1823–1824)
Philadelphia, Pa.
Bibl. 3

Thomas McCollin
  (c. 1824–1833)
Philadelphia, Pa.
Bibl. 3, 15, 44

T. MCCOLLIN

McConky & Lebey
  (c. 1811–1812)
Savannah, Ga.
David Marion McConky
Christian David Lebey
Bibl. 17

David Marion McConky
  (c. 1808–1820, d. 1820)
Savannah, Ga.
Jackson & McConky
  (c. 1808–1809)
McConky & Lebey
  (c. 1811–1812)
Bibl. 17

—————— **McConnaghy**
  (before 1850)
Wayne County, Ky.
Bibl. 32, 68

Hugh McConnel(l)
  (c. 1811–1813)
Philadelphia, Pa.
*Bibl. 3, 23, 24, 25, 29, 36,
  44, 54, 114*

MCCONNEL		MCCONNELL

John McConnell (d. 1858)
Richmond, Va.
  (c. 1827–1850)
Bibl. 19

Thomas McConnell
  (b. 1768–d. 1825,
  c. 1790–1818)
Richmond, Va.
Wilmington, Del.
Bibl. 19, 25, 30, 44, 91, 114

T. MCCONNELL		MCCONNELL

H. McConnelly (c. 1811)
Philadelphia, Pa.
Bibl. 3, 23, 36

Milton McConothy
  (c. 1843–1848)
Louisville, Ky.
Bibl. 32, 54, 68, 93

Bernard McCormick
  (c. 1844–1850)
Philadelphia, Pa.
Bibl. 3

Henry McCormick
  (c. 1833)
Philadelphia, Pa.
Bibl. 3

John McCormick (c. 1837)
Philadelphia, Pa.
Bibl. 3, 23, 36, 44

Patrick McCosker
  (c. 1842–1846)
Philadelphia, Pa.
Bibl. 3

Coles McCoun
  (c. 1840–1841)
Whitehall, N.Y.
Bibl. 20, 124

Henry T. McCoun
  (c. 1837–1840)
Troy, N.Y.
Bibl. 20, 124

Thomas McCowat
(c. 1823–1853)
Jackson, Tenn.
Bibl. 54, 159   M♪COWAT

George W. McCoy
(c. 1837–1850)
Philadelphia, Pa.
Bibl. 3

Robert McCrea (c. 1785)
Philadelphia, Pa.
Schenectady, N.Y.
Bibl. 3, 23, 36

R. A. McCredie (d. 1839)
Savannah, Ga. (c. 1836)
Bibl. 17

Thomas McCrow (c. 1767)
Annapolis, Md.
Bibl. 38

George H. McCulley
(c. 1829–1850)
Philadelphia, Pa.
Bibl. 3

William McCulley
(c. 1828–1850)
Philadelphia, Pa.
Bibl. 3, 91

Francis McCutchen
(c. 1844–1846)
Philadelphia, Pa.
Bibl. 3

John McDaniel
(c. 1848–1849)
Philadelphia, Pa.
Bibl. 3, 23

Peter McDaniel (c. 1743)
New York, N.Y.
Bibl. 23, 36, 44, 124

William H. McDaniel
(c. 1825)
Philadelphia Pa.
Bibl. 3

George W. McDannold
(19th century)
Winchester, Ky.
Bibl. 32, 54, 68, 93

MCDANNOLD

Charles C. McDermott
(c. 1850)
Philadelphia, Pa.
Bibl. 3

Edward McDermott
(c. 1848)
Philadelphia, Pa.
Bibl. 3

James McDermott
(c. 1835)
Philadelphia, Pa.
Bibl. 3

Charles McDonald
(19th century)
Lexington, Ky.
Bibl. 32, 54, 93

Daniel McDonald
(McDonnell)
Philadelphia, Pa.
(c. 1828–1837)
Bibl. 3, 23, 36, 44

H. E. McDonald (1875)
Belfast, Me.
Bibl. 105

Jacob McDonald
(c. 1833–1834)
Troy, N.Y.
Bibl. 20

Richard McDonald
(McDonnell)
Philadelphia, Pa.
(c. 1820–1824)
Bibl. 3

William T. McDonald
Shepherdstown, Va.
(c. 1845)
Alexandria, Va. (c. 1846)
Harpers Ferry, Va. (c. 1850)
Bibl. 19

D. McDonnell
(See D. McDonald)

John McDonough
(McDonnough)
Philadelphia, Pa. (c. 1775)
Bibl. 3, 23, 36, 44

Patrick McDonough
(McDonnough)
Philadelphia, Pa. (c. 1811)
Bibl. 3, 23, 36, 44

William McDougall
(c. 1825)
Meredith, N.H.
Bibl. 25, 28, 44, 91, 114

WM MCDOUGALL

James McDowell
(c. 1794–1808)
Philadelphia, Pa.
Bibl. 3

John McDowell
(c. 1817)
Philadelphia, Pa.
Bibl. 3

William Hanse McDowell
(b. 1795–d. 1842)
Philadelphia, Pa.
Bibl. 25, 44, 114

WM H. MCDOWELL

H. H. McDuffee (1875)
Portland, Me.
Bibl. 105

John W. McDuffee (1875)
Lewiston, Me.
Bibl. 105

I. McE.
Alexandria, Va.
Bibl. 54

James McElwee
(c. 1813–1814)
Philadelphia, Pa.
Ferris & McElwee (c. 1813)
Bibl. 3

John McEwen (McEuen)
(c. 1830–1833)
Philadelphia, Pa.
Ansbey & McEwen (c. 1825)
Bibl. 3

J. B. McFadden (c. 1840)
Pittsburgh, Pa.
Bibl. 24, 25, 44, 78, 114

J. B. MCFADDEN

John McFarlane
(MacFarland)
(MacFarlane)
Salem, Mass. (c. 1790)
Boston, Mass. (c. 1796)
Bibl. 4, 23, 24, 25, 28, 29,
36, 44, 91, 110, 114, 157

J. McF

William McFarlane
(c. 1805)
Philadelphia, Pa.
Bibl. 3

McFee & Reeder   M & R
(c. 1793–1796)
Philadelphia, Pa.
John McFee
Abner Reeder
Bibl. 3, 15, 24, 25, 29, 36,
44, 46, 54, 91, 114

John McFee
(c. 1797–1800)
Philadelphia, Pa.
McFee & Reeder
(c. 1793–1796)
Bibl. 3, 23, 28, 36, 44, 46, 91

M. McFee (c. 1769)
Philadelphia, Pa.
Bibl. 3, 23, 36, 44

Patrick McGann
(c. 1799–1831)
Charleston, S.C.
Bibl. 5

John McGlensey
(c. 1845–1850)
Philadelphia, Pa.
Bibl. 3

Edward B. McGlynn
(c. 1931–1965)
Newark, N.J.
Bibl. 127   McGLYNN

Isaac D. McGoodwin
(c. 1870–1885)
Bowling Green, Ky.
Fuselli & McGoodwin
(c. 1873–1885)
Bibl. 54, 93

Daniel McGraw (c. 1772)
Chester, Pa.
Bibl. 3, 23, 36, 44

McGrew and Beggs
(c. 1850)
Louisville, Ky.
———— McGrew
William Beggs
Bibl. 32, 89, 91

Alexander McGrew
(d. 1843)
Cincinnati, Ohio
(1805–1836)
Bibl. 34, 90, 91, 152

W. McGrew & Son
(c. 1855–1859)
Cincinnati, Ohio
Wilson McGrew (?)
Bibl. 54, 90, 91

Wilson McGrew
(b. 1800–d. 1859)
Cincinnati, Ohio
(1825–1859)
W. McGrew & Son (?)
Bibl. 34, 90, 91, 152

Robert McGuire (c. 1803)
Martinsburg, Va.
Bibl. 19, 91

McHarg & Selkirk
(c. 1815)
Albany, N.Y.
Alexander McHarg
William Selkirk
Bibl. 20, 124

Alexander McHarg
(c. 1817–1849)
Albany, N.Y.
McHarg & Selkirk (c. 1815)
Bibl. 20, 28, 44, 124

Dennis McHenry
(c. 1827–1830)
Baltimore, Md.
Bibl. 38

William T. McHenry
(c. 1833)
Hawkinsville, Ga.
Bibl. 17

McIlhenney & West
(c. 1818–1822)
Philadelphia, Pa.
Joseph McIlhenney
Thomas G. West(?)
Bibl. 3

Joseph McIlhenney
(c. 1818–1825)
Philadelphia, Pa.
McIlhenney & West
Bibl. 3

John K. McIlvaine
(McIlwain)
(c. 1823–1837)
Philadelphia, Pa.
Bibl. 3

James McIntire (c. 1840)
Philadelphia, Pa.
Bibl. 3, 23, 36, 44

John McIntosh (c. 1761)
Ft. Stanwix, Pa.
Bibl. 3, 23, 36, 44, 124

Colin (?) McIver (c. 1785)
Alexandria, Va.
Dawe & McIver
Bibl. 19

Murdo McIvor (c. 1844)
Rochester, N.Y.
Bibl. 20, 124

J. R. McKay (c. 1837)
New York, N.Y.
Bibl. 15, 124, 138

William McKean (c. 1819)
Charleston, S.C.
Bibl. 5

Archibald B. McKee
Lexington, Kentucky
Vincennes, Ind.
Bibl. 54, 133

John McKee (c. 1816)
Chester, S.C.
Bibl. 5

Henry McKeen   H. MCKEEN
(c. 1823–1850)
Philadelphia, Pa.
Bibl. 3, 15, 24, 25, 44, 91,
114

James McKeever
(c. 1829–1850)
Philadelphia, Pa.
Bibl. 3

**Walter H. McKenna &
Co., Inc.** (1915–present)
Providence, R.I.
Bibl. 127

MK

Henry McKenney (1860)
Auburn, Me.
Bibl. 105

John McKenney (1875)
Wiscasset, Me.
Bibl. 105

S. C. McKenney
(1860–1875)
Gardiner, Me.
Bibl. 105

William F. McKenzie
(1875)
Addison, Me.
Bibl. 105

Edward McKinley
(c. 1830–1837)
Philadelphia, Pa.
Bibl. 3

C. F. McKinney (c. 1825)
Location unknown
Bibl. 24

| C. F. MCKINNEY |

John McKliment (c. 1804)
New York, N.Y.
Bibl. 23, 36, 44, 124, 138

R. McLain (c. 1855)
Murfreesboro, Tenn.
Bibl. 54

John McLawrence
(c. 1818)
New York, N.Y.
Bibl. 23, 36, 44, 124, 138

Daniel J. McLean
(c. 1850)
Philadelphia, Pa.
Bibl. 3

O. P. McLean (c. 1840)
Columbus, Ga.
Bibl. 17

William S. McLean
(c. 1845–1850)
Philadelphia, Pa.
Bibl. 3

Simon E. McLellan (1875)
Gorham, Me.
Bibl. 105

McLure and Fusselli
(19th century)
Bowling Green, Ky.
Bibl. 32, 54

McLure & Valenti
(c. 1867)
Bowling Green, Ky.
James McLure
Philip Valenti
Bibl. 54

James McLure
(c. 1840–1881)
Bowling Green, Ky.
McLure & Valenti (c. 1867)
Bibl. 32, 54

John McMahon
(c. 1803–1804)
Philadelphia, Pa.
Bibl. 3, 23, 36, 44

John McManus
(c. 1840)
Philadelphia, Pa.
Bibl. 3

Michael McManus
(c. 1839)
New York, N.Y.
Bibl. 15, 124, 138

Hugh A. McMaster(s)
(c. 1839–1850)
Philadelphia, Pa.
Bibl. 3, 24, 25, 44, 91, 114

| H. A. MCMASTER |

John McMaster (c. 1805)
Philadelphia, Pa.
Bibl. 3, 23, 36

John McMillen (c. 1820)
Cambridge, Ohio
Bibl. 34, 116

James McMinn
(c. 1846–1850)
Philadelphia, Pa.
Bibl. 3

McMullen
(See John McMullin,
William McMullin)

Edward McMullen
(c. 1846–1848)
Philadelphia, Pa.
Bibl. 3

James McMullen (c. 1814)
Philadelphia, Pa.
Bibl. 3, 23, 36

McMullin & Black
(c. 1811)
Philadelphia, Pa.
John McMullin
John Black
*Bibl. 3, 4, 23, 24, 25, 28, 29,
36, 44, 80, 91, 114*

| MCMULLIN AND BLACK |

**John McMullin
(McMullen)**
(b. 1765–d. 1843)
Philadelphia, Pa.
(c. 1795–1841)
McMullin & Black
(c. 1811)
*Bibl. 3, 4, 23, 24, 25, 28, 29,
36, 39, 44, 54, 72, 81, 91,
95, 114, 118*

**William McMullin
(McMullen)**
Philadelphia, Pa.
(c. 1791–1794)
Bibl. 3, 23, 36, 44

**Thomas McMurrey
(McMurray)**
Frankfort, Ky. (c. 1810)
Louisville, Ga. (c. 1811)
Bibl. 17, 32, 54, 68

John McMurry (c. 1809)
Athens, Ga.
Bibl. 17

John McMyers (c. 1799)
Baltimore, Md.
Bibl. 38

McN & S (c. 1830)
Pennsylvania (?)
Bibl. 89

McNamara (c. 1765)
Philadelphia, Pa.
Bibl. 3

William McNeare
(c. 1828–1833)
Philadelphia, Pa.
Bibl. 3

———— **McNeeley** (c. 1814)
Paris, Ohio
Bibl. 34

D. McNeil (c. 1818)
Greensboro, Ga.
Bibl. 17

E. McNeil (c. 1813–1839)
Binghamton, N.Y.
Troy, N.Y.
Bibl. 15, 20, 25, 44, 114, 124

E MCNEIL

William McNeir
(c. 1835–1848)
Philadelphia, Pa.
Bibl. 3

Ezra McNutt (c. 1848)
Philadelphia, Pa.
Bibl. 3

William McParlin
(b. 1780–d. 1850)
Annapolis, Md.
(c. 1803–1850)
Bibl. 24, 25, 29, 38, 44, 114

W. McP

John McPherson
(c. 1846–1850)
Philadelphia, Pa.
Bibl. 3

Robert McPherson
(c. 1828–1850)
Philadelphia, Pa.
Bibl. 3, 23, 36, 44

Hugh McQuarters
Cincinnati, Ohio
(1817–1819)
Bibl. 34, 90, 152

William McQuilkin
(c. 1845–1853)
Philadelphia, Pa.
Bibl. 54

Solomon McQuivey
(c. 1832–1841)
Utica, N.Y.
Bibl. 18, 20, 124, 158

James McRea (c. 1805)
Mecklenburg County, N.C.
Bibl. 21

Francis McStocker
(c. 1831–1850)
Philadelphia, Pa.
Bibl. 3

Walter P. McTeigue
(c. 1895–1925)
New York, N.Y.
Bibl. 126

A. McVicker (c. 1821)
Winchester, Va.
Bibl. 19

Mead
(See Phinney & Mead)

Mead & Adriance
(c. 1836–1852)
St. Louis, Mo.
Ithaca, N.Y.

Edward Edmund Mead
Edwin Adriance
*Bibl. 15, 20, 24, 25, 29, 36,
44, 54, 91, 114, 124, 134,
155*

MEAD & ADRIANCE

Mead, Adriance & Co.
(c. 1831–1832)
Ithaca, N.Y.
St. Louis, Mo.
Edward Edmund Mead
Edwin Adriance
Bibl. 20, 23, 28, 36, 91, 124

B. Mead
Massachusetts (?)
Bibl. 28

Daniel Mead
(c. 1845–1848)
Louisville, Ky.
Bibl. 32, 54, 68

**Edward Edmund Mead
(Meade)**
(c. 1831–1842)
Ithaca, N.Y.
(c. 1831–1832)
St. Louis, Mo.
(c. 1838–1870)
DeRiemer & Mead
(c. 1830–1831)
Mead, Adriance & Co.
(c. 1831–1832)
Mead & Adriance
(c. 1836–1852)
*Bibl. 20, 24, 25, 44, 54, 91,
114, 124, 134, 155*

E MEAD

John O. Mead (c. 1850)
Philadelphia, Pa.
Filley, Mead & Caldwell
Bibl. 3, 135

Meadows & Co. (c. 1831)
Philadelphia, Pa.
Bibl. 24, 25, 44, 54, 114

MEADOWS & CO.

Mealy Mfg. Co.
(c. 1900–1956)
Baltimore, Md.
Bibl. 127, 157

HAND /925\ WROUGHT
/1000\

Charles Mears
(c. 1828–1835)
Philadelphia, Pa.
Bibl. 3

Lewis Mears (c. 1848)
Philadelphia, Pa.
Bibl. 3

Lewis J. Mears (c. 1839)
Philadelphia, Pa.
Bibl. 3

**Mechanics Sterling
Company**
(c. 1896–1897)
Attleboro, Mass.
Became Watson, Newell Co.
Bibl. 127

     ⬥STERLING

MECHANICS STERLING CO.

John Mecke
(c. 1837–1850)
Philadelphia, Pa.
Bibl. 3

John Mecom (d. 1770)
New York, N.Y.
Bibl. 23, 28, 36, 44, 124, 138

George Mecum
(c. 1825–1836)
Boston, Mass.
*Bibl. 4, 15, 23, 25, 28, 36,
44, 110, 114*

≥G. MECUM≥

G MECUM

Medallic Art Company
(c. 1907–present)
Danbury, Conn.
Bibl. 127

J. Medberry (c. 1831)
Rochester, N.Y.
Bibl. 20, 124

John Medenhall
(c. 1841–1846)
Philadelphia, Pa.
Bibl. 3

George A. Meder
(1860–1875)
Foxcroft, Me.
Bibl. 105

Medford Cutlery Co.
(See A. R. Justice Co.)

Jacob Mediary Jr.
(b. 1791, c. 1808)
Location unknown
Bibl. 38

Andrew G. Medley
(c. 1832–1850)
Louisville, Ky.
Bibl. 32, 54, 68

Meek and Milam
(c. 1850–1852)
Frankfort, Ky.
Jonathan Fleming Meek
Benjamin F. Meek
Benjamin Cave Milam
Bibl. 32, 93

Benjamin F. Meek
(b. 1816–d. 1901)
Danville, Ky. (1832–1834)
Frankfort, Ky. (1834–1882)
Louisville, Ky. (1882–1901)
J. F. and B. F. Meek
(c. 1837–1846)
Meek & Milam
(c. 1850–1852)
Bibl. 32, 54, 93

J. F. Meek and Co.
(c. 1837–1852)
Frankfort, Ky.
Jonathan Fleming Meek
Bibl. 32, 93

J. F. and B. F. Meek
(c. 1837–1846)
Frankfort, Ky.
Jonathan Fleming Meek
Benjamin F. Meek
Bibl. 32, 93

Jonathan Fleming Meek
(b. 1809)
Frankfort, Ky.
(c. 1837–1852)
Louisville, Ky.
J. F. and B. F. Meek
(c. 1837–1846)
J. F. Meek and Co.

(c. 1837–1852)
Meek and Milam
(c. 1850–1852)
Bibl. 32, 54, 93

**Thomas J. Megear
(Megar)** (b. 1809)
Philadelphia, Pa.
(c. 1830–1850)
Wilmington, Del.
*Bibl. 3, 15, 25, 30, 44, 91,
114*

≥T.J.MEGEAR≥

F. Megonegal
(c. 1841–1842)
Philadelphia, Pa.
Bibl. 3

W. H. Megonegal (c. 1844)
Philadelphia, Pa.
Bibl. 3

Jacob Mehrlust (c. 1900)
New York, N.Y.
Bibl. 126

Meier
(See Jacob Mayer)

Michel Meilleur Jr.
(b. 1818–d. 1893)
New Orleans, La.
(1841–1846)
Bibl. 141

Michael Melhorn
(c. 1830–1832)
Harpers Ferry, Va.
Bibl. 19, 91

Melville & Co.
New Orleans, La.
(1849–1858)
New York, N. Y. (1852)
Bibl. 141

MELVILLE&CO.

Henry Melville (c. 1798)
Wilmington, N.C.
Bibl. 21

Alexander Menard
(c. 1828–1829)
Macon, Ga.
Garland & Menard
Bibl. 17

Stephen Menard (c. 1817)
Philadelphia, Pa.
Bibl. 3

John Mendenhall
(c. 1841)
Philadelphia, Pa.
Bibl. 23

Thomas Mendenhall
(c. 1772)
Lancaster, Pa.
Bibl. 3, 112

Benjamin Mends (Mens)
Philadelphia, Pa.
(c. 1796–1797)
Bibl. 3

James Mends (Mens)
Philadelphia, Pa. (c. 1795)
Bibl. 3

Menkens & Recordon
(c. 1842)
St. Louis, Mo.
Anthony H. Menkens
Charles Recordon
Bibl. 24, 54, 114

| MENKENS |

Anthony H. Menkens
(c. 1840–1866)
St. Louis, Mo.
Successor to Menkens &
Recordan (c. 1842)
Bibl. 134, 155

Mens
(See Mends)

John Menzies
(c. 1804–1850)
Philadelphia, Pa.
Bibl. 3

John Menzies Jr.
(c. 1835–1850)
Philadelphia, Pa.
Bibl. 3

J. Merchant (c. 1795)
New York, N.Y.
*Bibl. 23, 24, 25, 36, 44, 78,
114, 124*

| J MERCHANT |

Meredith & Johnston
(c. 1827)
Winchester, Va.
James Meredith
William Johnston
Bibl. 19

J. Meredith & Son
(c. 1850)
Winchester, Va.
James Meredith
Bibl. 19

James Meredith (d. 1860)
Winchester, Va.
Meredith & Johnston
(c. 1827)
J. Meredith & Son (c. 1850)
Cambell & Meredith
(c. 1850)
Bibl. 19

Joseph P. Meredith
(c. 1824–1848)
Baltimore, Md.
Bibl. 15, 24, 25, 38, 44, 114

| J MEREDITH |

J. Merick (c. 1800)
Location unknown
Bibl. 54

J. B. Merick
Location unknown
Bibl. 28, 29

| J. B. MERICK |

Meriden Britannia Co.
(1852–1898)
Meriden, Conn.
Horace C. and Dennis C.
Wilcox
Merged International Silver
Company (1898)
Marks used until c. 1930
Bibl. 114, 127, 135, 157

**Meriden Cutlery
Company** (1855–1866)
South Meriden, Conn.
Became Landers, Frary &
Clark (1866–c. 1960)
Mark continued in use
Bibl. 127

MERIDEN CUTLERY CO

Meriden Jewelry Mfg. Co.
(c. 1915–1922)
Meriden, Conn.
Became Meriden Jewelry Co.
(c. 1922)
Bibl. 127

Meriden Sterling Co.
(c. 1896–1915)
Meriden, Conn.
Bibl. 114, 127, 157

Perry (Parry) Merkle
(c. 1840–1848)
Philadelphia, Pa.
Bibl. 3

John H. Merkler
(c. 1780–1791)
New York, N.Y.
*Bibl. 23, 24, 25, 28, 36, 44,
114, 124, 138*

| I H M |

**Mermod, Jaccard & King
Jewelry Company**
(1905–present)
St. Louis, Mo.
Successor to Mermod
Jaccard & Company
(c. 1845–1883)
Mermod & Jaccard Jewelry
Co. (1883–1905)
Became division of Scruggs,
Vandevoort & Barney
(c. 1917)
*Bibl. 114, 126, 127, 134, 152,
155*

Merrick (c. 1815–1820)
Location unknown
Bibl. 15, 44, 114

Merrick, Walsh & Phelps Jewelry Co. (1879–1901)
St. Louis, Mo.
Bibl. 155

John P. Merrie (c. 1833)
Utica, N.Y.
Bibl. 18, 20, 124

James Merrifield (c. 1850)
New York, N.Y.
Bibl. 23, 124, 138

Thomas V. Z. Merrifield
(d. 1845)
Albany, N.Y. (c. 1817–1845)
Hall, Hewson & Co.
(c. 1836–1842)
Hall, Hewson & Merrifield
(c. 1840)
Bibl. 20, 23, 28, 36, 44, 124

Merrill Shops (c. 1931)
New York, N.Y.
Successor to J. M. Merrill &
Co. (c. 1893–1896)
Merrill Brothers & Co.
(c. 1896–1922)
The Merrill Co.
(c. 1922–1931)
Bibl. 114, 127, 157

J. Ambrose Merrill (1860)
Portland, Me.
Bibl. 83, 105, 114

**Merrimac Valley
Silversmiths**
(c. 1939–1945)
Concord, N.H.
Division of Concord
Silversmiths, Ltd.
Became Ellmore Silver Co.,
Inc. (c. 1945)
Dies purchased by Crown
Silver Co.
Bibl. 127, 147

———— **Merriman** (c. 1855)
Memphis, Tenn.
Bibl. 54

Merriman & Bradley
(c. 1817–1826)
New Haven, Conn.
Marcus Merriman
Zebul Bradley
*Bibl. 15, 16, 23, 24, 25, 28,
36, 61, 92, 94, 102, 110,
114, 143*

Merriman & Tuttle
(c. 1802)
New Haven, Conn.
Marcus Merriman
Bethuel Tuttle
*Bibl. 16, 23, 28, 36, 44, 110,
143*

C. Merriman (c. 1825)
New York, N.Y.
Bibl. 23, 36, 44

C. G. Merriman
(c. 1850–1851)
Memphis, Tenn.
Bibl. 159

James E. Merriman
(c. 1845–1860)
Memphis, Tenn.
Bibl. 159

Marcus Merriman
(b. 1762–d. 1850,
c. 1787–1817)
New Haven, Conn.
(c. 1802–1820)
Cheshire, Conn.
Merriman & Tuttle (c. 1802)
Marcus Merriman & Co.
(c. 1802–1817)
Merriman & Bradley
(c. 1817–1826)
*Bibl. 15, 16, 23, 24, 25, 28,
36, 44, 54, 91, 92, 94, 102,
110, 114, 143*

Marcus Merriman & Co.
(c. 1802–1817)
New Haven, Conn.
Marcus Merriman
Zebul Bradley
Bethuel Tuttle
*Bibl. 16, 21, 23, 24, 25, 28,
36, 44, 61, 72, 91, 92, 94,
110, 122, 143*

Marcus Merriman Jr.
(c. 1826)
New Haven, Conn.
Bradley & Merriman
(c. 1826–1847)
Bibl. 19, 23, 28, 54, 110, 143

Reuben Merriman
(b. 1783–d. 1866)
Cheshire, Conn.
Litchfield, Conn.
*Bibl. 16, 24, 25, 28, 36, 44,
61, 91, 92, 110, 114*

Samuel Merriman
(b. 1769–d. 1805)
New Haven, Conn.
*Bibl. 15, 16, 23, 24, 25, 28,
29, 36, 44, 61, 92, 94, 110,
114, 143*

Silas Merriman
(b. 1734–d. 1805)
Cheshire, Conn.
New Haven, Conn.
*Bibl. 15, 16, 23, 28, 36, 44,
61, 92, 94, 110, 143*

Nathan Merrow
(b. 1758–d. 1825)
East Hartford, Conn.
*Bibl. 16, 23, 28, 36, 44, 92,
110*

Teapots

When teapots were first introduced into Europe they were very small. Since tea was very expensive, the teapot was designed to hold only one cup of tea. As tea became less expensive and easier to buy, the size of the teapot increased until it reached its present size. The shape of the teapot changed from round to pear-shaped, to inverted pear-shape to the classical straight-sided designs. About 1825 the bulbous belly pots were made. Victorian designers tried a variety of shapes, including some with upward sloping bodies and angular handles or oval bodies and sticklike legs and animal feet. The Art Nouveau teapots made in the early 1900s were irregularly shaped and covered with flowing raised designs. About 1910 the Colonial Revival pots appeared that had very classical lines but differed from the eighteenth-century pot because it had a pedestal foot. Designs after 1920 favored very rectangular or tubelike bodies and unusual spouts and handles.

1700

1710

1730

1730-60

1760–75

1790

1800

1810

1810–20

1820

1825

1850

1875–90

1900

1930

1930

F. Merry (c. 1799)
Philadelphia, Pa.
Bibl. 3

Mesick Mfg. Co. (c. 1950)
Los Angeles, Calif.
Bibl. 127

Mesker
(See Mexter)

S. Messinger (c. 1800)
Location unknown
Bibl. 15, 44, 91, 114

| S MESSINGER |

B. Mestier (c. 1817)
Philadelphia, Pa.
Bibl. 3

Metallurgic Art Co.
(c. 1895–1900)
Baltimore, Md.
Bibl. 127

Metten and Muller
(c. 1839)
St. Louis, Mo.
Lorens Metton
Bibl. 54, 155

Lorens Metten
(1839–1851)
St. Louis, Mo.
Bibl. 155

John G. D. Meurset
(c. 1778–1810)
Charleston, S.C.
Monk & Meurset
(c. 1804–1807)
Bibl. 5   J Meurset

Godfrey Mexter (Mesker)
(c. 1837–1840)
Philadelphia, Pa.
Bibl. 3

Gottlieb Meyer
(See Gottlieb Myer)

John C. Meyer
(1860–c. 1880)
New Orleans, La.
Bibl. 141
                J.C. MEYER

Joseph Meyer (c. 1840)
Canton, Ohio
Bibl. 34, 44

Matthew Meyer
(c. 1858–1859)
Utica, N.Y.
Bibl. 18, 124, 158

Maurice Meyer (c. 1849)
Philadelphia, Pa.
Bibl. 3

Max Meyer (c. 1866)
St. Charles, Mo.
Bibl. 134

Albert G. Meyers
(c. 1837–1846)
Philadelphia, Pa.
Bibl. 3

Elijah Meyers
(c. 1829–1830)
Philadelphia, Pa.
Bibl. 3

T. Meyers (c. 1802–1807)
Norfolk, Va.
Bibl. 19

William B. Meyers Co.
(c. 1907–1958)
Newark, N.J.
Bibl. 127

Richard Meyrick (c. 1729)
Philadelphia, Pa.
Bibl. 3, 28

James Michaels
(c. 1820–1826)
New York, N.Y.
Bibl. 15, 23, 36, 44, 124, 138

Adrian L. Michel
(c. 1820–1858)
Charleston, S.C.
Bibl. 5

John E. Michel
(c. 1819–1844)
Charleston, S.C.
Bibl. 5

John E. Michel
(1829–1830)
New Oleans, La.
Bibl. 141

Lewis C. Michel (c. 1822)
Charleston, S.C.
John Michel
Bibl. 5

William B. Middlebrook
(c. 1842)
Middletown, N.Y.
Bibl. 20, 124

Thomas F. Midlam
(b. 1828)
Utica, N.Y. (c. 1850–1860)
Bibl. 18, 20, 124, 158

P. Miedzielski (c. 1837)
Columbus, Ga.
Bibl. 17

Lewis Mignard
(c. 1829–1835)
Philadelphia, Pa.
Bibl. 3

James Mikles
(c. 1828–1841)
New York, N.Y.
Bibl. 15, 124, 138

John Matthew Miksch
(b. 1754–d. 1823)
Bethlehem, Pa.
Bibl. 3, 23, 24, 25, 29, 36, 44

| I M MIKSCH |

Benjamin Cave Milam
(b. 1821–d. 1904)
Frankfort, Ky.
Meek & Milam
(c. 1850–1852)
Bibl. 32, 93

Harold A. Milbrath
(1952–present)
Milwaukee, Wisc.
Bibl. 127

John Miler (19th century)
Cincinnati, Ohio
Bibl. 34

John Miles (c. 1785–1796)
Philadelphia, Pa.
Bibl. 3, 23, 28, 36, 44

Robert Miles
   (c. 1828–1850)
Philadelphia, Pa.
Bibl. 3

John Miley (c. 1829–1850)
Philadelphia, Pa.
Bibl. 3

Stephen Milhe (d. 1798)
Philadelphia, Pa. (c. 1780)
Bibl. 3, 23, 36, 44

Thomas Milk (b. 1753)
Maryland (c. 1775)
Bibl. 38

R. P. Milks (c. 1840)
Mansfield, Ohio
Bibl. 34

James Millar
   (c. 1825)
Boston, Mass.
Bibl. 23, 28, 36, 44, 110

George Millard (c. 1816)
Philadelphia, Pa.
Bibl. 3, 23, 36, 44, 110

Miller & Powers
   (c. 1799–1801)
Savannah, Ga.
Francis S. Miller
William Powers
Bibl. 17

Miller & Son
   (c. 1833–1835)
Philadelphia, Pa.
Bibl. 3, 23, 36, 44

Miller Brothers & Co.
   (1875)
Camden, Me.
Bibl. 105

The Miller Jewelry Co.
   (c. 1915–1922)
Cincinnati, Ohio
Bibl. 127

M Sterling

A. Miller (c. 1825)
Location unknown
Bibl. 15, 44, 114

A. H. Miller (1860–1880)
Chicago, Ill.
Successor to A. H. Miller &
   Bros. (c. 1854–1860)
Bibl. 98

D. B. Miller (c. 1850)
Boston, Mass.
Bibl. 24, 25, 44, 91, 114

D. B. MILLER

E. F. Miller (1825)
Providence, R.I.
Bibl. 108

Francis S. Miller
   (c. 1798)
Savannah, Ga.
Miller & Powers
   (c. 1799–1801)
Bibl. 17

Frederick A. Miller
   (c. 1946–present)
Brecksville, Ohio
Cleveland, Ohio
Bibl. 127

George Miller (c. 1809)
Philadelphia, Pa.
Bibl. 3

George Miller
   (c. 1829–1853)
Philadelphia, Pa.
Bibl. 3

H. Miller (c. 1815)
Schenectady, N.Y.
I. S. & H. Miller
Bibl. 20, 124

I. R. Miller (c. 1810)
Philadelphia, Pa.
Bibl. 24, 25, 44, 114

I. S. Miller (c. 1813–1822)
Schenectady, N.Y.
I. S. & H. Miller (c. 1815)
I.S. Miller & Co.
   (c. 1822–1826) (?)
Bibl. 20, 124

I. S. Miller & Co.
   (c. 1822–1826)
Schenectady, N.Y.
Bibl. 20, 124

I. S. & H. Miller (c. 1815)
Schenectady, N.Y.
Bibl. 20, 124

James Miller (c. 1812)
Cadiz, Ohio
Bibl. 34

John Miller (c. 1834)
Bellefontaine, Ohio
Bibl. 34, 152

John Miller (c. 1840–1841)
New York, N.Y.
Bibl. 15, 124

John David Miller
   (c. 1780–1815)
Charleston, S.C.
Bibl. 5, 25, 44, 54, 114

J D Miller		I D M

John Paul Miller
   (1937–present)
Brecksville, Ohio
Cleveland, Ohio
Bibl. 117, 127

Joseph Miller (c. 1837)
Milledgeville, Ga.
Bibl. 17

Julius Miller (c. 1850)
Prattsville, N.Y.
Bibl. 20, 124

L. H. Miller & Co.
   (c. 1840)
Baltimore, Md.
Bibl. 25, 44, 114

Martha Miller
  (c. 1807–1819)
Charleston, S.C.
Bibl. 5, 54

Matthew Miller
  (b. 1780–d. 1840)
Charleston, S.C.
  (c. 1805–1840)
Bibl. 5, 25, 44, 54, 91, 114

| M MILLER |

Mordecai Miller
  (b. 1763–d. 1832)
Alexandria, Va.
  (c. 1791–1795)
Bibl. 19, 54, 91

P. Miller (c. 1810)
Philadelphia, Pa.
Bibl. 24 | P MILLER |

Pardon Miller
  (b. 1797–d. 1852)
Providence, R.I.
Bibl. 15, 28, 44, 56, 91, 102, 110, 114

Philip Miller (c. 1763)
New York, N.Y.
Bibl. 3, 124

S. W. Miller (c. 1843)
Philadelphia, Pa.
Bibl. 3

Thomas Miller
  (c. 1819–1841)
Philadelphia, Pa.
Bibl. 3

William Miller (c. 1758)
Winchester, Va.
Bibl. 19

William Miller
  (c. 1810–1847)
Philadelphia, Pa.
Ward & Miller
  (c. 1822–1824)
Bibl. 3, 23, 24, 25, 29, 36, 44, 95, 114

William Miller (c. 1819)
Charleston, S.C.
Bibl. 5, 44, 91

William S. Miller
  (c. 1844–1848)
Philadelphia, Pa.
Bibl. 3

Thomas Millner
  (b. 1690–d. 1745)
Boston, Mass.
Bibl. 2, 15, 23, 24, 25, 28, 29, 36, 72, 94, 110, 114

Thomas Millner (c. 1825)
Ashtabula, Ohio
Bibl. 34

Peter Millon
  (c. 1820–1832)
New York, N.Y.
Bibl. 23, 36, 124, 138

Phillippe Milloudon
  (c. 1811)
Philadelphia, Pa.
Bibl. 3, 23, 36

Edmund Mills (c. 1785)
Philadelphia, Pa.
Bibl. 3, 23, 36

Edward Mills (c. 1794)
Philadelphia, Pa.
Bibl. 3, 23, 36

George F. Mills
  (c. 1834–1837)
New York, N.Y.
Bibl. 15, 124, 138

John Mills (c. 1793–1815)
Philadelphia, Pa.
Bibl. 3

John Bryant Mills
  (c. 1830)
Fayetteville, N.C.
Bibl. 21

Robert Mills (c. 1790)
Winchester, Va.
Bibl. 19

Moses Millum (c. 1819)
Baltimore, Md.
Bibl. 38

Edmund (Edward) Milne
  (b. 1724–d. 1822)
Philadelphia, Pa.
Bibl. 2, 3, 15, 24, 25, 28, 29, 39, 44, 54, 81, 91, 95, 102, 114, 116, 122

F. Milne (c. 1800)
New York, N.Y.
Bibl. 23, 36, 44, 124, 138

John Milne (c. 1817)
Morristown, Ohio
Bibl. 34

Robert Milne (c. 1817)
Philadelphia, Pa.
Bibl. 3

Stephen Milne (c. 1817)
Morristown, Ohio
Bibl. 34

Thomas Milne
  (c. 1795–1815)
New York, N.Y.
Bibl. 15, 23, 25, 36, 44, 91, 114, 124

| T. MILNE |

Gustavus Mindel (c. 1850)
Philadelphia, Pa.
Bibl. 3

Joseph Miner (c. 1840)
Burton, Ohio
Bibl. 34

Minott & Austin
  (c. 1760–1769)
Boston, Mass.
Samuel Minott
Josiah John Austin
Bibl. 15, 23, 24, 25, 29, 44,
  91, 110

Minott & Simpkins
  (c. 1750–1760)
Boston, Mass.
William Simpkins
Samuel Minott
Bibl. 23, 24, 25, 29, 36, 44,
  91, 110, 114

Samuel Minott
  (b. 1732–d. 1803)
Boston, Mass.
Minott & Simpkins
  (c. 1750–1760)
Minott & Austin
  (c. 1760–1769)
Bibl. 2, 15, 24, 25, 28, 29,
  36, 44, 54, 91, 94, 102,
  110, 114, 142, 143, 149

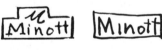

William Minshall (c. 1773)
Philadelphia, Pa.
Bibl. 3, 23, 36, 44

Vermont Mint
  (c. 1785–1788)
Rupert, Vt.
Bibl. 54

George W. Minter
Indianapolis, Ind.
Shelbyville, Ky. (after 1859)
Bacon & Minter
  (c. 1855–c. 1859)
Bibl. 133

Minton & Mayer
  (c. 1840–1842)
Norfolk, Va.
Joseph B. Minton
Gotlieb A. Mayer
Bibl. 19

MINTON & MAYER

Joseph B. Minton
  (c. 1840–1847)
Norfolk, Va.
Minton & Mayer
  (c. 1840–1842)
Bibl. 15, 19, 44

MINTON

John Miot (Myot)
  (b. 1740–d. 1791)
Charleston, S.C.
  (c. 1773–1791)
Bibl. 5, 54

Charles Missing (c. 1847)
Philadelphia, Pa.
Bibl. 3

Mitchell & Tyler
  (c. 1845–1866)
Richmond, Va.
Samuel Phillips Mitchell
William Mitchell Jr. (?)
John Henry Tyler
Bibl. 19, 54, 91

MITCHELL & TYLER

Benjamin Mitchell
  (c. 1799–1800)
Alexandria, Va.
Bibl. 19

Henry Mitchell
  (c. 1837–1844)
New York, N.Y.
Gunn & Mitchell
  (c. 1832) (?)
Bibl. 15, 124, 138

Henry Mitchell
  (c. 1844–1850)
Philadelphia, Pa.
Bibl. 3, 23, 24, 25, 44, 114

MITCHELL

James Mitchell (c. 1799)
Baltimore, Md.
Bibl. 38

James Mitchell
  (c. 1845–1846)
Philadelphia, Pa.
Bibl. 3, 23

Jesse C. Mitchell
  (c. 1835–1836)
Buffalo, N.Y.
Bibl. 20, 124

John Mitchell (c. 1816)
Charleston, S.C.
Bibl. 5

Phineas Mitchell (c. 1812)
Boston, Mass.
Bibl. 23, 28, 36, 44, 110

Samuel Phillips Mitchell
  (b. 1815–d. 1866)
Richmond, Va.
Mitchell & Tyler
  (c. 1845–1866)
Bibl. 19, 91

William Mitchell (c. 1820)
Boston, Mass.
Bibl. 15, 23, 24, 25, 29, 36,
  44, 110

W MITCHELL

William Mitchell Jr.
  (b. 1795–d. 1852)
Richmond, Va.
Taft & Mitchell
  (c. 1818–1819)
Mitchell & Tyler (?)
Bibl. 19, 44, 91, 114

WM.JR

Willis Mitchell (1875)
Liberty, Me.
Bibl. 105

James Mix (b. 1793)
Albany, N.Y. (c. 1817–?)
*Bibl. 4, 20, 23, 28, 36, 44,
124*

James Mix Jr.
(c. 1846–1881)
Albany, N.Y.
Bibl. 20, 91, 114, 124

Thomas Mix (c. 1803)
Philadelphia, Pa.
Bibl. 3

Vischer (Visscher) Mix
(c. 1840–1848)
Albany, N.Y.
Bibl. 20, 23, 28, 44, 124

William Mobbs
(c. 1835–1838)
Albany, N.Y.
Black Rock, N.Y.
Buffalo, N.Y.
Bibl. 20, 23, 36, 44, 124

Peter Moeller (c. 1849)
Cleveland, Ohio
Bibl. 54

Moellinger
(See Mollinger)

Moffat & Chase (c. 1839)
Buffalo, N.Y.
Bibl. 20, 124

Charles H. Moffat
(c. 1830–1835)
New York, N.Y.
Bibl. 15, 36, 44, 124, 138

F. W. Moffat (c. 1853)
Albany, N.Y.
Bibl. 4, 28, 124

John L. Moffat
(c. 1815–1835)
New York, N.Y.
*Bibl. 15, 23, 24, 25, 36, 44,
102, 114, 124, 138*

[J.L.MOFFAT]

[J.L. MOFFAT]

William Moffat
(c. 1832–1848)
Buffalo, N.Y.
Larzelere & Moffat (c. 1835)
Bibl. 20, 124

Benjamin Moffett
(c. 1839)
Philadelphia, Pa.
Bibl. 3

Jacob Mohler   [I M]
(b. 1744–d. 1773)
Baltimore, Md.
Bibl. 29, 38, 44

David Molan
(c. 1835–1841)
Troy, N.Y.
Albany, N.Y.
Bibl. 20, 124, 138

Jacob A. Moller
(c. 1907–1915)
New Rochelle, N.Y.
Bibl. 127, 157

**Henry Mollinger
(Moellinger)
(Moollinger)**
Philadelphia, Pa.
(c. 1794–1804)
Bibl. 3

Lawrence Mollyneux
(c. 1830)
New York, N.Y.
Bibl. 23, 124

Daniel Molyneaux
(c. 1828–1832)
New York, N.Y.
Bibl. 15, 124, 138

Monell & Williams
(c. 1825)
New York, N.Y.
John I. (J.) Monell
Charles M. Williams
Bibl. 25, 44, 114, 124, 138

[J J Monell]

John I. (J.) Monell
(c. 1824–1829)
New York, N.Y.
Monell & Williams
Bibl. 15, 23, 35, 83, 124, 138

Benedict Monfay
(c. 1828–1835)
Philadelphia, Pa.
Bibl. 3

Benjamin Monger
(c. 1806)
Poughkeepsie, N.Y.
Field & Monger
(c. 1805–1806)
Bibl. 20, 124

David Mongin Sr.
(c. 1765–1767)
Purysburgh, Ga.
Bibl. 17

Daniel Monier
(c. 1825–1850)
Philadelphia, Pa.
Bibl. 3

I. Monil & M. Williams
(c. 1835)
Location unknown
Bibl. 24

Monk & Co. (c. 1805)
Charleston, S.C.
James Monk
Bibl. 5   MONK & CO.

Monk & Meurset
(c. 1804–1807)
Charleston, S.C.
James Monk
John G. D. Meurset
Bibl. 5

James Monk   [MONK]
(c. 1797–1808)
Charleston, S.C.
(c. 1797–1799,
c. 1804–1807)
Manchester, S.C.
Atmar & Monk
(c. 1797–1799)
Monk & Meurset
(c. 1804–1807)
Monk & Co. (c. 1805)
Bibl. 5, 25, 44, 54, 114

Monroe and Defriez
(c. 1854–1859)
St. Louis, Mo.
Bibl. 155

E. P. Monroe (c. 1830s)
Mogadore, Ohio
Bibl. 34

J. S. Monroe (c. 1830s)
Mogadore, Ohio
Bibl. 34

James F. Monroe
  (1848–1900)
St. Louis, Mo.
Bibl. 54

C. J. Monson (c. 1815)
Location unknown
Bibl. 24

[C. J. MONSON]

Albert Montandon
  (c. 1824)
Clarksburg, Va.
Bibl. 19

William R. Montcastle
  (c. 1844–1856)
Warrenton, N.C.
Bibl. 21

Monteith & Co.
  (c. 1845)
Philadelphia, Pa.
Bibl. 3

Monteith & Shippen
  (c. 1817)
Philadelphia, Pa.
———— Monteith
William A. Shippen
Bibl. 3

Benjamin Monteith
  (c. 1847–1848)
Philadelphia, Pa.
Bibl. 3

Charles Monteith
  (c. 1847–1848)
Philadelphia, Pa.
Bibl. 3

I. & R. Monteith
  (c. 1814–1849)
Baltimore, Md.
John Monteith
Robert Montcith
Bibl. 15, 38, 44, 114

John Monteith
  (c. 1814–1849)
Baltimore, Md.
I. & R. Monteith
Bibl. 38, 44

John & Robert Monteith
(See I. & R. Monteith)

Robert Monteith
  (c. 1814–1849, d. 1849)
Baltimore, Md.
I. & R. Monteith
Bibl. 3, 25, 29, 44   [R M]

Montgomery Bros.
  (c. 1888–1915)
Los Angeles, Calif.
James Montgomery
George Montgomery
Bibl. 127, 157

Andrew Montgomery
  (c. 1822–1830)
Norfolk, Va. (c. 1822–1823)
Baltimore, Md.
  (c. 1824–1830)
Bibl. 19, 38

Edwin Montgomery
  (c. 1850)
Syracuse, N.Y.
Bibl. 20, 124

**Summerfield
  Montgomery**
  (c. 1856–1872, d. 1872)
Newberry, S.C.
Bibl. 5

Mood & Ewan (c. 1824)
Charleston, S.C.
———— Mood
John Ewan
Bibl. 44

[MOOD & EWAN]

Christian Adam Mood
  (b. 1799–d. 1858)
Charleston, S.C.
  (w. 1819–1831)
Bibl. 5

J. & P. Mood
  (c. 1834–1841)
Charleston, S.C.
John Mood
Peter Mood Jr.
*Bibl. 5, 15, 25, 44, 54, 91,
  95,*

John (I.) Mood   [I]
  (b. 1792–d. 1864)
Charleston, S.C.
  (c. 1810, c. 1834–1841)
Athens, Ga.
Peter Mood & Son
  (c. 1816–1819)
Peter Mood & Sons
  (c. 1819)
J. & P. Mood
  (c. 1834–1841)
*Bibl. 5, 17, 25, 28, 44, 54,
  89, 91, 95, 104*

Joseph Mood (c. 1806)
Charleston, S.C.
Philadelphia, Pa.
Bibl. 23, 24, 29, 44

I MOOD   J MOOD

P. Mood & Co.
  (c. 1823–1834)
Charleston, S.C.
Peter Mood Jr.
John Ewan
Bibl. 5

Peter Mood Sr.
  (b. 1766–d. 1821)
Charleston, S.C.
  (c. 1785–1821)
Peter Mood & Son
  (c. 1816–1819)
Peter Mood & Sons
  (c. 1819)

Bibl. 5, 15, 24, 25, 44, 54, 91, 95, 114

Peter Mood Jr.
 (b. 1796–d. 1879)
Charleston, S.C.
Peter Mood & Sons
 (c. 1819)
P. Mood & Co.
 (c. 1823–1834)
J. & P. Mood
 (c. 1834–1841)
Bibl. 5, 15, 54, 91, 95

P. Mood Jr

Peter Mood & Son
 (c. 1816–1819)
Charleston, S.C.
Peter Mood Sr.
John Mood
Bibl. 5, 91

P MOOD & SON

Peter Mood & Sons
 (c. 1819)
Charleston, S.C.
Peter Mood Sr.
Peter Mood Jr.
John Mood
Bibl. 5, 91

Thomas S. Mood (d. 1871)
Athens, Ga. (c. 1821)
Charleston, S.C. (1824)
Orangeburg, S.C. (c. 1849)
Sumter, Ga. (c. 1857)
Columbia, Ga. (c. 1860)
Augusta, Ga.
Bibl. 5, 17

Moollinger
(See Mollinger)

Moore & Brewer
 (c. 1824–1837)
New York, N.Y.
Jared L. Moore
Charles Brewer
Bibl. 15, 23, 25, 36, 44

MOORE & BREWER

Moore & Brown
 (c. 1832–1835)
New York, N.Y.
Jared L. Moore (?)
Francis Brown (?)
Bibl. 4, 15, 23, 28, 36, 44, 91, 114, 124, 138

Moore & Ferguson
 (c. 1801–1805)
Philadelphia, Pa.
Charles Moore
John Ferguson
Bibl. 3, 23, 24, 25, 28, 36, 39, 44, 91

MOORE & FERGUSON

Moore & Hibbard
 (c. 1820)
Location unknown
Bibl. 15, 44, 114

M & H

Moore & Hofman
 (c. 1915–1922)
Newark, N.J.
Successor to Schmitz, Moore
 & Co. (c. 1915)
Became Moore & Son
 (c. 1922–1943)
Bibl. 127

MH

**Moore & Leding,
Silversmiths**
 (c. 1882–1899)
Washington, D.C.
Became Robert Leding
 (1900–1902)
Bibl. 127

Moore & Son
 (c. 1922–1943)
Newark, N.J.
Successor to Moore &
 Hofman (c. 1915–1922)
Bibl. 157

M⊢X

Moore Bros. (1907–1940)
Attleboro, Mass.
John F. Moore
Thomas H. Moore
Charles E. Moore
Bibl. 127

M. B.

Apollos Moore
 (1842–1850)
Albany, N.Y.
Bibl. 20, 91, 124, 135

Charles Moore
 (c. 1801–1809)
Philadelphia, Pa.
Moore & Ferguson
 (c. 1801–1805)
Bibl. 3, 15, 23, 25, 36, 44, 91, 114, 122

C. MOORE

E. C. Moore (c. 1850)
New York, N.Y.
Bibl. 23, 28, 97, 122

H. Moore (c. 1850)
Philadelphia, Pa.
Bibl. 15, 44, 114

H. MOORE

Hoffard S. Moore (1875)
Rockland, Me.
Bibl. 105

Jared (John) L. Moore
 (c. 1825–1852)
New York, N.Y.
Moore & Brewer
 (c. 1824–1837)
Moore & Brown
 (c. 1832–1835) (?)
Jared L. Moore & Co.
 (c. 1837–1844)
Bibl. 4, 15, 23, 24, 25, 30, 35, 36, 44, 83, 91, 114, 124, 135, 138

J. L. MOORE MOORE
J L MOORE MOORE

Jared L. Moore & Co.
 (c. 1837–1844)
New York, N.Y.
Jared L. Moore
Charles Brewer
Francis Brown
Bibl. 15, 23, 91, 135, 138

John C. Moore J. C. M
 (c. 1832–1844)
New York, N.Y.
Eoff & Moore (c. 1835)
Bibl. 15, 23, 24, 28, 36, 44, 114, 116, 124, 138

John C. Moore & Son
  (c. 1827–1868)
New York, N.Y.
Became Tiffany & Co.
Bibl. 97, 127   J. C. M.

John L. Moore (c. 1810)
Philadelphia, Pa.
Bibl. 28, 29   J. L. MOORE

Robert Moore (b. 1736)
Baltimore, Md. (c. 1774–1778)
Bibl. 23, 28, 36, 38

Robert Moore
  (c. 1829–1840)
Philadelphia, Pa.
Bibl. 3

Sylvanus Moore (c. 1847)
Oxford, N.Y.
Bibl. 20, 124

Thomas Moore (c. 1805)
Philadelphia, Pa.
Bibl. 3, 23, 36, 44

William V. Moore & Co.
  (c. 1854 1860)
Mobile, Ala.
Bibl. 148

W. V. MOORE & CO.

MOBILE

R. L. Moorehead & Co.
  (c. 1918–1919)
Providence, R.I.
Bibl. 127

Morand, Alleoud & Co.
  (?–1820)
Augusta, Ga.
J. Morand
Marc Alleoud
J. Martiniere
Bibl. 17

J. Morand (c. 1820)
Augusta, Ga.
Morand, Alleoud & Co.
Bibl. 17

Thomas F. Moreland
  (c. 1850)
Philadelphia, Pa.
Bibl. 3, 23

Nicholas Morell (c. 1816)
Charleston, S.C.
Bibl. 5

Morgan
(See Hooker & Morgan)

Morgan (c. 1860)   MORGAN
Location unknown
Bibl. 15, 28, 44, 114

Morgan & Cook
  (c. 1806–1807)
Poughkeepsie, N.Y.
Elijah Morgan
———— Cook
Bibl. 20, 25, 124

Morgan & Gibson
  (c. 1841–1843)
Camden, N.J.
John Morgan
———— Gibson
Bibl. 3

Morgan & Kennedy
  (c. 1807)
Poughkeepsie, N.Y.
Elijah Morgan
———— Kennedy
Bibl. 20, 124

Aaron Morgan
  (c. 1842–1850)
Philadelphia, Pa.
Bibl. 3

Arthur Morgan (c. 1849)
Philadelphia, Pa.
Bibl. 3

Chauncey Morgan
  (c. 1850)
Hartford, Conn.
Bibl. 23

E. Morgan & Son
  (c. 1832–1835)
Poughkeepsie, N.Y.
Elijah Morgan (?)
Bibl. 20, 124

Elijah Morgan
  (b. 1783–d. 1857)
Poughkeepsie, N.Y.
Sadd & Morgan (c. 1806)
Morgan & Cook
  (c. 1806–1807)

Morgan & Kennedy
  (c. 1807)
E. Morgan & Son
  (c. 1832–1835) (?)
Bibl. 15, 20, 24, 25, 44, 114, 124   E. MORGAN

Jeremiah Morgan
  (c. 1743–1744)
Charleston, S.C.
Bibl. 5, 54

John Morgan (Morin)
  (c. 1808–1831)
Philadelphia, Pa.
Bibl. 3, 23, 36, 38, 44

John Morgan
  (c. 1844–1848)
Camden, N.J.
Morgan & Gibson
  (c. 1841–1843)
Bibl. 3

Lewis Morgan (c. 1847)
Hartford, Conn.
Bibl. 23

M. Morgan (c. 1876)
New York, N.Y.
Became George W. Shiebler
  & Co. (c. 1876–1915)
Bibl. 127

Thomas Morgan
  (c. 1771–1782)
Baltimore, Md.
Philadelphia, Pa.
Bibl. 3, 38

William S. Morgan
  (c. 1837–1847)
Poughkeepsie, N.Y.
Bibl. 20, 124

John Morin
(See John Morgan,
  Philadelphia)

Alexander C. Morin
  (c. 1813–1850)
Philadelphia, Pa.
Bibl. 3

Anthony Morin
  (c. 1849–1850)
Philadelphia, Pa.
Bibl. 3

Augustus Morin (c. 1835)
Philadelphia, Pa.
Bibl. 3

Pierre Morin (c. 1796)
Baltimore, Md.
Bibl. 38

Michael Mormagea
   (c. 1817)
Philadelphia, Pa.
Bibl. 3, 23, 36, 44

Angelo Morozzi
   (c. 1839–1842)
Philadelphia, Pa.
Bibl. 3

John Morrell
   (c. 1822–1823)
Baltimore, Md.
Bibl. 38

Joseph Morrell
   (c. 1840–1844)
Buffalo, N.Y.
Castle & Morrell
Bibl. 20, 124

William M. Morrell
   (c. 1828–1834)
New York, N.Y.
*Bibl. 14, 15, 25, 114, 124,
138*

W. M ORRELL

Morrie
(See Eagles & Morris)

S. S. Morrill (c. 1850)
Fulton, N.Y.
Bibl. 20, 124

Benjamin Morris
   (c. 1800–1802)
Petersburg, Va.
Bibl. 19

James Morris (b. 1754)
Maryland (c. 1775)
Bibl. 28, 38

James Morris (c. 1844)
Philadelphia, Pa.
Bibl. 3

John Morris (c. 1796)
New York, N.Y.
Bibl. 23, 28, 36, 44, 124, 138

John Morris
   (c. 1817–1842)
Philadelphia, Pa.
Bibl. 3

Sylvester Morris
   (b. 1708–d. 1783)
New York State
   (c. 1759–1783)
*Bibl. 4, 23, 24, 25, 28, 36,
   44, 114, 124, 138*

William Morris
   (c. 1832–1833)
Utica, N.Y.
Bibl. 18, 20, 124, 158

William Morris
   (c. 1837–1850)
Philadelphia, Pa.
Bibl. 3

William Morris Jr.
   (c. 1844–1850)
Philadelphia, Pa.
Bibl. 3

William C. Morris
   (c. 1850)
Penn Yan, N.Y.
Bibl. 20, 124

William Henry Morris
   (c. 1801–1805)
New York, N.Y.
Bibl. 23, 36, 44, 124

Wollaston Morris
   (b. 1753)
Maryland (c. 1774)
Bibl. 38

Morrisgreen
(See Jacob Marius Groen)

Israel Morrison
   (c. 1823–1824)
Philadelphia, Pa.
Bibl. 3, 23, 36, 44

J. A. Morrison (1895)
Bangor, Me.
Bibl. 105

Norman Morrison
   (d. 1783)
Hartford, Conn.
Bull & Morrison (c. 1780)
Bibl. 23, 110

William Morrison
   (c. 1834–1835)
New York, N.Y.
Bibl. 15, 124, 138

C. R. Morrissey (c. 1837)
Philadelphia, Pa.
Bibl. 3

Morrow & Barnard
   (c. 1805)
Philadelphia, Pa.
B. Morrow
———— Barnard
Bibl. 3

B. Morrow (c. 1806–1808)
Philadelphia, Pa.
Morrow & Barnard (c. 1805)
Bibl. 3

Obadiah Mors(e) (c. 1733)
Boston, Mass.
*Bibl. 15, 44, 70, 102, 110,
   114*

MORS

Morse & Mosely (c. 1823)
Albany, N.Y.
Bibl. 20, 124

David Morse
   (b. 1752–d. 1818)
Boston, Mass. (c. 1798)
Bibl. 4, 23, 28, 36, 44, 110

Hazen Morse
   (b. 1790–d. 1874)
Boston, Mass.
   (c. 1813–1815)
*Bibl. 4, 23, 28, 36, 44, 94,
   110*

J. H. Morse (c. 1792–1820)
Boston, Mass.
*Bibl. 23, 24, 29, 36, 44, 88,
   91, 94, 110, 114*

J H MORSE

Moses Morse
   (c. 1813–1825)

Boston, Mass.
*Bibl. 4, 15, 23, 24, 28, 29,
36, 44, 94, 110, 114*

M. Morse	Morse

Nathaniel Morse
(b. 1685–d. 1748)
Boston, Mass.
*Bibl. 2, 15, 23, 24, 25, 28,
29, 36, 44, 54, 69, 91, 94,
102, 104, 110, 114, 119,
151*

Obadiah Morse
(See Mors(e))

Stephen Morse
(b. 1743, c. 1764–1796)
Boston, Mass.
Newbury, Mass.
Portsmouth, N.H.
*Bibl. 23, 28, 29, 36, 44, 54,
110, 125*

MORSE

H. R. Morss & Co., Inc.
(c. 1930–1940)
North Attleboro, Mass.
Bibl. 127

MORSS
Trade Ⱉ Mark

Caleb Morton (1875)
Windham, Me.
Bibl. 105

George Morton
(c. 1829–1850)
Philadelphia, Pa.
Bibl. 3

David Moseley
(b. 1753–d. 1812)
Boston, Mass.
*Bibl. 15, 23, 24, 25, 28, 29,
36, 44, 69, 88, 110, 114*

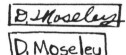

D. Moseley	DM

Joseph Moseley
(c. 1828–1838)
New York, N.Y.

Gale & Moseley
(c. 1828–1833)
*Bibl. 15, 23, 36, 44, 91, 114,
124, 135, 138*

———— **Moses** (c. 1821)
Richmond, Va.
Bibl. 19

Isaac N. Moses (c. 1781)
Derby, Conn.
Bibl. 44

Jacob Moses (d. 1785)
Savannah, Ga.
(c. 1768–1769)
Birmingham, Ga.
Baltimore, Md.
Sime & Moses
(c. 1768–1769)
Bibl. 17, 24, 25, 29, 36, 44

MOSES

Jacob Moses
(c. 1817–1822)
Baltimore, Md.
Philadelphia, Pa.
Bibl. 3, 38

M. Moses (c. 1830)
Boston, Mass.
Bibl. 36

O. H. Moses
Location unknown
Bibl. 21

S. Moses (c. 1830)
Boston, Mass.
Bibl. 23

Mosher & Davis (c. 1834)
Hamilton, N.Y.
S. Mosher
———— Davis
Bibl. 20, 124

S. Mosher (c. 1830)
Hamilton, N.Y.
Mosher & Davis (c. 1834)
Bibl. 20, 124

John Moshore (c. 1805)
New York, N.Y.
Bibl. 23, 36

Jacob Mosiman
(c. 1810–1812)
Baltimore, Md.

Bibl. 38

Barnet Moss (c. 1840)
Warrenton, Va.
Bibl. 19   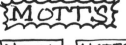

Isaac Nichols Moss
(b. 1761–d. 1840)
Derby, Conn.
Bibl. 16, 23, 28, 36, 110

George Moton
(c. 1849–1850)
Philadelphia, Pa.
Bibl. 3

Mott Bros. (c. 1840)
New York, N.Y.
Bibl. 15, 124, 138

J. & W. Mott
(See John S. & William
Mott)

James S. Mott
(c. 1812–1845)
New York, N.Y.
Bibl. 15, 24, 25, 91, 124, 138

J S MOTT
COR. PEARL & FULTON ST NY

John S. Mott (c. 1790)
New York, N.Y.
*Bibl. 23, 24, 25, 28, 29, 36,
44, 124*

J·Mott

J Mott	J.S. MOTT

John S. & William Mott
(c. 1789)
New York, N.Y.
*Bibl. 15, 23, 24, 25, 28, 29,
36, 44, 114, 124*

MOTT'S

MOTT'S	MOTTS

Jordan Mott
(b. 1768–d. 1840)
New York, N.Y.
(c. 1815–1835) | J. MOTT |
Schenectady, N.Y.
*Bibl. 15, 44, 91, 114, 124,
138*

Jordan Mott Jr. (c. 1836)
New York, N.Y.
Bibl. 15, 124

W. & J. S. Mott
(See John S. & William
Mott)

Benjamin Motteux
(c. 1725)
Charleston, S.C.
Bibl. 5

E. L. Mottley & Co.
(c. 1857)
Bowling Green, Ky.
Bibl. 54, 93

John Moulinar   I. M
(b. 1722, c. 1761)   I M
Albany, N.Y.
New York, N.Y.
*Bibl. 4, 15, 23, 24, 25, 28,
29, 30, 35, 36, 44, 78, 91,
95, 114, 124, 138*

Moulton & Bradbury
(c. 1830)
Newburyport, Mass.
Joseph Moulton IV
Theophilus Bradbury
Bibl. 23, 28, 36, 44, 110

MOULTON   B

Moulton & Davis
(c. 1824–1830)
Newburyport, Mass.
Abel Moulton
John D. (W. ?) Davis
*Bibl. 15, 23, 25, 36, 44, 110,
114*

M & D

Moulton & Lunt (c. 1870)
Newburyport, Mass.
William Moulton V
———— Lunt
Bibl. 28

Abel Moulton
(b. 1784–d. 1840)
Newburyport, Mass.
Moulton & Davis
(c. 1824–1830)
*Bibl. 15, 23, 24, 25, 28, 29,
36, 110, 114, 135*

A. MOULTON

**Ebenezer (Eben Noyes) S.
Moulton**
(b. 1768–d. 1824)
Boston, Mass.
Newburyport, Mass.
*Bibl. 24, 25, 28, 29, 44, 54,
91, 102, 110, 114, 122,
135, 149*

Edmund Moulton
(c. 1780)
Marietta, Ohio
Bibl. 34

Edward Moulton
(b. 1846–d. 1907)
Newburyport, Mass.
Bibl. 28

**Edward Sherburne
Moulton**
(b. 1778–d. 1855)
Rochester, N.H. (1801)
Saco, Me. (1815)
Bibl. 25, 44, 110, 114, 125

Enoch Moulton
(b. 1780–d. 1820)
Portland, Me. (c. 1801)
*Bibl. 15, 23, 24, 25, 28, 29,
36, 44, 91, 110, 114*

E. MOULTON

Joseph Moulton I   J. M
(b. 1694–d. 1756)
Newburyport, Mass.
Bibl. 2, 28, 29, 36, 110, 114

Joseph Moulton II
(b. 1724–d. 1795)
Newburyport, Mass.
Marietta, Ohio (?)
Bibl. 91

Joseph M. Moulton III
(b. 1744–d. 1816)
Newburyport, Mass.
*Bibl. 2, 15, 23, 24, 25, 28,
29, 36, 44, 54, 91, 94, 110,
114*

Joseph Moulton IV
(b. 1814–d. 1903)
Newburyport, Mass.
Moulton & Bradbury
*Bibl. 15, 23, 24, 25, 28, 29,
36, 44, 91, 110, 114*

J MOULTON   J M

William Moulton I
(b. 1617–d. 1664)
Hampton, N.H. (c. 1638)
Bibl. 15, 28

William Moulton II
(b. 1664–d. 1732)
Newburyport, Mass.
*Bibl. 15, 23, 24, 28, 36, 94,
110*

William Moulton III
(b. 1720–d. 1793)
Newburyport, Mass.
Marietta, Ohio (c. 1788)
*Bibl. 15, 23, 25, 28, 34, 36,
44, 91, 94, 110*

W M   W MOULTON

William Moulton IV
(b. 1772–d. 1861)
Newburyport, Mass.
*Bibl. 15, 23, 28, 29, 36, 91,
94, 110*

W MOULTON   W M

MOULTON   MOULTON

William Moulton V
(b. 1851–d. 1940)
Newburyport, Mass.
Moulton & Lunt (c. 1870)
Bibl. 28

Mount Vernon
(See Harris & Schafer)

Mt. Hood
(See Feldenheimer)

Mt. Vernon Company Silversmiths, Inc.
(c. 1903–1913)
Mount Vernon, N.Y.
Successor to Hayes &
  MacFarland (c. 1903)
Became Gorham Corp.
  (c. 1913)
Bibl. 127, 147, 152

Samuel P. Mountain
(c. 1842)
Philadelphia, Pa.
Bibl. 3

John Mountford
(c. 1818–1819)
Philadelphia, Pa.
Bibl. 3

John Hugan Moyston
(b. 1772–d. 1844)
Schenectady, N.Y. (c. 1798)
Bibl. 20, 124

Robert R. Mucklow
(c. 1970–1977)
Chicago, Ill.
Bibl. 98

Mudge & Co. (c. 1848)
New York, N.Y.
Bibl. 23

M. A. Mudge (c. 1837)
Philadelphia, Pa.
Bibl. 3

Mueck-Cary Co., Inc.
(c. 1940–1950)
New York, N.Y.
Mark is now owned by
  Towle Silversmiths
Bibl. 127

$$\langle M \rangle$$

Louis Müh (1822–1870)
New Orleans, La.
Bibl. 141

Mulen
(See Mullin)

Mulford & Wende(a)ll
(c. 1843–1850)
Albany, N.Y.
John H. Mulford
William Wendell
Bibl. 15, 20, 23, 24, 25, 28, 44, 91, 114, 124

John H. Mulford
(c. 1841–1843)
Albany, N.Y.
Boyd & Mulford
  (c. 1832–1842)
Mulford & Wendell
  (c. 1843–1850)
Bibl. 20, 23, 28, 36, 44, 91, 124

Mulholland Silver Company (1924–1934)
Chicago, Ill.
Successor to
Walter Mulholland & David
  Edward Mulholland
  (1912–1915)
Mulholland Brothers
  (1916–1919)
Mulholland Brothers, Inc.
  (1919–1924)
Bibl. 98

William Mulholland
(c. 1837–1844)
Philadelphia, Pa.
Bibl. 3

William Mulhollen
(c. 1817–1818)
Philadelphia, Pa.
Bibl. 3

Robert Mullan (c. 1764)
Baltimore, Md.
Bibl. 38

Muller
(See Metten & Muller)

Charles Muller
(19th century)
Winnsboro, S.C.
Bibl. 5

Ferdinand Muller
(c. 1844)
New York, N.Y.
Bibl. 23, 124, 138

Fred Will Muller (c. 1739)
Ebenezer, Ga.
Bibl. 17

Gustave Müller
(b. 1825; 1858–1870)
New Orleans, La.
Bibl. 141

Rudolphe Müller
(1877–c. 1930)
New Orleans, La.
Bibl. 141

H. Mulligan (c. 1840)
Philadelphia, Pa.
Bibl. 24, 25, 44, 114

William (W. J.) Mullin (Mulen)
(c. 1829–1833)
Philadelphia, Pa.
Bibl. 3

Multisilver
(See E. H. H. Smith Silver
  Co.)

Mumford
(See Barker & Mumford)

Henry (G.) (B.) Mumford
(c. 1813)
Providence, R.I.
Frost & Mumford
  (c. 1810) (?)
George C. (G.) Clark
  (c. 1813–1824)
Jabez Gorham
Bibl. 15, 23, 25, 28, 36, 110, 114

J. T. Munds
(c. 1855–1859)
Sumter, S.C.
Bibl. 5

Munger & Benedict
  (c. 1826–1828)
Auburn, N.Y.
Asa Munger
J. H. Benedict
Bibl. 20, 25, 114, 124

Munger & Dodge
  (c. 1824–1825)
Ithaca, N.Y.
Sylvester Munger (?)
Abraham Dodge Jr.
Bibl. 20, 124

Munger & Pratt (c. 1832)
Ithaca, N.Y.
Sylvester Munger (?)
Daniel Pratt
Bibl. 20, 124

A. Munger & Son
  (c. 1840)
Auburn, N.Y.
Asa Munger (?)
Bibl. 15, 20, 25, 44, 114, 124

A. MUNGER & SON

Asa Munger
  (b. 1778–d. 1851)
Herkimer, N.Y.
  (c. 1810–1818)
Auburn, N.Y.
  (c. 1818)
Munger & Benedict
  (c. 1826–1828)
A. Munger & Son
  (c. 1840) (?)
Bibl. 15, 20, 25, 44, 114, 124

A. MUNGER

Austin E. Munger
  (b. 1811–d. 1892)
Syracuse, N.Y. (c. 1847)
Bibl. 20, 124

James E. Munger
  (c. 1839–1845)
Ithaca, N.Y.
Bibl. 20, 114, 124

Sylvester Munger
Onondaga, N.Y. (c. 1822)
Elmira, N.Y. (c. 1835)
Ithaca, N.Y. (c. 1835–1845)
Munger & Dodge (?)
Munger & Pratt (?)
Bibl. 20, 124

John Munro   Munro
  (c. 1785–1809)
Charleston, S.C.
Bibl. 5, 15, 114

Munroe & Holman
  (c. 1826–1829)
Baltimore, Md.
Nathaniel Munroe
D. Holman
Bibl. 38

C. A. Munroe
Location unknown
Bibl. 28, 110

D. Munroe
Location unknown
Bibl. 28

D. MUNROE

James Munroe
  (b. 1784–d. 1879)
Barnstable, Mass.
*Bibl. 15, 23, 24, 25, 28, 29,
  36, 44, 110, 114*

J. MUNROE

J MONROE

JAMES MONROE

J. MUNROE

John Munroe
(See James Munroe; he is
  James Munroe)

Nathaniel Munroe
  (b. 1777–d. 1861)
Norfolk, Va. (c. 1805)
Massachusetts (before 1815)
Baltimore, Md.
  (c. 1815–1840)
Munroe & Holman
  (c. 1826–1829)
*Bibl. 19, 24, 25, 29, 38, 44,
  95, 114*

N MUNROE

G. C. Munsell
  (c. 1835–c. 1836)
Northampton, Mass.
Bibl. 15, 44, 84, 114

G.C. MUNSELL COIN PURE

Allen Munson (1861)
Houlton, Me.
Bibl. 105

Amos Munson
  (b. 1753–d. 1785)
New Haven, Conn.
*Bibl. 16, 23, 28, 36, 44, 91,
  110, 143*

Cornelius Munson
  (b. 1742–d. 1776)
Wallingford, Conn.
*Bibl. 16, 23, 28, 36, 44, 92,
  110*

A. H. Munyan (c. 1848)
Northampton, Mass.
Bibl. 84

Murdoch
(See Murdock)

Murdock & Andrews
  (c. 1822–1826,
   c. 1838–1849)
Utica, N.Y.
James Murdock
Elon Andrews
Selden Collins Jr.
*Bibl. 18, 20, 25, 44, 91, 124,
  135, 158*

M & A

MURDOCK & ANDREWS

Murdock & Collins
  (c. 1849–1850)
Utica, N.Y.
James Murdock
Selden Collins Jr.
Bibl. 18, 20, 91, 124

David A. Murdock
  (c. 1812)
New Bern, N.C.
Bibl. 21

H. & S. Murdock & Co.
   (c. 1830)
Philadelphia, Pa. (?)
Bibl. 89

H & S MURDOCK

James Murdock
   (b. 1792–d. 1850)
Utica, N.Y.
Murdock & Andrews
   (c. 1822–1826,
   c. 1838–1849)
James Murdock & Co.
   (c. 1826–1838)
Murdock & Collins
   (c. 1849–1850)
Bibl. 15, 18, 20, 91, 114,
124, 158

James Murdock & Co.
   (c. 1826–1838)
Utica, N.Y.
James Murdock
Elon Andrews
Selden Collins Jr.
Julius A. Spencer
Bibl. 15, 18, 20, 44, 91, 114,
124, 135, 158

JAMES MURDOCK & CO

James Murdock of
   Philadelphia
(See John Murdock)

John Murdock
   (b. 1748–d. 1786)
Philadelphia, Pa.
   (c. 1779–1785)
Woodbury, N.J.
   (c. 1785–1786)
Bibl. 3, 15, 23, 24, 25, 29,
36, 39, 44, 46, 54, 81, 114

IM

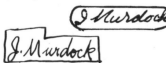

Murphy & Pollard
   (c. 1818–1820)
Norfolk, Va.
John Murphy (?)
Lewis R. Pollard
Bibl. 19

James Murphy
Boston, Mass. (c. 1816)
Philadelphia, Pa.
   (c. 1828–1846)
Bibl. 3, 15, 23, 24, 25, 29,
36, 44, 91, 110, 114

John Murphy
   (c. 1798–1810)
Norfolk, Va.
Murphy & Pollard (?)
Bibl. 19

John B. Murphy
Norfolk, Va. (c. 1830–1833)
Augusta, Ga. (c. 1834–1845)
Bibl. 17, 19

J. B. Murphy

Robert (R. E.) Murphy
   (c. 1849–1850)
Philadelphia, Pa.
Bibl. 3, 91

Murray, Draper, Fairman
   & Co. (c. 1830)
Philadelphia, Pa.
Jacob Perkins
Gideon Fairman (?)
Bibl. 28

Alexander Murray
   (c. 1814–1816)
Philadelphia, Pa.
Bibl. 3

Elijah Murray (c. 1829)
Sandy Hill, N.Y.
Bibl. 20, 124

John Murray (c. 1776)
New York, N.Y.
Bibl. 28, 124

William Murray (c. 1850)
Louisville, Ky.
Bibl. 32, 93

John N. Murrell (c. 1816)
Charleston, S.C.
Bibl. 5

Robert Murrey (c. 1805)
Baltimore, Md.
Bibl. 38

Perry Murtel (c. 1839)
Philadelphia, Pa.
Bibl. 3

Musgrave & James
   (c. 1797–1811)
Philadelphia, Pa.
(Could be incorrect listing
   for James Musgrave.)
Bibl. 28, 89

Musgrave.

Musgrave & Kelly
   (c. 1812)
Buffalo, N.Y.
Bibl. 20, 124

James Musgrave
   (c. 1793–1813)
Philadelphia, Pa.
Parry & Musgrave
   (c. 1793–1796)
Bibl. 3, 4, 23, 24, 25, 29, 36,
39, 44, 81, 91, 114

Musgrave   Musgrave

S. Musgrove (b. 1800)
Cincinnati, Ohio
   (1820–1840)   S. MUSGROVE
Bibl. 72, 90, 91, 93

Samuel Musgrove
   (c. 1853–1855)
Nashville, Tenn.
Bibl. 54

Myer & McClanan
   (c. 1836–1837)
Buffalo, N.Y.
Henry B. Myer
James McClanan
Bibl. 20, 91, 124

Gottlieb Myer (Meyer)
Norfolk, Va.
Bibl. 28

H. B. Myer (c. 1810)
New York, N.Y.
Bibl. 23, 24, 36, 91

H. B. Myer & Co.
(c. 1832–1835)
Newburgh, N.Y.
Henry B. Myer
Bibl. 20, 91, 124

H B MYER

Henry B. Myer
Newburgh, N.Y.
(c. 1818–1835)
Buffalo, N.Y. (c. 1836–1848)
H. B. Myer & Co.
(c. 1832–1835)
Myer & McClanan
(c. 1836–1837)
*Bibl. 15, 20, 25, 29, 44, 91,
114, 124*

John A. Myer (c. 1832)
Charleston, S.C.
Bibl. 5

**Myers and Holsted
(Halsteaad)**
New York, N.Y.
Myer Myers
(b. 1723–d. 1795)
Benjamin Holsted
*Bibl. 2, 15, 23, 24, 25, 29,
30, 35, 36, 40, 44, 54, 61,
91, 124, 135, 138*

Myers & Jacob (c. 1839)
Philadelphia, Pa.
Albert G. Myers
Celestin Jacob (?)
Bibl. 3, 23, 36, 44

Albert G. Myers
Philadelphia, Pa. (c. 1837)
Camden, N.J. (c. 1847)
Myers & Jacob
Bibl. 3, 23, 36, 44

Christalar Myers (c. 1844)
Philadelphia, Pa.
Bibl. 3

Jacob Myers
(See Jacob Mayer)

John Myers (b. 1757)
Philadelphia, Pa.
(c. 1785–1804)
*Bibl. 3, 4, 15, 23, 24, 25, 28,
29, 36, 39, 44, 54, 81, 91,
102, 114*

Leon Myers (1849–1859)
New Orleans, La.
Bibl. 141

Merrick Myers (1874)
Newport, R.I.
Bibl. 108

Myer Myers
(b. 1723–d. 1795)
Norwalk, Conn.
Stamford, Conn.
Underhill, Vt.
New York, N.Y. (c. 1770)
Hays & Myers (c. 1770)
Myers & Holsted
*Bibl. 2, 15, 23, 24, 25, 29,
30, 35, 36, 40, 44, 54, 61,
91, 92, 95, 102, 104, 110,
114, 116, 118, 119, 122,
124, 135, 138, 142, 151*

Paulette Myers
(c. 1968–1980)
St. Louis, Mo.
Bibl. 155

Comfort Starr Mygatt
(b. 1763–d. 1823)
Danbury, Conn. (c. 1804)
Canfield, Ohio (c. 1807)
*Bibl. 16, 28, 36, 44, 92, 94,
110*

David Mygatt
(b. 1777–d. 1822)
Danbury, Conn.

South East, N.Y.
*Bibl. 16, 23, 24, 25, 28, 29,
36, 44, 61, 92, 94, 110,
114*

Eli Mygatt
(b. 1742–d. 1807)
Danbury, Conn.
Daniel Noble Carrington
(c. 1793)
Najah Taylor (c. 1793)
Bibl. 16, 23, 28, 36, 44, 110

Noadiah Mygatt
New Milford, Conn.
Isaac Beach (c. 1788–1794)
Bibl. 89

J. P. Mylius (c. 1838)
St. Louis, Mo.
Bibl. 54, 155

John P. Mylius
(c. 1835–1836)
Harpers Ferry, Va.
Bibl. 19

Myot (See Miot)

Myre
(See Jacob Mayer)

**Myrick, Roller &
Holbrook**
(c. 1890–1904)
Philadelphia, Pa.
Bibl. 114, 127, 157

Joseph Myring
(c. 1811–1825)
Philadelphia, Pa.
Bibl. 3

———— **Mysendhender**
(c. 1813)
Philadelphia, Pa.
Bibl. 23, 36, 44

Jacob Mytinger
Newtown, Va. (c. 1827)
Warrenton, Va.
(c. 1848–1860)
Bibl. 19

J. MYTINGER

N

N
(See Napier Company,
  Nevius Company, E.
  Newton & Co., William
  Nost Co., Inc.)

N & D O
(See N & D Onderdonk)

N & H
(See Nussbaum & Hunold)

N. & Pratt
Location unknown
Bibl. 15

N & PRATT

N & S
(See Nichols & Salisbury)

N A
(See Nathaniel Austin)

N B
(See Nathaniel Bartlett,
  Nicholas Burdock,
  Nathaniel Burr)

N. B. Co.
(See N. Barstow & Co.)

N C
(See Nathaniel Coleman)

N H
(See Nathaniel Helme,
  Nicholas Hutchins)

N H & Co.
(See N. Harding & Co.)

N L
(See Nathaniel Leach)

N N
(See Nehemiah Norcross)

N R
(see Nicholas Roosevelt)

N S
(See Nathaniel Shipman)

N. S. C.
(See Newburyport Silver
  Co.)

N S C O
(See Newburyport Silver
  Co.)

N V
(See Nicholas Van
  Rensselaer, Nathaniel
  Vernon)

Nagel
(See also Nagle)

William Nagel (c. 1865)
Paducah, Ky.
Bibl. 54, 93

D. Nagin (Mfg. Corp.)
  (1957–present)
East Rutherford, N.J.
Bibl. 127

George P. Nagle
  (c. 1823–1850)
Philadelphia, Pa.
Bibl. 3

R. Nagle (c. 1828)
Philadelphia, Pa.
Bibl. 3

R. C. Nagle (c. 1828–1833)
Philadelphia, Pa.
Bibl. 3

John Naglee (Nagles)
  (d. 1780)
Philadelphia, Pa.
  (c. 1748–1755)
Bibl. 3, 23, 28, 36, 44

Martin Nangle (c. 1842)
Philadelphia, Pa.
Bibl. 3, 23

William Nangle
  (c. 1833–1837)
Philadelphia, Pa.
Bibl. 3

Napier Company
  (1922–present)
Meriden, Conn.   **DU BARRY**
Successor to Carpenter &
  Bliss (1875–1882)
Carpenter & Bliss, Inc.
  (1882–1883)
E. A. Bliss Co. (1883–1890)
E. A. Bliss, Inc. (1891–1920)
Napier-Bliss Co.
  (1920–1922)
Bibl. 127

NACO   **TRIANON**

NAPIER   **SUREFIRE**

PALM BEACH

Evolution   BLISS

John F. Nardier
  (c. 1819–1822)
Philadelphia, Pa.
Bibl. 3

F. J. Nardin
  (c. 1823–1824)
Philadelphia, Pa.
Bibl. 3

Coleman Nash (1925)
Cincinnati, Ohio
Bibl. 34, 90, 152

Nassau Lighter Co.
  (c. 1915–1922)
New York, N.Y.
Bibl. 127, 157

National Silver Company
  (1890–present)
New York, N.Y.
Samuel E. Bernstein   S.E.B.
Bibl. 127, 135, 147

National **STERLING**

Martin Naugh (c. 1833)
New York, N.Y.
Bibl. 15, 124

Joseph Neagt (c. 1816)
Philadelphia, Pa.
Bibl. 3

Daniel Neall
　(b. 1784–d. 1846) .
Milford, Del.
Bibl. 15, 25, 30, 44, 91, 114

Needels
(See Needles)

Joseph Needham
Richmond, Va. (c. 1799)
Lynchburg, Va. (c. 1814)
Bibl. 19, 54

**William Needles
　(Needels)**
Easton, Md. (c. 1798–1818)
Bowdle & Needles (c. 1798)
Bibl. 25, 29, 38, 44, 114

W. NEEDELS

Samuel Neely (c. 1842)
Philadelphia, Pa.
Bibl. 3

Paul Negrin
Charlottesville, Va.
　(c. 1820–1823)
Nashville, Tenn.
　(c. 1829–1844)
Bibl. 19, 54, 159

Neiderer & Moore
　(c. 1855)
Baltimore, Md.
Bibl. 127

Daniel Neill
　(c. 1823–1833)
Philadelphia, Pa.
Bibl. 3

T. E. Neill Co.　　TENCO
Brooklyn, N.Y.
Bibl. 127

George Neilson
　(d. 1736)
Annapolis, Md.
　(c. 1716–1736)
Bibl. 3, 38

Neise
(See Kneass)

George Neiser
　(c. 1823–1824)
Philadelphia, Pa.
Bibl. 3

Augustine Neisser
　(c. 1764–1772, d. 1780)
Philadelphia, Pa.
Bibl. 3

George B. Neisser
　(c. 1829–1839)
Philadelphia, Pa.
Bibl. 3

Joseph Neitt (c. 1813)
Philadelphia, Pa.
Bibl. 3

Ambrose Nelson
Charleston, S.C. (c. 1795)
Savannah, Ga.
　(c. 1795–1801)
Bibl. 5, 17

John Nelson
　(b. 1735–d. 1789)
Portsmouth, N.H. (c. 1755)
*Bibl. 25, 44, 54, 110, 114,
　125*

R. & J Nelson (c. 1850)
Dunkirk, N.Y.
Bibl. 20, 124

Richard W. Nelson
　(c. 1829–1837)
Philadelphia, Pa.
Bibl. 3

Neuill
(See Nevill)

Jan Neuss (Nys) (Nice)
　(d. 1719)
Philadelphia, Pa. (c. 1698)
Bibl. 3, 23, 44

William H. Nevers (1875)
Cornish, Me.
Bibl. 105

Richard Nevill (Neuill)
Boston, Mass. (c. 1674)
Bibl. 4, 23, 28, 36, 44, 110

Rufus Nevins
New York, N.Y.
Hyde & Nevins
　(c. 1798–1819)
*Bibl. 15, 23, 24, 25, 28, 29,
　36, 44*

Nevius Company
　(c. 1897–1915)
New York, N.Y.
Bibl. 127

**New England
　Silversmiths** (c. 1950)
New York, N.Y.
Bibl. 127

New Orleans Silversmiths
　(c. 1938–1966)
New Orleans, La.
Bibl. 127

Edwin C. Newberry
Brooklyn, N.Y. (c. 1828)
Bibl. 16, 23, 28, 44, 91, 124

J. & R. Newberry
　(c. 1816)
Philadelphia, Pa.
Bibl. 3, 91

James Newberry (c. 1748)
Annapolis, Md.
Bibl. 38

James W. Newberry
　(c. 1819–1850)
Philadelphia, Pa.
Bibl. 3, 91

Newburyport Silver Co.
　(1904–1914)
Keene, N.H.
Bibl. 127, 157

N. S. C.　　　NSCO

Newcomb
(See Palmer & Newcomb)

H. K. Newcomb
　(c. 1821–1850)
Watertown, N.Y.
Bibl. 20, 25, 44, 114, 124

Henry Newcomb (d. 1843)
Cooperstown, N.Y.
　(c. 1842–1843)
Bibl. 20, 124

J. N. Newell (c. 1834)
Petersburg, Va.
Bibl. 19

James J. Newell (c. 1834)
Utica, N.Y.
Bibl. 18, 20, 124, 158

Norman Newell (c. 1844)
Rochester, N.Y.
Bibl. 20, 124

Dudley Newhall (c. 1730)
Salem, Mass.
Bibl. 23, 28, 36, 44, 110

William F. Newhall
  (c. 1872–1957)
Lynn, Mass.
Bibl. 127, 157

**Joseph Newkirke
(Niewkerk) (Van Nieu
Kirke) (Van Niewkirke)**
New York, N.Y. (c. 1716)
*Bibl. 15, 23, 25, 28, 29, 35,
  36, 44, 54, 95, 102, 114,
  116, 124, 138, 151*

Newland & Jones
  (c. 1825–1827)
Albany, N.Y.
Luke F. Newland
—— Jones
Bibl. 20, 124

Luke F. Newland
  (c. 1824–1847)
Albany, N.Y.
Newland & Jones
  (c. 1825–1827)
Bibl. 20, 124

Edward G. Newlin
  (c. 1848)
Philadelphia, Pa.
Warner & Newlin
  (c. 1848–1850)
Bibl. 3

John Newman
  (c. 1833–1837)
Philadelphia, Pa.
Bibl. 3

John A. Newman
  (c. 1833–1850)
Philadelphia, Pa.
Witham & Newman
  (c. 1837–1850)
Bibl. 3

Thomas Newman
  (c. 1858–1877)
Crawfordsville, Ind.
Bibl. 133   T. NEWMAN

**Timothy Harrington
Newman**
  (c. 1778–1812)
Groton, Mass.
Lancaster, Pa.
New York, N.Y.
*Bibl. 15, 24, 25, 28, 29, 36,
  44, 91, 110*

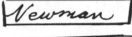

William Newth
Little Falls, N.Y.
  (c. 1832–1834)
Schenectady, N.Y.
  (c. 1837–1842)
Utica, N.Y. (c. 1842–1843)
Bibl. 18, 20, 124, 158

Newton & Reed (c. 1850)
Location unknown
Bibl. 15, 44, 114

NEWTON & REED

E. Newton & Co.   sterling N
  (c. 1896–1915)
New York, N.Y.
Bibl. 114, 127, 157

Neys
(See Johannis Nys)

Nice
(See Jan Neuss)
(See Johannis Nys)

Nicherson
(See Nickerson)

Casper Nicholas (c. 1837)
Philadelphia, Pa.
Bibl. 3

Michael Nicholas
  (c. 1793)
Philadelphia, Pa.
Bibl. 3

Nichols
(See Graves & Nichols)

—— **Nichols** (c. 1840)
Albany, N.Y. (?)
Bibl. 28   NICHOLS

Nichols and Perkins
  (c. 1831)
Charleston, N.C.
David Nichols
Leonard Perkins
Bibl. 89

Nichols and Salisbury
  (c. 1844–1846)
Charleston, S.C.
Bibl. 5, 44, 54

N & S   Nichols & Salisbury

Basset(t) Nichols (c. 1815)
Providence, R.I.
*Bibl. 15, 23, 24, 25, 28, 29,
  36, 39, 44, 54, 114*

NICHOLS

D. B. Nichols & Co.
  (c. 1820–1830)
Savannah, Ga.
David B. Nichols
John P. Smith
Bibl. 17

David B. Nichols
  (b. 1791–d. 1860)
Savannah, Ga. (c. 1815)
D. B. Nichols & Co.
  (c. 1820–1830)
Nichols and Perkins
Bibl. 17

H. Nichols (c. 1850)
Location unknown
Bibl. 15, 44, 114, 125

H. NICHOLS

H. M. Nichols (Nickols)
 (c. 1840)
Concord, N.H.
Bibl. 15, 24, 72, 91, 114, 125

H. M. NICHOLS

James Nichols (b. 1750)
Charleston, S.C. (c. 1774)
Bibl. 5

Nathaniel B. Nichols
 (d. 1831)
Petersburg, Va.
 (c. 1817–c. 1831)
Bibl. 19, 91

N. B. Nichols

Susanna E. Nichols
Petersburg, Va.
C. Lumsden & Co. (c. 1834)
Bibl. 19

Wilham Nichols
 (c. 1819–1832)
Cooperstown, N.Y.
Bibl. 20, 124

William S. Nichols
 (1808–1860)
Newport, R.I.
Bibl. 108

William Stoddard Nichols
 (b. 1785–d. 1871)
Newport, R.I.
 (1808–1860)   NICHOLS
*Bibl. 6, 23, 24, 25, 28, 29,
 36, 39, 44, 54, 91, 108,
 110, 114*

W S N   W. S. NICHOLS

Casper Nickels
 (c. 1823–1824)
Philadelphia, Pa.
Bibl. 3

**Baty (Batey) Nickerson
 (Nicherson)**
Harwich, Mass. (c. 1825)
Bibl. 23, 28, 36, 110

Nickols
(See H. M. Nichols)

Julian Nicolet
 (c. 1819–1831)
Baltimore, Md.
Bibl. 38

Julian Nicolet
 (c. 1842–1848)
St. Louis, Mo.
Bibl. 54, 155

———— **Nicolette** (c. 1793)
Philadelphia, Pa.
Bibl. 3

Joseph Marce Nicollett
 (c. 1797)
Philadelphia, Pa.
Bibl. 3

Joseph W. Nicollett
 (c. 1798)
Philadelphia, Pa.
Bibl. 3

Mary Nicollett (c. 1799)
Philadelphia, Pa.
Bibl. 3

Henry Niel (c. 1811)
Edenton, N.C.
Bibl. 21

Niewkerk
(See Newkirke)

Joseph Nihet (Nitch)
 (c. 1817–1819)
Philadelphia, Pa.
Bibl. 3

James Ninde
 (c. 1799–1835)
Baltimore, Md.
Bibl. 38

Nitch
(See Nihet)

Richard Nixon
 (c. 1820–1835)
Philadelphia, Pa.
*Bibl. 3, 15, 23, 25, 36, 44,
 114*

R. NIXON

Thomas J. Nixon
 (c. 1835–1858)
Salem, Ind.

Charlestown, Ind.
Bibl. 133   T.J. NIXON

George Noble
 (c. 1846–1850)
Philadelphia, Pa.
Bibl. 3

Joseph Noble
 (b. 1793–d. 1865)
Portland, Me. (c. 1823)
Wyer & Noble
Bibl. 23, 36, 44, 105, 110

Alpheus (Alpherrs) Noe
 (c. 1850)
Philadelphia, Pa.
Bibl. 3, 23

Beverly Noel
 (c. 1838–1839)
Louisville, Ky.
Bibl. 32, 54, 93

Washington Noel (c. 1836)
Louisville, Ky.
Bibl. 32, 93

William Noggle (c. 1822)
Baltimore, Md.
Bibl. 38

Gifford Beare Noland
 (c. 1970–1980)
St. Louis, Mo.
Bibl. 155

Norbert Mfg. Co. (c. 1950)
New York, N.Y.
Bibl. 127

Nehemiah Norcross
 (c. 1765–1804)
Boston, Mass.
*Bibl. 4, 23, 24, 25, 28, 29,
 36, 44, 72, 110, 114*

N·N   N N

Charles Nordmeyer
 (c. 1845–1850)
Richmond, Va.
Bibl. 19

Chas Nordmeyer

Norman & Bedwell
(c. 1779)
Philadelphia, Pa.
John Norman
——— Bedwell
Bibl. 3

Norman & Ward (c. 1774)
Philadelphia, Pa.
John Norman
——— Ward
Bibl. 3

James S. Norman
(c. 1840)
Lincolnton, N.C.
Bibl. 21

John Norman
(b. 1748?–d. 1817)
Philadelphia, Pa. (c. 1780)
Boston, Mass.
Norman & Ward (c. 1774)
Norman & Bedwell (c. 1779)
Bibl. 3, 28, 110, 119

George Norris (b. 1752)
Philadelphia, Pa. (c. 1775)
Bibl. 3, 23, 28, 36, 44

Patrick Norris
(c. 1844–1845)
Philadelphia, Pa.
Bibl. 3

North & Co.
(See W. B. North & Co.)

Linus North (c. 1830)
Palmyra, N.Y.
Bibl. 20, 124

Owen North
(c. 1827–1829)
New York, N.Y.
Bibl. 15, 124

William B. North
(b. 1787–d. 1838)
New Haven, Conn. (c. 1810)
New York, N.Y.
(c. 1818–1826)
New Britain, Conn.
(c. 1827–1831)
William B. North & Co.
(c. 1822–1826)
Mather & North
(c. 1827–1829)

*Bibl. 15, 23, 24, 25, 28, 29,
36, 44, 91, 92, 110, 114,
124, 138, 143*

W B N

**W(illiam). B. North & Co.
(North & Co.)**
(c. 1822–1826)
New York, N.Y.
*Bibl. 15, 24, 25, 28, 35, 44,
83, 91, 114, 124, 138, 143*

W B NORTH & CO

David I. Northee | D. N. |
(Northey)
(b. 1709–d. 1778)
Salem, Mass (c. 1748)
*Bibl. 15, 24, 25, 28, 29, 36,
44, 55, 72, 94, 102, 110,
114*

D. NORTHEE		D I NORTHEE

Abijah Northey (Northee)
(b. 1741?–d. 1817)
Salem, Mass. (c. 1775)
Bibl. 28, 29, 36, 44, 91, 110

A N

Elijah Northey
(c. 1844–1850)
Philadelphia, Pa.
Bibl. 3

Norton & Hotchkiss
(See also Hotchkiss &
Norton)
(c. 1849–1850)
Syracuse, N.Y.
Benjamin R. Norton
David Hotchkiss
Bibl. 20, 114

**Norton & Pitkin (Pitkin
& Norton)**
(c. 1820–1825)
Hartford, Conn.
C. C. Norton
Walter M. Pitkin
*Bibl. 23, 24, 25, 29, 36, 44,
92, 110, 114*

C C NORTON & PITKIN

W PITKIN   C C NORTON

Norton & Seymour
(c. 1850)
Syracuse, N.Y.
Benjamin R. Norton
Joseph Seymour
*Bibl. 15, 20, 44, 89, 114,
124, 135*

NORTON & SEYMOUR

Norton, Seymour & Co.
(c. 1850)
Syracuse, N.Y.
Benjamin R. Norton
Joseph Seymour
Bibl. 15, 20, 44, 91, 124, 130

Andrew Norton
(b. 1765–d. 1838)
Goshen, Conn.
*Bibl. 16, 23, 25, 28, 36, 44,
92, 110, 114*

B. R. Norton & Co.
(c. 1844–1849)
Syracuse, N.Y.
Benjamin R. Norton
Bibl. 20, 44, 124, 135

Benjamin Norton
(c. 1810–1813)
Boston, Mass.
*Bibl. 4, 23, 28, 36, 44, 110,
114*

Benjamin R. Norton
Palmyra, N.Y.
(c. 1841)
Syracuse, N.Y.
(c. 1845–1850)
Hotchkiss & Norton
(c. 1841–1842)
B. R. Norton & Co.
(c. 1844–1849)
Norton & Hotchkiss
(c. 1849–1850)
Norton & Seymour (c. 1850)
Norton, Seymour & Co.
(c. 1850)
*Bibl. 15, 20, 25, 44, 91, 114,
124*

B R NORTON

C. C. Norton | C C NORTON |
Hartford, Conn.
(c. 1820–1825)
Norton & Pitkin
*Bibl. 23, 24, 25, 28, 29, 36,
44, 91, 110, 114*

Henry D. Norton
(1860–1875)
Norridgewock, Me.
Bibl. 105

John F. Norton
(c. 1820–1822)
Philadelphia, Pa.
Bibl. 3

Jonathan Norton (c. 1783)
Savannah, Ga.
Papot & Norton
(c. 1790)
Bibl. 17

Joseph Norton
(1860–1875)
Baldwin, Me.
Bibl. 105

Samuel Norton (c. 1790)
Hingham, Mass.
Bibl. 23, 28, 36, 44, 110

Thomas Norton
(b. 1773–d. 1834)
Farmington, Conn.
(c. 1827–1834)
Norrisville, N.Y. (c. 1827)
Albion, N.Y.
Bibl. 16, 20, 23, 24, 25, 28,
29, 36, 44, 91, 92, 110,
124

Thomas Norton
(c. 1786–1811)
Philadelphia, Pa.
Waage & Norton (c. 1798)
Bibl. 3

Richard Norwood
(c. 1774)
New York, N.Y.
Bibl. 23, 36, 44, 124

William Nost Co., Inc.
(c. 1915–1922)
New York, N.Y.
Bibl. 127, 157

Palick Novick (1909–1957)
Chicago, Ill.
Bibl. 98, 144

Nowlan & Co.
(c. 1866–1908)
Richmond, Va.
Thomas Nowlan
Bibl. 19

NOWLAN & CO

Thomas Nowlan
Petersburg, Va.
(c. 1848–1865)
Richmond, Va.
(c. 1866–1908)
Nowlan & Co.
(c. 1866–1908)
Bibl. 19

Thomas Nowland
(c. 1806–1808)
Philadelphia, Pa.
Bibl. 3

Martin Noxon   NOXON
(c. 1780–1814)
Edenton, N.C.
(c. 1800)
Oswego, N.Y.
Bibl. 21, 25, 28, 29, 44, 114

John Noyes
(b. 1674–d. 1749)
Boston, Mass.
Bibl. 2, 15, 23, 25, 28, 29,
36, 44, 54, 66, 69, 72, 94,
102, 110, 114, 116, 118,
119

Joseph Noyes (d. 1719)
Philadelphia, Pa.
Bibl. 24

N & T. F. Noyes
Norwich, Conn. (?)
Bibl. 36

Samuel Noyes
(b. 1747–d. 1781)
Norwich, Conn.
Bibl. 16, 23, 28, 36, 44, 110

Nussbaum & Hunold
(c. 1920)
Providence, R.I.   **NUSSHOLD**
Walter Hunold
N & H

B. Nussbaum
J. Nussbaum
Bibl. 127, 157

Nusshold
(See Nussbaum & Hunold)

Frederick Nusz (c. 1819)
Fredericktown, Md.
Bibl. 25, 29, 38, 44

F NUSZ

John C. Nutman
(Nuttman) (c. 1818)
Lexington, Ky.
January & Nutman
Bibl. 32, 54, 90, 93

Aaron Nutting
(1860–1875)
Lisbon, Me.
Bibl. 105

Joseph Nuttall (b. 1738)
Maryland (c. 1774)
Bibl. 23, 28, 36, 38, 44

Stuart Nye Silver Shop
(c. 1933–present)
Asheville, N.C.
Uses trade name Stuart Nye
Handwrought Jewelry
Bibl. 89, 146

Jan Nys
(See Jan Neuss)

Johan Nys
(See John Denise)

Johannis Nys (Neys)
(Nice) (Dennis) (De
Noys)
(b. 1671–d. 1734)
Philadelphia, Pa.
(c. 1700–1723)
Bibl. 3, 15, 24, 25, 30, 39,
44, 81, 95, 114, 116, 119

O

O & S
(See Oakes & Spencer)

O. & W.
(See Oviatt & Warner)

O. N. C.
(See The Old Newbury
Crafters)

O P
(See Otto Paul de Parisien)

O P O P
(See Otto Paul de Parisien &
Son)

O R
(See Otto Reichardt Co.)

O Y B
(See Hibbard, Spencer,
Bartlett & Co.)

Oakes & Spencer
(c. 1811–1820)
Hartford, Conn.
Frederick Oakes
James Spencer
*Bibl. 15, 16, 23, 24, 25, 28,
29, 36, 44, 91, 92, 110,
114*

| O & S |

Edward Everett Oakes
(c. 1940)
Boston, Mass.
Detroit, Mich.
Bibl. 89, 117, 120

Frederick Oakes
(b. 1782–d. 1855)
Hartford, Conn.
(c. 1804–1825)
Oakes & Spencer
David Greenleaf Jr.
*Bibl. 15, 16, 23, 24, 25, 28,
29, 36, 44, 91, 92, 110,
114*

H. Oakes (c. 1850)
Hartford, Ct.
Bibl. 15, 44, 114 | H Oakes |

L. O. Oakes (1875)
Carland, Me.
Bibl. 105

John Oathret (c. 1843)
Philadelphia, Pa.
Bibl. 3

James O'Brien (c. 1850)
Philadelphia, Pa.
Bibl. 3

John O'Brien
(c. 1844–1849)
Philadelphia, Pa.
Bibl. 3

M. Isabella O'Brien
(d. 1808)
Charleston, S.C.
(c. 1802–1808)
Bibl. 5

Patrick O'Brien
(c. 1848–1850)
Philadelphia, Pa.
Bibl. 3

Joseph Obrihim (c. 1784)
Annapolis, Md.
Bibl. 36

Narcis O'Clair (c. 1819)
Albany, N.Y.
Bibl. 20, 124

Perry O'Daniel
(c. 1837–1850)
Philadelphia, Pa.
Bibl. 3, 91

Lawrence Odell
(c. 1827–1835)
New York, N.Y.
Bibl. 15, 23, 36, 44, 124, 138

Charles E. Oertelt
(O'Ertell)
Philadelphia, Pa.
(c. 1830–1850)
Bibl. 3, 23, 36, 44

Charles G. Oertelt
(c. 1847–1849)

Philadelphia, Pa.
Bibl. 3, 44

E. C. Oertelt (c. 1833)
Philadelphia, Pa.
Bibl. 3, 44

Oertle
(See Oretle)

Travis Ogden
(c. 1976–1980)
St. Louis, Mo.
Bibl. 155

John Ogier
(b. 1761–d. 1814)
New York, N.Y. (c. 1791)
Baltimore, Md.
(c. 1796–1799)
Norfolk, Va. (c. 1799–1806)
Savannah, Ga.
(c. 1808–1814)
*Bibl. 17, 19, 23, 28, 38, 44,
124, 138*

Gabriel Ogilvie
(c. 1791–1802)
New York, N.Y.
Bibl. 23, 36, 138

John Ogilvie
(c. 1732–1764)
New York, N.Y.
Bibl. 25, 44, 114, 138

William Ogle
(c. 1828–1829)
Philadelphia, Pa.
Bibl. 3

Charles O'Hara
(c. 1799–1800)
Philadelphia, Pa.
Bibl. 3

John O'Hara
(c. 1844–1849)
Philadelphia, Pa.
Bibl. 3

W. A. O'Hara, Jr. (c. 1856)
Connersville, Ind.
Bibl. 133   W.A. O'HARA, JR.

Old Constitution
(See J. H. Hutchinson &
Co.)

Old New England Craftsmen, Inc.
(c. 1931)
Newburyport, Mass.
Bibl. 127

PILLSBURY   **PORTSMOUTH**

The Old Newbury Crafters (1915–present)
Amesbury, Mass.
Became a subsidiary of
  Michele Silverware and
  Jewelry Company
Bibl. 127, 128, 147

 O. N. C. Handwrought

Franklin Olds (c. 1842)
Providence, R.I.
Bibl. 23

D. F. Olendorf
(c. 1849–1850)
Cooperstown, N.Y.
Bibl. 20, 124

Oliphant & Henderson
(c. 1767)
Charleston, S.C.
James Oliphant
Logan Henderson
Bibl. 5

James Oliphant
(c. 1767–1777)
Charleston, S.C.
Oliphant & Henderson
(c. 1767)
Bibl. 5

Oliver & Graham
(c. 1823–1824)
Philadelphia, Pa.
Bibl. 3

Oliver Mfg. Co. (c. 1950)
Los Angeles, Calif.
Bibl. 127

Andrew Oliver
(b. 1724–d. 1776)
Boston, Mass. (c. 1740)
*Bibl. 15, 25, 28, 29, 36, 44,
  91, 94, 110, 114*

| A. OLIVER | A O |

Daniel Oliver (c. 1805)
Philadelphia, Pa.
*Bibl. 23, 24, 25, 29, 36, 44,
  114*

| D. OLIVER |

Frederick Oliver
(c. 1840–1842)
Buffalo, N.Y.
Bibl. 20, 124

Griffith Oliver (c. 1785)
Philadelphia, Pa.
Bibl. 3

Peter Oliver
(b. 1682–d. 1712)
Boston, Mass.
*Bibl. 2, 15, 23, 24, 25, 28,
  29, 36, 39, 44, 54, 110,
  114, 116, 119*

William G. Oliver
(c. 1839–1848)
Buffalo, N.Y.
Bibl. 20

Peter Olivier (d. 1798)
Philadelphia, Pa. (c. 1797)
*Bibl. 3, 15, 23, 24, 25, 28,
  29, 36, 44, 114, 124*

Gideon Olmstead
(c. 1832)
Charlotte, N.C.
Bibl. 21

N. Olmstead & Son
(c. 1847)
Farmington, Conn.
New Haven, Conn.
Nathaniel Olmsted
*Bibl. 16, 23, 28, 44, 91, 92,
  143*

| N. OLMSTED & SON |

P. H. Olmstead (c. 1830)
Columbus, Ohio
Bibl. 34

Nathaniel Olmste(a)d
(b. 1785–d. 1860)
Farmington, Conn. (c. 1808)
New Haven, Conn. (c. 1826)

N. Olmstead & Son
(c. 1847)
*Bibl. 15, 16, 23, 24, 25, 28,
  29, 36, 44, 91, 94, 110,
  114, 143*

| N. OLMSTED |

Henry Olwine
(c. 1840–1850)
Philadelphia, Pa.
Bibl. 3

**Gerrit (Garrett)
Onclebagh
(Onkelbag)**
(b. 1670–d. 1732)
New York, N.Y.
*Bibl. 2, 4, 15, 23, 24, 25, 28,
  29, 30, 35, 36, 44, 54, 95,
  102, 114, 116, 119, 124,
  135, 138, 142, 151*

N. & D. Onderdonk
New York, N.Y.
(c. 1896–1915)
Bibl. 28, 124, 157

N & D O

N. & D. O.

Oneal
(See Oneille)

Oneida Silversmiths
(1877–present)
Sherrill, N.Y.
Sterling silver begun 1946
Bibl. 127, 135, 146, 147

ONEIDA COMMUNITY (O) (C) STERLING

Heirloom Sterling

Ⓞ Ⓒ STERLING

Oneida Sterling "HEIRLOOM"

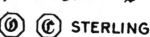

Oneil
(See Oneille)

Charles O'Neil (c. 1823)
New Haven, Conn.
Bibl. 28, 92, 110, 143

Thomas O'Neil
(c. 1837–1842)
Philadelphia, Pa.
Bibl. 3

John O'Neill (c. 1841)
Philadelphia, Pa.
Bibl. 3

**Antoine Oneille (Oneil)
(Oneal) (Onelle) (Onel)**
(b. 1764–d. 1820)
Detroit, Mich. (c. 1797)   **A O**
Vincennes, Ind.
(c. 1803–1817)   **A O**
Missouri Territory (c. 1820)
Bibl. 54, 58, 133

Onel
(See Oneille)

Onelle
(See Oneille)

Onkelbag
(See Onclebagh)

John Oram (Ouram)
Philadelphia, Pa.
(c. 1809–1811)
Bibl. 3

Joseph Orbrihim (c. 1784)
Annapolis, Md.
Bibl. 23

Ordway (c. 1840)
Location unknown
Bibl. 89   **ORDWAY**

Francis Oretle (Oertle)
(c. 1832)
New York, N.Y.
Bibl. 15, 124

Spencer Orgell
(c. 1950–1960)
Los Angeles, Calif.
Bibl. 89

Orleans Silver Co.
(1970–1981)
New Orleans, La.
Divison of United China &
Glass Co.
Bibl. 89, 146

Orleans Silver Co

Daniel D. R. Ormsby
(c. 1812–1834)
Cortland, N.Y.
Boon & Ormsby
(c. 1832–1834)
Bibl. 20, 124

Henry Ormsby
(c. 1839–1861)
Philadelphia, Pa.
Bibl. 3, 91

James Ormsby (c. 1771)
Baltimore, Md.
Bibl. 3

Thomas Orr
(c. 1809–1817)
Philadelphia, Pa.
Bibl. 3

Thomas Orr
(c. 1848–1849)
Louisville, Ky.
Bibl. 32, 54, 68, 93

C. E. Ortelett
(c. 1828–1831)
Philadelphia, Pa.
Bibl. 3

Osborn & Hammond
(c. 1804)
Utica, N.Y.
John Osborn
Seneca Hammond
Bibl. 20, 124

John Osborn
(c. 1805–1807)
Utica, N.Y.
Rugg & Osborn (c. 1804)
Osborn & Hammond
(c. 1804)
Butler & Osborn
(c. 1805–1807)
Bibl. 18, 20, 124, 158

OSBORN

John Osborn (1860–1875)
Bangor, Me.
Bibl. 105

Robert Osborn (c. 1847)
Rochester, N.Y.
Bibl. 20, 124

W. R. Osborn (c. 1850)
Watertown, N.Y.
Bibl. 20, 124

William Osborn (c. 1840)
Providence, R.I.
Bibl. 15, 25, 44, 91, 114

William Osborn

Henry J. Osborne
Milledgeville, Ga. (c. 1848)
Augusta, Ga. (c. 1860)
Bibl. 17

Orlando C. Osborne
(c. 1827)
Baltimore, Md.
Bibl. 38

Osborn
(See Stone & Osburn)

Clement Oscamp
(b. 1822–d. 1882)
Cincinnati, Ohio
(c. 1849–1865)
Bibl. 54, 114

H. A. Osgood & Son
(1875)
Lewiston, Me.
Bibl. 105

J. K. Osgood (1875)
Houlton, Me.
Bibl. 105

John Osgood
(b. 1770–d. 1840)
John Osgood (Jr.)
(c. 1795–1817)
Boston, Mass.
Haverhill, Mass.
Salem, Mass.
New Hampshire
*Bibl. 15, 23, 25, 28, 29, 36,
44, 91, 110, 114, 125*

J: OSGOOD

Andrew Osthoff
(c. 1809–1814)
Pittsburgh, Pa. (c. 1815)
Baltimore, Md.
*Bibl. 23, 24, 25, 36, 38, 44,
114*   A. OSTHOFF

Ralph Ostrom
Troy, N.Y. (c. 1830)
Schenectady, N.Y.
   (c. 1838–1842)
Bibl. 20, 124

John Otis (c. 1706)
Barnstable, Mass.
Bibl. 23, 36, 44, 110

Jonathan Otis
   (b. 1723–d. 1791)
Sandwich, Mass.
Middletown, Conn. (c. 1775)
Newport, R.I. (c. 1778)
*Bibl. 2, 15, 16, 23, 24, 25,
   28, 36, 39, 44, 61, 69, 91,
   92, 94, 110, 114*

Ott & Cluff (c. 1803–1806)
Norfolk, Va.
George Ott
Matthew Cluff
Bibl. 19

Daniel Ott (c. 1792)
New York, N.Y.
Bibl. 23, 36, 44

Daniel Ott (c. 1812)
Chillicothe, Ohio
Bibl. 34

David Ott (Otto)
Philadelphia, Pa.
   (c. 1797–1809)
Bibl. 3

George Ott (d. 1831)
Norfolk, Va. (c. 1801–1822)
Ott & Cluff (c. 1803–1806)
*Bibl. 19, 23, 24, 25, 29, 36,
   44, 114*

G. Ott	Ott

H. & S. M. Ott
   (c. 1845–1848)
Harrisonburg, Va.
Bibl. 19

Henry Ott (c. 1837–1850)
Harrisonburg, Va.
Bibl. 19

Jacob Ott (c. 1812)
Chillicothe, Ohio
Bibl. 34

Michael Ott (c. 1812)
Chillicothe, Ohio
Bibl. 34

Philip Ott (c. 1792)
Fayetteville, N.C.
Bibl. 21

Otto
(See David Ott)

Joseph Oudin (c. 1814)
Philadelphia, Pa.
Bibl. 3

Our Very Best
(See Hibbard, Spencer,
   Bartlett & Co.)

Ouram
(See Oram)

Ephraim Outten (d. 1825)
Maysville, Ky.
   (c. 1816–1825)
Bibl. 32, 54, 68, 93

Richard Overin (b. 1668)
New York, N.Y. (c. 1702)
*Bibl. 4, 23, 28, 36, 44, 124,
   138*

Oviatt & Warner (c. 1894)
Portland, Ore.
Bibl. 114, 127, 157

Owen
(See Palmer & Owen)

Owen and Read (Reed)
   (c. 1840)
Cincinnati, Ohio
Bibl. 34, 152

Ann Owen (c. 1837)
Philadelphia, Pa.
Bibl. 3

Griffith Owen
   (c. 1790–1814)
Philadelphia, Pa.
Bibl. 3

I. Owen
(See John Owen)

J. Owen & Co.
   (c. 1839–1840)
Philadelphia, Pa.
Bibl. 3

J. T. Owen (c. 1859–1860)
Abbeville, S.C.
M. T. & J. T. Owen
Bibl. 5

Jesse Owen (c. 1801–1816)
Philadelphia, Pa.
Bibl. 3, 23, 25, 29

JSE. OWEN

Jesse Owen (c. 1841–1848)
Philadelphia, Pa.
Bibl. 3

Jesse E. Owen (d. 1794)
Philadelphia, Pa. (c. 1790)
*Bibl. 3, 15, 23, 24, 29, 36,
   39, 44, 54, 79, 114*

OWEN	JSE. E. OWEN

John Owen (I. Owen)
   (c. 1804–1831)
Philadelphia, Pa.
*Bibl. 3, 15, 23, 24, 25, 28,
   29, 36, 44, 89, 90, 104,
   114*

I. OWEN	OWEN

M. T. Owen
   (c. 1848–1860)
Abbeville, S.C.
Bailey & Owen
   (c. 1848–1850)
M. T. & J. T. Owen
   (c. 1859–1860)
Bibl. 5

M. T. & J. T. Owen
   (c. 1859–1860)
Abbeville, S.C.
M. T. Owen
J. T. Owen
Bibl. 5

Owens & Currin
   (c. 1846–1850)
Philadelphia, Pa.
Samuel W. Owens
James W. Currin
Bibl. 3

Jesse Owens (c. 1836)
Philadelphia, Pa.
Bibl. 3

Samuel H. Owens
(c. 1857)
Anderson, S.C.
Bibl. 5

Samuel W. Owens
(c. 1846–1850)
Philadelphia, Pa.
Owens & Currin
Bibl. 3

William Owens
(c. 1839–1860)
Utica, N.Y.
Bibl. 18, 20, 124, 158

Aloysius Owings (c. 1800)
Baltimore, Md.
Bibl. 38

P

P
(See Pairpoint Corporation,
G. W. Parks Company,
Philadelphia Silversmithing
Co., Franklin Porter, S. C.
Powell)

P & B
(See Pangborn & Brinsmaid,
Paye & Baker Mfg. Co.)

P & M
(See Parry & Musgrave,
Phinney & Mead)

P & P
(See Palmer & Peckham)

P & U
(See Pelletreau & Upson)

P A
(See Pygan Adams)

P B
(See Phillip Becker, Phineas
Bradley)

P B & C
(See Pelletreau, Bennett &
Cooke)

P C
(See Phelps & Cary Co.)

P D
(See Phillip Dally, Peter
David, Peyton Dana)

P G
(See Philip Goelet)

P. G. H.
(See Heeren Bros. & Co.)

P H
(See Philip Hulbeart, Phil
Huntington)

P K
(See Peter Kirkwood)

P L
(See Peter Leret, Peter Lupp)

P L K
(See Peter L. Krider)

P M
(See Francois Paul Malcher,
Peter Martin, Peter Mood
Sr.)

P O
(See Peter Oliver, Peter
Olivier)

P P
(See Peter Perraux)

P Q
(See Peter Quintard)

P R
(See Paul Revere Sr., Paul
Revere II)

P S
(See Philip Benjamin Sadtler,
Philip Syng Sr., Philip
Syng Jr.)

P. S. Co.
(See Poole Silver Co.,
Preisner Silver Company)

P V
(See Peter Vergerau)

P V B
(See Peter Van Inburgh)

F. W. Pachmann
(c. 1850–1865)
New York, N.Y.
Bibl. 54, 91

William Pack (b. 1817)
Utica, N.Y.
(c. 1850–c. 1860)
Bibl. 18, 20, 158

Packard & Brown
(c. 1815)
Albany, N.Y.
Jonathan Packard
———— Brown
Bibl. 20, 41, 124

Packard & Scofield
(c. 1818–1819)
Rochester, N.Y.
Jonathan Packard
Salmon Scofield
Bibl. 20, 41, 124

Jonathan Packard
(b. 1789–d. 1854)
Springfield, Mass. (c. 1811)
Albany, N.Y. (c. 1815)
Rochester, N.Y.
(c. 1818–1854)
Huntington & Packard
(c. 1811)
Packard & Brown (c. 1815)
Packard & Scofield
(c. 1818–1819)
Bibl. 20, 41, 110, 124

L. H. Packard (c. 1847)
Potsdam, N.Y.
Bibl. 20, 91, 124

Samuel Paddy (b. 1645)
Boston, Mass. (c. 1679)
*Bibl. 23, 28, 36, 44, 102,
110, 119*

Lewis Pagaud
Norfolk, Va. (c. 1815)
Petersburg, Va.
(c. 1815–1846)
Bibl. 19

Charles Page
(c. 1801–1802)
Staunton, Va.
Bibl. 19

John Page (1860)
New Portland, Me.
Bibl. 105

Jacob Pain (c. 1793)
Philadelphia, Pa.
Bibl. 3

P. L. Painchaud (1895)
Biddeford, Me.
Bibl. 105

(James?) Paine
(c. 1835–?)
Waynesboro, Va.
Bibl. 19

John O. Paine (1875)
Providence, R.I.
Bibl. 108

Stephen Paine
(1870–1875)
Providence, R.I.
Bibl. 108

Thomas D. Paine
(1855–1865)
Cumberlain, R.I.
Bibl. 108

Washington Paine
(c. 1841–1850)
Philadelphia, Pa.
Bibl. 3

Isaac Painter
(c. 1837–1842)
Philadelphia, Pa.
Bibl. 3

Isaac Painter Jr.
(c. 1845–1850)
Philadelphia, Pa.
Bibl. 3

John Painter (c. 1735)
Philadelphia, Pa.
Bibl. 23, 36, 44

John S. Painter
(c. 1835–1848)
Philadelphia, Pa.
Bibl. 3

Pairpoint Corporation
(1880–present)
New Bedford, Mass.
Successor to Pairpoint Mfg.
Co. (1880–1900)
Flatware department bought
by Niagara Silver Co.
(1900)
Now a glass manufacturer.
Bibl. 127, 135

PAIRPOINT TRADE ❖ MARK.
FLAT 1880 WARE.
BEST

Daniel H. Pallais
(c. 1835–1842)
Mobile, Ala.
Coan and Pallais
(c. 1833–1835)
Bibl. 148
| PALLAIS MOBILE |

Palm Beach
(See Napier Company)

**Palmer & Batchelder
(Bachelder)
(Bachlader)
(Bachlander)**
Boston, Mass. (c. 1850)
New York, N.Y. (?)
James Palmer
———— Batchelder
*Bibl. 23, 24, 25, 28, 29, 36,
44, 91, 94, 114*

| PALMER & BACHELDER |

Palmer & Clapp
(c. 1823)
New York, N.Y.
James Palmer
H. W. Clapp
Bibl. 23, 36, 44, 124, 138

Palmer, Davis & Co.
(See Davis, Palmer & Co.)

Palmer & Hinsdale
(c. 1815)
New York, N.Y.
James Palmer
Horace Hinsdale
Bibl. 23, 36, 44, 124, 135, 138

Palmer & Newcomb
(c. 1850)
Location unknown
Bibl. 15, 44, 114, 138

Palmer & Owen
(1850–1859)
Cincinnati, Ohio
Bibl. 54, 90

Palmer & Peckham
(c. 1896–1904) **P. & P.**
North Attleboro, Mass. STERLING
Bibl. 114, 127, 157

Palmer & Ramsay
(c. 1847–1855)
Raleigh, N.C.
John C. Palmer
Walter J. Ramsay
Bibl. 21

Abraham Palmer
(b. 1811-d. 1880)
Cincinnati, Ohio (c. 1849)
Bibl. 54, 91

E. H. P. Palmer (c. 1865)
Richmond, Va.
Bibl. 54

G. W. Palmer & Son
(1875)
Rockland, Me.
Bibl. 105

James Palmer
(c. 1815–1823, c. 1850)
New York, N.Y.
(c. 1815–1823)
Philadelphia, Pa.
(c. 1831–1835)
Boston, Mass. (c. 1850)
Palmer & Hinsdale (c. 1815)
Palmer & Clapp (c. 1823)
Palmer & Batchelder
(c. 1850)
Bibl. 23, 36, 44, 91, 124, 138

John Palmer
(c. 1795–1796)
Philadelphia, Pa.
Bibl. 3

John C. Palmer
(b. 1806–d. 1893)
Salisbury, N.C.
(c. 1830–1832)
Raleigh, N.C. (c. 1840–?)
Hampton & Palmer
(c. 1830–1832)
Palmer & Ramsay
(c. 1847–1855)
Bibl. 21

Thomas Palmer (c. 1845)
Rochester, N.Y.
Bibl. 20, 124

William H. Palmer
(c. 1837–1840)
Philadelphia, Pa.
Bibl. 3

Samuel Pancoast (S P)
(c. 1785–1795)
Philadelphia, Pa.
Bibl. 3, 23, 25, 36, 39, 44,
81, 91, 114

PANCOAST

Stacy Pancoast (c. 1835)
Philadelphia, Pa.
Bibl. 3, 138

Pangborn & Brinsmaid
(c. 1833–1843)   **P & B**
Burlington, Vt.
Bibl. 25, 29, 44, 62, 91, 110,
114

Papot & Norton
(c. 1790)
Savannah, Ga.
——— Papot
Jonathan Norton
Bibl. 17

William Anthony
Paradice (c. 1799)
Philadelphia, Pa.
Bibl. 3, 23, 36, 44

William Paraset (c. 1811)
Philadelphia, Pa.
Bibl. 3, 23, 36, 44

William V. Pardee
(c. 1834)
Albany, N.Y.
Bibl. 20, 124

Earl Pardon (b. 1926)
Saratoga Springs, N.Y.
Bibl. 89, 156

William Parham (d. 1794)
Philadelphia, Pa.
(c. 1785–1794)   **W P**
Bibl. 3, 15, 23, 25, 36, 44,
81, 114

Joseph Parie (c. 1811)
Philadelphia, Pa.
Bibl. 3, 23, 36, 44

David (de) Parisien
(Parisen)   PARISIEN
(c. 1780–1817)
New York, N.Y.
Bibl. 28, 72, 124

Otto (Paul) de Parisien
(de Perrizang)
(w. 1757–1797)
New York, N.Y.
Otto Paul de Parisien & Son
(c. 1789–1791)
Bibl. 4, 15, 23, 24, 25, 28,
29, 35, 36, 44, 54, 83, 91,
114, 124, 138

O P | O P D P
PARISIEN

Otto Paul de Parisien &
Son (c. 1789–1791)
New York, N.Y.
Otto de Parisien   O P D P
Paul de Parisien
Bibl. 23, 25, 28, 29, 36, 44,
91, 124, 138

Paul de Parisien
(c. 1780–1817)
New York, N.Y.
Otto Paul de Parisien & Son
(c. 1789–1791)
Bibl. 23, 25, 28, 29, 36, 44

John Francis Parisot
(c. 1828–1836)
Savannah, Ga.
Bibl. 17

Park
(See Vernon & Park)

John Park (d. 1858)
Louisville, Ky. (c. 1848)
Bibl. 32, 93

Jonas Park (c. 1785–1786)
Bennington, Vt.
Bibl. 54, 110

Parke & Son (c. 1806)
Philadelphia, Pa.
Bibl. 3

Augustus W. Parke
(c. 1817–1822)
Philadelphia, Pa.
Bibl. 3

Charles B. Parke
(c. 1806–1810)
Philadelphia, Pa.
Bibl. 3

Solomon Parke
(c. 1791–1822)
Philadelphia, Pa.
Southampton, Bucks
County, Pa. (c. 1782)
Bibl. 3

Solomon Parke & Co.
(c. 1797–1801)
Philadelphia, Pa.
Bibl. 3

Parker & Co.
(c. 1818–1819)
Philadelphia, Pa.
Isaac Parker (?)
Bibl. 3

Allen Parker
(c. 1817–1819)
New York, N.Y.
Bibl. 15, 25, 44, 114, 124,
138   A PARKER

B. T. Parker
(1860–1875)
Phillips, Me.
Bibl. 105

Caleb Parker
(c. 1731–1770)
Boston, Mass.
Bibl. 28, 110

Charles H. Parker
(c. 1793–1819)
Salem, Mass.
Philadelphia, Pa.
Bibl. 28

Daniel Parker
(b. 1726–d. 1785) ⬭ D: P
Boston, Mass.
*Bibl. 2, 15, 23, 24, 25, 28,
29, 36, 44, 55, 91, 94, 110,
114*
D: PARKER

George Parker
(c. 1804–1831)
Baltimore, Md.
*Bibl. 23, 24, 25, 28, 29, 36,
38, 44, 91, 114*
G. PARKER

George Parker
(c. 1828–1834)
Utica, N.Y.
Storrs & Parker
Bibl. 18, 20, 91, 124, 158
G. PARKER

Isaac Parker
(b. 1749–d. 1805)
Deerfield, Mass. (c. 1780)
*Bibl. 23, 24, 25, 28, 29, 36,
44, 94, 110, 114*
I PARKER

Isaac Parker
(c. 1818–1850)
Philadelphia, Pa.
Parker & Co.
(c. 1818–1819) (?)
Bibl. 3

J. Parker
Location unknown
Bibl. 54

James Parker
(See George Parker)

John Parker (b. 1750)
Maryland (c. 1774)
Bibl. 38

Joseph Parker (c. 1785)
Princeton, N.J.
Bibl. 44, 46, 54

Richard Parker (c. 1785)
Philadelphia, Pa.
Bibl. 3, 23, 36, 44

T. E. Parker (c. 1840?)
Location unknown
Bibl. 89   T. E. Parker

T. H. Parker (c. 1833)
Philadelphia, Pa.
Bibl. 3

Thomas Parker
(c. 1785–1817)
Philadelphia, Pa.
Bibl. 3

Thomas Parker Jr.
(c. 1817–1822)
Philadelphia, Pa.
Bibl. 3

William Parker (c. 1733)
Savannah, Ga.
Bibl. 17

William Parker (c. 1777)
Newport, R.I.
Bibl. 28

William Parker (c. 1778)
Lewes, Del.
Bibl. 30

William Parker
(c. 1823–1824)
Philadelphia, Pa.
Bibl. 3

William Parker (c. 1834)
New York, N.Y.
Bibl. 15, 44, 124

William Parker Jr.
(c. 1835)
Philadelphia, Pa.
Bibl. 3

William B. Parker
(c. 1821)
Camden, S.C.
Bibl. 5

William H. Parker
New York, N.Y. (c. 1835)
Brooklyn, N.Y.
(c. 1837–1843)
Bibl. 23, 36

Nelson Parkes
(c. 1846–1847)
Utica, N.Y.
Bibl. 18, 124, 158

Joseph Parkins (c. 1837)
Philadelphia, Pa.
Bibl. 3

Charles Parkman (c. 1790)
Boston, Mass.
*Bibl. 23, 25, 29, 36, 44, 91,
110, 114*
C PARKMAN

Henry D. Parkman
(c. 1820–1823)
Hudson, N.Y.
Bibl. 20, 124

John Parkman
(c. 1716–1748)
Boston, Mass.
*Bibl. 15, 23, 24, 25, 28, 29,
36, 44, 110, 114*
PARKMAN

Thomas Parkman
(c. 1793)
Boston, Mass.
*Bibl. 23, 24, 25, 29, 36, 44,
110, 114*

Parks Bros. & Rogers
(1892–c. 1930)
Providence, R.I.
New York, N.Y.
Bibl. 114, 127

Asa Parks (c. 1852–1867)
Oswego, N.Y.
Bibl. 20, 91

G. W. Parks Company
(c. 1909–1922)
Providence, R.I.
Successor to Hayden Mfg.
Co.
Bibl. 127, 157

John Parks (c. 1791)
New York, N.Y.
Bibl. 23, 36, 44, 124, 138

James Parmele
(b. 1763–d. 1828)
Durham, Conn.
Bibl. 16, 23, 28, 36, 110

Samuel Parmele
(b. 1737–d. 1807)
Guilford, Conn.
*Bibl. 15, 16, 24, 25, 28, 29,
36, 44, 61, 91, 92, 94, 110,
114, 151*

Parmenter
(See Bailey & Parmenter)

John Peter Parmier
(c. 1793)
Philadelphia, Pa.
Bibl. 3

**Frederick W. Parrot
(Perrott)**
Philadelphia, Pa.
(c. 1847–1850)
Bibl. 3

Joseph Parrot (Perrot)
Philadelphia, Pa.
(c. 1835–1843)
Bibl. 3

T. Parrot(t)
Philadelphia, Pa. (c. 1770)
Boston, Mass.
(c. 1760–1775)
*Bibl. 15, 25, 28, 29, 44, 50,
110, 114, 139*

Parry
(See Leslie & Parry)

Parry & Musgrave
(c. 1793–1796)
Philadelphia, Pa.
Rowland Parry
James Musgrave | P & M |
*Bibl. 3, 15, 23, 24, 25, 36,
39, 44, 54, 91, 114*

Francis Parry
(c. 1846–1850)
Philadelphia, Pa.
Bibl. 3, 23

John Parry (c. 1795–1797)
Philadelphia, Pa.
Bibl. 3

John F. Parry (c. 1824)
Philadelphia, Pa.
Bibl. 3

John J. Parry (c. 1810)
Philadelphia, Pa.
Bibl. 46

Martin Parry
(b. 1737–d. 1802)
Portsmouth, N.H. (c. 1760)
Kittery, Me.
*Bibl. 15, 23, 24, 25, 28, 29,
36, 44, 91, 110, 114, 125*

| PARRY |

Rowland Parry
(c. 1790–1796)
Philadelphia, Pa.
Parry & Musgrave
(c. 1793–1796)
*Bibl. 3, 23, 25, 36, 39, 44,
95, 114*

Thomas Parry
(c. 1848–1850)
Philadelphia, Pa.
Bibl. 3

———— **Parsons** (c. 1770)
Philadelphia, Pa.
Bibl. 28, 29, 36

| PARSONS |

Henry R. Parsons
(c. 1840–1850)
Philadelphia, Pa.
Bibl. 3

John Parsons (c. 1780)
Boston, Mass.
Bibl. 15, 24, 25, 44, 114

| I. PARSONS |

Peterson Partin
Richmond, Va.
(c. 1819–1828)
Norfolk, Va. (c. 1819)
Bibl. 19

**William Paschall (Pascall)
(Pascal)** (d. 1696)
Philadelphia, Pa. (c. 1675)
Bibl. 3, 23, 36, 44, 119

Joseph Passano (c. 1827)
Location unknown
Bibl. 38

Blovet Pasteur
(c. 1759–c. 1782)
Williamsburg, Va.
Bibl. 19, 153

Pat Jane
(See York Silver Co.)

T. A. Patchin (c. 1846)
Syracuse, N.Y.
Bibl. 20, 124

Nancy Lumpee Pate
(1966–c. 1980)
St. Louis, Mo.
Bibl. 155

George Paterson (c. 1835)
New York, N.Y.
Bibl. 23, 36, 138

A. Paton (c. 1850)
Boston, Mass.
Bibl. 4, 23, 28, 44

B. F. S. Patten (1860)
Bangor, Me.
Bibl. 105

George Patterson (c. 1835)
New York, N.Y.
Bibl. 44, 124

James Patterson
(c. 1837–1848)
Philadelphia, Pa. | I. P |
Bibl. 3

James Patterson (d. 1773)
Williamsburg, Va. (c. 1767)
Richmond, Va.
   (c. 1772–1773)
Bibl. 19, 153

James Patterson
   (c. 1858–1867)
Crawfordsville, Ind.
Bibl. 133

J. PATTERSON

John Patterson (c. 1751)
Annapolis, Md.
Bibl. 28, 38, 44, 114

I. P

John Patterson (c. 1814)
Alexandria, Va.
Pittsburgh, Pa.
Potter & Patterson
   (c. 1814–1815)
Bibl. 19, 54

Wilson M. Patterson
   (c. 1840)
Mansfield, Ohio
Bibl. 34

Joseph Pattison (c. 1751)
Philadelphia, Pa.
Bibl. 3

Pattit
(See Pettit)

Patton
(See McBryde & Patton)

Patton & Jones
   (c. 1799–1815)
Baltimore, Md.
   (c. 1799–1815)
Philadelphia, Pa.
   (c. 1804–1814)
Abraham Patton
Samuel G. Jones
Bibl. 3, 38

Abraham Patton
   (c. 1795–1815)
Baltimore, Md.
   (c. 1795–1796)
Philadelphia, Pa.
   (c. 1799–1819)
Leslie & Price
   (c. 1793–1800)

Robert Leslie & Co.
   (c. 1795–1796)
Patton & Jones
   (c. 1799–1815)
Bibl. 3, 38

Thomas Patton (c. 1824)
Philadelphia, Pa.
Bibl. 3, 23, 36, 44

Philip Paul (c. 1835–1840)
Philadelphia, Pa.
S. & P. Paul (c. 1839–1840)
Bibl. 3

S. & P. Paul
   (c. 1839–1840)
Philadelphia, Pa.
Simon & Philip Paul
Bibl. 3

Simon Paul (c. 1839–1840)
Philadelphia, Pa.
S. & P. Paul
Bibl. 3

Cornelius Paulding
New York, N.Y.
   (c. 1801–1802)
Savannah, Ga.
   (c. 1802–1810)
New Orleans, La. (c. 1810)
Marquand & Paulding
   (c. 1801–1810)
H. Lord & Co.
   (c. 1805)
Marquand, Harriman & Co.
   (c. 1809–1812)
Cornelius Paulding & Co.
   (c. 1810)
Marquand, Paulding &
   Penfield (c. 1810–1816)
Bibl. 17, 124, 138

Cornelius Paulding & Co.
   (c. 1810)
New Orleans, La.
Cornelius Paulding
Bibl. 17

Paulgreen
(See Polgrain)

Anthony R. Paulin
   (c. 1778–1824)
Savannah, Ga.
Bibl. 17

Peter Paulson (c. 1800)
Wilmington, Del.
Bibl. 30

**John A. (J. I.) Paxson
   (Paxton)**
Philadelphia, Pa.
   (c. 1807–1811)
Bibl. 3, 23, 36, 44, 91

Isaac Paxton (c. 1821)
Hamilton, Ohio
Bibl. 34

John A. Paxton
(See John A. Paxson)

John W. Paxton
   (c. 1814–1815)
Danville, Va.
John W. Paxton & Son
   (c. 1815)
Bibl. 19

John W. Paxton & Son
   (c. 1815)
Danville, Va.
Bibl. 19

Paye & Baker Mfg. Co.
   (c. 1891–1935)
North Attleboro, Mass.
Successor to Simmons &
   Paye
Bibl. 127, 130, 157

William D. Paylor (c. 1823)
Macon, Ga.
Bibl. 17

Payn & Heroy (c. 1813)
Albany, N.Y.
Bibl. 20, 124

C. S. Payn (c. 1815)
Albany, N.Y.
Bibl. 20, 124

Hiram Payn
   (c. 1815–1818)
Albany, N.Y.
Bibl. 20, 124

Chauncey S. Payne
   (b. 1795–d. 1877)
Detroit, Mich.
Levi Brown (c. 1866)
Bibl. 58

Asa Peabody
Wilmington, N.C. (c. 1821)
New York, N.Y. (c. 1915)
Bibl. 21, 138

John Peabody
(c. 1823)
Fayetteville, N.C.
Bibl. 21, 91

John Peabody
(1836–1849)
Nashville, Tenn.
Bibl. 89

John Tyng Peabody
(b. 1756–d. 1822)
Enfield, Conn. (c. 1779)
Wilmington, N.C. (c. 1787)
Bibl. 16, 21, 23, 24, 25, 28,
29, 36, 44, 92, 110, 114

J. PEABODY

Nathaniel Prentiss
Peabody
(b. 1806–d. 1883)
Bennettsville, S.C.
(c. 1830–1870)
Bibl. 5

C. D. Peacock
(1837–present)
Chicago, Ill.
Became division of
Dayton-Hudson
Corporation (1970)
Bibl. 98, 126, 127

Emily Peacock (c. 1907)
Boston, Mass
Bibl. 89

Richard G. Peacock Jr.
(c. 1819)
Fredericksburg, Va.
Weidemeyer & Peacock
Bibl. 19

Thomas Peacock (b. 1818)
Lancaster, Ky.
(c. 1845–1879)
Louisville, Ky.
Bibl. 32, 54, 93

Daniel Peake
(c. 1837–1840)
Philadelphia, Pa.
Bibl. 3

Daniel Peake Jr.
(c. 1839–1850)
Philadelphia, Pa.
Bibl. 3

Edward Peake
(c. 1829–1850)
Philadelphia, Pa.
Bibl. 3

Thomas Peake (c. 1850)
Philadelphia, Pa.
Bibl. 3

Charles Willson Peale
(b. 1741–d. 1827)
Annapolis, Md.
(c. 1761–1764)
Philadelphia, Pa. (c. 1765)
Bibl. 2, 3, 23, 28, 36, 38, 44,
116

James Peale
(c. 1814–1817)
Philadelphia, Pa.
Bibl. 3

Pear & Bacall (c. 1850)
Boston, Mass.
Edward Pear
Thomas Bacall
Bibl. 4, 23, 28, 44, 91

PEAR & BACALL

Edward Pear
(c. 1836–1850)
Boston, Mass.
Pear & Bacall (c. 1850)
Bibl. 4, 23, 24, 25, 28, 29,
36, 91, 114

Pearce & Spratley
(c. 1833)
Norfolk, Va.
Walter Pearce
James H. Spratley
Bibl. 19

Hamett A. Pearce
(c. 1845–1850)
Richmond, Va.
Kersey & Pearce
Bibl. 19

Hart Pearce (c. 1833–1835)
New York, N.Y.
Bibl. 15, 124, 138

Samuel Pearce (c. 1783)
New York, N.Y.
Bibl. 28, 44, 124

Walter (William) Pearce
(c. 1831–1833)
Norfolk, Va.
Pearce & Spratley (c. 1833)
Bibl. 19, 23, 25, 29, 36, 44,
95, 114

W. PEARCE

William Pearman
Petersburg, Va. (c. 1832)
Williamsburg, Va.
(after 1832)
Richmond, Va.
Bibl. 19

Pearse
(See also Hunter & Pearse)

Samuel Pearse (c. 1783)
New York, N.Y.
Bibl. 23, 36

Isaac Pearson
(b. 1685–d. 1749)
Burlington, N.J.
(c. 1710–1749)
Bibl. 46, 54

John Pearson
(c. 1789–1807)
New York, N.Y.
(c. 1791)
Savannah, Ga. (c. 1802)
Letourneau & Pearson
(c. 1802–1803)
Bibl. 17, 23, 24, 25, 28, 29,
36, 39, 44, 114, 124, 138

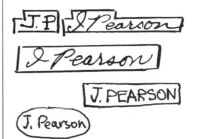

John Pearson
  (c. 1815–1817)
New York, N.Y.
Bibl. 15, 91, 124

Widow of John Pearson
  (c. 1819–1824)
New York, N.Y.
Bibl. 15, 124

M. & T. Pearson
  (c. 1825–1850)
Portland, Me.
Bibl. 15, 44, 91, 105, 114

| M & T. PEARSON |

Moses Pearson
  (1860–1875)
Portland, Me.
Bibl. 105

Nathaniel Pearson
  (1858–1877)
Portland, Me.
Bibl. 105

Peck & Co. (1860–1868)
Providence, R.I.
Bibl. 108

Peck & Porter (c. 1827)
Bridgeport, Conn.
Bibl. 23

A. G. Peck (c. 1823)
Ashtabula, Ohio
Bibl. 15, 24, 34, 44, 114

| A. G. PECK |

B. Peck (c. 1820)
Connecticut or R.I.
Bibl. 28, 29, 44, 92, 110

| B. PECK |

George Peck Jr. (c. 1850)
New York, N.Y.
Bibl. 23, 124

Isaac C. Peck (1873–1878)
Providence, R.I.
Bibl. 108

J. H. Peck & Co. (1858)
Providence, R.I.
Bibl. 108

Lawrance M. Peck
  (c. 1837)
Philadelphia, Pa.
Bibl. 3, 23, 36, 44

Moses Peck
  (b. 1718–d. 1801)
Boston, Mass. (c. 1780)
Bibl. 3, 110

Timothy Peck
  (b. 1765–d. 1818)
Middletown, Conn.
  (c. 1791)
Litchfield, Conn. (after 1791)
Boston, Mass. (c. 1810?)
Bibl. 16, 23, 28, 36, 44, 110

James Peckham
  (c. 1830–1847)
Charleston, S.C.
Peckham & George
Bibl. 5

S. Pedosy (c. 1810)
Philadelphia, Pa.
Bibl. 3, 23, 36, 44

Peebles & Wilson (c. 1840)
Philadelphia, Pa.?
Bibl. 89

| PEEBLES & WILSON |

Allen T. Peebles
Charlottesville, Va.
  (before 1837)
Staunton, Va. (c. 1839)
Leesburg, Va.
  (c. 1843–1848)
Richmond, Va.
  (c. 1849–1857)
Bibl. 19

John Pegg (c. 1830)
Albany, N.Y.
Bibl. 20, 124

W. H. Peiffer (c. 1890)
Niagara Falls, N.Y.
Bibl. 127

John Peirce
(See John Pierce)

William S. Peirce (c. 1841)
Philadelphia, Pa.
Bibl. 3

Joseph Peiri (c. 1811)
Philadelphia, Pa.
Bibl. 3, 23, 36, 44

Peirse
(See J. Pierce)

William Pelham (c. 1846)
Fishkill, N.Y.
Bibl. 20, 124

Emmett (Emmet) T. Pell
  (c. 1824–1841)
New York, N.Y.
*Bibl. 15, 25, 44, 95, 114,
124, 138*

| E. T. PELL |

Pelletrau
(See William Smith
  Pelletreau)

Pelletreau & Richards
  (Richards & Pelletreau)
  (c. 1825)
New York, N.Y.
William Smith Pelletreau
Thomas Richards (?)
Samuel R. Richards Jr.
*Bibl. 24, 25, 44, 91, 114,
124, 135*

| W S P | | T R |

Pelletreau & Upson
  (c. 1818)
New York, N.Y.

| P & U |

William Smith Pelletreau
Stephen Upson
*Bibl. 23, 24, 25, 44, 91, 114,
124, 135, 138*

Pelletreau & Van Wyck
  (c. 1815)
New York, N.Y.
William Smith Pelletreau
Stephen Van Wyck
*Bibl. 24, 25, 44, 91, 114,
124, 138*

| S.VANWYCK |

| S. VAN WYCK |

| W.S. PELLETREAU |

Pelletreau, Bennett & Co.
  (c. 1827–1829)
New York, N.Y.

John Bennett Sr.
D. C. Cooke
Maltby Pelletreau
Bibl. 15

**Pelletreau, Bennett &
  Cooke** (c. 1826–c. 1827)
New York, N.Y.
John Bennett Sr.
D. C. Cooke   P B & C
Maltby Pelletreau
*Bibl. 15, 25, 44, 91, 114,
  124, 135, 138*

Elias Pelletreau
  (b. 1726–d. 1810,
  c. 1776–1782)
Southampton, L.I., N.Y.
Simsbury, Conn.
Saybrook, Conn.
*Bibl. 4, 15, 20, 23, 24, 25,
  28, 29, 30, 35, 44, 54, 61,
  64, 91, 92, 95, 102, 110,
  114, 116, 118, 119, 124,
  135, 138, 151*

John Pelletreau
  (b. 1755 d. 1822)
Southampton, N.Y.
Bibl. 20, 23, 36, 44, 124

Maltby Pelletreau
  (c. 1815–1840)
Charleston, S.C.
New York, N.Y.
Pelletreau, Bennett & Cooke
  (c. 1826–c. 1827)
Clark & Pelletreau (c. 1819)
Bennett, Cooke & Co.
  (1823–c. 1826)
Pelletreau, Bennett & Co.
  (c. 1827–1829)
*Bibl. 15, 23, 25, 36, 44, 89,
  91, 114, 124, 135, 138*

**William Smith Pelletreau
  (Pelletrau)**
  (b. 1786–d. 1842)
Southampton, N.Y.
Pelletreau & Van Wyck
  (c. 1815)
Pelletreau & Upson (c. 1818)
Pelletreau & Richards
  (c. 1825)
*Bibl. 15, 20, 23, 24, 25, 28,
  29, 36, 44, 91, 124, 135*

W S PELLETREAU

W S P   W. S. PELLETREAU

Jean Baptiste Pellissier
  (b. 1792)
Charleston, S.C. (c. 1815)
Bibl. 5

James S. Pemberton
  (c. 1842–1850)
Albany, N.Y.
Bibl. 20, 124

**William F. Pendrell
  (Pendren)**
Philadelphia, Pa.
  (c. 1843–1846)
Bibl. 3, 23

Penfield (Pennfield)
  (c. 1810)
Location unknown
Bibl. 89

J. Penfield & Co.
  (c. 1820–1828)
Savannah, Ga.
Josiah Penfield
Moses Eastman
Frederick Marquand
Bibl. 17, 91

PENFIELD & CO.

Josiah Penfield
  (b. 1785–d. 1828)
Savannah, Ga.
Marquand, Paulding &
  Penfield (c. 1810–1816)
J. Penfield & Co.
  (c. 1820–1828)
Bibl. 17, 91

PENFIELD

**John Pennefather
  (Pennyfeather)**
  (d. 1745)
Charleston, S.C.
  (c. 1736–1740)
Bibl. 5

Charles D. Pennell
  (c. 1847)
Providence, R.I.
Bibl. 23

J. C. Penney Co. Inc.
  (c. 1925–present)
New York, N.Y.
Bibl. 127

PAT. 72786 J. C. PENNEY CO. INC.

Pennfield
(See Penfield)

A. C. Pennington
  (c. 1849)
Wellsburg, Va.
Bibl. 19

Joshua S. Pennington
  (c. 1825–1834)
Eatonton, Ga.
Bibl. 17

Harvey Pennoyer
  (c. 1818)
Sing Sing, N.Y.
Bibl. 20, 124

Pennyfeather
(See Pennefather)

Penot & Brother (c. 1821)
Charleston, S.C.
Bibl. 5

**Scarboro (Scarborough)
  Pentecost**
  (c. 1822–1852)
Evansville, Ind.
Mt. Vernon, Ind.
Henderson County, Ky.
Bibl. 32, 54, 68, 93, 133

S. PENTECOST

Henry Pepin
  (c. 1854–1858)
New Orleans, La.
Bibl. 141

H. S. Pepper (c. 1837)
Philadelphia, Pa.
Bibl. 3

Henry J. Pepper (c. 1766)
Philadelphia, Pa.
Henry J. Pepper & Son
  (c. 1846–1850)
*Bibl. 28, 29, 30, 44, 79, 95,
  104, 114*

H. I. PEPPER   H. J. PEPPER

Henry J. (I.) Pepper
(b. 1789–d. 1853)
Wilmington, Del.
(before 1814)
Philadelphia, Pa.
(c. 1828–1850)
Bibl. 3, 15, 23, 24, 25, 30,
36, 39, 44, 91, 104

H. J. PEPPER

H. I. PEPPER

Henry J. Pepper & Son
(c. 1846–1850)
Philadelphia, Pa.
Bibl. 3, 15, 25, 44, 91, 114

H.I. PEPPER & SON

Joel S. Pepper (c. 1850)
Philadelphia, Pa.
Bibl. 3

Samuel W. Pepper
(c. 1848–1850)
Philadelphia, Pa.
Bibl. 3, 91

Thomas Percival (c. 1840)
Albany, N.Y.
Bibl. 20, 124

S. Perdriaux
(c. 1829–1833)
Philadelphia, Pa.
Bibl. 3

William Peres
(c. 1820–1822)
Philadelphia, Pa.
Bibl. 3

Elsa Peretti (1969–present)
New York, N.Y.
Worked at Tiffany (c. 1974)
Bibl. 126

Period Silver
(See Tuttle Silversmiths)

Houghton Perkins
(b. 1735–d. 1778)
Boston, Mass.
Taunton, Mass.
Bibl. 23, 25, 28, 36, 44, 54,
91, 110, 114, 119

Isaac Perkins
(b. 1676–d. 1737)
Boston, Mass.
(c. 1707–1737)
Charlestown, Mass.
Bibl. 23, 28, 29, 36, 44, 110

Jacob Perkins
(b. 1766–d. 1849)
Newburyport, Mass.
(c. 1781–1815)
Philadelphia, Pa.
(c. 1816–1819)
Murray, Draper, Fairman &
Co.
Bibl. 3, 14, 15, 23, 24, 25,
28, 29, 36, 44, 102, 110,
114

Joseph Perkins
(b. 1749–d. 1789)
South Kingston, R.I.
(c. 1789)
Bibl. 15, 24, 25, 28, 44, 56,
91, 94, 110, 114

J PERKINS

Leonard Perkins (b. 1796)
Sparta, Ga. (c. 1818–1820)
Milledgeville, Ga.
(c. 1820–1831)
Wilcox & Perkins
(c. 1818–1820)
Nichols & Perkins
Bibl. 17, 91

L. PERKINS

T. Perkins (c. 1810)
Boston, Mass.
Bibl. 24, 25, 44, 110, 114

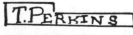

T PERKINS

Thomas Perkins
(c. 1785–1799)
Philadelphia, Pa.
Bibl. 3

Isaac Peronneau (c. 1743)
Charleston, S.C.
Bibl. 5

I P

James Perot (c. 1753)
Bermuda
Bibl. 3

Peter Perpignan
(c. 1809–1825)
Philadelphia, Pa.
Bibl. 3, 23, 36, 44

S. Perpignan & J. Varnier
(c. 1800–1801)
Philadelphia, Pa.
Bibl. 3, 23

Peter Perraux (Perreaux)
(c. 1797)
Philadelphia, Pa.
Bibl. 3, 4, 15, 23, 24, 25, 28,
29, 36, 44, 54, 95, 114

Perret & Sandoz (Sander)
(c. 1810–1811)
New York, N.Y.
Augusta Perret
——— Sandoz
Bibl. 23, 36, 44, 124, 138

August(a)(e) Perret
(c. 1811–1819)
New York, N.Y.
Perret & Sandoz
(c. 1810–1811)
Bibl. 15, 23, 36, 44, 124, 138

Phillip H. Perret
(d. 1826)
Cincinnati, Ohio
(1819–1826)
Bibl. 34, 90, 152

W. D. Perrine (c. 1850)
Lyons, N.Y.
Bibl. 20, 91, 124

Perrot
(See Joseph Parrot)

Perrott
(See Frederick W. Parrot)

Elias Perry (c. 1804)
Philadelphia, Pa.
Bibl. 3

Felicity Perry
(c. 1820–1822)
Philadelphia, Pa.
Bibl. 3

J. J. Perry (19th century)
Location unknown
Bibl. 54

John J. Perry (1875)
Oxford, Me.
Bibl. 105

Thomas Perry
(b. 1814–d. 1898)
Westerly, R.I.
(c. 1828–1865)
Bibl. 15, 28, 36, 44, 74, 91, 114

[T. PERRY]

Jefferson Peterman
(c. 1841)
Rochester, N.Y.
Boss & Peterman
Bibl. 20, 124

William Peterman
(c. 1837)
Philadelphia, Pa.
Bibl. 3

—— **Peters** (c. 1813)
Philadelphia, Pa.
Bibl. 3

Frederick R. Peters
(1854–1874)
New Orleans, La.
Bibl. 141

J. Peters & Co. (c. 1830)
Philadelphia, Pa.
James Peters
Bibl. 15, 25, 44, 91, 114

[J. PETERS & CO]

James Peters   J. PETERS
(c. 1821–1850)
Philadelphia, Pa.

J. Peters & Co. (c. 1830)
Bibl. 3, 15, 23, 25, 36, 44, 91, 114

R. Peters (c. 1807–1809)
Philadelphia, Pa.
Bibl. 3, 23, 36, 44

William S. Peters
(c. 1833–1850)
Philadelphia, Pa.
Bibl. 3

Henry Peterson (c. 1783)
Philadelphia, Pa.
Bibl. 25, 28, 44, 102, 114

[H P]

Henry Peterson Jr.
(c. 1787)
Alexandria, Va.
Bibl. 19

L. S. Peterson Co.   L. S. P.
(c. 1940–present)
North Attleboro, Mass.
Bibl. 127   L. S. P. Co.

Matthew Petit (Pettit)
(c. 1811)   [M P]
New York, N.Y.
Bibl. 23, 24, 25, 29, 36, 44, 114, 124

Alexander Petrie
(c. 1745–1765, d. 1768)
Charleston, S.C.
Bibl. 5, 25, 44, 54, 74, 104, 114   [A P]

Petterson Studio
(c. 1914–1920)
Chicago, Ill.
Became John P. Petterson
(c. 1920–1949)
Bibl. 98, 127

John P. Petterson
(c. 1920–1949)   J. P. P.
Chicago, Ill.
Successor to Petterson Studio
(c. 1914–1920)
Bibl. 98, 127

E. P. Pettes (c. 1850)
Location unknown
Bibl. 89, 91   [E. P. Pettes]

Pettit
(See also Borde & Pettit)

—— **Pettit** (c. 1803)
Charleston, S.C.
Borde & Pettit (c. 1803)
Bibl. 5

Matthew Pettit
(See Petit)

Thomas Pettit (Petit)
(Pattit)
New York, N.Y. (c. 1796)
Bibl. 23, 28, 36, 44, 124

Henry Petty
(c. 1829–1833)
Philadelphia, Pa.
Bibl. 3

Lewis Peyssou
(c. 1807–1810)
South Carolina
Bibl. 5

Widow Peyssou (c. 1810)
South Carolina
Bibl. 5

Peter Pezant
(b. 1786–d. 1843)
Charleston, S.C. (c. 1816)
Bibl. 5

August Pfaff
(c. 1829–1833)
Philadelphia, Pa.
Bibl. 3

Henry Pfaff (c. 1829–1833)
Philadelphia, Pa.
Bibl. 3

John William Pfaltz
(c. 1800–1812)
Baltimore, Md.
(c. 1800–1806)
Alexandria, Va.
Sadtler & Pfaltz
(c. 1800–1806)
Bibl. 19, 38, 91

F. Pfeiffer (c. 1839–1847)
St. Louis, Mo.
Bibl. 54, 155

Hermann Pfluefer
  (c. 1849–1850)
Philadelphia, Pa.
Bibl. 3

David Pheil (File)
  (c. 1798–1817)
Philadelphia, Pa.
Bibl. 3

Phelph & Cary Co.
  (c. 1904)
New York, N. Y.
Became Hartford Sterling
  Company
Bibl. 127, 157

Phelps & Holland
  (c. 1827–1828)
Northampton, Mass.
E. S. Phelps
Nelson Holland
Bibl. 84

Phelps & Strong
  (c. 1823–1826)
Northampton, Mass.
Ebenezer S. Phelps
———— Strong
Bibl. 44, 110

Phelps & White
  (c. 1828–1830)
Northampton, Mass.
Ebenezer S. Phelps
G. W. White
Bibl. 84

Phelps
(See Bowles & Phelps)

Charles H. Phelps
  (c. 1825)
Bainbridge, N.Y.
Bibl. 25, 44, 114, 124

[C H PHELPS]

Ebenezer S. Phelps
  (c. 1815–1831)
Northampton, Mass.
Phelps & Strong
  (1823–1826)
Phelps & Holland (1827)
Phelps & White (1828–1830)
Bibl. 84, 110

Jedediah Phelps (c. 1781)
Great Barrington, Vt.
Rome, N.Y. (1785–1800)
Bibl. 23, 28, 36, 44, 110, 124

Samuel F. Phelps
  (c. 1834–1838)
Troy, N.Y.
Bibl. 20, 95, 124

Silas Phelps
  (b. 1788–d. 1825)
Newark, N.J. (c. 1815)
New York, N.Y. (c. 1825)
Downing & Phelps
*Bibl. 46, 54, 91, 114, 124,
  138*

George M. Phenix (1875)
Alfred, Me.
Bibl. 105

**Philadelphia
  Silversmithing Co.**
  (c. 1890–1935)
Philadelphia, Pa.
Bibl. 127, 157

George Philbrick
  (1860–1875)
Skowhegan, Me.
Bibl. 105

Helen Porter Philbrick
  (c. 1926)   **H L P**
Danvers, Mass.
Daughter of Franklin Porter
Bibl. 127

Philibert
(See Philobad)

Philip & Yver (c. 1796)
Philadelphia, Pa.
Bibl. 36, 44

**Ranard Guyeon & Yver
  Philip** (c. 1796)
Philadelphia, Pa.
Bibl. 23

———— **Philipe** (c. 1794)
Philadelphia, Pa.
Georgeon & Philipe
Bibl. 3

Philippe & Le Gras
  (c. 1796)

Baltimore, Md.
Joseph Phillippe
John Francis LeGras
Bibl. 38

J. Philippe
(See Phillippe)

**James D. Philips
  (Phillips)**
  (c. 1824–1829)
Cincinnati, Ohio
Bibl. 24, 25, 29, 34, 36, 44

[JAS. D. PHILIPS]

Jasper D. Philips
(Incorrect name for James D.
  Philips)

Edward Philley (c. 1846)
Philadelphia, Pa.
Bibl. 3

**Joseph Phillippe
  (Phillyss) (Phillips)
  (Philippe)**
Baltimore, Md.
  (c. 1796–1802,
  c. 1819–1823)
Philippe & LeGras (c. 1796)
Bibl. 29, 38, 44

Phillips
(See Richard & Phillips)

———— **Phillips** (c. 1817)
Winchester, Va.
Phillips & Foster
Bibl. 19

Phillips & Foster (c. 1817)
Winchester, Va.
———— Phillips
John Foster
Bibl. 19

Phillips & Frazer (c. 1799)
Paris, Ky.
Thomas Phillips
Alexander Frazer
Robert Frazer
Bibl. 32, 54, 68

A. Phillips (c. 1829)
Cincinnati, Ohio
Bibl. 54

James Phillips (c. 1839)
Philadelphia, Pa.
Bibl. 3

James D. Phillips
(See also James D. Philips)

James D. Phillips
   (b. 1804–d. 1835)
Cincinnati, Ohio (c. 1829)
Bibl. 23, 90, 91, 114, 152

John W. Phillips
   (c. 1842–1850)
Philadelphia, Pa.
Bibl. 3, 15

J. W. P

Joseph Phillips
(See Joseph Phillippe)

Samuel Phillips   S P
   (b. 1658–d. 1722)
Boston, Mass.
Salem, Mass.
*Bibl. 23, 25, 28, 29, 36, 44,
   114*

Thomas Phillips
   (1774–1843)
Glasgow, Scotland
Paris, Ky.
   (c. 1792–1818,
   c. 1820–1827)
Hopkinsville, Ky.
   (c. 1818–1820)
Lawrenceburg, Ky.
   (c. 1827–1831)
Phillips and Frazer (c. 1799)
Bibl. 32, 54, 68, 91, 93

Phillyss
(See Joseph Phillippe)

**Augustus Philobad
   (Philibert)** (c. 1839)
St. Louis, Mo.
Bibl. 54, 155

William H. C. Philpot
   (c. 1846–1849)
Philadelphia, Pa.
Bibl. 3, 23

Phinney & Mead (c. 1825)
Location unknown
Bibl. 28, 29, 44   P & M

D. S. Phinney (1875)
Wilton, Me.
Bibl. 105

Gotthold Benjamin Phole
   (b. 1812)
Columbus, Ga. (c. 1842)
Bibl. 17

William Phyfe
Boston, Mass. (c. 1830)
New York, N.Y.
   (c. 1840–1850)
Eoff & Phyfe (c. 1844–1850)
*Bibl. 15, 23, 36, 44, 91, 124,
   135, 138*

W. A. Piatt & Co.
   (c. 1840–1847)
Columbus, Ohio
Bibl. 34

Picadilly
(See Henry Wiener & Son)

Richard Pickadick
   (c. 1770–1776)
Norfolk, Va.
Bibl. 19

Charles Pickering
   (b. 1683–d. 1749)
Philadelphia, Pa.
Bibl. 3, 23, 36, 44

John Pickering
   (c. 1823–1824)
Philadelphia, Pa.
Bibl. 3, 90

Joseph Pickering
   (c. 1816–1846)
Philadelphia, Pa.
Bibl. 3

J. L. Pickrell (c. 1851)
Greenville, S.C.
Bibl. 5

E. R. Pierce (1875)
Auburn, Me.
Bibl. 105

Hart Pierce (c. 1835)
New York, N.Y.
Bibl. 23, 36, 44, 138

**John Pierce (Peirce)
   (Peirse)**   Peirce
Boston, Mass.
   (c. 1810–1816)
*Bibl. 23, 24, 25, 28, 29, 36,
   44, 110, 114*

O. Pierce (c. 1824)
Boston, Mass.
*Bibl. 15, 23, 25, 29, 36, 44,
   110, 114*

Benjamin Pierpont
   (b. 1730–d. 1797)
Boston, Mass.
Roxbury, Mass.
*Bibl. 2, 4, 15, 23, 24, 25, 28,
   29, 36, 44, 91, 94, 110,
   114, 151*

Matthey Pierret
   (c. 1795–1796)
Philadelphia, Pa.
Bibl. 3

Phillip Pierson (c. 1798)
New York, N.Y.
*Bibl. 23, 35, 36, 44, 83, 124,
   138*

John Peter Pignolet
   (c. 1814–1816)
Philadelphia, Pa.
Bibl. 3

John Pigott (c. 1798)
Savannah, Ga.
Bibl. 17

H. Pike (19th century)
Location unknown
Bibl. 15, 44, 114

H. PIKE

George P. Pilling (c. 1845)
Philadelphia, Pa.
Bibl. 3, 23

Pillsbury
(See Old New England
 Craftsmen, Inc.)

E. F. Pillsbury (1860–1875)
Lewiston, Me.
Bibl. 105

Stephen Pilly (c. 1816)
Raleigh, N.C.
Bibl. 21

Amos Pilsbury
 (b. 1772–d. 1812,
 c. 1798)
Location unknown
Bibl. 5

E. F. Pilsbury
 (c. 1850)
Biddeford, Me.
Bibl. 89

Pincheon
(See Pinchon)

William Pinchin
 (c. 1818–1824)
Philadelphia, Pa.
Bibl. 3, 23, 28, 36, 44

**William Pinchon
(Pincheon)**
 (c. 1779–1809)
Philadelphia, Pa.
Bibl. 3

Charles Pine
 (c. 1844–1850)
Philadelphia, Pa.
Bibl. 3

David Pine (c. 1772)
Strasburg, Pa.
Bibl. 3

Edwin Pine (c. 1850)
Philadelphia, Pa.
Bibl. 3

H. S. Pine (c. 1849)
Philadelphia, Pa.
Bibl. 3

Edward Pink (c. 1843)
Philadelphia, Pa.
Bibl. 3

Pinkerd & Brown (c. 1774)
Savannah, Ga.
Jonathan Thomas Pinkerd
Robert Brown
Bibl. 17

**Jonathan Thomas
 Pinkerd**
Philadelphia, Pa. (c. 1773)
Savannah, Ga.
 (c. 1774–1776)
Pinkerd & Brown
 (c. 1774)
Bibl. 3, 17

Charles Pinkney (c. 1795)
Richmond, Va.
Bibl. 19

George Pinney (c. 1849)
Philadelphia, Pa.
Bibl. 3

E. J. Pinson (c. 1856)
Greenville, S.C.
Bibl. 5

Joseph Pinto (c. 1758)
New York, N.Y.
*Bibl. 4, 23, 28, 36, 44, 124,
 138*

Harrison Piper (1875)
Lincoln, Me.
Bibl. 105

James Piper
 (b. 1749–d. 1802)
Chestertown, Md.
Baltimore, Md.
 (c. 1772–1791)
Bibl. 38

John Piper (c. 1791)
Alexandria, Va.
Bibl. 19, 54

John H. Pippen
 (c. 1855–1881)
Mobile, Ala.
Bibl. 54, 148

Joseph N. Piquet
 (c. 1835–1850)
Philadelphia, Pa.
Bibl. 3

Charles Piquette
 (b. 1813–d. 1859)
Detroit, Mich.
Bibl. 58

Jean-Baptiste Piquette
 (b. 1781–d. 1813)
Montreal, Canada
Detroit, Mich.
 (c. 1803–1813)
Pierre-Jean Desnoyers
Bibl. 58

Jean Baptiste Piquette
 (b. 1809–d. 1851)
Detroit, Mich.
Bibl. 58

Vera E. Pirie (1930–1979)
St. Louis, Mo.
Bibl. 155

Henry Pitcher
 (c. 1833–1834)
Troy, N.Y.
Bibl. 20, 124

Pitkin & Norton
(See Norton & Pitkin)

Henry Pitkin (b. 1811)
Hartford, Conn. (c. 1834)
*Bibl. 15, 24, 25, 28, 29, 36,
 44, 92, 114*

Henry Pitkin
 (c. 1832–1834)
Troy, N.Y.
Bibl. 20, 23, 124

Horace E. Pitkin (b. 1832)
Hartford, Conn.
Bibl. 28, 44

J. O. & W. Pitkin
Philadelphia, Pa.
  (c. 1811–1831)
East Hartford, Conn.
  (c. 1826–1840)
John O. Pitkin
Walter M. Pitkin
*Bibl. 15, 23, 24, 25, 28, 29,
  36, 44, 91, 92*

| J O & W PITKIN |

James F. Pitkin (c. 1834)
East Hartford, Conn.
Bibl. 15, 23, 36

Job O. Pitkin
(See John Owen Pitkin)

John Owen Pitkin
  (b. 1803–d. 1891)
East Hartford, Conn.
Vicksburg, Tenn.
  (c. 1834–1837)
J. O. & W. Pitkin
*Bibl. 15, 16, 24, 25, 28, 36,
  44, 72, 91, 92, 110, 114*

| J. O. PITKIN | (PITKIN)

Joseph F. Pitkin
  (c. 1844–1848)
Buffalo, N.Y.
Mather & Pitkin
Bibl. 20, 124

Levi Pitkin
  (b. 1774–d. 1854)
Ogdensburg, N.Y. (c. 1811)
Rochester, N.Y.
Bibl. 20, 124

Walter M. Pitkin
  (b. 1808–d. 1885)
East Hartford, Conn.
  (c. 1825)
Vicksburg, Tenn.
  (c. 1834–1837)
Norton & Pitkin
J. O. & W. Pitkin
*Bibl. 15, 16, 23, 24, 25, 28,
  29, 36, 44, 72, 91, 92, 114*

| W. PITKIN |

William J. Pitkin (c. 1820)
East Hartford, Conn.
*Bibl. 23, 24, 29, 36, 44, 92,
  94*

| WM J. PITKIN |

William L. Pitkin
  (d. 1886)
East Hartford, Conn.
  (c. 1825)
*Bibl. 23, 24, 25, 28, 29, 36,
  44, 91, 92*

| WM L PITKIN |

James F. Pitkins (b. 1812)
Hartford, Conn.
Bibl. 28, 44

Pitman & Dodge (c. 1790)
Providence, R.I.
Sanders Pitman
Nehemiah Dodge
Bibl. 23, 36, 44, 91, 110

Pitman & Dorrance
  (c. 1795–1800)
Providence, R.I.
Sanders Pitman
Samuel Dorrance
Bibl. 23, 28, 36, 44, 91, 110

Benjamin Pitman
  (b. 1728–d. 1814)
Providence, R.I.
*Bibl. 15, 24, 25, 28, 29, 36,
  44, 91, 94, 110, 114*

| B. PITMAN |

I. Pitman
(See John K. Pitman)

John K. Pitman
  (b. 1779–d. 1819)
Providence, R.I.
  (c. 1805–1812)
Bibl. 28, 36, 44, 110

Sa(u)nders Pitman
  (b. 1732–d. 1804)
Providence, R.I.
Pitman & Dodge (c. 1790)
Pitman & Dorrance
  (c. 1795–1800)
*Bibl. 2, 15, 24, 25, 28, 29,
  36, 44, 54, 56, 91, 94, 110,
  114*

William Robinson Pitman
  (b. 1804–d. 1891)
New Bedford, Mass.
  (c. 1835)
*Bibl. 15, 23, 25, 28, 36, 44,
  91, 110, 114*

Richard Pitt(s) (c. 1744)
Philadelphia, Pa.
Bibl. 23, 44

John Pittman
Falmouth, Va. (c. 1792)
Alexandria, Va. (c. 1797)
Philadelphia, Pa.
  (c. 1801–1818)
Bibl. 3, 19, 25, 28, 29, 44, 91

A. Pitts (c. 1790)
Philadelphia, Pa.
Bibl. 23, 36, 44

Abner Pitts
Berkeley, Mass.
Bibl. 28, 91

Albert Pitts
Berkeley, Mass.
Bibl. 28, 91

Richard Pitts
Philadelphia, Pa.
  (c. 1732–1745)
Charleston, S.C. (c. 1746)
*Bibl. 3, 24, 25, 28, 29, 30,
  36, 44, 95, 114*

Daniel Place
Rochester, N.Y. (c. 1827)
Ithaca, N.Y. (c. 1832–1845)
Bibl. 20, 41, 44, 91, 114, 124

William L. Place (1875)
Charleston, Me.
Bibl. 105

Edward Plain
New York, N.Y.
 (c. 1836–1838)
Philadelphia, Pa.
 (c. 1841–1850)
Bibl. 3, 15, 23, 36, 44, 124, 138

Gregory Planquet
 (c. 1797)
New York, N.Y.
Bibl. 23, 36, 44, 124, 138

Platt & Brother (c. 1825)
New York, N.Y.
Bibl. 15, 24, 25, 36, 44, 89, 91, 114, 124, 135, 138

Platt & Brother

Platt & Bro.

George W. Platt (c. 1820)
New York, N.Y.
Bibl. 23, 36, 44, 91, 114, 124, 135, 138

George W. & N. C. Platt
 (c. 1816–1820)
New York, N.Y.
Bibl. 29, 35, 36, 44, 83, 88, 91, 114, 124, 135, 138

GW.NC PLATT

PLATT & BROTHER

James Platt (c. 1834–1837)
New York, N.Y.
Bibl. 15, 23, 36, 44, 124, 138

John Platt (c. 1843)
Philadelphia, Pa.
Bibl. 3

Nathan C. Platt (c. 1820)
New York, N.Y.
Bibl. 23, 36, 44, 91, 124, 138

William Platt (c. 1817)
Columbus, Ohio
Bibl. 34, 91, 110

John Frederick Plint
 (c. 1839)
Philadelphia, Pa.
Bibl. 3

P. S. Plowman (c. 1838)
Wheeling, Va.
Bibl. 19

John F. Plummer
Baltimore, Md.
Bibl. 15, 44

J F PLUMMER

Gustavus A. Pohlman
 (c. 1903)
Baltimore, Md.
Bibl. 127

Francis Poincignon
 (c. 1794–1799)
Philadelphia, Pa.
Bibl. 3, 23, 36, 44

Peter Poincy (d. 1815)
Philadelphia, Pa.
 (c. 1813–1814)
Bibl. 3, 23, 36, 44

W. Poindexter and Son
 (c. 1838–1839)
Lexington, Ky.
Bibl. 32, 54, 91

William A. Poindexter
 (b. 1818–d. 1884)
Lexington, Ky.
 (c. 1838–1859)
Bibl. 32, 91, 93

William P. Poindexter
 (b. 1792–d. 1869)
Lexington, Ky.
 (c. 1820–1859)
Bibl. 32, 91, 93

Pointe & Tanguy (c. 1811)
Philadelphia, Pa.
James Pointe (?)
——— Tanguy
Bibl. 3, 23, 36, 44

James Pointe
 (c. 1811–1814)
Philadelphia, Pa.
Pointe & Tanguy
 (c. 1811) (?)
Bibl. 3, 23, 36, 44

N. J. Poissenot (c. 1806)
Philadelphia, Pa.
Bibl. 3, 23, 36, 44

F. Poissonier (c. 1797)
Philadelphia, Pa.
Bibl. 3, 23, 28, 36, 44

Peter Poitevin (c. 1813)
Philadelphia, Pa.
Bibl. 3

D. R. Poland (c. 1837)
Philadelphia, Pa.
Bibl. 3

P. Poland (c. 1837)
Philadelphia, Pa.
Bibl. 3, 23, 36, 44

**Quom Polgrain
(Polegreen) (Paulgreen)**
Philadelphia, Pa.
 (c. 1797–1799)
Bibl. 3, 23, 28, 36

**John Polhemus
(Polhamus)**
 (c. 1833–1837)
New York, N.Y.
Bibl. 4, 15, 23, 28, 36, 44, 114, 124, 138

Robert Isaac Watts Polk
 (b. 1818–d. 1861)
Winchester, Va.
Campbell & Polk
 (c. 1850–1858)
Bibl. 19

POLK

Horatio N. Pollard
Boston, Mass.
 (c. 1798–1820?)
New Orleans, La.
Bibl. 15, 110

H. N. POLLARD

H. N. Pollard & Co.
 (c. 1825)
New Orleans, La.?
Bibl. 15, 44, 114

Lewis R. Pollard
(c. 1818–1832)
Norfolk, Va.
Murphy & Pollard
(c. 1818–1820)
Freeman & Pollard
(c. 1832–1834)
Bibl. 19

William Pollard
(b. 1690–d. 1740)
Charleston, S.C.
(c. 1738–1740)
Bibl. 5, 110, 114, 116, 119

William Pollard
(b. 1687–d. 1746)
Boston, Mass.
*Bibl. 2, 15, 23, 24, 25, 29,
36, 44, 54*

Jonas Polley (c. 1823)
Steubenville, Ohio
Bibl. 34

Hyman Pollock
(c. 1841–1850)
Philadelphia, Pa.
Bibl. 3

Hunt Pomeroy
Ithaca, N.Y. (c. 1828–1829)
Elmira, N.Y. (c. 1832)
Bibl. 20, 124

Lewis Joseph Poncet
(c. 1800–1822)
Baltimore, Md.
*Bibl. 24, 25, 28, 29, 36, 38,
44, 91, 114*

Elijah T. Pond (1875)
Guilford, Me.
Bibl. 105

Thomas Pons
(b. 1757–d. 1827)
Boston, Mass. (c. 1789)
*Bibl. 4, 23, 24, 25, 28, 29,
36, 44, 91, 94, 110*

Peter Ponson (c. 1796)
Philadelphia, Pa.
Bibl. 3

John Baptiste Pontier
(c. 1801)
Baltimore, Md.
Bibl. 38

Pontifex
(See R. Blackinton & Co.)

Pontran
(See Poutrau)

David L. Pool
(b. 1810–d. 1861)
Philadelphia, Pa.
(before 1832)
Salisbury, N.C.
Bibl. 21

James Pool (c. 1837–1844)
Philadelphia, Pa.
Bibl. 3

James M. Pool (c. 1846)
Washington, N.C.
Bibl. 21

Thomas Pool
(c. 1842–1850)
Philadelphia, Pa.
Bibl. 3

Poole Silver Co.
(1893–present)
Taunton, Mass.
Successor to Poole & Rocke
Became division of Towle
Mfg. Co. in 1971
Bibl. 127

Charles Poole
(c. 1819–1835)
New York, N.Y.
Bibl. 35, 83, 124

Henry Poole
(b. 1754, c. 1775)
Maryland
Bibl. 28, 38

J. Poole (c. 1850)
Leesburg, Va.
Bibl. 19

Nicholas Poole
(c. 1770–1776)
Norfolk, Va.
Bibl. 19

Thomas Poole (c. 1776)
Norfolk, Va.
Bibl. 19

William Poole
(b. 1764–d. 1846)
Wilmington, Del.
Bibl. 25, 30, 44, 54, 91, 114

WP	W P

William W. Poole
(c. 1828–1843)
Philadelphia, Pa.
Bibl. 3

Pooley & Barnum
(c. 1850)
New Albany, Ind.
Bibl. 133

POOLEY & BARNUM

James Pooley
(c. 1848–1858)
New Albany, Ind.
Bibl. 133

JAMES POOLEY

J. POOLEY

Nathaniel C. Poor
(b. 1808–d. 1895)
Boston, Mass.
Bibl. 23, 28, 36, 44, 91, 104

Porter
(See also Peck & Porter)

Porter (c. 1927)			E S D P
Danvers, Mass.
Son of Franklin Porter
Bibl. 127

Porter & White
(c. 1808–1809)
Canandaigua, N.Y.
Joseph S. Porter
——— White
Bibl. 20, 91, 124

B. F. Porter (1875)
Pittsfield, Me.
Bibl. 105

F. W. Porter (c. 1820)
New York, N.Y.
Bibl. 23, 24, 25, 29, 36, 44,
114, 124, 138

F. W. PORTER

Franklin Porter (b. 1869)
Danvers, Mass. (c. 1925)
Bibl. 89, 127

Sterling F. Porter ℞

Freeman Porter (1860)
Westbrook, Me.
Bibl. 105

George E. Porter
Utica, N.Y. (c. 1834–1840)
Syracuse, N.Y. (c. 1841)
Boston, Mass. (c. 1848)
Bibl. 18, 20, 124, 158

Henry C. Porter (c. 1820)
New York, N.Y.
Henry C. Porter & Co.
  (c. 1830)
Bibl. 23, 36, 44, 124, 138

Henry C. Porter & Co.
  (c. 1830)
New York, N.Y.
Bibl. 15, 23, 24, 25, 28, 29,
36, 44, 114, 124, 138

H PORTER & CO

H Porter & Co

John Porter (c. 1842)
Philadelphia, Pa.
Bibl. 3

Joseph S. Porter
  (b. 1783–d. 1862)
Canandaigua, N.Y.
Utica, N.Y. (c. 1805–1849)
Porter & White
  (c. 1808–1809)
Barton & Porter
  (c. 1811–1816)
Doolittle, Norris, & Co.
  (1842–1846)
Nicholas N. Weaver
Bibl. 15, 18, 20, 25, 28, 44,
72, 91, 114, 124, 158

I. S. PORTER

I. S. PORTER

I·S Porter

M. S. Porter (c. 1830)
Location unknown
Bibl. 28

M S PORTER

William S. Porter (c. 1835)
Philadelphia, Pa.
Bibl. 3

Abraham Portram
  (c. 1727)
New York, N.Y.
Bibl. 23, 29, 36

Portsmouth
(See Old New England
  Craftsmen, Inc.)

Frederick J. Posey
Hagerstown, Md.
  (c. 1820–1842)
Shepherdstown, Va.
  (c. 1842)
Bibl. 19, 25, 29, 38, 44, 114

F. J. POSEY

J. Posner & Sons, Inc.
  (c. 1960)
New York, N.Y.
Bibl. 127

J. Post (before 1800)
Location unknown
Bibl. 28

Samuel Post
  (b. 1736, c. 1783)
New London, Conn.
Norwich, Conn.
Cleveland & Post (c. 1799)
Bibl. 16, 23, 28, 36, 44, 110

Potter
(See Redman & Potter)

Potter & Briggs (1830)
Providence, R.I.
Bibl. 108

Potter & Mellen, Inc.
  (c. 1933–present)

Cleveland, Ohio
Horace E. Potter
Louis Mellen
Bibl. 120, 144

POTTER MELLEN

Potter & Patterson
  (c. 1814–1815)
Alexandria, Va.
John Potter
John Patterson
Bibl. 19

Potter-Bentley Studios
  (c. 1929–c. 1933)
Cleveland, Ohio
Horace E. Potter
Gordon W. Bentley
Bibl. 89

Potter Studio
  (c. 1900–c. 1929)
Cleveland, Ohio
Became Potter-Bentley
  Studios
  (c. 1929–c. 1933)
Potter and Mellen, Inc.
  (c. 1933–present)
Horace E. Potter
Louis Mellen   POTTER
Bibl. 120, 144   STUDIO

A. S. Potter (1870–1876)
Providence, R.I.
Bibl. 108

A. V. Potter (1857–1863)
Providence, R.I.
Bibl. 108

C. C. Potter (1863)
Providence, R.I.
Bibl. 108

C. C. Potter & Co.
  (1870–1878)
Providence, R.I.
Bibl. 108

Horace E. Potter
  (b. 1873–d. 1948)
Cleveland, Ohio
Potter Studio
  (c. 1900–c. 1929)

Potter-Bentley Studios
(c. 1929–c. 1933)
Potter & Mellen, Inc.
(c. 1933–present)
Bibl. 89, 120, 144

H. E. POTTER

J. O. & J. R. Potter
(c. 1810–1824)
Providence, R.I.
Bibl. 23, 24, 25, 36, 44, 110, 114

John Potter
(c. 1813–1821)
Alexandria, Va.
(c. 1814–1815)
Norfolk, Va. (c. 1818)
Redman & Potter
(c. 1819–1821)
Potter & Patterson
(c. 1814–1815)
Bibl. 19, 54   J. POTTER

Niles Potter
(c. 1780–1790)
Westerly, R.I.
Bibl. 28, 44, 91, 110

William Potter (c. 1827)
New York, N.Y.
Bibl. 15, 138

Francis Pottier
(b. 1794–d. 1818)
Savannah, Ga.
Avice & Pottier (c. 1818)
Bibl. 17

Potwine & Whiting
(c. 1735–1762)
Hartford, Conn.
John Potwine
Captain Charles Whiting
Bibl. 23, 28, 36, 44, 91

John Potwine
(b. 1698–d. 1792)
Hartford, Conn.
(c. 1735–1762)
Coventry, Conn.
East Windsor, Conn.
Boston, Mass.

Potwine & Whiting
(c. 1735–1762)
Bibl. 2, 4, 15, 16, 23, 24, 25, 28, 29, 36, 54, 61, 91, 92, 94, 102, 104, 110, 114, 116

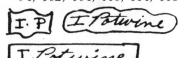

**James Poupard
(Poussard)**
(c. 1772–1814)
Boston, Mass. (?)
Philadelphia, Pa.
Bibl. 3, 23, 28, 36, 44, 110, 124

Auguste Poupon
(c. 1813–1814)
Philadelphia, Pa.
Bibl. 3

Poussard
(See Poupard)

**Abraham Poutrau
(Pontran)** (b. 1701)
New York, N.Y. (c. 1726)
Bibl. 15, 25, 28, 44, 71, 114, 124, 138

**Christopher Frederick
Powell** (c. 1764)
Philadelphia, Pa.
Boston, Mass. (?)
Bibl. 3, 23, 36, 44

John Powell (c. 1745)
Annapolis, Md.
Bibl. 38

John B. Powell (c. 1850)
Philadelphia, Pa.
Bibl. 3, 124

S. C. Powell
(c. 1900–1909)
New York, N.Y.
Bibl. 127, 157

W. S. Powell (c. 1839)
Honeoye Falls, N.Y.
Bibl. 20, 124

Charles Powelson (c. 1841)
Albany, N.Y.
Bibl. 3, 20, 30, 36, 44, 124

Henry Power
(b. 1797–d. 1867)
Poughkeepsie, N.Y.
(c. 1822–1850)
Bibl. 20, 91, 124

Gilbert Powers
(c. 1832)
Utica, N.Y.
Bibl. 18, 20, 124, 158

Titus Powers (c. 1832)
Utica, N.Y.
Bibl. 18, 20, 124, 158

William Powers
(c. 1799–1801)
Savannah, Ga.
Miller & Powers
Bibl. 17

John Praefelt
(c. 1797–1798)
Philadelphia, Pa.
Bibl. 3

Pratt & Lockwood
(c. 1841)
Newburgh, N.Y.
George W. Pratt
———— Lockwood
Bibl. 20, 124

Pratt & Reath
Location unknown
Bibl. 54

A. B. Pratt (c. 1837–1840)
Brookville, Ind.
Bibl. 133   **PRATT**

Azariah Pratt (c. 1788)
Marietta, Ohio
Bibl. 34

Daniel Pratt
(c. 1832–c. 1839)
Ithaca, N.Y.
Munger & Pratt (c. 1832)
Bibl. 20, 41, 124

E. P. Pratt
(b. 1801–d. 1866)
Cincinnati, Ohio
(c. 1828–1829)
Chillicothe, Ohio
(c. 1830–c. 1861)
Bibl. 34, 54, 90, 91

Elisha Pratt (c. 1828)
Marietta, Ohio
Bibl. 34

George W. Pratt
(c. 1839–1845)
Newburgh, N.Y.
Pratt & Lockwood
(c. 1841)
Bibl. 20

Henry Pratt
(c. 1709–1749)
Philadelphia, Pa.
*Bibl. 3, 23, 25, 36, 44, 81,
114, 119*

Katharine Pratt
(c. 1930–1947)
Dedham, Mass.
Bibl. 89, 144

Nathan Pratt
(b. 1772–d. 1842)
Essex, Conn.
*Bibl. 16, 23, 24, 25, 28, 29,
36, 44, 92, 110, 114*

N. PRATT

Nathan Pratt Jr. (b. 1802)
Essex, Conn. (c. 1823)
Bibl. 16, 23, 28, 110

Phineas Pratt
(b. 1747–d. 1813)
Lyme, Conn. (c. 1772)
Westbrook, Conn.
Bibl. 16, 23, 28, 36, 44, 110

Seth Pratt
(b. 1741–d. 1802)
Lyme, Conn.
Bibl. 16, 23, 28, 36, 44, 110

William T. Pratt (c. 1828)
Black Rock, N.Y. (c. 1826)
New York, N.Y.
Bibl. 15, 20, 114, 124

William T. Pratt
(c. 1834)
Washington, N.C.
Bibl. 21

Charles F. Pray (1875)
Millbridge, Me.
Bibl. 105

Charles Pree
(c. 1818–1822)
Philadelphia, Pa.
Bibl. 3

Preisner Silver Company
(c. 1935–present)
Wallingford, Conn.　　P S CO.
Bibl. 127

Premier Silver Co.
(c. 1920)
Brooklyn, N.Y.
Bibl. 127

——— **Prentice** (w. 1788)
Baltimore, Md.
Joseph Morgan Bowene
Bibl. 38

Alanzo T. Prentice
(c. 1826–1850)
Buffalo, N.Y. (c. 1821)
Lockport, N.Y.
Bibl. 20, 124

W. W. Prentice
(c. 1827–1831)
Lockport, N.Y.
Bibl. 20, 124

John H. Prentiss (c. 1832)
Little Falls, N.Y. (c. 1838)
Utica, N.Y.
Bibl. 18, 20, 124, 158

Henry Prescot(t)
(b. 1781–d. 1810)
Springfield, Mass.
*Bibl. 20, 25, 44, 91, 110,
114, 124*

Henry Prescott
(c. 1828–1831)
Keeseville, N. Y.
Bibl. 20, 25, 44, 114, 124

**Presto Cigarette Case
Corp.** (c. 1920–1930)

North Attleboro, Mass.
Bibl. 127

James B. Preston (c. 1819)
Baltimore, Md.
Bibl. 38

James Bond Preston
(b. 1790–d. 1833)
Alexandria, Va.
(c. 1817–1819)
Baltimore, Md. (c. 1819)
Bibl. 19

Jessie Preston
(c. 1900–1918)
Chicago, Ill.
Bibl. 98, 120

Stephen L. Preston
(c. 1825–c. 1849)
Philadelphia, Pa.
Newburgh, N.Y.
Wallkill, N.Y.
Curry & Preston
*Bibl. 3, 13, 20, 25, 44, 91,
114, 124*

S. L. PRESTON

Prevear & Harrington
(c. 1841–1842)
Amherst, Mass.
Edward Prevear
Samuel Harrington
Bibl. 84, 91

Edward Prevear (c. 1841)
Amherst, Mass.
Prevear & Harrington
(c. 1841–1842)
Bibl. 84, 91, 114

Benjamin Price (c. 1767)
Philadelphia, Pa.
Bibl. 23, 28, 36, 44, 112

Henry M. Price
(c. 1860–1862)
Newark, N.J.
Successor to his father, John
Price
Bibl. 127

Henry P. Price (c. 1810)
Philadelphia, Pa.
Bibl. 44　　H·P·PRICE

Isaac Price (c. 1793–1800)
Philadelphia, Pa.
Leslie & Price
Bibl. 3

John Price (c. 1764)
Lancaster, Pa.
Bibl. 23, 28, 36, 44, 112

John Price (c. 1840–1860)
Newark, N.J.
Bibl. 127

Joseph Price
(See Joseph Rice)

Philip Price (c. 1824)
Philadelphia, Pa.
Bibl. 3

Philip Price Jr.
(c. 1813–1825)
Philadelphia, Pa.
Bibl. 3

William Price (c. 1806)
Cincinnati, Ohio
Bibl. 34, 152

William H. Price
(c. 1818–1822)
Philadelphia, Pa.
Bibl. 3

Prichard
(See Burger & Prichard)

P. Prie (c. 1780)
Location unknown
Bibl. 10, 28, 29, 44

Joseph Priest (b. 1756)
Maryland (c. 1775)
Bibl. 38

Prill Silver Co., Inc.
(c. 1940–present)
New York, N.Y.
Successor to Edward Prill,
Inc.
Bibl. 127

Edward Prill, Inc.
(c. 1936)
New York, N.Y.
Became Prill Silver Co.
(c. 1940–present)
Bibl. 127

Prime & Roshore
(1832–1834)
New York, N.Y.
————— Prime
John Roshore
Became Roshore & Prime
(1834–1848)
(See Ketcham & McDougall)
Bibl. 15, 124

Prime, Roshore & Co.
(1848–1850)
New York, N.Y.
(See Ketcham & McDougall)
Bibl. 127

Peter Primrose
(c. 1811–1816)
Augusta, Ga.
Bibl. 17

Abraham Prince (c. 1825)
Boston, Mass.
Bibl. 24, 91 | A. PRINCE |

Job Prince | I. P |
(b. 1680–d. 1704)
Milford, Conn.
Boston, Mass.
Hull, Mass.
Bibl. 16, 23, 24, 25, 28, 29,
36, 44, 61, 92, 94, 102,
110, 143

Samuel Prioleau
(b. 1690–d. 1752)
Charleston, S.C. (c. 1721)
Bibl. 5

E. Priollaud (1860–1870)
New Orleans, La.
Bibl. 141

John N. Prior
Fayetteville, N.C.
Warren Prior & Son
(after 1887)
Bibl. 21, 91

Warren Prior
(b. 1811–d. 1909,
c. 1833–1887)
Fayetteville, N.C.
(c. 1834–1836,
after 1887)
Northfield, Mass.
Campbell & Prior
(c. 1834–1836)

Warren Prior & Son
(after 1887)
Bibl. 21, 91

Warren Prior & Son
(after 1887)
Fayetteville, N.C.
Warren Prior
John N. Prior
Bibl. 21, 91

Priscilla
(See Simons, Bro. & Co.)

Jacob Probasco (c. 1822)
Philadelphia, Pa.
Bibl. 3

Emile Profilet
(b. 1801–d. 1868)
New Orleans, La. (1822)
Natchez, Miss. (1823–1868)
Bibl. 141

G. Promise (c. 1816–1817)
Philadelphia, Pa.
Bibl. 3

William Promise
(c. 1810–1818)
Philadelphia, Pa.
Bibl. 3

Prouhet & Witt
(1850–1858)
St. Louis, Mo.
Bibl. 155

J. N. Provenzano
(c. 1896–1904)
New York, N.Y.
Bibl. 114, 127   TRADE (L) MARK.

Providence Stock Co.
(c. 1896–1950)
Providence, R.I.
Bibl. 114, 127

Pryor Mfg. Co., Inc.
Newark, N.J. (c. 1915)
Became B. M. Shanley, Jr.,
Co. (c. 1915–1922)
Bibl. 127, 157

Charles Pryse (c. 1824)
Baltimore, Md.
Bibl. 38

Jonathan H. Pugh
(c. 1845–1850)
Philadelphia, Pa.
Bibl. 3

Richard Pugh (c. 1845)
Cleveland, Ohio
Bibl. 54, 65

Robert Pullen
(c. 1798–1811)
Philadelphia, Pa.
Bibl. 3

Charles Purcell (d. 1815)
Richmond, Va.
(c. 1791–1795)
Bibl. 19

Charles Purcell II
(c. 1819–1820)
Richmond, Va.
Bibl. 19

Elisha Purdy
(c. 1803–1804)
Kingston, N.Y.
Bibl. 20, 124

J. H. Purdy
(19th century)
Location unknown
Bibl. 54

J. H. Purdy & Co.
(c. 1896–1924)
Chicago, Ill.
(See Guild; U. S. Jewelers'
Guild)
Bibl. 157

Woodbury M. Purington
(1875)
Rockland, Me.
Bibl. 105

John Purkis
(c. 1732, d. 1741)
Charleston, S.C.
Bibl. 5

Samuel B. Purple
(b. 1813–d. 1857)
Columbus, Ga.
Foster & Purple

(c. 1844–1845)
Bibl. 17, 91

John Purse (c. 1803)
Philadelphia, Pa.
Bibl. 3

Thomas Purse
(b. 1776–d. 1823)
Baltimore, Md.
(c. 1795, c. 1812)
Winchester, Va. (c. 1801)
Charleston, S.C. (c. 1813)
Bibl. 19, 38

| T P |

William Purse
(b. 1760–d. 1844)
Charleston, S.C.
(c. 1785–1825)
Bibl. 5, 25, 44, 114

| PURSE |

| Purse |

Henry Pursell (c. 1775)
Philadelphia, Pa.
(c. 1783–1785)
New York, N.Y.
Bibl. 3, 28, 29, 44, 124

| H. P. |

Putnam & Low (c. 1822)
Boston, Mass.
Edward Putnam
John J. Low
*Bibl. 15, 28, 44, 91, 110,
114, 157*

| Putnam & Low |

Edward Putnam
Salem, Mass. (c. 1810)
Boston, Mass.
(c. 1822–1825)
Putnam & Low (c. 1822)
*Bibl. 23, 25, 28, 29, 36, 91,
110, 114*

| E. P |

| E. PUTNAM |

F. H. Putnam (c. 1830)
Worcester, Mass.
Bibl. 89

| F. H. PUTNAM |

Gen. Putnam
(See George E. Shaw)

**George Washington
Putnam** (b. 1820)
Roxbury, Mass. (c. 1842)
Bibl. 23

John S. Putnam
(c. 1835–1848)
Albany, N.Y.
Buffalo, N.Y.
Wright & Putnam (c. 1836)
Bibl. 20, 124

Rufus Putnam (c. 1815)
Albany, N.Y.
Selkirk & Putnam
Bibl. 20, 23, 36, 124

Putney & Howe
(c. 1816–1817)
Sackets Harbor, N.Y.
Reuben H. Putney
Otis Howe
Bibl. 20, 124

Reuben H. Putney
Sackets Harbor, N.Y.
(c. 1816)
Watertown, N.Y.
(c. 1821–1828)
Putney & Howe
(c. 1816–1817)
*Bibl. 20, 25, 44, 110, 114,
124, 125*

| R PUTNEY |

Benjamin Pyle (d. 1812)
Washington, N.C.
Bibl. 21

Benjamin Pyle II
(c. 1837–1841)
Fayetteville, N.C.
Selph & Pyle (c. 1837–1838)
Bibl. 21, 91

George Pyle (c. 1850)
Philadelphia, Pa.
Bibl. 3

Q

Q. S. Co.
(See Quaker Silver Co., Inc.)

Quaker Silver Co., Inc.
(c. 1926–1959)
North Attleboro, Mass.

Became Gorham Corp.
(1959)   **QUAKER**
Bibl. 127   **VOGUE**

Lewis Quandale
(c. 1813–1845)
Philadelphia, Pa.
Bibl. 3, 104

Frederick Quaritus
(c. 1833–1835)
New York, N.Y.
Bibl. 15, 23, 36, 124, 138

Thomas Quayle
(1873–1876)
Providence, R.I.
Bibl. 108

**J. V. D. Quereau
(Quercau)**
(c. 1841–1845)
Philadelphia, Pa.
Bibl. 3

M. Quimby
(19th century)
Location unknown
Bibl. 15, 44, 114, 125

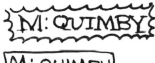

M. T. Quimby (1869–1875)
Providence, R.I.
Bibl. 108

Abrilla Quinby
(early 19th century)
Warren, Ohio
Bibl. 34

Captain Ephraim Quinby
(c. 1799)
Warren, Ohio
Bibl. 34

Daniel Quincy
(c. 1651–1690)

Braintree, Mass.
Qunicy, Mass.
Bibl. 2, 23, 28, 36, 44, 110

Joseph Quinn
(c. 1849–1850)
Philadelphia, Pa.
Bibl. 3

F. F. Quintard (c. 1843)
New York, N.Y.
Bibl. 23, 114, 124

Peter Quintard
(b. 1699–d. 1762)
New York, N.Y. (c. 1731)
Norwalk, Conn.
(c. 1737–1762)
*Bibl. 4, 15, 16, 23, 24, 25,
28, 29, 30, 35, 36, 44, 61,
91, 92, 94, 95, 110, 114,
124, 138, 139*

R

R
(See Richter Mfg. Co., Chas.
M. Robbins, C. F. Rumpp
& Sons)

R & B
(See Chas. M. Robbins)

R & G
(See Riggs & Griffith)

R. & K.
(See Roeder & Kiersky)

R & L
(See Roberts & Lee)

R & S
(See Ritter & Sullivan)

R & W
(See Roger Williams Silver
Co.)

R A
(See Radar Silversmiths,
Inc.)

R B
(See Roswell Bartholomew,
Robert Brookhouse,
Reeves & Browne)

R C
(See Robert Campbell)

R. D.
(See Richard Dimes
Company)

R D
(See Robert Douglas)

R E
(See Robert Evans)

R F
(See Robert Fairchild, Rufus
Farnam)

R G
(See Robert Gray, Rufus
Green, Rene Grignon)

R H
(See Richard Humphrey)

R. J. B. & Co. (c. 1830)
Location unknown
Bibl. 89

R. J. B. & Co.

R. L. & B. Co.
(See Rogers, Lunt & Bowlen
Co.)

R M
(See Reuben Merriman,
Robert Monteith)

R P
(see Richard Pitts)

R R
(See Richard Riggs, Richard
Ritter, Robert Ross)

R. S. Co.
(See Rockwell Silver
Company)

R V
(See Richard Vincent)

R W
(See Richard Ward, Richard
Waynes, Roger Williams
Silver Co., Robert Wilson)

R W M
(See Richard M. Woods &
Co.)

James Rabbeth (Rabeth)
Albany, N.Y. (c. 1834–1835)
New York, N.Y.
(c. 1836–1838)
Bibl. 15, 23, 36, 44, 124, 138

James Rabbith (c. 1834)
Albany, N.Y.
Bibl. 20

Rabeth
(See Rabbeth)

Rach
(See Anthony Rasch)

Nicholas Racich
(1853–1870)
New Orleans, La.
Bibl. 141

Daniel Racine (c. 1799)
Baltimore, Md.
Bibl. 38

George Rackett (d. 1852)
Augusta, Ga.
Clark, Rackett & Co.
(c. 1840–1852)
Bibl. 17

Radar Silversmiths, Inc.
(c. 1950)
Brooklyn, N.Y.   **R A**
Bibl. 127

Radcliffe & Guignard
(c. 1856–1858)
Columbia, S.C.
Thomas W. Radcliffe
James S. Guignard
Bibl. 5

Thomas W. Radcliffe
(d. 1870)
Columbia, S.C.

(c. 1827–1833,
c. 1848–1870)
Camden, S.C. (c. 1833)
Glaze & Radcliffe
(c. 1848–1851)
Thomas W. Radcliff(e) & Co.
(c. 1852–1856)
Radcliffe & Guignard
(c. 1856–1858)
Bibl. 5

**Thomas W. Radcliffe &
Co.** (c. 1852–1856)
Columbia, S.C.
Bibl. 5

William T. Rae
(c. 1856–1864)
Newark, N.J.
Successor to A. J. Williams
Bibl. 127

Joseph Rafel
(c. 1842–1861)
New York, N.Y.
Cincinnati, Ohio
New Orleans, La.
Bibl. 141

J. RAFEL

Raimond Silver Mfg. Co.
(1966–present)
Chelsea, Mass.
Bought W. & S. Blackinton
Co., Inc. in 1966
Bibl. 127

*Raimond
SILVER
MFG CO*

Nathaniel Raine (c. 1773)
Philadelphia, Pa.
Bibl. 3

David Rait (c. 1833–1850)
New York, N.Y.
Bibl. 23, 36, 44, 124

Robert Rait (c. 1830–1855)
New York, N.Y.
*Bibl. 15, 23, 24, 25, 29, 35,
36, 83, 91, 114, 124, 138*

R RAIT

Ralph
(See Loomis and Ralph)

William Ralston
(c. 1840–1850)
Ashland, Ohio
Bibl. 34

John Rambo (c. 1837)
Philadelphia, Pa.
Bibl. 3

Peter Rambo
(c. 1837–1841)
Philadelphia, Pa.
Bibl. 3

William Rambo (c. 1837)
Philadelphia, Pa.
Bibl. 3

John Rampp
(c. 1848–1849)
Louisville, Ky.
Bibl. 32

William Rampp
(c. 1848–1859)
Louisville, Ky.
Bibl. 32, 93

Ramsay & Beckwith
(c. 1840–1843)
New Bern, N.C.
Raleigh, N.C.
Walter J. Ramsay
Robert W. Beckwith
Bibl. 21

W. J. Ramsay & Co.
(c. 1833–1836)
Raleigh, N.C.
Walter J. Ramsay
Bibl. 21

Walter J. Ramsay
(b. 1802–d. 1856)
Raleigh, N.C.
(c. 1826, c. 1833–1855)
New Bern, N.C.
(c. 1840–1843)
W. J. Ramsay & Co.
(c. 1833–1836)
Ramsay & Beckwith
(c. 1840–1843)
Palmer & Ramsay
(c. 1847–1855)
Bibl. 21

Rand & Crane
(1886–c. 1922)

Boston, Mass.
Successor to C. W. Kennard
   & Co.
Bibl. 127, 144, 157 **HOLMES**

C. A. Rand (c. 1846)
Haverstraw, N.Y.
Bibl. 20, 124

Joseph Rand
   (b. 1762–d. 1836)
Medford, Mass.
Bibl. 28, 110

Randahl Shop
   (1911–present)
Park Ridge, Ill.
   (1911–c. 1915)
Chicago, Ill.
   (c. 1915–present)
Division of Reed & Barton
   since 1965
(See Cellini Shop)
Bibl. 98, 127, 144

Randall & Fairchild
   (1837–1843)
New York, N.Y.
Became LeRoy W. Fairchild
   (1843–1867)
LeRoy W. Fairchild & Co.
   (1867–1873)
L. W. Fairchild (1873–1886)
L. W. Fairchild & Sons
   (1886–1889)
LeRoy Fairchild & Co.
   (1889–1898)
Fairchild & Johnson
   (1898–1919)
Fairchild & Co.
   (1919–c. 1922)
Bibl. 127

C. Ray Randall & Co.
   (c. 1915–1935)
North Attleboro, Mass.
Bibl. 127, 157

STERLING R. R.

Randle & Harwell
   (c. 1833)
Eatonton, Ga.
Bibl. 17

James H. Randolph
   (c. 1827–1857)
Greensville, S.C.
Bibl. 5

Alexander Rankin
   (c. 1829–1833)
Philadelphia, Pa.
Bibl. 3

Elijah Ranney
   (c. 1804–c. 1805)
Utica, N.Y.
Bibl. 18, 20, 124, 158

Asa Ransom
   (b. 1767–d. 1837)
Buffalo, N.Y. (c. 1797–1812)
Bibl. 20, 124

Solomon Raphael
   (c. 1796)
Philadelphia, Pa.
Bibl. 3

William D. Rapp
   (c. 1828–1850)
Philadelphia, Pa.
Bibl. 3, 15, 25, 44, 114

Rasch (Rach) (Roush) &
   Willig (Jr.) (c. 1819)
Philadelphia, Pa.
Anthony Rasch
George Willig Jr.
Bibl. 3, 4, 23, 28, 36, 44, 91

Anthony Rasch (Rach)
   (Roush)
   (c. 1807–1819)
Philadelphia, Pa.
   (c. 1815–1820)
New Orleans, La.
   (c. 1822–1851)
Chaudron & Rasch
Rasch & Willig (c. 1819)
Anthony Rasch & Co.
   (c. 1820)
Bibl. 3, 4, 15, 23, 24, 25, 28,
   29, 36, 44, 54, 91, 104,
   114, 116, 122 A RASCH

ANTY RASCH (A R)

Anthony Rasch & Co.
   (c. 1820)
Philadelphia, Pa.
Bibl. 24, 25, 28, 44, 91, 102,
   122
A. RASCH & CO.

W. A. Rasch (c. 1830)
New Orleans, La.
Bibl. 25, 44 W A RASCH

Frederick Rath (c. 1840)
New York, N.Y.
Bibl. 15, 25, 44, 91, 114,
   124, 138

Rathbun & Hudson
   (1857–1863)
Providence, R.I.
Bibl. 108

Rathbun, Leonard & Co.
   (1874)
Providence, R.I.
Bibl. 108

Anthony R. Raulin
   (d. 1824)
Savannah, Ga.
   (c. 1818–1824)
Avice & Raulin
   (c. 1818–1819)
Bibl. 17

Francis Raulin
   (c. 1805–1822)
Savannah, Ga.
Bibl. 17

Xavier Ravee (Ravel)
   (c. 1796–1797)
Philadelphia, Pa.
Bibl. 3, 23, 36, 44

Benjamin Rawls
   (b. 1772–d. 1866)
Columbia, S.C.
   (c. 1816–1866)
Bibl. 5

E. Raworth (c. 1783)
Location unknown
Bibl. 28

E. RAWORTH

Egbert Raworth (c. 1802)
Nashville, Tenn.
Bibl. 54

Asa Rawson (c. 1808)
Charlton, N.Y.
Bibl. 20, 124

Newton Rawson
(c. 1850–1858)
Utica, N.Y.
Bibl. 18, 124, 158

Henry Raymond
(c. 1833–1840)
Albany, N.Y.
Bibl. 20, 124

John Raymond
(b. 1731–d. 1775)
Boston, Mass.
Bibl. 28, 44, 110

**Peter Elizabeth Benjamin
Raynal** (c. 1806–1831)
Charleston, S.C.
Bibl. 5

William Thomas Raynal
(c. 1831)
Columbia, S.C.
Bibl. 5

Joseph Raynes
(b. 1810–d. 1896)
Lowell, Mass. (c. 1835)
Portsmouth, N.H.
Bibl. 15, 25, 44, 91, 114, 125

| JOSEPH RAYNES |

Read (and Owen?)
(c. 1840)
Cincinnati, Ohio
Bibl. 34, 90, 152

Daniel I. Read (c. 1798)
Philadelphia, Pa.
Bibl. 3

Isaac Read (c. 1819–1822)
Philadelphia, Pa.
Bibl. 3

Jacob Read
(b. 1741–d. 1783)
Burlington, N.J.
(1763–1783)
Bibl. 46

John Read (c. 1835–1848)
Buffalo, N.Y.
Bibl. 20, 124

Thomas (Culbert) Read
(c. 1759)
Annapolis, Md.
Bibl. 38

William H. J. Read
(c. 1831–1850)
Philadelphia, Pa.
Bibl. 3

—— **Reade**
New York, N.Y.
Gibney & Reade (c. 1847)
Bibl. 23

S. B. Reading (1875)
Saco, Me.
Bibl. 105

Thomas Reak (c. 1835)
Philadelphia, Pa.
Bibl. 3

John Reasnors (c. 1841)
Rochester, N.Y.
Bibl. 20, 124

James Reat
(b. 1782–d. 1815)
Richmond, Va.
Johnson & Reat
(c. 1810–1815)
James Reat & Co.
Bibl. 19

James Reat & Co.
Richmond, Va.
Bibl. 19

Reath
(See Pratt & Reath)

Charles Recordon
(c. 1838–1842)
St. Louis, Mo.
Menkens & Recordon
(c. 1842)
Bibl. 54, 155

Red Cross
(See J. B. & S. M. Knowles
Co.)

Reddall & Co., Inc.
(c. 1896–1909)
Newark, N.J.
Successor to John W.
Reddall & Co.
Bibl. 127, 157

Henry Reddell
(1858–1863)
Providence, R.I.
Bibl. 108

Redfield & Rice
New York, N.Y.
(c. 1865–1872)
Successor to Bancroft,
Redfield & Rice
(c. 1857–1865)
(See also Bernard Rice's
Sons)
Bibl. 54, 124, 127

Jacob Redifer
(c. 1844–1850)
Philadelphia, Pa.
Bibl. 3

Redlich & Co.
(1895–1946)
New York, N.Y.
Successor to Ludwig &
Redlich
Became Elgin Silversmith
Co., Inc. (1946)
Bibl. 114, 127, 157

Redman & Potter
(c. 1819–1821)
Norfolk, Va.
Henry H. Redman
John Potter
Bibl. 19

| R & POTTER |

Henry H. Redman
(d. 1840)
Norfolk, Va.
Redman & Potter
(c. 1819–1821)
Bibl. 19   REDMAN

Claudius Redon (c. 1828)
New York, N.Y.
*Bibl. 15, 25, 44, 114, 124,
138*

| C. REDON |

Reed
(See Bleasom & Reed,
  Lincoln and Reed, Newton
  & Reed)

Reed & Barton
  (1840–present)
Taunton, Mass.
(Started making sterling in
  1889)
Bibl. 104, 113

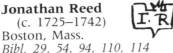

YEAR MARKS

1928	🔔	1941	🔔
	🦅	1942	V
1929	🕯	1943	🗡
1930	⚜	1944	✈
1931	⚓	1945	Ⓐ
1932	🎩		🪂
1933	👄		
1934	🦆	1946	⭐
1935	✚	1947	⚖
1936	🎯	1948	♪
1937	⛵	1949	🪐
1938	🎺	1950	🥁
1939	✽	1951	🔔
1940	🔫	1952	🐘

1953	⌛	1956	♡
1954	⚗	1957	✈
1955	🕯		

Reed & Slater (c. 1830?)
Nashua, N.H.
Bibl. 28, 91, 125

**Augustus Gardiner Reed
& Co.** (c. 1835)
Nashua, N.H.
Bibl. 36, 44, 91, 114, 125

Frederick Reed
  (c. 1814–1823)
Philadelphia, Pa.
Bibl. 3

G. Washington Reed
  (c. 1839–1850)
Philadelphia, Pa.
Bibl. 3

Isaac Reed (b. 1746)
Stamford, Conn. (c. 1776)
Bibl. 16, 28, 36, 44

Isaac Reed (c. 1820–1846)
Philadelphia, Pa.
Bibl. 3, 15, 91

Isaac Reed & Son
  (c. 1830–1850)
Philadelphia, Pa.
*Bibl. 3, 15, 24, 25, 29, 36,
  44, 91, 110, 114*

| I REED & SON |

| I R & S |

John W. Reed
  (c. 1846–1847)
Philadelphia, Pa.
Bibl. 3

Jonathan Reed
  (c. 1725–1742)
Boston, Mass.
Bibl. 29, 54, 94, 110, 114

| I. R |

Joseph Reed (c. 1847)
St. Louis, Mo.
Bibl. 54

Lewis Reed (c. 1810)
New York, N.Y.
Bibl. 23, 36, 44, 124, 138

Osmon Reed | O REED |
  (c. 1831–1841)
Philadelphia, Pa.
Osmon Reed & Co.
  (c. 1841–1850)
*Bibl. 3, 23, 24, 28, 29, 36,
  44, 91, 114, 116, 122*

Osmon Reed & Co.
  (c. 1841–1850)
Philadelphia, Pa.
*Bibl. 3, 15, 23, 24, 25, 29,
  44, 91, 114*

| O REED & CO |

| REED & CO |

Robert W. Reed
Winchester, Va. (c. 1837)
Baltimore, Md.
  (c. 1849–1852)
Bibl. 19

Samuel Reed (c. 1827)
New York, N.Y.
Bibl. 15, 124, 138

Stephen Reed (b. 1805)
Philadelphia, Pa.
  (c. 1846–1850)
*Bibl. 3, 15, 23, 24, 25, 44,
  114, 124*

| S. REED |

Abner Reeder
  (b. 1766–d. 1841)
Philadelphia, Pa.
  (c. 1793–1800)
Trenton, N.J. (c. 1798–1830)
McFee & Reeder
  (c. 1793–1796)
*Bibl. 3, 4, 23, 24, 25, 28, 29,
  36, 46, 54, 91, 114, 139*

| A. REEDER |

John Reeder (c. 1835)
Philadelphia, Pa.
Bibl. 3, 23, 36, 44

William Windor Rees
(1852–1861)
New Orleans, La.
Bibl. 141

Philip Louis Reese
(c. 1857–1897)
Mt. Sterling, Ky.
Bibl. 54, 93

William Reese
(b. 1786, c. 1802)
Baltimore, Md.
Bibl. 38

Reeve & Clark (1818)
Newburgh, N.Y.
Bibl. 20, 124

Reeve & Heroy
(c. 1813–1815)
Newburgh, N.Y.
Isaac Heroy
Joseph Reeve
Bibl. 20, 124

Charles Reeve
(c. 1826–1840)
Newburgh, N.Y.
Charles Reeve & Co.
(c. 1835–1837)
Bibl. 20, 91, 124

Charles Reeve & Co.
(c. 1835–1837)
Newburgh, N.Y.
Bibl. 20, 124

G. Reeve (c. 1825)
Location unknown
Bibl. 28, 29, 44

George Reeve
(c. 1804–1805)
Philadelphia, Pa.
Richard & George Reeve
(c. 1804)
Bibl. 3

J. Reeve
(See James Reeves)

Joseph Reeve (d. 1828)
Newburgh, N.Y. (c. 1813)
New York, N.Y. (c. 1828)
Reeve & Heroy
Bibl. 20, 24, 25, 91, 95, 114, 124

Richard Reeve
(c. 1803–1807)
Philadelphia, Pa.
Richard & George Reeve
(c. 1804)
Bibl. 3

Richard & George Reeve
(c. 1804)
Philadelphia, Pa.
Bibl. 3

Y. Reeve (c. 1808)
Philadelphia, Pa.
Bibl. 3

Reeves & Browne
(c. 1904–1915)
Newark, N.J.
Successor to Reeves &
Sillcocks (c. 1896–1904)
Browne, Jennings & Lauter
(c. 1915–1922)
Jennings & Lauter (c. 1922)
Bibl. 127, 157

Reeves & Sillcocks
(c. 1896–1904)
New York, N.Y.
Became Reeves & Browne
Bibl. 114, 127, 157

Abner Reeves
(c. 1832–1838)
Louisville, Ky.
Bibl. 32, 93

David S. Reeves
(c. 1830–1835)
Philadelphia, Pa.
Bibl. 3

Enos Reeves
(b. 1753–d. 1807)
Charleston, S.C.
(c. 1784–1807)
Bibl. 5, 24, 25, 28, 29, 36, 46

E R REEVES

James Reeves (J. Reeve)
(c. 1837–1838)
New York, N.Y.
Bibl. 15, 44, 114

Joseph F. Reeves
(c. 1835–1840)
Baltimore, Md.
Bibl. 15, 25, 44, 91, 114

J.F. REEVES

J.F. REEVES

Joseph James Reeves
(c. 1831–1837)
New York, N.Y.
Bibl. 15, 114, 124

L. R. Reeves
(c. 1839–1840)
New Albany, Ind.
Bibl. 133   REEVES

Stephen Reeves
(b. 1738–d. 1776)
Bridgeton, N.J.
(before 1754)
Philadelphia, Pa.
(c. 1754–1774)
Burlington, N.J. (1766)
Georgetown, Md. (c. 1775)
New York, N.Y. (c. 1776)
*Bibl. 24, 25, 28, 29, 36, 44,
46, 54, 72, 114, 124, 138*

Referendum
(See Joseph Lesher)

M. A. Regensburg
(c. 1821)
Lovingston, Va.
Bibl. 19

Abraham Regin
(c. 1820–1822)
Philadelphia, Pa.
Bibl. 3

Maria Regnier
(1938–1963)
St. Louis, Mo.
Bibl. 155

Joseph Reibley (Rively)
Philadelphia, Pa.
(c. 1845–1846)
Bibl. 3

Reibling-Lewis, Inc.
(c. 1950)
Providence, R.I.
Bibl. 127   GOLDEN WHEEL

John Reich (c. 1803–1808)
Philadelphia, Pa.
Bibl. 3

Otto Reichardt Co.
(c. 1925–1960)
New York, N.Y.
Bibl. 127

F. R. Reichel (c.1890)
San Francisco, Ca.
Bibl. 89

**Frederick Reicke (Richie)
(Ritchie)**
Philadelphia, Pa.
(c. 1794–1798)
Bibl. 3

Elisha Reid (c. 1814–1816)
Milledgeville, Ga.
T. & E. Reid (c. 1814–1815)
Bibl. 17

Elisha Reid (c. 1836)
Columbus, Ga.
Bibl. 17

Jacob Reid (c. 1763–1783)
Burlington, N.J.

Bibl. 54

James Reid (c. 1825)
Philadelphia, Pa.
Bibl. 3

Josephus Reid (c. 1821)
Milledgeville, Ga.
Bibl. 17

T. & E. Reid
(c. 1814–1815)
Milledgeville, Ga.
Templeton Reid
Elisha Reid
Bibl. 17

Templeton Reid
(b. 1765–d. 1851)
Milledgeville, Ga.
(c. 1813–1815)
Columbus, Ga.
(c. 1836–1851)
T. & E. Reid (c. 1814–1815)
Bibl. 17

Bernard Reilly
(See Rielly)

John C. Reilly and Co.
Louisville, Ky. (c. 1816)
Vincennes, In.
(c. 1817–1830)
Bibl. 32, 54, 68, 133

John Reilly (c. 1783–1818)
Philadelphia, Pa.
Bibl. 3

John Reilly
Richmond, Va. (c. 1785)
Bibl. 19

John C. Reilly (c. 1833)
Philadelphia, Pa.
Bibl. 3

J. H & R. J. Relay
(c. 1848)
Albany, N.Y.
Bibl. 20, 124

P. de Remier
(See DeRiemer)

John Renaud (Renowd)
Philadelphia, Pa.
(c. 1811–1817)
Bibl. 3

**John M. Renaud
(Renowd)**
Philadelphia, Pa. (c. 1811)
Bibl. 3

Renommee Mfg. Co.
(c. 1896–1904)
Newark, N.J.
Bibl. 114, 127, 157

R. M. CO.

Renowd
(See Renaud)

Rentz Bros. (c. 1896–1935)
Minneapolis, Minn.
Bibl. 127

⬡ STERLING ⬡

William Renville
(c. 1837–1839)
New York, N.Y.
Bibl. 15, 124, 138

Revere & Son (c. 1796)
Boston, Mass.
Paul Revere (II)
Paul Revere (III)
*Bibl. 4, 15, 23, 28, 36, 44,
110*

Revere Silver Co.
(c. 1960–1978)
Brooklyn, N.Y.
Successor to Revere
Silversmiths, Inc.
Became division of Crown
Silver, Inc.
Bibl. 127, 146

Edward Revere
(b. 1768–d. 1803)
Boston, Mass.
Bibl. 4, 23, 28, 36, 44, 110

Joseph Warren Revere
Boston, Mass. (c. 1796)
Canton, Ohio (c. 1801)
Bibl. 23, 28, 36, 44

**Paul Revere Sr. (Apollos
Rivoire)**
(b. 1702–d. 1754)
Boston, Mass.
(c. 1702–1754)   P.R

Bibl. 4, 15, 23, 24, 25, 26, 28, 29, 36, 43, 44, 54, 77, 91, 94, 102, 110, 114, 116, 118, 119, 122, 135, 151

Paul Revere (II)
(b. 1735–d. 1818)
Boston, Mass.
Revere & Son (c. 1796)
Bibl. 4, 15, 23, 24, 25, 26, 28, 29, 36, 43, 54, 77, 91, 94, 104, 110, 114, 116, 118, 119, 122, 135, 139, 142, 151

Paul Revere (III)
(b. 1760–d. 1813)
Boston, Mass.
Revere & Son (c. 1796)
Bibl. 4, 15, 23, 28, 29, 36, 44, 110

Paul Revere Silver Co., Inc.
(1912–1922)
Boston, Mass.
Bibl. 135

Thomas Revere
(b. 1738–d. 1817)
Boston, Mass.
Bibl. 4, 23, 24, 25, 28, 29, 36, 44, 110, 114

Rev-O-Noc
(See Hibbard, Spencer, Bartlett & Co.)

Henry Reymond (c. 1842)
St. Louis, Mo.
Bibl. 54, 155

A. G. Reynolds
(1868–1873)
Pawtucket, R.I.
Bibl. 108

George W. Reynolds
(c. 1837–1843)
Philadelphia, Pa.
Bibl. 3

Henry A. Reynolds
(c. 1847)
Rochester, N.Y.
Bibl. 20, 124

John Reynolds
(b. 1770–d. 1832)
Hagerstown, Md.
(c. 1790–1832)
Bibl. 25, 29, 38, 44, 91, 114

S. R. Reynolds (c. 1800)
Boston, Mass.
Bibl. 28

Theodore J. Reynolds
(b. 1806)
Philadelphia, Pa.
(c. 1830–1833)
New York, N.Y.
Utica, N.Y. (c. 1850–1851)
Bibl. 3, 15, 20, 23, 24, 44, 124, 138, 158

Thomas Reynolds
(c. 1784, d. 1785)
Philadelphia, Pa.
Bibl. 3, 28

William Reynolds
(c. 1770)
Exeter, R.I. (w. 1747)
Bibl. 54, 110

John Rheinhart (c. 1839)
Buffalo, N.Y.
Bibl. 20, 124

James F. Rhodes (c. 1837)
Cincinnati, Ohio
Bibl. 34, 152

Thomas F. Rhodes
(1832–1836)
Cincinnati, Ohio
Bibl. 54, 90

Rhododendron
(See G. B. Stocking)

Isaac Riboulau (c. 1726)
Location unknown
Bibl. 2

———— **Rice** (c. 1780)
Location unknown
Bibl. 28, 29

Rice & Barry
(c. 1785–1787)
Baltimore, Md.
Joseph Rice
Standish Barry
Bibl. 38

Rice & Burnett (c. 1860)
Cleveland, Ohio
Bibl. 89

Rice & Rutter (c. 1794)
Baltimore, Md.
Joseph Rice
Richard Rutter
Bibl. 38, 91

A. W. Rice (c. 1850)
Hamilton, N.Y.
Bibl. 20, 124

Arthur Rice
(b. 1785–d. 1808)
Savannah, Ga.
Bibl. 17

Henry P. Rice
(c. 1815–1830)
Saratoga Springs, N.Y.
(c. 1827–1830)
Albany, N.Y.
Bibl. 15, 20, 23, 24, 25, 36, 44, 91, 114, 124

J. J. Rice (c. 1849)
Auburn, N.Y.
Bibl. 20, 124

Joseph Rice
 (b. 1761–d. 1808)
Baltimore, Md.
 (c. 1784–1787, c. 1794)
Savannah, Ga.
 (c. 1799–1801)
Augusta, Ga. (c. 1802)
Rice & Barry (c. 1785–1787)
Rice & Rutter (c. 1794)
*Bibl. 3, 17, 23, 24, 25, 36,
 38, 39, 44, 91, 114*

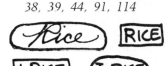

Joseph T. Rice (d. 1854)
Albany, N.Y. (c. 1813–1850)
*Bibl. 4, 15, 20, 23, 24, 25,
 28, 29, 44, 91, 114, 122,
 124, 135*

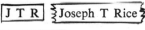

William C. Rice
 (c. 1835–1850)
Philadelphia, Pa.
Bibl. 3

William H. Rice (c. 1839)
Albany, N.Y.
Bibl. 20, 124

Bernard Rice's Sons
 (c. 1899–1959)
New York, N.Y.
Successor to Bray & Redfield
 (c. 1850–1855)
Bancroft, Redfield & Rice
 (1857–1871)
Redfield & Rice Mfg. Co.
 (1871–1872)
Merged Apollo Silver Co.,
 Redfield & Rice, Shepard
 & Rice
Bibl. 127

APOLLO STERLING

Joseph Rich (c. 1790)
Philadelphia, Pa.
Bibl. 28

Obadiah Rich
 (c. 1832–1850)

Boston, Mass.
Ward & Rich (c. 1832–1835)
*Bibl. 4, 23, 24, 25, 28, 29,
 36, 44, 94, 102, 104, 114,
 116, 122, 135*

O. RICH   O. RICH
☆BOSTON☆

Richard & Phillips
 (c. 1832–1836)
New York, N.Y.
Bibl. 15, 124, 138

Richard & Williamson
(See Richards & Williamson)

Augustus Richard
 (c. 1818–1819)
Philadelphia, Pa.
Bibl. 3, 23, 36

George E. Richard & Co.
 (c. 1828–1832)
New York, N.Y.
Bibl. 15, 124, 138

Stephen Richard
 (c. 1815–1829)
New York, N.Y.
*Bibl. 4, 28, 29, 35, 83, 91,
 104, 114, 124, 138*

S RICHARD   RICHARD

Richards
(See also Rickards, Boyd &
 Richards)

——— **Richards** (c. 1819)
Baltimore, Md.
Richards & Campbell
Bibl. 38

Richards & Campbell
 (c. 1819)
Baltimore, Md.
——— Richards
Robert Campbell
Bibl. 25, 38

Richards & Pelletreau
(See Pelletreau & Richards)

Richards & Williamson
 (c. 1797–1800)
Philadelphia, Pa.
Samuel R. Richards Jr.
Samuel Williamson
*Bibl. 3, 4, 15, 23, 24, 25, 28,
 29, 36, 39, 44, 91, 114*

RICHARDS & WILLIAMSON   RICHARD & WILLIAMSON
S.Richards   SW
S.Richard

A. Richards (c. 1809)
Philadelphia, Pa.
Bibl. 3

George Richards
 (c. 1829–1840)
Philadelphia, Pa.
Bibl. 3

Hervey M. Richards
 (c. 1839–1842)
Philadelphia, Pa.
Bibl. 3

John Richards
(See John Rickards)

Samuel Richards, Jr.
 (1860)
Paris, Me.
Bibl. 105

Samuel R. Richards Jr.
 (c. 1791–1818)
Philadelphia, Pa.
Richards & Williamson
 (c. 1797–1800)
*Bibl. 3, 24, 25, 28, 36, 39,
 44, 46, 81, 91, 95, 114*

S.Richards
S.Richards
S.RICHARDS
S.Richards
S. Richards

Stephen Richards
  (c. 1815–1825)
New York, N.Y.
Pelletreau & Richards
  (c. 1825)
Bibl. 23, 24, 25, 44

Thomas Richards
  (c. 1815–1834)
New York, N.Y.
Sayre & Richards
  (1802–1811)
Foster & Richards (c. 1815)
Pelletreau & Richards
  (c. 1825)
*Bibl. 15, 24, 25, 28, 30, 36,
  44, 91, 95, 114, 122, 124,
  135, 138*

| T RICHARDS | T R |

W. & S. Richards
  (c. 1818–1829)
Philadelphia, Pa.
Bibl. 3, 23, 36

William Richards
  (c. 1823–1824)
Philadelphia, Pa.
Bibl. 3

William Richards
  (c. 1842–c. 1843)
Utica, N.Y.
Bibl. 18, 20, 124, 158

William Richards Jr.
  (c. 1813)
Philadelphia, Pa.
Bibl. 3, 23, 36

Richardson & Delleker
(See Delleker & Richardson)

Colin Richardson
  (c. 1819)
Charleston, S.C.
Bibl. 5

Francis Richardson
  (b. 1681–d. 1729)
Philadelphia, Pa.
*Bibl. 3, 4, 23, 24, 25, 28, 29,
  36, 39, 44, 54, 81, 102,
  103, 104, 114, 116, 118,
  119*

**Francis Richardson II
(Jr.)** (b. 1706–d. 1782)
Philadelphia, Pa.
  (c. 1736–1745)
*Bibl. 3, 25, 39, 44, 81, 103,
  114, 119*

| F R |

George Richardson
  (b. 1761, c. 1782–c. 1793)
Richmond, Va.
William & George
  Richardson
  (c. 1782–1793)
Bibl. 19

George Richardson
  (c. 1818–1828)
Boston, Mass.
Bibl. 54

| G RICHARDSON |

George Richardson
  (c. 1845–1848)
Louisville, Ky.
Bibl. 32, 93

James Richardson
  (c. 1840–1850)
Mansfield, Ohio
Bibl. 34

John Richardson
  (c. 1793–1831)
Philadelphia, Pa.
Delleker & Richardson
  (c. 1819)
Bibl. 3

Joseph Richardson Sr.
  (b. 1711–d. 1784)
Philadelphia, Pa.

*Bibl. 3, 4, 15, 23, 24, 25, 28,
  29, 39, 54, 81, 95, 102,
  103, 104, 114, 118, 119,
  122, 142, 151*

Joseph Richardson Jr.
  (b. 1752–d. 1831)
Philadelphia, Pa.
  (c. 1777–1805)
Joseph & Nathaniel
  Richardson
*Bibl. 3, 15, 23, 24, 25, 28,
  29, 36, 39, 54, 81, 91, 95,
  102, 103, 104, 114, 116,
  118, 119, 122, 124, 151*

| I R | J R |

**Joseph & Nathaniel
Richardson**
  (c. 1785–1791)
Philadelphia, Pa.
Joseph Richardson Jr.
Nathaniel Richardson
*Bibl. 3, 15, 24, 25, 29, 36,
  39, 44, 54, 72, 81*

| I N R | I N R |

Martin Richardson
  (c. 1837–1839)
Little Falls, N.Y.
Bibl. 20, 124

Nathaniel Richardson
  (c. 1785–1791)
Philadelphia, Pa.
Joseph & Nathaniel
  Richardson
  (c. 1785–1791)
*Bibl. 44, 91, 95, 102, 103,
  116, 118, 119, 151*

Richard Richardson
  (c. 1793–1796)
Philadelphia, Pa.
Bibl. 23, 36, 44

Thomas Richardson
  (c. 1769)
New York, N.Y.
Bibl. 28, 124, 139

Capt. William Richardson
(b. 1757–d. 1809)
Richmond, Va.
William and George
Richardson
(c. 1782–1793)
Bibl. 19

William Richardson
(c. 1782–c. 1789)
Winchester, Va.
Bibl. 19

William Richardson
(c. 1796)
Norfolk, Va.
Bibl. 19

William Richardson Jr.
(c. 1808)
Richmond, Va.
Bibl. 19

**William & George
Richardson**
(c. 1782–1793)
Richmond, Va.
Captain William Richardson
George Richardson
Bibl. 19

W & G R

C. Richet (1848–1851)
New Orleans, La.
Bibl. 141

Richie
(See Reicke)

Isaac Richman (c. 1850)
Philadelphia, Pa.
Bibl. 3

Richmond & Flint
(c. 1816–1823)
Nashville, Tenn.
Barton Richmond
F. P. Flint
Bibl. 159

RICHMOND & FLINT

Franklin Richmond
(b. 1792–d. 1869)
Providence, R.I.
(c. 1815–1820)
*Bibl. 23, 24, 25, 29, 36, 91,
102, 110, 114*

F. RICHMOND

G. & A. Richmond
(c. 1815)
Providence, R.I.
Bibl. 28, 36, 44, 110

Horace Richmond
(c. 1814–1825)
Canandaigua, N.Y.
Bibl. 20, 91, 124

Thomas Richmond
(c. 1806–1808)
Waterford, N.Y.
New York, NY (c. 1817)
Bibl. 15, 20, 44, 114, 124

RICHMOND

William Richmond
(c. 1835–1848)
Philadelphia, Pa.
Bibl. 3

Richter Mfg. Co.
(c. 1915–1920)
Providence, R.I.
Bibl. 127, 157

Charles William Richter
(c. 1842–1867)
Madison, Ga.
Bibl. 17, 91

**Joseph Rickard
(Rickardus)**
(c. 1796–1797)
Philadelphia, Pa.
Bibl. 3

Rickards & Dubosq
(c. 1828–1833)
Philadelphia, Pa.
Bibl. 3

Rickards & Lancaster
(c. 1817)
Philadelphia, Pa.
——— Rickards
Richard Lancaster
Bibl. 3

Rickards & Snyder
(c. 1842)
Philadelphia, Pa.
Bibl. 3

John Rickards (Richards)
(c. 1841–1850)

Philadelphia, Pa.
Bibl. 3

Nutter Rickards (Rickett)
Philadelphia, Pa.
(c. 1829–1850)
Bibl. 3

William Rickards
(c. 1825–1845)
Philadelphia, Pa.
William Rickards & Son
(c. 1850)
Bibl. 3

William Rickards & Son
(c. 1850)
Philadelphia, Pa.
William Rickards
William D. Rickards
Bibl. 3

William D. Rickards
(c. 1841–1850)
Philadelphia, Pa.
William Rickards & Son
(c. 1850)
Bibl. 3

Rickardus
(See Rickard)

Ricketson Company
(c. 1955–1961)
Taunton, Mass.
Bibl. 127

Rickett
(See Nutter Rickards)

Israel Ricksecker
(c. 1834–1872)
Dover, Ohio
Bibl. 34

Arthur Rider
(c. 1822–1824)
Baltimore, Md.
Bibl. 38

J. J. Rider (c. 1830)
Salem, Mass.
Bibl. 89

James (John) Ridg(e)way
(b. 1780–d. 1851)
Boston, Mass. (1789)
Groton, Mass. (1793)

Worcester, Mass.
*Bibl. 15, 23, 24, 25, 28, 29,
  36, 39, 44, 89, 110, 114*

I. RIDGWAY

J. RIDGWAY

John Ridgway Jr.
  (c. 1813–1869)
Boston, Mass.
Bibl. 28, 91, 110

George Ridout (Rydout)
  (c. 1745)
New York, N.Y.
*Bibl. 4, 15, 23, 24, 25, 28,
  29, 30, 35, 36, 44, 54, 91,
  95, 102, 104, 114, 124,
  138, 142, 151*

G R

Johan Ried (b. 1784)
Philadelphia, Pa. (1810)
Bibl. 23, 36, 44

George Riehl (c. 1805)
Philadelphia, Pa.
Bibl. 3

Bernard Rielly (Reilly)
  (c. 1835)
New York, N.Y.
Bibl. 23, 36, 44, 124

—— **Riggs** (d. 1819)
Philadelphia, Pa.
Bibl. 28

Riggs   Riggs

Riggs & Griffith
  (c. 1816–1818)
Baltimore, Md.
George W. Riggs
Henry Griffith or C.
  Greenberry Griffith
Bibl. 24, 25, 29, 38, 44, 54

R & G

Benjamin McKenny Riggs
  (b. 1799–d. 1839)
Paris, Ky.

*Bibl. 15, 25, 32, 44, 54, 68,
  93, 114*

BM RIGGS

David H. Riggs (c. 1840)
Paris, Ky.
Bibl. 32, 54, 68, 93

George W. Riggs
  (b. 1777–d. 1864)
Baltimore, Md.
Georgetown, Va.
Washington, D.C.
Riggs & Griffith
  (c. 1816–1818)
*Bibl. 15, 29, 38, 39, 44, 54,
  91, 95, 114*

RIGGS
Riggs   G R   G W RIGGS

Richard Riggs (d. 1819)
Philadelphia, Pa.
*Bibl. 15, 23, 24, 25, 36, 44,
  114*

R.R.   RIGGS
RR   Riggs

William H. C. Riggs
  (c. 1819–1850)
Philadelphia, Pa.
Bibl. 3

Albert M. Rihl
  (c. 1849–1850)
Philadelphia, Pa.
Bibl. 3

—— **Rikeman**
Savannah, Ga.
Horton & Rikeman
  (c. 1850–1856)
Bibl. 17

**Riker & Alexander
(Alexander & Riker)**
  (c. 1797–1798)
New York, N.Y.
Peter Riker
—— Alexander
*Bibl. 4, 23, 25, 28, 36, 44,
  114, 124, 138*

A & RIKER

Peter Riker (c. 1797–1814)
New York
Riker & Alexander
Clapp & Riker
  (c. 1802–1808)
*Bibl. 4, 23, 25, 28, 29, 36,
  44, 54, 114, 124, 138*

P. RIKER

—— **Riley** (c. 1786)
Baltimore, Md.
Johnson & Riley
Bibl. 38

Bernard Riley
  (c. 1845–1850)
Philadelphia, Pa.
Bibl. 3, 23

Conrad Riley
  (c. 1837–1841)
Philadelphia, Pa.
Bibl. 3

John H. Riley
  (c. 1876–1883)
Baltimore, Md.
Bibl. 127

Robert Riley (c. 1806)
Philadelphia, Pa.
Bibl. 3

William Riley
  (c. 1818–1822)
Philadelphia, Pa.
Bibl. 3

Roger Lee Rimel
  (1975–present)
St. Louis, Mo.
Bibl. 155

Elijah M. Ringo
  (c. 1830–1850)
Fayetteville, Tenn.
Bibl. 89

Ritchie
(See Reicke)

Benjamin Ritchie
  (b. 1751)
Maryland (c. 1774)
Bibl. 38

George Ritchie
(b. 1785–d. 1811)
Philadelphia, Pa.
Bibl. 3

Benjamin Rittenhouse
(c. 1760)
Norriton, Pa.
Bibl. 3

David Rittenhouse
(c. 1768, d. 1796)
Philadelphia, Pa.
Bibl. 3

Ritter & Sullivan
(1900–1915)
Baltimore, Md.
Successor to Gottlieb Ritter
Bibl. 127, 157   

Gottlieb Ritter
(c. 1895–1900)
Baltimore, Md.
Became Ritter & Sullivan
Bibl. 127

John Peter Ritter
(c. 1786)
New York, N.Y.
Bibl. 23, 124, 138

Michael Ritter
(c. 1786–1800)
New York, N.Y.
*Bibl. 4, 23, 28, 36, 44, 91,
124, 138*

Richard Ritter
(c. 1790–1800)
New York, N.Y.
Bibl. 15, 23, 44, 124, 138

Rively
(See Reibley)

P. Napoleon Rivera
(b.c. 1820–d. 1872)
New Orleans, La.
Bibl. 141

Riverton Silver Co.
(See A. R. Justice Co.)

Apollos Rivoire
(c. 1702–1754)
Boston, Mass.

Changed name; Paul Revere
Sr.

**Roswell Walston
(Walsten) Roath**
(b. 1805)
Norwich, Conn. (c. 1826)
Denver, Col.
Bibl. 16, 28, 36, 44

Amos Robbins
(c. 1846–1849)
Philadelphia, Pa.
Bibl. 3

Chas. M. Robbins
(1892–present)
Attleboro, Mass.
Became subsidiary of
Continental
Communications
Corporation (1963)
Bibl. 114, 127, 135, 157

E. Robbins (c. 1846–1848)
Camden, N.J.
Bibl. 3

Elisha Robbins
(c. 1831–1843)
Philadelphia, Pa.
Bibl. 3, 23, 36, 44

George Robbins (Robins)
Philadelphia, Pa.
(c. 1833–1850)
Bibl. 3

**Jeremiah Robbins
(Robins)**
Philadelphia, Pa.
(c. 1847–1850)
New York, N.Y. (c. 1835)
Bibl. 3, 138

John Robbins (Robins)
Philadelphia, Pa.
(c. 1835–1850)
Bibl. 3

Samuel F. Robbins (1875)
Portland, Me.
Bibl. 105

———— **Robbs** (c. 1788)
New York, N.Y.
Bibl. 28, 124

Robert
(See James S. H. Robert[s])

Christopher Robert
(b. 1708–d. 1783)
New York, N.Y.
*Bibl. 4, 23, 24, 25, 28, 29,
33, 35, 36, 44, 54, 56, 83,
114, 119, 124, 138*

James Robert
(See next entry)

James S. H. Robert(s)
Lexington, Ky. (c. 1806)
Frankfort, Ky. (c. 1807)
Bibl. 32, 54, 68, 93

Roberts
(See Wendell & Roberts)

Roberts & Atmore
(c. 1850)
Philadelphia, Pa.
Bibl. 3

Roberts & Lee
(c. 1772–1775)
Boston, Mass.
Frederick Roberts (?)
———— Lee
*Bibl. 23, 24, 25, 36, 44, 110,
114*

Daniel F. Roberts & Co.
(c. 1840–1850)
Philadelphia, Pa.
Daniel F. Roberts & Co.
(c. 1850)
Bibl. 3

Daniel F. Roberts
(c. 1850)
Philadelphia, Pa.
Bibl. 3

E. M. Roberts & Son
(1825–1890)
Hartford, Conn.
Bibl. 127

Enoch Roberts (c. 1816)
Philadelphia, Pa.
Bibl. 3

F. Roberts (c. 1828–1829)
Philadelphia, Pa.
Bibl. 3

Frederick Roberts
(c. 1770)
Boston, Mass.
Roberts & Lee
(c. 1772–1775) (?)
Bibl. 23, 28, 36, 44, 110

George Roberts
(c. 1835–1843)
Philadelphia, Pa.
Bibl. 3

John Roberts
(c. 1797–1799)
Philadelphia, Pa.
Bibl. 3

John Roberts
(c. 1841–1849)
Philadelphia, Pa.
Bibl. 3

L. D. Roberts (c. 1850)
Hartford, Conn.
Chapell & Roberts
Bibl. 89

Michael Roberts
(c. 1786)
New York, N.Y.
Bibl. 28, 44, 138

Michael Roberts
(c. 1791–1796)
Philadelphia, Pa.
Bibl. 3, 23

N. H. Roberts
(c. 1848–1850)
Philadelphia, Pa.
Bibl. 3

S. & E. Roberts (c. 1830)
Trenton, N.J.
Bibl. 28

Samuel Roberts
(c. 1833–1850)
Fredericksburg, Va.
Bibl. 19

Thomas Roberts (b. 1744)
Philadelphia, Pa. (c. 1774)
Bibl. 28

Thomas Roberts (c. 1842)
Philadelphia, Pa.
Bibl. 3

William Roberts (c. 1745)
Annapolis, Md.
Bibl. 38

William Roberts (c. 1802)
Charleston, S.C.
Bibl. 5

William Roberts (c. 1821)
Philadelphia, Pa.
Bibl. 3

Alexander Robertson
(d. 1751)
Philadelphia, Pa.
(c. 1740–1750)
Bibl. 3, 23, 36, 44

Robert Robertson
(c. 1777)
Philadelphia, Pa.
Bibl. 3, 23, 36, 44

Isaac Robeson (Robinson)
(c. 1843–1846)
Philadelphia, Pa.
Bibl. 3

J. C. Robie (c. 1835)
Binghamton, N.Y.
Bibl. 20, 124

John Robie (c. 1817)
Plattsburg, N.Y.
Bibl. 20, 124

Robins
(See Robbins)

Robinson
(See Robeson)

Robinson & Dixon
(c. 1845–1846)
Portsmouth, Va.

Andrew Robinson
D. L. Dickson
Bibl. 19

Robinson & Harwood
(c. 1814–1822)
Philadelphia, Pa.
John Harwood
——— Robinson
Bibl. 3, 4, 23, 28, 36, 44

A. Robinson & Co.
(c. 1839–1842)
Charlottesville, Va.
Staunton, Va.
Alexander Robinson
J. C. La Grange
Bibl. 19

A. J. Robinson
(1872–1876)
Providence, R.I.
Bibl. 108

Alexander Robinson
(c. 1839–1842)
Charlottesville, Va.
Staunton, Va.
A. Robinson & Co.
Bibl. 19

Andrew Robinson
(c. 1845–1846)
Portsmouth, Va.
Robinson & Dixon
Bibl. 19

Anthony W. Robinson
(c. 1788–1803)
Trenton, N.J.
Philadelphia, Pa.
Bibl. 3, 23, 24, 25, 29, 36, 39, 44, 46, 54, 114

A ROBINSON

Benjamin Robinson
(c. 1818–1844)
Philadelphia, Pa.
Bibl. 3, 23, 36, 44

E. Robinson
(c. 1780?, c. 1820?)
Rhode Island (?)
Bibl. 15, 28, 29, 44, 110

E. ROBINSON

E. F. Robinson (1875)
Ellsworth, Me.
Bibl. 105

G. E. Robinson (c. 1850)
Nashua, N.Y.
Bibl. 89

| G E. ROBINSON |

Hannah Robinson
(b. 1803)
Wilmington, Del. (c. 1865)
Bibl. 25, 30, 44, 114

| H. ROBINSON |

Isaac Robinson
(c. 1829–1835)
Philadelphia, Pa.
Bibl. 3

Israel Robinson (c. 1840)
Philadelphia, Pa.
Bibl. 23, 36, 44

James Robinson
(c. 1827)
Montgomery, N.Y.
Bibl. 20, 124

James Robinson
(c. 1831–1833)
Philadelphia, Pa.
Bibl. 3

John F. Robinson
(b. 1812–d. 1867)
Wilmington, Del.
Bibl. 15, 25, 30, 91, 114

| J. F. ROBINSON |

O. Robinson
(c. 1790–c. 1800)
New Haven, Conn.
Bibl. 24, 25, 44, 61, 92, 110, 114

| O. ROBINSON |

William Robinson
(c. 1810)
Chillicothe, Ohio
Bibl. 34

William Robinson
(c. 1840)
Baltimore, Md. (1844)
Portsmouth, Va.
North Carolina (?)
Bibl. 19

William D. Robinson
(c. 1846–1850)
Philadelphia, Pa.
Bibl. 3

William F. Robinson
(c. 1835)
Philadelphia, Pa.
Bibl. 3

William F. Robinson
(c. 1850)
Wilmington, Del.
Bibl. 30

William K. Robinson
Brownville, N.Y. (c. 1828)
Fayetteville, N.Y. (c. 1834)
Bibl. 20, 124

Wm. H. Robinson & Co.
(1873–1888)
Providence, R.I.
(See Kent & Stanley Co.,
Ltd.)
Bibl. 127

Desire Roby (1895)
Biddeford, Me.
Bibl. 105

Thomas Rochead
(c. 1833–1844)
Albany, N.Y.
Bibl. 20, 124

William B. Rock (c. 1850)
Philadelphia, Pa.
Bibl. 3, 23

Rockford Silver Plate Co.
(1873–c. 1925)
Rockford, Ill.
Successor to Racine Silver
Plate Co.
Became Sheets-Rockford
Silver Plate Co.
Bibl. 127, 157

J.♀♀G STERLING

Rockwell & Garland
(c. 1829)
Macon, Ga.
Peter P. Rockwell
John R. Garland
Bibl. 17

Rockwell Silver Company
(1905–1978)
Meriden, Conn.
Merged Silver City Glass Co.
(1978)
Became Decorex Industries,
Inc.
Bibl. 127, 146, 157

**Rockwell, Smith &
Whitney**
(c. 1788–1789)
Lansingburgh, N.Y.
John Rockwell
David Smith
Henry Whitney
Bibl. 20, 124

———— **Rockwell** (c. 1839)
Bridgeport, Conn. (?)
Bibl. 28 | ROCKWELL |

Edward Rockwell
(c. 1807–1846)
New York, N.Y.
Edward & Samuel Rockwell
(c. 1815–1841)
*Bibl. 15, 23, 24, 25, 29, 35,
36, 44, 54, 83, 91, 95, 114,
122, 124, 138*

| ROCKWELL |
| ROCKWELL |

**Edward & Samuel
Rockwell**
(c. 1815–1841)
New York, N.Y.
Edward Rockwell
Samuel D. Rockwell
Bibl. 15, 91, 124, 138

John Rockwell
(c. 1789–1795)
Lansingburgh, N.Y.
Yates & Rockwell
(c. 1787–1788)

Rockwell, Smith & Whitney
(c. 1788–1789)
Bibl. 20, 91, 124

Peter P. Rockwell
(c. 1826–1833)
Macon, Ga.
Rockwell & Garland
(c. 1829)
Bibl. 17

R. Rockwell (c. 1825)
New York, N.Y.
Bibl. 23, 124

Samuel D. Rockwell
(c. 1815–1841)
New York, N.Y.
Edward & Samuel Rockwell
*Bibl. 15, 24, 25, 44, 91, 119,
124, 138*

S. D. ROCKWELL

Thomas Rockwell
(c. 1775, d. 1795)
New London, Conn.
Norwalk, Conn.
*Bibl. 15, 16, 24, 28, 29, 36,
44, 92, 110, 114, 143*

William Rode (c. 1795)
Philadelphia, Pa.
Bibl. 3

William Rodgers (c. 1824)
Philadelphia, Pa.
Bibl. 3

Peter C. (G.) Rodier
(c. 1810–1825)
New York, N.Y.
Bibl. 15, 23, 36, 44, 124, 138

(W.) Roe & Stollenwerck
(c. 1805)
Kingston, N.Y.
William Roe
——— Stollenwerck
*Bibl. 20, 23, 25, 29, 36, 44,
72, 91, 114, 124*

W ROE

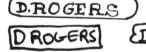

James Roe (c. 1770)
Kingston, N.Y.
Bibl. 25, 91, 124

I·ROE   I.ROE

William Roe
(c. 1795–1805)
Kingston, N.Y.
Roe & Stollenwerck
(c. 1805)
*Bibl. 15, 20, 21, 23, 25, 28,
29, 44, 54, 78, 91, 114,
124, 138*

W.ROE   WR

Roeder & Kiersky
(c. 1896)
New York, N.Y.
Bibl. 127

R. & K.
STERLING.

——— **Roff** (c. 1813)
New York, N.Y.
Bibl. 23, 44, 138

Rogers
(See Leonard & Rogers)

Rogers & Brittin
(c. 1880–1882)
West Stratford, Conn.
Became Holmes & Edwards
(c. 1882–1898)
Bibl. 127, 135

Rogers & Brother
(1858–present)
Waterbury, Conn.
Bibl. 135

Rogers & Cole
(1830–1832)
New Britain, Conn.
Asa Rogers, Jr.
John A. Cole
Bibl. 121, 127, 157

Rogers & Hamilton Co.
(1886–present)
Waterbury, Conn.
Bibl. 135

Rogers & Spurr Mfg. Co.
(c. 1879)
Greenfield, Mass.
Successor to George W.

Spurr & Co.
Bibl. 127

Rogers & Wendt (c. 1850)
Boston, Mass.
Bibl. 4, 23, 28, 44

**Rogers, Lunt & Bowlen
Co.** (1902–present)
Greenfield, Mass.
(See Lunt Silversmiths)
Bibl. 127, 135, 157

**Rogers, Wendt &
Wilkinson** (1860)
New York, N.Y.
Bibl. 127

Augustus Rogers
(c. 1831–1832)
New York, N.Y.
Leonard & Rogers
Bibl. 15

Augustus (Aug.) Rogers
(c. 1840–1850)
Boston, Mass.
*Bibl. 4, 15, 23, 28, 36, 44,
124, 138*

Daniel Rogers
(b. 1753–d. 1792)
Ipswich, Mass.
*Bibl. 2, 5, 15, 23, 25, 29, 36,
39, 44, 54, 72, 80, 91, 94,
102, 110, 114*

DR

D.ROGERS   D ROGERS   D.R

**F. B. Rogers Silver
Company**
(1883–present)
Boston, Mass.
Became division of National
Silver (1955)
Bibl. 135, 146

G. S. & G. L. Rogers
  (1860–1875)
Gardiner, Me.
Bibl. 105

Henry Rogers
  (c. 1838–c. 1850)
Troy, N.Y.
Bibl. 20, 124

James M. Rogers
  (c. 1836–1840)
Troy, N.Y.
Bibl. 20, 124

Joseph Rogers
  (b. 1753–d. 1825)
Newport, R.I. (c. 1760)
Hartford, Conn.
  (c. 1808–1825)
Church & Rogers
Tanner & Rogers
  (c. 1825–1828)
*Bibl. 15, 16, 23, 24, 25, 28,
  29, 36, 44, 54, 89, 92, 110,
  114, 124*

S. B. Rogers
  (b. 1800–d. 1855,
  c. 1840–1855)
Charleston, S.C.
Bibl. 5

Simeon Rogers
Hartford, Conn.
Wm. Rogers & Co.
  (1841–1847)
Bibl. 121, 127, 157

William Rogers
  (b. 1801–d. 1873)
Hartford, Conn.
Church & Rogers
  (1825–1836)
William Rogers & Son
*Bibl. 15, 16, 24, 25, 28, 29,
  36, 44, 91, 92, 121, 127,
  157, 110, 114*

WM ROGERS

William Rogers & Co.
  (1841–1847)
Hartford, Conn.

Continued making silver
  plate
Bibl. 15, 24, 25, 44, 92, 127

William Rogers & Son
  (c. 1850–1865)
Hartford, Conn.
William Rogers
William Henry Rogers
  (William Rogers, Jr.)
Became William Rogers Mfg.
  Co. (c. 1865–1898)
International Silver
  Company (c. 1898)
*Bibl. 15, 24, 25, 44, 91, 92,
  114, 121, 127, 157*

WM. ROGERS & SON

John A. Rohr   I ROHR
  (c. 1807–1813)
Philadelphia, Pa.
Bibl. 3, 24, 25, 44, 114, 121

Henry J. Rohrbach
  (c. 1893)
Chicago, Ill.
Bibl. 127

Rokesley Shop
  (c. 1907–1916)
Cleveland, Ohio
Rorimer-Brooks Studios
Louis Rorimer
Mary Blakeslee
Ruth Smedley
Carolyn Hadley (Vinson)
Bibl. 89

William Rollin(g)son
  (b. 1762–d. 1842)
New York, N.Y.
Bibl. 23, 28, 36, 44, 124

John Romney (Rominie)
New York, N.Y. (c. 1770)
Bibl. 4, 23, 28, 36, 44, 124

Nicholas Roosevelt
  (b. 1715–d. 1769)
New York, N.Y.
  (c. 1735–1763)
*Bibl. 2, 4, 15, 23, 24, 28, 29,
  35, 44, 54, 91, 95, 102,
  114, 119, 124, 135, 138*

Root & Chaffee
  (c. 1826–1880)
Hartford, Conn.
Bibl. 72, 91, 92

Charles Boudinot Root
  (b. 1818–d. 1903)
Raleigh, N.C.
Bibl. 25, 44, 114

C. B. ROOT

L. M. & A. C. Root
  (c. 1830)
Pittsfield, Mass.
Bibl. 15, 25, 44, 91, 114

L M & A C ROOT

W. N. Root & Brother
  (c. 1850)
New Haven, Conn.
Bibl. 25, 44, 92, 114

W. N. ROOT & BROTHER

Washington M. Root
  (c. 1840)
Pittsfield, Mass.
Bibl. 25, 91, 114

Anthony Rose (b. 1731)
New York, N.Y. (c. 1755)
Bibl. 23, 36, 44, 124

William E. Rose
  (c. 1839–1844)
New York, N.Y.
Bibl. 23, 124, 138

William Rosenteel
  (c. 1801)
Baltimore, Md.
Bibl. 38

Rosenthal U. S. A. Ltd.
  (1879–present)
New York, N.Y.
Bibl. 127

Roshore & Ketcham
  (1853–1854)
New York, N.Y.
(See Ketcham & McDougall)
Bibl. 127

Roshore & Prime
  (c. 1834–1848)
New York, N.Y.
John Roshore
———— Prime
(See Ketchum & McDougall)
Bibl. 23, 36, 44, 127, 138

Roshore & Wood
  (1850–1853)
New York, N.Y.
(See Ketchum & McDougall)
Bibl. 127

John Roshore
  (c. 1792–1835)
New York, N.Y.
Roshore & Prime
Bibl. 15, 23, 28, 36, 44, 124, 138

Alexander Coffin Ross
  (c. 1812)
Zanesville, Ohio
Bibl. 34

James Ross (c. 1829)
Zanesville, Ohio
Bibl. 34

John Ross   I R
  (b. 1756–d. 1798)
Baltimore, Md.
  (c. 1790–1798)
Bibl. 25, 29, 38, 44, 91, 114

Robert Ross (c. 1789)
Frederica, Del.
Bibl. 25, 30, 36, 44, 95, 114

  R. ROSS   R R

William Ross
  (c. 1838–1839)
Troy, N.Y.
Bibl. 20, 124

Bartholomew Roswell
Hartford, Conn.
(See Roswell Bartholomew)
Bibl. 25, 44, 114, 124, 158

Nelson Roth
  (c. 1837–1853)
Utica, N.Y.
Bibl. 15, 18, 20, 25, 44

N ROTH UTICA

Volkert Roth
  (c. 1846–1847)
Utica, N.Y.
Bibl. 18, 20, 124, 158

John Round (c. 1634)
Portsmouth, N.H.
Bibl. 36, 44

B. H. Rounds & Son
  (c. 1880)
Rockport, Ind.
Bibl. 133

B.H. ROUNDS & SON

Victor Rouquette
  (c. 1817–1824)   **V. R.**
Detroit, Mich.
Bibl. 58

Anthony Rouse (c. 1807)
Philadelphia, Pa.
Bibl. 23, 36, 44

Emanuel Rouse
  (c. 1747–1768)
Philadelphia, Pa.
Bibl. 3

Michael Rouse (b. 1687)
Boston, Mass. (c. 1711)
Bibl. 23, 28, 36, 110

Sidney Rouse
  (c. 1849–1850)
Rochester, N.Y.
Bibl. 20, 41, 44, 124

William Rouse (Rowse)
  (b. 1639–d. 1705)
Boston, Mass.
*Bibl. 15, 23, 25, 28, 29, 36,
  44, 54, 69, 70, 94, 102,
  104, 110, 114, 116, 119,
  151*

William Madison Rouse
  (b. 1812–d. 1888)
Charleston, S.C.
Bibl. 5, 25, 44, 114

W. M. ROUSE

Roush
(See Rasch)

Pierre Casimir Rouyer
  (1850–1877)
New Orleans, La.
Bibl. 141

C.ROUYER

Rowan
(See Holmes & Rowan)

Rowan & Wilcox
  (c. 1889–1892)
New York, N.Y.
Became Wilcox & Evertsen
  (c. 1892–1896)
Bibl. 127

Thomas T. Rowe
  (c. 1832–1834)
Utica, N.Y.
Bibl. 18, 20, 124, 158

John H. Rowell
  (1860–1875)
Solon, Me.
Bibl. 105

David S. Rowland
  (c. 1831–1839)
Utica, N.Y.
Storrs & Cooley
Bibl. 18, 20, 124, 158

John & William Rowsay
  (c. 1774)
Williamsburg, Va.
Bibl. 19, 153

William Rowse
(See William Rouse)

**Royal Silver
  Manufacturing Co.**
  (c. 1918–1931)
Newark, N.J.
Bibl. 127

John (I.) Royalston
  (c. 1725–1770)
Boston, Mass.
Bibl. 23, 28, 29, 36, 44, 50

Harvey Royce
(c. 1834–1850)
Morrisville, N.Y.
Bibl. 20, 124

John Rubel & Co.
(c. 1939–1947)
New York, N.Y.
Bibl. 126

Roy Rubens Silversmith
(c. 1961)
Beverly Hills, Calif.
Bibl. 127

Antón Rubesch
(c. 1968–present)
Alexandria, Va.
Bibl. 89, 127

J. Rudd & Co.
(c. 1831–1841)
New York, N.Y.
Bibl. 15, 25, 44, 114, 124,
138
　　　　J. RUDD & CO

William Rudell
(c. 1844–1848)
Buffalo, N.Y.
Bibl. 20, 124

Samuel Rudolph (c. 1803)
Philadelphia, Pa.
Bibl. 3

Henry Rue (c. 1835)
Philadelphia, Pa.
Bibl. 3

William E. Ruff (c. 1829)
Halifax, N.C.
Bibl. 21

Rugg & Osborn (c. 1804)
Utica, N.Y.
Samuel Rugg
John Osborn
Bibl. 20, 124

Samuel Rugg
(c. 1800–1811)
Utica, N.Y.
Rugg & Osborn (c. 1804)
Bibl. 18, 20, 124, 158

Israel Ruland
Detroit, Mich. (c. 1772)

Vincennes, Ind.
(c. 1779–1812)
Bibl. 58, 133

——— **Rule** (c. 1780)
Massachusetts (?)
Bibl. 28, 29, 44, 110

C. F. Rumpp & Sons
(1850–present)
Philadelphia, Pa.
Bibl. 114, 127, 157

A. Rumrill & Co.
(c. 1831–1832)
New York, N.Y.
Alexander Rumrill
Bibl. 15, 44, 91, 114, 124

　　A.　RUMRILL　&　CO.

Alexander Rumrill
(c. 1831–1832)
New York, N.Y.
A. Rumrill & Co.
Bibl. 15, 91, 124, 138

Alexander Rumrill Jr.
(c. 1840)
New York, N.Y.
Bibl. 15, 91, 124, 138

Lucius Rumrill
(c. 1832–c. 1833)
Utica, N.Y.
Bibl. 18, 20, 24, 158

Charles Rumsey
(b. 1819–d 1841)
Salem, N.J.
Bibl. 15, 44, 46, 54, 114

| C RUMSEY | C RUMSEY |

William Ruser
(c. 1947–1960)
Los Angeles, Calif.
Bibl. 126

John H. Russel　
(c. 1792–1798)
New York, N.Y.
Bibl. 23, 25, 28, 29, 36, 44

Jonathan Russel (b. 1770)
Auburn, N.Y.
(c. 1807–1817)
Geneva, N.Y.
Bibl. 20, 92, 124

Jonathan Russel(l)
(b. 1770, c. 1807)
Ashford, Conn.
Bibl. 16, 24, 25, 28, 29, 36,
44, 114

Moody Russel(l)
(b. 1694–d. 1761)
Barnstable, Mass.
Bibl. 2, 15, 24, 25, 28, 29,
36, 44, 55, 72, 78, 94, 110

Russelier
(See Russellier)

Russell
(See also Russel)

Arthur Russell
(19th century)
Bardstown, Ky.
Bibl. 32, 54, 93

Daniel Russell
(b. 1698–d. 1771)
Newport, R.I.
Bibl. 2, 15, 23, 24, 25, 28,
29, 36, 44, 54, 55, 56, 72,
91, 94, 102, 110, 114, 119

Eleazer Russell
(c. 1663–1691)
Boston, Mass.
Bibl. 15, 28, 110

George Russell
(c. 1831–1850)

Philadelphia, Pa.
Bibl. 3, 28, 44, 91

John H. Russell (c. 1795)
New York, N.Y.
Bibl. 44, 114, 124

Joseph Russell
(b. 1702–d. 1780)
Barnstable, Mass.
Bristol, R.I.
Bibl. 15, 44, 72, 91, 110

S. A. Russell (1895)
Augusta, Me.
Bibl. 105

Thomas Russell
(c. 1855–1856)
Charleston, S.C.
Columbia, S.C.
Bibl. 5

William Russell (c. 1830)
Columbus, Ga.
Bibl. 17, 68

William Russell
(19th century)
Nelson County, Ky.
Bibl. 32

William Russell & Son
(c. 1840–1865)
Bardstown, Ky.
Bibl. 32, 54, 93

William A. Russell
(c. 1842–1843)
Utica, N.Y.
Bibl. 18, 20, 124, 158

Peter Russellier
(Russelier) (c. 1794)
New York, N.Y.
Bibl. 23, 36, 44, 124, 138

George W. Ruth (c. 1853)
Shelbyville, Tenn.
Bibl. 54

John W. Ruth
(c. 1858–1886)
Shelbyville, Tenn.
Bibl. 159

J.W. RUTH

James Rutherford
(c. 1751–1752)
Charleston, S.C.
Bibl. 5, 54, 118

Benjamin Rutledge
(c. 1809)
Charleston, S.C.
Bibl. 5

Moses Rutter (c. 1811)
Denton, Md.
Bibl. 38

Peter Rutter
(c. 1837–1850)
Philadelphia, Pa.
Bibl. 3

Richard Rutter
(c. 1790–1798)
Baltimore, Md.
Rice & Rutter (c. 1794)
Bibl. 24, 25, 29, 38, 44, 78, 91, 114

Samuel Rutter
(c. 1807–1812)
Baltimore, Md.
Bibl. 38

James Ryan
(b. 1838)
New Orleans, La. (c. 1860)
Bibl. 141

Frank J. Ryder & Charles Wilmarth (1908)
Attleboro, Mass.
Bibl. 135

Rydout
(See Ridout)

Lou Ryerson
(b. 1771–d. 1855)
Manchester (Hawthorne),
N.J.
York, Pa.
Bibl. 15, 18, 23, 24, 25, 28, 29, 36, 54, 91, 114

S

S
(See Frank Kursch & Son
Co., George B. Sharp,
Victor Siedman Mfg. Co.,
Inc., Simons, Bro. & Co.,
Sinclair Mfg. Co., E. H. H.
Smith Silver Co., Webster
Company)

S & A
(See Simmon & Alexander)

S & B
(See Sheperd & Boyd)

S & C
(See Storrs & Cooley)

S & H
(See Seymour & Hollister)

S & L
(See Stevens & Leithoff)

S & M
(See Sibley & Marble)

S. & P.
(See Simmons & Paye)

S & R
(See Sayre & Richards)

S & T
(See Shethar & Thomson)

S A
(See Samuel Alexander,
Samuel Avery)

S B
(See Standish Barry, Samuel
Bartlett, Stephen Bourdet,
Samuel Buel, Samuel
Burrill, Samuel Burt)

S. B. & Co.
(See Simons, Bro. & Co.)

S B C
(See The Steel-Brussel Co.)

S C
(See Samuel Casey, S. Cottle Co.)

S C & Co.
(See Stephen Castan & Co., Simon Chaudrons & Co.)

S D
(See Samuel Drown, Shem Drowne)

S E
(See Stephen Emery)

S. E. B.
(See National Silver Company)

S E Co.
(See Strong & Elder Co.)

S F
(See Samuel Ford)

S G
(See S. Garre, Samuel Gilbert, Samuel Gray)

S H
(See Stephen Hardy, Stephen Hopkins Jr., Samuel Hough, Silberstein, Hecht & Co.)

S J
(See Samuel Johnson)

S K
(See Samuel Kirk)

S L
(See Samuel Leach)

S M
(See Samuel Merriman, Silas Merriman, Samuel Minott, Sylvester Morris)

S. M. L. & Co.
(See S. M. Lewis & Co.)

S P
(See Samuel Pancoast, Samuel Parmele, Samuel Phillips)

S R
(See Samuel Richards Jr.)

S S
(See Silas Sawin, Simon Sexnine, Samuel Soumain, Simeon Soumaine)

S S M C
(See The Sterling Silver Mfg. Co.)

S S S
(See Stone Sterling Silver Co.)

S S S Co.
(See Sterling Silver Souvenir Co.)

S T
(See Samuel Tingley, S. Townsend)

S V
(See Samuel Vernon)

S W
(See Samuel Warner, Samuel Waters, Simon Wedge Sr., S. White, Silas White, Samuel Williamson)

S W L
(See Samuel W. Lee)

Saart Bros. Company
(c. 1915–1983)
Attleboro, Mass.
William H. Saart
Albert Saart
Herman Saart
Successor to W. M. Saart Co.
Bibl. 127, 147

W. H. Saart Co.
(c. 1906–1915)
Attleboro, Mass.
Became Saart Bros. Company
Bibl. 127, 157

John Sacheverel(l)
(c. 1732–1733)
Philadelphia, Pa.
Bibl. 3, 28

Sackett & Co., Ltd.
(c. 1893–1904)
Philadelphia, Pa.
Successor to Mead & Robbins (c. 1860–1893)
Bibl. 114, 127, 157

Sackett & Willard
(c. 1815–1823)
Providence, R.I.
Adnah Sackett
———— Willard
Bibl. 23, 28, 36, 44, 110

Sackett, Davis & Co.
(1873)
Providence, R. I.
Bibl. 108

Adnah Sackett
(b. 1796–d. 1860)
Providence, R.I.
(c. 1815–1823)
Sackett & Willard
Bibl. 23, 110

Sadd & Morgan (c. 1806)
Poughkeepsie, N.Y.
Henry Sadd
Elijah Morgan
Bibl. 20, 124

Harvey Sadd
(b. 1776–d. 1840)
New Hartford, Conn.
(c. 1776–1829)
Austinburg, Ohio
(after 1829)
Bibl. 16, 23, 24, 25, 28, 29, 36, 44, 92, 110, 114

H. SADD

F. H. Sadler Co., Inc.
(c. 1930)
Attleboro, Mass.
Bibl. 127

Sadtler (c. 1790)
Baltimore, Md.
Bibl. 54

Sadtler & Pfaltz
   (c. 1800–1806)
Baltimore, Md.
Philip Benjamin Sadtler
John William Pfaltz
Bibl. 38, 44, 91

G. T. Sadtler & Sons
   (1800–1923)
Baltimore, Md.
Bibl. 127

Philip B. Sadtler & Son
   (b. 1680–d. 1923)
Baltimore, Md.
Bibl. 24, 25, 38, 44, 91, 114

P B SADTLER & SON

Philip Benjamin Sadtler
   (b. 1771–d. 1860)
Baltimore, Md.
Sadtler & Pfaltz
   (c. 1800–1806)
*Bibl. 4, 15, 23, 25, 28, 29,
   36, 38, 44, 91, 114*

 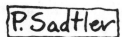

H. (Henry) Harry Safford
   (c. 1800–1812)
Gallipolis, Ohio
Marietta, Ohio
Zanesville, Ohio
Bibl. 15, 25, 34, 44, 114

H SAFFORD

H. Sage (c. 1840)
Location unknown
Bibl. 89

William P. Sage
   (c. 1833–1852)
Athens, Ga.
Benjamin B. Lord
Bibl. 17

G. A. Sagendorph & Co.
   (1858–1864)
Providence, R.I.
Bibl. 108

Washington Sailor
   (c. 1825–1833)
Philadelphia, Pa.
Bibl. 3

S. L. St. Cyr (1820–1860)
New Orleans, La.
Bibl. 23, 36, 44, 141

C. G. St. John (c. 1834)
Saratoga Springs, N.Y.
Bibl. 20, 124

**Charles Grandison St.
   John** (1834–1846)
Macon, Ga.
Bibl. 17

Gould St. John (c. 1817)
Sing Sing, N.Y.
Bibl. 20

De St. Leger (c. 1790)
New Bern, N.C.
Bibl. 21

St. Louis Metalcrafts, Inc.
   (c. 1945–1953)
St. Louis, Mo.
Bibl. 127, 155

St. Louis Metalsmiths
   (1938–1945)
St. Louis, Mo.
Bibl. 155

St. Louis Silversmiths
   (c. 1953)
St. Louis, Mo.
Bibl. 155

Anthony Saint-Martin
   (c. 1794–1796)
Philadelphia, Pa.
Bibl. 3, 23, 28, 36

James Saint-Maurice
   (c. 1748)
Philadelphia, Pa.
Bibl. 3

Salisbury
(See Nichols and Salisbury)

Salisbury & Co. (c. 1835)
New York, N.Y.
Henry Salisbury
Bibl. 25, 28, 91

H. T. Salisbury & Co.
   (1872–1878)
Providence, R.I.
Bibl. 108

Henry Salisbury
   (c. 1830–1838)
New York, N.Y.
Salisbury & Co. (c. 1835)
*Bibl. 15, 24, 25, 28, 44, 91,
   114, 124, 138*

H SALISBURY		SALISBURY

Owen Salisbury (c. 1847)
Providence, R.I.
Bibl. 23

Jacob Salm (1851–1888)
New Orleans, La.
Bibl. 141

Alfred Salmon
Cincinnati, Ohio
   (1825–1844)
Bibl. 34, 90, 152

William H. Salmon
   (c. 1830–1850)
Cazenovia, N.Y.
Morrisville, N.Y.
Troy, N.Y.
Bibl. 20, 124, 138

William Salomon
   (b. 1822–d. 1881)
New Orleans, La.
Bibl. 141

Henry Salsbury
   (c. 1831–1838)
New York, N.Y.
Bibl. 78

Nathaniel Saltonstall
   (c. 1821)
Eatonton, Ga.
Daniel B. Hempsted & Co.
Bibl. 17

S. A. Saltonstall (c. 1830)
Augusta, Ga.
Victor Crepu
Bibl. 17

William Sampson
(c. 1802–1803)
Philadelphia, Pa.
Bibl. 3

Hyman Samuel
(c. 1791–1809)
Petersburg, Va. (c. 1791)
Norfolk, Va. (c. 1803)
Charleston, S.C.
(c. 1806–1809)
Richmond, Va.
Baltimore, Md. (?)
Bibl. 5, 19

A. Sanborn & Co. (1860)
Lowell, Mass.
Bibl. 106

Amos Sanborn (c. 1850)
Lowell, Mass.
*Bibl. 15, 23, 24, 25, 28, 44,
91, 114*

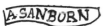

J. G. Sanborn (1860)
Cherryfield, Me.
Bibl. 105

**Jacob Sandbuhler (Jacobi
Cembuhler)**
Utica, N.Y. (c. 1854–1860)
Bibl. 18, 124, 158

Edward Sandell (d. 1822)
Baltimore, Md.
(c. 1816–1822)
Bibl. 25, 29, 38, 44, 114

E. S

Charles Sanders
(c. 1833–1845)
Schenectady, N.Y.
Bibl. 20, 124

James Sanders (c. 1850)
Schenectady, N.Y.
Bibl. 20, 91, 124

Benjamin Sanderson
(b. 1649–d. 1678) B S
Boston, Mass.
*Bibl. 2, 15, 23, 24, 25, 28,
29, 36, 44, 69, 94, 110,
114, 119*

Joseph Sanderson
(b. 1642–d. 1687)
Boston, Mass.
Bibl. 2, 15, 28, 110

Robert Sanderson
(b. 1608–d. 1693)
Boston, Mass.
Hull & Sanderson
(c. 1652–1683)
*Bibl. 15, 23, 24, 25, 28, 29,
36, 44, 69, 94, 102, 104,
110, 114, 116, 118, 119,
125, 135, 142, 151*

Robert Sanderson Jr.
(b. 1652–d. 1714)
Boston, Mass.
Watertown, Mass.
*Bibl. 2, 15, 23, 28, 36, 54,
94, 110*

William Sanderson
(c. 1799–1801)
New York, N.Y.
Bibl. 23, 36, 44, 124, 138

Sandford
(See Frederick C. Sanford,
William Sanford)

F. S. Sandford (c. 1830)
Location unknown
Bibl. 89

F. S. Sandford

Sandland, Capron & Co.
(c. 1896–1909)
North Attleboro, Mass.
Bibl. 114, 127, 157 **S. C. & CO.
STERLING**

F. A. Sandon (c. 1809)
Charleston, S.C.
Bibl. 5

Peter Sandose (Sandoz)
(c. 1824)
Baltimore, Md.
Bibl. 38

Sandoz & Brother
(c. 1811)
New York, N.Y.
Bibl. 36, 44, 124

Charles H. Sandoz
(c. 1800–1802)
Philadelphia, Pa.
Bibl. 3

Louis Sandoz (c. 1845)
Philadelphia, Pa.
Bibl. 3

Peter Sandoz
(See Sandose)

Philip Augustus Sandoz
(c. 1814–1822)
Philadelphia, Pa.
Bibl. 3, 23, 36, 44, 124

D. Sands (c. 1840)
Location unknown
Bibl. 89

Stephen Sands
(c. 1771–1774)
New York, N.Y.
Bibl. 23, 36, 44, 124

Sanford & Beach
(See Beach & Sanford)

Abel Sanford
(b. 1798–d. 1843)
Hamilton, N.Y.
Bibl. 20, 124

Edward Sanford (d. 1814)
Alexandria, Va. (c. 1773)
Bibl. 19, 54

Edward N. Sanford
(c. 1855–1859)
Utica, N.Y.
B. F. & T. M. Davies
Bibl. 18

Frederick C. (S.) Sanford
(Sandford) (d. 1890)
Nantucket Island, Mass.
  (c. 1828–1830)
Easton & Sanford
  (c. 1830–1838)
Bibl. 12, 23, 24, 25, 28, 36,
44, 114

Isaac Sanford (d. 1842)
Hartford, Conn.
  (c. 1783–1824)
Providence, R.I.
Beach & Sanford
  (c. 1785–1788)
Bibl. 15, 16, 23, 28, 36, 44,
91, 92, 110

Judson Sanford
  (c. 1843–1844)
Hamilton, N.Y.
Bibl. 20, 124

William Sanford
(Sandford)
  (c. 1817–1818)
Nantucket Island, Mass.
Bibl. 12, 15, 23, 24, 25, 44,
110, 114, 138

| W Sandford |

Sanger
(See Hall & Sanger)

Michael Sardo (c. 1817)
Baltimore, Md.
Bibl. 23, 28, 36, 44

Ensign Sargeant
  (b. 1761–d. 1843)
Hartford, Conn.
Mansfield, Conn.
Boston, Mass.
Bibl. 23, 24, 25, 28, 29, 36,
44, 110, 114

H. Sargeant
  (b. 1796–d. 1864)
Springfield, Mass. (1825)
Hartford, Conn. (?)
Bibl. 15, 25, 44, 92, 94, 110,
114

H. Sargent

H. Sargeant

Jacob Sargeant
  (b. 1761–d. 1843,
  c. 1785–1838)
Hartford, Conn.
Mansfield, Conn.
Springfield, Mass.
Bibl. 2, 15, 16, 23, 24, 25,
28, 29, 36, 44, 61, 88, 91,
92, 94, 110, 114

| J SARGEANT |

Thomas Sargeant
  (b. 1773–d. 1834)
Springfield, Mass.
  (c. 1810–1816)
Connecticut
Bibl. 15, 25, 28, 44, 91, 110,
114

Sargent & Gaylord
  (c. 1822)
Batavia, N.Y.
Bibl. 20, 124

A. G. Sargent (c. 1830's)
Milan, Ohio
Bibl. 34

J. E. Sargent (1875)
Portland, Me.
Bibl. 105

John Sargent
  (c. 1821)
Wilmington, N.C.
Bibl. 21

Sarrazin & Wright
  (c. 1746)
Charleston, S.C.
Moreau Sarrazin
William Wright
Bibl. 54

Jonathan Sarrazin
  (c. 1754–1790)
Charleston, S.C.
Moreau & Jonathan Sarrazin
  (c. 1754–1761)
Bibl. 5, 44, 54

| I S |

Moreau Sarrazin
  (b. 1710–d. 1761)
Charleston, S.C.
Sarrazin & Wright (c. 1746)
Moreau & Jonathan Sarrazin
  (c. 1754–1761)
Bibl. 5, 25, 44, 54, 114

Moreau & Jonathan
Sarrazin
  (c. 1754–1761)
Charleston, S.C.
Bibl. 54

Christopher Saur (c. 1724)
Philadelphia, Pa.
Bibl. 3

William S. Saurman
  (c. 1829)
Philadelphia, Pa.
Bibl. 3

Richard Sause
New York, N.Y. (c. 1771)
Philadelphia, Pa. (c. 1778)
Bibl. 3, 124, 138

Savage and Eubank
  (c. 1805–1820)
Glasgow, Ky.
William M. Savage
James Eubank
Bibl. 32, 54

Savage & Kunsman
  (c. 1823)
Salisbury, N.C.
—— Savage
Henry Kunsman
Bibl. 21

Savage & Lyman
Location unknown
Bibl. 15, 44

| SAVAGE | & | LYMAN |

Savage & Stedman
  (c. 1819–1820)
Raleigh, N.C.
John Y. Savage
John C. Stedman
Bibl. 21

Benjamin Savage
(b. 1699–d. 1750)
Boston, Mass.
Charleston, S.C. (?)
Bibl. 5, 110

Daniel Savage (1860)
Eastport, Me.
Bibl. 105

Edward Savage
(c. 1761–1817, d. 1817)
Philadelphia, Pa.
New York, N.Y.
Bibl. 3, 23, 28, 36, 44, 124

John Y. Savage
(c. 1818–1820)
Raleigh, N.C.
New York, N.Y. (c. 1839)
Savage & Stedman
(c. 1819–1820)
Bibl. 21, 25, 44, 124, 138

Thomas Savage
(b. 1664–d. 1749)
Boston, Mass.
*Bibl. 2, 15, 23, 24, 28, 29,
36, 44, 94, 102, 110, 114,
116, 119, 151*

Thomas Savage Jr.
(b. 1692)
Boston, Mass.
Bibl. 23, 36, 44

William Savage
(c. 1808)
Liberty, (now Bedford), Va.
Bibl. 19

William M. Savage
(c. 1805–1820)
Glasgow, Ky.
Savage & Eubank
*Bibl. 15, 25, 32, 44, 54, 68,
91, 93, 114*

William Savil (Saville)
Philadelphia, Pa.
(c. 1820–1837)
Bibl. 3

Silas Sawin (c. 1811–1838)
Boston, Mass.
*Bibl. 2, 15, 23, 24, 28, 29,
36, 110, 114, 124, 135*

Silas W. Sawin
(c. 1825–1838)
New York, N.Y.
*Bibl. 23, 25, 36, 44, 124,
135, 138*

H. L. Sawyer (c. 1840)
New York, N.Y.
Hartford, Conn. (?)
Coe & Upton
*Bibl. 15, 23, 24, 25, 28, 29,
36, 44, 91, 92, 114, 124*

Joseph Saxton
(c. 1823–1824)
Philadelphia, Pa.
Bibl. 3

Saya
Southampton, L.I., N.Y.
Bibl. 54

Sayre & Richards
(c. 1802–1811)
New York, N.Y.
John Sayre
Thomas Richards
*Bibl. 15, 23, 24, 25, 29, 35,
44, 54, 91, 95, 114, 124,
135, 138*

David A. (E.) Sayre
(b. 1793–d. 1870)
Lexington, Ky.
Bibl. 32, 68, 93

Joel Sayre (c. 1778–1818)
New York, N.Y.
*Bibl. 15, 23, 24, 25, 28, 29,
30, 35, 36, 44, 54, 91, 114,
122, 124, 135, 138*

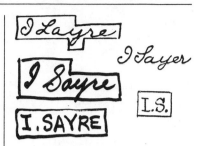

John Sayre
(b. 1771–d. 1852)
New York, N.Y.
Sayre & Richards
(c. 1802–1811)
*Bibl. 2, 3, 4, 15, 23, 24, 25,
35, 36, 54, 91, 95, 114,
122, 124, 135, 138*

I SAYRE   SAYRE

L. Sayre (19th century)
Lexington, Ky.
Bibl. 32, 68, 90   L. Sayre

Paul Sayre (b. 1762)
Southampton, N.Y. (c. 1785)
*Bibl. 15, 20, 25, 44, 91, 114,
124, 135*

P SAYRE

Scarret
(See Skerret)

Scerad
(See Serad)

Bartholomew Schaats
(Schatts) (Skaats)
(Staats)
(b. 1670–d. 1758)
New York, N.Y.
*Bibl. 2, 4, 15, 23, 24, 25, 28,
30, 35, 36, 44, 50, 91, 95,
102, 114, 116, 119, 124,
138*

Murray L. Schacter & Co.
(c. 1950)
New York, N.Y.
Bibl. 127

HAMPSHIRE HOUSE

Rudolph Schaeffer
  (c. 1910)
San Francisco, Calif.
Bibl. 89, 140

M. Schafer (c. 1840)
Location unknown
Bibl. 89

Jeremiah Schaffield
  (c. 1785)
Philadelphia, Pa.
Bibl. 3, 23, 36, 44

J. Schanck
(See J. Schank)

Schank
(See also Van Voorhis,
  Schanck & McCall)

Garret (Gerrit) Schank
  (d. 1795)
New York, N.Y. (c. 1791)
Van Voorhis & Schank
  (c. 1791–1792)
*Bibl. 15, 23, 24, 25, 29, 35,
44, 72, 91, 95, 114, 116,
124, 138*

G SCHANK

John A. Schank
  (Schanck)
  (c. 1792–1797)
New York, N.Y.
*Bibl. 15, 23, 24, 25, 28, 29,
36, 44, 72, 91, 95, 114,
124, 138*

J SCHANK	SCHANK
I SCHANK	W

Scharling & Co.
  (c. 1885–1931)
Newark, N.J.
Bibl. 127, 157

Schatts
(See Schaats)

Bernard Scheer (c. 1855)
Charleston, S.C.
Bibl. 5

John C. Scheer
  (c. 1835–1850)
Philadelphia, Pa.
Bonsall & Scheer
  (c. 1845–1847) (?)
Dubosq & Scheer
  (c. 1849–1850) (?)
Bibl. 3

William Scheer, Inc.
  (c. 1910)
New York, N.Y.
Bibl. 126

Samuel F. Schell
  (c. 1829–1835)
Philadelphia, Pa.
Bibl. 3

Nicholas Schelnin Co.
  (c. 1904–1909)
New York, N.Y.
Bibl. 127, 157

Seaman Schepps (b. 1881)
New York, N.Y. (c. 1921)
Bibl. 117

Frederick Schern
  (Shehum)
  (c. 1848–1850)
Philadelphia, Pa.
Bibl. 3, 23

Lewis Scherr
  (c. 1843–1850)
Philadelphia, Pa.
Bibl. 3

William Schimper & Co.
  (c. 1896–1927)
Hoboken, N.J.
Successor to William
  Schimper (c. 1841)
Bibl. 114, 127, 157

John Schimpf & Sons
  (c. 1890–1897)
New York, N.Y.
Became Adelphi Silver Plate
  Co.
Bibl. 114, 127

Jonas (Joseph) Schindler
  (c. 1776–1792)
Montreal, Canada

Detroit, Mich.   I S
Bibl. 58

John Schinkle (c. 1810)
Philadelphia, Pa.
Bibl. 3

Jerome N. Schirm
  (c. 1901)
Baltimore, Md.
Bibl. 127

Jean Schlumberger
  (b. 1907)
New York, N. Y.
Bibl. 117

John G. Schmid (c. 1850)
Philadelphia, Pa.
Bibl. 3

Christian Schmidt
  (Smith) (c. 1819–1840)
New Philadelphia, Ohio
Winesburg, Ohio
Bibl. 34

E. Schmidt & Co.
  (c. 1918–1919)
Philadelphia, Pa.
Bibl. 127

John Schmitt (Smith)
  (c. 1846–1850)
Philadelphia, Pa.
Bibl. 3, 23

Schmitz, Moore & Co.
  (c. 1915)
Newark, N.J.
Became Moore & Hofman
Bibl. 127, 157

Schofield & DeWyngaert
  (c. 1904–1922)
Newark, N.J.
Became F. P. Scofield &
  Company (c. 1922)
Bibl. 127

(Frank M.) Schofield Co.
  (Inc.) (c. 1928–1967)
Baltimore, Md.
(See Heer-Schofield Co.)
Bibl. 127, 147

Solomon Schofield
(c. 1815–1827)
Albany, N.Y.
Rochester, N.Y.
Bibl. 36

Schoolfield (c. 1855)
Location unknown
Bibl. 15, 44, 90, 114

SCHOOLFIELD

Gerrit Van Schoonhoven
(c. 1830)
Albany, N.Y.
Bibl. 20

H. Schoonmater (c. 1810)
Location unknown
Bibl. 24

F. V. Schrader & Co.
(c. 1837)
Philadelphia, Pa.
Bibl. 3

Charles W. Schreiner
(c. 1813–1833)
Philadelphia, Pa.
Bibl. 3

Andrew B. Schreuder
(Schroeder) b. 1828,
c. 1852–1895)
Utica, N.Y.
Syracuse, N.Y.
Successor to Hotchkiss &
Schreuder (c. 1850–1871)
Became Syracuse Silver Mfg.
Co. (1895)
Bibl. 18, 20, 91, 124, 127,
158

Schroeder & Wangelin
(c. 1844–1850)
Cleveland, Ohio
A. Schroeder
Edward Wangelin
Lewis Wangelin
Bibl. 54

A. Schroeder (c. 1844)
Cleveland, Ohio
Schroeder & Wangelin
(c. 1844–1850)
Bibl. 54

Andrew B. Schroeder
(See Schreuder)

J. Schuller (c. 1845–1846)
Philadelphia, Pa.
Bibl. 3

Schultz & Fischer
(c. 1874–1883)
San Francisco, Calif.
Successor to Schultz, Fischer
& Mohrig (1868–1869)
Fischer & Schultz
(1869–1874)
Became Schultz, Fischer &
McCartney (1883–1888)
Schultz & McCartney
(1888–1893)
Shreve & Co., San Francisco,
acquired some flatware
dies
Bibl. 127

A. G. Schultz & Co.
(c. 1899–1950)
Baltimore, Md.
Successor to Schultz
Tschudy & Co.
Bibl. 127, 157

Gottlieb Schultz (Shultz)
(c. 1821–1844)
Philadelphia, Pa.
Bibl. 3

Gustav A. Schultz
Location unknown
Bibl. 54, 93

Saunders Schultz
(b. 1927)
Chesterfield, Mo.
Bibl. 89, 155

Thomas Schumo
(c. 1824–1825)
Philadelphia, Pa.
Bibl. 3

Jodocus Schutte (c. 1800)
Baltimore, Md.
Bibl. 38

J. Phillip Schwalb
(b. c. 1840) (1860–1880)
New Orleans, La.
Bibl. 141

Michael Schwartz
(c. 1824–1825)
Philadelphia, Pa.
Bibl. 3

Peter Schwartz (c. 1770)
York, Pa.
Bibl. 3

Schweitzer Silver Corp.
(c. 1950–1968)
Brooklyn, N.Y.
Division of Lord Silver, Inc.
Bibl. 127

B. Schwekert (c. 1842)
Philadelphia, Pa.
Bibl. 3

Godfrey Schwing
(See Shiving)

John G. Schwing
(b. 1783–d. 1868)
Louisville, Ky.
Bibl. 32, 54, 68, 93

Scientific Silver SVC
Corp. (c. 1957–1961)
New York, N.Y.
Bibl. 127

Scofield & Lee (c. 1822)
Rochester, N.Y.
Salmon Scofield
Samuel W. Lee
Bibl. 20, 41, 124

Salmon (Solomon)
Scofield
(b. 1792–d. 1831,
c. 1815–1831)
Albany, N.Y.
(c. 1815–1817)
Rochester, N.Y.
Packard & Scofield
(c. 1818–1819)
Scofield & Lee (c. 1822)
Bibl. 4, 20, 23, 28, 41, 91,
124

Gabriel Scooler
(1857–1870)
New Orleans, La.
Bibl. 141

G. SCOOLER

Maurice Scooler
(1842–1900)
New Orleans, La.
Bibl. 141

Jehu Scot(t)
(c. 1806, d. 1819)
Raleigh, N.C.
Bibl. 21, 24, 25, 44, 91

Robert Scot
(c. 1775–1779)
Fredericksburg, Va.
Bibl. 19

Robert Scot
(c. 1781–1822)
Philadelphia, Pa.
Bibl. 3

Scott & Anderson
(c. 1829)
Greensboro, N.C.
David Scott
——— Anderson
Bibl. 21

Scott & Kitts
(c. 1843–1845)
Louisville, Ky.
William D. Scott
John Kitts
Bibl. 32, 68

Scott, Combs & Co.
(1872)
Providence, R.I.
Bibl. 108

Charles Scott (c. 1839)
Penn Yan, N.Y.
Bibl. 20, 124

David Scott
(b. 1797–d. 1875)
Greensboro, N.C.
Scott & Anderson (c. 1829)
Bibl. 21

David Scott
(c. 1819–1823)
Martinsburg, Va.
Bibl. 19

Edward Scott (1857–1868)
Providence, R.I.
Bibl. 108

I. (J.) Scott (c. 1750)
Albany, N.Y.
Bibl. 25, 44, 124

Jehu Scott
(See Jehu Scot)

John Scott (c. 1803–1809)
Charleston, S.C.
Bibl. 5

John Scott (c. 1838–1847)
St. Louis, Mo.
Bibl. 54, 134, 155

John B. Scott
(1840)
Pittsfield, Mass.
Bibl. 106

John B. Scott
(c. 1820–1850)
New York, N.Y.
*Bibl. 23, 24, 25, 28, 36, 44,
114, 124*

Samuel Scott (c. 1825)
Concord, N.C.
Bibl. 21

W. B. Scott & Co.
(1858–1865)
Providence, R.I.
Bibl. 108

W. D. Scott and Co.
(c. 1848–1849)
Louisville, Ky.
William D. Scott
Bibl. 32, 93

William D. Scott
(c. 1841–1849)
Louisville, Ky.
Scott & Kitts
(c. 1843–1845)
W. D. Scott and Co.
(c. 1848–1849)
Bibl. 32, 54, 93

——— **Scotthorn** (c. 1799)
Shelby County, Ky.
Bibl. 32, 54, 68, 93

Scovil & Co. (c. 1836)
Cincinnati, Ohio
Bibl. 54, 90, 91

Scovil & Kinsey (c. 1830)
Cincinnati, Ohio
Pulaski Scovil
*Bibl. 15, 25, 29, 44, 54, 90,
91, 114*

Scovil, Willey & Co.
(1836–1837)
Cincinnati, Ohio
Bibl. 54, 90, 91, 122

Scovil-Willey & Co.
(c. 1815–1836)
Cincinnati, Ohio
Bibl. 54, 78, 90

——— **Scovill** (c. 1816)
Cincinnati, Ohio
Bibl. 152

Edward Scranton
(c. 1847)
Philadelphia, Pa.
Bibl. 3, 23

**James Scrymageour
(Scrymgeour)**
(c. 1835)
New York, N.Y.
Bibl. 23, 36, 138

Andrew Scudder
(c. 1850–1851)
Utica, N.Y.
Bibl. 18, 20, 124, 158

Egbert Scudder
(c. 1827–1837)
New York, N.Y.

Benedict & Scudder
Bibl. 15, 124, 135, 138

Thomas Scummo
(c. 1823–1824)
Philadelphia, Pa.
Bibl. 3

John Scwind (c. 1790)
New York, N.Y.
Bibl. 23, 36, 124

Charles Seager
(c. 1840–c. 1842)
Utica, N.Y.
Tanner & Cooley
(c. 1840–1842)
Bibl. 18, 20, 124, 158

William Seal(e) (Jr.)
(c. 1810–1819)
Philadelphia, Pa.
Browne & Seal(e)
(c. 1810–1811)
*Bibl. 3, 4, 15, 24, 25, 29, 36,
44, 91, 114, 116*

| W SEAL |

J. W. Sealey (Suley)
(c. 1846–1849)
Charleston, S.C.
Bibl. 5

Thomas Seaman
(c. 1790–1802)
Edenton, N.C.
Bibl. 21

J. M. Seamans
(c. 1848–c. 1850)
Troy, N.Y.
Bibl. 20, 124

Joseph Searl
(c. 1840–1850)
Philadelphia, Pa.
Bibl. 3

Henry Sears & Son
(c. 1865–1895)
Chicago, Ill.
Bibl. 89

John Sears (c. 1805–1817)
Cambridge, Ohio
Chillicothe, Ohio
Bibl. 34

Mathew Sears (c. 1835)
New York, N.Y.
Bibl. 23, 36, 44, 124, 138

Samuel Sears
(c. 1839–1850)
Philadelphia, Pa.
Bibl. 3

Jeanne L. Sebastien
(c. 1814)
New York, N.Y.
Bibl. 23, 36, 44, 124, 138

John Seccombe (c. 1850)
Cobleskill, N.Y.
Bibl. 20, 124

John D. Seckle (Seckler)
(c. 1837–1850)
Philadelphia, Pa.
Bibl. 3

Margaret Seddinger
(c. 1846)
Philadelphia, Pa.
Bibl. 3

Matthias Seddinger
(c. 1819–1850)
Philadelphia, Pa.
Bibl. 3

**Conrad F. (Frederick C.)
Seeger** (c. 1823–1850)
Philadelphia, Pa.
Bibl. 3

H. Seely & Co. (c. 1830)
Staunton, Va.
Horace Seely
Bibl. 19

Horace Seely (c. 1830)
Staunton, Va.
H. Seely & Co.
Bibl. 19, 28

———— Seewald
(18th century)
Seneca, Huron, Muskingum
Counties, Ohio
Bibl. 34

Philip B. Segee (c. 1840)
Location unknown
Bibl. 24

George Segn
(c. 1820–1822)
Philadelphia, Pa.
Bibl. 3, 23, 36, 44

J. N. Sehorn (c. 1853)
Shelbyville, Tenn.
Bibl. 54

William M. Sehorn
(c. 1855)
Athens, Tenn.
Bibl. 54

Sehro
(See Sekro)

Lawrence Sekel
(c. 1841)
Philadelphia, Pa.
Bibl. 3

William C. Sekro (Sehro)
(c. 1837–1850)
Philadelphia, Pa.
Bibl. 3

Lemuel T. Selby
(c. 1842–1850)
Philadelphia, Pa
Bibl. 3, 23

Samuel Selby (c. 1841)
Philadelphia, Pa.
Bibl. 3, 23

Selkirk & Putnam
(c. 1814)
Albany, N.Y.
William Selkirk
Rufus Putnam
Bibl. 20, 124

William Selkirk
Albany, N.Y.
Selkirk & Putnam
(c. 1814–1815)
McHarg & Selkirk (c. 1815)
Bibl. 15, 20, 23, 36, 44, 124

J. Sell (c. 1800)
New York, N.Y.
Bibl. 23, 36, 44, 124

Joseph Sellers
(c. 1828–1850)
Philadelphia, Pa.
Bibl. 3

Selph & Campbell
(c. 1827–1829)
Fayetteville, N.C.
John Selph
John Campbell
Bibl. 21, 25, 91

Selph & Pyle
(c. 1837–1838)
Fayetteville, N.C.
John Selph
Benjamin Pyle II
Bibl. 21, 91

John Selph
(c. 1807–1836, d. 1838)
Fayetteville, N.C.
Selph & Campbell
(c. 1827–1829)
Selph & Pyle (c. 1837–1838)
Bibl. 21, 54, 91

Mathew Semple
(1851–1860)
New Orleans, La.
Bibl. 141

John B. Sénémaud
(Sénémand)
Philadelphia, Pa.
(c. 1798–1822)
Bibl. 3, 23, 36

Louis Senneshac (c. 1804)
Baltimore, Md.
Bibl. 38

William Senter (1850)
Portland, Me.
Bibl. 105

William Senter & Co.
(1875)
Portland, Me.
Bibl. 105

E. Sepes (c. 1851–1852)
Utica, N.Y.
Bibl. 18, 20, 124, 158

Heikki Seppä
(1945–present)
St. Louis, Mo.
Bibl. 155

John Serad (Scerad)
(c. 1835–1850)
Philadelphia, Pa.
Bibl. 3

Thomas Serre
(c. 1810–1812)
Baltimore, Md.
Bibl. 38

J. Serrill (c. 1837)
Philadelphia, Pa.
Bibl. 3

Charles Servoss (c. 1849)
Philadelphia, Pa.
Bibl. 3

Joseph S. Servoss
(c. 1850)
Philadelphia, Pa.
Bibl. 3

Lewis Sestie
(c. 1796–1800)
Richmond, Va.
Philadelphia, Pa. (?)
Bibl. 19

Benjamin Settle (b. 1840)
Russellville, Ky. (c. 1867)
Bibl. 54, 93

———— Setzler
(date unknown)
Newberry, S.C.
Bibl. 5

E. P. Seveignes
(1846–1858)
New Orleans, La.
Bibl. 141

Jacques Seveignes
(c. 1822)
New Orleans, La.
Bibl. 23, 36, 44

Lewis Sevrin (Sivrin)
(c. 1837–1840)
Philadelphia, Pa.
Bibl. 3, 23, 36, 44

Simon Sexnine (c. 1772)
New York, N.Y.
Bibl. 23, 28, 29, 36, 44, 78

| S S | ? |

Pliny Sexton
(c. 1819–1820)
Palmyra, N.Y.
Bibl. 20, 124

Joseph Seydell
(c. 1848–1849)
Philadelphia, Pa.
Bibl. 3

William H. Seyfer
(c. 1884)
Baltimore, Md.
Bibl. 127

Seymour & Holister
(Hollister)
(c. 1843–1850)
Hartford, Conn.
Oliver D. Seymour
Julius Hol(l)ister
Bibl. 15, 23, 24, 25, 44, 92,
94, 114, 158

| S & H |

SEYMOUR & HOLLISTER

Seymour & Williston
(c. 1816–1819)
Cincinnati, Ohio
Bibl. 34, 90

Edward Seymour
(c. 1839–1850)
Philadelphia, Pa.
Bibl. 3

Henry P. Seymour
(c. 1840)
Hartford, Conn.
Bibl. 15, 44, 91, 114

| H. P. Seymour |

Holister A. Seymour
Hartford, Conn.
Bibl. 23

Jeffrey Seymour
(b. 1793–d. 1865)
Cincinnati, Ohio
(1816–1820)
Bibl. 34, 90, 152

Joseph Seymour
(c. 1835–1863)
Syracuse, N.Y. (c. 1850)
New York, N.Y.
Utica, N.Y.

Norton & Seymour (c. 1850)
Norton, Seymour & Co.
  (c. 1850)
Joseph Seymour & Co.
  (c. 1851–1887)
Bibl. 15, 18, 20, 23, 36, 44,
  91, 114, 122, 124, 135,
  138, 158

Joseph Seymour & Co.
  (c. 1851–1887)
Syracuse, N.Y.
Successor to Joseph
  Seymour   J.S. & Co.
  (c. 1835–1844)
Willard & Hawley
  (c. 1844–1850)
Norton & Seymour
  (c. 1850–1851)
Became Joseph Seymour,
  Sons & Co.
  (c. 1887–1900)
Bibl. 15, 20, 25, 44, 114,
  124, 127
         J. S. & Co.

Joseph Seymour Mfg. Co.
  (c. 1900–1909)
Syracuse, N.Y.   ★ S ★
Successor to Joseph
  Seymour, Sons & Co.
  (c. 1887–1900)
Bibl. 127, 130, 135, 157

Joseph Seymour, Sons &
  Co. (c. 1887–1900)
Syracuse, N.Y.
Successor to Joseph
  Seymour & Co.   • S •
  (c. 1850–1887)
Bibl. 114, 127, 130, 135

Oliver D. Seymour
  (c. 1850)
Hartford, Conn.
Seymour & Hol(l)ister
  (c. 1843–1850)
Bibl. 15, 23, 25, 29, 44, 92,
  94

O.D. Seymour

O. D. Seymour

John V. Shade
  (c. 1845–1847)
Philadelphia, Pa.
Bibl. 3

Whitaker Shadforth
  (b. 1754–d. 1802)
Petersburg, Va. (c. 1791)
Richmond, Va. (c. 1795)
Georgia
Folwell, Shadforth & Co.
Bibl. 19

J. Shakespeare (c. 1850)
Nyack, N.Y.
Bibl. 20, 124

Francis Shallus
  (c. 1797–1822)
Philadelphia, Pa.
Bibl. 3, 102, 122

B. M. Shanley, Jr. Co.
  (c. 1915–1922)
Newark, N.J.
Became Pryor Mfg. Co.
  (c. 1922–1935)
Bibl. 127

Robert Shannon
  (c. 1841–1842)
Philadelphia, Pa.
Ashburn & Shannon
  (c. 1841)
Hattrick & Shannon
  (c. 1844)
Bibl. 3

George Sharp(e)
  (c. 1850–1870)
Danville, Ky.
Bibl. 32, 44, 54, 68, 93

G SHARP   G S

George B. Sharp   Ⓢ
  (c. 1844–1850)
Philadelphia, Pa.
William & George Sharp
Bibl. 3, 15, 23, 114

George Sharp Jr. &
  ——Floyd (c. 1871)
Atlanta, Ga.
Bibl. 89

William Sharp
  (c. 1835–1850)
Philadelphia, Pa.
William & George Sharp
  (c. 1848–1850)
Bibl. 3, 23, 36, 44, 114

William & George Sharp
  (c. 1848–1850)
Philadelphia, Pa.
William Sharp   W. & G. SHARP
George B. Sharp
Bibl. 3, 4, 23, 25, 28, 29, 44

William H. Sharpe
  (c. 1843)
Philadelphia, Pa.
Bibl. 3

R. Sharpley (c. 1855)
Location unknown
Bibl. 15, 44, 114

R SHARPLEY

Sharrard and Ewing
  (c. 1840)
Shelbyville, Ky.
Warren B. Ewing
James S. Sharrard
Bibl. 32, 54

James S. Sharrard
Scott County, Ky. (1836)
Paris, Ky. (1841)
Shelbyville, Ky.
  (c. 1840–1861)
Henderson, Ky.
Owensboro, Ky.
Paducah, Ky.
Sharrard and Ewing
  (c. 1840)
Bibl. 24, 25, 32, 44, 54, 68,
  93, 114

J S SHARRARD

Judson Sharrard (c. 1848)
Shelbyville, Ky.
Bibl. 25, 32, 93

William M. Sharrard
  (c. 1839–1850)
Harrodsburg, Ky.
Bibl. 32, 54, 93

Jacob A. Shartle (c. 1844)
Philadelphia, Pa.
Bibl. 3

Charles C. Shaver
  (d. 1900)   C C S
Utica, N.Y. (c. 1854)
Bibl. 15, 18, 20, 44, 91, 114,
  124, 158
©©Ⓢ   C C SHAVER

Michael Shaver
(b. 1775–d. 1859)
Abingdon, Va.
Bibl. 19

M. SHAVER

Shaw & Clark(e) (c. 1840)
Biddleford, Me.?
Bibl. 89, 91

Shaw & Dunlevy (c. 1833)
Philadelphia, Pa.
———— Shaw
Robert Dunlevy (?)
*Bibl. 3, 15, 23, 24, 25, 36,
44, 114*

SHAW & DUNLEVY

Benjamin Shaw
(c. 1828–1829)
New York, N.Y.
Bibl. 15, 124

Edward Shaw (c. 1837)
Philadelphia, Pa.
Bibl. 3

Edward G. Shaw
(c. 1825–1830)
Philadelphia, Pa.
Bibl. 3, 23, 36, 44

Foster Shaw (c. 1793)
Fair Haven, Vt.
Bibl. 54, 110

George E. Shaw
(c. 1896–1922)
Putnam, Mass.
Bibl. 127, 157

GEN. PUTNAM

James Shaw
(c. 1839–1841)
Philadelphia, Pa.
Bibl. 3

James W. Shaw (c. 1854)
Winnsboro, S.C.
Bibl. 5

John Shaw (c. 1819)
Philadelphia, Pa.
Bibl. 3

John Shaw & Co.
(c. 1842–1851)
St. Louis, Mo.
Bibl. 54, 91, 155

J SHAW & CO

John A. Shaw
(c. 1802–1819)
Newport, R.I.
*Bibl. 15, 23, 24, 25, 28, 29,
36, 44, 91, 110, 114*

Josephine Hartwell Shaw
(c. 1900–1935)
Duxbury, Mass.
Bibl. 89

Shearman
(See Robert Sherman)

Alex Shears (c. 1850)
Baltimore, Md.
Bibl. 89

Walter Sheed
(c. 1831–1833)
Philadelphia, Pa.
Bibl. 3

William W. Sheed
(c. 1840)
Philadelphia, Pa.
Bibl. 3

———— **Sheets** (c. 1697)
Henrico, Va.
Bibl. 28

James H. Shegogg
(c. 1855)
Nashville, Tenn.
Bibl. 54

Shehum
(See Schern)

Alonzo D. Sheldon
(c. 1851–1852)
Utica, N.Y.
Bibl. 18, 20, 124, 158

Shepard Mfg. Co.
(c. 1892–1923)
Melrose Highlands, Mass.
Chester Shepard
Chester Burdelle Shepard
Bibl. 127, 130, 157

S   SMCO

**Alpheus Xavier Francis
Shepard** (b. 1795)
Georgetown, Ky.
(c. 1815–1831)
Bibl. 32, 68, 93

E. R. Shepard (c. 1866)
New Orleans, La.
Bibl. 141

G. Shepard (c. 1831–1832)
Lockport, N.Y.
Bibl. 20, 124

**Thomas Jefferson
Shepard**
(b. 1801–d. 1875)
Georgetown, Ky.
(c. 1817–1828)
Louisville, Ky.
(c. 1828–1831)
Georgetown, Ky.
(c. 1831–1875)
Beard & Ayres
(c. 1828–1831)
Bibl. 32, 54, 68, 93

T J SHEPARD GEORGETOWN KY

Timothy B. Shepard
(c. 1834)
Utica, N.Y.
Bibl. 18, 20, 91, 124, 158

**Sheperd (Shepherd) &
Boyd** (c. 1810–1830)
Albany, N.Y.
Robert Sheperd   S & B
William Boyd
*Bibl. 15, 20, 23, 24, 28, 29,
36, 44, 54, 91, 98, 102,
114, 122, 124, 135*

•SHEPHERD & BOYD

Cumberland Sheperd
   (c. 1850)
Philadelphia, Pa.
Bibl. 3

Ephraim Sheperd
   (c. 1834–1836)
Newport, Ky.
Bibl. 32, 90

**Robert Sheperd
   (Shepherd)**
   (b. 1781–d. 1853)
Albany, N.Y. (c. 1800–1810)
Sheperd & Boyd
   (c. 1810–1830)
*Bibl. 20, 23, 24, 25, 28, 29,
   36, 44, 72, 91, 95, 102,
   119, 124, 135*

Shepherd
(See also Sheperd)

Humphrey M. Shepherd
   (c. 1824–1826)
New York, N.Y.
Bibl. 15, 124, 138

George L. Sheppard
   (c. 1846–1848)
Philadelphia, Pa.
Bibl. 3, 23

George M. Sheppard
   (c. 1837)
Philadelphia, Pa.
Bibl. 3

John Sheppard (c. 1798)
Easton, Me.
Bibl. 38, 105 | I S |

John D. Shepper
   (c. 1818–1819)
Philadelphia, Pa.
Bumm & Shepper
   (c. 1818–1823)
Bibl. 3, 4, 23, 28, 36, 44

Edward Sherman
   (c. 1850)
Hartford, Conn.
Bibl. 23

James Sherman (c. 1770)
Boston, Mass.
Bibl. 28, 110

**Robert Sherman
   (Shearman)** (c. 1799)
Philadelphia, Pa.
Bibl. 3

John Shermer
   (c. 1803–1813)
Philadelphia, Pa.
Bibl. 3

Sherwood & Whatley
   (c. 1849–1854)
Chicago, Ill.
Successor to Smith J.
   Sherwood (c. 1836–1849)
Eli Whatley
Bibl. 98

John Sherwood (c. 1832)
Buffalo, N.Y.
Bibl. 20, 124

Smith J. Sherwood
Buffalo, N.Y.
   (c. 1835–1836)
Chicago, Illinois
   (c. 1836–1849)
Bibl. 20, 98, 124

Sheth(e)ar & Gorham
   (c. 1806–1808)
New Haven, Conn.
Samuel Sheth(e)ar
Richard Gorham
*Bibl. 15, 16, 23, 36, 44, 110,
   143*

Sheth(e)ar & Thom(p)son
   (c. 1796–1805)
Litchfield, Conn. | S&T |
Samuel Sheth(e)ar
Isaac Thompson
*Bibl. 15, 16, 23, 25, 36, 44,
   91, 92, 114, 143*

Samuel Sheth(e)ar
   (b. 1755–d. 1815)
Litchfield, Conn. (c. 1801)
New Haven, Conn.
   (c. 1806)
Shethar & Thom(p)son
Shethar & Gorham
*Bibl. 15, 16, 23, 36, 44, 91,
   92, 110, 114, 143*

Walter D. Shewell
   (c. 1829–1840)
Philadelphia, Pa.
Bibl. 3

George W. Shiebler & Co.
   (c. 1876–1915)
New York, N.Y.
Bibl. 114, 120, 127, 135, 157

Shields, Inc.
   (c. 1936–1939)
Attleboro, Mass.
Successor to Fillkwik
   Company
   (c. 1920–1936)
Became division of Rex
   Products Corporation
   (1939)
Bibl. 127

Caleb Shields | C S |
   (c. 1773–1782)
Baltimore, Md.
*Bibl. 3, 23, 24, 36, 38, 44,
   54, 114*

Francis Shields (c. 1818)
Cincinnati, Ohio
Bibl. 34, 152

Jesse C. Shields (c. 1845)
Philadelphia, Pa.
Bibl. 3

Thomas Shields | T S |
   (c. 1765–1794)
Philadelphia, Pa.
*Bibl. 3, 15, 23, 24, 25, 28,
   29, 36, 49, 44, 54, 81, 95,
   151*

Anthony Shimer (c. 1850)
Auburn, N.Y.
Bibl. 20, 124

John Shimer (c. 1811)
Philadelphia, Pa.
Bibl. 3

John T. Shinkle
(c. 1824–1825)
Philadelphia, Pa.
Bibl. 3

Shinn (?) and Baldwin
(c. 1860)
Location unknown
Bibl. 79

Arthur Shipherd (c. 1764)
New York, N.Y.
Bibl. 3, 124

Nathaniel Shipman
(b. 1764–d. 1853)
Norwich, Conn. (c. 1790)
*Bibl. 15, 16, 23, 24, 25, 28,
29, 36, 44, 91, 92, 110,
114*

Shipp & Collins
(1829–1834)
Cincinnati, Ohio
Bibl. 15, 25, 44, 90, 114

Shipp & Woodbridge
(c. 1842)
St. Louis, Mo.
Horace P. Woodbridge
Bibl. 54, 155

SHIPP & WOODBRIDGE

S. A. M. Shipp
(d. 1843)
Cincinnati, Ohio
(1819–1835)
Bibl. 34, 90, 152

William A. Shippen
(c. 1818–1824)
Philadelphia, Pa.
Monteith & Shippen
(c. 1817)
Bibl. 3

**Godfrey Shiving
(Schwing)** (c. 1779)
Philadelphia, Pa.
*Bibl. 3, 23, 25, 36, 39, 44,
81, 95, 114*

G S

Frank Shizmuller
(c. 1860)
New Orleans, La.
Bibl. 141

**Shoemaker, Pickering &
Co.** (c. 1896–1915)
Newark, N.J.
Same mark as Frank Kursch
& Son Co.
Bibl. 114, 127, 157

Abraham Shoemaker
(c. 1846)
Philadelphia, Pa.
Bibl. 3

Charles Shoemaker
(c. 1825–1832)
New York, N.Y.
Bibl. 15, 23, 36, 44, 124, 138

Joseph Shoemaker
(b. 1764–d. 1829)
Philadelphia, Pa.
(c. 1793–1829)
New York State (?)
*Bibl. 3, 4, 15, 23, 24, 25, 28,
29, 36, 39, 44, 54, 81, 91,
95, 114*

J. SHOEMAKER   J S

George Shonnard
(c. 1797)
New York, N.Y.
Bibl. 23, 36, 44, 124

Shopshire
(See Shropshire)

John Short (c. 1792)
Halifax, N.C.
Bibl. 21

John Short (c. 1783–1792)
Alexandria, Va.
Norfolk, Va.
Bibl. 19

Martin Shreiner
(b. 1767–d. 1866)
Lancaster, Pa.
Bibl. 3

Philip Shreiner (c. 1760)
Lancaster, Pa.
Bibl. 3

Shreve & Co.
(c. 1852–present)
San Francisco, Calif.
George C. Shreve
S. S. Shreve
*Bibl. 114, 120, 127, 140, 144,
152, 157*

GEO.C.SHREVE&CO

SHREVE & CO.

*SHREVE & CO. SAN
FRANCISCO STERLING*

Shreve, Brown & Co.
(c. 1857)
Boston, Mass.
Benjamin Shreve
———— Brown
Bibl. 15, 122, 157

**Shreve, Crump & Low
Co.** (c. 1869–1888)
Boston, Mass.
Benjamin Shreve
Charles H. Crump
John J. Low
*Bibl. 15, 102, 104, 114, 126,
127, 135, 157*

**Shreve, Crump & Low
Co., Inc.** (1888–present)
Boston, Mass.
(See Jones, Shreve, Brown &
Co., Shreve, Crump &
Low Co.)
*Bibl. 15, 102, 104, 114, 126,
135, 157*

S. C. & L. CO.
STERLING

Shreve, Stanwood & Co.
(c. 1860)
Boston, Mass.
Benjamin Shreve
Henry B. Stanwood
Bibl. 15, 122, 157

Shreve, Treat & Eacret
(1912–1940)
San Francisco, Calif.
Bibl. 127

Benjamin Shreve
  (b. 1813; to 1896)
Boston, Mass.
  (c. 1834, c. 1854)
Salem, Mass.
Jones, Shreve, Brown & Co.
  (c. 1854)
Shreve, Brown & Co.
  (c. 1857)
Shreve, Stanwood & Co.
  (c. 1860)
Shreve, Crump & Low Co.
Bibl. 23, 28, 36, 44

Thomas H. Shriver
  (c. 1837–1843)
Philadelphia, Pa.
Baker & Shriver
  (c. 1837–1841)
Bibl. 3

Charles Shroeter
  (c. 1807–1818)
Baltimore, Md.
Bibl. 38

**Robert Shropshire
(Shopshire)** (b. 1748)
Baltimore, Md.
  (c. 1774–1778)
Bibl. 28, 38

————— **Shuber** (c. 1837)
Philadelphia, Pa.
Gregory & Shuber
Bibl. 3

Shuire
(See Suire)

John Shuler (c. 1849)
Philadelphia, Pa.
Bibl. 3

Shultz
(See Gottlieb Schultz)

Gustavus Shultz
  (c. 1825–1833)
Philadelphia, Pa.
Bibl. 3

John Shultz
  (c. 1813–1822)
Philadelphia, Pa.
Bibl. 3

Frederick Shuman
  (c. 1818)
Philadelphia, Pa.
Bibl. 3

John Shuman
  (c. 1818–1837)
Philadelphia, Pa.
Bibl. 3

John Shurley
  (c. 1839–1840)
Albany, N.Y.
Bibl. 20, 124

Sibley & Adams
  (c. 1847–1848)
Buffalo, N.Y.
O. E. Sibley
Nathaniel W. Adams
Bibl. 20, 124

Sibley & Marble `S & M`
  (c. 1801–1806)
New Haven, Conn.
Clark Sibley
Simeon Marble
*Bibl. 16, 23, 24, 25, 28, 29,
  36, 44, 91, 92, 110, 114,
  143*

Asa Sibley
  (b. 1764–d. 1829)
Woodstock, Conn. (c. 1787)
Walpole, N. H.
  (c. 1807–1808)
Rochester, N.Y. (c. 1827)
*Bibl. 41, 44, 91, 92, 110,
  124, 125*

Clark Sibley
  (b. 1778–d. 1807)
New Haven, Conn.
Sibley & Marble `SIBLEY`
  (c. 1801–1806)
*Bibl. 15, 16, 23, 24, 25, 28,
  36, 44, 91, 92, 110, 114,
  143*

James Sibley
  (b. 1779–d. 1865)
Great Barrington, Mass.
  (c. 1799–1801)
Albany, N.Y. (c. 1801–1803)
Canandaigua, N.Y.
  (c. 1803–1836)
Ann Arbor, Mich.
  (c. 1843–1846)

Rochester, N.Y.
  (c. 1847–1850)
Detroit, Mich.
Bibl. 20, 40, 41, 124

John Sibley (c. 1801–1810)
New Haven, Conn.
*Bibl. 23, 24, 25, 29, 36, 44,
  92, 110, 114, 143*

`J. SIBLEY`

O. E. Sibley (c. 1836–1848)
Buffalo, N.Y. (c. 1847–1848)
Canandaigua, N.Y.
Sibley & Adams
  (c. 1847–1848)
Bibl. 20, 79, 124

R. J. Sibley (c. 1850)
Genesee, N.Y.
Bibl. 20, 124

Stephen Sibley
  (b. 1759–d. 1829)
Great Barrington, Mass.
  (c. 1795)
Bibl. 41, 110

Joseph Siddall
  (c. 1846–1847)
Philadelphia, Pa.
Bibl. 3

John Siddons
  (c. 1841–1850)
Philadelphia, Pa.
Bibl. 3

Josiah C. Siddons
  (c. 1835–1837)
Philadelphia, Pa.
Bibl. 3

Lawrence L. Siddons
  (c. 1852–1855)
Charleston, S.C.
Bibl. 5

Michael Siebenlist
  (c. 1846–1850)
Camden, N.J.
Bibl. 3

**Victor Siedman Mfg. Co.,
  Inc.** (c. 1920–1930)
Brooklyn, N.Y.
Bibl. 127

`S`

Amos Sigler
 (c. 1847–1850)
Philadelphia, Pa.
Bibl. 3, 23

Sigourney & Hitchcock
 (after 1850)
Watertown, N.Y.
Bibl. 20, 124

Sigourney & Turner
 (c. 1838–1842)
Watertown, N.Y.
————— Sigourney
Alonzo B. Turner
Bibl. 20, 124

Alanson P. Sigourney
 (c. 1839–?)
Watertown, N.Y.
W. H. & A. P. Sigourney
Bibl. 20, 124

W. H. Sigourney & Co.
 (c. 1851–?)
Watertown, N.Y.
William H. Sigourney
Bibl. 20, 124

W. H. & A. P. Sigourney
 (c. 1839–?)
Watertown, N.Y.
Alanson P. Sigourney
William H. Sigourney
Bibl. 20, 124

William H. Sigourney
 (c. 1842–after 1850)
Watertown, N.Y.
W. H. & A. P. Sigourney
 (c. 1839–?)
W. H. Sigourney & Co.
 (c. 1851–?)
Bibl. 20, 124

William Sikler (c. 1850)
Philadelphia, Pa.
Bibl. 3

Silberstein, Hecht & Co.
 (c. 1904)
New York, N.Y.
Bibl. 127, 157

Silberstein, LaPorte & Co.
 (c. 1897)
Providence, R.I.
New York, N.Y.
Bibl. 127

A. L. Silberstein
 (c. 1904–1915)
New York, N.Y.
Successor to Silberstein,
 Hecht & Co.
Became Griffon Cutlery
 Works
Bibl. 127

Silbro
(See Silver Brothers)

H. Sill (c. 1840–1850)
New York, N.Y.
Bibl. 15, 25, 44, 114, 124

H. & R. W. Sill
 (c. 1840–1841)
New York, N.Y.
*Bibl. 15, 25, 44, 114, 124,
138*

Silliman
 (See Wilmot & Stillman)

Hezekiah Silliman
 (b. 1738–d. 1804)
New Haven, Conn.
Cutler, Silliman, Ward & Co.
 (c. 1767)
*Bibl. 15, 16, 23, 24, 25, 28,
36, 44, 61, 91, 92, 94, 110,
114*

Silver Brothers (c. 1950)
Atlanta, Ga.
Bibl. 127

Silver By Citra (present)
Division of Citra Trading
 Corp.
New York, N.Y.
Bibl. 146

**Silver Counselors of
 Home Decorators, Inc.**
 (c. 1943–1950)
Newark, N.Y.
Successor to Home
 Decorators, Inc.
Bibl. 127

Silverart (c. 1957–1961)
New York, N.Y.
Bibl. 127

Silvercraft Co. Inc.
 (c. 1950)
Boston, Mass.
Became Raimond Silver
 Manufacturers
Bibl. 127

SILVERCRAFT

Silvercryst
(See F. A. Hermann Co.)

Silvergrams
(See Chicago Monogram
 Studios)

Silverthorn & Clift
 (c. 1857–c. 1860)
Lynchburg, Va.
Henry Silverthorn
Josiah Clift
Bibl. 19

Silverthorn & Clift

Henry Silverthorn
 (b. 1810–d. 1900)
Baltimore, Md. (1832–1837)
Lynchburg, Va. (1842–1897)
Silverthorn & Clift
 (c. 1857–1860)
Bibl. 19, 54

SILVERTHORN

H SILVERTHORN

Henry T. Silverthorn
 (c. 1850)
Lynchburg, Va.
Bibl. 19

Sime & Moses
(c. 1768–1769)
Savannah, Ga.
Birmingham, Ga. (?)
William Sime
Jacob Moses
Bibl. 17, 23, 36

William Sime
(c. 1768–1778)
Savannah, Ga.
Birmingham, Ga. (?)
Sime & Moses
(c. 1768–1769)
Wright & Sime (c. 1774)
Bibl. 17, 23, 44

William Cadogan Simes
(b. 1773–d. 1824)
Portsmouth, N.H.
*Bibl. 15, 23, 24, 25, 28, 29,
36, 44, 91, 110, 114, 125*

**Simmon(s) & Alexander
(Alexander &
Simmons)**
(c. 1798–1804)
Philadelphia, Pa.
Anthony Simmons
Samuel Alexander
*Bibl. 15, 22, 23, 24, 25, 28,
29, 36, 44, 54, 91, 114*

Simmonds
(See Andrew Simmons)

Simmons & Paye (c. 1897)
North Attleboro, Mass.
Became Paye & Baker
Sold some patterns and dies
to Wendell Mfg. Co.
Bibl. 127   S. & P.

Simmons & Williamson
(c. 1797–1798)
Philadelphia, Pa.
Anthony Simmons
Samuel Williamson (?)
Bibl. 25, 44, 91, 114

Abel Simmons (c. 1836)
Buffalo, N.Y.
Bibl. 20, 124

**Andrew Simmons
(Simmonds)**
(c. 1795–1798)
Philadelphia, Pa.
Bibl. 3, 23, 28, 36

Anthony Simmons
(c. 1797–1808)
Philadelphia, Pa.
Simmons & Williamson
(c. 1797–1798)
Simmon(s) & Alexander
(c. 1798–1804)
*Bibl. 3, 4, 15, 23, 24, 28, 29,
36, 39, 44, 54, 81, 91, 102,
114*

J. & A. Simmons
(c. 1805–1813)
New York, N.Y.
*Bibl. 15, 23, 24, 28, 29, 36,
44, 46, 54, 91, 114, 124*

James Simmons
(c. 1815–1820)
New York, N.Y.
*Bibl. 15, 23, 24, 25, 28, 29,
36, 44, 91, 114, 124, 138*

Joseph Simmons (c. 1765)
Philadelphia, Pa.
Bibl. 3, 44

Joseph Simmons
(c. 1828–1833)
Philadelphia, Pa.
Bibl. 3, 23, 36, 44

Peter Simmons (c. 1817)
New York, N.Y.
Bibl. 15, 23, 36, 44, 124

Robert H. Simmons
(c. 1837–1850)
Philadelphia, Pa.
Bibl. 3

S. Simmons (c. 1797)
Philadelphia, Pa.
Simmons & Alexander
(c. 1798–1804)
Bibl. 23, 24, 25, 28, 36, 44

John Simnet (c. 1783)
Albany, N.Y.
New York, N.Y.
Bibl. 20, 124, 138

**Dominique Leopold
Simonin** (1838–1868)
New Orleans, La.
Bibl. 141

Simons, Bro. & Co.
(1840–1908)
Philadelphia, Pa.   S. B. & CO.
Variations in name
Successors to Peter L.
Krider Co. (1903)
Bibl. 114, 127, 157

Elijah Simons
(c. 1804–1810)
Sag Harbor, N.Y.
Bibl. 20, 124

George W. Simons
(c. 1844–1850)
Philadelphia, Pa.
Bibl. 3, 23

Leon Simons (1870–1880)
New Orleans, La.
Bibl. 141

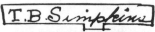

Simpkins
(See Minott & Simpkins)

James Simpkins
  (c. 1845–1846)
Louisville, Ky.
Bibl. 32, 93

Thomas Barton Simpkins
  (b. 1728–d. 1804)
Boston, Mass.
Bibl. 2, 4, 15, 23, 24, 25, 28,
  29, 36, 44, 110, 114

William Simpkins
  (b. 1704–d. 1780)
Boston, Mass.
Minott & Simpkins
  (c. 1750–1760)
Bibl. 2, 15, 23, 24, 25, 28,
  29, 36, 44, 54, 70, 91, 102,
  110, 114

Simpson & Beckel
  (c. 1848)
Albany, N.Y.
Moses Simpson
Moses Beckel
Bibl. 20, 23, 28, 44, 124

Simpson & Bro.
  (c. 1846–1850)
Philadelphia, Pa.
Bibl. 3

Simpson, Hall, Miller &
  Co. (1866–1898)
Wallingford, Conn.
Sterling from 1895
Became International Silver
  Co.
Bibl. 114, 127, 135, 152, 157

Alexander Simpson
  (c. 1799–c. 1805)
Hagerstown, Md.
Bibl. 38

David Simpson
  (c. 1807–1850)
Philadelphia, Pa.
Bibl. 3

J. Alexander Simpson
  (c. 1848–1850)
Philadelphia, Pa.
Bibl. 3

James Simpson (c. 1840)
Philadelphia, Pa.
Bibl. 3

John W. Simpson
  (c. 1832)
Charleston, S.C.
Bibl. 5

John W. Simpson
  (c. 1839–1850)
Philadelphia, Pa.
Bibl. 3

Jonathan Simpson
Bardstown, Ky.
  (c. 1830–1861)
Madison, Ind.
  (c. 1861–1863)
Bardstown, Ky. (c. 1863)
Bibl. 32, 54, 68, 133

Moses Simpson
  (c. 1848–1850)
Albany, N.Y.
Simpson & Beckel (c. 1848)
Bibl. 20, 124

S. Simpson (19th century)
Hopkinsville, Ky.
Bibl. 32, 54, 93

Samuel Simpson
  (c. 1840–1860)
Clarksville, Tenn.
Bibl. 54, 159   S. SIMPSON

Thomas W. Simpson
  (c. 1839–1841)
Philadelphia, Pa.
Bibl. 3

William Simpson
  (c. 1801)
Philadelphia, Pa.
Bibl. 3

William Simpson
  (c. 1830–1844)
Philadelphia, Pa.
Bibl. 3

Sinclair Mfg. Co. (c. 1950)
Chartley, Mass.
Bibl. 127

William Sinclair (c. 1837)
Philadelphia, Pa.
Bibl. 3

Louis Singer (c. 1846)
New York, N.Y.
Bibl. 23, 124, 138

Singleton & Young
  (c. 1800)
New York, N.Y.
Bibl. 23, 36, 44, 114, 124,
  138

Anthony Singleton
  (b. 1750–d. 1795)
Richmond, Va.
  (c. 1787–1795)
Newport, R.I.
Williamsburg, Va.
Bibl. 19, 153

Ripley Nichols Singleton
  (b. 1754–d. 1799)
Charleston, S.C.
  (c. 1779–1787)
Bibl. 5

Robert Singleton (c. 1839)
Greensboro, N.C.
Bibl. 21

Patrick Sinnott (c. 1761)
Baltimore, Md.
Bibl. 38

Sivrin
(See Sevrin)

Joseph A. Sixte
(c. 1837–1850)
Philadelphia, Pa.
Bibl. 3, 23, 36, 44

Vincent B. Sixte
(c. 1837–1840)
Philadelphia, Pa.
Bibl. 3, 23, 36, 44

Skaats
(See Schaats)

John Skates
(c. 1668–1680)
Boston, Mass.
Bibl. 28, 110

Skeplinger
(See Samuel Keplinger)

Joseph Skerret (Scarret)
(c. 1797–1798, d. 1804)
Philadelphia, Pa.
Bibl. 3, 28, 44

Joseph Skerret (Scarret)
(c. 1804–1850).
Philadelphia, Pa.
Bibl. 3, 23, 36, 44

George W. Skerry
(d. 1842)
Boston, Mass. (c. 1837)
Bibl. 23, 28, 36, 44, 91

Thomas Skidmore
(c. 1767)
Lancaster, Pa.
Bibl. 3

Skinker & Ballantine
(c. 1772–?)
Norfolk, Va.
William Skinker
James Ballantine
Bibl. 19

William Skinker
(b. 1741, c. 1766–c. 1776)
Norfolk, Va. (c. 1772–?)

Easton, Md.
Skinker & Ballantine
(c. 1772)
Bibl. 19

Abraham Skinner
(c. 1756–1773)
New York, N.Y.
*Bibl. 4, 15, 23, 24, 25, 28,
29, 36, 44, 114, 124, 138*

Benjamin Skinner
Easton, Md. (c. 1801)
Baltimore, Md. (c. 1804)
Norfolk, Va. (c. 1804)
Bibl. 19, 38

Elizer Skinner (d. 1858)
Hartford, Conn.
(c. 1826)
Bibl. 16, 23, 28, 36, 44, 110

Matt Skinner (c. 1752)
Philadelphia, Pa.
Bibl. 23, 29, 36, 44, 114

| MATT SKINNER |

Thomas Skinner
(b. 1712–d. 1761)
Marblehead, Mass.
New York, N.Y.
*Bibl. 2, 15, 23, 24, 25, 28,
29, 36, 44, 72, 83, 91, 104,
110, 114*

| Skinner | | T S |

William Skinner
(c. 1789–1790)
Easton, Md.
Bibl. 38

Josiah U. Slack
(c. 1837–1839)
Norfolk, Va.
Bibl. 19

William Slack (c. 1850)
Philadelphia, Pa.
Bibl. 3

Joseph P. Slade (b. 1784)
Augusta, Ga. (c. 1794–1805)
Bibl. 17

William Slater (c. 1792)
Baltimore, Md.
Bibl. 38

John Slattery (c. 1850)
Hartford, Conn.
Bibl. 23

Sleeper & Jeannert
(c. 1850)
Philadelphia, Pa.
Bibl. 3

Joshua Slidell (Slydell)
(c. 1765)
New York, N.Y.
*Bibl. 4, 23, 24, 25, 28, 36,
44, 114, 124, 138*

| SLIDELL | SLIDELL |

William Sloan (c. 1794)
Hartford, Conn.
Bibl. 23, 36, 44, 110

Warrington L. Sloat
(c. 1819–1839)
Mobile, Ala.
Bibl. 148

| SLOAT. MOBILE |

Slydell
(See Slidell)

Scott Small
(c. 1980–present)
St. Louis, Mo.
Bibl. 155

Williams Small
(c. 1795–1796)
Philadelphia, Pa.
Bibl. 3

George Smart (c. 1794)
Lexington, Ky.
Bibl. 32, 54, 68, 93

John Smart (c. 1839–1850)
Philadelphia, Pa.
Bibl. 3

Elisha Smartt (c. 1810)
Mecklenburg County, N.C.
Bibl. 21

Peter Smick
 (c. 1846–1848)
Philadelphia, Pa.
Bibl. 3

Martin B. Smiley (1875)
Athens, Me.
Bibl. 105

Smith
(See also Hattrick & Smith,
 Hull & Smith, List &
 Smith, Lovell & Smith)

Smith & Bean (c. 1844)
Skaneateles, N.Y.
S. Smith
H. L. Bean
Bibl. 20, 124

Smith & Beggs
(See Beggs & Smith)

Smith & Bro.
 (c. 1843–1844)
Philadelphia, Pa.
Bibl. 3

Smith & Chamberlain
 (c. 1846–1853)
Salem, Mass.
Bibl. 89, 91, 110

SMITH & CHAMBERLAIN

Smith & Goodrich
 (c. 1850)
Philadelphia, Pa.
Bibl. 3

**Smith & Grant (Grant &
 Smith)** (c. 1827–1831)
Louisville, Ky.
Richard Ewing Smith
William Grant (?)
*Bibl. 24, 25, 32, 44, 54, 68,
 91*

Smith & Grant

Smith & Grant

Smith & Kitts
 (c. 1844–1845)
Louisville, Ky.
———— Smith
John Kitts
Bibl. 32

**Smith & List (List &
 Smith)** (c. 1848–1850)
Philadelphia, Pa.
———— Smith
John List
Bibl. 3

Smith & Patterson
 (c. 1860)
Boston, Mass.
Bibl. 89

Smith & Smith (c. 1956)
Attleboro, Mass.
Became division of Wallace
 Silversmiths, Inc. (1956)
Bibl. 127

Smith & Whitney
 (c. 1787–1793)
Lansingburgh, N.Y.
David Smith
Henry Whitney
Bibl. 20, 91, 124

Smith Metal Arts Co.
 (c. 1920)
Buffalo, N.Y.
Bibl. 120

———— **Smith** (c. 1815)
Batavia, N.Y.
Hull & Smith
 (c. 1815–1816)
Bibl. 20

A. Smith (19th century)
Location unknown
Bibl. 89

A Smith

Allen Smith (c. 1841)
Philadelphia, Pa.
Bibl. 3

Alvin Smith (c. 1846)
Port Chester, N.Y.
Bedford, N.Y.
Bibl. 20, 124

B. Smith (c. 1835)
Philadelphia, Pa.
Bibl. 3

Benjamin C. Smith
 (c. 1850)
Philadelphia, Pa.
Bibl. 3

B. H. Smith & Co.
 (c. 1836–1838)
Fredericksburg, Va.
Benjamin H. Smith
William K. Smith
William H. White
Bibl. 19

Benjamin H. Smith
 (c. 1834)
Fredericksburg, Va.
William H. White & Co.
B. H. Smith & Co.
 (c. 1836–1838)
Bibl. 19

C. C. Smith (c. 1841–1843)
Fayetteville, N.C.
Bibl. 21

Charles Smith
 (c. 1848–1850)
Philadelphia, Pa.
Bibl. 3

Charles Smith
Pendleton, S.C. (c. 1848)
Laurens, S.C. (c. 1849)
Spartanburg, S.C. (c. 1851)
Greenville, S.C.
 (c. 1852–1857)
Lancaster, Pa. (c. 1853)
Bibl. 5

Charles A. Smith (c. 1850)
Auburn, N.Y.
Harbottle & Smith
Bibl. 20, 124

Charles R. Smith
 (c. 1837–1850)
Philadelphia, Pa.
Bibl. 3, 23

Christian Smith (Ohio)
(See Christian Schmidt)

Christian Smith
(c. 1820–1833)
Philadelphia, Pa.
Bibl. 3, 23, 36, 44

D. S. Smith (c. 1831)
Columbus, Ga.
Bibl. 17

David Smith (b. 1751)
Virginia (c. 1774)
Bibl. 15, 23, 28, 29, 36, 114

D. SMITH

David Smith
Philadelphia, Pa.
(c. 1778–1793)
Lansingburgh, N.Y.
(c. 1787–1793)
Smith & Whitney
(c. 1787–1793)
Rockwell, Smith & Whitney
(c. 1788–1789)
Bibl. 20, 24, 25, 44, 91, 114, 124

D S	D. SMITH

E. H. H. Smith Silver Co.
(c. 1904–1914)
Bridgeport, Conn.
Became Blackstone Silver
Co. (1914–1943)
Bibl. 127

◁ S ▷

Ebenezer Smith
(b. 1745–d. 1830)
Brookfield, Conn.
(c. 1775–1790)
Bibl. 16, 23, 28, 36, 44, 110

Edwin Smith (c. 1837)
Albany, N.Y.
Bibl. 20, 124

Ernest Smith
(c. 1830–1833)
Philadelphia, Pa.
Bibl. 3

Eugene O. Smith (1875)
Bath, Me.
Bibl. 105

F. C. Smith (c. 1844)
Philadelphia, Pa.
Bibl. 3

Floyd Smith
(c. 1815–1836)
New York, N.Y.
Bibl. 15, 25, 44, 91, 114, 124, 138

FLOYD SMITH

Francis Smith
(b. 1720, c. 1743)
New York, N.Y.
Bibl. 23, 124

Francis W. Smith (c. 1837)
Philadelphia, Pa.
Bibl. 3

**Frank W. Smith Silver
Co., Inc.** (1886–1958)
Gardner, Mass.
Frank W. Smith
(b. 1848–d. 1904)
Became division of Webster
Company,
North Attleboro, Mass.
(1958)
Bibl. 114, 127, 146, 147, 157

Frederick L. Smith
(1894–1895)
Denver, Colo.
Successor to C. H. Green
Jewelry Company
(1889–1892)
Green-Smith Watch and
Diamond Company
(1892–1894)
Became John W. Knox
(1895)
Bibl. 127

George Smith
(c. 1823–1849)
Philadelphia, Pa.
Bibl. 3, 23, 36, 44

George Smith
(c. 1824)

New York, N.Y.
Lord & Smith
Bibl. 15, 124, 138

George C. Smith
(c. 1839–1845)
Philadelphia, Pa.
Bibl. 3

George E. Smith
(c. 1848–1849)
Louisville, Ky.
Bibl. 32, 93, 133

George H. Smith (c. 1850)
Watertown, N.Y.
Bibl. 20, 124

George M. Smith
(c. 1845–1849)
Philadelphia, Pa.
Bibl. 3

George O. Smith
(c. 1825–1850)
New York, N.Y.
Bibl. 23, 36, 124, 138

Gerritt Smith (c. 1840)
New York, N.Y.
Bibl. 15, 124, 138

Hartley Taliaferro Smith
(c. 1850–1860)
Bowling Green, Ky.
Bibl. 32, 54, 93

Hezekiah Smith (c. 1845)
Philadelphia, Pa.
Bibl. 3

I. Smith
(c. 1742, d. 1789)
Boston, Mass.
Bibl. 23, 36, 114

I S

I. (Joseph?) Smith
(c. 1842)
Boston, Mass.
Bibl. 4, 15, 23, 25

I. SMITH

Isaac Smith (c. 1840–1843)
Philadelphia, Pa.
Bibl. 3

J. & T. Smith
(See John & Thomas Smith)

J. W. W. Smith (c. 1847)
Shelbyville, Ky.
Bibl. 32, 54, 68, 93

Jacob Smith
(c. 1809–1822)
Philadelphia, Pa.
Bibl. 3, 23, 36, 44

Jacob C. Smith
(c. 1839–1850)
Philadelphia, Pa.
Bibl. 3

James Smith
(c. 1794–1797)
New York, N.Y.
Bibl. 23, 28, 36, 44, 124, 138

James Smith
(c. 1807–1808)
Philadelphia, Pa.
Bibl. 3, 36, 44

James E. Smith (c. 1839)
Albany, N.Y.
Bibl. 20, 124

James S. Smith
(c. 1837–1850)
Philadelphia, Pa.
Bibl. 3

Joel M. Smith
(1820–1825)
Carthage, Tenn.
Nashville, Tenn.
Bibl. 89

John Smith (c. 1814–1825)
Baltimore, Md.
Hart & Smith
(c. 1814–1816)
Kirk & Smith
(c. 1818–1823)
John & Thomas Smith
(c. 1817–1818)
Bibl. 25, 29, 38

| I SMITH |

John Smith (c. 1818–1822)
Philadelphia, Pa.
Bibl. 3, 23, 36

John Smith
Winchester, Va. (c. 1790)
Alexandria, Va. (c. 1792)
Bibl. 19

John Smith (c. 1846–1850)
Philadelphia, Pa.
(See John Schmitt)

John Smith (c. 1850)
Camden, N.J.
Bibl. 3

John Creagh Smith
(c. 1839–1850)
Philadelphia, Pa.
Bibl. 3

John E. Smith (c. 1825)
Philadelphia, Pa.
Bibl. 3

John Leonard Smith
(c. 1850–1855)
Syracuse, N.Y.
Bibl. 15, 20, 25, 44, 91, 114, 124

| J. L. SMITH |

John M. Smith (c. 1835)
Nashville, Tenn.
Bibl. 54

John P. Smith
(c. 1799–1820)
Savannah, Ga.
D. B. Nichols & Co.
(c. 1820–1830)
Bibl. 17

**John & Thomas Smith
(J. & T. Smith)**
(c. 1817–1818)
Baltimore, Md.
Bibl. 23, 28, 38, 44

Joseph Smith
(c. 1742–1789, d. 1789)
Boston, Mass.
*Bibl. 2, 4, 23, 24, 25, 28, 29,
36, 44, 102, 110, 114*

| I. SMITH | | I. S. |

Joseph Smith
(c. 1804–1810)
Philadelphia, Pa.
Bibl. 3, 23, 36, 44, 91

Joseph E. Smith
(c. 1839–1850)
Philadelphia, Pa.
Bibl. 3

Lawrence B. Smith Co.
(1887–1958)
Boston, Mass.
Bibl. 127, 157

Lemuel F. Smith (1875)
Biddeford, Me.
Bibl. 105

Levin H. Smith
(c. 1837–1843)
Philadelphia, Pa.
Bibl. 3, 23, 36, 44

Nathaniel W. Smith
Wheeling, Va.
(c. 1829–1838)
Clarksburg, Va. (c. 1846)
Bibl. 19

Nathaniel W. Smith
(c. 1814)
Columbus, Ohio
Bibl. 34

Nicholas Smith
(c. 1762–1782)
Charleston, S.C.
Bibl. 5

O. W. Smith (1875)
Winn, Me.
Bibl. 105

Philip Smith
(c. 1847–1850)
Philadelphia, Pa.
Bibl. 3

R. H. Smith (1875)
Moscow, Me.
Bibl. 105

Richard Smith
(1850–1853)
Newark, N.J.
Baldwin & Smith
Bibl. 91, 135

Richard Ewing Smith
(b. 1800–d. 1849)
Louisville, Ky.
(c. 1821–1849)
Peter Daumont
(c. 1843–1846)

Smith & Grant
(c. 1827–1831)
*Bibl. 25, 32, 44, 54, 68, 91,
93*

R E SMITH

Robert Smith
(c. 1818–1822)
Philadelphia, Pa.
Bibl. 3, 23

Robert E. Smith
(c. 1820–1831)
Philadelphia, Pa.
Bibl. 3, 24, 29, 36

R E SMITH

Roderick D. Smith
(c. 1846–1850)
Philadelphia, Pa.
Bibl. 3

Rufus R. Smith
(c. 1823–1833)
Troy, N.Y. (c. 1823–1826)
Macon, Ga. (c. 1829–1833)
Bibl. 17, 20, 124

S. Smith (c. 1844)
Skaneateles, N.Y.
Saratoga Springs, N.Y.
(c. 1846)
Smith & Bean
Bibl. 20, 124

Samuel Smith (c. 1785)
Philadelphia, Pa.
Bibl. 3, 23, 36, 44

Samuel Smith (c. 1845)
Philadelphia, Pa.
Bibl. 3, 23

Thomas Smith
(b. 1790–d. 1850)
Lexington, Ky. (c. 1818)
Bibl. 32, 93

Thomas Smith
(c. 1817–1818)
Baltimore, Md.
John & Thomas Smith
(c. 1817–1818)
Bibl. 38

Truman Smith (c. 1815)
Utica, N.Y.

Nathaniel Butler
Bibl. 89, 124

Walter C. Smith
(c. 1850–1860)
Bowling Green, Ky.
Bibl. 32, 54, 68, 93, 114

William Smith (c. 1770)
New York, N.Y.
*Bibl. 23, 25, 28, 44, 91, 124,
138*

William Smith
(c. 1817–1840)
New York, N.Y.
*Bibl. 15, 44, 91, 114, 124,
138*

WM SMITH

William Smith
(c. 1818–1825)
Philadelphia, Pa.
Bibl. 3

William Smith (c. 1837)
Philadelphia, Pa.
Bibl. 3

William Smith & Co.
(c. 1837)
Wellsburg, Va.
Bibl. 19

William A. Smith
(c. 1840)
Leesburg, Va.
Bibl. 19

William K. Smith
Fredericksburg, Va.
B. H. Smith & Co.
(c. 1836–1838)
Bibl. 19

Zebulon Smith
(b. 1786–d. 1865)
Bangor & Ellsworth
Maine (c. 1820–1830)
*Bibl. 15, 25, 44, 91, 94, 105,
110, 114, 151*

Z.SMITH

Z.Smith

James Smither
(c. 1768–1819)

Philadelphia, Pa.
(c. 1768–1777)
New York, N.Y. (?)
Bibl. 3, 28, 102, 116

George Smithson
(c. 1775–1778)
Charleston, S.C.
Bibl. 5, 118

R. T. Smitten
(c. 1844–1847)
Philadelphia, Pa.
Bibl. 3

John Smoker
(c. 1846–1847)
Philadelphia, Pa.
Bibl. 3, 23

Albert Smyth Co., Inc.
(c. 1965–1974)
Baltimore, Md.
Bibl. 127

John L. Snedeker
(c. 1837–1841)
New York, N.Y.
Bibl. 15, 124, 138

Lewis Snell (c. 1831–1835)
Philadelphia, Pa.
Bibl. 3

Henry Snelling
(c. 1776–1777)
Philadelphia, Pa.
Bibl. 3

Philip Snider
(c. 1831–1833)
New York, N.Y.
Bibl. 15, 124, 138

Ebenezer Snow (1860)
Westbrook, Me.
Bibl. 105

I. Snow (c. 1810)
(See Jeremiah Snow Jr.)
Bibl. 15, 28, 39

Jeremiah Snow Jr.
(b. 1764) (c. 1808–?)
Williamstown, Mass.
*Bibl. 15, 25, 29, 44, 84, 91,
110, 114*

I. Snow   J: SNOW

William H. Snow
Cleveland, Ohio
(c. 1833–1839)
Troy, N.Y. (c. 1840–1842)
Hall & Snow (c. 1835)
Bibl. 20, 54, 124, 138

Snyder
(See Rickards & Snyder)

Snyder & Bros.
(c. 1847–1850)
Philadelphia, Pa.
Bibl. 3

Charles F. Snyder
(c. 1801)
Philadelphia, Pa.
Bibl. 3

Edwin V. Snyder (c. 1918)
Philadelphia, Pa.
Bibl. 127

G. K. Snyder (1823–1830)
New Orleans, La.
Bibl. 141

George Snyder
(c. 1801)
Philadelphia, Pa.
Bibl. 3, 44

George (H.) Snyder
(c. 1816–1818)
Philadelphia, Pa.
Bibl. 3, 23, 36

George W. Snyder Sr.
(c. 1803–1813, d. 1813)
Paris, Ky.
Bibl. 32, 54, 68, 93

George W. Snyder Jr.
(c. 1821–1848)
Paris, Ky.
J. C. and G. W. Snyder
(c. 1845–1848)
Bibl. 32, 93

J. C. and G. W. Snyder
(c. 1845–1848)
Paris, Ky.
James C. Snyder
George W. Snyder Jr.
Bibl. 32

James C. Snyder
(b. 1815–d. 1852)
Paris Ky. (1845–1852)
J. C. and G. W. Snyder
(c. 1845–1848)
Bibl. 32, 54, 68, 93

Joseph H. Snyder
(c. 1848–1850)
Philadelphia, Pa.
Bibl. 3

Robert Snyder (c. 1850)
Philadelphia, Pa.
Bibl. 3

A. M. Soffel Co., Inc.
(c. 1920–1930)
Newark, N.J.
Bibl. 127

Abner Solcher (c. 1819)
Cincinnati, Ohio
Bibl. 34, 152

Daniel H. Solliday
(c. 1829–1850)
Philadelphia, Pa.
Bibl. 3

Solomon
(See also Parke, Solomon, &
Co.)

Lewis Solomon
(c. 1840–1841)
Philadelphia, Pa.
Bibl. 3

Samuel Solomon (c. 1800)
Baltimore, Md.
Bibl. 38

Samuel Solomon (c. 1811)
Philadelphia, Pa.
Bibl. 3, 23, 36, 44

Robert Somerby
(c. 1794–1821)
Boston, Mass.
Bibl. 28, 44

William Somerdike
(c. 1848–1850)
Philadelphia, Pa.
Bibl. 3

Somers & Crowley
(c. 1828–1833)
Philadelphia, Pa.
——— Somers
E. Crowley (?)
Bibl. 3

Albertus Somers (d. 1863)
Woodstown, N.J. (c. 1820)
Gloucester County, N.J.
(c. 1821)
Bibl. 3, 46, 54

**John Somerville
(Sommerville)**
(c. 1844–1846)
Philadelphia, Pa.
Bibl. 3

Joseph Sonnece (c. 1816)
Philadelphia, Pa.
Bibl. 3

Joseph Sonnier
(c. 1811–1818)
Philadelphia, Pa.
Lagazze & Sonnier
(c. 1814–1816)
Bibl. 3, 23, 36, 44

Samuel Soumain(e)
(b. 1718–d. 1765)
Annapolis, Md.
(c. 1740–1754)
Philadelphia, Pa.
(c. 1754–1765)
*Bibl. 2, 3, 23, 24, 25, 28, 36,
38, 81, 91, 114*

Simeon Soumaine
(b. 1685–d. 1750)
New York, N.Y.
*Bibl. 2, 15, 23, 24, 25, 28,
29, 30, 35, 36, 44, 54, 95,
102, 104, 114, 116, 119,
124, 135, 138, 142, 151*

Peter Sounalet
Norfolk, Va. (c. 1806–1822)
Richmond, Va. (c. 1812)
Bibl. 19

Michael Soque
(c. 1794–1819)
New York, N.Y.
Bibl. 15, 23, 36, 44, 124, 138

George South
(c. 1823–1824)
Philadelphia, Pa.
Bibl. 3

William South
(c. 1828–1850)
Philadelphia, Pa.
Bibl. 3

A. S. Southwick & Co.
(c. 1892)
Providence, R.I.
Successor to Vose &
Southwick
(c. 1874–1892)
Bibl. 127

Elijah Southworth
(c. 1788)
Kingston, N.Y.
Bibl. 20, 124, 138

A. Souty (c. 1811)
Philadelphia, Pa.
Bibl. 3

Samuel Souza (c. 1819)
Philadelphia, Pa.
Bibl. 3, 44

**Anthony Sowerall
(Sowerlt)**
(c. 1811–1824)
Philadelphia, Pa.
Bibl. 3, 23, 36, 44

Sowerlt
(See Sowerall)

George Spackman
(c. 1824–1825)
Philadelphia, Pa.
Bibl. 3

John Spalding (c. 1801)
Baltimore, Md.
Bibl. 38

Rudolph Spangler
(c. 1774)
York, Pa.
Bibl. 3

J. E. Sparks (c. 1920)
Brooklyn, N.Y.
Bibl. 127 $ Spark $

Henry Sparrow (c. 1811)
Philadelphia, Pa.
Bibl. 3, 23, 36, 44

Thomas Sparrow
(b. 1746, c. 1764–1784?)
Philadelphia, Pa.
(before 1765)
Annapolis, Md.
*Bibl. 25, 29, 38, 44, 54, 91,
114*

Spaulding & Co.
(1888–1929;
1943–present)
Chicago, Ill.
Successor to S. Hoard & Co.
(1855–1888)
Spaulding-Gorham, Inc.
(1929–1943)
Bibl. 98, 120, 126, 127

D. S. Spaulding
(c. 1896–1922)
Mansfield, Mass.
Bibl. 114, 127, 157

George N. Spaulding
(1860)
Fairfield, Me.
Bibl. 105

W. W. Spaulding (1860)
Fairfield, Me.
Bibl. 105

William M. Spaulding
(1875)
Norridgewock, Me.
Bibl. 105

Spear & Co. (c. 1849)
Charleston, S.C.
James E. Spear
J. Charles Wood
Bibl. 5, 91

Spear & Jones (c. 1841)
Savannah, Ga.
———— Spear
James M. Jones
Bibl. 17

E. R. Spear (1860)
Rockland, Me.
Bibl. 105

E. R. Spear & Co. (1875)
Rockland, Me.
Bibl. 105

Isaac Spear (Speer)
Boston, Mass. (c. 1836)
Newark, N.J. (c. 1837)
Bibl. 2, 23, 25, 36, 44, 114

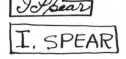

James E. Spear
(b. 1817–d. 1871)
Charleston, S.C.
(c. 1846–1871)
Spear & Co. (c. 1849)
Bibl. 5, 54, 91

J. E. SPEAR

Thomas S. Spear
(c. 1858)
Columbus, Ga.
Bibl. 17

T S SPEAR	T Spear

David Huston Spears
(1815–1876)
Washington County, Ky.
Springfield, Ky. (?)
Bibl. 32, 54, 68, 93

Speer
(See also Isaac Spear)

Speer & Cosper
(1852–1853)
Chicago, Ill.
Became I. & E. W. Speer
(1861–1879)
Bibl. 98
SPEER & COSPER

Isaac Speer
(b. 1809–d. 1879)
Chicago, Ill. (1842–1852,
1853–1857)
Became Speer & Cosper
(1852–1853)
I. & E. W. Speer
(1861–1879)
Bibl. 98

SPEER

Speigelhalder & Sons
(c. 1865–1867)
Louisville, Ky.
John F. Speigelhalder
Bibl. 32

**Speigelhalder and Werne
(Werne and
Speigelhalder)**
(c. 1836–1858)
Louisville, Ky.
Ferdinand Speigelhalder
Joseph Werne Sr.
Bibl. 32, 54, 93

Ferdinand Speigelhalder
(c. 1836–1858)
Louisville, Ky.
Speigelhalder & Werne
Bibl. 32, 68, 93

John F. Speigelhalder
(c. 1844–1867)
Louisville, Ky.
Speigelhalder & Sons
(c. 1865–1867)
Bibl. 32, 93

Gaven Spence
(c. 1830–1840)
Newark, N.J.
Bibl. 15, 25, 44, 91, 114, 138

Gaven Spence & Co.
(c. 1859–1916)
Newark, N.J.
Bibl. 127

Spencer & Hand (c. 1843)
Philadelphia, Pa.
Oliver Spencer
Joseph S. K. Hand
Bibl. 3

Spencer & Marshall
(c. 1829–1833)
Philadelphia, Pa.
Oliver Spencer
——— Marshall
Bibl. 3

George Spencer
(b. 1787–d. 1878)
Essex, Conn.
Bibl. 16, 23, 28, 44

George W. Spencer
(b. 1824–d. 1876)
Charleston, S.C. (c. 1860)
Bibl. 5

James Spencer
(b. 1775?–d. 1817?)
Hartford, Conn. (c. 1793)
Oakes & Spencer
Bibl. 16, 23, 28, 36, 44, 110

James Spencer Jr.
(c. 1843)
Hartford, Conn.
Bibl. 23, 44

Julius A. Spencer
(b. 1802–d. 1874)
Utica, N.Y.
James Murdock & Co.
(c. 1826–1838)
*Bibl. 15, 18, 20, 124, 135,
158*

Oliver Spencer
(c. 1833–1843)
Philadelphia, Pa.
Spencer & Marshall
(c. 1829–1833)
Spencer & Hand (c. 1843)
Bibl. 3

William Sperry
(c. 1843–1849)
Philadelphia, Pa.
Bibl. 3

Spier & Forsheim
(c. 1896–1909)
New York, N.Y.
Became Ben Spier Co.
(c. 1909)
Bibl. 114, 127

Ben. Spier Co. (c. 1909)
New York, N.Y.
Successor to Spier &
Forsheim
(c. 1896–1909)
Bibl. 127

H. S. Sprague (c. 1825)
Location unknown
Bibl. 24

> H. S. Sprague

James H. Spratley
(c. 1833–1835)
Norfolk, Va.
Pearce & Spratley (c. 1833)
Bibl. 19

William Spratling
(1931–1967)
New Orleans, La.
Taxco, Mexico
Bibl. 127, 144

mark used
after his death

John Spring
(c. 1807, d. 1827)
Charleston, S.C.
Bibl. 5

George F. Springer (1875)
Westbrook, Me.
Bibl. 105

Gwen Springette
(c. 1960–1980)
St. Louis, Mo.
Bibl. 155

John Sprogell
(c. 1765–1794)
Philadelphia, Pa.
Bibl. 3

John Sprogell Jr. (c. 1771)
Philadelphia, Pa.
Bibl. 3

Peter Spurck
(c. 1794–1806)
Philadelphia, Pa.
Bibl. 3

David M. Spurgin (b. 1814)
Mt. Sterling, Ky. (c. 1829)
Carlisle, Ky. (c. 1833–1847)
Winchester, Ky.
(c. 1847–1852)

Greencastle, Ind.
(c. 1852–1892)
Bibl. 32, 54, 68, 93, 133

Peter Spurk (c. 1812)
Chillicothe, Ohio
Bibl. 34

Moses Spyers (c. 1830)
Philadelphia, Pa.
Bibl. 3

Squire & Bros. (c. 1846)
New York, N.Y.
*Bibl. 23, 25, 28, 44, 89, 91,
114, 124, 138*

SQUIRE & BROS

Squire & Lander (c. 1840)
New York, N.Y.
*Bibl. 23, 25, 29, 36, 44, 91,
114, 124*

SQUIRE & LANDER

Bela S. Squire Jr. (c. 1839)
New York, N.Y.
Benedict & Squire
(c. 1825–1839)
Bibl. 15, 91, 124, 135, 138

Seth P. Squire (c. 1835)
New York, N.Y.
*Bibl. 25, 29, 36, 44, 91, 95,
114, 124*

S. P. SQUIRE

R. Squires (c. 1845)
Binghamton, N.Y.
Bibl. 20, 124

Staats
(See Schaats)

Jacob Stackel (c. 1825)
Philadelphia, Pa.
Bibl. 3

Philemon Stacy Jr.
(c. 1798–1829)   P. STACY
Boston, Mass.
*Bibl. 4, 23, 24, 25, 28, 29,
36, 44, 110, 114*

Joseph Stall
(c. 1802–1812)

Baltimore, Md.
Bibl. 23, 28, 36, 38, 44

Standard
(See E. Borhek)

Standish
(See S. Barry)

John Staniford
(b. 1737–d. 1811)
Windham, Conn.
Elderkin & Staniford
(c. 1790–1792)
*Bibl. 15, 16, 23, 24, 25, 28,
29, 36, 44, 61, 91, 92, 94,
102, 110, 114*

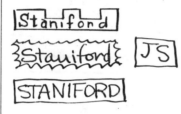

———— **Stanley** (c. 1807)
Chillicothe, Ohio
Bibl. 34

Frank Stanley (1875)
Dixfield, Me.
Bibl. 105

Joseph E. Stanley
Zanesville, Ohio
(c. 1804–1848)
Cleveland, Ohio (c. 1848)
Probably Joseph M. Stanley
Bibl. 54

Joseph M. Stanley
Zanesville, Ohio
(c. 1804–1848)
Cleveland, Ohio (c. 1848)
Bibl. 34, 65

Salmon Stanley (c. 1831)
Cazenovia, N.Y.
Bibl. 20, 124

I. Stanniford (c. 1788)
Bennington, Vt.
Bibl. 54, 110

J. J. Stansbury (?)
Leesburg, Va.
Bibl. 89

Stanton & Brother
(c. 1845–c. 1850)
Rochester, N.Y.
William P. Stanton (?)
Henry Stanton (?)
Bibl. 20, 124

D. E. & Z. Stanton
(c. 1775–1780)
Stonington, Conn.
Daniel Stanton
Enoch Stanton
Zebulon Stanton
Bibl. 44, 91, 110

Daniel Stanton
(b. 1755–d. 1781)
Stonington, Conn.
D. E. & Z. Stanton
(c. 1775–1780)
*Bibl. 16, 23, 24, 25, 28, 36,
44, 91, 92, 110, 114*

D. Stanton

Enoch Stanton
(b. 1745–d. 1781)
Stonington, Conn.
D. E. & Z. Stanton
(c. 1775–1780)
*Bibl. 16, 25, 28, 36, 44, 91,
92, 110, 114*

Henry Stanton
(b. 1803–d. 1872)
Rochester, N.Y.
(c. 1825–1850)
W. P. & H. Stanton
(c. 1826–1841)
Stanton & Brother
(c. 1845–1850) (?)
Bibl. 20, 41, 124

W. P. & H. Stanton
(c. 1826–1841)
Rochester, N.Y.
William P. Stanton
Henry Stanton
*Bibl. 15, 20, 25, 41, 44, 114,
124*

W.P.& H STANTON

William Stanton
(b. 1772–d. 1850)
Hudson, N.Y.
(c. 1801–1802)
Providence, R.I.
Bibl. 20, 28, 41, 44, 110, 124

William P. Stanton
   (c. 1821)
Nantucket Island, Mass.
Bibl. 12

William P. Stanton
   (b. 1794–d. 1878)
Rochester, N.Y.
W. P. & H. Stanton
   (c. 1826–1841)
Stanton & Brother
   (c. 1845–1850) (?)
Bibl. 20, 41, 110, 124

Zebulon Stanton
   (b. 1753–d. 1828)
Stonington, Conn.
D. E. & Z. Stanton
   (c. 1775–1780)
*Bibl. 6, 23, 24, 25, 28, 29,
   36, 44, 91, 92, 110, 114*

Stanwood
(See also Shreve, Stanwood
   & Co.)

Stanwood & Halstrick
   (c. 1850)
Boston, Mass.
———Stanwood
Joseph Halstrick
Bibl. 4, 23, 28, 44

Henry B. Stanwood
   (b. 1818–d. 1869)
Boston, Mass.
Harris & Stanwood (c. 1835)
Shreve, Stanwood & Co.
*Bibl. 15, 23, 24, 25, 28, 29,
   36, 44, 114, 157*

Henry B. Stanwood

J. E. Stanwood (c. 1850)
Philadelphia, Pa.
Bibl. 23, 24, 25, 44, 114

J E STANWOOD

James D. Stanwood
   (c. 1846)
Boston, Mass.
Bibl. 4, 23, 28, 44

George Staple (Staples)
   (c. 1848–1850)

Philadelphia, Pa.
Bibl. 3, 23

Ezra Staples (1860)
Skowhegan, Me.
Bibl. 105

John J. Staples Jr.
   (c. 1788)
New York, N.Y.
*Bibl. 23, 24, 25, 28, 29, 36,
   44, 114, 124, 138*

E. F. Starbuck
   (c. 1833, d. 1848)
Nantucket Island, Mass.
Bibl. 12

Erastus Charles Starin
   (c. 1832–c. 1834)
Utica, N.Y.
Storrs & Cooley
   (c. 1831–1839)
Bibl. 18, 20, 124, 158

W. T. Stark (c. 1832)
Xenia, Ohio
Bibl. 34

Henry Starke (b. 1835)
New Orleans, La. (1860)
Bibl. 141

Starr & Marcus
   (19th century)
New York, N.Y. (c. 1864)
Theodore B. Starr
Herman Marcus
Bibl. 89

Starr & Marcus

Jasper Starr
   (b. 1709–d. 1792)
New London, Conn.
Bibl. 28, 44, 110, 151

Richard Starr
   (b. 1785–d. 1849)
Boston, Mass.
   (c. 1807–1813)
Philadelphia, Pa.
*Bibl. 3, 24, 25, 28, 29, 44,
   91, 110, 114*

R STARR

1750

1790–1810

1900

COFFEEPOTS

The coffeepot was similar in design to the teapot but was much taller. It went through a series of shape changes. About 1715 the pot was straight sided. The pear shape, the inverted pear, then the straight-sided pot came into fashion by 1790. By 1800 a fatter pot was made which by 1820 was on a pedestal base. By 1835 it had a footed base. Victorian pots were designed with shapes that were different from anyone else's, the more unusual the better. Next came the Colonial Revival styles of the early 1900s, then the straight-sided, angular, Deco designs. The handle of the coffee or teapot had an insulating piece of bone or wood until about 1850 when the all-metal handle was in use and was hot to hold.

1760	1760	1760–1770	1790
1815–1825	1870–1890	1875–1890	1900
1920	1920–1930	1930	1930

Theodore B. Starr
  (c. 1900–1924)
New York, N.Y.
Starr & Marcus
Became Reed & Barton
Bibl. 89, 114, 127, 151

James Starrett (c. 1796)
Brandywine, Mass.
Bibl. 3

State House Sterling
(See Silver Counselors of
  Home Decorators, Inc.)

P. M. Statzell
  (c. 1845–1850)
Philadelphia, Pa.
Bibl. 3

Stebbins & Co.
  (c. 1845–1856)
New York, N.Y.
  (c. 1836–1841)
William Stebbins
Bibl. 15, 78, 91, 114

STEBBINS & CO

Stebbins & Howe
  (c. 1830–1832)
New York, N.Y.
Edwin Stebbins
George C. Howe
*Bibl. 24, 25, 29, 36, 44, 54,
  91, 95, 114, 124, 138*

STEBBINS & HOWE

E. Stebbins & Co.
  (c. 1835–1845)
New York, N.Y.
Edwin Stebbins
*Bibl. 4, 23, 24, 28, 29, 35,
  36, 83, 91, 114, 116, 124,
  138*

E. STEBBINS & CO

Edwin Stebbins
New York, N.Y.
Stebbins & Howe
E. Stebbins & Co.
Bibl. 15, 91, 95, 124, 138

N. W. Stebbins (c. 1848)
Seneca, Huron, Muskingum
  Counties, Ohio
Bibl. 34

Thomas E. Stebbins
  (c. 1828–1833)
New York, N.Y.
Thomas E. Stebbins & Co.
  (c. 1810–1835)
Bibl. 15, 24, 29, 44, 124

T STEBBINS   T. E. S.

STEBBINS

Thomas E. Stebbins & Co.
  (c. 1810–1835)
New York, N.Y.
Bibl. 23, 24, 25, 36, 44, 124

Stebbins

**Valentine Steckell
  (Stickell)** (d. 1796)
Fredericktown, Md.
  (c. 1793)
Bibl. 38

Alexander Stedman
  (c. 1793–1814)
Philadelphia, Pa.
Bibl. 3, 23, 36, 44

John C. Stedman
  (c. 1819–1822, d. 1833)
Raleigh, N.C.
Savage & Stedman
  (c. 1819–1820)
Bibl. 21

John Stedmetz
  (c. 1829–1833)
Philadelphia, Pa.
Bibl. 3

Steel & Field
  (c. 1814–1825)
Philadelphia, Pa.
Robert Steel
Samuel Field
Bibl. 3, 23

The Steel-Brussel Co.
  (c. 1896–1904)
New York, N.Y.
Bibl. 114, 127, 157

S·B·C

James Steel (c. 1812)
Baltimore, Md.
Bibl. 3

Robert Steel
  (c. 1811–1831)
Philadelphia, Pa.
Steel & Field (c. 1814–1825)
Bibl. 3

Steele and Carr (c. 1836)
Louisville, Ky.
Robert Steele
——— Carr
Bibl. 32, 54, 93

Steele & Hocknell
  (c. 1830)
Location unknown
Bibl. 89

STEELE & HOCKNELL

J. H. Steele (1875)
Portland, Me.
Bibl. 105

James P. Steele
  (b. 1811–d. 1893)
Rochester, N.Y.
  (c. 1838–1855)
Bibl. 20, 41, 44, 91, 124

John Steele
  (c. 1720–1722, d. 1722)
Annapolis Md.
Bibl. 23, 36, 38, 44

Robert Steele
  (c. 1832–1848)
Louisville, Ky.
Steele and Carr (c. 1836)
Bibl. 32, 54, 93

Samuel Steele
  (c. 1829–1850)
Baltimore, Md.
Bibl. 38

T. Steele & Co. (c. 1840)
Hartford, Conn.
Bibl. 88, 91, 110

T. Steele & Co

T. S. Steele (c. 1800)
Hartford, Conn.

T. S. Steele & Co. (c. 1815)
Bibl. 24, 25, 44

(T. Steele)

T. Steele

T. S. Steele & Co.
(c. 1815)
Hartford, Conn.
Bibl. 24, 25, 44, 91, 92

T Steele & Co

The Rev. William Steele
(c. 1780–1844)
Henderson County, Ky.
Bibl. 32, 54, 68

Haldor S. Steen
(c. 1844–c. 1850)
Rochester, N.Y.
Bibl. 20

Ole S. Steen (c. 1847)
Rochester, N.Y.
Bibl. 20

John Steeper (c. 1762)
Philadelphia, Pa.
Bibl. 3

I. Steer (c. 1835)
Location unknown
Bibl. 24

I STEER

John Steikleader
(c. 1791–1793)
Hagerstown, Md.
Bibl. 38

Abraham Stein
(c. 1795–1828)
Philadelphia, Pa.
Bibl. 3

Charles K. Stellwagen
(c. 1840–1848)
Philadelphia, Pa.
Bibl. 3

W. S. Stenson
Location unknown
Bibl. 28

Gothelf Stephanis
(c. 1791–1795)
New York, N.Y.
Bibl. 23, 36, 91, 124

Stephen
(See Thomas H. Stevens)

Stephens & Doud
(c. 1841–?)
Utica, N.Y.
David Stephens
William Gaylord Doud
Bibl. 18, 20, 124

David Stephens (c. 1840)
Utica, N.Y.
T. C. & D. Stephens
(c. 1840–1841)
Stephens & Doud
(c. 1841–?)
Bibl. 18, 20, 124, 158

George Stephens (c. 1790)
New York, N.Y.
(May be Gothelf Stephanis)
*Bibl. 23, 24, 25, 28, 29, 35,
36, 44, 83, 114, 124*

Joseph Lawrence
Stephens
(b. 1764–d. 1848)
Paris, Ky. (c. 1810–1827)
Bibl. 32, 93

J STEPHENS   PARIS

T. C. & D. Stephens
(c. 1840–1841)
Utica, N.Y.
Thomas C. Stephens
David Stephens
Bibl. 18, 20, 124, 158

Thomas C. Stephens
(b. 1819)
Utica, N.Y.
T. C. & D. Stephens
(c. 1840–1841)
Bailey & Brothers
Bibl. 18, 20, 124

William Stephens
(c. 1840–1842)
Albany, N.Y.
Bibl. 20, 124

Thomas Stephenson
(c. 1835–1848)
Buffalo, N.Y.
Bibl. 20, 25, 44, 91, 114, 124

Thomas Stephenson &
Co. (c. 1839–1848)
Buffalo, N.Y.
Bibl. 20, 24, 91, 124

STEPHENSON

SterlinE
(See James E. Blake Co.)

Sterling
(See also Haight & Sterling)

———— Sterling
Newburgh, N.Y.
Haight & Sterling
(c. 1841–1843)
Bibl. 20

Sterling Co. (1886–1891)
Providence, R.I.
Became Howard Sterling Co.
(1891–1901)
Bibl. 127

TRADE
SSMC
MARK

Sterling Silver Mfg. Co.
(c. 1894–1932)
Baltimore, Md.
Successor to Klank Mfg. Co.
Dies purchased by Saart
Bros.
Bibl. 127, 147, 157

Sterling Silver Souvenir
Co. (c. 1890–1915)
Boston, Mass.
Bibl. 114, 127, 157

S⬩S

Louis Stern Co., Inc.
(c. 1871–1950)
Providence, R.I.
Bibl. 127

L.S. & Co.

William Stern
(c. 1820–1822)
Philadelphia, Pa.
Bibl. 3

Sterne Brothers (c. 1850)
Syracuse, N.Y.
Baruch Sterne
Abraham Sterne
Bibl. 20

Abraham Sterne (c. 1850)
Syracuse, N.Y.
Sterne Brothers
Bibl. 20, 124

Baruch Sterne (c. 1850)
Syracuse, N.Y.
Sterne Brothers
Bibl. 20, 124

Sterret & Lewis (c. 1822)
Leesburg, Va.
Samuel Sterret
—— Lewis
Bibl. 19

Samuel Sterret
(c. 1822–c. 1834)
Leesburg, Va.
Sterret & Lewis (c. 1822)
Bibl. 19

T. W. Sters (c. 1850)
Location unknown
Bibl. 24

George Steven (c. 1719)
New York, N.Y.
Bibl. 23, 36, 44, 124

—— **Stevens** (c. 1815)
Chillicothe, Ohio
Bibl. 34

Stevens & Lakeman
(c. 1825)
Salem, Mass.
John Stevens
Ebenezer Knowlton
Lakeman
*Bibl. 15, 23, 24, 25, 28, 29,
36, 44, 91, 110, 114*

STEVENS+LAKEMAN

Stevens & Leithoff
(c. 1915–1922)
Irvington, N.J.
Bibl. 127, 157

S&L

B. F. Stevens
(19th century)
Location unknown
Bibl. 89

Charles C. Stevens (1875)
Kennebunk, Me.
Bibl. 105

Eben Stevens (1875)
Bangor, Me.
Bibl. 105

George Stevens
(c. 1845–1848)
Philadelphia, Pa.
Bibl. 3

J. C. Stevens
(c. 1837–1838)
Utica, N.Y.
Bibl. 18, 20, 124, 158

John Stevens
(c. 1819–1830)
Salem, Mass.
Stevens & Lakeman
(c. 1825)
Bibl. 15, 91, 110

Joseph Stevens (c. 1810)
Paris, Ky.
Bibl. 54, 68

Robert Stevens (c. 1808)
Petersburg, Va.
Cohen & Stevens
Bibl. 19

Thomas H. Stevens
(Stephen)
(c. 1839–1846)
Philadelphia, Pa.
Bibl. 3, 23, 44

Charles Stevenson
(c. 1823–1825)
Philadelphia, Pa.
Bibl. 3

John Stevenson (c. 1850)
Pittsburgh, Pa.?
Bibl. 89, 91, 124

John Stevenson (c. 1777)
New Bern, N.C.
Bibl. 21

Steward
(See James Stuart, Thomas
Stuart)

Aaron Steward (c. 1843)
Philadelphia, Pa.
Bibl. 3

Stewart
(See Marrs & Stewart,
James Stuart,
Thomas Stuart)

—— **Stewart** (c. 1830)
(May be mark of John
Stewart)
Bibl. 15, 44

STEWART

Stewart & Co. (c. 1824)
Philadelphia, Pa.
George Stewart (?)
Bibl. 3

Alexander Stewart
(c. 1850)
New York, N.Y.
Bibl. 23, 138

B. Stewart (1861)
Skowhegan, Me.
Bibl. 105

B. Stewart & Son (1860)
Skowhegan, Me.
Bibl. 105

C. Stewart (19th century)
Location unknown
Bibl. 79

C. W. Stewart (c. 1840)
New York, N.Y.
Bibl. 23, 36

C. W. Stewart (c. 1850)
Lexington, Ky.
Bibl. 24, 25, 44, 54

C W STEWART

Charles Stewart (b. 1805)
Albany, N.Y. (c. 1837–1848)
Utica, N.Y. (c. 1848–1851)
Bibl. 18, 20, 124, 158

Charles G. Stewart
(c. 1820–1849)
Charles Town, Va.
Charles G. Stewart & Son
Bibl. 19

Charles G. Stewart & Son
(c. 1847–1849)
Charles Town, Va.
Charles G. Stewart
George L. Stewart
Bibl. 19

George Stewart (c. 1837)
Philadelphia, Pa.
Stewart & Co. (c. 1824) (?)
Bibl. 3

George L. Stewart
Charles Town, Va.
Charles G. Stewart & Son
(c. 1847–1849)
Bibl. 19

George W. Stewart
(c. 1846–1852)
Lexington, Ky.
Garner & Stewart (c. 1850)
Bibl. 32, 68, 91, 114

James Stewart
(c. 1787–1811)
Savannah, Ga.
Bibl. 17

James D. Stewart
(c. 1836–1841)
New York, N.Y.
Bibl. 15, 124, 138

John Stewart
New York, N.Y. (c. 1791)
Baltimore, Md. (c. 1810)
Bibl. 23, 25, 36, 44, 124, 138

STEWART

T. M. Stewart (1860–1875)
Anson, Me.
Bibl. 105

Warner W. Stewart
(c. 1837–1838)

Utica, N.Y.
Bibl. 18, 20, 124, 158

William Stewart
(c. 1790–1851)
Russellville, Ky.
Bibl. 32, 93

William Stewart (c. 1845)
St. Louis, Mo.
Bibl. 54, 155

Worthington Stewart
(c. 1842–1847)
St. Louis, Mo.
Bibl. 54, 155

Stickell
(See Steckell)

John Stickler (c. 1823)
New York, N.Y.
Gale & Stickler
*Bibl. 23, 36, 44, 114, 124,
135, 138*

Stickles
(See Connor & Stickles)

Jonathan Stickney (Jr.)
(b. 1760–d. 1808)
Newburyport, Mass.
(c. 1770–1798)
*Bibl. 23, 24, 25, 28, 29, 36,
44, 91, 110, 114*

I. STICKNEY

Moses Peck Stickney
(d. 1832)
Newburyport, Mass. (1820)
New Orleans, La.
(1830–1832)
*Bibl. 23, 24, 25, 29, 36, 44,
91, 110, 114, 141*

M P STICKNEY

B. H. Stief (c. 1858)
Nashville, Tenn.
Bibl. 159

B.H.STIEF

Stieff Company
(1904–1979)
Baltimore, Md.
Baltimore Sterling Silver

Company (1892–1904)
(See Kirk Stieff Company)
Bibl. 127, 128, 131, 146, 147

Stieff-Orth Co.
(c. 1909–1915)
Baltimore, Md.
Bibl. 127, 157

Stiles & Baldwin
(c. 1791–1792)
Northampton, Mass.
Samuel Stiles
Jedediah Baldwin
Bibl. 41, 84, 110

Benjamin Stiles (c. 1825)
Woodbury, Conn.
Curtis(s), Candee & Stiles
(c. 1831–1835)
Curtis(s) & Stiles (c. 1835)
Bibl. 16, 23, 28, 36, 44

George Keith Stiles
(b. 1805, c. 1834–1844)
Cortland, N.Y.
Bibl. 20, 124

John Stiles (c. 1792–1798)
Augusta, Ga.
John & Joseph Stiles
Bibl. 17

John & Joseph Stiles
(c. 1792–?)
Augusta, Ga.
Bibl. 17

Joseph Stiles (d. 1838)
Augusta, Ga.
John & Joseph Stiles
Bibl. 17

Samuel Stiles
(c. 1785–1795)
Northampton, Mass.
Stiles & Baldwin
(c. 1791–1792)
Bibl. 41, 84, 110

John Stillas
(c. 1784–1793, d. 1793)
Philadelphia, Pa.
Bibl. 3

Stillman (Silliman)
(See Wilmot & Stillman)

Alexander Stillman
(c. 1806)
Philadelphia, Pa.
Bibl. 3, 23, 36, 44

Barton Stillman
(b. 1767–d. 1858)
Westerly, R.I.
Bibl. 28, 44

E. Stillman (c. 1800–1825)
Stonington (?), Conn.
Bibl. 23, 24, 25, 28, 29, 36, 44, 92, 110, 114

(E.Stillman)

[E Stillman]

Paul Stillman
(b. 1782–d. 1810)
Westerly, R.I.
Bibl. 28, 44, 110

Richard Stillman (c. 1805)
Philadelphia, Pa.
Bibl. 23, 24, 25, 29, 36, 44, 114

[R STILLMAN]

Samuel W. Stillman
(c. 1850)
Hartford, Conn.
Bibl. 23, 44

Willet Stillman (c. 1804)
Utica, N.Y.
Bibl. 20, 124, 158

William Stillman
(See Stilman)

Mortimer F. Stillwell
(c. 1845–1859)
Rochester, N.Y.
Cook & Stillwell
(c. 1847–1859)
Bibl. 20, 41, 124

William Stilman
(b. 1767–d. 1858)
Hopkinton, R.I.
Bibl. 2, 28, 36, 44, 110

George F. (A.) Stinger
(b. 1812)
Cincinnati, Ohio
(1836–1883)
Bibl. 34, 90, 152

S. J. Stinger (c. 1850)
Cincinnati, Ohio
Bibl. 34, 152

David T. Stinson (1860)
Bath, Me.
Bibl. 105

William Stinson
(c. 1813–1815)
New York, N.Y.
Bibl. 23, 36, 44, 124

Stockerman & Pepper
(See Stockman & Pepper)

Stocking & Kipp (c. 1833)
Wheeling, Va.
Philo W. Stocking
R. M. Kipp
Bibl. 19

G. B. Stocking
(c. 1893–1896)
Tacoma, Wash.
Bibl. 127   RHODODENDRON

Philo W. Stocking
(c. 1833–1839)
Wheeling, Va.
Stocking & Kipp (c. 1833)
Forking & Kipp
(c. 1835–1839)
Bibl. 19

Reuben Stocking (c. 1831)
Batavia, N.Y.
Keyes & Stocking
Bibl. 20, 124

Stock(er)man & Pepper
(c. 1828–1831)
Philadelphia, Pa.
Bibl. 3, 24, 25, 28, 29, 36, 44, 114

[STOCKERMAN & PEPPER]

Jacob Stockman
(c. 1828–1850)
Philadelphia, Pa.
Bibl. 3, 15, 23, 25, 36, 44, 91, 114

[J. STOCKMAN]

(J. STOCKMAN)

S. Stockman (c. 1837)
Philadelphia, Pa.
Bibl. 3

Samuel W. Stockton
(c. 1823–1831)
Philadelphia, Pa.
Bibl. 3

Stodder & Frobisher
(c. 1816–1825)
Boston, Mass.
——— Stodder
Benjamin C. Frobisher (?)
Bibl. 4, 15, 23, 25, 28, 29, 36, 39, 44, 110, 114

[Stodder & Frobisher]

Jonathan Stodder (Jr.)
(c. 1826–1829)
New York, N.Y.
Bibl. 15, 25, 44, 114, 124, 138

[J. STODDER]

George Stokeberry
(c. 1837)
Philadelphia, Pa.
Bibl. 3

T. Stokes (c. 1832)
Cazenovia, N.Y.
Willard & Stokes (c. 1833)
Bibl. 20, 124

Stollenwerck & Bros.
(c. 1805)
New York, N.Y.
Bibl. 23, 24, 25, 36, 44, 91, 114, 124, 138

Stollenwerck & Co.
(c. 1800)
New York, N.Y.
Bibl. 23, 25, 29, 36, 44, 114, 124

Stollenwerck

Stollenwerck & Roe
(See Roe & Stollenwerck)

P. M. Stollenwerck
Philadelphia, Pa.
  (c. 1813–1816)
New York, N.Y. (c. 1820)
Bibl. 3, 124, 138

Stone & Ball (c. 1850)
Syracuse, N.Y.
Seymour H. Stone
Calvin S. Ball Jr.
Bibl. 20, 124

Stone & Osburn (Osborn)
  (c. 1796)
New York, N.Y.
Bibl. 23, 28, 36, 44, 124, 138

Stone Associates
  (1937–1957)
Gardner, Mass.
Successor to Arthur J. Stone
Bibl. 127, 135

Stone Sterling Silver Co.
  (c. 1896–1904)
New York, N.Y.
Bibl. 114, 127, 157

Adam Stone
  (c. 1803–1812)
Baltimore, Md.
Bibl. 23, 25, 28, 36, 44, 114

   A S

Arthur J. Stone
  (b. 1847–d. 1938)
Gardner, Mass.
Became Stone Associates
  (1937–1957)
Bibl. 120, 127, 135, 144, 157

Charles F. Stone
  (1860–1875)
Machias, Me.
Bibl. 105

John Stone (c. 1831)
Baltimore, Md.
Bibl. 38

John A. Stone (c. 1817)
Baltimore, Md.
Bibl. 38

Seymour H. Stone
  (c. 1850)
Syracuse, N.Y.
Stone & Ball
Bibl. 20, 124

William G. Stone (c. 1809)
Somers, N.Y.
Bibl. 20, 124

William R. Stone
  (c. 1845–1846)
Louisville, Ky.
Bibl. 32, 93

Rudy Stoner (c. 1764)
Lancaster, Pa
Bibl. 3

A. Stoops (c. 1825)
Location unknown
Bibl. 24

A STOOPS

Max H. Storch (c. 1950)
New York, N.Y.
Bibl. 127

Storer & Wilmot
  (c. 1796–1800)
Rutland, Vt.
William Storer
Thomas Wilmot
Bibl. 54, 110

William Storer
  (b. 1763–d. 1842)
Rutland, Vt. (c. 1792–1796)
Storer & Wilmot
  (c. 1796–1800)
Bibl. 54, 110

Storm & Son (c. 1830)
Albany, N.Y. (?)
Abraham G. Storm (?)
Bibl. 15, 114

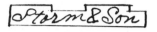

Storm & Wilson
  (c. 1802–1818)
Poughkeepsie, N.Y.
James Wilson
Abraham G. Storm
*Bibl. 15, 20, 25, 44, 91, 95,
  114, 124*

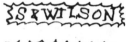

A. G. Storm & Son
  (c. 1823–1826)
Poughkeepsie, N.Y.
Abraham G. Storm
Bibl. 20, 25, 44, 91, 124

Storm & Son

Abraham G. Storm
  (b. 1779–d. 1836)
Albany, N.Y. (c. 1830)
Poughkeepsie, N.Y.
Storm & Wilson
  (c. 1802–1818)
A. G. Storm & Son
  (c. 1823–1826)
Storm & Son (c. 1830) (?)
Fellows & Storm
  (c. 1839–1844)
*Bibl. 15, 20, 23, 24, 25, 29,
  91, 95, 114, 124*

A. G. STORM

E. C. Storm (c. 1815)
Rochester, N.Y.
Bibl. 25, 44, 124

E. C. STORM

Storrs & Chubbuck
 (c. 1847–c. 1849)
Utica, N.Y.
Henry S. Storrs
Samuel W. Chubbuck
Bibl. 18, 20, 114, 124, 158

| STORRS & CHUBBUCK |

Storrs & Cook
 (c. 1827–1833)
Amherst, Mass.
Northampton, Mass.
Nathan Storrs
Benjamin E. Cook
Bibl. 25, 44, 84

| Storrs & Cook |

Storrs & Cooley
 (c. 1831–1839)
Utica, N.Y.
Charles Storrs
Oliver B. Cooley
Horace P. Bradley
David S. Rowland
Erastus Charles Starin
*Bibl. 15, 18, 20, 23, 25, 28,
  29, 36, 89, 114, 124, 158*

Storrs & Davies
 (c. 1829–1830)
Utica, N.Y.
Charles Storrs
Thomas Davies
Bibl. 18, 20, 124, 158

| Storrs & Davies Utica |

Storrs & Parker (c. 1828)
Utica, N.Y.
Charles Storrs
George Parker
Bibl. 18, 20, 124

Charles Storrs
 (c. 1828, d. 1839)
Utica, N.Y.
Storrs & Parker (c. 1828)
Storrs & Davies
 (c. 1829–1830)

Storrs & Cooley
 (c. 1831–1839)
Bibl. 18, 20, 114, 124, 158

Eli A. Storrs
 (c. 1832–1833)
Utica, N.Y.
Bibl. 18, 20, 124, 158

Henry S. Storrs
 (b. 1826–d. 1862)
Utica, N.Y. (c. 1846–1849)
Storrs & Chubbuck
 (c. 1847–c. 1849)
Bibl. 18, 20, 124, 158

Nathan Storrs
 (b. 1768–d. 1839)
Amherst, Mass.
Northampton, Mass.
New York, N.Y. (?) (c. 1825)
Baldwin & Storrs
 (c. 1792–1794)
Storrs & Cook
 (c. 1827–1833)
*Bibl. 15, 23, 24, 25, 28, 29,
  41, 44, 84, 91, 94, 102,
  110, 114*

| N. STORRS |

Shubael Storrs (d. 1847)
Utica, N.Y. (c. 1803–1828)
Bibl. 18, 20, 124, 158

| STORRS |

E. F. Story (c. 1872)
Wilmington, N.C.
T. W. Brown & Sons
Bibl. 21

S. N. Story (c. 1845)
Worcester, Mass.
Bibl. 15, 25, 44, 114

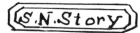

Edwin Stott (c. 1850)
Philadelphia, Pa.
Bibl. 3

John Stott (d. 1749)
Williamsburg, Va. (c. 1737)
Bibl. 19

Samuel Stott
 (c. 1846–1850)
Philadelphia, Pa.
Bibl. 3

Stout
(See Brown & Stout)

James D. Stout
 (c. 1817–1836)
New York, N.Y.
*Bibl. 15, 24, 25, 28, 44, 72,
  114, 124, 138*

Samuel Stout
 (b. 1756–d. 1795)
Princeton, N.J.
 (c. 1779–1795)
Bibl. 3, 23, 36, 44, 46, 54

**Luke (Lucas)
 Stoutenburgh Sr.**
 (b. 1691–d. 1743)
Charleston, S.C.
 (c. 1718–1743)
Bibl. 5, 25, 44, 114

**Luke (Lucas)
 Stoutenburgh Jr.**
 (b. 1691–d. 1743)
Charleston, S.C. (c. 1765)
Bibl. 5, 95, 151

Tobias Stoutenburgh
 (b. 1700–d. 1759)
New York, N.Y.
*Bibl. 2, 4, 23, 24, 25, 28, 29,
  35, 36, 44, 54, 87, 91, 114,
  119, 124, 138*

John Stow
 (b. 1748–d. 1802,
  c. 1772)
Wilmington, Del
*Bibl. 3, 23, 25, 30, 36, 39,
  44, 91*

L. S. Stowe (c. 1855–1900)
Gardner, Mass.
 (c. 1855–1864)
Springfield, Mass.
 (c. 1864–1900)

Became H. J. Webb & Co.
Bibl. 127

Frederick Stowee
(c. 1802–1803)
Philadelphia, Pa.
Bibl. 3

A. Stowell Jr.
Baltimore, Md. (c. 1855)
Charlestown, Mass.
Gould, Stowell & Ward
(c. 1855–1858)
Bibl. 24, 28, 44

(A STOWELL JR)

Avery W. Stowell
(d. 1844)
Syracuse, N.Y.
(c. 1842–1844)
Bibl. 20, 124

David C. Stoy
(c. 1844–1849)
Louisville, Ky.
Kitts & Stoy (c. 1851–1852)
Bibl. 32, 93

Frederick Stoy
(c. 1807–1822)
Augusta, Ga.
(may be Frederick Stowee of
Philadelphia, Pa.)
Bibl. 17

Pierce Stoy (c. 1803–1827)
Savannah, Ga.
Bibl. 17

C. Strade (c. 1838)
Richmond, Va.
Bibl. 19

Samuel Stradley (c. 1857)
Greenville, S.C.
Bibl. 5

Strathmore Co.
(c. 1915–1927)
Providence, R.I.
Bibl. 127, 157

SOLID STRATHMORE SILVER

Strauss Silver Co., Inc.
(c. 1920–1930)
New York, N.Y.
Bibl. 127

**George Streepey
(Strieby)(Strebe)
(Streepy)**(c. 1799–1847)
Greensburg, Pa.
Charlestown, Ind.
Salem, Ind.
Bibl. 133

George Wesley Streepey
(c. 1858–1916)
New Albany, Ind.
Charlestown, Ind.
Columbus, Ind.
Hot Springs, Ark.
Bibl. 133

Michael Streepey
(b. 1805–d. 1889)
Salem, Ind.
New Albany, Ind.
Bibl. 133

Streepy
(See Streepey)

Jacob Strembeck
(c. 1820–1822)
Philadelphia, Pa.
Bibl. 3

Isaac Stretch
(c. 1732–1752)
Philadelphia, Pa.
Bibl. 3

Peter Stretch
(c. 1708–1738, d. 1746)
Philadelphia, Pa.
Bibl. 3

Samuel Stretch
(c. 1715, d. 1732)
Philadelphia, Pa.
Bibl. 3

Thomas Stretch
(c. 1754–1764, d. 1765)
Philadelphia, Pa.
Bibl. 3

John E. Stretcher
(c. 1828–1866)
Cincinnati, Ohio
Columbus, Ohio
Hillsboro, Ohio
Indianapolis, Ind.
Greenwood, Ind.
Bibl. 133

Strieby
(See Streepey)

George W. Striker
(c. 1825–1833)
New York, N.Y.
*Bibl. 15, 25, 44, 114, 124,
138*

(G W STRIKER)

George A. Stringer
(c. 1849)
Cincinnati, Ohio
Bibl. 54

Samuel Stringfellow
(c. 1816–1837)
Augusta, Ga.
Virgin(s) & Stringfellow(?)
Bibl. 17

Strobel & Crane (c. 1907)
Newark, N. J.
Bibl. 89

D. H. Strock (c. 1853)
Paris, Tenn.
Bibl. 54

Edmund Strock (c. 1850)
Philadelphia, Pa.
Bibl. 3

Strom & Son (c. 1835)
Albany, N.Y.
(May be Storm & Son)
A. G. Strom
Bibl. 36

STROM & SON

A. G. Strom (c. 1830)
Albany, N.Y.
(May be A. G. Storm)
Strom & Son (c. 1835)
Bibl. 36

Strong
(See Phelps & Strong)

Strong & Elder Co.
(c. 1896)
Address unknown
Bibl. 114, 127, 157

J.E. STRETCHER

John Strong
 (b. 1749, c. 1774)
Maryland
Bibl. 23, 28, 36, 38, 44

Peter Strong
 (b. 1764–d. 1797)
Fayetteville, N.C.
Bibl. 21

William Strong
 (c. 1807–1811)
Philadelphia, Pa.
Bibl. 3, 23, 36, 44

———— Strother
Cincinnati, Ohio
Bibl. 54

Nelson Strout (1875)
Limerick, Me.
Bibl. 105

A. Strub (c. 1847)
St. Louis, Mo.
Bibl. 54, 155

Alexander C. Stuart
 (c. 1834–1841)
New York, N.Y.
Bibl. 15, 124, 138

Arthur Stuart Company
 (1949–1960)
Albuquerque, N.M.
Bibl. 127

Hugh Stuart
 (c. 1800–1808)
New York, N.Y.
Bibl. 23, 36, 44, 124, 138

I. (J.) Stuart (c. 1700)
(probably John Stuart)
Bibl. 28

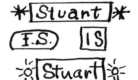

James Stuart (Steward)
 (Stewart)
 (c. 1837–1850)

Philadelphia, Pa.
Bibl. 3

John Stuart   (Stuart)
 (c. 1720, d. 1737)
Providence, R.I.
Bibl. 23, 24, 25, 29, 36, 44,
 110, 114

[J. S.] [J. S.]

Robert Stuart (c. 1931)
Cincinnati, Ohio
Bibl. 127

Thomas Stuart (Steward)
 (Stewart)
Philadelphia, Pa.
 (c. 1839–1850)
Bibl. 3

F. Stubenrauch
 (1857–1866)
New Orleans, La.
Bibl. 141

Isaac Stuckert (c. 1809)
Philadelphia, Pa.
Bibl. 3, 23, 36, 44

D. F. Studley (c. 1830)
Location unknown
Bibl. 28, 29, 44

[D. F. STUDLEY]

L. Studley (19th century)
Location unknown
Bibl. 89

Joseph Gordon Bonner
 Stukes (c. 1788)
Charleston, S.C.
Bibl. 5

Sturdy & Marcy
 (1870–1880)
Providence, R.I.
Bibl. 108

Thomas Sturgeon
 (c. 1830)
Lancaster, Ohio
Bibl. 34

Timothy Sturgeon
 (c. 1812)
Lancaster, Ohio
Bibl. 34

Joseph Sturgis
 (c. 1813–1817)
Philadelphia, Pa.
Bibl. 3

James Stutson (c. 1838)
Rochester, N.Y.
Bibl. 20, 124

James Styles (b. 1772)
Rhinebeck, N.Y. (c. 1780)
Kingston, N.Y. (c. 1784)
Bibl. 20, 124

William J. Styles (c. 1823)
Rhinebeck, N.Y.
Bibl. 20, 124

Suire & Deloste
 (c. 1822–1826)
Baltimore, Md.
Joseph Suire
Francis Deloste
Bibl. 38

Joseph Suire (Shuire)
 (Suiro)
Baltimore, Md.
 (c. 1799–1826)
Suire & Deloste
 (c. 1822–1826)
Bibl. 38

Suley
(See also Sealey)

John Suley (c. 1810–1812)
Baltimore, Md.
Bibl. 38

Cornelius D. Sullivan
 (c. 1842–1868)
St. Louis, Mo.
Bibl. 24, 25, 54, 91, 114, 155

[C D Sullivan]

D. Sullivan & Co.
 (c. 1820)
New York, N.Y.
Bibl. 3, 23, 24, 29, 36, 44,
 114, 124

Enoch Sullivan
(c. 1800–1816)
Richmond, Va.
Bibl. 19

 E SULLIVAN

George Sullivan
(c. 1802–1806)
Lynchburg, Va.
Bibl. 19, 54, 90, 93

J. T. Sullivan (1850–1851)
St. Louis, Mo.
Bibl. 155

Martin Sullivan (1875)
Portland, Me.
Bibl. 105

Owen Sullivan (c. 1748)
Boston, Mass.
Bibl. 54, 110

J. F. B. Sumner (1875)
Damariscotta, Me.
Bibl. 105

Sunderlin & Weaver
(before 1864)
Brooklyn, N.Y. (?)
Rochester, N.Y. (?)
Bibl. 41, 124

Jacob Supplee (c. 1790)
Philadelphia, Pa.
Bibl. 3, 23, 36, 44

Supreme Silver Co.
(c. 1930)
New York, N.Y.
Bibl. 127

S

Surefire
(See Napier Company)

George Sutherland
(d. c. 1845)
Boston, Mass. (c. 1810)
Bibl. 4, 23, 28, 36, 44, 110

Robert Sutton
(c. 1800–1825)
New Haven, Conn.
Bibl. 16, 23, 28, 36, 44, 92, 110, 143

Sutton Hoo Jewelers
(1972–present)
Colorado Springs, Colo.
Bob Newell
Charles Lamoreaux
Lewis Ridenour
Bibl. 127

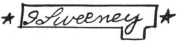

Swaine
(See Robert Swan)

Benjamin Swan
(b. 1792–d. 1867)
Augusta, Me. (c. 1825)
Bibl. 23, 29, 91, 110

B. SWAN

Caleb Swan
(b. 1754–d. 1816)
Boston, Mass.
Charlestown, Mass.
Bibl. 2, 23, 28, 36, 44, 110

Fred C. Swan (1875)
Augusta, Me.
Bibl. 105

Robert Swan (Swaine)
Worcester, Mass. (c. 1775)
Andover, Mass. (c. 1795)
Philadelphia, Pa.
(c. 1799–1831)
Bibl. 3, 15, 23, 24, 25, 28, 29, 36, 39, 44, 54, 78, 81, 104, 110, 114

R Swan   R SWAN

R SWAN

William Swan
(b. 1715–d. 1774)
Boston, Mass.
Worcester, Mass.
Bibl. 2, 15, 23, 24, 25, 28, 29, 36, 44, 54, 72, 102, 110, 114, 118, 119

John Sweeney
(c. 1814–1827)
Geneva, N.Y.
Giffing & Sweeney
(c. 1809–1814)
Bibl. 15, 20, 24, 25, 44, 114, 124

E. C. Sweet & Co. (1875)
Bangor, Me.
Bibl. 105

J. P. Sweet (1872–1877)
Providence, R.I.
Bibl. 108

Sweetser Co.
(c. 1900–1915)
New York, N.Y.
Bibl. 120, 127, 157

S & E

Henry Philips Sweetser
(b. 1742–d. 1792)
Worcester, Mass. (c. 1768)
Bibl. 23, 36, 44, 110

T. J. Swett (1860)
Cornish, Me.
Bibl. 105

Swift & Jones (c. 1810)
Canandaigua, N.Y.
John D. Swift
Harlow Jones
Bibl. 20, 124

Amos B. Swift (c. 1846)
Earlville, N.Y.
Bibl. 20, 124

Chas. N. Swift & Co.
(c. 1904–1915)
New York, N.Y.
Bibl. 127, 157

John D. Swift (c. 1810)
Manlius, N.Y. (c. 1811–1813)
Canandaigua, N.Y.
Cazenovia, N.Y.
(c. 1816–1821)
Swift & Jones
Bibl. 20, 124

R. B. Swift (1875)
Portland, Me.
Bibl. 105

George J. Swortfiguer
(c. 1840–1842)
Schenectady, N.Y.
Bibl. 20, 114, 124

Christopher Syberry
(c. 1769–?)
Savannah, Ga.
Bibl. 17

Philip Syderman (c. 1785)
Philadelphia, Pa.
Bibl. 3

J. Sylvester (c. 1838–1861)
St. Louis, Mo.
Bibl. 54, 155

William Sylvester
(19th century)
Nixonton, N.C.
Bibl. 21

Celadon (Cleadon) Symmes
(b. 1770–d. 1837)
Cincinnati, Ohio
(c. 1789–1790)
Bibl. 34, 46, 90, 152

Daniel Symmes
(b. 1772–d. 1827,
c. 1792–1793)
Cincinnati, Ohio (c. 1793)
Newton, N.J.
Bibl. 46, 54

John Symmes (c. 1766)
Boston, Mass.
*Bibl. 15, 23, 25, 28, 36, 44,
91, 110, 114*

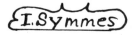

(Judge) Timothy Symmes
(b. 1744–d. 1797)
Newton, N.J.
Walpack, N.J.
Bibl. 46, 54

Daniel Syng
(b. 1713–d. 1745)
Lancaster, Pa. (c. 1734)
*Bibl. 15, 23, 25, 36, 44, 112,
114*

 *(D.S.)*

John Syng
Philadelphia, Pa. (c. 1734)
Wilmington, Del.
(c. 1772) (?)
Bibl. 3, 15, 25, 44, 114

I S

Philip Syng Sr.
(b. 1676–d. 1739)
Philadelphia, Pa.
(c. 1714–1730)
Cape May, N.J.
(after 1723–1728)
Annapolis, Md.
(c. 1728–1739)
*Bibl. 2, 3, 4, 15, 23, 24, 25,
28, 29, 38, 44, 54, 74, 81,
91, 102, 114, 116, 118,
119, 122*

Philip Syng Jr.
(b. 1703–d. 1789)
Philadelphia, Pa.
(c. 1726–1785)
*Bibl. 2, 3, 4, 15, 23, 25, 28,
29, 36, 44, 54, 74, 81, 91,
95, 104, 114, 116, 118,
119, 122, 142, 151*

Syracuse Silver Mfg. Co.
(c. 1895–1904)
Syracuse, N.Y.
Successor to A. B. Schreuder
and A. Lesser's Sons
Bibl. 114, 127, 157

T

T
(See Tennant Company,
Eugene S. Toner Co.,
Towle Silversmiths, Tuttle
Silversmiths)

T & B
(See Trott & Brooks)

T & C
(See Trott & Cleveland)

T & Co
(See Edward Todd & Co.)

T & H
(See Taylor & Hinsdale)

T & R
(See Tanner & Rogers)

T A
(See Thomas Arnold)

T.A.L.C.O
(See Talbot Mfg. Co.)

T B
(See Thauvet Besley,
Timothy Bontecou,
Timothy Bontecou Jr.,
Theophilus Bradbury,
Timothy Brigden, Thomas
Burger, Thomas Bentley)

T B C
(See Thomas Boyle
Campbell)

T C
(See The Thomae Co.,
Thomas Carson)

T C & H
(See Carson & Hall, Thomas
Chadwick & Heims)

T C C
(See Thomas Chester Coit)

T Co
(See Thiery & Co.)

T Co. P
(See Tucker & Parkerhurst
   Co.)

T. C. Shop
   (1910–1913)
Chicago, Ill.
Emery W. Todd
   (1923–1928)
Clemencia C. Cosio
Bibl. 98, 120, 127, 144

T D
(See Timothy Dwight)

T D D
(See Tunis D. Dubois)

T. D. & V. Co.
(See Townsend, Desmond &
   Voorhis Co.)

T E
(See Thomas Stevens Eayres,
   Thomas Edwards, Thomas
   Knox Emery)

T E & Co
(See Theo. Evans & Co.)

T E S
(See Thomas E. Stebbins)

T F
(See Thomas Fletcher)

T G
(See Timothy Gerrish)

T H
(See Thomas Hammersley)

T K
(See Thomas Kettel, Thomas
   Kinney)

T K E
(See Thomas Knox Emery)

T M
(See Thomas Millner)

T N
(See Thomas Norton)

T P
(See Thomas Purse)

T P S
(See Petterson Studio)

T R
(See Thomas Revere,
   Thomas Richards, Thiery
   & Co.)

T S
(See Thomas Savage,
   Thomas Shields, Thomas
   Skinner, Thomas Sparrow,
   Tobias Stoutenburgh, A. F.
   Towle & Son Co.)

T T
(See Thomas Townsend,
   Thomas Trott)

T U
(See Thomas Underhill)

T V R
(See Tunis Van Riper)

T W
(See Thomas H. Warner,
   Thomas Whartenby)

T Y
(See Thomas You)

S. M. Taber & Co.
   (c. 1835)
Providence, R.I.
*Bibl. 15, 44, 91, 108, 110,
114*

Samuel M. Taber (c. 1835)
Providence, R.I.
Bibl. 89, 110, 114

W. E. Taber (1873)
Providence, R.I.
Bibl. 108

W. E. Taber & Son (1875)
Providence, R.I.
Bibl. 108

William Taber (c. 1835)
Philadelphia, Pa.
Bibl. 3, 23, 36, 44

William Taber (1859)
Providence, R.I.
Bibl. 108

John James Taf (c. 1794)
Philadelphia, Pa.
Bibl. 3

Taft & Mitchell
   (c. 1818–1819)
Richmond, Va.
Elisha Taft
William Mitchell Jr.
Bibl. 19

Elisha Taft (c. 1817)
Richmond, Va.
Taft & Mitchell
   (c. 1818–1819)
Bibl. 19, 91

R. Taft (19th century)
Location unknown
Bibl. 15, 44, 114

R. TAFT

Thomas E. Taggart
   (c. 1839)
Columbus, Ga.
Bibl. 17

Talbot Mfg. Co. (c. 1920)
Providence, R.I.
Bibl. 127   TALCO

Talbott, Bailey & Co.
   (c. 1852)
Indianapolis, Ind.
Bibl. 133

TALBOTT, BAILEY & CO.
          INDIANAPOLIS

C. H. Talbot & Co. (1875)
Plymouth, Me.
Bibl. 105

Charles H. Talbot (1860)
Plymouth, Me.
Bibl. 105

Washington Houston Talbot
(b. 1817–d. 1873)
Indianapolis, Ind.
(c. 1855–1865)
Kentucky (c. 1840–1860)
Bibl. 32, 91, 133

A. G. Talcott (c. 1840)
Oswego, N.Y.
Bibl. 20

C. Talcott (19th century)
Location unknown
Bibl. 89

Louis Tamis & Son
(1930–present)
New York, N.Y.
Bibl. 126

H. H. Tammen Curio Co.
(c. 1881–1962)
Denver, Colo.
Became Thrift Novelty
Company
(c. 1962–present)
Bibl. 127

Tanguy
(See also Desquet & Tanguy)

John Tanguy (Tanguey) (Tanguay)
(b. 1780–d. 1858)
Philadelphia, Pa.
(c. 1801–1822)
John & Peter Tanguy
(c. 1808)
*Bibl. 3, 15, 23, 24, 25, 28,
36, 39, 44, 80, 91, 95, 114*

John & Peter Tanguy (Tanguey) (Tanguay)
Philadelphia, Pa. (c. 1808)
Bibl. 3, 23, 44, 91

J & P TANGUY

Peter Tanguy (Tanguey) (Tanguay)
(c. 1810–1819)
Philadelphia, Pa.
John & Peter Tanguy
(c. 1808)
Bibl. 3, 23, 44, 91

Rebiton Tanguy (c. 1806)
Philadelphia, Pa.
Bibl. 3, 23

Yves Tanguy
(b. 1900–d. 1955)
Woodbury, Conn.
Bibl. 89, 117

Theodore Tankey
(b. 1841)
Utica, N.Y. (c. 1859–1860)
Bibl. 18, 124, 158

Tanner & Cooley
(c. 1840–1842)
Utica, N.Y.
Perry G. Tanner
Oliver B. Cooley
Horace P. Bradley
Nathan M. Christian
William Gaylord Doud
Charles Seager
Bibl. 18, 20, 124, 158

TANNER & COOLEY

Tanner & Rogers (c. 1750)
Newport, R.I.
John Tanner
Joseph & Daniel Rogers
Bibl. 25, 44, 110

T & R

Benjamin Tanner
(c. 1800)
Philadelphia, Pa.
Bibl. 3

John Tanner
(b. 1713–d. 1785)
Newport, R.I.
Tanner & Rogers
*Bibl. 15, 24, 28, 36, 44, 54,
56, 91, 94, 110, 114*

Perry G. Tanner
(b. 1842–d. 1878)
Utica, N.Y. (c. 1840–1844)
Cooperstown, N.Y.
(c. 1844–?)
Tanner & Cooley
*Bibl. 18, 20, 24, 25, 44, 114,
124, 158*

P G TANNER

Richard Tape (c. 1844)
Rochester, N.Y.
Bibl. 20, 124, 138

Tappan & Whitney
(c. 1809)
Northampton, Mass.
Benjamin Tappan
——— Whitney
Bibl. 84

Benjamin Tappan
(b. 1742–d. 1831)
Northampton, Mass.
(c. 1768–1809)
Tappan & Whitney (c. 1809)
Bibl. 84, 91, 110

William Tappan (c. 1806)
Geneva, N.Y.
Bibl. 20, 124

William B. Tappan
(c. 1818–1819)
Philadelphia, Pa.
Lemist & Tappan
Bibl. 3

E. Tarbell (c. 1830)
Location unknown
Bibl. 24, 28, 44

E. TARBELL

John Targee
(c. 1797–1841)
New York, N.Y.
John & Peter Targee
(c. 1798–1811)
*Bibl. 15, 23, 24, 25, 26, 36,
44, 91, 122, 124, 138*

I T

John & Peter Targee
(c. 1798–1811)
New York, N.Y.

Bibl. 4, 15, 23, 24, 25, 28, 29, 30, 35, 36, 39, 44, 83, 89, 91, 114, 122, 124

I & P T

I & P TARGEE

Peter Targee (c. 1811)
New York, N.Y.
John & Peter Targee
  (c. 1798–1811)
Bibl. 23, 36, 44, 91, 124, 138

William Targee (c. 1807)
New York, N.Y.
Bibl. 23, 36, 44, 124

Anne Taussig
  (c. 1975–1980)
St. Louis, Mo.
Bibl. 155

Taylor
(See Fairchild & Taylor)

Taylor & Gilpin (c. 1843)
Philadelphia, Pa.
Bibl. 3

Taylor & Hinsdale
  (Hinsdale & Taylor)
  (1807–1817)
Newark, N.J.
New York, N.Y.
John Taylor
Horace Seymour Hinsdale
Bibl. 15, 23, 24, 25, 29, 35, 36, 44, 46, 78, 83, 91, 114, 124, 135, 138

T & H

Taylor & Lawrie (Lowrie)
  (c. 1837–1850)
Philadelphia, Pa.
—— Taylor
Robert D. Lawrie
Bibl. 3, 4, 23, 24, 25, 28, 36, 44

TAYLOR & LAWRIE

Taylor, Baldwin & Co.
  (c. 1817–1840)
Newark, N.J.
John Taylor
Isaac Baldwin
Bibl. 46, 54, 127

Taylor, Lawrie & Wood
  (after 1841)
Philadelphia, Pa.
—— Taylor
Robert D. Lawrie
—— Wood
Bibl. 23

Andrew A. Taylor
  (c. 1930–1973)
Newark, N.J.
Bibl. 127

David Taylor Jewelry Co.
  (c. 1945)
New York, N.Y.
Bibl. 127

E. A. Taylor
  (c. 1810–1820)
New Orleans, La.
Bibl. 54

Edward Taylor
  (c. 1828–1837)
New York, N.Y.
Bibl. 15, 124, 138

George Taylor (b. 1825)
Mobile, Ala. (c. 1850)
Bibl. 54, 148

George W. Taylor
  (c. 1823–1850)
Philadelphia, Pa.
Bibl. 3, 23, 36, 44

John Taylor
Philadelphia, Pa.
  (c. 1786)
Charleston, S.C. (c. 1790)
Bibl. 3, 5, 124

John Taylor
  (c. 1801–1829)
New York, N.Y.
Newark, N.J.
Hempstead, L.I., N.Y.
Taylor & Hinsdale
  (1807–1817)
E. Hinsdale & Co.
  (before 1810)
Taylor, Baldwin & Co.
  (1817–1840)
Bibl. 36, 44, 54, 91, 102, 124, 138

John G. Taylor
  (c. 1837–1843)
Philadelphia, Pa.
Bibl. 3

Luther Taylor
  (c. 1823–1835)
Philadelphia, Pa.
Bibl. 3

N. Taylor & Co. (c. 1825)
New York, N.Y.
Bibl. 24, 25, 44, 110, 114, 124, 138

N TAYLOR & CO

Najah Taylor (c. 1793)
Danbury, Conn.
New York, N.Y.
Eli Mygatt
Daniel Noble Carrington
Bibl. 23, 28, 36, 44, 110, 124, 138

Noah C. Taylor (c. 1844)
Salisbury, N.C.
Bibl. 21

Richard Taylor
  (c. 1834–1841)
New York, N.Y.
Bibl. 15, 124, 138

Robert Taylor
  (c. 1839–1850)
Philadelphia, Pa.
Bibl. 3

Samuel Taylor
  (c. 1798–1799)
Philadelphia, Pa.
Bibl. 3

Thomas Taylor
  (d. c. 1742)
Providence, R.I.
Bibl. 23, 36, 44, 110

W. S. Taylor & Co.
  (c. 1858–?)
Utica, N.Y.
William S. Taylor
Theodore M. Timms
Bibl. 20, 124

W. S. TAYLOR & CO.

William Taylor
(c. 1772–1778)
Philadelphia, Pa.
*Bibl. 3, 15, 23, 25, 28, 44,
54, 81, 95, 114*

William Taylor
(c. 1829–1850)
Philadelphia, Pa.
Bibl. 3

William Taylor (c. 1835)
Buffalo, N.Y.
Bibl. 20, 124

William S. Taylor
(c. 1847–1849)
Troy, N.Y.
Bibl. 20, 124

William S. Taylor
(b. 1829–d. 1905)
Utica, N.Y.
Davies & Taylor
(c. 1851–1852)
Maynard & Taylor
(c. 1852–1858)
W. S. Taylor & Co.
(c. 1858–?)
Bibl. 18, 20, 91, 124, 158

WM S. TAYLOR

Tebbetts & Appleton
(1840)
Lowell, Mass.
Bibl. 106

Robert Tempest
(c. 1814–1816, d. 1816)
Philadelphia, Pa.
Marshall & Tempest
(c. 1813–1830)
Bibl. 3, 23, 44, 91

Robert Tempest
(c. 1814–1850)
Philadelphia, Pa.
Bibl. 3, 36

William Templeman
(b. 1746)
Charleston, S.C. (c. 1774)
Bibl. 5

Barent Ten Eyck B. E
(b. 1714–d. 1795)
Albany, N.Y.
*Bibl. 15, 20, 44, 54, 95, 102,
114, 116, 119, 124*

Jacob Ten Eyck
(b. 1705–d. 1793)
Albany, N.Y.
*Bibl. 2, 15, 20, 23, 24, 25,
28, 29, 36, 95, 102, 104,
114, 116, 119, 124*

Koenraet Ten Eyck
(b. 1678–d. 1753)
Albany, N.Y. (c. 1703–1753)
*Bibl. 4, 15, 20, 23, 24, 28,
29, 30, 35, 36, 44, 54, 95,
102, 114, 119, 124, 138,
151*
K E

Tenco
(See T. E. Neill Co.)

Tennant Company
(c. 1896–1901)
New York, N.Y.
Became Hartford Sterling Co.
(c. 1901–1924)
Bibl. 114, 127, 157

William I. Tenney
(c. 1831–1852)
New York, N.Y.
*Bibl. 15, 24, 25, 29, 44, 91,
114, 122, 124, 138*

TENNEY   W I TENNEY

Terfloth & Kuchler
(1858–1866)
New Orleans, La.
Bibl. 141

Geer Terry
(b. 1775–d. 1858)
Enfield, Conn.

Worcester, Mass.
*Bibl. 15, 16, 23, 24, 25, 28,
36, 44, 54, 91, 92, 94, 110,
114*

G TERRY   TERRY

John Terry
Savannah, Ga.
(c. 1741–c. 1746)
Frederick, Va. (c. 1742)
Charleston, Va. (c. 1746)
Bibl. 5, 17

John Terry (c. 1819)
New York, N.Y.
Bibl. 15, 23, 36, 44, 124, 138

L. B. Terry (c. 1810)
Enfield, Conn.
Bibl. 23, 29, 36, 44, 92, 110

L. B. TERRY

Lucien B. Terry
(c. 1830–1835)
Albany, N.Y.
Bibl. 20, 124

Wilbert Terry
(c. 1785–1810)
Enfield, Conn.
*Bibl. 23, 24, 25, 29, 36, 44,
91, 92, 114, 124*

W. TERRY   WM TERRY

William Terry (c. 1799)
Mechanic Town, N.Y.
Bibl. 20, 91

David Tew (c. 1785)
Philadelphia, Pa.
Bibl. 3

George Tharp
(c. 1807–1820)
Baltimore, Md.
Bibl. 38

Joseph Blake Thaxter
(b. 1791–d. 1863)
Hingham, Mass.
*Bibl. 15, 23, 25, 28, 36, 44,
91, 110, 114*

J B THAXTER

Amos Thayer (c. 1809)
Troy, N.Y.
Gragg & Thayer
Bibl. 20, 124

William Theofile (c. 1822)
New Orleans, La.
Bibl. 23, 36, 44

Thibarult
(See Thibault & Co., Felix
Thibault)

Thibault & Brothers
(c. 1810–1835)
Philadelphia, Pa.
*Bibl. 3, 23, 24, 25, 29, 36,
44, 91*

THIBAULT BROTHERS

**Thibault & Co. (Thibarult
& Co.)**
Philadelphia, Pa.
(c. 1797–1798)
Bibl. 3, 23, 28, 36, 44, 91

Felix Thibault (Thibarult)
Philadelphia, Pa.
(c. 1814–1837)
Bibl. 3, 15, 23, 36, 44, 91

**Francis Thibault
(Thibout)** (d. 1802?)
Philadelphia, Pa.
(c. 1800–1802)
Bibl. 3, 15, 23, 91

Francis Thibault
(c. 1816–1850)
Philadelphia, Pa.
Bibl. 3, 15, 91

**Francis, Frederick & Felix
Thibault**
Philadelphia, Pa. (c. 1813)
Bibl. 3, 15, 91

Frederick Thibault
(c. 1818–1835)
Philadelphia, Pa.
Bibl. 3, 15, 23, 36, 44, 91

**Frederick (Francis) &
Felix Thibault**
(c. 1813)
Philadelphia, Pa.

*Bibl. 15, 23, 24, 25, 29, 36,
44, 54, 91, 114*

F & F THIBAULT

THIBAULT

Thibout
(See Francis Thibault)

John Thiele (c. 1847)
St. Louis, Mo.
Bibl. 54, 155

Thiery & Co. (c. 1909)
Newark, N.J.
Bibl. 127

Thirion & Hinkle
(c. 1850)
Philadelphia, Pa.
Lewis Thirion
Benjamin Hinkle
Bibl. 3

Lewis Thirion
(c. 1828–1850)
Philadelphia, Pa.
Thirion & Hinkle (c. 1850)
Bibl. 3

George E. Thoits (1875)
Yarmouth, Me.
Bibl. 105

The Thomae Co.
(1920–present)
Attleboro, Mass.
Charles Thomae
Bibl. 127, 157

Thomas, Griswold & Co.
(1861–1865)
New Orleans, La.
Bibl. 141

August Thomas (c. 1838)
Piqua, Ohio
Bibl. 34

Benjamin Thomas
(c. 1813–1850)
Philadelphia, Pa.
Bibl. 3

Ebenezer Thomas
(c. 1802–1819)
Petersburg, Va.
Bennett & Thomas
(c. 1812–1819)
John W. Thomas & Co.
(c. 1819)
Bibl. 19

John W. Thomas & Co.
(c. 1819)
Petersburg, Va.
John Warren Thomas
Ebenezer Thomas
John Bennett
Bibl. 19

John Warren Thomas
(c. 1817–?)
Petersburg, Va.
Bennett & Thomas
(c. 1812–1819)
John W. Thomas & Co.
(c. 1819)
Bibl. 19

Joseph Thomas
(c. 1805–1808)
Philadelphia, Pa.
Bibl. 3

Richard Thomas
(c. 1802–1808)
Philadelphia, Pa.
Bibl. 3

Richard Thomas (1807)
New Orleans, La.
Bibl. 141

Thomas Thomas (c. 1784)
New York, N.Y.
Bibl. 23, 36, 44, 124

Walter Thomas (c. 1769)
New York, N.Y.
*Bibl. 4, 23, 24, 25, 28, 36,
44, 114, 124*

W·T

William Thomas
Elizabethtown, N.J.
(before 1780)
Trenton, N.J. (c. 1780)
Bibl. 23, 36, 44, 46, 54

Peter Thomeguex
 (c. 1802)
Northampton, Mass.
Bibl. 84, 110

Peter Thomison (c. 1817)
Boston, Mass.
Bibl. 36, 44

Thompson & Benjamin
 (c. 1803)
Canandaigua, N.Y.
Seth Thompson
Luther W. Benjamin
Bibl. 20, 124

Thompson & Griffith
 (c. 1785–1786)
Savannah, Ga.
John Thompson
Edward Griffith
Bibl. 17

Thompson, Hayward &
 Co. (1851–1855)
Mechanicsville, Mass.
Became C. E. Hayward Co.
 (1855–1887)
Hayward & Sweet
 (1887–c. 1904)
Walter E. Hayward Co., Inc.
 (c. 1904–present)
Bibl. 127, 135

B. S. Thompson (1861)
Kennebunk, Me.
Bibl. 105

D. B. Thompson (c. 1825)
Litchfield, Conn.
Bibl. 23, 25, 36, 44, 92, 114

> D B THOMPSON

Henry Thompson
 (c. 1847–1850)
Philadelphia, Pa.
Bibl. 3

Isaac Thompson
(Thomson)
 (c. 1801–1817)
Litchfield, Conn.
Brattleboro, Vt.
Shethar & Thom(p)son
Bibl. 15, 16, 23, 24, 25, 28,
 29, 36, 44, 91, 92, 110,
 114, 143

> I THOMPSON

> I THOMSON

Isaac Thompson Jr.
 (c. 1831–1833)
Kingston, N.Y.
Bibl. 20, 124

Isaac P. Thompson
 (c. 1857)
Orangeburg, S.C.
Bibl. 5

James Thompson
 (c. 1796)
Baltimore, Md.
Bibl. 38

James Thompson
 (c. 1834)
Brooklyn, N.Y.
Bibl. 36, 124

James S. Thompson
 (c. 1832)
Louisville, Ky.
Bibl. 54

Jeremiah Thompson
 (c. 1840–1841)
Philadelphia, Pa.
Bibl. 3

John Thompson (c. 1786)
Savannah, Ga.
Thompson & Griffith
 (c. 1785–1786)
Bibl. 17

John P. Thompson
 (c. 1819–1824)
Philadelphia, Pa.
Bibl. 3

Joseph S. Thompson
 (c. 1832)
Louisville, Ky.
Bibl. 32, 93

Peter Thompson
 (c. 1835–1850)
Philadelphia, Pa.
Bibl. 3, 23, 110

Robert Thompson
 (c. 1840–1841)
Philadelphia, Pa.
Bibl. 3

Seth Thompson (c. 1803)
Canandaigua, N.Y.
Thompson & Benjamin
Bibl. 20, 124

William Thompson
Abingdon, Md.
 (before 1774)
Port Tobacco, Md.
 (c. 1762–1772)
Bibl. 29, 38

> W T

William Thompson
 (c. 1795–1824)
Baltimore, Md.
Bibl. 25, 38, 44, 95, 114

> W T

William Thompson
 (c. 1809–1845)
New York State
Bibl. 54, 116, 122

Thompsons (1959–present)
Damariscotta, Me.
Ernest Thompson, Jr.
Evelyn Thompson
Bibl. 89, 127

> E.T.THOMPSON

THOMPSON

E.T.

> THOMPSONS
> STUDIO INC.

Charles F. Thoms (1875)
Bangor, Me.
Bibl. 105

Thomson & Beckwith
 (c. 1837–1839)
Raleigh, N.C.
William Thomson
Robert W. Beckwith
Bibl. 21

F. Thomson (c. 1835)
Boston, Mass.(?)
Bibl. 15, 44, 114

| F THOMSON |

H. Thomson
Location unknown
Bibl. 89

Isaac Thomson
(See Isaac Thompson)

James Thomson
(c. 1834–1841)
New York, N.Y.
Bibl. 4, 15, 23, 24, 25, 28, 36, 44, 91, 124, 138

| Jas Thomson |

John L. Thomson
(c. 1849)
Philadelphia, Pa.
Bibl. 3

Peter Thomson (c. 1817)
Boston, Mass.
Philadelphia, Pa. (c. 1835)
Bibl. 23, 28, 36, 44, 91

W. Thomson (c. 1804)
New York, N.Y.
Bibl. 54

William Thomson
(c. 1810–1834)
New York, N.Y.
Bibl. 4, 15, 24, 25, 28, 29, 35, 36, 39, 44, 78, 83, 91, 95, 114, 124, 138

| Wm Thomson |

| W. THOMSON |

William Thomson
(b. 1800–d. 1850)
Raleigh, N.C. (c. 1837–1839)
Wilmington, N.C.
Thomson & Beckwith
(c. 1837–1839)
Bibl. 21

C. B. Thorn (c. 1834–1835)
Troy, N.Y.
Bibl. 20, 124

John Thorn (c. 1837)
Philadelphia, Pa.
Bibl. 3

Thornton & Company
(c. 1896)
New York, N.Y.
Successor to Holbrook &
Simmons and Holbrook &
Thornton
Bibl. 114, 127, 157

Thornton Brothers
(c. 1877–1927)
New York, N.Y.
Bibl. 127

Andrew Thornton
(c. 1811)
Philadelphia, Pa.
Bibl. 3

Henry Thornton
(b. 1798–d. 1824)
Providence, R.I. (c. 1824)
Bibl. 23, 36

John Thornton Jr.
(c. 1825–1847)
Philadelphia, Pa.
Bibl. 3

Joseph Thornton (c. 1819)
Philadelphia, Pa.
Bibl. 3

Joseph Thornton (c. 1825)
Cincinnati, Ohio
Bibl. 34, 90, 152

Thran
(See Trahn)

Orramel Hinckley Throop
(b. 1798)
New Orleans, La.
(1831–1834)
Bibl. 141

Charles Thum
(c. 1828–1833)
Philadelphia, Pa.
Bibl. 3

Thurber
(See Gorham & Thurber)

Robert Thurmer (d. 1758)
Yorktown, Va.
Bibl. 19

Jacob Thurston
(c. 1797–1815)
Schenectady, N.Y.
Bibl. 20, 122, 124

William N. Tibbets
(c. 1837–1838)
Utica, N.Y.
Buffalo, N.Y. (c. 1842)
Bibl. 18, 20, 124, 158

Tibolt
(See Thibault)

Philip Tidyman (d. 1780)
Charleston, S.C.
(c. 1764–1776)
Bibl. 5

Cornelius Tiebout
(c. 1770–1830)
New York, N.Y.
Bibl. 28, 102, 124

John Tierney
(c. 1820–1824)
Philadelphia, Pa.
Bibl. 3

John Tierney (1860–1875)
Portland, Me.
Bibl. 105

A. Tiers (c. 1790)
Location unknown
Bibl. 24 | A. TIERS |

Tiffany & Co. (Inc.)
(1848–present)
New York, N.Y.
Bibl. 35, 97, 104, 111, 114, 116, 122, 124, 127, 135, 157

TIFFANY & CO

Tiffany & Young
(c. 1837–1853)
New York, N.Y.
Bibl. 35, 88, 97, 124, 138

Tifft & Whiting
(c. 1840–1858)
North Attleboro, Mass.
Became Whiting, Fessenden
& Cowan (c. 1858)
Whiting Manufacturing
Company (1866)
Became Gorham Company
(1926) and moved to
Providence, R.I.
Bibl. 127

Tilden-Thurber & Co.
(1880–1892)
Providence, R.I.
Successor to Henry T. Brown
& Co.
Became Tilden-Thurber
Corporation
Bibl. 127

Tilden-Thurber Corporation
(1892–present)
Providence, R.I.
Successor to Gorham Co. &
Brown (1856–1878)
Henry T. Brown & Co.
(1878–1880)
Tilden-Thurber & Co.
(1880–1892)
Bibl. 127

James Tiley
(b. 1704–d. 1792)
Hartford, Conn.
Norfolk, Va.
*Bibl. 16, 23, 24, 25, 28, 29,
36, 44, 61, 92, 110, 114,
122*

I TILEY	TILEY

Tillinghast Silver Co.
(c. 1920–1935)
Meriden, Conn.
Bibl. 127

TILLINGHAST SILVER CO.

James R. Tillotson
(c. 1859–1877)
Terre Haute, Ind.
Bibl. 133

J.R. TILLOTSON

A. F. Tilton (1875)
Waterville, Me.
Bibl. 105

Theodore M. Timms
Utica, N.Y.
W. S. Taylor & Co.
(c. 1858–?)
Bibl. 20, 124

Charles Tinges
(b. 1765–d. 1816)
Annapolis, Md.
(c. 1788–1794)
Baltimore, Md. (1794–1816)
Bibl. 38

Samuel Tingley
(c. 1765–1790)
New York, N.Y.
Philadelphia, Pa.
*Bibl. 15, 23, 24, 25, 28, 35,
36, 44, 50, 54, 83, 91, 95,
114, 116, 124, 138*

F. Tinkham & Co.
(c. 1840–1850)
New York, N.Y.
Foster Tinkham
Bibl. 15, 25, 114, 124, 138

F. TINKHAM & CO.

B. H. Tisdale & Son
(1865)
Newport, R.I.
Bibl. 108

Benjamin H. Tisdale
(c. 1825)
Newport, R.I.
Providence, R.I.
*Bibl. 15, 23, 24, 25, 28, 29,
36, 39, 44, 56, 91, 94, 110,
114*

B·H· Tisdale

B.H. TISDALE

Nathan Tisdale
(c. 1795–1829)
New Bern, N.C.
Bibl. 21

William Tisdale I
(c. 1771–1796)

New Bern, N.C.
Bibl. 21, 110

William Tisdale II
   (b. 1791–d. 1861)
New Bern, N.C.
Bibl. 21

Titcomb & Chick (1860)
Lincoln, Me.
Bibl. 105

Francis Titcomb
   (b. 1790–d. 1832,
   c. 1815)
Newburyport, Mass.
*Bibl. 14, 23, 24, 25, 28, 29,
   36, 44, 110, 114*

F TITCOMB	TITCOMB

Titlow & Fry
   (c. 1844–1847)
Philadelphia, Pa.
J. Titlow
N. L. Fry
Bibl. 3, 23

J. Titlow (c. 1844–1850)
Philadelphia, Pa.
Titlow & Fry (c. 1844–1847)
Bibl. 3, 23

Charles T. Tittle
   (c. 1841–1847)
Philadelphia, Pa.
Bibl. 3, 23

James Titus (c. 1833)
Philadelphia, Pa.
Bibl. 3, 25, 44, 91, 114

I TITUS

Peter N. Titus (c. 1843)
Albany, N.Y.
Bibl. 20, 124

Robert Titus (c. 1817)
Petersburg, Va.
Bibl. 19

Tobey
(See Hood & Tobey)

William Tod(d)
   (c. 1794, d. 1836)
Lexington, Ky.
Bibl. 32, 54, 68, 93

Edward Todd & Co.
   (c. 1869–1927)
New York, N.Y.
Bibl. 114, 127, 157

Richard Todd (c. 1769)
Strasburg, Pa.
Bibl. 3

William F. Todd (1875)
Portland, Me.
Bibl. 105

Elijah Tollotson Jr.
   (c. 1815)
West Bloomfield, N.Y.
Bibl. 20

Tompkins & Morris
   (1860)
Bangor, Me.
Bibl. 105

C. Tompkins (c. 1822)
Clarksville, Ga.
Monticello, Ga.
Bibl. 17

Edmund Tompkins
   (b. 1757)
Waterbury, Conn. (c. 1779)
Bibl. 16, 23, 28, 36, 44, 110

Erastus O. Tompkins
   (c. 1836)
New York, N.Y.
Marquand & Co.
   (c. 1834–1839)
Ball, Tompkins & Black
   (c. 1839–1851)
Bibl. 15, 91, 124, 138

Daniel Toncry (c. 1799)
Martinsburg, Va.
Bibl. 19

Eugene S. Toner & Co.
   (c. 1909)
New York, N.Y.
Bibl. 127, 157

Silas Tonkrey (c. 1812)
Shelbyville, Ky.
Bibl. 32, 68

James Took
   (c. 1842–1847)
St. Louis, Mo.
Bibl. 54, 155

Benjamin Toppan
   (c. 1760)
Northampton, Mass.
Bibl. 28

Peter Torlay
   (c. 1813–1819)
Charleston, S.C.
Bibl. 5

Tounshendt
(See Thomas Townsend)

John Touzell (Towzell)
   (b. 1726–d. 1785)
Salem, Mass.
*Bibl. 15, 23, 24, 25, 28, 29,
   36, 91, 94, 110, 114*

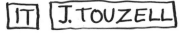

Towle Silversmiths
   (1882–present)
Newburyport, Mass.
Successor to Towle & Jones
   (c. 1857–1873)
Towle, Jones & Co.
   (c. 1873)
A. F. Towle & Son Co.,
   Newburyport, Mass.
   (1873–1880)
A. F. Towle & Son Co., Inc.
   (1880–1882)
Towle Manufacturing Co.
   (1882)
*Bibl. 104, 114, 127, 128, 131,
   146, 147*

Towle & Jones
(c. 1857–1873)
Newburyport, Mass.
Anthony F. Towle
William P. Jones
Became Towle, Jones & Co.
(c. 1873)
A. F. Towle & Son Co.
(1873–1902)
Bibl. 89, 122, 127

A. F. Towle & Son Co.
Newburyport, Mass.
(1873–1880)
Greenfield, Mass.
(1890–1902)
Anthony F. Towle
(b. 1816–d. 1897)
Successor to Towle & Jones
(c. 1855)
Towle, Jones & Co.
(c. 1873)
From this company, A. F.
Towle & Son Co., Inc.,
was formed in 1880, and
became Towle
Manufacturing Company
in 1882.
Bibl. 114, 127, 131

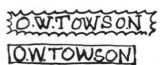

**E. J. Towle
Manufacturing Co.**
(c. 1938–present)
Seattle, Wash.
Successor to Joseph Mayer &
Bros. (c. 1897–1920)
Joseph Mayer, Inc.
(c. 1920–1945)
Northern Stamping &
Manufacturing Co.
Bibl. 127

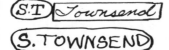

Henry Towle
(b. 1788–d. 1862)
Haverhill, N.H. (c. 1835)
Bibl. 24, 110, 125

Town & Witherall
(c. 1825)
Location unknown
Bibl. 89

Ira Strong Town
(b. 1809–d. 1902)
Montpelier, Vt. (c. 1825)
Bibl. 15, 25, 44, 91, 110, 114

IRA S TOWN

Townsend (c. 1775)
Location unknown
Bibl. 24

**Townsend, Desmond &
Voorhis Co.**
(c. 1896–1908)
New York, N.Y.
Bibl. 114, 127, 157

**T. D. & V. CO.
STERLING.**

Charles Townsend
(c. 1799–1850)
Philadelphia, Pa.
Bibl. 3

Charles Townsend Jr.
(c. 1829–1850)
Philadelphia, Pa.
Bibl. 3

Elisha Townsend
(c. 1828–1829)
Philadelphia, Pa.
Bibl. 3

James Townsend
(b. 1750, c. 1774)
Maryland
Bibl. 38

John Townsend
(c. 1849)
Philadelphia, Pa.
Bibl. 3

John Townsend
(before 1820)
Lancaster, Ohio
Bibl. 34

John Townsend Jr.
(c. 1813–1833)
Philadelphia, Pa.
Bibl. 3

S. Townsend (c. 1775)
Delaware (?)
Bibl. 24, 28, 29, 30, 44, 91

**Thomas Townsend
(Townshend)
(Tounshendt)**

(b. 1701–d. 1777)
Boston, Mass. (c. 1725)
Bibl. 25, 44, 91, 94, 110, 114

James Townsley
(c. 1772–1790)
Salisbury, N.C.
Bibl. 21

Obadiah W. Towson
(b. 1791)
Baltimore, Md.
(c. 1813–1819)
Philadelphia, Pa.
(c. 1819–1824)
*Bibl. 3, 23, 24, 25, 29, 36,
38, 44, 114*

O.W.TOWSON

O.W.TOWSON

Philemon Towson
(b. 1769–d. 1843)
Baltimore, Md.
(c. 1790–?)
Bibl. 38

Towzell
(See Touzell)

Toy & Wilson (c. 1790)
Abingdon, Md.
Joseph Toy
William Wilson
Bibl. 25, 44

I. T		W. W.

Isaac Nicholas Toy
(b. 1771–d. 1830)
Abingdon, Md.
(c. 1790–1795)
Bibl. 24, 25, 29, 38, 44, 114

I. N. TOY

I.N.TOY

Joseph Toy
  (b. 1748–d. 1826,
  c. 1776–1795)
Hartford, Conn.
Abingdon, Md.
Candy, Md.
Toy & Wilson (c. 1790)
Bibl. 25, 29, 38, 44, 54, 114

J. F. Tozer (c. 1850)
Binghamton, N.Y.
Bibl. 20

Junius F. Tozer
  (c. 1847–?)
Binghamton, N.Y. (c. 1850)
Rochester, N.Y.
Bibl. 20, 41, 44, 124

Tracy & Hawley
  (c. 1848–1850)
Cazenovia, N.Y.
A. Fayette Tracy
Bibl. 20, 124

A. Fayette Tracy
Oswego, N.Y. (c. 1844)
Cazenovia, N.Y. (c. 1848)
Tracy & Hawley
Bibl. 20, 124

C. & E. Tracy
  (c. 1847–1850)
Philadelphia, Pa.
Charles Tracy
E. Tracy
Bibl. 3

Charles Tracy
  (c. 1842–1850)
Philadelphia, Pa.
C. & E. Tracy
  (c. 1847–1850)
Bibl. 3

E. Tracy (c. 1841–1850)
Philadelphia, Pa.
C. & E. Tracy
  (c. 1847–1850)
Bibl. 3

Elisha C. Tracy (c. 1810)
Cooperstown, N.Y.
Bibl. 20, 124

Erastus Tracy
  (b. 1768–d. 1795)
New London, Conn.
Norwich, Conn.
Bibl. 16, 23, 28, 36, 44

Gurdon (Gordon) Tracy
  (b. 1767–d. 1792)
Norwich, Conn.
  (1781–1791)
New London, Conn.
  (after 1791)
*Bibl. 16, 23, 24, 25, 28, 36,
  44, 67, 92, 110, 114*

W. J. Tracy
  (1872–1876)
Burrillville, R.I.
Bibl. 108

William Tracy
  (c. 1843–1850)
Philadelphia, Pa.
Bibl. 3

Peter C. Trahn (Thran)
  (c. 1843–1849)
Philadelphia, Pa.
Bibl. 3

J. Trast (c. 1850)
Syracuse, N.Y.
Bibl. 20, 124

Traux
(See Henry R. Truax)

Samuel Treadway
  (c. 1848)
St. Louis, Mo.
Bibl. 54, 155

——— Treadwell
New York, N.Y.
Gelston & Treadwell
  (c. 1836)
*Bibl. 23, 25, 28, 35, 36, 44,
  83*

Isaac Treadwell
Boston, Mass.
Churchill & Treadwell
  (c. 1805–1813)
Bibl. 4, 24, 25, 28, 29, 36, 44

Oren B. Treadwell
  (c. 1847–1849)
Philadelphia, Pa.
Bibl. 3

Treasure
(See Lunt Silversmiths)

Arthur Trench (d. 1838)
Raleigh, N.C. (c. 1833–1838)
Bibl. 21

Trenchard & Watson
  (c. 1800)
Philadelphia, Pa.
James Trenchard (?)
——— Watson
Bibl. 3

James Trenchard
  (c. 1777–1793)
Philadelphia, Pa.
Trenchard & Watson
  (c. 1800) (?)
Bibl. 3, 102

John Trenson (c. 1817)
Philadelphia, Pa.
Bibl. 3

**Daniel Trezevant
  (Trezvant)** (d. 1768)
Charleston, S.C.
  (c. 1757–1768)
Bibl. 5, 28, 44, 54

Trianon
(See Napier Company)

Christian Tripler
  (c. 1794–1797)
New York, N.Y.
Bibl. 23, 36, 44, 138

William Troll
  (c. 1810–1811)
Philadelphia, Pa.
Bibl. 3, 23, 36, 44

Peter Trone (c. 1844)
Philadelphia, Pa.
Bibl. 3

Jerimiah Trotater
  (1821–1844)
Cincinnati, Oh.
Bibl. 152

James Troth
Easton, Md. (c. 1802)
Pittsburgh, Pa.
Bibl. 3, 23, 36, 38, 44

William Troth
(c. 1804–1819)
Philadelphia, Pa.
Bibl. 3, 23

William Troth
(c. 1833–1835)
Philadelphia, Pa.
Bibl. 3

Trott & Brooks | T & B |
(c. 1798–?)
New London, Conn.
John Proctor Trott
———— Brooks
*Bibl. 16, 23, 25, 28, 29, 36,
44, 92, 114*

Trott & Cleveland
(c. 1792–?)
New London, Conn.
John Proctor Trott
William Cleveland
*Bibl. 16, 23, 25, 28, 29, 36,
44, 91, 92*

| T. & C. |

George Trott (c. 1765)
Boston, Mass.
Bibl. 28, 44

John P. Trott & Son
(c. 1820)
New London, Conn.
*Bibl. 23, 24, 25, 36, 44, 91,
92, 114*

| J. P. T. & SON |

John Proctor Trott
(b. 1769–d. 1852)
New London, Conn.
Trott & Cleveland
(c. 1792–?)
Trott & Brooks
(c. 1798–?)
John P. Trott & Son
(c. 1820)
Currier & Trott
(c. 1823–1857)
*Bibl. 2, 15, 23, 24, 25, 28,
29, 36, 44, 91, 92, 114*

| J: P. TROTT | | J. P. T. |

Jonathan Trott
(b. 1730–d. 1815)
Boston, Mass. (before 1772)
Norwich, Conn. (after 1772)
New London, Conn.
(c. 1790–1815)
*Bibl. 2, 15, 16, 23, 24, 25,
28, 29, 36, 44, 91, 92, 114*

Jonathan Trott Jr. | I. T. |
(b. 1771–d. 1813)
New London, Conn.
(c. 1800)
*Bibl. 15, 16, 23, 25, 28, 29,
36, 44, 91, 92, 110, 114*

Thomas Trott | T. T. |
(b. 1701–d. 1777)
Boston, Mass.
Bibl. 23, 24, 28, 29, 44

Trotter & Alexander
(c. 1837–1838)
Charlotte, N.C.
Thomas Trotter
Samuel P. Alexander
Bibl. 21

Trotter & Huntington
(c. 1828–1832)
Charlotte, N.C.
Thomas Trotter
John Huntington
Bibl. 21

Jeremiah Trotter
(c. 1836–1868)
Cincinnati, Ohio
Bibl. 34, 90, 138

Thomas Trotter
(b. 1800–d. 1865)
Charlotte, N.C.
Thomas Trotter & Co.
(c. 1827–1828)
Trotter & Huntington
(c. 1828–1832)
Trotter & Alexander
(c. 1837–1838)
Bibl. 21

Thomas Trotter & Co.
(c. 1827–1828)
Charlotte, N.C.
Bibl. 21

A. W. Trou
(b. 1818–d. 1854)
Charleston, S.C.
(c. 1846–1854)
Bibl. 5

George Trout
(c. 1837–1843)
Philadelphia, Pa.
Bibl. 3

Truax & Clench
(c. 1813–?)
Albany, N.Y.
Henry R. Truax (?)
Benjamin Clench
Bibl. 20, 124

Dewitt Truax
(c. 1842–1843)
Utica, N.Y.
Bibl. 18, 20, 124, 158

Henry R. Truax (Traux)
(b. 1760–d. 1834)
Albany, N.Y. (c. 1815–?)
Isaac & Henry Truax
Truax & Clench
(c. 1813–?)
*Bibl. 4, 15, 20, 23, 24, 25,
28, 29, 36, 44, 114, 124*

Isaac Truax
Albany, N.Y.
Isaac & Henry Truax
(c. 1796)
Bibl. 20, 124

Isaac & Henry Truax
(c. 1796)

Albany, N.Y.
Isaac Truax
Henry R. Truax
Bibl. 20, 124

**Richard Trumbul
(Trumbull)**
   (b. 1742–d. 1815)
Boston, Mass.
Bibl. 23, 36, 44, 110

Armistead Truslow
   (c. 1813–1825)
Lynchburg, Va.
Bibl. 19, 54

| A. T. |

Tucker & Parkerhurst Co.
   (c. 1898–1904)
Ogdensburg, N.Y.
Successor to Bell Bros.
Bibl. 127, 157

Benoni Tucker
   (c. 1858–1860)
Utica, N.Y.
Bibl. 18, 124, 158

Daniel Tucker
   (b. 1760–d. 1824)
Portland, Me. (c. 1781)
Bibl. 23, 36, 44, 105, 110

John Walter Tucker
   (c. 1803)
New York, N.Y.
Bibl. 21, 44, 124

| J W TUCKER |

M. Tucker (c. 1840)
Location unknown
Bibl. 24

Silas G. Tucker (1874)
Providence, R.I.
Bibl. 108

Tuel & Ellis (1848–1849)
Windsor, Vt.
Bibl. 89

Tuells
(See Johonnot & Tuells)

B. Tuells (c. 1818)
Palmyra, N.Y.
Bibl. 20, 124

Susan Turk (1856–1860)
New Orleans, La.
Bibl. 141

S.TURK

Alonzo B. Turner
   (c. 1838–1844)
Watertown, N.Y.
Sigourney & Turner
   (c. 1838–1842)
Bibl. 20, 124

Ansel Turner
   (b. 1789–d. 1814)
Savannah, Ga.
Bibl. 17

Charles Turner (d. 1776)
Alexandria, Va.
   (c. 1760–1766)
Bibl. 19, 54

Franklin Turner
   (c. 1812–1823)
Cheraw, N.C.
Fayetteville, N.C.
Wadesboro, N.C.
Clark & Turner
   (c. 1820–1823)
Bibl. 5, 21, 44, 54

| TURNER |

J. A. S. Turner & Co.
   (c. 1833)
Columbus, Ga.
Bibl. 17

James Turner (d. 1759)
Boston, Mass. (c. 1748)
Philadelphia, Pa. (c. 1758)
*Bibl. 3, 24, 25, 28, 29, 44,
   94, 110, 114*

William Turner
   (c. 1847–1850)
Philadelphia, Pa.
Bibl. 3

Jacques Turpia (b. 1812)
   (1842–1855)
New Orleans, La.
Bibl. 141

Thomas M. Turpin
   (c. 1813)
Richmond, Va.
Bibl. 19

A. B. Turrell
   (c. 1827–1828)
Penn Yan, N.Y.
Bibl. 20, 124

Septimus Tustin (c. 1814)
Baltimore, Md.
Bibl. 38

Christopher Tuthill
   (c. 1730)
Philadelphia, Pa.
Bibl. 3, 23, 28, 36, 44

John Tuthill (c. 1831)
New York, N.Y.
Bibl. 15, 124, 138

Tuttle Silversmiths
   (1890–present)
Boston, Mass.
Timothy Tuttle
Tuttle Silver Co., Inc.
   (corporate name)
Became division of R.
   Wallace & Sons Mfg. Co.
   (1955), which became
   Wallace Silversmiths and
   was acquired by Hamilton
   Watch Company (1959)
*Bibl. 127, 128, 135, 146, 147,
   157*

Date Letter System
Letters are initials of incumbent
   U.S. president

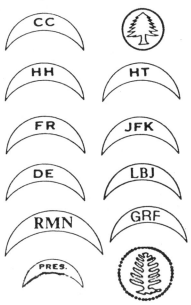

TUTTLE

Bethuel Tuttle
(b. 1779–d. 1813)
New Haven, Conn.
(c. 1802–1818)
Merriman & Tuttle (c. 1802)
Marcus Merriman & Co.
(c. 1802–1817)
*Bibl. 16, 23, 28, 36, 44, 91,
110, 143*

William Tuttle
(b. 1800–d. 1849)
New Haven, Conn.
Suffield, Conn.
*Bibl. 16, 23, 28, 36, 44, 110,
143*

Weston Weed Tuxford
(c. 1837)
Clarksville, Ga.
Bibl. 17

Twambley & Cleaves
(1870)
Biddeford, Me.
Bibl. 105

Charles Twambley & Son
Saco, Me.
Bibl. 105

G. E. Twambley (1895)
Saco, Me.
Bibl. 105

R. K. Twambley (1875)
Saco, Me.
Bibl. 105

S. G. Twambley & Son
(1895)
Biddeford, Me.
Bibl. 105

Samuel G. Twambley
(1880)
Biddeford, Me.
Bibl. 105

Twedy & Barrowss
Location unknown
Bibl. 15, 44, 114

TWEDY & BARROWSS

M. Twelbib (c. 1828–1833)
Philadelphia, Pa.
Bibl. 3

**Spencer Twitchel
(Twitchell)** (c. 1832)
New York, N.Y.
Bibl. 15, 124, 138

Marcus Twitchell
(c. 1829–?)
Utica, N.Y.
Bibl. 18, 20, 124, 158

William Twybill (c. 1841)
Philadelphia, Pa.
Bibl. 3

Albert Tyler & Co.
(1870–1875)
Providence, R.I.
Bibl. 108

Andrew Tyler
(b. 1692–d. 1741)
Boston, Mass.
*Bibl. 2, 4, 15, 23, 24, 25, 28,
29, 33, 36, 44, 50, 54, 70,
94, 102, 110, 114, 119,
139, 151*

Coleman J. Tyler (1875)
S. Berwick, Me.
Bibl. 105

D. M. Tyler (c. 1810)
Boston, Mass.
*Bibl. 23, 24, 25, 29, 36, 44,
110, 114*

D. M. TYLER

David Tyler
(b. 1760–d. 1804)
Boston, Mass.
*Bibl. 4, 15, 23, 24, 25, 28,
29, 36, 44, 54, 91, 102,
110, 114*

D T   D T

Edward A. Tyler
(b. 1815–d. 1879)
Belfast, Me. (1834–1838)
New Orleans, La.
(1838–1879)
Bibl. 141

George Tyler   G T
(b. 1740–d. 1785)
Boston, Mass.
*Bibl. 15, 23, 24, 25, 28, 29,
36, 44, 110, 114, 139*

John H. Tyler & Co.
(c. 1840)
Boston, Mass.
John Henry Tyler
Bibl. 24, 25, 44, 114

JOHN H. TYLER & CO.

John Henry Tyler
(d. 1883)
Richmond, Va.
John H. Tyler & Co.
(c. 1840)
Mitchell & Tyler
(c. 1845–1866)
Bibl. 19, 91

John H. Tyler & Co.

A. B. Tyrrel(l) (c. 1840)
Location unknown
Bibl. 15, 44, 114

A·B·TYRREL

Leech Tyson
(c. 1823–1831)
Philadelphia, Pa.
Bibl. 3

U

U
(See Unger Brothers)

U & B
(See Ufford & Burdick)

U B
(See Unger Brothers)

U C
(See Unger & Christl)

Frederick Ubelin (c. 1773)
Philadelphia, Pa.
Bibl. 3, 23, 36, 44

———— Udall
(early 19th century)
Garrettsville, Ohio
Hiram, Ohio
Bibl. 34

Ufford & Burdick
(c. 1812–c. 1814)
New Haven, Conn.
Thomas Ufford
William S. Burdick
*Bibl. 16, 23, 24, 25, 28, 29,
36, 44, 92, 110, 114, 143*

A. & J. Ulman
(c. 1829–1835)
Philadelphia, Pa.
Bibl. 3

J. Ulman (c. 1829–1830)
Philadelphia, Pa.
A. & J. Ulman
(c. 1829–1835)
Bibl. 3

Jacob Ulman (c. 1843)
Philadelphia, Pa.
Bibl. 3

Uncle Remus
(See Julius R. Watts & Co.)

Underhill & Vernon
(c. 1786)

New York, N.Y.
Thomas Underhill
John Vernon
*Bibl. 4, 15, 24, 25, 28, 29,
36, 44, 54, 91, 95, 114,
124, 138*

Andrew Underhill
(b. 1749–d. 1800)
New York, N.Y.
(c. 1780–1788)
*Bibl. 15, 23, 24, 28, 29, 35,
36, 44, 72, 91, 95, 114,
124, 138*

Thomas Underhill
(c. 1787)
New York, N.Y.
Underhill & Vernon
(c. 1786)
*Bibl. 4, 15, 23, 24, 25, 28,
29, 35, 36, 44, 83, 91, 95,
114, 124, 138*

John Underwood
(c. 1797–1798)
Philadelphia, Pa.
Bibl. 3, 23, 36, 44

Unger & Christl
(c. 1906–1909)
Newark, N.J.
Bibl. 128, 157

Unger Brothers
(1872–1919)
Newark, N.J.
H. Unger and Co.
*Bibl. 111, 114, 120, 127, 128,
135, 157*

George M. Updike
(c. 1848)
Philadelphia, Pa.
Bibl. 3

Upson
(See also Pelletreau &
Upson)

Upson & Hart (1895)
Unionville, Conn.
Bibl. 89

George Urwiler
(c. 1814–1844)
Philadelphia, Pa.
Bibl. 3

J. Urwiler (c. 1831)
Philadelphia, Pa.
Bibl. 3

U. S. Jewelers' Guild
(See Guild)

Austin Usher (c. 1842)
Philadelphia, Pa.
Bibl. 3

**Utopian Silver Deposit &
Novelty Co.** (c. 1922)
New York, N.Y.
Bibl. 127, 157

V

V
(See Geo. L. Vose Mfg. Co.,
Inc.)

V & C
(See Van Voorhis & Coley)

V & Co.
(See W. K. Vanderslice,
Vansant & Co.)

V & S
(See Van Voorhis &
Schanck)

V & W
(See Van Ness & Waterman)

V. Co.
(See Geo L. Vose Mfg. Co.,
Inc.)

V L
(See V. Lollo)

V L & B
(See Vincent LaForme &
   Brother)

V R
(See Victor Rouquette)

V V & S
(See Van Voorhis &
   Schanck)

Elijah M. Vail
   (c. 1835–1850)
Albany, N.Y.
Troy, N.Y.
Bibl. 20, 23, 36, 44, 124

Victor Vaissiere
   (c. 1816–1819)
New York, N.Y.
Bibl. 15, 23, 36, 44, 124, 138

Philip Valenti
   (c. 1860–1879)
Bowling Green, Ky.
Fuselli & Valenti
McLure & Valenti (c. 1867)
Bibl. 54, 93

Dennis Valentine
   (c. 1850)
Syracuse, N.Y.
Barney & Valentine
Bibl. 20, 124

Peter Valet (c. 1787)
New York, N.Y.
Bibl. 23, 36, 44

William Vallant (c. 1752)
Philadelphia, Pa.
Bibl. 44

Vallee & Co. (c. 1817)
New York, N.Y.
Bibl. 15, 124, 138

Antonie Valleé
   (1810–1822)
New Orleans, La.
Bibl. 23, 36, 44, 141

F. D. Vallee (c. 1835)
Philadelphia, Pa.
Bibl. 3

Benjamin F. Vallet
   (c. 1833–1850)

Kingston, N.Y.
Bibl. 20, 91, 124

John Vanall
   (c. 1749–1752)
Charleston, S.C.
Bibl. 5, 25, 44, 114

James Vanarsdale
   (c. 1849)
Philadelphia, Pa.
Bibl. 3

John Van Bergen
   (c. 1813–1822)
Albany, N.Y.
*Bibl. 4, 20, 23, 28, 36, 44,
   124*

Peter Van Beuren
   (c. 1795–1798)
New York, N.Y.
*Bibl. 4, 23, 24, 25, 28, 29,
   36, 44, 114, 124, 138*

William Van Beuren
   (c. 1790–1796)
Newark, N.J.
New York, N.Y.
*Bibl. 15, 23, 24, 28, 29, 36,
   44, 46, 102, 114, 124, 138*

Peter Van Bomell
   (c. 1792–1803)
Poughkeepsie, N.Y.
Bibl. 20, 124

Van Cleef & Arpels
   (1939–present)
New York, N.Y.
Bibl. 126

Clarence A. Vanderbilt
   (c. 1909–1935)
New York, N.Y.
Bibl. 127, 157

STERLING   STERLING—V

Cornelius Vander Burgh
(Van der Burch)
(Vanderbrugh)
   (b. 1653–d. 1699)
New York, N.Y.
*Bibl. 15, 23, 24, 25, 29, 35,
   44, 54, 95, 102, 104, 114,
   119, 124, 138, 142, 151*

J. Vanderhan
(Venderhaul) (c. 1740)
Philadelphia, Pa.
Bibl. 23, 24, 28, 29, 36

John G. Vanderleyden
(Van der Heyden)
   (c. 1842–1845)
Utica, N.Y.
Bibl. 18, 20, 124, 158

Vanderslice & Co.
   (c. 1860–1908)
San Francisco, Cal.
W. K. Vanderslice
Bibl. 54, 122, 127, 157

W. Vanderslice (c. 1840)
Philadelphia, Pa.
Bibl. 3, 122

Jacobus Van Der Spiegel
   (b. 1668–d. 1708)
Albany, N.Y.
New York, N.Y.
*Bibl. 2, 3, 15, 23, 24, 25, 28,
   29, 30, 35, 36, 39, 44, 54,
   91, 95, 102, 104, 114, 116,
   118, 119, 124, 138, 139,
   142, 151*

Johannes Van Der
Spiegel (b. 1666–d. 1716)
New York, N.Y.
Bibl. 4, 23, 28, 29, 30, 36,
124

Peter Van Dyck (Van
Dyke) (b. 1684–d. 1751)
New York, N.Y.
Bibl. 2, 4, 15, 23, 24, 25, 28,
29, 30, 35, 36, 44, 50, 54,
91, 95, 102, 104, 114, 116,
118, 119, 124, 138, 139,
142, 151

Richard Van Dyck
  (b. 1717–d. 1770)
New York, N.Y.
Bibl. 15, 23, 24, 25, 28, 29,
30, 35, 36, 91, 95, 114,
116, 118, 124, 138

Van Dyke
(See Van Dyck)

George Vane
  (c. 1752–1781)
Charleston, S.C.
Bibl. 5, 54

John Van Hook Jr.
  (c. 1816–1820)
Hillsboro, N.C.
William Huntington & Co.
Bibl. 21

David Vanhorn (c. 1801)
Philadelphia, Pa.
Bibl. 3, 23, 36, 44

Shelby Van Hoy
  (19th century)
Shelbyville, Ky.
Bibl. 54

Peter Van Inburgh
  (b. 1689–d. 1740)
New York, N.Y.
Bibl. 25, 35, 44, 83, 95, 114,
119, 124, 151

James Vanlone (c. 1775)
Philadelphia, Pa.
Bibl. 3

Jan Van Loon (c. 1678)
Albany, N.Y.
Bibl. 54, 124

Van Ness & Bwistrand
  (Burstrand) (c. 1844)
New York, N.Y.
Peter Van Ness
——— Bwistrand
Bibl. 23, 138

Van Ness & Waterman
  (c. 1835)
(Waterman & Van Ness)
New York, N.Y.
Peter Van Ness
——— Waterman
Bibl. 23, 24, 25, 28, 29, 36,
44, 114, 124, 138

V & W

Van Ness, Wood & Co.
  (c. 1846)
New York, N.Y.
Peter Van Ness
——— Wood
Bibl. 23, 124, 138

Peter Van Ness (Vanness)
  (c. 1833–1841)
New York, N.Y.
Van Ness & Waterman
  (c. 1835)
Van Ness & Bwistrand
  (c. 1844)

Van Ness, Wood & Co.
  (c. 1846)
Bibl. 15, 23, 124, 138

Van Nieu Kirke
Van Niewkirke
(See Newkirke)

Kiliaen van Rensselaer
  (b. 1663–d. 1719)
Albany, N.Y.
Watervliet, N.Y.
Bibl. 20, 54, 102, 116, 119,
124

Nicholas Van Rensselaer
  (c. 1760–1770)
New York, N.Y.   N V
Albany, N.Y. (?)
Bibl. 15, 25, 44, 91, 95, 114,
124, 138

Tunis Van Riper
  (c. 1813–1829)
New York, N.Y.
Bibl. 15, 23, 25, 36, 44, 114,
124, 138

T V R

Van Sanford & Cluet
  (c. 1725)
Albany, N.Y.
John Cluet
Bibl. 20

Richard Vansant
(See Richard Vincent)

Vansant & Company
  (c. 1850–1880)
Philadelphia, Pa.   V&Co
Bibl. 15, 25, 44, 114

G. Van Schaick
  (c. 1800–1840)
Albany, N.Y.
Bibl. 25, 28, 29, 44, 102, 114

G V Schaick

James Vanstavoren
  (c. 1818)
Philadelphia, Pa.
Bibl. 3

**John Van Steenbergh
(Jr.)** (c. 1772–1782)
Kingston, N.Y.
Bibl. 15, 20, 25, 44, 114, 124

John S. Van Steenbergh
(c. 1820)
Kingston, N.Y.
Bibl. 20, 124

Peter Van Steenbergh
(c. 1780)
Kingston, N.Y.
Lansing Burgh, N.Y.
Bibl. 20, 124

John L. Vantine
(c. 1829–1847)
Philadelphia, Pa.
Bibl. 3

Henry Van Veghten
(c. 1760, d. 1787)
Albany, N.Y.
*Bibl. 20, 23, 25, 36, 44, 114,
124*

Van Vliet & Cromwell
(c. 1844)
Poughkeepsie, N.Y.
B. C. Van Vliet
——— Cromwell
Bibl. 20

Benjamin C. Van Vliet
(b. 1805–d. 1851)
Poughkeepsie, N.Y.
(c. 1830–1847)
Van Vliet & Cromwell
(c. 1844)
Bibl. 20, 23, 29, 36, 114, 124

B VAN VLEIT

Van Voorhis & Coley
(c. 1786)
New York, N.Y.
Daniel Van Voorhis
William Coley
Reuben Harmon
*Bibl. 4, 23, 24, 25, 28, 36,
54, 91, 95, 110, 114, 124,
135, 138*

V & C

Van Voorhis & Schanck
(c. 1791–1792)
New York, N.Y.
Daniel Van Voorhis
Garret Schanck
*Bibl. 23, 24, 25, 29, 35, 36,
91, 95, 114, 124, 138*

V V & S	V & S

**Van Voorhis, Schanck &
McCall** (c. 1800)
Albany, N.Y.
Bibl. 25, 44, 114

V.V.SCHANK& MCCALL

Van Voorhis & Son
(c. 1798)
New York, N.Y.
*Bibl. 23, 24, 25, 29, 35, 36,
124, 135, 138*

V. V. & S

——— Van Voorhis
(c. 1843)
Utica, N.Y.
Brooks & Van Voorhis
(c. 1843)
Bibl. 18, 20

Daniel Van Voorhis
(b. 1751–d. 1824)
Princeton, N.J.
New York, N.Y.
Philadelphia, Pa.
Burlington, Vt.
Rupert, Vt.
Underhill, Vt.
Van Voorhis & Coley
(c. 1786)
Van Voorhis & Schanck
(c. 1791–1792)
*Bibl. 3, 4, 15, 23, 28, 29, 30,
35, 36, 46, 54, 74, 81, 91,
95, 102, 110, 114, 116,
122, 124, 135, 138, 139,
151*

Van Wyck & Pelletreau
(See Pelletreau & Van Wyck)

Stephen Van Wyck
(c. 1825)
New York, N.Y.
Pelletreau & Van Wyck
*Bibl. 24, 25, 44, 114, 124,
138*

S VAN WYCK

John Van Zandt
(c. 1842–1848)
Albany, N.Y.
Bibl. 20, 124

Joseph Varley (b. 1809)
Utica, N.Y. (c. 1858–1860)
Bibl. 18, 124

John Varney (d. 1802)
Philadelphia, Pa.
Bibl. 3, 23, 36, 44

Leon Varney (1895–1935)
East Aurora, N.Y.
Bibl. 120

J. Varnier (c. 1800–1801)
Philadelphia, Pa.
S. Perpignan & J. Varnier
Bibl. 3, 23

Robert Varrick
(c. 1844–1845)
Philadelphia, Pa.
Bibl. 3, 23

Vaughn & Merrill
(1873–1878)
Providence, R.I.
Bibl. 108

D. Vaughan (c. 1695)
Philadelphia, Pa.
Bibl. 3

George C. Vaughn
(c. 1840–1849)
Buffalo, N.Y.
Chase & Vaughn
Bibl. 20, 114, 124

Vautroit
(See Vautrot)

Vautroit & Ackley
(See Vautroma & Ackley)

Vautroit and Meyers
(c. 1860–?)
Warren, Ohio
Bibl. 89

Vautroma (Vautroit) & Ackley (c. 1850)
Warren, Ohio
Bibl. 89

Vautrot (Vautroit)
(c. 1850)
Warren, Ohio
Bibl. 89, 114

Veal & Glaze
(c. 1838–1841)
Columbia, S.C.
John Veal (Sr.)
William Glaze
Bibl. 5, 44, 54

John Veal (Sr.)
(c. 1827–1857)
Columbia, S.C.
Veal & Glaze (c. 1838–1841)
Bibl. 5, 44

Joseph E. Veal
(c. 1848–c. 1853)
Madison, Ga.
Bibl. 17

Joseph Veazie (c. 1774)
Boston, Mass.
Bibl. 2

Joseph Veazie
(c. 1815–1824)
Providence, R.I.
Samuel & Joseph Veazie
(c. 1820)
Bibl. 23, 28, 36, 44, 110

Samuel & Joseph Veazie
(c. 1820)
Providence, R.I.
Bibl. 28, 110

Anthony Veeter (c. 1825)
Shelbyville, Ky.
Bibl. 32, 54, 68

Venderhaul
(See Vanderhan)

Emanuel Vener (c. 1826)
Madison, Ga.
Bibl. 17

Bordo Vensal (c. 1850)
Philadelphia, Pa.
Bibl. 3

John F. Vent (c. 1810)
Boston, Mass.
Bibl. 24, 102, 110, 125

Peter Vergereau
(b. 1700–d. 1755)
New York, N.Y.
*Bibl. 4, 15, 24, 25, 28, 29,
35, 36, 44, 54, 83, 91, 95,
114, 124, 138*

Vernay & Lincoln (c. 1877)
Attleboro, Mass.
Bibl. 127

Vernon & Co.
(c. 1806–1807)
Charleston, S.C.
Nathaniel Vernon
Bibl. 25

Vernon & Park (c. 1815)
Pittsburgh, Pa.
Nathaniel Vernon
———— Park
Bibl. 23, 36, 44

Daniel Vernon (b. 1716)
Newport, R.I.
Bibl. 28, 110

John (I.) Vernon
(c. 1768–1815)
New York, N.Y.
Underhill & Vernon (c. 1786)
John Vernon & Co. (c. 1796)
*Bibl. 4, 15, 23, 24, 25, 28,
29, 35, 36, 39, 44, 54, 83,*

*91, 95, 104, 114, 116, 124,
138*

John Vernon & Co.
(c. 1796)
New York, N.Y.
Bibl. 23, 28, 36, 91, 124, 138

Nathaniel Vernon
(b. 1777–d. 1843)
Charleston, S.C.
(w. 1808–1835)
Nathaniel Vernon & Co.
(c. 1802–1808)
Vernon & Co.
(c. 1806–1807)
Vernon & Park
*Bibl. 5, 23, 24, 25, 28, 29,
54, 91, 114*

Nathaniel Vernon & Co.
(c. 1802–1808)
Charleston, S.C.
*Bibl. 5, 23, 24, 25, 36, 44,
91, 95, 104, 114*

Samuel Vernon
(b. 1683–d. 1737)
Newport, R.I.
*Bibl. 2, 15, 23, 25, 28, 29,
36, 39, 44, 50, 54, 69, 91,
94, 110, 114, 116, 119*

Samuel Verree
(c. 1804–1816)
Charleston, S.C.
Bibl. 5

P. O. Vickery (1890)
Augusta, Me.
Bibl. 105

P. O. Vickery & Co.
(1875)
Augusta, Me.
Bibl. 105

Edward William Victor
(b. 1819)
Lynchburg, Va.
(c. 1844–1850)
Bibl. 19

John Victor
(b. 1793–d. 1845)
Lynchburg, Va.
Williams & Victor
(c. 1814–1845)
Bibl. 9, 54

John Vignes
(c. 1820–1859)
Kingston, N.Y.
Bibl. 20, 91

| J. VIGNES |

Vilant
(See Vivant)

R. H. L. Villard
(c. 1833–1835)
Washington, D.C.
Georgetown, Md.
*Bibl. 15, 23, 24, 25, 29, 36,
44, 91, 114*

| Villard | VILLARD |

| VILLARD | Villard |

L. Villenjer (c. 1845)
St. Louis, Mo.
Bibl. 54, 155

**Joseph J. Villio
(Villot)(Villiod)
(Villiot)**
(b.c. 1822–d. 1889)
New Orleans, La.
Bibl. 141

**(Monsieur) Antoine
Claude Vincent**
(c. 1790)
Gallipolis, Ohio
Bibl. 34

**Richard Vincent
(Vansant)** (c. 1799)
Baltimore, Md.

*Bibl. 23, 25, 28, 29, 36, 38,
44, 114*

| R: V |

Vinegar Bros. (c. 1927)
New York, N.Y.
Bibl. 127

David Vinton
(c. 1790–1792)
Boston, Mass.
Providence, R.I.
*Bibl. 23, 24, 25, 28, 36, 54,
91, 94, 110, 114*

| D. V |

J. A. & S. S. Virgin
(c. 1834–1837)
Macon, Ga.
Jonathan Ambrose Virgin
Samuel Stanley Virgin
Bibl. 17

| J A & S S VIRGIN |

Virgin(s) & Stringfellow
(c. 1837)
Macon, Ga.
Samuel Stanley Virgin(s)
Samuel Stringfellow (?)
Bibl. 17

Jonathan Ambrose Virgin
(b. 1808–d. 1881)
Macon, Ga.
J. A. & S. S. Virgin
(c. 1834–1837)
Bibl. 17

Samuel Stanley Virgin(s)
(b. 1810–d. 1887)
Macon, Ga.
(c. 1833, c. 1840–1849)
Columbus, Ga.
J. A. & S. S. Virgin
(c. 1834–1837)
Bruno & Virgin(s)
(c. 1840–1849)
Virgin(s) & Stringfellow
Bibl. 17

William M. Virgin
(b. 1796–d. 1861)
Concord, N.H. (c. 1830)
Bibl. 24, 28, 44, 110, 125

| W. M. VIRGIN |

—— **Virney**
(c. 1844–1845)
Louisville, Ky.
Bibl. 32, 93

Jacques Vitant
(1830–1834)
New Orleans, La.
Bibl. 141

William Vivant (Vilant)
(c. 1725)
Philadelphia, Pa.
*Bibl. 3, 15, 23, 24, 25, 28,
29, 36, 39, 44, 54, 78, 81,
91, 114, 118, 119*

Elias Alexander Vogler
(b. 1825–d. 1876)
Salem, N.C.
Bibl. 21

John Vogler
(b. 1783–d. 1881)
Salem, N.C.
Bibl. 21, 25, 44, 91, 102, 114

| J. VOGLER |

John Utzmann Vogler
(c. 1812–1856)
Salisbury, N.C.
Bibl. 21

Ignatius Christian Vogt
(c. 1764)
New York State
Bibl. 3

Henry Voight (Voigt)
(c. 1785–1791, d. 1814)
Philadelphia, Pa.
Bibl. 3

Sebastian Voight
(c. 1793–1800)
Philadelphia, Pa.
Bibl. 3

Henry Voigt
(See Henry Voight)

Thomas H. Voigt
(c. 1811–1835)
Philadelphia, Pa.
Bibl. 3

Frederick C. Von Borstel
(d. 1876)
Anderson, S.C.
(c. 1848–1876)
Athens, Ga.
Bibl. 5, 17

Hermanus Vondyk
(c. 1820–1822)
Philadelphia, Pa.
Bibl. 3

Jacob Vonneida
(c. 1837–1840)
Philadelphia, Pa.
Bibl. 3

L. Von Praag (1859)
New Orleans, La.
Bibl. 141

Abraham Voorhees
(c. 1840)
New Brunswick, N.J.
Bibl. 15, 44, 46, 91, 114

A. VOORHEES

John O. Vorse (c. 1841)
Palmyra, N.Y.
Bibl. 20

John Hobart Vosburgh
(b. 1830)
Utica, N.Y. (c. 1852–1860)
Bibl. 18, 91, 158

Vose, Southwick & Co.
(1872–1878)
Providence, R.I.
Bibl. 108

**Geo. L. Vose Mfg. Co.,
Inc.** (c. 1904–1920)
Providence, R.I.
Successor to Geo. L. Vose &
Co.
Bibl. 127, 157   G V   Ⓥ

Lewis C. Voute (Vouty)
(d. 1886)
Bridgeton, N.J.
(c. 1826–1850)

Philadelphia, Pa.
Bibl. 3, 46, 54, 91

Jacob I. Vrooman
(c. 1814)
Ithaca, N.Y.
Bibl. 20

Alexander Vuille (c. 1766)
Baltimore, Md.
Bibl. 3

W
(See Graff, Washbourne &
Dunn, J. Wagner & Son,
Inc., Wallace Silversmiths,
Inc., Watrous Mfg. Co.,
Watson Company, E. G.
Webster & Son, Weidlich
Bros. Mfg. Co., Weidlich
Sterling Spoon Co.,
Wendell Mfg. Co., Frank
M. Whiting & Co.,
Whiting Manufacturing
Company, F. G. Whitney
& Co., Wm. Wilson &
Son, Woodside Sterling
Co.)

W & B
(See Ward & Bartholomew)

W. & Co.
(See Wallace Silversmiths,
Inc.)

W. & D.
(See Whiting & Davis Co.,
Inc.)

W & G
(See Woodward & Grosjean)

W & G R
(See William & George
Richardson)

W & H
(See Wood & Hughes)

W & V
(See Williams & Victor)

W A
(See William Anderson)

W B
(See William Ball, William
Ball Jr., William Barton,
William Breed, William
Byrd, Weizennegger Bros.)

W. B. Mfg. Co.
(See Weidlich Bros. Mfg.
Co.)

W B N
(See William B. North)

W. B. & T. (c. 1800)
Location unknown
Bibl. 24, 72

W. B. & T.

W C
(See William Clark, William
Cleveland, William
Cowell, William Cross,
Wiley-Crawford Co., Inc.)

W Co
(See Webster Company,
Wendell Mfg. Co.)

W E B
(See Web Silver Co., Inc.)

W E R
(See Wm. R. Elfers Co., Inc.)

W F
(See William Forbes, William
Faris Jr.)

W G
(See William Gale, William
Ghiselin, William W.
Gilbert, William Gowen,
William Grant Jr., William
Gurley)

W H
(See William Haverstick, W.
Hayes, William Heurtin,
William Hollingshead,
William Homes, William
Hughes)

W. H.
(See Walter Hunold)

W H W
(See William W. Hayden
 Co.)

W I
(See William Jones)

W J
(See William B. Johonnot)

W J B & Co.
(See W. J. Braitsch & Co.)

W K
(See William H. Kimberly)

W L
(See William Little)

W M
(See William Moulton III,
 William Moulton IV)

W. M. Co.
(See Watrous Mfg. Co.)

W M Jr.
(See William Mitchell Jr.)

W Mc P
(See William McParlin)

W P
(See William Parham,
 William Pollard, William
 Poole)

W R
(See Wilcox-Roth Co., Capt.
 William Richardson,
 William Roe, William
 Rouse)

W R P
(See William R. Pitman)

W S
(See Wallace Sterling Co.,
 Wayne Silversmith, Inc.,
 William Simes, William
 Simpkins, William Swan)

W. S. Co.
(See Wayne Silver Co.)

W S N
(See William Stoddard
 Nichols)

W S P
(See William Smith
 Pelletreau)

W T
(See William Taylor, Walter
 Thomas, William
 Thompson)

W V
(See Wortz & Voorhis,
 William Vivant)

W W
(See William Ward, William
 Whetcroft, William
 Whittemore, William
 Wightman, Wilcox &
 Wagoner, William Wilson)

W W G
(See W. W. Gaskins, William
 Waddell Geddy)

W Y
(See William Young)

Waage & Norton (c. 1798)
Philadelphia, Pa.
——— Waage
Thomas Norton
Bibl. 3

F. W. Wachner
  (c. 1791–1819)
New York, N.Y.
Bibl. 23, 36, 44

Noel Waddill
  (b. 1753–d. 1833)
Petersburg, Va.
Hill & Waddill
  (c. 1780–1782)
Bibl. 19, 23, 36

William Waddill
Williamsburg, Va.
  (c. 1767–1772)
Richmond, Va.
  (c. 1785)
Petersburg, Va.
  (c. 1785–1795)
Bibl. 19, 153

Wade
(See Hogan & Wade)

Jacob B. Wade
  (c. 1820–1822)
Philadelphia, Pa.
Bibl. 3

Nathaniel Wade (c. 1793)
Newfield, Conn.
Bibl. 61, 110

Thomas Waglin
  (c. 1818–1819)
Philadelphia, Pa.
Bibl. 3, 23, 36

A. L. Wagner & Son, Inc.
  (1931–1950)
New York, N.Y.
Successor to Central Sterling
  Company
  (c. 1909–1914)
Weber-Wagner Co. (c. 1915)
Weber-Wagner & Benson
  Co. (c. 1915–1927)
A. L. Wagner Mfg. Co., Inc.
  (1927–1931)
Became J. Wagner & Son,
  Inc. (c. 1950–1967)
Bibl. 127

Henry Wagner
  (c. 1853–1855)
Nashville, Tenn.
Bibl. 54

J. Wagner & Son, Inc.
  (c. 1950–1967)
New York, N.Y.
Successor to Central Sterling
  Company
  (c. 1909–1915)
Weber-Wagner Co. (c. 1915)
Weber-Wagner & Benson
  Co. (c. 1915–1927)
A. L. Wagner Mfg. co., Inc.
  (1927–1931)
A. L. Wagner & Son, Inc.
  (1931–1950)
Mark used since 1909
Bibl. 127

Thomas Wagstaff (c. 1791)
New York, N.Y.
Bibl. 36, 44

Isaiah Wagster
(c. 1776–1793)
Baltimore, Md.
Bibl. 25, 29, 38, 44, 114, 118

| I W |

Wait & Wright (c. 1837)
Philadelphia, Pa.
Bibl. 3, 23, 36, 44

Edgar A. Wait (c. 1848)
Louisville, Ky.
Bibl. 32, 93

L. D. Wait (c. 1838–1847)
Skaneateles, N.Y.
Bibl. 20, 124

Waite, Smith & Co.
(1868–1876)
Providence, R.I.
Bibl. 108

Alva Waite (c. 1840)
Ravenna, Ohio
Bibl. 34

Edwin F. Waite (c. 1840)
Ravenna, Ohio
Bibl. 34

George Waite (c. 1847–1850)
Philadelphia, Pa.
Bibl. 3

John Waite
(b. 1742–d. 1817)
Kingston, R.I.
*Bibl. 24, 25, 28, 29, 39, 91,
94, 102, 114, 124*

| J W |

| I. WAITE | | J WAITE |

Jonathan Waite
(b. 1730–d. 1822)
Wickford, R.I.
Bibl. 28

William Waite
(b. 1730–d. 1826)
Cambridge, N.Y.
Little Rest, R.I.
Wickford, R.I.
*Bibl. 21, 24, 25, 28, 29, 44,
91, 114, 124*

| W: WAITE |

Frederick Waitt
(c. 1843–1850)
Philadelphia, Pa.
Bibl. 3

Wakefield & Woodward
Great Falls, N.H.
Bibl. 15, 44, 114

| WAKEFIELD & WOODWARD |

A. Wakefield
(c. 1846–1857)
Great Falls, N.H.
Bibl. 89

Charles Wakefield
(c. 1835)
Philadelphia, Pa.
Bibl. 3

Thomas Wakefield
(c. 1837)
Philadelphia, Pa.
Bibl. 3

**Walcott (Wolcott) &
Gelston** (c. 1820–1830)
Boston, Mass.
Henry D. Walcott
Maltby Gelston
George P. Gelston
*Bibl. 24, 25, 28, 29, 44, 91,
110, 114*

| WOLCOTT & GELSTON |

**Henry D. Walcott
(Wolcott)**
(b. 1797?–d. 1830)
Boston, Mass.
Walcott & Gelston
Bibl. 28, 91, 110

D. Waldron (c. 1789)
New York, N.Y.
*Bibl. 23, 24, 25, 29, 36, 44,
114, 124*

| D. WALDRON |

N. H. Wales (1871–1874)
Providence, R.I.
Bibl. 108

S. H. Wales (1857–1863)
Providence, R.I.
Bibl. 108

S. H. Wales & Co.
(1873–1875)
Providence, R.I.
Bibl. 108

Walker
(See Barnhurst & Walker)

Walker & Peak (c. 1843)
Philadelphia, Pa.
Bibl. 3

Walker & Son
(1870–1874)
Providence, R.I.
Bibl. 108

A. K. P. Walker
(1860–1875)
Richmond, Me.
Bibl. 107

Albert Walker
Brockport, N.Y. (c. 1831)
Rochester, N.Y. (c. 1834)
Bibl. 20, 124

Calvin Walker (c. 1831)
Philadelphia, Pa.
New York, N.Y. (c. 1839)
Bibl. 3, 124

Gardiner Walker (1860)
Wiscasset, Me.
Bibl. 105

George Walker
(c. 1797–1822)
Philadelphia, Pa.
William & George Walker
(c. 1795–1796)
*Bibl. 3, 15, 23, 24, 25, 28,
29, 36, 44, 46, 91*

| G. WALKER |

Hannah Walker
(c. 1816–1817)
Philadelphia, Pa.
*Bibl. 3, 23, 24, 25, 29, 36,
44, 91, 114*

| H.WALKER |

James Walker
Fredericksburg, Va.
(c. 1791–1802)
Richmond, Va. (c. 1805)
McCabe & Walker
(c. 1805–1806)
Bibl. 19

John Walker Jr.
(c. 1798–1833)
Philadelphia, Pa.
Bibl. 3, 23, 36

Jonathan Walker
(b. 1797, c. 1812)
Baltimore, Md.
Bibl. 38

Julius Walker
(c. 1840–1848)
Buffalo, N.Y.
Bibl. 20

L. (I.) Walker (c. 1825)
Boston, Mass.
Bibl. 24, 25, 44, 110, 114

> L. Walker

> Joys Building

Richard Walker
(c. 1837–1846)
Philadelphia, Pa.
Bibl. 3

William Walker
(c. 1793–1816)
Philadelphia, Pa.
William & George Walker
(c. 1795–1796)
*Bibl. 3, 15, 23, 24, 25, 28,
29, 36, 44, 80, 91*

> W WALKER

William & George Walker
(c. 1795–1796)
Philadelphia, Pa.
*Bibl. 3, 15, 23, 36, 44, 91,
114*

Wallace Silversmiths
(1956–1984)
Wallingford, Conn.
(See Wallace Silversmiths,
Inc.)
*Bibl. 114, 127, 130, 135, 147,
152*

WALLACE ✶ STERLING

WALLACE ✶ STERLING

Wallace Silversmiths, Inc.
(1984–present)
Wallingford, Conn.
Successor to Robert Wallace
(1834–1855)
Robert Wallace & Co.
(1855–1865)
Wallace, Simpson & Co.
(1865–1871)
R. Wallace & Sons Mfg. Co.
(1871–1956)
Wallace Silversmiths
(1956–1984)
Became division of H. M. W.
Industries (1971–1983)
Became division of Katy
Industries, Inc.
(1983–present)
*Bibl. 114, 127, 130, 135, 147,
152*

Wallace, Simpson & Co.
(1865–1871)
Wallingford, Conn.
(See Wallace Silversmiths,
Inc.)
*Bibl. 114, 127, 130, 135, 147,
152*

James Wallace Jr.
(c. 1739)
Edenton, N.C.
Bibl. 21

R. Wallace & Sons Mfg.
Co. (1871–1956)
Wallingford, Conn.
(See Wallace Silversmiths,
Inc.)
*Bibl. 104, 114, 127, 130, 135,
147, 152, 157*

Robert Wallace
(1834–1855)
Wallingford, Conn.
(See Wallace Silversmiths,
Inc.)
*Bibl. 114, 127, 130, 135, 147,
152*

Robert Wallace & Co.
(1855–1865)
Wallingford, Conn.
(See Wallace Silversmiths,
Inc.)
*Bibl. 114, 127, 130, 135, 147,
152*

W. F. Wallace (1875)
Westerly, R. I.
Bibl. 108

William F. Wallace
Westerly, R.I.
Bibl. 28, 44, 110

John Wallen
(c. 1763)
Philadelphia, Pa.
Bibl. 25, 44, 114

> J. WALLEN

John Waller (c. 1763)
Philadelphia, Pa.
Bibl. 3, 23, 36

Robert Wallin
(c. 1845–1850)
Philadelphia, Pa.
Freeman & Wallin
Bibl. 3, 91

Thomas Wallis
(c. 1804–1808)
Philadelphia, Pa.
Bibl. 3, 23, 36, 44

Richard Waln (c. 1837)
Philadelphia, Pa.
Bibl. 3

John Walraven
(b. 1771–d. 1814)
Baltimore, Md.
Bibl. 15, 24, 25, 28, 29, 38,
44, 91, 114

Walsh (c. 1780)
Location unknown
Bibl. 24, 28

WALSH

Noemi Walsh
(c. 1928–1976)
St. Louis, Mo.
Bibl. 155

Abm. Walter
(c. 1849–1850)
Philadelphia, Pa.
Bibl. 3

H. N. Walter
(c. 1833–1850)
Norwich, N.Y.
Bibl. 20, 124

Jacob Walter
(b. 1782–d. 1869)
Baltimore, Md. (c. 1815)
Bibl. 15, 24, 25, 29, 38, 91,
114

J. WALTER

John J. Walter (c. 1837)
Canton, Ohio
Bibl. 34

Joseph M. Walter
(c. 1835)
Baltimore, Md.
Bibl. 15, 44, 114

JOS M. WALTER

Edward Walters (c. 1847)
Philadelphia, Pa.
Bibl. 3

John Walters
(c. 1779–1784)
Philadelphia, Pa.
Bibl. 3

John J. Walto
(c. 1849–1850)
Philadelphia, Pa.
Bibl. 3

Benjamin Walton
(1860–1875)
Paris, Me.
Bibl. 105

Daniel Walton
(c. 1816–1817)
Philadelphia, Pa.
Bibl. 3, 23, 36, 44

Simeon Walton (1860)
Paris, Me.
Bibl. 105

Daniel Walworth
(b. 1760–d. 1830)
Middletown, Conn.
(c. 1785)
Bibl. 16, 23, 28, 36, 44, 110

Wanamaker & Brown
(1861–1870)
Philadelphia, Pa.
Became John Wanamaker
Bibl. 127

John Wanamaker
(1870–present)
Philadelphia, Pa.
Successor to Wanamaker &
Brown
Bibl. 127, 157

Edward Wangelin
Cleveland, Ohio
Schroeder & Wangelin
(c. 1844–1850)
Bibl. 89

Lewis Wangelin
Cleveland, Ohio
Schroeder & Wangelin
(c. 1844–1850)
Bibl. 89

Edward Wanton
(c. 1799–1810, d. 1811)
Richmond, Va.
Bibl. 19

Nathaniel Waples
(c. 1816–1819)
Philadelphia, Pa.
Bibl. 3

Ward
(See Foster & Ward, Norman
& Ward)

————**Ward** (c. 1774-1810)
Philadelphia, Pa.
Bibl. 15, 28   WARD

Ward & Bartholomew
(c. 1804–1809)
Hartford, Conn.
James Ward
Roswell Bartholomew
Bibl. 15, 16, 23, 24, 25, 28,
29, 36, 39, 61, 91, 92, 94,
110, 114, 116, 143

WARD&BARTHOL
OMEW.HARTFORD

WARD&BARTHOLOMEW

W&B

Ward & Cox
(c. 1811–1818)
Philadelphia, Pa.
John Ward
John Cox
Bibl. 3, 4, 23, 28, 36, 44, 54,
91, 95

Ward & Cox

Ward & Govett (Gavett)
(c. 1813–1814)
Philadelphia, Pa.
John Ward
———— Govett
Bibl. 3, 23, 36, 44

Ward & Hughes (c. 1806)
Middletown, Conn.
John Ward
Edmund Hughes
Bibl. 16, 23, 36, 44, 110

Ward & Jones
(19th century)
Location unknown
Bibl. 28

Ward & Miller
(c. 1822–1824)
Philadelphia, Pa.
John Ward
William Miller
Bibl. 3, 23, 44

Ward & Rich
(c. 1832–1835)
Boston, Mass.
—— Ward
Obadiah Rich
Bibl. 4, 23, 25, 28, 36, 102

Ward, Bartholomew &
Brainard
(c. 1809–1830)
Hartford, Conn.
James Ward
Roswell Bartholomew
Charles Brainard
Bibl. 16, 23, 25, 28, 36, 44,
110

Ambrose Ward
(b. 1735–d. 1808)
New Haven, Conn.
Cutler, Silliman, Ward & Co.
(c. 1767)
Bibl. 16, 23, 25, 28, 36, 44,
91, 92, 110, 114, 143

Anthony Ward (c. 1717)
Philadelphia, Pa.
Bibl. 3

Benjamin Ward
(c. 1787)
Pasquotank County, N.C.
Bibl. 21

Benjamin Ward
(c. 1845–1846)
Troy, N.Y.
Bibl. 20, 124

Bil(l)ious Ward
(b. 1729–d. 1777)
Guilford, Conn.
Middletown, Conn.

Bibl. 2, 15, 16, 23, 24, 25,
28, 29, 36, 44, 91, 92, 94,
110, 114, 122

Charles Ward
(c. 1824)
Philadelphia, Pa.
Bibl. 3

Charles Ward
(c. 1839–1840)
Philadelphia, Pa.
Bibl. 3

David B. Ward (1860)
Oldtown, Me.
Bibl. 105

Edward Ward (1875)
Presque Isle, Me.
Bibl. 105

Edward H. Ward
(c. 1839–1842)
Philadelphia, Pa.
Bibl. 3

Isaac Ward (c. 1811–1818)
Philadelphia, Pa.
Bibl. 3

J. Ward & Co. (c. 1843)
Philadelphia, Pa.
Bibl. 3

James Ward
(b. 1768–d. 1856)
Guilford, Conn.
Hartford, Conn.
Beach & Ward
(c. 1790–1797)
Ward & Bartholomew
(c. 1804–1809)
Ward, Bartholomew &
Brainard (c. 1809–1830)
Bibl. 15, 16, 23, 24, 25, 28,
29, 36, 44, 61, 78, 91, 92,
94, 110, 114

Jehu Ward (c. 1808–1848)
Philadelphia, Pa.
Jehu & W. L. Ward & Co.
(c. 1839–1850)
Bibl. 3, 80, 91, 114

Jehu & W. L. Ward & Co.
(c. 1839–1850)
Philadelphia, Pa.
Bibl. 3, 15, 25, 79, 91

John Ward
Middletown, Conn (c. 1805)
Ward & Hughes (c. 1806)
Bibl. 16, 23, 25, 28, 36, 110,
114

John Ward (c. 1803–1839)
Philadelphia, Pa.
Ward & Cox
(c. 1811–1818)
Ward & Govett
(c. 1813–1814)
Ward & Miller
(c. 1822–1824)
Bibl. 3, 23, 28, 29, 36, 39, 44

WARD, 67 MARKET ST.

Joshua Ward
(c. 1826–1828)
Auburn, N.Y.
Bibl. 20, 124

Macock Ward
(b. 1702–d. 1783)
Wallingford, Conn.
Bibl. 28, 110

Richard Ward (c. 1815)
Boston, Mass.
Jones & Ward (c. 1809)
Bibl. 23, 28, 36, 44, 72, 91,
110

R W

Samuel L. Ward
(c. 1830–1835)
Boston, Mass.
Ward & Rich (c. 1832–1835)
Bibl. 23, 28, 36, 44, 102

Thomas Ward (c. 1755)
Baltimore, Md.
Bibl. 38

Timothy Ward
(b. 1742–d. 1768)
Middletown, Conn.
Bibl. 16, 23, 28, 36, 44, 110

W. W. Ward (c. 1841)
Winnsboro, S.C.
Bibl. 5

William Ward
(b. 1678–d. 1768)
Wallingford, Conn.
Bibl. 2, 28, 29, 92, 110

William Ward
(b. 1705–d. 1761)
Guilford, Conn.
*Bibl. 2, 15, 16, 23, 24, 28,
36, 44, 92, 110*

W. W.   W. WARD

W. Ward

William Ward
(c. 1797–1798)
New Windsor, N.Y.
Bibl. 20

William Ward (Jr.)
(b. 1763–d. 1826)
Litchfield, Conn. (c. 1757)
*Bibl. 15, 16, 23, 25, 28, 29,
36, 44, 54, 61, 91, 94, 110,
114, 143*

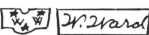

William H. Ward
Baltimore, Md.
Gould & Ward (c. 1850)
Gould, Stowell & Ward
(c. 1855–1858)
Bibl. 23, 36, 38, 44

William L. Ward
(c. 1831–1850)
Philadelphia, Pa.
Bibl. 3

Warden
(See Ayres & Warden)

—— **Warden**
Philadelphia, Pa.
Ayres & Warden (c. 1817)
Bibl. 3

Abijah B. Warden
(c. 1842–1850)
Philadelphia, Pa.
Bibl. 3, 15, 25, 44, 114

WARDEN

Daniel Wardin (c. 1811)
Bridgeport, Conn.
Bibl. 16, 23, 28, 36, 44, 110

J. Wardwool (c. 1791)
New York State
Bibl. 4

J. H. Warfield (c. 1827)
Baltimore, Md.
Bibl. 38, 91

Warford
(See Bassett & Warford)

Joseph Warford (c. 1810)
Albany, N.Y.
*Bibl. 15, 20, 25, 44, 91, 114,
124*

WARFORD

G. Waring (c. 1848)
Hudson, N.Y.
Bibl. 20, 114, 124

William Wark
(c. 1848–1850)
Philadelphia, Pa.
Bibl. 3

Warner & Fellows
(See Werner & Fellows)

Warner & Keating
(c. 1840–1843)
Philadelphia, Pa.
Bibl. 3

Warner & Newlin
(c. 1848–1850)
Philadelphia, Pa.
—— Warner
Edward G. Newlin
Bibl. 3

**A. E. & T. H. Warner
(Thomas & A. E.
Warner)** (c. 1805–1812)
Baltimore, Md.
Andrew Ellicott & Thomas
H. Warner
*Bibl. 4, 23, 24, 28, 29, 36,
38, 39, 44, 48, 91, 114,
160*

Andrew Ellicott Warner
(b. 1786–d. 1870)
Baltimore, Md.
A. E. & T. H. Warner
(c. 1805–1812)
*Bibl. 4, 15, 23, 24, 25, 28,
29, 36, 38, 44, 54, 72, 78,
91, 95, 102, 104, 114, 122,
135, 149, 160*

A.E.WARNER

A.E.W   A.E.W

A.E. WARNER

ANDᵂ E. WARNER

C. & J. Warner (c. 1825)
Salem, Mass.
Bibl. 24, 25, 28, 29, 44

C & J WARNER

Cuthbert Warner
(b. 1760–d. 1838)
Baltimore, Md.
Bibl. 38, 160

C. WARNER

Cuthbert Warner
(c. 1837–1850)
Philadelphia, Pa.
Bibl. 3, 15

Daniel Warner
(c. 1810–1820)
Salem, Mass.
Ipswich, Mass. (?)
Bibl. 23, 24, 25, 28, 29, 36,
110, 114

D. WARNER

J. Warner
Norfolk, Va. (before 1801)
Richmond, Va.
(c. 1801–1803)
Bibl. 19

John S. Warner
(c. 1825–1846)
Philadelphia, Pa.
Baltimore, Md. (b.c. 1795)
Bibl. 3, 38

Joseph Warner
(b. 1742–d. 1800)
Wilmington, Del.
Bibl. 3, 15, 23, 24, 25, 30,
36, 44, 91, 95, 104

J. WARNER   I W

I WARNER

Joseph Warner
(c. 1811–1850)
Philadelphia, Pa.
Bibl. 3, 4, 23, 28, 29, 36, 72

J WARNER

Joseph P. Warner
(b. 1811–d. 1862)
Baltimore, Md.
(c. 1830–1862)
Bibl. 24, 25, 29, 38, 44, 114

J P W

Joseph P. Warner
(c. 1839)
Philadelphia, Pa.
Bibl. 3

Philip Warner (c. 1835)
Philadelphia, Pa.
Bibl. 3

Robert P. Warner
(c. 1839–1850)
Philadelphia, Pa.
Bibl. 3

Samuel Warner
Philadelphia, Pa. (c. 1797)
Baltimore, Md. (c. 1812)
Bibl. 3, 23, 24, 25, 28, 29,
44, 114

S W   S. Warner

WARNER

T. Warner
(19th century)
Location unknown
Bibl. 28

T WARNER

Thomas & A. E. Warner
(See A. E. & T. H. Warner)

Thomas H. Warner
(c. 1780–1828)
Baltimore, Md.
A. E. & T. H. Warner
(c. 1805–1812)

Bibl. 15, 23, 24, 25, 28, 29,
36, 38, 54, 86, 91, 102,
122, 135, 160

T. WARNER

T W

William Warner
(c. 1814–1850)
Philadelphia, Pa.
William Warner & Co.
(c. 1844–1850)
Bibl. 3

William Warner & Co.
(c. 1844–1850)
Philadelphia, Pa.
Bibl. 3

Benjamin Warren
(c. 1809–1817)
Philadelphia, Pa.
Bibl. 3, 23, 36, 44

Chauncey Warrener
(1875)
Fryeburg, Me.
Bibl. 105

S. W. Warriner
(c. 1845–1848)
Louisville, Ky.
J. N. Alrich & S. W.
Warriner (c. 1848)
Bibl. 32, 54, 68, 93

—— **Warrington**
(c. 1840)
Philadelphia, Pa.
Bibl. 15, 91, 114

WARRINGTON

John Warrington
Philadelphia, Pa.
John Warrington & Co.
(c. 1828–1831)
John & S. R. Warrington
Bibl. 3, 91

John Warrington & Co.
(c. 1828–1831)
Philadelphia, Pa.
Bibl. 3, 91

John & S. R. Warrington
(c. 1841–1850)
Philadelphia, Pa.
John Warrington
Samuel R. Warrington
Bibl. 3, 91

Samuel R. Warrington
(c. 1841–1850)
Philadelphia, Pa.
John & S. R. Warrington
Samuel R. Warrington & Co.
Bibl. 3, 91

**Samuel R. Warrington &
Co.** (c. 1841–1850)
Philadelphia, Pa.
Bibl. 3, 91

William Warrock
(c. 1795–1804)
Richmond, Va. (c. 1803)
Norfolk, Va.
Brooks & Warrock
(c. 1795?)
Bibl. 19

F. A. Wart (c. 1841)
Philadelphia, Pa.
Bibl. 3

Warwick
(See W. Bell & Company)

Warwick Sterling Co.
(c. 1913–1922)
Providence, R.I.
Bibl. 127, 157

William Warwick (c. 1837)
Philadelphia, Pa.
Bibl. 3

Charles Washburn
(c. 1844–c. 1850)
Rochester, N.Y.
Bibl. 20, 124

Washington
(See Harris & Schafer Co.,
Inc.)

Charles H. Waterhouse
(c. 1847)
Providence, R.I.
Bibl. 23

Waterman & Van Ness
(See Van Ness & Waterman)

Waterman & Whalen
(c. 1849)
Albany, N.Y.
George Waterman
James Whalen
Bibl. 20, 124

George Waterman
(c. 1848–1850)
Albany, N.Y.
Waterman & Whalen
(c. 1849)
Bibl. 20, 23, 28, 44, 124

Henry Waters (c. 1738)
Yorktown, Va.
Bibl. 19

Samuel Waters
(c. 1790–1805)
Boston, Mass.
*Bibl. 2, 15, 23, 24, 25, 28,
29, 36, 91, 114*

James Watkins (c. 1819)
New York, N.Y.
Bibl. 23, 36, 44, 124, 138

John Watkins
(c. 1831–1837)
Philadelphia, Pa.
Bibl. 3, 44

Mildred G. Watkins
(b. 1883–d. 1968)
Cleveland, Ohio
Bibl. 89

O. C. Watkins (c. 1850)
Unadilla, N.Y.
Bibl. 20, 124

James Watling
(c. 1837–1850)
Philadelphia, Pa.
Bibl. 3, 23, 36

Watrous Mfg. Co.
(1896–1898)
Wallingford, Conn.
Successor to Maltby, Stevens
& Company
Maltby, Stevens and Curtiss
Became International Silver
Co. (1898)
Bibl. 114, 127, 157

Watson & Briggs Co.
(c. 1934)
Attleboro, Mass.
Bibl. 127

Watson & Brown
(c. 1820–1830)
Philadelphia, Pa.
Boston, Mass. (?)
*Bibl. 23, 24, 25, 28, 29, 36,
44, 91, 114*

**Watson & Hildeburn
(Hildeburn & Watson)**
(c. 1833–1849)
Philadelphia, Pa.
Bibl. 3, 91

Watson Company
(1919–1955)
Attleboro, Mass.
Successor to Cobb, Gould &
Co. (1874–1880)
Watson & Newell
(1880–1886)
Watson, Newell & Co.
(1886–1895)
Watson, Newell Co.
(1895–1919)

Souvenir spoon dies sold to
Whiting & Davis (1964)
Rest of business purchased
by R. Wallace & Sons
(now Wallace
Silversmiths)
*Bibl. 114, 127, 135, 146, 147,
152, 154, 157*

Edward E. (J.) Watson
(d. 1839)
Boston, Mass.
Davis & Watson (c. 1815)
Davis, Watson & Co.
(c. 1820)
*Bibl. 2, 15, 23, 24, 25, 28,
29, 36, 39, 54, 91*

E. WATSON

E. Watson

Isaac S. Watson
(c. 1843–1846)
Philadelphia, Pa.
Bibl. 3, 23

James Watson
(c. 1820–1850)
Philadelphia, Pa.
*Bibl. 3, 23, 24, 25, 29, 36,
39, 54, 91*

J. WATSON

Joseph H. Watson
(c. 1844–1878)
Warrenton, Va.
Bibl. 19

WATSON

Joshua Watson
(c. 1819–1824)
Philadelphia, Pa.
Bibl. 3

L. Watson (19th century)
Location unknown
Bibl. 54

Robert Watson
(c. 1842–1850)
Philadelphia, Pa.
Bibl. 3

William Watt
(c. 1767–1789)
Savannah, Ga.
Bibl. 17

Charles Watts
(c. 1844–c. 1850)
Rochester, N.Y.
Bibl. 20, 124

J. & W. Watts
(c. 1839–1845)
Philadelphia, Pa.
James & William Watts
Bibl. 3, 4, 23, 28, 36

James Watts
(c. 1835–1850)
Philadelphia, Pa.
J. & W. Watts
(c. 1839–1845)
Bibl. 3, 23, 36, 44, 114

John W. Watts (c. 1794)
New York, N.Y.
Bibl. 23, 36, 44, 124, 138

Julius R. Watts & Co.
(c. 1888–1959)
Atlanta, Ga.
Bibl. 127, 157

William Watts
(c. 1841–1850)
Philadelphia, Pa.
J. & W. Watts
(c. 1839–1845)
Bibl. 3, 23

John Waugh (c. 1803)
Schenectady, N.Y.
Bibl. 20, 124

Thomas Waugh (1875)
Starks, Me.
Bibl. 105

Wayne Silver Co.
(c. 1895–1904)
Honesdale, Pa.
Bibl. 114, 127, 157

Wayne Silversmith, Inc.
(c. 1950–present)
Yonkers, N.Y.
Bibl. 127

Richard Waynes (c. 1750)
Philadelphia, Pa.
Bibl. 23, 28, 29, 36, 44

William Wearer (c. 1825)
Augusta, Ga.
Brelet, Wearer & Co.
Bibl. 17

David Weatherly
(c. 1805–1850)
Philadelphia, Pa.
Bibl. 3

Michael Weathers
(c. 1794)
New York, N.Y.
Bibl. 23, 36, 44, 124, 138

J. P. Weatherstone
(c. 1892)
Chicago, Ill.
Bibl. 127

Weaver
(See Sunderlin & Weaver)

Emmor T. Weaver
(b. 1786–d. 1860)

Philadelphia, Pa.
*Bibl. 3, 23, 24, 25, 29, 36,
39, 44, 95, 104, 114*

Joseph S. Weaver
(c. 1846–c. 1849)
Utica, N.Y.
N. N. Weaver & Son
(c. 1846–1847)
Bibl. 18, 20, 91, 95, 124, 158

Joshua Weaver
(b. 1753–d. 1827)
West Chester, Pa.
Bibl. 24, 25, 39, 114

N. N. Weaver & Son
(c. 1846–1847)
Utica, N.Y.
Joseph S. Weaver
Nicholas N. Weaver
William N. Weaver
Bibl. 18, 20, 91, 124

N. N. & W. Weaver
(c. 1817)
Utica, N.Y.
Nicholas N. Weaver
William Weaver
Bibl. 18, 20, 124

Nicholas N. Weaver
(b. 1791–d. 1853)
Utica, N.Y.
Cleveland, Ohio
N. N. Weaver & Son
(c. 1846–1847)
N. N. & W. Weaver
Joseph S. Porter
*Bibl. 15, 18, 20, 25, 44, 91,
114, 124, 158*

N. N. WEAVER

William Weaver (b. 1794)
Utica, N.Y. (1817–1825)
N. N. & W. Weaver
Bibl. 18, 20, 124, 158

William N. Weaver
(b. 1822)

Utica, N.Y.
N. N. Weaver & Son
(c. 1846–1847)
Bibl. 18, 20, 124, 158

Web Silver Co., Inc.
(c. 1950–present)
Philadelphia, Pa.
Successor to Web Jewelry
Manufacturing Co.
Bought dies & patterns of
Weidlich Sterling Spoon
Company (1952)
Bibl. 127, 146

Webb & Boon (c. 1785)
Philadelphia, Pa.
Bibl. 3, 23, 36, 44

Webb & Britain (c. 1835)
Nashville, Tenn.
Bibl. 54

Webb & Company
(c. 1865–1877)
Baltimore, Md.
Became Geo. W. Webb &
Co. (c. 1877–1886)
Bibl. 127

Webb & Cowell (c. 1739)
Boston, Mass.
Edward Webb
Bibl. 70

W₽BB ₽ COWELL

Webb & Johannes
(c. 1827–1835)
Baltimore, Md.
James Webb
John M. Johannes
Bibl. 38

**Barnabas (Barnebus)
Webb** (b. 1729–d. 1795)
Thomaston, Me.
(c. 1756–1786)
Boston, Mass.
*Bibl. 15, 23, 25, 28, 29, 36,
91, 105, 110, 114*

B W

Charles Webb (c. 1738)
Philadelphia, Pa.
Bibl. 3, 23, 36, 44

Charles Webb (c. 1850)
Philadelphia, Pa.
Bibl. 3

Christopher Webb
(c. 1737)
Charleston, S.C.
Bibl. 5

Daniel A. Webb (c. 1835)
Nashville, Tenn.
Bibl. 54

David Webb (Inc.)
(c. 1925–present)
New York, N.Y.
Bibl. 117, 126

Edward Webb
(b. 1665–d. 1718)
Boston, Mass.
*Bibl. 15, 24, 25, 44, 54, 55,
69, 70, 91, 94, 102, 110,
114, 116, 118, 119, 151*

E W

WEBB

Frederick I. Webb (1860)
Damariscotta, Me.
Bibl. 105

George W. Webb
(b. 1812–d. 1890)
Baltimore, Md.
*Bibl. 4, 15, 23, 24, 25, 28,
38, 44, 114*

G W WEBB

GEO W WEBB

H. J. Webb & Co.
(c. 1900–1915)
Springfield, Mass.
Successor to L. S. Stowe &
Co.
Bibl. 127

James Webb
  (c. 1788–d. 1844)
Baltimore, Md. (w. 1817)
Webb & Johannes
  (c. 1827–1835)   J WEBB
James Webb & Son
Bibl. 15, 23, 24, 25, 28, 29,
38, 114

James Webb & Son
  (c. 1835)
Baltimore, Md.
Bibl. 38

John Webb (c. 1827–1842)
Baltimore, Md.
Bibl. 38

Lewis Webb
  (c. 1827–1830)
Baltimore, Md.
Bibl. 38

Robert Webb
  (c. 1791–1817)
Philadelphia, Pa.
Bibl. 3, 23, 36

Thomas Webb
  (c. 1818–1819)
Philadelphia, Pa.
Bibl. 3

William Webb (c. 1801)
Philadelphia, Pa.
Bibl. 3

Weber-Wagner & Benson
  Co. (1915–1927)
New York, N.Y.
(See J. Wagner & Son, Inc.)
Bibl. 127

Weber-Wagner Co.
  (c. 1915)
New York, N.Y.
(See J. Wagner & Son, Inc.)
Bibl. 127

Kem Weber
  (c. 1928–1939)
New York, N.Y.
Hollywood, Calif
Bibl. 120

Phylis Weber (c. 1980)
St. Louis, Mo.
Bibl. 155

Webster & Knowles
  (c. 1852–1865)
Boston, Mass.
Providence, R.I.
Became Knowles & Ladd
  (c. 1864–1875)
J. B. & S. M. Knowles
  (1875–1905)
Mauser Mfg. Co.
Bibl. 127

Webster Brother & Co.
  (c. 1886)
Brooklyn, N.Y.
Successor to Frederick S.
  Hoffman
Became A. A. Webster & Co.
Clarence B. Webster
Bibl. 127

Webster Company
  (c. 1894–present)
North Attleboro, Mass.
Successor to G. K. Webster
  (c. 1869–1894)
Became division of Reed &
  Barton (1950)
Bibl. 114, 120, 127, 135

Webster Mfg. Co.
  (1859–1873)
Brooklyn, N.Y.
Became E. G. Webster &
  Bros. (1873–1886)
E. G. Webster & Son
  (1886–1928)
Became International Silver
  and moved to Meriden,
  Conn. (1928)
Bibl. 114, 127, 157

A. A. Webster & Co.
  (c. 1886–1904)
Brooklyn, N.Y.
Successor to Frederick S.
  Hoffman
Webster Brother & Co.
Became Clarence B. Webster
Bibl. 127

Clarence B. Webster
  (c. 1904)
Brooklyn, N.Y.
Successor to Frederick S.
  Hoffman
Webster Brother & Co.
A. A. Webster & Co.
Bibl. 127

E. G. Webster & Bros.
  (1873–1886)
Brooklyn, N.Y.
Successor to Webster Mfg.
  Co. (1859–1873)
Became E. G. Webster &
  Son (1886–1928)
Bibl. 114, 127, 157

E. G. Webster & Son
  (1886–1928)
Brooklyn, N.Y.
Successor to Webster Mfg.
  Co. (1859–1873)
E. G. Webster & Bros.
  (1873–1886)
Became International Silver
  Co. and moved to
  Meriden, Conn. (1928)
Bibl. 114, 127, 157

G. K. Webster
  (c. 1869–1894)
George K. Webster
North Attleboro, Mass.
Became Webster Company
  (c. 1894–present)
Became division of Reed &
  Barton (1950)
Bibl. 114, 127, 157

Henry L. Webster
  (c. 1831–1841)
Providence, R.I.
  (c. 1831–1841)
Boston, Mass.
Gorham & Webster
Henry L. Webster & Co.
Gorham, Webster & Price

Bibl. 15, 23, 24, 25, 28, 44, 91, 114

H L WEBSTER

Henry L. Webster & Co.
(c. 1831–1841)
Providence, R.I.
Boston, Mass.
Bibl. 15, 23, 24, 25, 29, 36, 91, 114

H L W & Co

H L Webster & Co

W. E. Webster Co.
(c. 1895–1904)
Providence, R.I.
Bibl. 114, 127, 157

P. M. Weddell (c. 1845)
Cleveland, Ohio
Bibl. 89

Simon Wedge Sr.
(b. 1774 d. 1823)
Baltimore, Md.
(c. 1798–1823)
Bibl. 15, 23, 25, 28, 29, 36, 38, 44, 91, 114

Simon Wedge Jr.
(b. 1799–d. 1887)
Baltimore, Md.
(c. 1823–1869)
Bibl. 15, 38, 91

Wee Cherub Mfg. Co.
(c. 1950)
Houston, Tex.
Bibl. 127

WEE CHERUB

George Weedaman
(c. 1807)
Philadelphia, Pa.
Bibl. 3

Peleg Weeden
(b. 1759?–d. 1840)
North Kingston, R.I.
(c. 1803)
Bibl. 23, 28, 36, 44, 110

Jason Weeks (1860)
Bangor, Me.
Bibl. 105

John Weeks (c. 1835)
Philadelphia, Pa.
Bibl. 3

W. F. Weeks (1875)
Bangor, Me.
Bibl. 105

Solomon Weida (c. 1847)
Rochester, N.Y.
Bibl. 20, 124

Weidemeyer & Peacock
(c. 1819)
Fredericksburg, Va.
John M. Weidemeyer
Richard G. Peacock Jr.
Bibl. 19

John M. Weidemeyer
Baltimore, Md.
(c. 1800–1801)
Fredericksburg, Va.
(c. 1806–1819)
Charlottesville, Va.
(c. 1823)
Weidemeyer & Peacock
Bibl. 19

Lewis Weidemeyer
(c. 1828–1829)
New York, N.Y.
Bibl. 15, 138

Louis Weidemeyer
(c. 1817)
Lynchburg, Va.
Bibl. 19, 54

Weidlich Bros. Mfg. Co.
(1901–1950)
Bridgeport, Conn. **EVER DRY**
Bibl. 127
AVON

THE WARNER SILVER CO.

Weidlich Sterling Spoon Co. (c. 1915–1952)
Bridgeport, Conn.
Dies and patterns acquired by Web Silver Co., Inc. (1952)
Bibl. 127, 147, 157

John Wein (c. 1811)
Philadelphia, Pa.
Bibl. 3

George Weiss (c. 1847)
Philadelphia, Pa.
Bibl. 3, 23

Jedediah Weiss
(b. 1798–d. 1870)
Bethlehem, Pa.
(c. 1777–1815)
Philadelphia, Pa.
Bibl. 3, 91

Weizennegger Bros.
(c. 1909–1922)
Newark, N.J.
Bibl. 127, 157

Enoch Welborn
(1826–1855)
Nashville, Tenn.
Memphis, Tenn.
Bibl. 54, 89

John Welch
Boston, Mass.
Bibl. 44

John Welch (c. 1823)
Fincastle, Va.
Bibl. 19

Francis Weller
(c. 1777–1778)
Philadelphia, Pa.
Bibl. 3

James M. Welles
(See James M. Wells)

Welles & Co.
(c. 1800–1821)
Boston, Mass.
George I. Welles
Hugh Gelston
*Bibl. 2, 23, 24, 25, 28, 29,
36, 44, 110, 114*

| WELLES & CO. |

Welles & Gelston (c. 1840)
New York, N.Y.
Bibl. 24, 25, 28, 114

| Welles & Gelston |

| WELLES & GELSTON |

Alfred George Welles
(c. 1804–1810)
Boston, Mass.
*Bibl. 23, 24, 25, 28, 29, 39,
44, 72, 91, 110*

| A + G WELLES |

| A. & G. W. |

Andrew (Alfred) Welles
(b. 1783–d. 1860)
Hebron, Conn. (c. 1804)
*Bibl. 15, 16, 25, 28, 36, 44,
92, 110, 114*

| A Welles |

George I. Welles
(c. 1784–1827)
Boston, Mass.
Hebron, Conn.
Welles & Co.
*Bibl. 2, 4, 15, 23, 25, 28, 29,
36, 44, 54, 110, 114*

| WELLES | | WELLES |

J. M. Welles
(See J. M. Wells)

Wells & Horace
(See Lemuel & Horace
Wells)

Wells, Inc. (c. 1970)
Attleboro, Mass.
Became Wells Benrus Corp.
(1977)
Bibl. 127, 146

| W |

Wells Inc

Wells, Tain & Hall
(after 1800)
Location unknown
Bibl. 28

| A S Tain | | L T Welles |
| D G Hall |

D. Wells (c. 1813)
Ogdensburg, N.Y.
Bibl. 20, 124

D. A. Wells (c. 1833)
Medina, Ohio
Bibl. 34

Horace Wells (c. 1790)
New York, N.Y.
Lemuel & Horace Wells
(c. 1794)
Bibl. 36, 44, 91, 124

James M. Wells (Welles)
(c. 1827–1835)
New York, N.Y.
Bibl. 15, 23, 36, 124, 138

L. & C. Wells
(c. 1794–1798)
New York, N.Y.
Bibl. 36, 44

Lemuel Wells | L W |
(c. 1790–1820)
New York, N.Y.
Lemuel Wells & Co.
(c. 1794)
Lemuel & Horace Wells
(c. 1794)
*Bibl. 23, 24, 25, 29, 44, 91,
114, 124, 138*

Lemuel Wells & Co.
(c. 1794–1798)
New York, N.Y.
*Bibl. 23, 24, 25, 44, 91, 124,
138*

| L W & Co |

Lemuel Wells & Horace
(See Lemuel & Horace
Wells)

Lemuel & Horace Wells
(c. 1794)
New York, N.Y.
Bibl. 23, 25, 36, 91, 124, 138

Richard Wells (c. 1775)
Sunbury, Ga.
Bibl. 17

Robert Wells
(c. 1787–c. 1804)
Winchester, Va.
Bibl. 19

William Wells
(b. 1766, c. 1828)
Hartford, Conn.
Bibl. 16, 23, 28, 36, 44

John Wellwood
(c. 1751–?)
Edenton, N.C.
Bibl. 21

William Welscher
(c. 1783–1789)
Savannah, Ga.
Bibl. 17

Alexander Welsh
(c. 1800–1801)
Baltimore, Md.
Bibl. 38

Beta Welsh (c. 1808)
Northampton, Mass.
Bibl. 84

David Welsh
(c. 1848–1851)
Lincanton, N.C.
Bibl. 21

John Welsh
(b. 1730–d. 1812)
Boston, Mass.
Bibl. 28, 110

Wendell & Roberts
(c. 1850)
Albany, N.Y.
William Wendell
——— Roberts
Bibl. 23, 124

Wendell Mfg. Co.
(c. 1885–1909)
Chicago, Ill.
Successor to Charles Wendell
(c. 1850–1885)
New York outlet, Wendell &
Co. (1904–1909)
Bibl. 114, 127, 152, 157

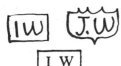

William Wendell
(c. 1839–1842)
Albany, N.Y.
Mulford & Wendell
(c. 1843–1850)
Wendell & Roberts (c. 1850)
Bibl. 20, 23, 91, 124

John (Jan) Wendover
(Windover) (Windeford)
(d. 1727, c. 1694–1727)
New York, N.Y.
Bibl. 23, 24, 25, 28, 29, 30,
36, 44, 72, 114, 124, 138

Wendt
(See Rogers & Wendt)

J. R. Wendt & Co.
(c. 1855–1870)
New York, N.Y.
Sold to Whiting Mfg. Co.
and to Adams & Shaw Co.
(later Dominick & Haff)
Bibl. 28, 127

Bernard Wenman
(c. 1789–1834)
New York, N.Y.

Bibl. 4, 15, 23, 24, 25, 28,
29, 35, 36, 39, 44, 54, 72,
83, 91, 114, 124, 138

Widow of Bernard
Wenman
(c. 1834–1835)
New York, N.Y.
Bibl. 15, 91, 138

Wentworth & Co.
(c. 1850)
New York, N.Y.
Bibl. 24, 25, 44, 124

WENTWORTH & CO.

C. K. Wentworth & Co.
(c. 1847)
Macon, Ga.
Cyrus King Wentworth
B. L. Burnett
Bibl. 17

Cyrus King Wentworth
(c. 1816–1847)
Milledgeville, Ga. (c. 1840)
Macon, Ga. (c. 1847)
Boston, Mass.
New York, N.Y.
C. K. Wentworth & Co.
(c. 1847)
Bibl. 17

G. E. Wentworth (1875)
Appleton, Me.
Bibl. 105

Jason Wentworth
(c. 1846)
Boston, Mass.
Bibl. 25, 44, 114

J. WENTWORTH

Hilary (Henry) Wentz
(c. 1822–1824)
Philadelphia, Pa.
Bibl. 3

Benjamin Wenzell
(Winzel) (Winson)
(c. 1839–1850)
Philadelphia, Pa.
Bibl. 3

Werne & Speiglehalder
(See Speiglehalder & Werne)

Joseph Werne Sr.
(c. 1808–1858)
Louisville, Ky.
Speiglehalder & Werne
(c. 1836–1858)
Bibl. 32, 54, 68, 93

Joseph Werne Jr.
(b. 1837–d. 1903)
Louisville, Ky.
Kitts & Werne
(c. 1865–1874)
Bibl. 32, 54, 68, 93

Werner (Warner) &
Fellows (c. 1824)
Portsmouth, N.H.
Caleb Werner
John F. Fellows
Bibl. 23, 36, 44, 91

Caleb Werner (Warner)
(b. 1784–d. 1861)
Portsmouth, N.H. (c. 1824)
Portland, Me.
Salem, Mass.
Werner & Fellows (c. 1824)
Bibl. 15, 23, 24, 25, 28, 29,
38, 44, 91, 102, 105, 110,
114

C. Warner

I. Wescoat (c. 1830)
Location unknown
Bibl. 15, 24, 44, 114

I. Wescoat

Benjamin West
(c. 1770–1830)
Boston, Mass.
Bibl. 23, 25, 28, 29, 36, 110,
114, 116

B. WEST

Charles West (c. 1830)
Boston, Mass.
Bibl. 23, 28, 36, 44

Edward West Sr. (c. 1765)
Stafford County, Va.
Bibl. 19

Edward West Jr.
(b. 1757–d. 1827)
Stafford County, Va.
(c. 1785–1788)
Lexington, Ky.
(c. 1788–1827)
Bibl. 19, 32, 54, 68, 93

James L. West
(c. 1829–1833)
Philadelphia, Pa.
Bibl. 3

Joseph West
(d. 1780, c. 1776)
Philadelphia, Pa.
Bibl. 3, 23, 36, 44

Josiah West
(c. 1798–1808)
Philadelphia, Pa.
Bibl. 3

S. W. West (c. 1859)
Laurens, S.C.
Bibl. 5

Thomas G. West
(c. 1819–1822)
Philadelphia, Pa.
McIlhenney & West
(c. 1818–1822) (?)
Bibl. 3

William E. West
(19th century)
Lexington, Ky.
Bibl. 54

Westerling Company
(1974–present)
Chicago, Ill
Sterling inventory and
pattern rights purchased
from Easterling Co.
(1974); patterns
manufactured by Gorham
Bibl. 127

Andrew Westermeyer
(c. 1790–1807)
Charleston, S.C.
Bibl. 5

Henry Westermeyer
(c. 1790)
Charleston, S.C.
Bibl. 5, 44

| H W |

**John L. Westervelt
(Westervell)** (b. 1826)
Newburgh, N.Y.
(c. 1826–1850)
*Bibl. 20, 23, 24, 25, 28, 29,
44, 114, 124*

| J. L. W. |

**Westmoreland Sterling
Co.** (1940–present)
Wallingford, Conn.
Bibl. 127

Westmorland

Benjamin Weston
(c. 1797)
Philadelphia, Pa.
Bibl. 3, 19, 36, 44

Charles Westphall
(c. 1801)
Philadelphia, Pa.
Bibl. 3

**Charles William
Westphall**
(c. 1802–1822)
Philadelphia, Pa.
*Bibl. 3, 23, 24, 25, 28, 29,
44, 114*

| C. WEST PHAL |
| C. WESTPHAL |
| C. WESTPHAL |

Ferdinand Westphall
(c. 1814–1824)
Philadelphia, Pa.
Bibl. 3

C. A. Wetherell & Co.
(c. 1892–1897)
Attleboro, Mass.
Bibl. 127

| CAW&CO |

Wetmore & Dikeman
(c. 1817)
Bath, N.Y.
Bibl. 20, 124

Edward A. Wetmore
(c. 1839–1843)

Troy, N.Y.
Bibl. 20, 124

Jacob G. Weyman
(c. 1844–1846)
Philadelphia, Pa.
Bibl. 3

James Whalen (c. 1849)
Albany, N.Y.
Waterman & Whalen
Bibl. 20, 124

Joseph Wharfe (c. 1804)
Baltimore, Md.
Bibl. 38

Joseph Wharfe
(b. 1789, c. 1819)
Fredericktown, Md.
Bibl. 38

Whartenby and Bumm
(c. 1816–1818)
Philadelphia, Pa.
Thomas Whartenby
Peter Bumm
Bibl. 3, 36, 39, 44, 91, 122

James Whartenby
(c. 1847–1848)
Philadelphia, Pa.
Bibl. 3, 23

John Whartenby
(c. 1829–1835)
Philadelphia, Pa.
Bibl. 3, 4, 23, 28, 36, 44

Thomas Whartenby
(c. 1811–1850)
Philadelphia, Pa.
Whartenby & Bumm
(c. 1816–1818)
Thomas Whartenby & Co.
(c. 1847–1850)
*Bibl. 3, 4, 23, 24, 25, 28, 29,
44, 54, 91, 102, 114, 122*

| T.W | TW |
| WHARTENBY |

Thomas Whartenby & Co.
(c. 1847–1850)
Philadelphia, Pa.
Bibl. 3, 4, 23, 28, 44, 91, 114

William Whartenby
   (c. 1844)
Philadelphia, Pa.
Bibl. 3, 23

Eli Whatley (c. 1849–1855)
Chicago, Ill.
Sherwood & Whatley
Bibl. 98

Frederick G. Wheatley
   (c. 1805–1824)
New York, N.Y.
Fourniquet & Wheatley
   (c. 1815)
Bibl. 15, 23, 36, 44, 124, 138

Benjamin Wheaton
   (c. 1835)
Philadelphia, Pa.
Bibl. 3

Calvin (Caleb) Wheaton
   (b. 1764)
Providence, R.I.
   (c. 1784–1827)
*Bibl. 23, 24, 25, 28, 29, 36,
   56, 91, 110, 114*

Joseph Whedbee
   (c. 1771–1779)
Edenton, N.C.
Bibl. 21

I. Wheeler (Wheelen)
   (c. 1810)
Location unknown
Bibl. 15, 24, 44

Wheeler(s) & Brooks
   (c. 1830)
Livonia, N.Y.
*Bibl. 15, 25, 44, 91, 92, 114,
   124*

WHEELERS & BROOKS

Wheeler, Brooks & Co.
   (c. 1835)

Livonia, N.Y.
Bibl. 20, 124

A. Elliot Wheeler (1875)
Winthrop, Me.
Bibl. 105

Ralph Wheeler (c. 1838)
Hudson, N.Y.
Bibl. 20, 124

Richard C. Wheeler
   (c. 1800–1831)
Savannah, Ga.
Bibl. 17

Samuel Wheeler Jr.
   (c. 1844)
Rochester, N.Y.
Bibl. 20, 124

Selden Wheeler (1875)
Canaan, Me.
Bibl. 105

Wheelers & Brooks
(See Wheeler & Brooks)

Franklin A. Whelan
   (c. 1885–1926)
Mt. Vernon, Va.
Bibl. 130

Samuel H. Wheritt
   (c. 1860)
Richmond, Ky.
Bibl. 54, 93

Whetcroft & Higginson
   (c. 1774)
Annapolis, Md.
William Whetcroft
Samuel Higginson
Bibl. 38

William Whetcroft
   (b. 1735–d. 1799)
Annapolis, Md.
   (c. 1766–1769)   W W
Baltimore, Md.
Whetcroft & Higginson
   (c. 1774)
*Bibl. 24, 25, 28, 29, 38, 44,
   114*

William G. Whilden
   (c. 1855)
Charleston, S.C.

Hayden & Whilden
   (c. 1855–1863) (?)
Bibl. 54

Arnold Whipple
   (b. 1788–d. 1848)
Providence, R.I. (c. 1825)
Bibl. 28, 44, 110

Whit(t)aker & Green(e)
   (c. 1825)
Providence, R.I.
Bibl. 23, 28, 36, 44

John Whitaker
   (c. 1814–1822)
Philadelphia, Pa.
Bibl. 3, 91

White
(See also Porter & White,
   White & William Matlack)

White & Cooke
(See Cooke & White)

Alfred White
   (c. 1807–1809)
Boston, Mass.
Philadelphia, Pa.
Bibl. 3, 23, 36, 44

Alphine White (c. 1805)
Philadelphia, Pa.
Bibl. 3

Amos White
   (b. 1745–d. 1825)
East Haddam, Conn.
Meriden, Conn.
Maryland
*Bibl. 16, 23, 24, 25, 28, 29,
   36, 44, 54, 91, 92, 110,
   114*

WHITE | A WHITE

Andrew White
   (c. 1817–1833)
Lynchburg, Va.
   (c. 1817–1818)
Petersburg, Va.
   (after 1818–c. 1833)
Norfolk, Va. (c. 1829–1833)
Marshall & White
   (c. 1817–?)
Cooke & White (c. 1833)
Bibl. 15, 19, 25, 72, 91

Charles White
(c. 1825–1840)
Mobile, Ala.
Bibl. 15, 25, 72, 114, 143,
148

| C WHITE MOBILE |

| C WHITE |

E. White (1875)
Union, Me.
Bibl. 105

Edward White (c. 1757)
Ulster County, N.Y.
Bibl. 23, 24, 25, 28, 29, 44,
114, 124

| E: WHITE | | E W |

Francis White (c. 1849)
Philadelphia, Pa.
Bibl. 3

G. W. White
(c. 1828–1830)
Northampton, Mass.
Phelps & White
Bibl. 84

George L. (A.) White
(1827–1843)
Cincinnati, Ohio
Woodruff & White (c. 1829)
Bibl. 23, 34, 36, 54, 90, 91,
133, 152

H. White & Son
(c. 1818–1822)
Fredericksburg, Va.
Henry White
William H. White
Bibl. 19

H. M. White (1860)
Frankfort, Me.
Bibl. 105

Henry White (d. 1827)
Fredericksburg, Va. (c. 1788)
H. White & Son
(c. 1818–1822)
Bibl. 19

| H. W | | H. WHITE |

J. White & Co.
(c. 1830–1831)
Athens, Ga.
Joel White
Bibl. 17

Joel White (c. 1830–1831)
Athens, Ga.
J. White & Co.
(c. 1830–1831)
B. B. Lord & Co.
(c. 1830–1839)
Bibl. 17

Joseph White
(c. 1808–1818)
Philadelphia, Pa.
Bibl. 3

Moses White (c. 1811)
Buffalo, N.Y.
Bibl. 20, 124

Peregrine White
(b. 1747–d. 1834)
Woodstock, Conn.
Bibl. 16, 23, 24, 25, 28, 29,
36, 41, 44, 61, 91, 92, 94,
110, 114, 143

| P WHITE |

Peter White
(b. 1718–d. 1803)
Norwalk, Conn.
Bibl. 16, 23, 28, 36, 44, 110

| P. WHITE |

Peter White (c. 1832)
Louisville, Ky.
Bibl. 32, 54, 68, 93

Philo White
(c. 1843–1844)
Utica, N.Y.
Bibl. 18, 20, 124, 158

S. White
Delaware (?)
Bibl. 30

| S. WHITE | | S W |

S. White & Co. (c. 1830)
New York, N.Y.

Samuel White
Bibl. 15, 44, 91, 114, 124,
138

Samuel White (d. 1833)
New York, N.Y.
(c. 1805–1833)
S. White & Co. (c. 1830)
Bibl. 15, 23, 36, 44, 91, 124,
138

Sebastian White
(c. 1795–1796)
Philadelphia, Pa.
Bibl. 3

Silas White
(b. 1754–d. 1798)
New York, N.Y.
(c. 1791–1798)
Bibl. 23, 24, 25, 29, 35, 36,
54, 83, 124, 138

| S W | | S | | W |
| S WHITE |

Stephen White
(c. 1805–1815)
New York, N.Y.
Bibl. 15, 23, 36, 124, 138

T. P. White (1860)
Union, Me.
Bibl. 105

Thomas White (c. 1810)
Philadelphia, Pa.
Bibl. 3

Thomas Sturt White
(c. 1734)
Boston, Mass.
Bibl. 28

William H. White
(d. 1859)
Philadelphia, Pa.
(c. 1835–1837)
Fredericksburg, Va.
(c. 1836–1838)
H. White & Son
(c. 1818–1822)
William H. White & Co.
(c. 1835–1837)

B. H. Smith & Co.
(c. 1836–1838)
Bibl. 19

William H. White & Co.
Philadelphia, Pa.
(c. 1835–1837)
William H. White
Benjamin H. Smith
Bibl. 19

William J. White
(c. 1833–1838)
New York, N.Y.
Bibl. 15, 23, 36, 44, 124, 138

William Wilson White
New York, N.Y.
(c. 1827–1841)
Philadelphia, Pa.
(c. 1805–1806)
Bibl. 3, 15, 23, 24, 25, 29, 36, 44, 54, 91, 114, 124, 138

W. W. WHITE

WM. W. WHITE

John Whitehead
(b. 1791–d. 1875)
Haddenfield, N.J.
(c. 1821–1830)
Bibl. 46, 54

John Whitehead
(c. 1848–1849)
Philadelphia, Pa.
Bibl. 3

William W. Whitehead
(c. 1850)
Philadelphia, Pa.
Bibl. 3

Ira Whiteman
(c. 1761, b. 1740)
New York, N.Y.
Bibl. 23, 36, 44, 124

Nelson Whiteside
(c. 1832)
Wheeling, Va.
Bibl. 19

Samuel Whiteside
(c. 1802)
Staunton, Va.
Bibl. 19

Samuel H. Whiteside
(d. 1851)
Cincinnati, Ohio
(1819–1831)
Bibl. 34, 90, 152

Whiting & Davis Co., Inc.
(c. 1876–present)
Plainville, Mass.
Bibl. 114, 127, 135, 157

 **W. & D.**

Whiting & Marquand
(c. 1787)
Fairfield, Conn.
Bradford Whiting
Isaac Marquand
Bibl. 89, 110

Whiting Manufacturing Company (1866–present)
North Attleboro, Mass.
(1866–1910)
Bridgeport, Conn.
(1910–1926)
Providence, R.I.
(1926–present)
Successor to Tifft & Whitney
(1840)
Whiting, Fessenden & Cowan (c. 1858)
Became division of Gorham
Company (1926)
Bibl. 115, 120, 127, 147, 152, 157

Bradford Whiting
(b. 1751)
Norwich, Conn. (c. 1800)
Whiting & Marquand
Bibl. 15, 23, 25, 29, 36, 44, 92, 94, 110, 114

B: WHITING

Captain Charles Whiting
(b. 1725–d. 1765)
Norwich, Conn.
Potwine & Whiting
Bibl. 15, 16, 17, 23, 24, 25, 28, 29, 36, 44, 54, 61, 92, 94, 104, 110, 114

C W   WHITING   C W

Ebenezer Whiting
(b. 1735–d. 1794)
Savannah, Ga.
(c. 1786–1788)
Bibl. 17, 110

E Whiting

Frank M. Whiting & Co.
(1896–1940)
North Attleboro, Mass.
Successor to Holbrook,
Whiting & Albee
(c. 1878)
F. M. Whiting & Co.
(1878–1891)
F. M. Whiting (1891–1895)
Frank M. Whiting Co.
(1895–1896)
Became division of Ellmore
Silver Co. (c. 1940–1960)
Bibl. 114, 120, 127, 135, 147, 157

S. Whiting (c. 1700)
Norwich, Conn.
New York, N.Y.
Bibl. 23, 36, 44, 92, 110

Spencer Whiting
Rhinebeck, N.Y. (c. 1816)
Hudson, N.Y.
(c. 1819–1820)
Waterford, N.Y. (c. 1824)
Bibl. 20, 124

William Bradford Whiting
(c. 1788)
Savannah, Ga.
Bibl. 89

Frederick A. Whitlock
Augusta, Ga.
Woodstock & Whitlock
(c. 1850–1851)
Bibl. 17

Thomas B. Whitlock
(c. 1796–1805)
New York, N.Y.
*Bibl. 23, 24, 25, 28, 29, 36,
44, 114, 124, 138*

William H. Whitlock
(c. 1805–1827)
New York, N.Y.
*Bibl. 15, 23, 24, 25, 29, 36,
44, 91, 114, 124, 138*

Whitnery (c. 1846)
New York, N.Y.
Bibl. 89

Whitney
(See Tappan & Whitney)

Whitney & Hoyt
(c. 1827–1836)
New York, N.Y.
*Bibl. 15, 23, 24, 25, 29, 36,
44, 91, 114, 124, 138*

Whitney & Osgood (1890)
Lewiston, Me.
Bibl. 105

Amos Whitney
(c. 1800–1810)
New York, N.Y.
*Bibl. 15, 23, 24, 25, 35, 36,
44, 83, 114, 124*

E. A. Whitney Company
(1894–1911)
Boston, Mass.
Successor to Whitney
Brothers (c. 1882)
Whitney Jewelry Co.
(c. 1883–1894)
Bibl. 127, 135

Eben (W.) Whitney
(c. 1805–1828)
New York, N.Y.
*Bibl. 15, 23, 24, 25, 29, 36,
44, 91, 114, 124, 138*

Edward T. Whitney
(c. 1847)
Rochester, N.Y.
Bibl. 20, 124

F. G. Whitney & Co.
(c. 1881)
Attleboro, Mass.
Bibl. 127

Henry Whitney
(c. 1793–1798)
Lansingburgh, N.Y.
Smith & Whitney
(c. 1787–1793)
Rochwell, Smith & Whitney
(c. 1788–1789)
Bibl. 20, 91, 124

John Whitney
(c. 1839–1845)
Albany, N.Y.
Bibl. 20, 124

Lemuel Whitney
(b. 1764–d. 1847)
Newfane, Vt. (c. 1785–1790)
Brattleboro, Vt.
(c. 1790–1847)
Bibl. 54, 110

Leonard Whitney
(c. 1841–1842)
Philadelphia, Pa.
Bibl. 3

M. F. Whitney
(c. 1823–1824)
Schenectady, N.Y.
New York, N.Y. (c. 1826)
*Bibl. 15, 20, 25, 28, 29, 44,
114, 124, 138*

William H. Whitney
New York, N.Y. (c. 1838)
Rochester, N.Y. (c. 1845)
Binghamton, N.Y.
Bibl. 20, 124, 138

Ezza (Ebed) Whiton
(b. 1813–d. 1879)
Boston, Mass.
*Bibl. 4, 15, 23, 24, 25, 28,
29, 36, 44, 91, 110, 114*

Whittaker & Green
(See Whitaker & Green(e))

—— **Whitteker**
Charleston, Va.
Anderson & Whitteker
(c. 1831–1835)
Bibl. 19

Edward Whittemore
(d. 1772)
Boston, Mass.
Bibl. 28, 110

Edwin Whittemore
(1830–1867)
Natchez, Miss.
New Orleans, La.
Bibl. 141

William Whittemore
(b. 1710–d. 1770)
Portsmouth, N.H.
Kittery, Maine
*Bibl. 2, 13, 23, 25, 28, 29,
36, 91, 110, 114*

Whitten Brothers (1875)
Winterport, Me.
Bibl. 105

S. M. R. Whitten (1860)
Searsport, Me.
Bibl. 105

Samuel Whitten, Jr.
(1860)
Troy, Me.
Bibl. 105

L. M. B. Whitter (1861)
Searsport, Me.
Bibl. 105

John Whittier
(See H. G. Hudson)

Isaac Newton Whittlesey
(b. 1798–d. 1870)
Vincennes, Ind.
(c. 1819–1870)
Bibl. 28, 133

Daniel H. Wickham Jr.
(c. 1832–1841)
New York, N.Y.
Bibl. 15, 23, 36, 44, 124, 135

Widdifield & Gaw
(c. 1820–1822)
Philadelphia, Pa.
William Widdifield Jr.
William P. Gaw
Bibl. 3

William Widdifield
(c. 1817)
Philadelphia, Pa.
Bibl. 3

William Widdifield Jr.
Philadelphia, Pa.
(c. 1820–1822)
Fayetteville, N.C.
(c. 1820–1840)
Widdifield & Gaw
(c. 1820–1822)
Bibl. 21

Frederick W. Widman
(c. 1817–1848)
Philadelphia, Pa.
Bibl. 3

Henry P. Wiedemeyer
(c. 1830)
Lynchburg, Va.
Bibl. 19

J. M. Wiedemeyer
(c. 1800–1801)
Baltimore, Md.
Bibl. 38

Otto Wieders (1860)
Portland, Me.
Bibl. 105

Frederick Wieland
(c. 1848)
Philadelphia, Pa.
Bibl. 3

T. Wieland (c. 1835)
Philadelphia, Pa.
Bibl. 3

Henry Wiener & Son
(c. 1920)
New York, N.Y.
Bibl. 127   PICADILLY

Charles C. Wientge Co.
(c. 1891–1896)
Newark, N.J.
Bibl. 127, 157

Thomas Wiggins & Co.
(c. 1833)
Philadelphia, Pa.
Bibl. 3

William Wightman
(c. 1783–1825, d. 1835)
Charleston, S.C.
Bibl. 5, 44, 54

John Wilbank
(c. 1839–1841)
Philadelphia, Pa.
Bibl. 3

——— **Wilcke** (c. 1810)
Location unknown
Bibl. 28

Wilcox & Evertsen
(1892–1896)
New York, N.Y.
Successor to Rowan &
Wilcox

Became Meriden Britannia
Co. and moved to
Meriden, Conn. (1896)
Became International Silver
(1898)
Bibl. 114, 127, 157

Wilcox & Perkins
(c. 1818–1820)
Sparta, Ga.
Cyprian Wilcox
Leonard Perkins
Bibl. 17

Wilcox & Wagoner
(c. 1904)
New York, N.Y.
Bought by Watson Co.
(c. 1905)
Bibl. 127, 157

Wilcox-Roth Co. (c. 1909)
Newark, N.J.
Bibl. 127, 157

GEM SILVER CO.

Alanson D. Wilcox
(c. 1843–1850)
Albany, N.Y. (c. 1844)
Troy, N.Y. (c. 1847–1850)
Harris & Wilcox
Bibl. 20, 25, 44, 91, 114, 124

Alvan Wilcox (Willcox)
(b. 1783–d. 1870)
Norwich, Conn.
(1805–1807)
New Jersey
Fayetteville, N.C.
(c. 1819–1823)
New Haven, Conn.
(1824–1870)
Hart & Wilcox
(c. 1805–1807)
*Bibl. 16, 17, 21, 23, 28, 36,
44, 92, 110, 143*

Cyprian Wilcox (Willcox)
(b. 1795–d. 1875)
Sparta, Ga. (c. 1818–1821)
Berlin, Conn.
New Haven, Conn.
Wilcox & Perkins
(c. 1818–1820)
*Bibl. 15, 16, 17, 23, 25, 28,
36, 44, 92, 110, 114, 143*

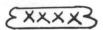

Michael Wilcox
(c. 1772–1799)
Dorchester County, Md.
Bibl. 29, 38, 44

L. H. Wilder & Co.
(c. 1845)
Philadelphia, Pa.
Bibl. 3

Wiley-Crawford Co., Inc.
(c. 1915–1922)
Newark, N.J.
Bibl. 127, 157

Samuel Wilham(s)
(c. 1795–1796)
Philadelphia, Pa.
Bibl. 3, 23, 28, 36

William Wilkings
(c. 1749–1751)
Charleston, S.C.
Bibl. 5

Wilkinson & Horah
(c. 1820–1821)
Salisbury, N.C.
Curtis Wilkinson
Hugh Horah
Bibl. 21

Curtis Wilkinson
(c. 1820–1823)
Salisbury, N.C.
Wilkinson & Horah
(c. 1820–1821)
Bibl. 21

E. Wilkinson (c. 1840)
Mansfield, Ohio
Bibl. 34

Wilson Wilkinson
(c. 1840)
Mansfield, Ohio
Bibl. 34

Willard
(See Willard & Stokes)

Willard & Hawley
(c. 1844–1851)
Syracuse, N.Y.
William W. Willard
John Dean Hawley
Bibl. 15, 20, 44, 91, 114, 124

Willard & Stokes (c. 1833)
Cazenovia, N.Y.
William W. Willard
T. Stokes
Bibl. 20, 124

A. Willard (c. 1810)
Utica, N.Y.
Bibl. 24, 25, 91, 114, 124

B. Willard (c. 1838)
Schenectady, N.Y.
Bibl. 20, 124

H. Willard (c. 1818)
Catskill, N.Y.
Bibl. 20, 124

James Willard (c. 1815)
East Windsor, Conn.
Bibl. 24, 25, 44, 92, 110, 114

William W. Willard
Cazenovia, N.Y.
(c. 1833–1834)
Syracuse, N.Y.
(c. 1841–1844)
Willard & Stokes (c. 1833)
Willard & Hawley
(c. 1844–1851)
Bibl. 20, 91, 124

Willcox
(See Alvan Wilcox, Cyprian
Wilcox)

Curtis R. Willett
(c. 1799–1820)
Savannah, Ga.
Bibl. 17

Willey
(See Scovil, Willey & Co.)

Willey & Blakesley
(c. 1830–1835)
Cincinnati, Ohio
Bibl. 54, 90, 114

Willey & Co. (c. 1836)
Cincinnati, Ohio
Bushnell Willey
Bibl. 54, 90

Bushnell Willey
(b. 1806–d. 1855)
Cincinnati, Ohio (c. 1836)
Willey & Co.
Bibl. 29, 44, 54, 90, 93, 114

George William
(c. 1843–1848)
Philadelphia, Pa.
Bibl. 3

Williams & Son
Lynchburg, Va.
Jehu Williams Sr.
Bibl. 19

Williams & Victor
(c. 1814–1845)
Lynchburg, Va.
Jehu Williams Sr.
John Victor
Bibl. 19, 54

———— **Williams**
Winchester, Va.
Bibl. 19

A. & R. Williams (c. 1812)
Philadelphia, Pa.
Bibl. 3

A. B. Williams (c. 1855)
Nashville, Tenn.
Bibl. 54

Alexander Williams
(c. 1807–1813)
Philadelphia, Pa.
Bibl. 3, 23, 36, 44

Andrew Williams
Location unknown
Bibl. 28

| ANDREW WILLIAMS |

Benjamin Williams
(c. 1788–1794)
Elizabeth, N.J.
New Brunswick, N.J.
Trenton, N.J.
Bibl. 46, 54

C. C. Williams
(1860–1875)
Bangor, Me.
Bibl. 105

Charles Williams
(c. 1827)
New York, N.Y.
Bibl. 15, 124, 138

Charles M. Williams
(c. 1837)
New York, N.Y.
Monell & Williams (c. 1825)
Bibl. 15, 23, 44

Deodat Williams (d. 1781)
Hartford, Conn. (c. 1776)
Bibl. 16, 23, 28, 36, 91, 92,
102, 110

E. Williams (c. 1829–1830)
Augusta, Ga.
Bibl. 17

George Williams
(c. 1847–1867)
Aurora, Ind.
Louisville, Ky.
Seymore, Ind.
Bibl. 133

WILLIAMS

Henry Williams (c. 1804)
Philadelphia, Pa.
Bibl. 3

J. Williams (c. 1795)
Alexandria, Va.
Philadelphia, Pa. (?)
Bibl. 15, 19, 91

Jehu Williams Sr.
(b. 1788–d. 1859)
Lynchburg, Va.
Williams & Victor
(c. 1814–1845)
Williams & Son
Bibl. 19, 54

| J WILLIAMS | William |

John Williams (c. 1793)
Philadelphia, Pa.
Bibl. 44, 114

John Williams (c. 1818)
Philadelphia, Pa.
Bibl. 3, 23, 25, 36

John Williams (c. 1836)
New York, N.Y.
Bibl. 15, 124, 138

John Williams
(c. 1858–c. 1860)
Utica, N.Y.
Bibl. 18, 124, 158

Joseph Williams (c. 1816)
Philadelphia, Pa.
Bibl. 3

Margery & Mary Williams
(c. 1823–1824)
Philadelphia, Pa.
Bibl. 3

Nicholas Williams
(c. 1792)
Liberty Town, Md.
Bibl. 38

Oliver S. Williams
(c. 1850)

Hartford, Conn.
Bibl. 23

Roger Williams Silver Co.
(c. 1900–1903)
Providence, R.I.
Successor to Howard Sterling
Silver Co.
Merged Mauser Mfg. Co.
and Hayes & McFarland to
form Mt. Vernon
Company Silversmiths,
Inc., which became
Gorham Corporation
(1913 ?)
Bibl. 127, 157

    R & W

Stephen Williams
(d. 1811)
Providence, R.I. (c. 1799)
Bibl. 23, 25, 28, 36, 44, 56,
91, 110, 114

| S. WILLIAMS |

W. H. Williams
(c. 1839–1844)
Hamilton, N.Y.
Bibl. 20, 124

W. W. Williams (c. 1829)
Alexandria, Va.
Bibl. 23, 36

William A. Williams
(b. 1787–d. 1846)
Alexandria, Va.
(c. 1809–1835)
Washington, D.C. (c. 1829)
Bibl. 19, 24, 25, 29, 36, 44,
54, 78, 91, 102, 114

| W. A. WILLIAMS |

Henry Williamson
(c. 1808)
Baltimore, Md.
Bibl. 38

Samuel Williamson
(b. 1772–d. 1843)
Philadelphia, Pa.
(c. 1794–1813)
Simmons & Williamson

(c. 1797–1798) (?)
Richards & Williamson
   (c. 1797–1800)
*Bibl. 2, 3, 15, 23, 24, 25, 29,
   36, 39, 44, 54, 72, 81, 91,
   95, 102, 116, 118, 139*

George Willig Jr.
   (c. 1819–1822)
Philadelphia, Pa.
Rasch & Willig (c. 1819)
Bibl. 3, 4, 23, 28, 36

Andrew Willis (c. 1842)
Boston, Mass.
Bibl. 15, 25, 44, 114

| Andrew Willis |

| Oppo. Old South |

J. Willis (c. 1820)
Boston, Mass.
Bibl. 23, 36, 44, 110

Stillman Willis
   (c. 1813–1825)
Boston, Mass.
*Bibl. 15, 23, 24, 25, 28, 29,
   36, 44, 94, 110, 114*

| S. Willis |

William S. Willis (c. 1830)
Boston, Mass.
Bibl. 24, 25, 91, 114

| Wm. S. Willis |

| Oppo. Old South |

Othniel Williston
   (1816–1820)
Cincinnati, Ohio
Bibl. 34, 90, 152

Seymour Williston
(See Seymour & Williston)

Benjamin Willmott
   (c. 1797–1816)
Easton, Md.
Bibl. 38

James Willock
   (b. 1793, c. 1811)
Baltimore, Md.
Bibl. 38

Henry Wills (c. 1774)
New York, N.Y.
Bibl. 23, 36, 44, 124

Joseph Wills
   (c. 1753, d. 1759)
Philadelphia, Pa.
Bibl. 3

J. Wilmer (c. 1849)
Philadelphia, Pa.
Bibl. 3

Wilmort Mfg. Co.
   (c. 1920–1930)
Chicago, Ill.
Bibl. 127   Wilmort

Wilmot & Richmond
Charleston, S.C.
Samuel Wilmot
——— Richmond
Bibl. 25

**Wilmot & Stillman
(Silliman)**
   (c. 1800–1808)
New Haven, Conn.
Samuel Wilmot
Benjamin Stillman (Silliman)
*Bibl. 16, 23, 28, 36, 44, 91,
   110, 143*

Samuel Wilmot
   (b. 1777–d. 1846)
New Haven, Conn.
   (c. 1800–1808)
Georgetown, S.C. (c. 1825)
Charleston, S.C. (c. 1837)
Wilmot & Stillman
   (Silliman) (c. 1800–1808)
Wilmot & Richmond
*Bibl. 5, 15, 16, 17, 23, 24,
   25, 28, 29, 36, 54, 61, 91,
   92, 94, 110, 114, 143*

| WILMOT |

| S. WILMOT |

**Samuel & Thomas T.
   Wilmot** (c. 1837–1841)
Charleston, S.C.
Bibl. 25, 114

| S. & T. T. WILMOT |

T. T. Wilmot (c. 1810)
New Haven, Conn.
Bibl. 23, 24, 29, 36, 143

| T. T. WILMOT |

Thomas Wilmot
   (b. 1774–d. 1813)
Rutland, Vt. (c. 1796–1800)
Fairhaven, Vt.
   (c. 1801–1813)
Storer & Wilmot
   (c. 1796–1800)
Bibl. 54, 110

Thomas T. Wilmot
Charleston, S.C.
   (c. 1837–1838)
Savannah, Ga. (1843–1850)
Columbus, Ga. (c. 1844)
Bibl. 5, 17, 25, 44, 91

| T T WILMOT |

Wilson
(See Leonard & Wilson)

Wilson & Toy
(See Toy & Wilson)

Albert Wilson
   (c. 1833–1850)
Albany, N.Y. (c. 1834)
Troy, N.Y.
*Bibl. 4, 20, 23, 28, 36, 44,
   124*

Alfred V. Wilson (c. 1842)
St. Louis, Mo.
Bibl. 54, 155

Andrew Wilson
   (c. 1844–1847)
Philadelphia, Pa.
Bibl. 3

D. W. Wilson
York, S.C.
J. N. Lewis & Co.
   (c. 1854–1856)
Bennet, Wilson & Co.
   (c. 1856)
Bibl. 5, 25

E. P. H. Wilson (1875)
Monmouth, Me.
Bibl. 105

Edwin Franklin Wilson
(b. 1813–d. 1904)
Rochester, N.Y. (c. 1838)
Bibl. 20, 41, 44, 91, 124

George Wilson
(c. 1848–1850)
Philadelphia, Pa.
Bibl. 3, 4, 23, 28, 44, 91, 112

Hosea Wilson
Philadelphia, Pa. (c. 1812)
Baltimore, Md.
(c. 1814–1819)
Hosea Wilson & Co.
(c. 1814–1816)
Bibl. 15, 23, 24, 25, 28, 29, 38, 44, 114

Hosea Wilson & Co.
(c. 1814–1816)
Baltimore, Md.
Bibl. 15, 24, 29, 38, 44, 114

J. Wilson (b. 1804–d. 1889)
Lexington, Ky.
(c. 1838–1839)
Bibl. 32, 54, 93

James Wilson
(b. 1745, c. 1768)
Trenton, N.J.
Bibl. 3, 23, 36, 44, 46, 54

James Wilson
(c. 1802–1818)
Poughkeepsie, N.Y.
Storm & Wilson
Bibl. 20, 91, 95, 124

John Wilson
(c. 1770, d. 1787)
Philadelphia, Pa.
Bibl. 3, 23, 36

John Wilson
(c. 1784–1791, d. 1795)
Richmond, Va.
Bibl. 19

P. G. Wilson (c. 1840)
Philadelphia, Pa.
Bibl. 3

Robert Wilson (d. 1846)
New York, N.Y. (c. 1805)
Philadelphia, Pa.
(c. 1814–1846)
Robert & William Wilson
(c. 1825–1846)
Bibl. 3, 4, 15, 24, 25, 28, 29, 36, 91, 95, 114, 124, 138, 151

R·W

Robert & William Wilson
(c. 1825–1846)
Philadelphia, Pa.
Bibl. 3, 4, 15, 23, 24, 28, 29, 36, 39, 44, 54, 72, 91, 95, 114, 116, 122, 151

R & W. WILSON

R & W. W

S. Wilson (c. 1805)
Philadelphia, Pa.
Bibl. 23, 36, 44

S. N. Wilson (c. 1800)
Connecticut
Bibl. 28

S. N. WILSON

S. & S. Wilson (c. 1805)
Philadelphia, Pa.
Bibl. 24, 25, 29, 36, 72, 114

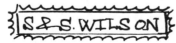

Thomas Wilson
(c. 1837–1839)
Philadelphia, Pa.
Bibl. 3, 23, 36, 44

William Wilson
(b. 1755–d. 1829)
Abingdon, Md.
(c. 1781–1829)
Toy & Wilson (c. 1790)
Bibl. 38, 114

W W

William Wilson
(c. 1829–1850)
Philadelphia, Pa.
Robert & William Wilson
(c. 1825–1846)
Bibl. 3, 4, 23, 28, 36, 91, 95, 151

William A. Wilson
(1856–1861)
New Orleans, La.
Bibl. 141

William Rowan Wilson
(b. 1821–d. 1866)
Salisbury, N.C.
Boger & Wilson
(c. 1846–1853)
Bibl. 21

Wm. Wilson & Son
(c. 1883–1909)
Philadelphia, Pa.
Bibl. 104, 114, 127, 157

WM. WILSON & SON

Wiltberger & Alexander
(c. 1797–1808)
Philadelphia, Pa.
Christian Wiltberger
Samuel Alexander
Bibl. 3, 23, 25, 36, 44, 91

Christian Wiltburger
(Wiltberger) (Jr.)
(b. 1766–d. 1851)
Philadelphia, Pa.
(c. 1793–1819)
Wiltberger & Alexander
Bibl. 3, 4, 15, 24, 25, 28, 29, 36, 54, 72, 91, 95, 114, 122

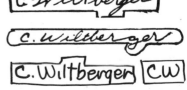

Frances Wilte (c. 1839)
St. Louis, Mo.
Bibl. 54

Andrew Wimer
(c. 1818–1819)
Philadelphia, Pa.
Bibl. 3

V. Winchell
Location unknown
Bibl. 15, 44, 114

V. Winchell

Daniel F. Winchester
Lexington, Ky.
Garner & Winchester
(c. 1842–1862)
Louisville, Ky. (c. 1841)
Bibl. 32, 54, 95, 104

James Edwin Winckler
(b. 1824–d. 1910)
Charleston, S.C.
(c. 1761–1763)
Mecklenburg County, Va.
(c. 1778–1801)
Bibl. 19

John Winckler
(b. 1730–d. 1803)
Charleston, S.C.
(c. 1761–1763)
Mecklenburg County, Va.
(c. 1778–1801)
Bibl. 5, 19, 54

John Winckler Jr.
(b. 1775–d. 1854)
Mecklenburg County, Va.
Bibl. 19

Jan Windeford
(See John Wendover)

John Windover
(See John Wendover)

Windsor Silver Co., Inc.
(c. 1966–1973)
Brooklyn, N.Y.
Bibl. 127

Rodney M. Winfield
(1945–present)
St. Louis, Mo.
Bibl. 155

Moses Wing
(b. 1760–d. 1809)
Windsor Locks, Conn.
Worcester, Mass.
Bibl. 15, 25, 44, 92, 110, 114

M WING

S. Wing & Co.
(c. 1850–1851)
Utica, N.Y.
Stephen Wing
Bibl. 18, 20, 124, 158

Stephen Wing
(b. 1828, c. 1845)
Utica, N.Y.
S. Wing & Co.
(c. 1850–1851)
Bibl. 18, 20, 124, 158

C. W. Wingate (1860)
Waterville, Md.
Bibl. 105

George W. Wingate
(c. 1816)
Baltimore, Md.
Bibl. 38

James H. Winn
(1895–1927)
Chicago, Ill.
Bibl. 98

Winship
(See Burwell & Winship)

Edward Winslow
(b. 1669–d. 1753)
Boston, Mass.
*Bibl. 2, 15, 23, 24, 25, 28,
29, 36, 39, 44, 54, 55, 69,
70, 91, 94, 102, 104, 110,
114, 116, 119, 139, 142,
151*

Isaac Winslow
(c. 1847–1848)
Philadelphia, Pa.
Bibl. 3

Winson
(See Wenzell)

William Winsor
(b. 1723, c. 1759)
Boston, Mass.
Bibl. 23, 36, 44, 110

Harry Winston
(1945–present)
New York, N.Y. & various
other cities
Bibl. 117

Stephen Winter (c. 1740)
Boston, Mass.
Bibl. 70, 110

Stephen Winter
(b. 1753, c. 1774)
Maryland
Bibl. 38

Isaac Winters
(c. 1844–1848)
Philadelphia, Pa.
Bibl. 3

Winthrop
(See Friedman Silver Co.,
Inc.)

Winzel
(See Wenzell)

Mary Wirlock (1901–1927)
Boston, Mass.
Bibl. 89

John Wirt (c. 1818)
Lexington, Ky.
Bibl. 32, 54, 93

William Wirth
(c. 1839–1845)
St. Louis, Mo.
Bibl. 54, 155

George K. Wise
(c. 1842–1850)
Philadelphia, Pa.
Butler, Wise & Keim
(c. 1850)
Dunlevy & Wise
(c. 1847–1850) (?)
Bibl. 3, 23

William M. Wise & Sons
(1890–1899)
Brooklyn, N.Y.
Bibl. 28, 91, 114, 124

Alexander Wishart
(c. 1808–1810)
New York, N.Y.
Bibl. 23, 44, 124, 138

B. Wishart (c. 1839–1840)
Philadelphia, Pa.
Bibl. 3

Daniel Wishart (c. 1825)
New York, N.Y.
Bibl. 23, 36, 44, 124, 138

Hugh Wishart
(c. 1784–1819)
New York, N.Y.
*Bibl. 4, 23, 24, 25, 29, 30,
35, 36, 44, 54, 91, 95, 104,
114, 116, 122, 124, 138*

H WISHART

WISHART

William Wishart (c. 1800)
New York, N.Y.
Bibl. 23, 36, 44, 124

Witch
(See Daniel Low & Co.)

Witham & Newman
(c. 1837–1850)
Philadelphia, Pa.
———— Witham
John A. Newman
Bibl. 3

A. Witham (c. 1828–1831)
Philadelphia, Pa.
Bibl. 3

Ebenezer Witham
(c. 1833–1850)
Philadelphia, Pa.
Bibl. 3

William Witham
(c. 1846–1850)
Philadelphia, Pa.
Bibl. 3

James Withers
(b. 1753–d. 1778)
Maryland (c. 1774)
Bibl. 28, 38

M. P. C. Withers
(1860–1875)
Bangor, Me.
Bibl. 105

Daniel Withington
(c. 1840)
Ashland, Ohio
Bibl. 34

James Withington
(c. 1823–1824)
Philadelphia, Pa.
Bibl. 3

Marlin A. Withington
(c. 1830)
Massillon, Ohio
Bibl. 34

Samuel Withington
(c. 1820–1841)
Philadelphia, Pa.
Bibl. 3

Hollis Witt (1860)
S. Berwick, Me.
Bibl. 105

Wittich & Beaver
(c. 1793)
Augusta, Ga.
John Wittich
Mathias Beaver
Bibl. 17

**Charles & Frederick
Wittich** (c. 1802–1807)
Charleston, S.C.
Bibl. 5, 25, 44, 54, 114

C F WITTICH

**Christian Charles Lewis
Wittich** (c. 1785–1804)
Charleston, S.C.
Charles & Frederick Wittich
(c. 1802–1807)
Bibl. 5, 54

C W

Frederick Wittich
(c. 1802–1807)
Charleston, S.C.
Charles & Frederick Wittich
(c. 1802–1807)
Bibl. 89

John Wittich
(c. 1791–c. 1793)
Augusta, Ga.
Wittich & Beaver (c. 1793)
Bibl. 17

Miguel Wodom
(1788–1790)
New Orleans, La.
Bibl. 141

Wolcott & Gelston
(See Walcott & Gelston)

Henry D. Wolcott
(See Henry D. Walcott)

S. B. Wolcott (c. 1840)
Massachusetts (?)
Bibl. 15, 44, 114

S.B WOLCOTT

S.B. WOLCOTT

Wolf & Knell
(c. 1900)
New York, N.Y.
Bibl. 127

Wolf(e) & Wriggins
(c. 1837)
Philadelphia, Pa.
*Bibl. 3, 23, 24, 25, 29, 36,
44, 114*

WOLFE & WRIGGINS

Francis H. Wolf(e)
(c. 1829–1849)
Philadelphia, Pa.
*Bibl. 3, 23, 24, 25, 36, 44,
114*

F. H. WOLFE

General James Wolf
Wilmington, Del (c. 1822)
Philadelphia, Pa.
  (c. 1830–1833)
*Bibl. 3, 15, 23, 25, 30, 36,
  89, 91, 114*

G. J. WOLF / I. WOLF

I. Wolf (c. 1828–1833)
Philadelphia, Pa.
Bibl. 15, 44, 114

I. WOLF

J. Wolf(f)
  (b. 1775, c. 1828–1833)
Philadelphia, Pa.
Bibl. 3

I. WOLFF

George Wolfe
  (c. 1870–1895)
Louisville, Ky.
Bibl. 54

**Wolfenden Silver
  Company** (1919–present)
North Attleboro, Mass.
Successor to J. W.
  Wolfenden Corp.
Now division of Crown
  Silver Inc.
Moved to New York (1955)
Bibl. 127

Beatrice S. Wolff
  (1939–1950)
St. Louis, Mo.
Bibl. 155

George Woltz
  (c. 1775?–1813, d. 1813)
Hagerstown, Md.
Bibl. 38

John Woltz (c. 1811–1814)
Shepherdstown, Va.
Bibl. 19   I. B WOLTZ

Wood
(See Taylor, Lawrie & Wood,
  Van Ness, Wood & Co.)

Wood & Dodge
  (c. 1816–1817)
Philadelphia, Pa.

———— Wood
Daniel H. Dodge
Bibl. 3

Wood & Force
  (c. 1839–1841)
New York, N.Y.
———— Wood
Jabez W. Force
Bibl. 15, 124

Wood & Hudson (c. 1773)
Mt. Holly, N.J.
Bibl. 3

Wood & Hughes
  (1845–1899)
New York, N.Y.
Jacob Wood
Jasper W. Hughes
*Bibl. 4, 23, 24, 25, 28, 29,
  44, 91, 104, 114, 122, 124,
  127, 135, 138, 148, 157*

A. H. Wood
Location unknown
Bibl. 89

A. & W. Wood
  (c. 1850–1860)
New York, N.Y.
Bibl. 23, 24, 25, 44, 114, 138

A & W WOOD

Wood, Bicknell & Potter
  (c. 1890)
Providence, R. I.
Bibl. 89

Abraham C. Wood
  (c. 1822)
Newburgh, N.Y.
Bibl. 20, 95, 124, 135

Alfred Wood (c. 1800)
New England (?)
Bibl. 28, 29, 44

WOOD

Bazel Wood
  (c. 1823–1833)
Philadelphia, Pa.
Bibl. 3

Benjamin B. Wood
  (c. 1794–1846)
New York, N.Y.
Ebenezer Cole
  (c. 1818–1826)
*Bibl. 15, 23, 24, 25, 28, 29,
  36, 44, 54, 91, 114, 124,
  135, 138*

B.BWOOD

B.WOOD

Charles Wood
  (c. 1829–1830)
Philadelphia, Pa.
Bibl. 3

J. Charles Wood (c. 1849)
Charleston, S.C.
Spear & Co.
Bibl. 5, 91

J. E. Wood (c. 1845)
New York, N.Y.
(May be Jacob Wood)
*Bibl. 4, 15, 24, 25, 28, 29,
  44, 114, 124*

J. WOOD

J.E. WOOD

Jacob Wood
  (c. 1834–1841)
New York, N.Y.
Gale, Wood & Hughes
Wood & Hughes
*Bibl. 44, 91, 114, 124, 135,
  138*

J. WOOD

John Wood
  (d. 1761, c. 1734)
Philadelphia, Pa.
Bibl. 3

John Wood
  (c. 1762–1793)

Philadelphia, Pa.
Bibl. 3

John Wood
New York, N.Y. (c. 1770)
Schenectady, N.Y.
  (c. 1780–1792)
Bibl. 25, 44, 91, 95, 114,
  124, 135, 138

J Wood

Landais Wood
  (c. 1832–1834)
Utica, N.Y.
Bibl. 18, 20, 124, 138, 158

N. G. Wood & Sons
  (c. 1891–1922)
Boston, Mass.
Bibl. 127, 157

Sarah B. Dickinson Wood
(See Sarah B. Dickinson)

T. S. Wood (c. 1849)
Laurens, S.C.
Bibl. 5

Thomas Wood
  (c. 1837–1848)
Philadelphia, Pa.
Bibl. 3

William Wood (c. 1799)
Newport, R.I.
Bibl. 56, 110

William S. Wood
  (c. 1810–1815)
Skaneateles, N.Y.
Bibl. 20, 124, 135

Horace P. Woodbridge
  (c. 1842–1845)
St. Louis, Mo.
Shipp & Woodbridge
Bibl. 54, 155

Woodbury & Curtis
  (1858–1865)
Providence, R.I.
Bibl. 108

Woodbury, Dix & Hartwell (c. 1836)
Location unknown
Bibl. 28

WOODBURY, DIX & HARTWELL

Samuel Woodbury
  (1856–1860)
Providence, R.I.
Bibl. 108

Woodcock & Byrnes
  (c. 1793)
Wilmington, Del.
Bancroft Woodcock
Thomas Byrnes
Bibl. 25, 44, 91, 114

Bancroft Woodcock
  (b. 1732–d. 1817)
Wilmington, Del.
  (c. 1735–1820)
Woodcock & Byrnes
  (c. 1793)
Bibl. 3, 15, 23, 24, 25, 28,
  29, 30, 36, 39, 44, 54, 91,
  95, 102, 114

Isaac Woodcock
  (b. 1764–d. 1849)
Hagerstown, Md. (c. 1795)
Wilmington, Del.
Bibl. 15, 25, 30, 38, 44, 91,
  114

William Woodcock
  (c. 1819–1829)
Baltimore, Md.
Bibl. 38

Woodford & Kimball
  (c. 1850)
Dunkirk, N.Y.
Bibl. 20, 124

S. D. Woodhill (b. 1831)
Utica, N.Y.
  (c. 1852–1853)
Bibl. 18, 20, 124

Woodruff & Deterly
  (1817–1821)
Cincinnati, Ohio
Enos Woodruff
Jacob Deterly
Bibl. 54, 91

Woodruff & White
  (c. 1829)
Cincinnati, Ohio
Enos Woodruff
George L. White
Bibl. 23, 36, 44, 54

Enos Woodruff
  (1820–1834)
Cincinnati, Ohio
Woodruff & Deterly
  (1817–1821)
Woodruff & White
Bibl. 23, 34, 36, 44, 90, 91,
  93, 152

Ezra Woodruff (c. 1815)
Lexington, Ky.
L. & W. (E.) Woodruff
  (c. 1811–1815)
Bibl. 54, 93

Jesse Woodruff
  (b. 1744–d. 1797)
Bridgeton, N.J.
Bibl. 46, 54

L. Woodruff (c. 1843)
Cincinnati, Ohio
Bibl. 34, 152

L. & W. (E.) Woodruff
  (c. 1811–1815)
Lexington, Ky.
Ezra Woodruff
Bibl. 32, 68, 93

Woods & Chatellier
  (c. 1904–1922)
New York, N.Y.
Successor to Stephen Woods
Bibl. 127, 157

Freeman Woods
(b. 1766–d. 1834)
New York State
(c. 1791–1794)
New Bern, N.C.
(c. 1794–1827)
Bibl. 2, 15, 21, 23, 24, 25,
28, 29, 30, 35, 36, 44, 54,
95, 114, 124, 138

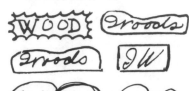

I. Woods (c. 1790)
Location unknown
Bibl. 15, 44, 114

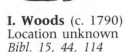

Richard M. Woods & Co.
(c. 1920–1940)
New York, N.Y.
Successor to Woodside
Sterling Company
Bibl. 127

Woodside Sterling Co.
(c. 1896–1920)
New York, N.Y.
Became Richard M. Woods
& Co.
Bibl. 127, 157

David Woodson (b. 1735)
Petersburg, Va. (c. 1766)
Salisbury, N.C.
(c. 1774–1807)
Bibl. 21

Richard Woodson
(c. 1736–1766)
Petersburg, Va.
Bibl. 19, 21

Woodstock & Whitlock
(c. 1850–1851)

Augusta, Ga.
William G. Woodstock
Frederick A. Whitlock
Bibl. 17

William G. Woodstock
(c. 1840–1853)
Augusta, Ga.
Woodstock & Whitlock
(c. 1850–1851)
Bibl. 17

Woodward
(See also Wakefield &
Woodward)

Woodward & Grosjean
(c. 1847–1852)
Boston, Mass.
Hartford, Conn. | W & G |
Eli Woodward
——— Grosjean
Bibl. 4, 15, 23, 24, 25, 28,
29, 44, 114

Antipas Woodward
(b. 1763–d. 1812)
Middletown, Conn.
Bibl. 16, 23, 24, 25, 28, 29,
36, 44, 92, 110, 114

| A W | | Woodward |

Charles Woodward
(c. 1825)
New York, N.Y.
Bibl. 23, 36, 44, 124, 138

Eli Woodward (c. 1812)
Boston, Mass.
Hartford, Conn.
Woodward & Grosjean
(c. 1847–1852)
Bibl. 23, 28, 36, 110

Thomas Woodward
(c. 1828)
New York, N.Y.
Bibl. 15, 124, 138

William Woodward
(b. 1700–d. 1774)
Annapolis, Md. (c. 1759)
Bibl. 38

E. Woodworth (c. 1800)
Location unknown

Bibl. 29, 44

Jeremiah Ward Wool
(b. 1769)
New York, N.Y. (c. 1791)
Bibl. 23, 25, 28, 36, 44, 95,
114, 124, 138

Wooldridge
(See Woolridge)

Charles Woolley
(c. 1848–1849)
Philadelphia, Pa.
Bibl. 3

James T. Woolley
(c. 1908)
Boston, Mass.
Bibl. 127

John W. Woolridge
(Wooldridge) (c. 1819)
Frankfort, Ky.
Bibl. 32, 54, 68

Woolworth & Anderson
(c. 1829–1830)
Greensboro, N.C.
Aaron Woolworth
——— Anderson
Bibl. 21

Aaron Woolworth
(b. 1801–d. 1856)
Salisbury, N.C.
(c. 1825–1826)
Greensboro, N.C. (c. 1829)
Woolworth & Anderson
(c. 1829–1830)
Bibl. 21

Charles Woolworth
(c. 1829)
Philadelphia, Pa.
Bibl. 3

Danforth Woolworth
(c. 1823–1824)
Philadelphia, Pa.
Bibl. 3

R. C. Woolworth
(c. 1816–1817)
Philadelphia, Pa.
Bibl. 3

R. C. Woolworth (c. 1835)
Philadelphia, Pa.
Bibl. 3

Richard Woolworth
(c. 1830–1839)
Philadelphia, Pa.
Bibl. 3

Worden-Munnis Co., Inc.
(1940–1964)
Boston, Mass.
Became Old Newbury
Crafters (1964)
Bibl. 127

**Wordley, Allsopp & Bliss
Co., Inc.** (c. 1915–1927)
Newark, N.J.
Became Allsopp & Allsopp
(c. 1927–1931)
Allsopp-Bliss
(c. 1927–1931)
Allsopp Bros.
(c. 1927–1931)
Allsopp-Bliss Co.
(c. 1931–1943)
Allsopp Bros.
(c. 1931–1943)
Allsopp-Steller, Inc.
(1943–1973)
Bibl. 127, 157

YAB

W. W. Wormwood
(c. 1850)
Lyons, N.Y.
Bibl. 20, 89, 124

W. W. WORMWOOD

James W. Worn
(c. 1849–1850)
Philadelphia, Pa.
Bibl. 3

Goodwin Worrell
(c. 1837–1849)
Philadelphia, Pa.
Bibl. 3

John Worrell (c. 1837)
Philadelphia, Pa.
Bibl. 3

Samuel Worthington
(c. 1833)
Philadelphia, Pa.
Bibl. 3

Worthley Brothers (1875)
Brunswick, Me.
Bibl. 105

N. T. Worthley (1860)
Bath, Me.
Bibl. 105

Robert Worton (c. 1849)
Philadelphia, Pa.
Bibl. 3

Wortz & Voorhis
(c. 1896–1915)
New York, N.Y.
Bibl. 114, 127, 157

Wriggins
(See Wolf & Wriggins)

Wriggin(s) & Co.
(c. 1831–1833)
Philadelphia, Pa.
Thomas Wriggins
Bibl. 3, 23, 36, 44, 91

T. Wriggins & Co.
(c. 1842–1846)
Philadelphia, Pa.
Thomas Wriggins
Bibl. 3, 91

Thomas Wriggins
(c. 1837–1846)
Philadelphia, Pa.
Wriggin(s) & Co.
(c. 1831–1833)
T. Wriggins & Co.
(c. 1842–1846)
Bibl. 3, 4, 23, 28, 36, 44, 91

Wright
(See Wait & Wright)

Wright & Putnam
(c. 1836)
Buffalo, N.Y.
William S. Wright
John S. Putnam
Bibl. 20, 124

Wright & Sime (c. 1774)
Savannah, Ga.

—— Wright
William Sime
Bibl. 17

Alexander Wright
(b. 1748, c. 1775)
Maryland
Bibl. 23, 28, 36, 38, 44

George B. Wright (c. 1849)
Staunton, Va.
Bibl. 19

H. C. Wright (c. 1850)
Cleveland, Ohio (?)
Bibl. 89

James Wright
(c. 1841–1844)
Philadelphia, Pa.
Bibl. 3

James R. Wright (c. 1846)
Lynchburg, Va.
Bibl. 19, 54

James R. Wright
(c. 1849–c. 1856)
Lexington, Va.
Bibl. 19   **WRIGHT**

John Wright
(c. 1845–1850)
Philadelphia, Pa.
Bibl. 3

John Austin Wright
(c. 1844–1846)
Leesburg, Va.
Bibl. 19

John F. Wright
(c. 1830–1833)
Philadelphia, Pa.
Bibl. 3, 23, 36, 44

John H. Wright
(c. 1841–1848)
Louisville, Ky.
Bibl. 32, 93

Joseph Wright (d. 1793)
Philadelphia, Pa.
Bibl. 3

M. Wright (c. 1815)
New York, N.Y.
Bibl. 15, 124, 138

Mary Ann Wright
(c. 1847–1850)
Leesburg, Va.
Bibl. 19

Sullivan Wright (1860)
Wiscasset, Me.
Bibl. 105

William Wright
(c. 1802–1803)
Baltimore, Md.
Bibl. 29, 38

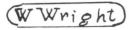

William Wright (d. 1746)
Charleston, S.C.
(before 1740)
Sarrazin & Wright (c. 1746)
Bibl. 5, 19, 28, 54, 118

W WRIGHT   W Wright

William Wright
(c. 1777–1799)
Petersburg, Va.
Bibl. 19

William S. Wright
(c. 1836)
Buffalo, N.Y.
Wright & Putnam
Bibl. 20, 124

Wrought Right
(See Marshall Field & Co.)

John Wyand (c. 1847)
Philadelphia, Pa.
Bibl. 3

John Wyant
(c. 1829–1833)
Philadelphia, Pa.
Bibl. 3

Joseph Wyatt
(c. 1797–1798)
Philadelphia, Pa.
Bibl. 3, 23, 24, 25, 28, 36, 44, 114

J.W.   J·W

Wyer & Farley
(c. 1828–1830)
Portland, Me.
Eleazer Wyer (Sr.)

Eleazer Wyer Jr.
Charles Farley
Bibl. 15, 23, 24, 25, 28, 29, 36, 110, 114

WYER & FARLEY

Wyer & Noble (c. 1823)
Portland, Me.
Eleazer Wyer (Sr.)
Eleazer Wyer Jr.
Joseph Noble
Bibl. 23, 25, 36, 44, 105, 110

Eleazer Wyer (Sr.)
(b. 1752–d. 1800)
Charlestown, Mass.
Boston, Mass.
Wyer & Noble (c. 1823)
Wyer & Farley
(c. 1828–1830)
Bibl. 15, 23, 28, 36, 44, 110

Eleazer Wyer Jr.
(b. 1786–d. 1848)
Portland, Me.
Wyer & Noble (c. 1823)
Wyer & Farley
(c. 1828–1830)
Bibl. 15, 24, 25, 28, 29, 44, 91, 110

Benjamin Wynkoop
(b. 1675–d. 1728)
New York, N.Y. (c. 1740)?
Bibl. 4, 15, 24, 25, 28, 30, 35, 36, 44, 54, 91, 102, 114, 119, 124, 138

Benjamin Wynkoop Jr.
(b. 1705–d. 1766)
Fairfield, Conn.
New Haven, Conn.
New York, N.Y.
Bibl. 15, 25, 29, 44, 54, 61, 91, 92, 95, 110, 114, 116, 124

Cornelius Wynkoop
(b. 1701)
New York, N.Y.
(c. 1727–1740)
Bibl. 4, 15, 23, 24, 25, 28, 29, 35, 36, 44, 91, 95, 114, 124, 138

Jacobus Wynkoop
(c. 1765)
Kingston, N.Y.
Bibl. 23, 25, 36, 44, 114, 124

WYNKOOP

Christopher Wynn
(b. 1795–d. 1883)
Baltimore, Md.
Bibl. 24, 25, 29, 38, 44, 114

C. WYNN

Madeline Yale Wynne
(b. 1847–d. 1918)
Chicago, Ill. (1893–1909)
Bibl. 89, 98

Robert Wynne
(c. 1827–1830)
Salisbury, N.C.
Huntington & Wynne
(c. 1827–1828)
Bibl. 21

Y

Y
(See W. F. Cory & Bro.,
Otto Young & Company)

Raymond C. Yard, Inc.
(1922–present)
New York, N.Y.
Bibl. 126

Yates & Clark
(c. 1788–1790)
Lansingburgh, N.Y.
Bibl. 20, 124

Yates & Kent (c. 1798)
Trenton, N.J.
Joseph Yates
—————— Kent
Bibl. 46, 54

Yates & Kimball
  (c. 1842–1843)
Elmira, N.Y.
William P. Yates
O. Kimball
Bibl. 20, 124

Yates & Rockwell
  (c. 1787–1788)
Lansingburgh, N.Y.
—————— Yates
John Rockwell
Bibl. 20, 124

Henry H. Yates
  (c. 1822–1831)
Albany, N.Y.
Bibl. 20, 124

Joseph Yates (c. 1798)
Trenton, N.J.
Yates & Kent
Bibl. 46

Samuel Yates (c. 1825)
Albany, N.Y.
Bibl. 24, 25, 28, 29, 44, 91,
  114, 124

William P. Yates
  (c. 1841–1850)
Elmira, N.Y.
Yates & Kimball
  (c. 1842–1843)
Bibl. 20, 124

Edward Yeager
  (c. 1844–1850)
Philadelphia, Pa.
Bibl. 3

J. M. Yeager
  (c. 1839–1846)
Philadelphia, Pa.
Bibl. 3

Joseph Yeager
  (c. 1816–1847)
Philadelphia, Pa.
Bibl. 3

William Yeager (c. 1837)
Philadelphia, Pa.
Bibl. 3

Frederick Yeiser
Danville, Ky. (c. 1814–1820)
Lexington, Ky. (c. 1857)
Bibl. 32, 54, 93

Philip Yeiser (d. 1859)
Danville, Ky. (c. 1814)
Lexington, Ky. (c. 1859)
Bibl. 32

Alexander Yeoman
  (c. 1837)
Philadelphia, Pa.
Bibl. 3

Elijah Yeomans
  (b. 1738–d. 1794)
Hartford, Conn.
Hadley, Mass.
Bibl. 16, 28, 36, 44, 91, 92,
  110

Randal (Randell) Yettons
  (c. 1739)
Philadelphia, Pa.
Bibl. 3, 28, 44

Robert A. Yongue
  (c. 1852–1857)
Columbia, S.C.
Cooper & Yongue (c. 1852)
Bibl. 5

York Silver Co. (c. 1950)
New York, N.Y.
Bibl. 127   **PAT JANE**

William Yost
  (c. 1846–1847)
Wheeling, Va.
Bibl. 19

Daniel You
  (c. 1743–1750, d. 1750)
Charleston, S.C.
Bibl. 5, 15, 24, 25, 44, 54,
  114

Thomas You
  (b. 1753–d. 1786)

Charleston, S.C. (c. 1775)
Bibl. 5, 15, 24, 25, 44, 54,
  91, 104

Young
(See also Singleton & Young,
  Tiffany & Young)

Young & Bockius
  (c. 1798)
Martinsburg, Va.
William Young
Daniel Bockius
Bibl. 19, 91, 114

Young & Co. (c. 1848)
Columbia, S.C.
Edward Young
Bibl. 5, 54

Young & Co. (1850–1853)
New Orleans, La.
Bibl. 141

YOUNG & Cº

Young & Delleker
  (c. 1823–1824)
Philadelphia, Pa.
—————— Young
Samuel Delleker
Bibl. 3

Young & Tiffany
(See Tiffany & Young)

—————— **Young**
  (c. 1829–1831)
Philadelphia, Pa.
Bibl. 3

A. Young & Co. (c. 1807)
Camden, S.C.
Alexander Young
Edward Young
Bibl. 5, 25, 114   A Young & Co.

A. Young & Son (c. 1848)
Camden, S.C.
Alexander Young
Bibl. 54, 114

Alexander Young
  (b. 1784–d. 1856,
  c. 1807–1856)
Baltimore, Md.

Camden, S.C.
A. Young & Co. (c. 1807)
A. Young & Son (c. 1848)
Bibl. 5, 23, 24, 25, 29, 36,
44, 54, 114

A. YOUNG	YOUNG

Daniel D. Young (c. 1841)
Schenectady, N.Y.
Bibl. 20, 124

Ebenezer Young
(b. 1756, c. 1778–1780)
Hebron, Conn.
Bibl. 16, 23, 24, 25, 28, 36,
44, 92, 110, 114

YOUNG

Edward Young
(b. 1816–d. 1848)
Columbia, S.C.
A. Young & Co.
Young & Co.
A. Young & Son (c. 1848)
Bibl. 5, 54

A YOUNG & SON

Francis Young (c. 1777)
Philadelphia, Pa.
Bibl. 3

J. T. Young (c. 1855)
Petersburg, Va.
Bibl. 19   J T YOUNG

Jacob Young
(b. 1752–d. 1791)
Hagerstown, Md.
(c. 1780–1791)
Bibl. 38

James Young
(c. 1829–1838)
Troy, N.Y.
Bibl. 20, 124

James H. Young
(c. 1817–1850)
Philadelphia, Pa.
Bibl. 3

John Henry Young
Albany, N.Y. (c. 1833)
Rochester, N.Y. (c. 1834)
Bibl. 20, 24

L. P. Young (1875)
Orono, Me.
Bibl. 105

Levi Young (c. 1827)
Bridgeport, Conn.
Bibl. 16, 23, 28, 36, 44, 110

Nicholas E. Young
(c. 1839–1846)
Saratoga Springs, N.Y.
Bibl. 20, 124

Otto Young & Company
(1880–1924)
Chicago, Ill.
Successor to William B.
Clapp, Young & Co.
(1865–1880)
Became A. C. Becken Co.
Bibl. 127, 135

Philip Young (c. 1792)
Martinsburg, Va.
William & Philip Young
Bibl. 20

Samuel Young
(c. 1811–1816)
Charles Town, Va.
Bibl. 19

Samuel E. Young (c. 1840)
Laconia, N.H.
Bibl. 4, 25, 44, 91, 114, 125

S E YOUNG

Thomas Young
Lexington, Ky.
(c. 1789–1793)
Danville, Ky. (after 1793)
Bibl. 32, 54, 68

Walter Young
(c. 1831–1832)
Rochester, N.Y. (c. 1834)
Albany, N.Y. (c. 1838–1839)
Bibl. 20, 124

William Young
(c. 1761–1778)
Philadelphia, Pa.

Bibl. 3, 15, 23, 25, 28, 36,
44, 81, 95, 102

William Young
Martinsburg, Va.
(c. 1792, c. 1798)
Staunton, Va.
(c. 1806–1807)
William & Philip Young
(c. 1792)
Young & Bockius (c. 1798)
Bibl. 19, 91

William & Philip Young
(c. 1792)
Martinsburg, Va.
Bibl. 19

P. J. Ysabelle (Isabel)
(1831–1832)
New Orleans, La.
Bibl. 141

Yver
(See Philip & Yver)

Z

Z B
(See Zalman Bostwick,
Zachariah Brigden)

Z S
(See Zebulon Stanton)

Zadek & Caldwell
(c. 1867–1870)
Mobile, Ala.
Bibl. 54, 148

Zahm & Jackson (c. 1830)
New York, N.Y.
Bibl. 24, 25, 44, 91, 114

ZAHM & JACKSON

George M. Zahm (d. 1895)
Lancaster, Pa. (c. 1840)
Bibl. 24, 25, 44, 112, 114

G. M. ZAHM

Isaac Zane (c. 1795)
Zanesfield, Ohio
Bibl. 25, 34, 44, 114

I. ZANE

Jacob Zane (c. 1837–1846)
Philadelphia, Pa.
Bibl. 3

Jesse Shenton Zane
(c. 1796)
Wilmington, Del.
Bibl. 25, 30, 44, 114

J. ZANE

John Zeibler (c. 1848)
St. Louis, Mo.
Bibl. 54

G. A. Zeissler (c. 1848)
Philadelphia, Pa.
Bibl. 3

Zell Bros. (c. 1950)
Portland, Ore.
Bibl. 127

William Zeller
(c. 1835–1850)
Philadelphia, Pa.
Bibl. 3

Samuel Zepp
(c. 1842–1850)
Philadelphia, Pa.
Bibl. 3

Zeuma Zeumer
(See Zumar)

**C. H. Zimmerman &
Company**
(c. 1866–1871)
New Orleans, La.
Bibl. 104, 127, 141

C.H. ZIMMERMAN

NEW ORLEANS

Marie Zimmerman
(b. 1878–d. 1972)
Chicago, Ill.
New York, N.Y.
Bibl. 89, 161

P. Zimmerman (1865)
New Orleans, La.
Bibl. 141

P. ZIMMERMAN

Zoomer
(See Zumar)

Philip R. Zulauf
(c. 1860–1909)
New Albany, Ind.
Owensboro, Ky.
Bibl. 133

PHIL. R. ZULAUF

**George A. Zumar (Zuma)
(Zumer) (Zeuma)
(Zeumer) (Zoomer)**
Louisville, Ky.
(c. 1831–1849)
E. C. Beard & Co.
(c. 1831–c. 1852)
Bibl. 32, 54, 93

BIBLIOGRAPHY

1. Avery, Clara Louise. *Early American Silver.* New York: The Century Company, 1930.

2. Bigelow, Francis Hill. *Historic Silver of the Colonies and Its Makers.* New York: Tudor Publishing Company, 1948.

3. Brix, Maurice, *List of Philadelphia Silversmiths and Allied Artificers, 1682–1850.* Philadelphia: Privately Printed, 1920.

4. Buck, J. H. *Old Plate, Its Makers and Marks.* New York: Gorham Manufacturing Company, 1914.

5. Burton, E. Milby. *South Carolina Silversmiths 1690–1860.* Charleston: The Charleston Museum, 1942.

6. Carpenter, Ralph E. Jr. *The Arts and Crafts of Newport, Rhode Island 1640–1820.* Newport, Rhode Island: Preservation Society of Newport County, Pittshead Tavern, 1954.

7. Clarke, Hermann Frederick, *John Coney, Silversmith 1655–1722.* Boston: Houghton Mifflin Company, 1932.

8. Clarke, Hermann Frederick and Foote, Henry Wilder. *Jeremiah Dummer, Colonial Craftsman and Merchant 1645–1718.* Boston: Houghton Mifflin Company, 1935.

9. Clarke, Hermann Frederick. *John Hull, Builder of the Bay Colony.* Portland, Me.: The Southworth-Anthoensen Press, 1940.

10. Clearwater, Alphonso T. *American Silver, List of Un-identified Makers and Marks.* New York, 1913.

11. Crosby, Everett Uberto. *Books and Baskets, Signs and Silver of Old Time Nantucket.* Nantucket, Mass.: Inquirer and Mirror Press, 1940.

12. Crosby, Everett Uberto. *95% Perfect.* Nantucket Island, Mass.: Tetaukimmo Press, 1953.

13. Crosby, Everett Uberto. *The Spoon Primer.* Nantucket, Mass.: Inquirer and Mirror Press, 1941.

14. Currier, Ernest M. *Early American Silversmiths, The Newbury Spoonmakers.* Cleveland, Ohio: The Potter Studio, Inc., 1930.

15. Currier, Ernest M. *Marks of Early American Silversmiths, List of New York City Smiths 1815–1841.* Privately printed, 1970.

16. Curtis, George Munson. *Early Silver of Connecticut and Its Makers.* Meriden, Conn.: International Silver Company, 1913.

17. Cutten, George Barton. *Silversmiths of Georgia.* Savannah, Ga.: Pigeonhole Press, 1958.

18. Cutten, George Barton, and Cutten, Minnie Warren. *The Silversmiths of Utica.* Hamilton, N.Y., 1936.

19. Cutten, George Barton. *Silversmiths of Virginia.* Richmond, Va.: The Dietz Press, 1952.

20. Cutten, George Barton. *The Silversmiths, Watchmakers, and Jewelers of The State of New York outside New York City.* Hamilton, New York: Privately printed, 1939.

21. ———. *Silversmiths of North Carolina.* Raleigh, N.C.: State Department of Archives & History, 1948.

22. Ensko, Robert. *Makers of Early American Silver.* New York: Trow Press, 1915.

23. Ensko, Stephen. *American Silversmiths and Their Marks.* New York: Privately printed, 1927.

24. Ensko, Stephen G. C. *American Silversmiths and Their Marks II.* New York: Robert Ensko, Inc., Privately printed, 1937.

25. Ensko, Stephen G. C. *American Silversmiths and Their Marks III.* New York: Dover Publications, Inc., 1983.

26. Forbes, Esther. *Paul Revere and the World He Lived in.* Boston: Houghton Mifflin Co., 1942.

27. French, Hollis. *Jacob Hurd and His Sons Nathaniel and Benjamin, Silversmiths.* Printed by the Riverside Press for the Walpole Society, 1939.

28. French, Hollis. *A List of Early American Silversmiths and Their Marks.* New York: Walpole Society, 1917.

29. Graham, James Jr. *Early American Silver Marks.* New York: James Graham Jr., 1936.

30. Harrington, Jessie. *Silversmiths of Delaware 1700–1850.* Delaware: National Society of Colonial Dames of America, 1939.

31. Heller, David. *History of Cape Silver, 1700–1750.* D. Heller, 1949.

32. Hiatt, Noble W. and Lucy F. *The Silversmiths of Kentucky.* Louisville, Ky.: The Standard Printing Co., 1954.

33. Jones, E. Alfred. *Old Silver of Europe and America.* Philadelphia: Lippincott Company, 1928.

34. Knittle, Rhea Mansfield. *Early Ohio Silversmiths and Pewterers 1787–1847.* (Ohio Frontier Series.) Cleveland, Ohio: Calvert-Hatch Company, 1943.

35. Miller, V. Isabelle. *Silver by New York Makers, Late Seventeenth Century to 1900.* New York: Women's Committee of the Museum of The City of New York, 1938.

36. Okie, Howard Pitcher. *Old Silver and Old Sheffield Plate.* New York: Doubleday, Doran and Company, 1928.

37. Phillips, John Marshall. *American Silver.* New York: Chanticleer Press, 1949.

38. Pleasants, J. Hall and Howard Sill. *Maryland Silversmiths, 1715–1830.* Privately printed, 1930.

39. Prime, Mrs. Alfred Coxe. *Three Centuries of Historic Silver.* Philadelphia: Pennsylvania Society of Colonial Dames of America, 1938.

40. Rosenbaum, Jeanette, *Myer Myers, Goldsmith.* Philadelphia: Jewish Publication Society of America, 1954.

41. Schild, Joan Lynn. *Silversmiths of Rochester.* Rochester, N.Y.: Rochester Museum of Arts and Sciences, 1944.

42. Semon, Kurt M. A. *Treasury of Old Silver.* New York: McBride Company, 1947

43. Taylor, Emerson. *Paul Revere.* New York: Dodd, Mead & Co., 1930.

44. Thorn, C. Jordan. *Handbook of American Silver and Pewter Marks*. New York: Tudor Publishing Company, 1949.

45. Wenham, Edward. *Practical Book of American Silver*. New York and Philadelphia: J. B. Lippincott Co., 1949.

46. Williams, Carl Mark. *Silversmiths of New Jersey 1700–1825*. Philadelphia: G. S. MacManus Co., 1949.

47. Wroth, Lawrence C. *Abel Buell of Connecticut, Silversmith, Typefounder, and Engraver*. 1926.

48. Wyler, Seymour B. *The Book of Old Silver*. New York: Crown Publishers, 1937.

49. *American Church Silver of 17th and 18th Centuries exhibited at the Museum of Fine Arts, July to December, 1911*. Boston: Boston Museum of Fine Arts, 1911.

50. *A Collection of Early American Silver*. Tiffany and Company, 1920.

51. *American Collector*. New York, 1933.

52. "American Silver." *American Magazine of Art*, August 1919, v. 10, p. 400.

53. *Antiquarian Magazine*, 1924–1933.

54. *Antiques Magazine*. 1922–1959.

55. *Boston Museum of Fine Arts Philip Leffingwell Spalding Collection of Early American Silver*. F. J. Hipkiss. Cambridge, Mass.: Harvard University Press, 1943.

56. *Catalog of an Exhibition of Paintings by Gilbert Stuart, Furniture by the Goodards and Townsends, Silver by Rhode Island Silversmiths*. Rhode Island School of Design, Providence, R.I., 1936.

57. *Descriptive Catalogue of Various Pieces of Silver Plate forming Collection of The New York Farmers 1882–1932*.

58. *Detroit Historical Society Bulletin*. November, 1952.

59. "Early American Silver," H. D. Eberlein. *Arts and Decoration*, XI (August 1919), 166.

60. "Early American Silver," W. A. Dyer. *Arts and Decoration*, VII (May 1917), 365.

61. *Early Connecticut Silver 1700–1830*. Gallery of Fine Arts, Yale University, New Haven, Conn.: Connecticut Tercentenary Commission, 1935.

62. *Early New England Silver lent from the Mark Bortman Collection*. Northampton, Mass.: Smith College Museum of Art, 1958.

63. "Early Philadelphia Silversmiths," H. F. Jayne and S. W. Woodhouse, Jr. *Art in America*, IX (October 1921), 248.

64. *Elias Pelletreau, Long Island Silversmith and his sources of Design*. Brooklyn, N.Y.: Brooklyn Institute of Arts and Sciences, Brooklyn Museum, 1959.

65. *Early Cleveland Silversmiths*, Muriel Cutten Hoitsma. Cleveland, Ohio: Gates Publishing Co., 1953.

66. *From Colony to Nation exhibit*. Chicago Art Institute, 1949.

67. "Jacob Boelen, Goldsmith of New York and his family circle." Howard S. F. Randolph. *New York Genealogical and Biographical Record*, October, 1941.

68. "Kentucky Silversmiths before 1850." M. M. Bridwell. *Filson Club History Quarterly*, XVI, No. 2 (April 1942), 111–126.

69. *Masterpieces of New England Silver 1650–1800*. Gallery of Fine Arts, Yale University, 1939.

70. "New England Silversmiths, news items gleaned from Boston newspapers, 1704–1705." G. F. Dow. *Art in America*, X (February 1922), 75.

71. "New York Metropolitan Museum of Art Exhibition of Early American Silver." C. Louise Avery. *Metropolitan Museum of Art Bulletin*, December 1931.

72. "New York Metropolitan Museum of Art American Silver of the 17th and 18th centuries." C. L. Avery. *Metropolitan Museum of Art Bulletin*, 1920.

73. "New York Metropolitan Museum Catalogue of Exhibition of Silver Used in New York, New Jersey, and the South." R. T. Haines Halsey. Metropolitan Museum of Art, 1911.

74. *New York Sun*, antiques section, 1938–1959.

75. "Old American Silver," *Country Life in America*. February 1913–January 1915.

76. "Old Silver." Prof. Theodore S. Woolsey. *Harper's Magazine*, 1896.

77. *Outline of the Life and Works of Col. Paul Revere (partial catalogue of silverware bearing his name)*. Newburyport, Mass.: Towle Manufacturing Co., 1901.

78. *Parke-Bernet Galleries catalogue*. January 1938–December 1959.

79. *Pennsylvania Museum and School of Industrial Art Exhibition of Old American and English Silver*. 1917.

80. "Pennsylvania Museum and School of Industrial Art Loan exhibition of Colonial Silver, special catalogue." *Pennsylvania Museum Bulletin*, No. 68, June 1921.

81. "Philadelphia Silver 1682–1800." *Philadelphia Museum Bulletin*, LI, No. 249 (Spring 1956).

82. "Silver." H. E. Gillingham. *Pennsylvania Magazine of History and Biography*, 1930–1935.

83. "Silver by New York Makers." *Museum of the City of New York*. New York, 1937. December 7, 1937–January 17, 1938.

84. *Silversmiths of Northampton, Massachusetts and Vicinity down to 1850*. George Barton Cutten. Pamphlet.

85. *The Story of Sterling*. New York: Sterling Silversmiths Guild of America, 1937.

86. *The Story of the House of Kirk*. Baltimore: Samuel Kirk and Son Co., 1914.

87. "Three Centuries of European and American Silver." San Francisco: *M. H. de young Memorial Museum Bulletin*. October 1938.

88. *Your Garden and Home*. 1931–1932.

89. Ralph and Terry Kovel.

90. Beckman, Elizabeth A. *Cincinnati Silversmiths, Jewelers, Watch and Clockmakers*, Cincinnati, Ohio: B.B. & Co., 1975.

91. Belden, Louise Conway. *Marks of American Silversmiths in the Ineson-Bissell Collection*. Charlottesville, Virginia: The University Press of Virginia, 1980.

92. Bohan, Peter, and Philip Hammerslough. *Early Connecticut Silver, 1700–1840*. Middletown, Connecticut: Wesleyan University Press, 1970.

93. Boultinghouse, Marquis. *Silversmiths, Jewelers, Clock and Watch Makers of Kentucky 1785–1900*. Privately printed, 1980 (900 North Broadway, Lexington, KY 40505).

94. Buhler, Kathryn C. *American Silver 1655–1825 in the*

Museum of Fine Arts Boston, Vols. I & II. Boston, Massachusetts: Museum of Fine Arts, 1972.

95. Buhler, Kathryn C., and Graham Hood. *American Silver in the Yale University Art Gallery,* Vols. I & II. New Haven: Yale University Press, 1970.

96. Carpenter, Charles H. Jr. *Gorham Silver 1831–1981.* New York: Dodd, Mead & Company, 1982.

97. Carpenter, Charles H. Jr. and Mary Grace. *Tiffany Silver.* New York: Dodd, Mead & Company, 1978.

98. Darling, Sharon S., and Gail Farr Casterline. *Chicago Metalsmiths.* Chicago, Illinois: Chicago Historical Society, 1977.

99. Divis, Jan. *Silver Marks Of The World.* New York: Hamlyn, 1976.

100. Duncan, Alastair. *American Art Deco.* New York: Harry N. Abrams, Inc., 1986.

101. *Encyclopedia of Early American Silversmiths and Their Marks with a Concise Glossary of Terms.* Harrisburg, Pennsylvania: Benson Gallery Press, 1966.

102. Fales, Martha Gandy. *Early American Silver.* New York: E. P. Dutton & Co., Inc., 1973.

103. ———. *Joseph Richardson and Family, Philadelphia Silversmiths.* Middletown, Connecticut: Wesleyan University Press, 1974.

104. Fennimore, Donald L. *The Knopf Collectors' Guides to American Antiques: Silver & Pewter.* New York: Alfred A. Knopf, 1984.

105. Fredyma, James P. *A Directory of Maine Silversmiths and Watch and Clock Makers.* Privately printed, 1972 (Marie-Louise Antiques, Lyme Rd., Hanover, NH 03755).

106. Fredyma, Paul J. and Marie-Louise. *A Directory of Massachusetts Silversmiths and Their Marks.* Privately printed, 1972. (Lyme Road, Hanover, NH 03755).

107. ———. *A Directory of Massachusetts Silversmiths and Their Marks.* Privately printed, 1971 (Lyme Road, Hanover, NH 03755).

108. ———. *A Directory of Rhode Island Silversmiths and Their Marks.* Privately printed, 1972 (Lyme Road, Hanover, NH 03755).

109. Freeman, Larry. *Victorian Silver.* Watkins Glen, New York: Century House, 1967.

110. Flynt, Henry, and Martha Gandy Fales. *The Heritage Foundation Collection of Silver with Biographical Sketches of New England Silversmiths, 1625–1825.* Old Deerfield, Massachusetts: The Heritage Foundation, 1968.

111. Gere, Charlotte. *American & European Jewelry 1830–1914.* New York: Crown Publishers, Inc., 1975.

112. Gerstell, Vivian S. *Silversmiths of Lancaster, Pennsylvania 1730–1850.* Lancaster, Pennsylvania: Lancaster County Historical Society, 1972.

113. Gibb, George S. *The Whitesmiths of Taunton: A History of Reed & Barton, Silversmiths, 1842–1943.* Cambridge, Massachusetts: Harvard University Press, 1943.

114. Green, Robert Alan. *Marks of American Silversmiths, Revised (1650–1900).* Privately printed, 1984 (214 Key Haven Road, Key West, FL 33040).

115. Haslam, Malcolm. *Marks and Monograms of The Modern Movement 1875–1930.* New York: Charles Scribner's Sons, 1977.

116. Hood, Graham. *American Silver: A History of Style, 1650–1900.* New York: Praeger Publishers, 1971.

117. Hughes, Graham. *Modern Jewelry.* New York: Crown Publishers, Inc., 1963.

118. Kauffman, Henry J. *The Colonial Silversmith: His Techniques & His Products.* Nashville, Tennessee: Thomas Nelson, 1969.

119. Kolter, Jane Bentley, editor. *Early American Silver and Its Makers.* New York: Mayflower Books, Inc., 1979.

120. Kovel, Ralph and Terry. *Kovels' Know Your Collectibles.* New York: Crown Publishers, Inc., 1981.

121. May, Earl Chapin. *Century of Silver, 1847–1947: Connecticut Yankees and a Noble Metal.* New York: Robert M. McBride & Company, 1947.

122. McClinton, Katharine Morrison. *Collecting American 19th Century Silver.* New York: Charles Scribner's Sons, 1968.

123. Metropolitan Museum of Art. *In Pursuit of Beauty: Americans And The Aesthetic Movement.* New York: Rizzoli International Publications, Inc., 1986.

124. *New York State Silversmiths.* Privately printed, 1964 (The Darling Foundation of New York State Early American Silversmiths and Silver, 790 Lebrun Road, Eggertsville, NY).

125. Parson, Charles S. *New Hampshire Silver.* Privately printed, 1983 (Adams Brown Company, Horological Literature, P.O. Box 357, Cranbury, NJ 08512).

126. Proddow, Penny, and Debra Healy. *American Jewelry: Glamour and Tradition.* New York: Rizzoli International Publications, Inc., 1987.

127. Rainwater, Dorothy T. *Encyclopedia of American Silver Manufacturers.* Third Edition Revised. West Chester, Pennsylvania: Schiffer Publishing, Ltd., 1986

128. ———. *Sterling Silver Holloware.* New York: Charles Scribner's Sons, 1973.

129. Rainwater, Dorothy T. and H. Ivan. *American Silverplate.* Nashville, Tennessee: Thomas Nelson, Inc., 1968.

130. Rainwater, Dorothy T., and Donna H. Felger. *American Spoons: Souvenir and Historical.* Camden, New Jersey: Thomas Nelson & Sons, 1968.

131. *Random House Collector's Encyclopedia: Victoriana to Art Deco.* New York: Random House, 1974.

132. Raulet, Sylvie. *Art Deco Jewelry.* New York: Rizzoli International Publications, Inc., 1984.

133. Redfearn, Jerome. *Indiana Silversmiths, Clock Makers and Watchmakers, 1779–1900.* Privately printed, 1984 (American Publications, Box 204, Georgetown, KY 40324).

134. Roach, Ruth Hunter. *St. Louis Silversmiths.* St. Louis, Missouri: Eden Publishing House, 1967.

135. Schwartz, Marvin D. *Collectors' Guide to Antique American Silver.* New York: Doubleday & Company, Inc., 1975.

136. Turner, Noel D. *American Silver Flatware 1837–1910.* San Diego, California: A. S. Barnes and Co., Inc., 1972.

137. Van Lenten, Howard H. *An American Heritage: A Book about the International Silver Company.* Dallas, Texas: Taylor Publishing Company, 1977.

138. Von Khrum, Paul. *Silversmiths of New York City 1684–1850*. Portland, Maine: The Anthoensen Press, 1978.

139. *American Silver and Pressed Glass*. The R. W. Norton Art Foundation, 4700 Block of Creswell Avenue, Shreveport, LA 71106, 1967.

140. *California Design 1910*. Timothy J. Anderson, Eudorah M. Moore and Robert W. Winter, editors, Pasadena, California: California Design Publications, 1974.

141. *Crescent City Silver*. The Historic New Orleans Collection, 533 Royal Street, New Orleans, LA 70130, 1980.

142. *Early American Silver Selected from the Mabel Brady Garvan Collection, Yale University*. John Marshall Phillips. Yale University Art Gallery, 1960.

143. *An Exhibition of New Haven Silver*. The New Haven Colony Historical Society, 1967.

144. *Fine, Handwrought Early 20th Century American Silver Plus Related Jewelry And Metalwork*. ARK Antiques, Box 3133, New Haven, CT 06515, 1987.

145. *Gorham Hollowware*. Gorham Textron, Gorham Division of Textron Inc., 333 Adelaide Avenue, Providence, RI 02907, 1979.

146. *Jewelers' Circular-Keystone Brand Name and Trademark Guide*. Jewelers' Circular-Keystone, Chilton Way, Radnor, PA 19089, 1984, updated periodically.

147. *Jewelers' Circular-Keystone Sterling Flatware Pattern Index*. Jewelers' Circular-Keystone, Chilton Way, Radnor, PA 19089, 1983, updated periodically.

148. *Mobile Silversmiths and Jewelers 1820–1867*. Sidney Adair Smith. Historic Mobile Preservation Society, 350 Oakleigh Place, Mobile, AL 36604, 1970.

149. *Presentation Pieces in The Museum of History and Technology*. Margaret Brown Klapthor. Smithsonian Institution, Washington, D.C., 1965.

150. *Samuel Kirk and Son: American Silver Craftsman Since 1815*. Samuel Kirk and Son, Baltimore, Maryland, 1966.

151. *Silver in American Life*. Barbara McLean Ward & Gerald W. R. Ward. The American Federation of Arts, 41 East 65th Street, New York, NY 10021, 1979.

152. *Silver Magazine* (formerly *Silver-rama*). P.O. Box, 1243, Whittier, CA 90609.

153. *The Silversmith in Eighteenth-Century Williamsburg*. William De Matteo. Colonial Williamsburg, Williamsburg, Virginia, 1956.

154. *Souvenirs In Sterling Silver: Spoons, Forks and Novelities*. Watson & Newell Co., 347 Fifth Avenue, New York, NY 10016, undated.

155. *St. Louis Silversmiths*. St. Louis Art Museum, St. Louis, Missouri, 1980.

156. *Structure and Ornament: American Modernist Jewelry 1940–1960*. Fifty-50, 793 Broadway, New York, NY 10003, 1984.

157. *Trade-Marks of the Jewelry and Kindred Trades*. New York: Jewelers' Circular Publishing Co., 1904, 1915, 1922, 1940–1975.

158. *Utica Silver*. Munson-Williams-Proctor Institute, 310 Genesee Street, Utica, NY 13502, 1972.

159. *A View of Tennessee Silversmiths*, Dixon Gallery and Gardens, Memphis, Tennessee, 1983.

160. *The Warner Family: Silversmiths to Baltimore*. Peale Museum, Baltimore, Maryland, 1971.